Selected Papers from the 14th Estuarine and Coastal Modeling Conference

Special Issue Editor
Richard P. Signell

Special Issue Editor
Richard P. Signell
United States Geological Survey, Woods Hole
USA

Editorial Office
MDPI AG
St. Alban-Anlage 66
Basel, Switzerland

This edition is a reprint of the Special Issue published online in the open access journal *Journal of Marine Science and Engineering* (ISSN 2077-1312) from 2016–2017 (available at: http://www.mdpi.com/journal/jmse/special_issues/ECM14).

For citation purposes, cite each article independently as indicated on the article page online and as indicated below:

Author 1; Author 2; Author 3 etc. Article title. *Journal Name*. **Year**. Article number/page range.

ISBN 978-3-03842-362-1 (Pbk)
ISBN 978-3-03842-363-8 (PDF)

Table of Contents

About the Guest Editor

Richard P. Signell is a research oceanographer at the US Geological Survey in Woods Hole, MA, USA. He holds his doctorate in physical oceanography from the MIT/Woods Hole Oceanographic Institution Joint Program (1989). He has over 28 years of experience in coastal ocean modeling and geoinformatics. He is author or co-author of more than 100 refereed articles, was the Chair of the 2011 Gordon Research Conference on Coastal Ocean Modeling, the Chair of the 13th and 14th International Estuarine and Coastal Modeling Conferences, and is the current Chair of the Earth System Information Partners (ESIP) Interoperability and Technology Committee.

Preface to "Selected Papers from the 14th Estuarine and Coastal Modeling Conference"

This Special Issue contains selected papers from the 14th International Conference on Estuarine and Coastal Modeling (ECM14), held June 13–15, 2016 in Kingston, RI, USA. The conference brings modelers from academic institutions, government and private industry together to present and discuss the latest developments in the field of marine environmental modeling. Begun in 1989 by Dr. Malcolm Spaulding, the conference is held every other year in a retreat-like setting with a maximum of about 125 people to encourage interaction and help strengthen ties between modeling communities. A wide range of modeling issues are encouraged, including advances in physical understanding, numerical algorithm development, model applications, and better tools. A wide range of modeling topics are encouraged as well, including storm surge, eutrophication, larval transport, search and rescue, oil spills, fisheries' issues, coastal erosion and contaminated sediment transport. The special theme of ECM14 was Coastal Flooding.

The 21 papers presented here cover a broad spectrum of topics, including development of regional forecast systems, storm surge impacts, improved numerical techniques, water quality, methods for distributing model output, and regional modeling applications.

Richard P. Signell
Guest Editor

Journal of
Marine Science and Engineering

Article

An Open-Access, Multi-Decadal, Three-Dimensional, Hydrodynamic Hindcast Dataset for the Long Island Sound and New York/New Jersey Harbor Estuaries

Nickitas Georgas [1,*], Lun Yin [1], Yu Jiang [1], Yifan Wang [1], Penelope Howell [2], Vincent Saba [3], Justin Schulte [1], Philip Orton [1] and Bin Wen [1]

1   Davidson Laboratory, Stevens Institute of Technology, Hoboken, NJ 07030, USA; lyin1@stevens.edu (L.Y.); yjiang14@stevens.edu (Y.J.); ywang152@stevens.edu (Y.W.); jschulte@stevens.edu (J.S.); porton@stevens.edu (P.O.); bwen1@stevens.edu (B.W.)
2   Marine Fisheries Division, Connecticut Department of Energy and Environmental Protection, Old Lyme, CT 06371, USA; Penny.Howell@ct.gov
3   NOAA, National Marine Fisheries Service, Northeast Fisheries Science Center, Geophysical Fluid Dynamics Laboratory, Princeton University, Princeton, NJ 08540, USA; vincent.saba@noaa.gov
*   Correspondence: nickitas.georgas@stevens.edu; Tel.: +1-201-216-8218

Academic Editor: Richard P. Signell
Received: 17 July 2016; Accepted: 11 August 2016; Published: 16 August 2016

Abstract: This article presents the results and validation of a comprehensive, multi-decadal, hindcast simulation performed using the New York Harbor Observing and Prediction System's (NYHOPS) three-dimensional hydrodynamic model. Meteorological forcing was based on three-hourly gridded data from the North American Regional Reanalysis of the US National Centers for Environmental Prediction. Distributed hydrologic forcing was based on daily United States Geologic Survey records. Offshore boundary conditions for NYHOPS at the Mid-Atlantic Bight shelf break included hourly subtidal water levels from a larger-scale model ran for the same period, tides, and temperature and salinity profiles based on the Simple Ocean Data Assimilation datasets. The NYHOPS model's application to hindcast total water level and 3D water temperature and salinity conditions in its region over three decades was validated against observations from multiple agencies. Average indices of agreement were: 0.93 for storm surge (9 cm RMSE, 90% of errors less than 15 cm), 0.99 for water temperature (1.1 °C RMSE, 99% of errors less than 3 °C), and 0.86 for salinity (1.8 psu RMSE, 96% of errors less than 3.5 psu). The model's skill in simulating bottom water temperature, validated against historic data from the Long Island Sound bottom trawl survey, did not drift over the years, a significant and encouraging finding for multi-decadal model applications used to identify climatic trends, such as the warming presented here. However, the validation reveals residual biases in some areas such as small tributaries that receive urban discharges from the NYC drainage network. With regard to the validation of storm surge at coastal stations, both the considerable strengths and remaining limitations of the use of North American Regional Reanalysis (NARR) to force such a model application are discussed.

Keywords: Long Island Sound; New York/New Jersey Harbor Estuary; NYHOPS model; multi-decadal hydrodynamic hindcast; North American Regional Reanalysis

1. Introduction

Every year since 1976 has had an average global temperature warmer than the long-term average. Over the 1979–2013 period, global temperature warmed at an average of 0.26 °C per decade over land and 0.10 °C per decade over the global ocean [1]. The recently signed Paris Agreement [2], adopted by 195 countries, has a long-term goal of keeping the increase in global average temperature to well below

2 °C above pre-industrial levels, and aims to limit the increase to 1.5 °C, as doing so is expected to significantly reduce risks and the impacts of climate change. Yet, the Northeast US shelf waters have experienced higher warming rates than the global ocean, deduced by the Sea Surface Temperature (SST) satellite record. Pershing et al. [3] reported that SST rose by 0.30 °C per decade between 1982 and 2013 in the Gulf of Maine. The sole long-term observation record for water temperatures within the Long Island Sound (LIS) estuary, a US Estuary of National Significance, at a location near Millstone CT [4] has measured a much more rapid increase in LIS water temperatures than the global average: an alarming 0.44 °C per decade between 1979 and 2013, over four times higher than the global average rate. Over coastal Connecticut counties, on LIS's northern coast, surface air temperatures for the same time period increased by 0.33 °C per decade; that rate was double if only the 1992–2012 period was considered, but has decreased somewhat since, to 0.28 °C per decade (1979–2015; [1]).

Over these last few decades, the LIS ecosystem has undergone profound changes. Ocean warming is suggested to be the most important factor associated with the observed shifts in the mean center of biomass in Northeast U.S. fisheries [3,5–7]. However, understanding what controls the observed trends in the Northeast U.S., and how such processes affect the LIS ecosystem, has been limited due to the paucity of available three-dimensional, physical data. In 2013, the New York and Connecticut Sea Grants and the US EPA Long Island Sound Study joined forces to fund a multi-disciplinary project to address this deficiency, spearheading collaborative research involving numerical modelers, climate scientists, and fishery biologists. The work evaluated conditions and identified warming, freshening, and estuarine circulation trends in Long Island Sound over the past three decades. This research also explored how global climate contributes to long-term and inter-annual variability in the LIS physical environment and its Living Marine Resources [8].

This research article, presented at the 14th Estuarine and Coastal Modeling Conference (ECM14, http://ecm.github.io/ECM14/), focuses on the validation and results of a comprehensive, multi-decadal, hindcast simulation performed using the New York Harbor Observing and Prediction System (NYHOPS) hydrodynamic model that generated a continuous, three-dimensional dataset for a coastal aquatic region that includes Long Island Sound and the New York/New Jersey Harbor (NYNJH) Estuaries, between 1981 and 2013. Section 2 describes the data and methods used to set up the multi-decadal hindcast and the data and methods used to validate it for LIS and NYNJH and to have it serve as an open access dataset. Section 3 presents validation results. Section 4 puts the importance of the validation in perspective and discusses identified or verified trends and climatologies based on the validated model. Conclusions are outlined in the last section. Supplementary material in the form of a comprehensive PowerPoint presentation configured in two parts is also provided.

An online THREDDS Data Server (http://colossus.dl.stevens-tech.edu/thredds/catalog.html) was set up to serve the NYHOPS model's results in oceanographic NetCDF format over the web using the OPENDAP protocol, enabling open access to daily averaged or monthly averaged time series for all the gridded hindcast physical variables in or over the NYHOPS region (including LIS and NYNJH). Simulated climatologies (mean simulated climate conditions averaged over the three decades of the NYHOPS hindcast period) for two- and three-dimensional fields such as water temperatures and salinities, were also generated, and included in THREDDS. The use of the validated results of the model to research global climate teleconnections to the LIS ecosystem and its living marine resources will be presented in subsequent papers that are presently under preparation.

2. Materials and Methods

The completed multi-decadal high-resolution three-dimensional hindcast simulation for LIS and NYNJH was based on a nested modeling concept utilizing two hydrodynamic domains (Figure 1): The Stevens North Atlantic Predictions model (SNAP) [9–11] and the New York Harbor Observing and Prediction System model (NYHOPS, www.stevens.edu/NYHOPS) [9,11–18]. Both domains were simulated in 3D with the Stevens Estuarine and Coastal Ocean Model code (sECOM) [11,14,19], a derivative of the Princeton Ocean Model [20]. The SNAP model was run first, in a diagnostic mode (clamping temperature and salinity at the initial condition), at its regular 5 km resolution grid for the complete 1979–2013 simulation. SNAP wave and water level results, along with observation-based temperature and salinity fields, were then used to derive NYHOPS offshore boundary conditions and force the NYHOPS prognostic hindcast simulation on its variable-resolution grid (4 km to 25 m horizontal resolution, 10 vertical sigma layers). This is the same nesting concept used operationally for the ensemble-based Stevens Flood Advisory System (www.stevens.edu/SFAS [11]).

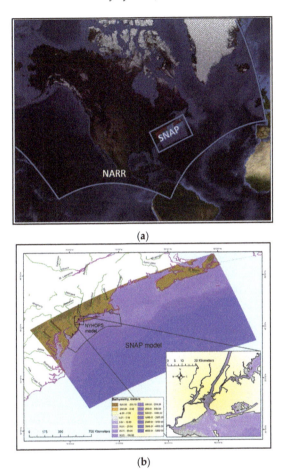

(a)

(b)

Figure 1. Hydrodynamic simulation domains used in this work: (**a**) The Stevens North Atlantic Prediction model (SNAP) domain embedded within the NCEP North-American Regional Reanalysis meteorological model; (**b**) The New York Harbor Observing and Prediction System model (NYHOPS) domain, embedded within the SNAP model domain. The insert highlights NYHOPS variable grid resolution in the NYNJH and Western LIS. Colors show bathymetry, in meters.

Surface meteorological forcing to both SNAP and NYHOPS was based on gridded data from the North American Regional Reanalysis (NARR [21]) created for the US National Centers for Environmental Prediction (NCEP). NARR (Figure 1) has been shown to have good skill for regional climate studies [22], but may be deficient for strong Atlantic precipitation events and Atlantic hurricanes [21]. Three-hourly surface meteorological variables provided by NARR at its 32 km grid were interpolated to the SNAP and NYHOPS grids and used to force the two models throughout the hindcast. Winds at 10 m above surface and barometric pressure reduced to mean sea level, total cloud cover, relative humidity and air temperature at 2 m above ground were used to compute locally dynamic surface heat flux terms, surface stress terms and surface wave growth terms with the methodology described in [14] and [23] as progressed by Orton et al. [17] based on internally calculated surface wave fields and explicit wave-steepness by Taylor and Yelland [24].

In the construction of the three dimensional NYHOPS hindcast, great care was put into creating high-fidelity lateral and internal boundary conditions for hydrodynamic forces included in the NYHOPS model, to complement the surface meteorological forcing provided by NARR. SNAP model results were used to provide hourly offshore boundary conditions to NYHOPS at the Mid-Atlantic Bight shelf break for surface waves and offshore tidal residuals (storm surge), the latter being used to provide the subtidal part to the tidal NYHOPS water level boundary conditions as in [14,15]. An attempt was made to account for steric and mean sea level rates across the NYHOPS simulations by adding the spatially and-seasonally averaged residual errors across SNAP coastal station predictions within the NYHOPS domain to the NYHOPS offshore water level boundary conditions [14,15]; average rates are listed in [25]. The observed water level records used in this step were tied to the geodetic NAVD88 datum.

Further, to provide offshore temperature and salinity profiles at the continental shelf break to NYHOPS for the hindcast, monthly data from the Simple Ocean Data Assimilation (SODA) climatology for water temperature (T) and salinity (S) were acquired beginning in 1959 on a global 0.5 degree geographic resolution grid with 40 standard depth levels in the vertical [26]. Some issues were identified with the continuity and versioning of the available SODA datasets that required significant effort in order to create a consistent monthly climatological dataset for the complete NYHOPS hindcast period of 1979–2013. A unified set of NYHOPS boundary conditions was created using SODA version 2.1.6 from 1979–1999, then SODA version 2.2.4 from 2000–2010, then results from a ROMS model run [18] generated at Rutgers University nested within a global HYCOM model for 2011–2012, and finally HYCOM global model results for 2013 [27]. To decrease climatologically relevant discrepancies between the last two datasets and SODA, bias correction for the last two datasets was performed both for the T/S means and their range. The native ROMS results for 2011–2012 were bias-corrected based on mean and range anomalies between the SODA version 2.2.4 datasets and the ROMS-with-HYCOM datasets for the common years of 2005–2008. HYCOM for 2013 was similarly bias-corrected based on the same debiasing factors. The assumption was that if the ROMS and HYCOM models were biased compared to SODA years 2005–2008 (shifted and inflated/deflated), they would continue being biased in a similar fashion in subsequent years. This assumption was validated by comparing the debiased datasets against SODA 2.2.4 for the last two SODA years, 2009–2010. Both means and ranges were significantly closer to SODA after debiasing (not shown). After the unified monthly T/S dataset from 1979 to 2013 was created at SODA resolution, it was interpolated in space and time along the NYHOPS offshore boundary, checked for vertical density stability, and used to force the NYHOPS 3D hindcast simulation.

Distributed hydrologic forcing to the NYHOPS estuarine model was based on daily United States Geologic Survey (USGS) records [25] with comparable but expanded results to other regional published studies [28,29]. As part of this work, a fluvial temperature study for rivers with long temperature time series across the Mid-Atlantic was completed to aid with the assignment of daily temperatures to riverine discharges in the NYHOPS hindcast (NYHOPS includes an extensive hydrologic input network [14]). That work was presented at the annual Mid-Atlantic Bight Oceanography and Meteorology Meeting (MABPOM 2013). Results indicated that river temperatures, and associated thermal inputs to Mid-Atlantic waters increased—similarly to, though somewhat less rapidly than, the regional air temperature trends—with variation in the positive rate values between different MAB watersheds (Figure 2). River flows also increased considering the 1979–2013 period as a whole. Based on linear trends estimated from the USGS discharge data, major freshwater river inflow rates to the LIS and NYNJH increased significantly: the Connecticut River at Thompsonville (USGS station

ID 01184000) by 17%—the Connecticut River contributes about 75% of total freshwater flow into LIS—the Housatonic River at Stevenson (USGS station ID 01205500) by 21%, and the Hudson River at Green Island by 33% (USGS station ID 01358000). The completed daily time series of estimated river flows and temperatures from 1979 to 2013 were used as distributed discharge forcing in the NYHOPS 3D hindcast. Ungauged tributaries in NYHOPS are included through basin-area scaling of observed hydrographs from proximal gauged rivers. Finally, distributed end-of-pipe Point Source forcing is also included in NYHOPS model runs based on monthly climatologies of waste water treatment plant effluent and power plant intake/outfall pairs [14].

The model hindcast simulation period started in 1979 and completed in 2013. The first two years were considered spin-up years for 3D hydrodynamics. Therefore, for consistency, results will be presented from 1981 on. This hypothesis was tested in LIS by considering different initial conditions updated every five years from the hindcast. It was found that the NYHOPS solution for T and S within the LIS estuary would converge well within two years from initiation.

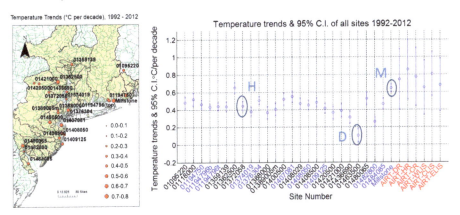

Figure 2. Linear temperature trends (°C per decade) for different NYHOPS river stations between 1992 and 2012 shown in the Mid-Atlantic Region map. The trend over the same time period at the LIS basin near Millstone, CT is also shown for comparison ("M" in the insert to the right). Also highlighted are the Hudson River at Poughkeepsie ("H") and the Delaware River at Trenton, NJ ("D"). Monthly NARR-based, watershed-area-averaged, surface air temperature linear trends are also included in the right panel as "AIRT-w" where watershed $w \in$ [DR, HR, CR, WLIS, CLIS, ELIS] = [Delaware River, Hudson River, Connecticut River, Western LIS, Central LIS, Eastern LIS]. 95% confidence intervals are included as vertical bars, with central estimates shown as circles.

The NYHOPS model's application to hindcast total water level, and 3D water temperature and salinity conditions in its region over three decades was validated extensively against various available observational datasets. Hourly total water levels collected by the National Ocean Service (NOS) at 12 coastal stations within the NYHOPS domain between 1979 and 2013 were used to quantify the model's performance to storm surge after subtraction of the NOS-predicted astronomical tide (Figure 3a). Near-surface and near-bottom T and S grab samples taken with variable frequency—weekly to biweekly, and mostly during summer—from a New York City Department of Environmental Protection (NYC DEP) boat between 1981 and 2012 were used to quantify the skill of the model for T and S at NYC DEP stations in NYNJH (Figure 3b). Vertical CTD casts from cruise surveys conducted for the Long Island Sound Study between 1991 and 2012 as provided by the Connecticut Department of Energy and Environmental Protection (CT DEEP) were used to quantify the skill of the model for T and S in LIS (Figure 3c). Near-bottom temperatures collected on a regular grid that covers most of the LIS bottom by CT DEEP fisheries as part of the Long Island Sound Trawl Survey between 1992 and 2013 were used to test whether the model's skill in simulating bottom water temperature showed signs of drift over the years in LIS (Figure 3d). Finally, an observations-based monthly three-dimensional temperature and salinity climatology dataset called MOCHA version-2 created at Rutgers University in New Jersey (http://tds.marine.rutgers.edu/thredds/catalog/other/climatology/mocha/catalog.html; [30] as updated in MOCHA's 2nd version in 2012) was used to quantify the skill of the NYHOPS hydrodynamic model for *T* and *S* against climatology. MOCHA is a three-dimensional climatological analysis of the temperature and salinity, with a 0.05 degree (~5 km) grid in the horizontal and 55 standard depths in the vertical that covers the MAB, from 45° N to 32° N, 77° W to 64° W. It is derived from all in situ data available from the NODC World Ocean Database 2005 and the NOAA North East Fisheries Science Center database. Comparisons to MOCHA were only made in LIS as the NYNJH is not well resolved in its grid.

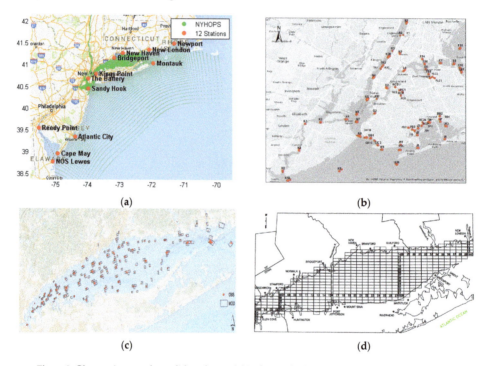

Figure 3. Observations used to validate the model in this study. (**a**) 12 NOS coastal stations; (**b**) NYC DEP Harbor Survey stations throughout the years; (**c**) Long Island Sound Study cruise stations through the years; (**d**) Long Island Trawl Survey Site grid.

Adopting NOS guidelines and prior literature used for validating the operational NYHOPS forecast model [11,15,16,31], the following metrics were used to quantify model skill in the Results section:

- Bias or mean error, *M.E.*: The mean error between model and observations.
- *RMSE*: The square root of the average error between model and observations squared.
- R-square, R^2: The square of the correlation coefficient between model and observations.
- Willmott Skill or Index of Agreement, *W.I.* [32]: A non-dimensional measure of how close the model's results are to observations. Values are between 0 and 1, with 1 being a perfect "skill core."
- Central frequency of error, *C.F.*: The percent of errors that are below a given threshold that is considered high for operational use. The larger the *C.F.*, the better the model. NOS usually

considers a *C.F.* $\geq$ 90% as accepted model performance against the following thresholds: 15 cm for total water level, 3.0 °C for *T*, and 3.5 psu for *S* [31].

- Taylor diagram, [33]. The Taylor Diagram provides a visual statistical summary of how well the model and observation patterns match each other in terms of their correlation coefficient (*R*), their root mean square error (*RMSE*), and their standard deviation (σ).

- Brier Skill Score, *B.S.S.* [34]: The Brier Skill Score essentially compares the magnitude of the difference between a model (NYHOPS here) and observations to that achieved by a reference model (the monthly MOCHA climatology here). The *B.S.S.* is written as

$$BSS = 1 - \frac{1}{N_i} \sum_{j=1}^{N_i} \left(d_{i,j} - p_{i,j} \right)^2 / \frac{1}{N_i} \sum_{j=1}^{N_i} \left(d_{i,j} - r_{i,j} \right)^2 \tag{1}$$

where the vector $d_{i,j}$ contains the $j = 1, 2, \ldots, N_j$ measurements (in situ observations). Similarly, $p_{i,j}$ are the model predictions at the same time and location of the data, $d_{i,j}$, and the vector $r_{i,j}$ contains the predictions of the reference climatology (MOCHA here). *BSS* compares the ratio of the variance in the observations not explained by the model to that not explained by the reference climatology. If *BSS* > 0, then the model is in better agreement with the data than the reference model. Conversely, if *BSS* < 0, it is not as good.

NYHOPS model results were interpolated from the native NYHOPS grid to the location and time of individual observations, before making comparisons. It is important to note that there are always discrepancies in the observations due not only to the precision of the instruments and analyses methods, but also due to the difference in the property simulated (the average over a model cell's volume and output time step) and that measured (sometimes a few samples from a bottle). Even a perfect model, therefore, should not be expected to have *BSS* = 1, (nor will *W.I.* and R^2 be equal to unity for that matter). Given however the comparison to average climatology, *BSS* for a skillful model should be consistently higher than 0, and hopefully closer to unity. Finally, binned histograms of model errors against observations were also used to show uncertainty in model results, and whether that uncertainty grew or decreased over the hindcast years.

3. Results

The model's grand-mean temperature and salinity bias against all Long Island Sound Study observations in the Sound was found to be 0.18 °C warmer for water temperature, and 1.31 psu saltier for salinity; these biases were assumed constant in time and space and were removed from all raw NYHOPS model gridded time series results. The local tidal correction procedure described in [16] was applied to the raw NYHOPS water level results for the 12 coastal stations. The astronomical tide predicted by NOS at these stations was used in that correction, and then removed from the total water level signals to calculate storm surge. The results used and shown below are after these treatments were put into effect.

3.1. Storm Surge Validation

Figure 4 shows example storm surge results at The Battery, NY, highlighting the storm surge validation that was performed at each of the 12 NOS stations. The highest storm surge (SS) and total water level (TWL) values at The Battery for the 1981–2013 time period shown were simulated by NYHOPS to have occurred during Hurricane Sandy in 2012. Although this is consistent with the observed record, the NARR-forced NYHOPS hindcast under-predicted surge during that storm by about 2 feet or ~20%.

Table 1 lists NYHOPS hindcast performance metrics for TWL and SS using the methods of Georgas and Blumberg [15] against NOS observations at 12 coastal stations. *RMSE* varied between 5.7 cm at Montauk, NY and 14.1 cm at Reedy Point, DE, the latter being in a region (Delaware Bay) not well resolved by the NYHOPS model's horizontal grid. R^2 for TWL that includes astronomical tide varied between 0.95 at Montauk and 0.99 at New Haven, Kings Point, and Bridgeport where the tide range is larger. Excluding astronomical tide, R^2 for SS was lowest where RMSE was highest. In addition to Delaware Bay, this relative degradation in storm surge prediction occurred in west-central LIS at Bridgeport and Kings Point. As expected, *W.I.* and R^2 for SS were positively correlated and showed similar qualitative results. *W.I.* for TWL was higher than 0.98 everywhere (not shown). Similar to the operational NYHOPS forecast validation [16], 8 out of the 12 stations had *C.F.* < 15 cm over 90%, with one more (The Battery, NY) coming also very close at 89.9%. Overall the results of the NYHOPS hindcast for water level and its storm surge component were good, providing confidence that the model was able to reproduce hydrodynamics reasonably well.

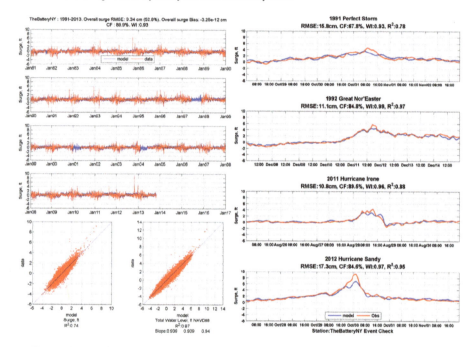

Figure 4. Observed (red) and NYHOPS-simulated (blue) SS (=TWL—astronomical tide) time series for the complete 1981–2013 series (left), as well as four regionally significant events. Correlograms, and their statistics, for both SS and TWL within the complete 1981–2013 period, are also shown on the bottom left.

Table 1. NYHOPS hindcast performance metrics for total water level (TWL) and storm surge (SS) at 12 NOS stations.

Station Name	Dates	RMSE, cm	CF ≤ 15 cm, %	R^2_{SS}	R^2_{TWL}	WI_{SS}
Lewes, DE	1979–2012	8.6	91.9	0.78	0.97	0.94
Reedy Point, DE	1996–2013	14.1	71.7	0.63	0.96	0.88
Cape May, NJ	1979–2013	7.8	94.6	0.80	0.98	0.95
Atlantic City, NJ	1985–2013	6.6	97.2	0.86	0.98	0.96
Sandy Hook, NJ	1979–2013	9.0	91.1	0.76	0.97	0.93
The Battery, NY	1979–2013	9.3	89.9	0.74	0.97	0.93
Kings Point, CT	1998–2013	12.8	76.4	0.65	0.99	0.90
Bridgeport, CT	1996–2013	11.6	79.8	0.65	0.98	0.89

Table 1. *Cont.*

Station Name	Dates	*RMSE*, cm	$CF \leq 15$ cm, %	R^2_{SS}	R^2_{TWL}	WI_{SS}
New Haven, CT	1999–2013	9.1	90.6	0.75	0.99	0.93
Montauk, NY	1979–2013	5.7	98.9	0.85	0.95	0.96
New London, CT	1979–2013	7.1	96.5	0.78	0.96	0.94
Newport, RI	1979–2013	7.4	95.6	0.72	0.97	0.92

3.2. Water Temperature and Salinity Validation

3.2.1. Against New York City Department of Environmental Protection (NYC DEP) Data in the New York/New Jersey Harbor (NYNJH) Estuary

The correlograms shown in the top row of Figure 5 summarize the comparison of the NYHOPS hindcast results against all observations for T and S taken by NYC DEP between 1981 and 2012 at the surface and bottom of the NYNJH at all Harbor Survey stations. For water temperatures, most points fell along the 1:1 line. Although this was also true for S, there were several observations that were not well-captured by the model, with most of these values being over-predicted by the model. Thorough station-by-station and event-by-event study, summarized in the Discussion section and in the Supplementary Material, revealed that these discrepancies are mostly associated with sewer overflow events and other wet-weather non-point source contributions at small tidal tributaries. Nevertheless, considering the whole estuary and NYC DEP dataset, *M.E.* was only −0.1 °C for T and 0.0 psu for S, *RMSE* was 1.2 °C for T and 2.3 psu for S, *W.I.* was 0.99 for T and 0.95 for S, while the central frequency of error was as high as 99% for T and 93% for S, revealing a very skillful hindcast. The Taylor Diagrams on the bottom row of Figure 5 further show that correlation coefficients were higher than 0.9 for both T and S, and reveal that the model was able to capture the range of variation both for T and S as shown by the concentric dotted black circles of standard deviation on the diagram. Further, the model's error standard deviation, approximated by the *RMSE* (also depicted with the green circles in the Taylor Diagram), was overall smaller than the standard deviation of the signal it simulated.

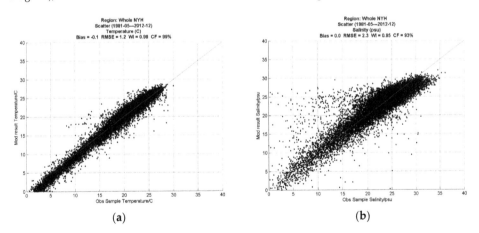

(a) **(b)**

Figure 5. *Cont.*

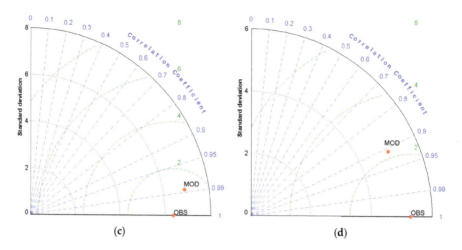

(c)   (d)

Figure 5. Correlograms (**a** and **b**), and Taylor Diagrams (**c** and **d**), summarizing the comparison between the NYHOPS results and NYC DEP Harbor Survey observations for T (**a,c**) and S (**b,d**). The Taylor Diagrams summarize *RMSE* (dotted green circles with the observations "OBS" as origin), correlation coefficient (dotted blue radials with 0 origin), and standard deviation (black dotted circles with 0 origin).

Figure 6 shows example time series for simulated surface and bottom *T* and *S* against observed surface and bottom *T* and *S* at Harbor Survey station N5, the station nearest to The Battery, NY. The model is seen to capture well the ranges and seasonal signals in both T and S and shows good skill in responding to events in the record. Surface measurements taken at station N5 in the early 1980s, mid-1990s, and 2002, revealed somewhat higher salinities during peak ocean salt intrusion summer seasons than those simulated by the model. Higher salinities were also observed but not simulated in 2002 near the bottom at station N5.

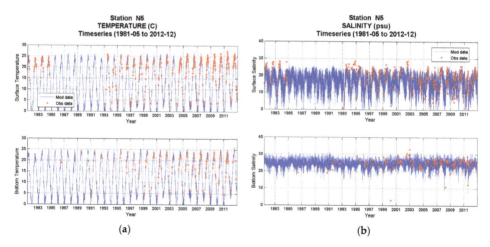

(a)   (b)

Figure 6. Time series of observer (red) and simulated (blue) *T* (**a**) and *S* (**b**) at NYC DEP Harbor Survey station N5 near The Battery, NY.

3.2.2. Against Connecticut Department of Energy and Environmental Protection (CT DEEP) Data in Long Island Sound (LIS)

Figure 7 shows correlograms summarizing the comparison of the NYHOPS hindcast results against all CTD casts during CT DEEP Long Island Sound Study cruises between 2001 and 2012. Results are summarized by LIS management basin. Most points fell along the 1:1 line, and the model results throughout LIS were overall reasonable. For *T*, *RMSE* was close to 1 °C in all three basins, *W.I.* was greater than 0.99, and model errors were less than 3 °C over 99% of the time (*C.F.* ≥ 99%, Figure 7). Salinity *RMSE* was 0.5 psu in the western and central management basins, but reached 1.0 psu in the eastern basin, largely because of a residual *M.E.* contribution there of 0.6 psu that was not found for the other two basins. Although the central frequency was greater than 99% for salinity in all three basins, the *W.I.* was significantly lower in the eastern basin too, at 0.77. It appears that the removal of the grand-mean bias of 1.31 psu from all raw NYHOPS hindcast results made the eastern basin of LIS slightly fresher than it should. This result will be discussed further in the Discussion section.

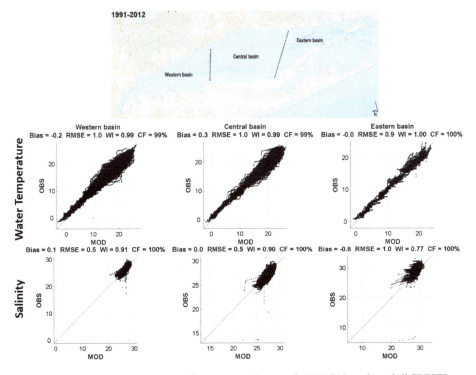

Figure 7. Correlograms, summarizing the comparison between the NYHOPS results and all CT DEEP Long Island Sound Study observations taken between 1991 and 2012 for *T* and *S* at the three LIS management basins.

3.2.3. Against MOCHA Climatology in LIS

Figure 8 compares the NYHOPS model's performance to hindcast LISS water temperatures and salinities against MOCHA monthly climatology. The top panels of the Figure compare overall performance throughout the LISS record using Taylor Diagrams, while year-to-year relative performance between 1991 and 2012 is depicted in the lower panel as a *B.S.S.* time series.

The Taylor diagrams show that the NYHOPS model ("M") is closer to the observed conditions ("O") compared to the MOCHA climatology ("C") for the correlation coefficient and the RMSE

(Figure 8). Thus the dynamic model exhibits significantly higher correlation and lower error in describing the data. Note that the correlation coefficient scale is logarithmic and that the correlation between the NYHOPS model and the observations is significantly higher especially for salinity where it grew from less than 0.7 (C) to over 0.9 (M). The standard deviation captured by the observation-based monthly MOCHA climatology appears closer to the one based on LISS observations than the NYHOPS model, consistently with the Taylor Diagrams for NY Harbor (Figure 5): In both the NYNJH and LIS, the model seems to somewhat over-predict the overall observed range in water temperature and under-predict the overall range in salinity. Even so, the NYHOPS model was overall significantly closer to observations that the climatology: the Taylor dot for the model (M) is closer to the Taylor dot for observations (O) than the Taylor dot for MOCHA climatology (C).

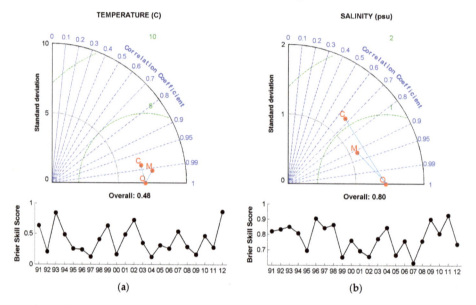

Figure 8. Taylor Diagrams and time series of *B.S.S.*, comparing the skill of the NYHOPS hydrodynamic model (M) to the climatological MOCHA model (C) in describing CT DEEP Long Island Sound Study observations (O) taken between 1991 and 2012 for *T* (a) and *S* (b) in LIS. Taylor Diagrams summarize RMSE (dotted green circles with the observations "O" as origin), correlation coefficient (dotted blue radials with 0 origin), and standard deviation (black dotted circles with 0 origin).

The lower panels in Figure 8 also show that the hydrodynamic NYHOPS model was a better predictor of the year-to-year water temperature and salinity observed in LIS than the static observation-based MOCHA climatology: During the whole LISS observation record from 1991 to 2012, the relative *B.S.S.* was always higher than 0, meaning NYHOPS had better skill than climatology each year. Peaks close to the optimal 1.0 value in relative *BSS* are seen in some years that were anomalously cold or hot compared to climatology, such as during 1993 and 2012, respectively. During these years the monthly mean MOCHA climatology would not have been a good descriptor of what happened in LIS, unlike the NYHOPS model that included three-hourly heat flux forcing based on NARR. Given the large seasonal signal in temperature causing higher correlation coefficients even between MOCHA climatology and observations, the relative *B.S.S.* for water temperature ranged more from year to year than the one for salinity, as seen in the smaller *y*-axis for salinity *B.S.S.* (Figure 8). Similarly, the 1991–2012 mean *B.S.S.* for water temperature (0.48) was also smaller than the one for salinity (0.80). For salinity, the *B.S.S.* ranged largely between 0.6 and 0.9, since the NYHOPS hydrodynamic model that included daily freshwater flows was, as expected, much more able to reproduce spatiotemporal salinity variations compared to the monthly climatological means of MOCHA. No statistically significant trend was found for either water temperature or salinity *B.S.S.* time series.

4. Discussion

The skill of the comprehensively-forced multi-decadal NYHOPS Hindcast presented in the previous paragraph was overall excellent: across all stations considered, the average Willmott Index of Agreement for storm surge (tidal departure) alone against NOS hourly observations was 0.93, (9 cm Root-Mean-Square-Error, *RMSE*, 90% of errors less than 15 cm). For water temperature against available NYC DEP and CTDEEP observations, *W.I.* was 0.99 (1.1 °C *RMSE*, 99% of errors less than 3 °C). For salinity against NYC DEP and CTDEEP observations, *W.I.* was 0.86 (1.8 psu *RMSE*, 96% of all errors less than 3.5 psu).

For water levels, model results were reasonable overall, though model errors against hourly observations increased as expected during major storm surge events and Atlantic hurricanes (Figure 9); Figure 9 can also be compared to [16] (Figure 7) and [11] (Figure 5). This error increase with surge magnitude is in part due to the resolution in time (3-hourly) and space (36 km) of the NARR dataset used to provide winds and barometric pressure to the NYHOPS model. Mesinger et al. in 2006 [21] stated expectations for relatively poorer NARR skill during Atlantic Hurricanes. This may in part be due to a presumed increase of the number of observations fed into NARR during the reanalysis process in later years compared to the beginning of the NARR record in 1979. Storm surges during some early events, the Nor'Easter of March 1984 and Hurricane Gloria in 1985 being examples, were under-predicted. The storm surge from the quick transit of Hurricane Bob that devastated New England in 1991 was also not captured. For example, the surge built from 0 to over 5 feet in 4 h at Newport, RI, but the 3-hourly, 36 km NARR record was not able to capture that hurricane well.

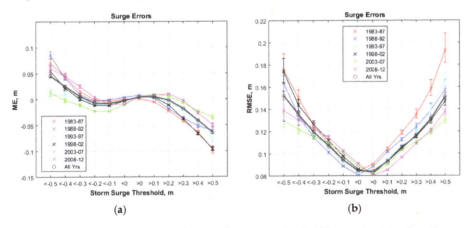

Figure 9. (a) M.E. and (b) RMSE as a function of storm surge threshold for negative (−) and positive (+) surges between different 5-year periods in the NYHOPS hindcast.

The residual water level errors during significant storm surge events appeared to decrease toward the second half of the simulation (Figure 9), even though these later years included some of the highest storm surge peaks in the region's history during Hurricanes Irene and Sandy. It is also important to note however that the NARR-forced NYHOPS still under-predicted Hurricane Sandy's peak surge at The Battery by ~2 feet, or ~20% of the observed ~10 feet surge (Figure 4). During the actual event in October 2012 the NYHOPS OFS forecast forced by the deterministic North American Mesoscale (NAM) model at 12 km resolution under-predicted Sandy's surge at The Battery by approximately 3 feet, while it was within 1 foot when, after the fact, the same model was forced with a more accurate forecast [9] or a high-fidelity reanalysis [10].

Another contributing reason to the apparent increase in the model's storm surge simulation skill over time may be due to changes in bathymetry and coastline over time, or other morphodynamic or anthropogenic (targeted channel dredging) changes not accounted for in the NYHOPS historic hindcast: the model's bathymetry is held fixed, and is based on a variety of datasets described in Georgas [14], meant to represent the configuration of the MAB estuaries in the beginning decade of the 21st century. Blumberg and Georgas [13] showed that water levels are quite sensitive to bathymetric uncertainties in the region. Further research is needed in creating a quantitative timeline for such changes, so that future model run versions can account for them.

Table 2 summarizes some skill metrics of the NYHOPS historic hindcast against water temperature and salinity datasets at different estuarine regions, and compares that skill to the overall skill of the NYHOPS OFS forecasts from Georgas [14] and Georgas and Blumberg [15]. The multi-decadal NYHOPS hindcast appears to have comparable or better skill than the validated NYHOPS OFS. Note however that the periods compared and the stations used to aggregate errors are not the same, nor is the forcing methodology: the NYHOPS Hindcast used estimates of daily river flows based on observed hydrographs by USGS and three-hourly heat fluxes based on the 36 km NARR, while the NYHOPS deterministic OFS used six-hourly NOAA AHPS river discharge forecasts and three-hourly heat fluxes based on the NAM 12 km forecasts.

Table 2. NYHOPS Hindcast Performance metrics summary for water temperature (*T*) and salinity (*S*) at regions within LIS and NYNJH.

Water Temperature	Region	Bias, °C	RMSE, °C	W.I.$_T$	CF ≤ 3 °C, %
Long Island Sound	Western Basin	−0.2	1.0	0.99	99
CT DEEP	Central Basin	+0.3	1.0	0.99	99
LISS Survey	Eastern Basin	+0.0	0.9	1.00	100
	Western LIS	−0.4	1.1	0.99	98
New York Harbor	Upper East River	−0.3	1.1	0.99	99
NYC DEP	Inner Harbor	+0.0	1.3	0.99	98
Surface/Bottom data	Lower NY Bay	+0.1	1.3	0.99	98
	Jamaica Bay	−0.2	1.2	0.99	98
NYHOPS OFS [1]	NYHOPS [2]	+0.0	1.4	0.98	95
Salinity	**Region**	**Bias, psu**	**RMSE, psu**	**W.I.$_S$**	**CF ≤ 3.5 psu, %**
Long Island Sound	Western Basin	+0.1	0.5	0.91	100
CT DEEP	Central Basin	+0.0	0.5	0.90	100
LISS Survey	Eastern Basin	−0.6	1.0	0.77	100
	Western LIS	+0.5	1.3	0.77	99
New York Harbor	Upper East River	+0.8	2.2	0.94	93
NYC DEP	Inner Harbor	−0.1	2.8	0.93	89
Surface/Bottom data	Lower NY Bay	−0.9	2.2	0.91	91
	Jamaica Bay	+0.0	1.8	0.71	96
NYHOPS OFS [1]	NYHOPS [2]	+0.0	2.8	0.77	87

[1] Georgas and Blumberg [15]; [2] All stations considered within the NYHOPS model domain, 2007–2009.

Overall hindcast results are well within NOAA standards and skill metrics for T and S (*CF* > 90%; Table 2). Both water temperatures and salinities were very well predicted. Given the greater seasonality in estuarine temperature compared to that of salinity, and the three-hourly meteorological forcing compared to the daily hydrological forcing, the relative *RMSE* (*RMSE* divided by the expected range as in Georgas [14]), was higher for salinity than temperature, at an across-station median of 30.9% versus 4.7%, respectively (Figure 10). Figure 10 highlights spatial differences in model skill (as described by the relative *RMSE*) within NYNJH, by comparing the quartiles of relative RMSE between the hindcast time series and observed time series at NYC DEP Harbor Survey stations. Even though the Hudson River is one of the most dynamic regions in the estuary, it is also one of the best predicted: larger circles in Figure 10 show that the relative *RMSE* is at its lowest quantile for both T and S there. On the other hand, the model had less skill simulating T and S within some small tributaries such as Newtown Creek and Flushing Creek in the lower and upper East River, respectively, and several tributaries in Jamaica Bay (Figure 10), especially for salinity. These tributaries receive Storm Water flows and occasional Combined Sewer Overflows from the NYC drainage system, non-point sources that are presently not directly simulated by the NYHOPS model but rather estimated as ungagged watersheds. The model's skill there would potentially benefit greatly through coupling to hydraulic forecast models developed for NYC DEP, although, for a multi-decadal hindcast, changes in the City's drainage system over time may also need to be accounted for: upgrades to two-times dry-weather-flow by the City's treatment plants, sewer separation in some areas, and increase in retention storage in others, for example, affect the spatial and temporal distribution of storm water and combined sewage discharged from the hundreds of the City's interconnected pipes and outfalls.

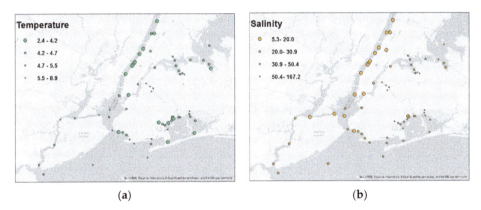

Figure 10. Quartiles of relative *RMSE* for (**a**) water temperature and (**b**) salinity in the NYNJH for the NYHOPS hindcast at NYC DEP Harbor Survey stations between 1981 and 2012.

The model's dynamics were able to capture more variability than the observation-based MOCHA v2 climatology as evident in relative Brier Skill Scores (*BSS*) that were positive: 0.48 for temperature and 0.8 for salinity sound-wide. The only exception was for salinity in the Sound's eastern basin, where the period-average relative *BSS* was −0.29, indicating that the MOCHA v2 climatology had higher skill than the debiased NYHOPS model there (not shown). Even for that region's salinity, however, the model's total RMSE was only 1 psu, of which the remaining bias was 0.6 psu, the average index of agreement 0.77, and the model's results were less than 3.5 psu away from observed more than 99% of the time. As a comparison, the NOS C.F. standard for simulated salinity is so that errors should be within 3.5 psu for at least 90% of the time [31]. It is important to note here that results in the Eastern LIS basin as well as the Lower NY Bay appear to have been degraded after debiasing (Table 2). The salinity bias correction in the NYHOPS model is consistent with, though slightly smaller than, earlier models in the region: Both the LISS 2.0 and SWEM models used climatological boundary conditions but subtracted 2.0 psu. It is possible that the SODA climatology is biased high for salinity, but the results from the two regions closest to the open boundary in Table 2 may indicate otherwise. Also, like earlier models, the NYHOPS Hindcast does not include the precipitation-evaporation imbalance over the Sound's waters, submarine groundwater discharge, or other aquifer-related freshwater sources. Although these diffuse sources have been estimated to contribute a total freshwater flow over the Sound that is an order of magnitude smaller than the Connecticut River [35,36], they may in any case contribute somewhat to the high-salinity bias in the models. Further research is needed to quantify these contributions, and explore the reason for that consistent bias in models of the region.

A very important finding of the research is that the NYHOPS model's skill in simulating water temperature, validated against historic data from the LIS bottom trawl survey, did not drift over the years. The error histograms and PDFs included in Figure 11 for four consecutive periods during both the (a) spring and (b) fall survey periods, show that there was no clear indication of an earlier period having greater error than a later one, or vice versa, unlike what was shown earlier for storm surge. A similar analysis against NYC DEP Harbor Survey data in NYNJH for subsequent five-year periods from 1983 to 2012 also did not indicate drift in skill for surface or bottom T nor S (Supplementary Material, Pages 10–18). This is a significant and encouraging finding for multi-decadal model applications used to identify and research climatic trends and causalities. Figure 11 also shows that the median error in simulated bottom temperature in LIS was low for both the spring (+0.1 °C) and the fall (−0.5 °C) surveys, with only few predictions being further than ±1.5 °C from observed samples.

The lack of model drift was further supported through comparison of the simulated water temperature time series to the one and only long-term water temperature record for Long Island Sound taken at a near-surface location just outside the Millstone Power Plant at Millstone, CT (Figure 12). The central estimate for the linear trend of the observations at Millstone (0.439 °C/decade) was somewhat higher than the linear trend of the NYHOPS hindcast there (0.313 °C/decade), and the simulated annual range was somewhat higher than observed (Figure 12), however the two trends were not different at the 95% confidence level. Figure 12 shows that water temperature was simulated very well throughout the hindcast period. It also shows clearly that temperatures have been increasing at the site and that 2012 was the warmest year in both the simulated and observed record.

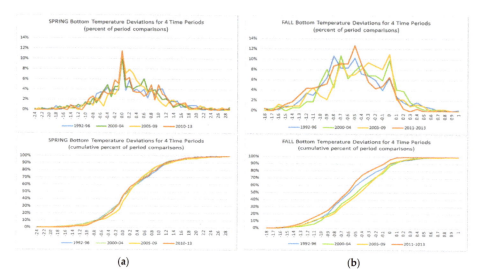

Figure 11. Error histograms (**top**) and probability density functions (**bottom**) between NYHOPS Hindcast bottom temperature results and LIS Trawl Survey bottom temperature samples for four subsequent spring (**a**) and fall (**b**) survey periods from 1992 to 2013.

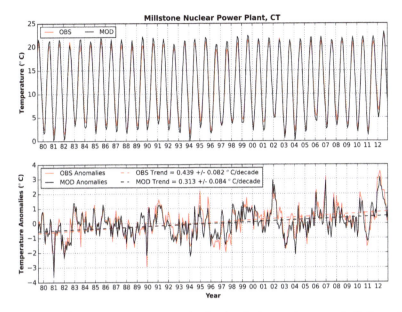

Figure 12. Monthly mean water temperature (**top**) and water temperature anomaly (**bottom**; after removal of seasonal signal) time series near the Millstone Nuclear Power Plant outfall location at Millstone, CT, as observed (OBS), and simulated (MOD).

NYHOPS model results were then used to quantify linear, water temperature, salinity, and stratification trends for LIS in the hindcast period between 1981 and 2013. Spatially averaged trends over the three Long Island Sound management basins (east, central, west), and the Sound as a whole are shown in Figure 13, with confidence intervals, while the spatial variation on the NYHOPS grid cell level is seen in Figure 14. Statistically significant warming and freshening trends (Figure 13), non-stationary trends in volumetric fluxes across the western and eastern basins of the Sound (Figure 15), and an associated statistically significant increase in stratification (Figures 13 and 14) have all occurred within the hindcast period. Based on the NYHOPS hindcast, in the Long Island Sound basin, surface air temperatures, contributing river temperatures, and receiving LIS-basin-wide water temperatures (0.34 ± 0.08 °C per decade) have all seen significant increases between 1981 and 2013, more so on the shallower north shore and western Sound than the south shore similar to [37]. The basin wide average is comparable to the 0.30 °C per decade rate reported for SST at the Gulf of Maine [3]. The increase in major freshwater rivers mentioned in Section 2 may have led to the Sound overall becoming somewhat fresher (a statistically significant trend of 0.12 ± 0.05 psu/decade), especially near river mouths at the surface (Figure 14), increasing stratification and changing long-term volumetric transport fluxes in the basin in a statistically significant, nonstationary way (Figure 15). Further research is needed to deduce whether these trends are expected to continue into the future.

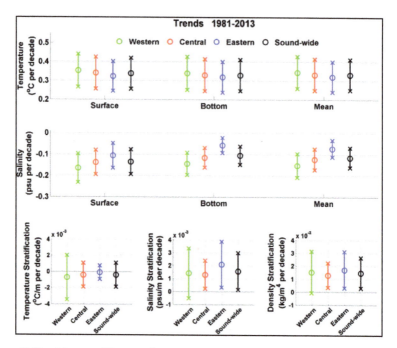

Figure 13. Decadal-averaged linear trends in water temperature (**top**), salinity (**middle**), and stratification (**bottom**), for the three LIS basins, and the whole Sound within the 1981–2013 NYHOPS Hindcast period. Circles show central estimates while vertical bars show the 95% confidence intervals.

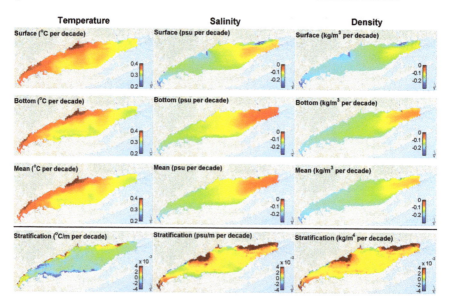

Figure 14. Spatial map of locally computed decadal-averaged linear trends in water temperature (**left**), salinity (**center**), density (**right**), and stratification (**bottom**) within the 1981–2013 NYHOPS Hindcast period. Surface and bottom are from the surface-most and bottom-most NYHOPS cells, mean is for the vertically averaged trends, and stratification is computed from surface to local bottom.

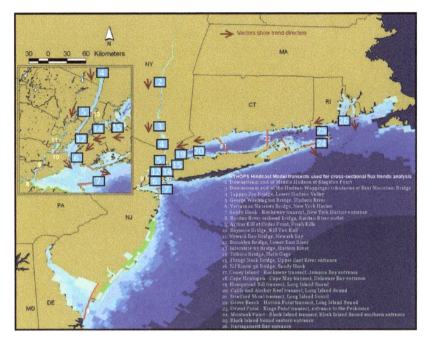

Figure 15. NYHOPS model transects across which linear trends in volumetric cross-channel transport were quantified. Transects for which statistically significant trends in volumetric fluxes between 1981 and 2013 were calculated (at the 95% confidence level) are highlighted with blue squares.

5. Conclusions

The NYHOPS model's application to hindcast storm surge and 3D water temperature and salinity conditions in its region over three-and-a-half decades was validated against observations from multiple agencies, as well as climatology: the average index of agreement for storm surge alone was 0.93 (9 cm *RMSE*, 90% of errors less than 15 cm); for water temperature, it was 0.99 (1.1 °C *RMSE*, 99% of errors less than 3 °C); and for salinity, it was 0.86 (1.8 psu *RMSE*, 96% of errors less than 3.5 psu). The model's skill in simulating bottom water temperature, validated against historic data from the Long Island Sound bottom trawl survey, did not drift over the years, a significant and encouraging finding for multi-decadal model applications used to identify climatic trends. However, the validation revealed residual biases in some areas, including small tributaries that receive urban discharges from the NYC drainage network. With regard to the validation of storm surge at coastal stations, both the considerable strengths and remaining limitations of the use of NARR to force such a model application were discussed.

Through the comprehensively forced, and herein extensively validated, multi-decadal simulation for Long Island Sound's physical environment performed using Stevens Institute of Technology's NYHOPS hindcast model, temperature increases in Long Island Sound over the past three-and-a-half decades have been confirmed and have been found to be statistically significant. The linear trends have also been found to be quite high (0.34 ± 0.08 °C per decade) and comparable to ones in the Gulf of Maine [3]. Further research is needed in identifying the cause for this increase in temperatures. Source allocation and further sensitivity runs using the NYHOPS model may aid in testing hypotheses in the future.

After extensive model validation and debiasing, an online THREDDS Data Server (http://colossus.dl.stevens-tech.edu/thredds/catalog.html) was set up to serve the NYHOPS model's results in NetCDF format over the web using the OPENDAP protocol, enabling similar analyses through open access to daily averaged or monthly averaged time series for all the gridded hindcast physical variables in or over the NYHOPS region that includes NYNJH and LIS.

Fisheries management has traditionally sought to reduce harvesting levels in response to low stock biomass, in its goal to maintain long-term fishery productivity [38]. More recently, accounting for non-stationary environmental forcing has started being considered in stock assessment and management ([39], pp. 131–147) with the realization that a failure to account for shifts in climate that can alter population dynamics can lead to stock collapse as with the Gulf of Maine cod fishery [3]. This progress has been facilitated by new population dynamics models that consider temperature-dependencies and an improved understanding in climate-fisheries teleconnections brought about through advances in environmental modeling.

NYHOPS Hindcast results are in demand to support this kind of fisheries research through coupling to habitat suitability indices, population models, water quality models, or to provide boundary conditions to higher resolution embayment or tributary circulation models. The datasets are also presently used to inform ongoing research in climate teleconnections and ecosystem change through exploratory statistical analyses linking regional fisheries abundance to global climate indices. The authors are encouraged by the early interest in these datasets.

Simulated climatologies (mean simulated climate conditions averaged over the three decades of the NYHOPS hindcast period) for two- and three-dimensional fields such as water temperatures and salinities, were also generated, and included in THREDDS. Included on the same THREDDS server is a "daily anomaly" dataset, comparing the latest operational forecast of the NYHOPS OFS model to the 1981–2013 debiased daily climatology, so that interested parties can see how different yesterday and the next three days are predicted to be from the climatological average, enabling near-term tracking of anomalous patterns in Long Island Sound. Fish-surveying strategies may also be improved through the use of the NYHOPS model forecasts: NYSDEC and NMFS routinely already use the model's predictions for adaptive sampling in the Hudson River estuary and the Mid-Atlantic Bight Apex. Visualization is easy with off-the-shelf free software, such as NASA's Panoply, accessing the datasets over the web.

Supplementary Materials: The following are available online at www.mdpi.com/2077-1312/4/3/48/s1, Comprehensive Validation and LIS Trend Presentation.

Acknowledgments: Financial support was provided by the US EPA Long Island Sound Study and NY and CT Sea Grants through the project R/CE-33-NYCT. Long-term NYHOPS model support has been provided through the NOAA Integrated Ocean Observing System program and many other projects. The authors appreciate the help of CT DEEP personnel and Nicholas Kim from HDR. Inc. in providing CT DEEP and NYC DEP temperature and salinity observations used in this work.

Author Contributions: Nickitas Georgas, Penny Howell, and Vince Saba conceived and designed the experiments. Yu Jiang, Larry Yin, and Nickitas Georgas performed the experiments. Larry Yin, Yifan Wang, Penny Howell, Yu Jiang, Bin Wen, and Nickitas Georgas analyzed the data; Philip Orton contributed the SNAP grid and provided model input guidance; Nickitas Georgas wrote the paper.

Conflicts of Interest: The authors declare no conflict of interest. The founding sponsors had no role in the design of the study; in the collection, analyses, or interpretation of data; in the writing of the manuscript, and in the decision to publish the results.

References

1. NCDC. Climate at a Glance. Time Series. Available online: http://www.ncdc.noaa.gov/cag/time-series/ (accessed on 15 July 2016).
2. United Nations. Paris Agreement. United Nations Treaty Collection. Available online: https://treaties. un.org/pages/ViewDetails.aspx?src=TREATY&mtdsg_no=XXVII-7-d&chapter=27&lang=en (accessed on 15 July 2016).
3. Pershing, A.; Alexander, M.A.; Hernandez, C.M.; Kerr, L.A.; le Bris, A.; Mills, K.E.; Nye, J.A.; Record, N.R.; Scannell, H.A.; Scott, J.D.; et al. Slow Adaptation in the Face of Rapid Warming Leads to Collapse of the Gulf of Maine Cod Fishery. *Science* **2015**. [CrossRef] [PubMed]

4. Dominion Resource Services. Monitoring the Marine Environment of Long Island Sound at Millstone Power Station. Annual Report 2002. Millstone Environmental Laboratory, April 2003. Available online: http://pbadupws.nrc.gov/docs/ML0409/ML040930039.pdf (accessed on 12 August 2016).
5. Nye, J.A.; Link, J.S.; Hare, J.A.; Overholtz, W.J. Changing spatial distribution of fish stocks in relation to climate and population size on the Northeast United States continental shelf. *Mar. Ecol. Prog. Ser.* **2009**, *393*, 111–129. [CrossRef]
6. Howell, P.; Auster, P. Phase shift in an estuarine finfish community associated with warming temperatures. *Mar. Coast. Fish. Dyn. Manag. Ecosyst. Sci.* **2012**, *4*, 481–495. [CrossRef]
7. Kleisner, K.M.; Fogarty, M.J.; McGee, S.; Barnett, A.; Fratantoni, P.; Greene, J.; Hare, J.A.; Lucey, S.M.; McGuire, C.; Odell, J.; et al. The Effects of Sub-Regional Climate Velocity on the Distribution and Spatial Extent of Marine Species Assemblages. *PLoS ONE* **2016**. [CrossRef] [PubMed]
8. Georgas, N.; Howell, P.; Saba, V.; Schulte, J.; Blumberg, A.F.; Orton, P.; Yin, L.; Jiang, Y.; Wang, Y. Analyzing History to Project and Manage the Future: Simulating the Effects of Climate on Long Island Sound's Physical Environment and Living Marine Resources. Final Report. NOAA Sea Grant Publications, Long Island Sound Study, 2016. Available online: http://longislandsoundstudy.net/wp-content/uploads/2013/08/Georgas-et-al-R-CE-33-NYCT-CR-Final-Report.pdf (accessed on 15 July 2016).
9. Georgas, N.; Orton, P.; Blumberg, A.F.; Cohen, L.; Zarrilli, D.; Yin, L. The impact of tidal phase on Hurricane Sandy's flooding around New York City and Long Island Sound. *J. Extreme Events* **2014**. [CrossRef]
10. Marsooli, R.; Orton, P.M.; Georgas, N.; Blumberg, A.F. Three-dimensional hydrodynamic modeling of coastal flood mitigation by wetlands. *Coast. Eng.* **2016**, *111*, 83–94. [CrossRef]
11. Georgas, N.; Blumberg, A.F.; Herrington, T.; Wakeman, T.; Saleh, F.; Runnels, D.; Jordi, A.; Ying, K.; Yin, L.; Ramaswamy, V.; et al. The Stevens Flood Advisory System: Operational H3-E flood forecasts for the greater New York/New Jersey metropolitan region. *Int. J. Saf. Secur. Eng.* **2016**, *6*, 1–15.
12. Georgas, N.; Blumberg, A.F.; Herrington, T. An operational coastal wave forecasting model for New Jersey and long Island waters. *Shore Beach* **2007**, *75*, 30–35.
13. Blumberg, A.F.; Georgas, N. Quantifying Uncertainty in Estuarine and Coastal Ocean Circulation Modeling. *J. Hydraul. Eng.* **2008**, *134*, 403–415. [CrossRef]
14. Georgas, N. Establishing Confidence in Marine Forecast Systems: The Design of a High Fidelity Marine Forecast Model for the NY/NJ Harbor Estuary and Its Adjoining Coastal Waters. Ph.D. Thesis, Stevens Institute of Technology, Hoboken, NJ, USA, August 2010; p. 272. Available online: http://web.stevens.edu/ses/documents/fileadmin/documents/pdf/PhD-dissertation_signed-o.pdf (accessed on 15 July 2016).
15. Georgas, N.; Blumberg, A.F. Establishing confidence in marine forecast systems: The design and skill assessment of the New York harbor observation and prediction system, Version 3 (NYHOPS v3). In Proceedings of the 11th International Conference in Estuarine and Coastal Modeling (ECM11), Seattle, WA, USA, 4–6 November 2010; pp. 660–685.
16. DiLiberto, T.; Colle, B.A.; Georgas, N.; Blumberg, A.F.; Taylor, A.A. Verification of a Multi-Model Storm Surge Ensemble Around New York City and Long Island During the Cool Season. *Weather Forecast.* **2011**, *26*, 922–939. [CrossRef]
17. Orton, P.M.; Georgas, N.; Blumberg, A.F.; Pullen, J. Detailed modeling of recent severe storm tides in estuaries of the New York City region. *J. Geophys. Res.* **2012**, *117*, C09030. [CrossRef]
18. Wilkin, J.L.; Hunter, E.J. An assessment of the skill of real-time models of Mid-Atlantic Bight continental shelf circulation. *J. Geophys. Res. Oceans* **2013**, *118*, 2919–2933. [CrossRef]
19. Blumberg, A.F.; Georgas, N.; Herrington, T.; Yin, L. Street Scale Modeling of Storm Surge Inundation along the New Jersey Hudson River Waterfront. *J. Atmos. Ocean. Technol.* **2015**, *32*, 1486–1497. [CrossRef]
20. Blumberg, A.F.; Mellor, G.L. A description of a three dimensional coastal ocean circulation model. In *Three-Dimensional Coastal Ocean Models*; Heaps, N.S., Ed.; American Geophysical Union: Washington, DC, USA, 1987; Volume 4, pp. 1–16.
21. Mesinger, F.; Dimego, G.; Kalnay, E.; Mitchell, K.; Shafran, P.C.; Ebisuzaki, W.; Jovic, D.; Woollen, J.; Rogers, E.; Berbery, E.H.; et al. North American Regional Reanalysis. *Bull. Am. Meteorol. Soc.* **2006**, *87*, 343–360. [CrossRef]
22. Choi, W.; Keuser, A.; Becker, S. Identification of mid-latitudinal regional and urban temperature variabilities based on regional reanalysis data. *Theor. Appl. Climatol.* **2012**, *107*, 87–98. [CrossRef]

23. Bhushan, S.; Blumberg, A.F.; Georgas, N. Comparisons of NYHOPS Hydrodynamic Model SST Predictions with Satellite Observations in the Hudson River Tidal, Estuarine and Coastal Plume Region. In Proceedings of the 11th International Conference in Estuarine and Coastal Modeling (ECM11), Seattle, WA, USA, 4–6 November 2010; pp. 11–26.

24. Taylor, P.K.; Yelland, M.A. The dependence of sea surface roughness on the height and steepness of the waves. *J. Phys. Oceanogr.* **2001**, *31*, 572–590.

25. Georgas, N. Analyzing History to Project and Manage the Future: Simulating the Effects of Climate on Long Island Sound's Physical Environment and Living Marine Resources. Supplementary Matter to Year 1 Report. Available online: http://www.stevens.edu/ses/documents/fileadmin/documents/pdf/R-CE-33-NYCT%20PR1%20supporting%20year%201%20PR.pdf (accessed on 15 July 2016).

26. Carton, J.A.; Giese, B.S. A reanalysis of ocean climate using Simple Ocean Data Assimilation (SODA). *Mon. Weather Rev.* **2008**, *136*, 2999–3017. [CrossRef]

27. Chassignet, E.P.; Hurlburt, H.E.; Metzger, E.J.; Smedstad, O.M.; Cummings, J.A.; Halliwell, G.R.; Bleck, R.; Baraille, R.; Wallcraft, A.J.; Lozano, C.; et al. US GODAE: Global Ocean Prediction with the HYbrid Coordinate Ocean Model (HYCOM). *Oceanography* **2009**, *22*, 64–75. [CrossRef]

28. Seekell, D.A.; Pace, M.L. Climate change drives warming in the Hudson River estuary, New York (USA). *J. Environ. Monit.* **2011**, *13*, 2321–2327. [CrossRef] [PubMed]

29. Kaushal, S.S.; Likens, G.E.; Jaworski, N.A.; Pace, M.L.; Sides, A.M.; Seekell, D.; Wingate, R.L. Rising stream and river temperatures in the United States. *Front. Ecol. Environ.* **2010**, *8*, 461–466. [CrossRef]

30. Fleming, N.E.; Wilkin, J. MOCHA: A 3-D climatology of the temperature and salinity of the Mid Atlantic Bight. *Eos Trans. AGU* **2010**, *91*, PO35G-08. Available online: http://abstractsearch.agu.org/meetings/2010/OS/PO35G-08.html (accessed on 15 August 2016).

31. NOAA Technical Report NOS CS 17. NOS Standards for Evaluating Operational Nowcast and Forecast Hydrodynamic Model Systems. Available online: www.nauticalcharts.noaa.gov/csdl/publications/TR_NOS-CS17_FY03_Hess_OFS-Standards.pdf (accessed on 12 August 2016).

32. Willmott, C.J. On the validation of models. *Phys. Geogr.* **1981**, *2*, 184–194.

33. Taylor, K.E. Summarizing multiple aspects of model performance in a single diagram. *J. Geophys. Res.* **2001**, *106*, 7183–7192. [CrossRef]

34. Von Storch, H.; Zwiers, F.W. *Statistical Analysis in Climate Research*; Cambridge University Press: Cambridge, UK, 1999; p. 494.

35. O'Donnell, J.; Wilson, R.E.; Lwiza, K.; Whitney, M.M.; Bohlen, W.F.; Codiga, D.; Fribance, D.B.; Fake, T.; Bowman, M.; Varekamp, J. The Physical Oceanography of Long Island Sound. In *Long Island Sound. Prospects for the Urban Sea*; Springer: New York, NY, USA, 2014; pp. 79–158.

36. Garcia-Orellana, J.; Cochran, J.K.; Bokuniewicz, H.; Daniel, J.W.R.; Rodellas, V.; Heilbrun, C. Evaluation of ^{224}Ra as a tracer for submarine groundwater discharge in Long Island Sound (NY). *Geochim. Cosmochim. Acta* **2014**, *141*, 314–330. [CrossRef]

37. Lee, Y.J.; Lwiza, K. Interannual variability of temperature and salinity in shallow water: Long Island Sound, New York. *J. Geophys. Res.* **2005**, *110*, C09022. [CrossRef]

38. Mahon, R.; McConney, P.; Roy, R.N. Governing fisheries as complex adaptive systems. *Mar. Policy* **2008**, *32*, 104–112. [CrossRef]

39. Northeast Fisheries Science Center Reference Document 14-04. 58th Northeast Regional Stock Assessment Workshop (58th SAW) Assessment Report. Available online: http://www.nefsc.noaa.gov/publications/crd/crd1404/crd1404.pdf (accessed on 15 August 2016).

Journal of
*Marine Science
and Engineering*

Article

Performance Assessment of NAMI DANCE in Tsunami Evolution and Currents Using a Benchmark Problem

Deniz Velioglu [1,*]**, Rozita Kian** [2]**, Ahmet Cevdet Yalciner** [3] **and Andrey Zaytsev** [4]

1   Civil Engineering Department, Middle East Technical University, Ankara 06800, Turkey
2   Ocean Engineering Department, University of Rhode Island, Narragansett, RI 02882, USA;
    kian.rozita@gmail.com
3   Civil Engineering Department, Middle East Technical University, Ankara 06800, Turkey;
    yalciner@metu.edu.tr
4   Department of Applied Mathematics, Nizhny Novgorod State Technical University,
    Nizhny Novgorod 603950, Russia; aizaytsev@mail.ru
*   Correspondence: denizcivil@gmail.com; Tel.: +90-541-211-10-49

Academic Editor: Richard P. Signell
Received: 5 July 2016; Accepted: 12 August 2016; Published: 18 August 2016

Abstract: Numerical modeling of tsunami evolution, propagation, and inundation is complicated due to numerous parameters involved in the phenomenon. It is important to assess the performance of numerical codes that solve tsunami motion, as well as flow and velocity patterns. NAMI DANCE is a computational tool developed for the modeling of long waves. It provides numerical modeling and efficient visualization of tsunami generation, propagation, and inundation mechanisms and computes the tsunami parameters. In the theory of long waves, the vertical motion of water particles has no effect on the pressure distribution. Based upon this approximation and neglecting vertical acceleration, the equations of mass conservation and momentum are reduced to two-dimensional depth-averaged equations. NAMI DANCE uses finite difference computational method to solve linear and nonlinear forms of depth-averaged shallow water equations in long wave problems. In this study, NAMI DANCE is applied to a benchmark problem which was discussed in the 2015 National Tsunami Hazard Mitigation Program (NTHMP) annual meeting in Portland, USA. The benchmark problem features a series of experiments in which a single solitary wave propagates up a triangular shaped shelf which has an offshore island feature. The problem provides detailed free surface elevation and velocity time series in the vicinity of the island. The comparison of the results showed that NAMI DANCE is able to satisfactorily predict long wave evolution, propagation, amplification, and tsunami currents.

Keywords: numerical modeling; tsunami currents; depth-averaged equation; benchmark

---

1. Introduction

Tsunamis are large waves that are generated by the abrupt movement of the ocean floor caused by undersea earthquakes, underwater landslides, volcanic eruptions, or large meteorite strikes. Tsunami waves are accepted as the most destructive parameter of this phenomenon; however, currents that are triggered by large wave movements may be very fatal in some cases. Basin resonance and geometric amplification are two reasonably well-understood mechanisms for local magnification of tsunami impact in closed basins, and are generally the mechanisms investigated when estimating the tsunami hazard potential in a port or harbor; on the other hand, the understanding of and predictive ability for currents is lacking [1]. This study aims to investigate the sufficiency of two-dimensional depth-averaged shallow water equations in the estimation of tsunami evolution, propagation, and amplification as well as tsunami currents by using a numerical tool; namely NAMI DANCE. Since the 1970s, solitary waves have commonly been used to model tsunamis, especially in experimental and mathematical studies [2]. In this respect, the numerical code is applied to a benchmark problem which focuses on the evolution and propagation of a single solitary wave over complex bathymetry. The problem describes a series of experiments that analyze the transformation of a single solitary wave as it propagates up a triangular shaped shelf with an island feature located at the offshore point of the shelf. The currents that are formed in the vicinity of the island are also investigated in the experiments. The benchmark problem used in this study is Benchmark Problem #5 of the 2015 National Tsunami Hazard Mitigation Program (NTHMP) workshop which was held in Portland, USA [3]. By comparing the benchmark data and the numerical results, it is observed that two-dimensional depth-averaged shallow water equations give satisfactory results regarding tsunami wave evolution and currents and thus are sufficient tools to use while determining tsunami mitigation strategies.

2. Materials and Methods

2.1. The Numerical Model: NAMI DANCE

Tsunami numerical modeling by NAMI DANCE is based on the solution of a nonlinear form of long wave equations with respect to related initial and boundary conditions [4]. In general, the explicit numerical solution of nonlinear shallow water (NSW) equations is preferred since it consumes reasonable computer time and memory, and also provides the results in acceptable error limits [4]. NAMI DANCE is a numerical model which is able to simulate tsunami evolution, propagation and inundation. It has been developed by the collaboration of Ocean Engineering Research Center, Middle East Technical University, Turkey, and Special Research Bureau for Automation of Marine Researches, Russia [5,6]. NAMI DANCE uses C++ programming language and solves NSW equations using a staggered leapfrog numerical solution procedure. In the theory of long waves, the vertical motion of water particles is not considered since it has a negligible effect on the pressure distribution. Based upon this approximation, using necessary dynamic and kinematic conditions and including the bottom friction terms, the fundamental equations of NAMI DANCE, which are given Equations (1)–(5), are obtained and these equations are discretized by following the staggered leapfrog scheme.

$$\frac{\partial \eta}{\partial t} + \frac{\partial M}{\partial x} + \frac{\partial N}{\partial y} = 0 \tag{1}$$

$$\frac{\partial M}{\partial t} + \frac{\partial}{\partial x}\left(\frac{M^2}{D}\right) + \frac{\partial}{\partial y}\left(\frac{MN}{D}\right) + gD\frac{\partial \eta}{\partial x} + \frac{gn^2}{D^{7/3}}M\sqrt{M^2 + N^2} = 0 \tag{2}$$

$$\frac{\partial N}{\partial t} + \frac{\partial}{\partial x}\left(\frac{MN}{D}\right) + \frac{\partial}{\partial y}\left(\frac{N^2}{D}\right) + gD\frac{\partial \eta}{\partial y} + \frac{gn^2}{D^{7/3}}N\sqrt{M^2 + N^2} = 0 \tag{3}$$

$$M = u\left(h + \eta\right) = uD \tag{4}$$

$$N = v\left(h + \eta\right) = vD \tag{5}$$

where x and y are the horizontal axes; t is time; h is undisturbed flow depth; η is the vertical displacement above the undisturbed water surface; M and N are the discharge fluxes in x and y directions; u and v are particle velocities in x and y directions, respectively; n is the Manning's roughness coefficient; g is the gravitational acceleration, and D is the total water depth given by $h + \eta$ [6].

NAMI DANCE is able to compute (i) tsunami source from either rupture characteristics or predetermined wave form; (ii) propagation; (iii) arrival time; (iv) coastal amplification; (v) inundation (according to accuracy and grid size); (vi) distribution of current velocities and their directions at selected time intervals; (vii) relative damage levels according to drag and impact forces; (viii) time histories of water surface fluctuations; (ix) 3D plots of sea state at selected time intervals from different camera and light positions; and (x) animations of tsunami propagation [7]. NAMI DANCE has been applied to analytical, experimental, and field benchmark problems [8,9] for validation and verification [10–14] and also applied to several tsunami events [7,15–18].

2.2. The Benchmark Problem

The benchmark problem describes a series of experiments which have a single solitary wave propagating up a triangular shaped shelf with an island feature located at the offshore point of the shelf. The series of experiments are conducted in a large wave basin which is 48.8 m long, 26.5 m wide and 2.1 m deep [19]. The basin is equipped with a piston-type wave maker powered by an electric motor and a wave board that consists of 29 independently functioning paddles, which is able to produce linear and nonlinear waves up to 0.8 m in height [19]. The walls and the underlying bathymetry of the basin are made of concrete in order to reduce the boundary effects due to friction [19]. The complex bathymetry is constructed symmetrically along the centerline of the basin. The water depth is kept constant at 0.78 m and hence the still water level (SWL) intersects the land at $X = 25.75$ m [19]. A single solitary wave with a height of 0.39 m is generated for each trial [19]. In the experiments, resistance and sonic wave gages are used to record the free surface elevation time series, and the velocity time series are recorded via acoustic Doppler velocimeters (ADVs) [19]. The bathymetry provided with the benchmark problem is given in Figure 1.

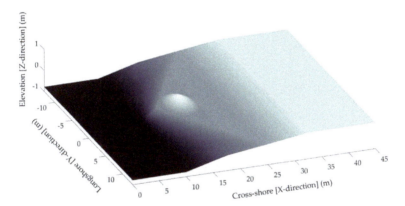

Figure 1. The bathymetry provided with the benchmark problem.

The free surface elevation time series are recorded at $Y = 0.0$ m at following X-locations: $X = 7.5$ m, 13.0 m, and 21.0 m; at $Y = 5.0$ m at following X-locations: $X = 7.5$ m, 13.0 m, and 21.0 m; and at $X = 25.0$ m at following Y-locations: $Y = 0.0$ m and 5.0 m. The velocity data are recorded at two locations: $X = 13.0$ m, $Y = 0.0$ m and $z = 0.75$ m and $X = 21.0$ m, $Y = -5.0$ m, and $z = 0.77$ m.

The input parameters that are necessary for numerical modeling are the XYZ dataset of the bathymetry and the free surface elevation time series of the incoming wave. The dimensions of these parameters are kept the same as the ones that are used in the experiments. Figure 2 shows the model bathymetry and the incoming wave, which is a single solitary wave with a height of 0.39 m. The free surface elevation time series of the incoming wave is inputted from the left border, i.e., $X = 0.0$ m along Y-axis. The model bathymetry is formed using structured grids. The spatial grid size, Δx, is selected as 0.05 m to achieve more accurate results. The time step, Δt, is selected as 0.001 s to ensure stability with 0.05 m grid size. The duration of each simulation is 20 s, which is sufficient to observe the maximum wave height and the effect of the island on the propagation of the solitary wave. It is observed that it takes approximately 1 h to complete each simulation using 12-Core CPUs.

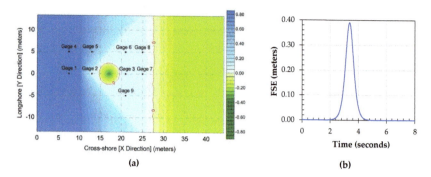

Figure 2. Model parameters: (**a**) bathymetry of the numerical model, NAMI DANCE; (**b**) incoming wave.

3. Results

3.1. Free Surface Elevation Time Series

The free surface elevation is measured via wave gages which are placed offshore, near shore and in the vicinity of the island. The gages placed in the vicinity of the island make it possible to record and analyze the effect of the island on the propagation of the single solitary wave and wave currents. The comparison of the results regarding the free surface elevation time series is given in Figure 3.

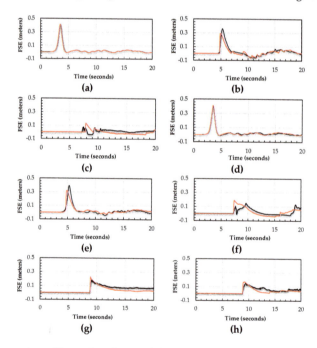

Figure 3. Comparison of free surface elevation (FSE) results: (**a**) $X = 7.5$ m and $Y = 0.0$ m at Gage 1; (**b**) $X = 13.0$ m and $Y = 0.0$ m at Gage 2; (**c**) $X = 21.0$ m and $Y = 0.0$ m at Gage 3; (**d**) $X = 7.5$ m and $Y = 5.0$ m at Gage 4; (**e**) $X = 13.0$ m and $Y = 5.0$ m at Gage 5; (**f**) $X = 21.0$ m and $Y = 5.0$ m at Gage 6; (**g**) $X = 25.0$ m and $Y = 0.0$ m at Gage 7; (**h**) $X = 25.0$ m and $Y = 5.0$ m at Gage 8. Black line represents benchmark data, red line represents numerical results.

The results revealed that depth-averaged NSW equations are able to satisfactorily predict the free surface elevation at gages 1, 4, 7, and 8. However, these equations fail to accurately estimate the free surface elevation in the vicinity of the island, i.e., at gages 2, 3, 5, and 6. It is known from the experimental observations that turbulence and relatively large wave currents are formed in the vicinity of the island; these are considered to play a role in the underestimation of maximum wave amplitudes.

3.2. Velocity Time Series

The velocity time series are measured via ADVs. The effect of the island on the direction and magnitude of wave currents is also recorded and analyzed. The comparison of the results regarding the wave currents is given in Figure 4.

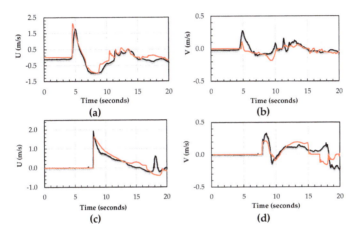

Figure 4. Comparison of results: (**a**) horizontal velocity in x-direction, U, recorded at $X = 13.0$ m, $Y = 0.0$ m and $Z = 0.75$ m at Gage 2; (**b**) horizontal velocity in y-direction, V, recorded at $X = 13.0$ m, $Y = 0.0$ m and $Z = 0.75$ m at Gage 2; (**c**) horizontal velocity in x-direction, U, recorded at $X = 21.0$ m, $Y = -5.0$ m and $Z = 0.77$ m at Gage 9; (**d**) horizontal velocity in y-direction, V, recorded at $X = 21.0$ m, $Y = -5.0$ m and $Z = 0.77$ m at Gage 9. Black line represents benchmark data, red line represents numerical results.

The results showed that depth-averaged NSW equations are able to satisfactorily predict the velocity components in x-direction. On the other hand, the maximum velocity values in y-direction are underestimated even though the predicted and measured velocity components show a similar trend.

3.3. Performance Assessment of the Model

The credibility of a numerical model is directly related to its performance. Using numerical models, it is impossible to obtain the same outcomes as those in natural systems since natural systems are never closed and model results are not always unique. The expected outcome is an acceptable level of agreement between analytical/experimental/field data and model prediction, as well as sufficient accuracy of the model. The performance of numerical models can be assessed by demonstrating the agreement between observation and prediction. Models can only be evaluated in relative terms, and their predictive value is always debatable. There is a variety of different methods to assess the performance of numerical models. Error statistics is one of these tools.

Different types of errors are introduced to determine the correlation between the analytical/experimental/field data and model results. In National Oceanic and Atmospheric Administration (NOAA), two common errors are emphasized; namely, normalized root mean square error, NRMSE, and the error of the maximum value, MAX [20]. The percent NRMSE is applied within a space segment or time period to all observed data points. The main use of NRMSE is to assess the accuracy of a model in predicting the entire set of observed data; in other words, it is used to define the overall model performance. NRMSE deals with an error of absolute values and does not show the bias of the code's prediction (i.e., underprediction or overprediction). MAX is used to quantify each model's predictive accuracy for the maximum data point regardless of the location and time.

The formulas to evaluate percent NRMSE and MAX error values are given in Equations (6) and (7):

$$\text{NRMSE} = 100 \times \frac{1}{f(x_i)_{max} - f(x_i)_{min}} \sqrt{\frac{\sum (f(x_i) - y_i)^2}{n}} \qquad (6)$$

$$\text{MAX} = 100 \times \frac{|f(x_i)_{max} - y_{i\,max}|}{f(x_i)_{max}} \qquad (7)$$

where $f(x_i)$ represents the observed data and y_i represents the predicted data.

The benchmark problem discussed in this study features a series of experiments collecting free surface elevation and velocity data. The velocity computations in numerical models differ at shallow water depths because of the nature and limit of two-dimensional depth-averaged shallow water equations. Therefore, larger error limits are accepted for velocity comparisons in shallow water depths. The NRMSE and MAX error limits for velocity values for experimental benchmarks can be selected as 15% and 25%, respectively [20]. For free surface elevation time series, NRMSE and MAX error limits may be reduced to 15% and 10%, respectively [20]. Statistical error analysis is applied to the results given in Sections 3.1 and 3.2. The results are listed separately for the free surface elevation time series, and velocity time series and are given in Tables 1 and 2.

Table 1. Error statistics of numerical results for free surface elevation time series recorded at each gage.

Free Surface Elevation (FSE)	% NRMSE	% MAX
Gage 1	0.60	0.02
Gage 2	7.30	19.30
Gage 3	15.00	17.60
Gage 4	2.60	2.60
Gage 5	7.20	18.80
Gage 6	8.70	8.20
Gage 7	4.50	7.30
Gage 8	5.00	6.80

Table 2. Error statistics of numerical results for horizontal velocity time series recorded at each gage.

Horizontal Velocity	% NRMSE	% MAX
Gage 2, U	8.25	18.90
Gage 2, V	16.00	27.90
Gage 9, U	10.75	15.00
Gage 9, V	16.00	28.60

4. Discussion

Nonlinear depth-averaged shallow water equations are commonly used to simulate the evolution and propagation of long waves offshore, near shore, and on the ground. These equations are solved using an explicit numerical scheme in which the staggered grid method in space and the leapfrog method in time are adopted. NAMI DANCE is one of many numerical tools that solve two-dimensional depth-averaged nonlinear shallow water equations to estimate the long wave behavior depending on bathymetry and topography. It is still controversial whether these equations predict tsunami currents accurately or not. In this study, the competence of depth-averaged NSW equations was tested using a benchmark problem. The results were analyzed in two aspects; free surface elevation and velocity time series. It is revealed that depth-averaged NSW equations satisfactorily predict the evolution, propagation, and amplification of long waves over complex bathymetry when turbulence effect is negligible. In the opposite case, the numerical results and observed data show a similar trend; however, the propagation and amplification of long waves are not accurately predicted. The turbulence and shoaling effects in the vicinity of the island, as well as the limitations of depth-averaged NSW equations, are considered to play a role in the underestimation of maximum wave amplitudes. The predicted and measured velocity components in x-direction are in good agreement with each other. The maxima of the velocity components in x-direction are reached. On the other hand, even though the predicted and measured velocity components in y-direction show a similar trend, the maximum velocity values are underestimated. Therefore, the prediction of the velocity components in y-direction needs improvement. Depth-averaged NSW equations may be a sufficient tool while developing tsunami mitigation strategies. However, long wave currents need further analysis in closed basins such as harbors and ports where they become a prominent parameter for the impact and drag on marine vessels, and also the resilience and endurance of coastal structures.

5. Conclusions

Numerical modeling of coastal hydrodynamics constantly gains importance in the world of coastal engineering due to the rapid development in computing technology. The modeling techniques have become more sophisticated and a large number of models can now be employed in a variety of coastal hydrodynamic problems. Accordingly, the performance assessment of numerical codes becomes crucial. The credibility of a numerical model has a direct relationship with its performance, which can be evaluated by indicating the level of agreement between observation and prediction. NAMI DANCE is one of many coastal models that solve two-dimensional depth-averaged NSW equations. This study investigated the performance of these equations in the estimation of long wave evolution, propagation, amplification, and long wave currents using NAMI DANCE. In this respect, the numerical code was applied to a benchmark problem which describes a series of experiments that analyze the transformation of a single solitary wave as it propagates up a triangular shaped shelf with an island feature located at the offshore point of the shelf. The results of this study indicate that depth-averaged NSW equations satisfactorily predict the evolution, propagation, and amplification of long waves over complex bathymetry when turbulence effect is negligible. On the other hand, NSW equations are not able to produce accurate results when the turbulence effects become dominant. Depth-averaged NSW equations may still be preferred while developing tsunami mitigation strategies. However, further studies on different benchmark problems are necessary to identify the performance and validity of depth-averaged NSW equations when the current behavior of long waves is investigated.

Author Contributions: This work is a part of the doctoral dissertation of Deniz Velioglu who analyzed the benchmark data and ran the numerical simulations. Rozita Kian contributed to the analysis of the model outcomes. Ahmet Cevdet Yalciner and Andrey Zaytsev took part in the development of the numerical tool NAMI DANCE. All authors contributed to the study.

Conflicts of Interest: The authors declare no conflict of interest.

References

1. Lynett, P.J.; Borrero, J.C.; Weiss, R.; Son, S.; Greer, D.; Renteria, W. Observations and modeling of tsunami-induced currents in ports and harbors. *EPSL* **2012**, *327*, 68–74.
2. Madsen, P.A.; Fuhrman, D.R.; Schaffer, H.A. On the solitary wave paradigm for tsunamis. *J. Geophys. Res.* **2008**, *113*. [CrossRef]
3. NTHMP Mapping & Modeling Benchmarking Workshop: Tsunami Currents. Benchmark #5. Available online: http://coastal.usc.edu/currents_workshop/problems/prob5.html (accessed on 2 August 2016).
4. Onat, Y.; Yalciner, A.C. Initial stage of database development for tsunami warning system along Turkish coasts. *Ocean Eng.* **2013**, *74*, 141–154. [CrossRef]

5. Kian, R.; Yalciner, A.C.; Aytore, B.; Zaytsev, A. Wave Amplification and Resonance in Enclosed Basins; A Case Study in Haydarpasa Port of Istanbul. In Proceedings of the 2015 IEEE/OES Eleventh Current, Waves and Turbulence Measurement, St. Petersburg, VA, USA, 2–6 March 2015; Volume 11, pp. 1–7.

6. Patel, V.M.; Dholakia, M.B.; Singh, A.P. Emergency preparedness in the case of Makran tsunami: A case study on tsunami risk visualization for the western parts of Gujarat, India. *Geomat. Nat. Hazards Risk* **2016**, *7*, 826–842. [CrossRef]

7. Yalciner, A.C.; Pelinovsky, E.; Zaytsev, A.; Kurkin, A.; Ozer, C.; Karakus, H.; Ozyurt, G. Modeling and visualization of tsunamis: Mediterranean examples. In *Tsunami and Nonlinear Waves*, 1st ed.; Kundu, A., Ed.; Springer: Berlin, Germany, 2007; pp. 273–283.

8. Synolakis, C.E.; Bernard, E.N.; Titov, V.; Kanoglu, U.; Gonzalez, F. Validation and verification of tsunami numerical models. *PAGEOPH* **2008**, *165*, 2197–2228. [CrossRef]

9. Yalciner, A.C.; Zaytsev, A.; Kanoglu, U.; Velioglu, D.; Dogan, G.G.; Kian, R.; Sharghivand, N.; Aytore, B. NTHMP Mapping and Modeling Benchmarking Workshop: Tsunami Currents. Available online: http://coastal.usc.edu/currents_workshop/presentations/Yalciner.pdf (accessed on 2 August 2016).

10. Ozer, C.; Yalciner, A.C. Sensitivity study of hydrodynamic parameters during numerical simulations of tsunami inundation. *PAGEOPH* **2011**, *168*, 2083–2095.

11. Sozdinler, C.O.; Yalciner, A.C.; Zaytsev, A. Investigation of tsunami hydrodynamic parameters in inundation zones with different structural layouts. *PAGEOPH* **2014**, *172*, 931–952. [CrossRef]

12. Sozdinler, C.O.; Yalciner, A.C.; Zaytsev, A.; Suppasri, A.; Imamura, F. Investigation of hydrodynamic parameters and the effects of breakwaters during the 2011 Great East Japan Tsunami in Kamaishi Bay. *PAGEOPH* **2015**, *172*, 3473–3491. [CrossRef]

13. Velioglu, D.; Kian, R.; Yalciner, A.C.; Zaytsev, A. Validation and Performance Comparison of Numerical Codes for Tsunami Inundation. In Proceedings of the 2015 American Geophysical Union Fall Meeting, San Francisco, CA, USA, 14–18 December 2015.

14. Velioglu, D.; Kian, R.; Yalciner, A.C.; Zaytsev, A. Validation and Comparison of 2D and 3D Codes for Nearshore Motion of Long Waves Using Benchmark Problems. In Proceedings of the 2016 European Geosciences Union, Vienna, Austria, 17–22 April 2016.

15. Dilmen, D.I.; Kemec, S.; Yalciner, A.C.; Düzgün, S.; Zaytsev, A. Development of a tsunami inundation map in detecting tsunami risk in Gulf of Fethiye, Turkey. *PAGEOPH* **2015**, *172*. [CrossRef]

16. Heidarzadeh, M.; Krastel, S.; Yalciner, A.C. The state-of-the-art numerical tools for modeling landslide tsunamis: A short review. In *Submarine Mass Movements and Their Consequences*, 6th ed.; Sebastian, K., Jan-Hinrich, B., David, V., Michael, S., Christian, B., Roger, U., Jason, C., Katrin, H., Michael, S., Carl, B.H., Eds.; Springer: Bern, Switzerland, 2013; Volume 37, pp. 483–495.

17. Yalciner, A.C.; Gülkan, P.; Dilmen, D. I.; Aytore, B.; Ayca, A.; Insel, I.; Zaytsev, A. Evaluation of tsunami scenarios for western Peloponnese, Greece. *Boll. Geofis. Teor. Appl.* **2014**, *55*, 485–500.

18. Zahibo, N.; Pelinovsky, E.; Kurkin, A.; Kozelkov, A. Estimation of far-field tsunami potential for the Caribbean Coast based on numerical simulation. *Sci. Tsunami Hazards* **2003**, *21*, 202–222.

19. Swigler, D.T. Laboratory Study Investigating the Three-dimensional Turbulence and Kinematic Properties Associated with a Breaking Solitary Wave. Master's Thesis, Texas A&M University, College Station, TX, USA, August 2009.

20. National Tsunami Hazard Mitigation Program. Proceedings and Results of the 2011 NTHMP Model Benchmarking Workshop. Available online: http://nws.weather.gov/nthmp/documents/nthmpWorkshopProcMerged.pdf (accessed on 21 July 2016).

Article

Application of an Unstructured Grid-Based Water Quality Model to Chesapeake Bay and Its Adjacent Coastal Ocean

Meng Xia * and Long Jiang

Department of Natural Sciences, University of Maryland Eastern Shore, Princess Anne, MD 21853, USA;
ljiang@umes.edu
* Correspondence: mxia@umes.edu; Tel.: +1-410-621-3551

Academic Editor: Richard P. Signell
Received: 11 July 2016; Accepted: 18 August 2016; Published: 1 September 2016

Abstract: To provide insightful information on water quality management, it is crucial to improve the understanding of the complex biogeochemical cycles of Chesapeake Bay (CB), so a three-dimensional unstructured grid-based water quality model (ICM based on the finite-volume coastal ocean model (FVCOM)) was configured for CB. To fully accommodate the CB study, the water quality simulations were evaluated by using different horizontal and vertical model resolutions, various wind sources and other hydrodynamic and boundary settings. It was found that sufficient horizontal and vertical resolution favored simulating material transport efficiently and that winds from North American Regional Reanalysis (NARR) generated stronger mixing and higher model skill for dissolved oxygen simulation relative to observed winds. Additionally, simulated turbulent mixing was more influential on water quality dynamics than that of bottom friction: the former considerably influenced the summer oxygen ventilation and new primary production, while the latter was found to have little effect on the vertical oxygen exchange. Finally, uncertainties in riverine loading led to larger deviation in nutrient and phytoplankton simulation than that of benthic flux, open boundary loading and predation. Considering these factors, the model showed reasonable skill in simulating water quality dynamics in a 10-year (2003–2012) period and captured the seasonal chlorophyll-a distribution patterns. Overall, this coupled modeling system could be utilized to analyze the spatiotemporal variation of water quality dynamics and to predict their key biophysical drivers in the future.

Keywords: FVCOM-ICM; Chesapeake Bay; water quality; nutrient; phytoplankton; dissolved oxygen

1. Introduction

As the largest and most biologically-diverse coastal plain estuary in North America [1], Chesapeake Bay (CB) is highly influenced by its vast watershed with a land-to-water ratio of 14.3 [2]. Following the population growth, industrial and agricultural development, CB has undergone severe eutrophication with symptoms of excessive nutrient loading, nuisance algal blooms, extensive summer hypoxia and declined seagrass coverage since the mid-1900s [3,4]. Typically, the overloading of cultural nutrients into CB directly drives its water quality deterioration, including bottom hypoxia/anoxia, overwhelming phytoplankton growth and diminished water clarity [2].

Biogeochemical cycles in CB and similar water bodies have been investigated using field investigation [5–7], retrospective long-term data analysis [8,9], remote sensing images [10], and numerical simulations [11,12]. Intra-seasonal and inter-annual observed data can effectively detect the dominant environmental factors driving water quality variations, but is usually limited by sparse spatiotemporal resolution [13]. Satellite imagery provides synoptic surface phytoplankton and suspended material distribution while it is incapable of exhibiting vertical variation [10]. Statistical empirical models and simplified oxygen models omitting nutrient cycles have been developed as substitutes for specific research goals, but it is impossible to reproduce the detailed internal spatiotemporal water quality variation and comparatively evaluate biophysical drivers [14]. In contrast, the three-dimensional physical-biogeochemical model could better resolve the biophysical interactions between circulation and water quality kinetics [11,12] and facilitate mechanistic analysis of internal water-column dynamics [15–17], making it an ideal tool to investigate nutrient dynamics and algal variability in eutrophic estuaries [18], synoptically assess estuarine biophysical processes and project future scenarios [19,20].

However, there exist several challenges and limitations in developing and applying sophisticated biophysical models [20]. For example, low-resolution models have difficulty following the coastline or investigating the tributary-estuary exchange very well. Unstructured grid models have the advantage of flexibility reaching fine resolution at areas of interest (e.g., nearshore, sills, deep channels and fronts) over the structured grid models [21]. Other key challenges and sources of uncertainty in configuring biophysical models lay in meteorological forcing, hydrodynamic simulation and nutrient loading [20]. For example, turbulent mixing and bottom roughness are key factors for the bay circulation [22], while their effects on the water quality dynamics are less investigated. In addition, uncertainties and errors originating from these processes have been poorly compared and discussed in any biophysical model application, and these limitations could be magnified when modeling a biologically-diverse estuary (e.g., CB) and cause biases when interpreting the model simulations and providing management suggestions [12,23].

Since high resolution would potentially benefit the water quality simulation, a three-dimensional biophysical model was configured for CB, its tributaries and adjacent coastal ocean based on the unstructured grid modeling framework FVCOM-ICM [24], which comprises the hydrodynamic model, the finite-volume coastal ocean model (FVCOM) and a water quality component, the modified Corps of Engineers Integrated Compartment Water Quality Model (FVCOM-ICM, [24]). During the model development, we tried to achieve a comprehensive understanding of various uncertainties for the model development and answer the following questions: (1) how will increased model resolution improve the simulation of water quality variables; (2) how sensitive is the model to different wind sources; and (3) what is the most significant physical and biological sources of uncertainty in our model? Sections 2 and 3 introduce the model frame and sensitivity experiments; model calibration results are depicted in Section 4; Section 5 lists the major conclusions.

2. Material and Methods

2.1. Study Site

CB, located adjacent to the Mid-Atlantic Bight on the east coast of United States (Figure 1), is a partially-mixed drowned river valley with a residence time of 90–300 days depending on the river flux [2,25]. A deep channel in the middle and shoals on both flanks (Figure 1 [2]) characterize the main stem of this large estuary with an area of 11,600 km^2 (323 km long, 48 km wide and 6.5 m deep on average), where the salinity typically ranges from 0–30 from the northern to the southern end. A two-layer estuarine circulation is subject to variation in river flux, local/remote winds, semidiurnal tides and other forces [26,27]. Receiving 337.3 kt/year (kt = thousand tons) nitrogen and 23.7 kt/year phosphorus inputs by 2010 [28], CB generates 2–12 km^3 bottom hypoxic waters every summer [29] and witnesses frequent occurrence of harmful algal blooms [30], which threatens the bay's living resources and ecological service to its recreational and commercial users.

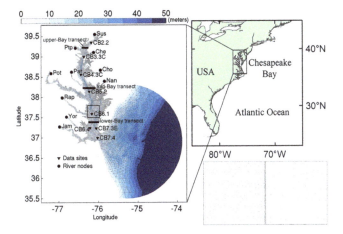

Figure 1. Model grid and bathymetry of Chesapeake Bay (CB) and its adjacent coastal ocean with river nodes, data sites and three transects. The bottom right panels are the zoom-in of the boxed area from two sets of grids generated for sensitivity experiments on spatial resolution. Sus, Susquehanna River; Ptp, Patapsco River; Che, Chester River; Pat, Patuxent River; Cho, Choptank River; Pot, Potomac River; Nan, Nanticoke River; Rap, Rappahannock River; Yor, York River; Jam, James River.

2.2. Model Description

An unstructured grid FVCOM-based hydrodynamic model was used to simulate the water level, temperature, salinity, circulation, eddy viscosity and other hydrodynamic information at an external and internal time step of 3 s and 12 s, respectively [31]. This work adopted this existing hydrodynamic model with the grid size ranging from 270 m–20.9 km (Figure 1). The major external forcing was comprised of daily river discharge, atmospheric forcing and open boundary conditions. The hydrodynamic data sources, calibration and validation processes and the justification of model settings could be retrieved in detail from [31].

The water quality kinetics, including nutrient cycles, sediment diagenesis and plankton growth, was simulated in the FVCOM-based water quality model FVCOM-ICM [24]. Integrated Compartment Model (ICM) was originally developed for the CB restoration and now works as part of the predictive model package CBEMP for the total maximum daily load plan [11,28]. A primary difference between CBEMP and FVCOM-ICM is our use of the unstructured grid and the sigma coordinate to accommodate the complex bay coastline and bathymetry. The mass balance of state variables in each control volume/cell [11] is solved as follows.

$$\frac{\partial VC}{\partial t} = \sum_{k=1}^{n} Q_k C_k + \sum_{k=1}^{n} A_k D_k \frac{\partial C}{\partial x} + VS \tag{1}$$

In Equation, V is the volume of a cell (m^3), C is the concentration or biomass in the cell (mg/L), t is the temporal coordinate (s), Q_k is the flux across the interface with the k-th neighbor cell (m^3/s), C_k is the concentration or biomass across the interface between two cells (mg/L), A_k is the interface area (m^2), D_k is the diffusion coefficient at the interface (m^2/s), n is the number of neighbor cells, i.e., the number of interfaces, x is the spatial coordinate (m) and S is the changing rate due to external loads and kinetic reaction in the cell (mg·L^{-1}·s^{-1}). To adapt to the sigma (σ) coordinate system, the transport of each state variable is modified as below [24].

$$\frac{\partial CD}{\partial t} + \frac{\partial CuD}{\partial x} + \frac{\partial CvD}{\partial y} + \frac{\partial C\omega}{\partial \sigma} = \frac{\partial}{\partial x}\left(A_h H \frac{\partial C}{\partial x}\right) + \frac{\partial}{\partial y}\left(A_h H \frac{\partial C}{\partial y}\right) + \frac{1}{D}\frac{\partial}{\partial \sigma}\left(A_v H \frac{\partial C}{\partial \sigma}\right) + DS \tag{2}$$

In the equation, D is total depth ($H + \zeta$, m), where H is the mean water depth and ζ is the water elevation, A_h is the horizontal diffusivity (m^2/s), A_v is the vertical diffusivity (m^2/s), u, v and ω are velocity components (m/s) in the directions of x, y and σ, respectively, and S is the biogeochemical changing rate (mg·L^{-1}·s^{-1}).

We simulated a total of 26 state variables in carbon, nitrogen, phosphorus, silicon and dissolved oxygen (DO) cycles (Figure 2), including total suspended solids (TSS), cyanobacteria, diatoms, dinoflagellates, microzooplankton (20–200 μm), mesozooplankton (0.2–20 mm), ammonia (NH4), nitrite and nitrate (NO23), phosphate (PO4), particulate inorganic phosphorus (PIP), labile/refractory dissolved/particulate organic carbon (LDOC, RDOC, LPOC, RPOC), labile/refractory dissolved/particulate organic nitrogen (LDON, RDON, LPON, RPON), labile/refractory dissolved/particulate organic phosphorus (LDOP, RDOP, LPOP, RPOP), chemical oxygen demand (COD), DO and particulate/dissolved silica (PSi/DSi). The sub-models of sediment diagenesis [32] and bivalve filtration [33] were turned on. ICM in CBEMP showed considerable model skills in representing the water quality variables for decades [11], so most of their model settings and parameters were followed (Table 1).

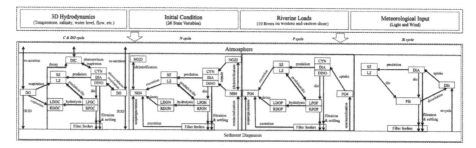

Figure 2. Schematic flow diagram of ICM set up for Chesapeake Bay. LDOC, RDOC, LPOC, RPOC, labile/refractory dissolved/particulate organic carbon; LDON, RDON, LPON, RPON, labile/refractory dissolved/particulate organic nitrogen; LDOP, RDOP, LPOP, RPOP, labile/refractory dissolved/particulate organic phosphorus; PSi/DSi, particulate/dissolved silica; COD, chemical oxygen demand; DO, dissolved oxygen; NO23, nitrite and nitrate; NH4, ammonia; PO4, phosphate; DIN, dissolved inorganic nitrogen.

Table 1. Key kinetic parameters used for the ICM for Chesapeake Bay. CHLA, chlorophyll = a.

Parameters	Value	Literature Range
Settling velocity W (CYN, m/day)	0	0–0.1 [11,14,34]
Settling velocity W (DIA, m/day)	0.2	0–0.5 [11,14,21,34]
Settling velocity W (DINO, m/day)	0.1	0–0.2 [21,34]
Max photosynthetic rate P_m (CYN, day^{-1})	150	100–270 [11,14,34]
Max photosynthetic rate P_m (DIA, day^{-1})	300	200–400 [11,14,21,34]
Max photosynthetic rate P_m (DINO, day^{-1})	200	200–350 [21,34]
C:CHLA ratio $CChl$ (CYN)	50	30–143 [11,14,34,35]
C:CHLA ratio $CChl$ (DIA)	37	30–143 [11,14,21,34,35]
C:CHLA ratio $CChl$ (DINO)	50	30–143 [21,34,35]
Half-saturation $K_{H\text{-}DIN}$ (CYN, mg/L)	0.02	0.01–0.03 [11,14,34]
Half-saturation $K_{H\text{-}DIN}$ (DIA, mg/L)	0.025	0.003–0.923 [11,14,21,34]
Half-saturation $K_{H\text{-}DIN}$ (DINO, mg/L)	0.025	0.003–0.923 [21]
Half-saturation $K_{H\text{-}DIP}$ (all, mg/L)	0.0025	0.001–0.195 [11,14,21,34]
Half-saturation $K_{H\text{-}DSi}$ (DIA, mg/L)	0.03	0.01–0.05 [11,14,21,34]
Photosynthesis T_{opt} (CYN, °C)	25	22–30 [11,14,34]
Photosynthesis T_{opt} (DIA, °C)	16	12–35 [11,14,21,34]
Photosynthesis T_{opt} (DINO, °C)	24	18–35 [21]

Table 1. *Cont.*

Parameters	Value	Literature Range
Respiration T_{ref} (°C)	20	20 [11,34]
Percentage of active respiration P_{res}	0.25	0.25 [11,14,21,34]
Basal metabolic rate M (CYN, day^{-1})	0.03	0.03–0.05 [11,14,34]
Basal metabolic rate M (DIA, day^{-1})	0.01	0.01–0.1 [11,14,21,34]
Basal metabolic rate M (DINO, day^{-1})	0.02	0.01–0.1 [21,34]
Herbivore predation rate F (CYN, day^{-1})	0.03	0.01–0.05 [14,34]
Herbivore predation rate F (DIA, day^{-1})	0.1	0.05–1 [14,21,34]
Herbivore predation rate F (DINO, day^{-1})	0.5	0.05–1 [21]
Max zooplankton predation ration (SZ, day^{-1})	2.25	0.8–2.25 [11,14]
Max zooplankton predation ration (LZ, day^{-1})	1.75	0.8–1.75 [11,14]
Settling velocity of particles (m/day)	0.25	0.03–0.8 [11,14,21,34]
Max nitrification rate (g·m^{-3}·day^{-1})	0.075	0.01–0.75 [11,14,21,34]
Optimal nitrification temperature (°C)	30	25–35 [11,14,21,34]

We simulated three major phytoplankton groups in CB [6]: diatoms (including other winter/spring groups), dinoflagellates (including other summer species) and cyanobacteria. Dinoflagellates were treated as autotrophs with their grazing capability not modeled. The time-dependent phytoplankton biomass governing equation [11] is given below.

$$\frac{\partial B}{\partial t} = (G - R)B - W\frac{\partial B}{\partial z} - F_z BZ - FB \tag{3}$$

In the equation, B is the biomass of a phytoplankton taxon (mg/L), G and R are the growth and respiration rate, respectively (day^{-1}), W is the settling velocity (m/day), z is the vertical coordinate converted from σ levels (m), F_z (L·mg^{-1}·day^{-1}) and F (day^{-1}) are the predation rate of zooplankton and other herbivores, respectively, and Z is the zooplankton biomass (mg/L). The growth rate is a function of temperature, nutrients and light, while the respiration rate is simply dependent on temperature. Equation (4) [11] is the depth-integrated net primary production (NPP) to manifest the detailed growth and respiration calculations.

$$NPP = \iint \left(\left(\frac{P_m}{CChl}\frac{I}{\sqrt{I^2 + I_k^2}}\frac{N}{K_h + N}e^{-K_T(T-T_{OPT})^2}\right)(1 - P_{res}) - Me^{-K_T(T-T_{ref})}\right)Gdzdt \tag{4}$$

In the equation, P_m is the maximum photosynthetic rate (day^{-1}), $CChl$ is the carbon to chlorophyll ratio, I and I_k are the instantaneous and reference radiation (mol·photons·m^{-2}·day^{-1}), N is the concentration of each nutrient (nitrogen, phosphorus and diatom-only silicon, mg/L), K_h is the half-saturation concentration in the Michaelis–Menten nutrient limitation function (mg/L), K_T (°C^{-2}) and $K_{T'}$ (°C^{-1}) are the temperature coefficients on photosynthesis and basal respiration, respectively, T_{opt} and T_{ref} are their corresponding optimal and reference temperature (°C), P_{res} is the percentage of active respiration in gross primary production and M is the basal respiration/metabolism rate (day^{-1}).

The light attenuation process is calculated with a subroutine computing the coefficient of diffuse light attenuation Ke (m^{-1}), which is controlled by the scattering and absorption to suspended solids and chlorophyll in the water column. In FVCOM-ICM, a look-up table along the visible spectrum (400–700 nm), derived based on field measurements in CB, is created to determine the six independent parameters, which feeds the subroutine for Ke calculation. The formulation and description of the light attenuation subroutine are detailed in [11,21].

2.3. Model Settings

For the simulation period 2003–2012, FVCOM-ICM off-line reads hourly hydrodynamic information from FVCOM. When the 30-min time interval in the water quality model was applied, simulated water quality variables reached over 90% correlations with those with a 5-min interval, while the computational time is only 22.4%; so we conducted water quality simulations at a time step of 30 min. We included 10 major riverine boundaries (Figure 1) for nutrient and TSS loading. The monitoring nutrients, TSS and phytoplankton maintained by the EPA Chesapeake Bay Program (CBP [36]) were the main data source of our model initialization, calibration and validation. The point-source and nonpoint-source loading of carbon, nitrogen, phosphorus and TSS were from the CBP's watershed model, Hydrological Simulation Program in Fortran (HSPF) in Phase 5.3.2 [36]. The deposition of nitrogen and phosphorus from the air-sea surface were estimated based on the observations (Stations MD13, MD15, MD99, VA10 and VA98) from National Atmospheric Deposition Program [37]. We referred to the monthly World Ocean Atlas 2005 data [38] for setting open boundary conditions. Meteorological data were downloaded from the National Center for Environmental Prediction (NCEP), North America Regional Reanalysis (NARR [39]). After model setup, major parameters were calibrated among literature ranges (Table 1) with data of 2010 to achieve the most reasonable and reliable model performance and verified with the other nine years' data. In order to validate our eutrophication model, we also compared our simulated chlorophyll-a (CHLA) distribution with the remote sensing images from the Chesapeake Bay Remote Sensing Program [40].

As suggested by Fitzpatrick, we computed the correlation coefficient (*CC*; Equation (5)) and the root mean squared error (*RMSE*; Equation (6)) to evaluate the fit between predicted (P_i) and observational (O_i) dissolved inorganic nitrogen (DIN) and phosphorus (DIP), TSS, DO and CHLA.

$$CC = \frac{\sum\limits_{i=1}^{n} (O_i - \overline{O})(P_i - \overline{P})}{\sqrt{\sum\limits_{i=1}^{n} (O_i - \overline{O})^2 \sum\limits_{i=1}^{n} (P_i - \overline{P})^2}} \tag{5}$$

$$RMSE = \sqrt{\frac{\sum\limits_{i=1}^{n} (P_i - O_i)^2}{n}} \tag{6}$$

2.4. Design of Numerical Experiments

In order to quantify the uncertainties in both hydrodynamic and water quality sub-models, we performed a variety of sensitivity tests along with the model calibration process (Table 2). These experiments were designed using the year 2010, which has been calibrated and has normal meteorological and hydrological conditions [31,41]. The effects of grid resolution on water quality simulation were examined using two model experiments with different spatial resolutions (the average grid size inside the bay is 1.43 km versus 1.74 km, respectively; see Figure 1). We also compared the water quality simulations with six, 11 and 21 sigma levels to determine the optimal vertical resolution. Given that the water quality simulation is sensitive to vertical mixing and bottom shear [20], the impacts of varied vertical eddy viscosity and bottom roughness length scale (Table 2) were discussed based on the calibrated hydrodynamic model [31]. We also examined the controls of two spatially-varying wind sources, NARR (spatial resolution of 30 km) and observation (data from 39 stations from National Data Buoy Center [42] and the National Centers for Environmental Information [43]), on DO variation. For the boundary loading, we altered the nutrient input from various sources (riverine, benthic and open boundary) to understand their influence on primary production. Additionally, the predation of zooplankton and suspension feeders was turned on and off to examine their controls on phytoplankton prey, respectively.

Table 2. A list of model sensitivity experiments.

Scenarios	Treatment
baseline	Described in Section 2 and [31]
coarse	Using a low-resolution model grid [a] (Figure 1)
sigma06, sigma20	Using 6 and 21 uniform sigma levels; i.e., each sigma layer represents 1/5 and 1/20 of the water depth, respectively
obs	Using wind data from National Data Buoy Center and National Centers for Environmental Information
obs + narr	Using observed wind to drive mixing and NARR wind to drive reaeration
az1, az2, az3, az4	Vertical eddy viscosity (az) computed in the hydrodynamic model was roughly 25%, 50%, 200% and 400% of the baseline scenario. The adjustment of vertical eddy viscosity is achieved by altering the Prandtl number
z01, z02, z03, z04	The bottom roughness length scale (z0) was 25%, 50%, 200% and 300% of the baseline scenario
r0.25, r0.50, r0.75, r0.80, r0.90, r0.95, r1.05, r1.10, r1.20	The riverine nutrient loading was 25%, 50%, 75%, 80%, 90%, 95%, 105%, 110% and 120% of the baseline scenario
bf0.25, bf0.50, bf0.75, bf0.8, bf0.9, bf1.1, bf1.2	The benthic nutrient flux was 80%, 90%, 110% and 120% of the baseline scenario
o0.25, o0.50, o0.75, o1.5, o2.0	The open boundary nutrient concentration was 25%, 50%, 75%, 150% and 200% of the baseline scenario
nzp and nsf	Predation of zooplankton (nzp) and suspension feeder (nsf) on phytoplankton was switched off, respectively

Note: a: the fine and coarse grid is presented in Figure 1 with the average inner-bay grid size of 1.43 km and 1.74 km, respectively.

3. Sensitivity Experiments

3.1. Sensitivity of Main Water Quality Variables to Grid Resolution

3.1.1. Effect of Horizontal Resolution

Two sets of model grids using different resolutions were applied in order to compare their performance and determine the optimal grid size. In the water quality simulation of 2010, both simulations represented the seasonal variation of nutrients, TSS, DO and CHLA at three stations located at the upper, middle and lower bay (Figures 1 and 3). Nitrogen, TSS and CHLA peaks appeared to be associated with the high-flow period in spring, and the concentration/biomass decreased with the distance from the northern end. Strong water-column and sediment respiration, as well as the low solubility in summer lowered the oxygen level at both the surface and bottom, and the lack of strong mixing ventilation contributed to the depletion of bottom oxygen at the upper and middle bay. Hypoxic conditions at the sediment-water interface favored the release of regenerated ammonia and phosphate, causing the "bump-ups" of their concentrations. The annual cycles of simulated nutrients, TSS, DO and CHLA by both models are in line with what were previously observed in CB (e.g., [5,29,35,44]).

However, there was discrepancy between them. For instance, the nitrate concentration in the low-resolution model was higher than that of the high-resolution one at the upper-bay and mid-bay stations, particularly in late spring and summer; the difference in phosphate concentration reached around 0.003 mg/L at the mid-bay station in summer; TSS simulation was also impacted by the model resolution at the upper and middle bay. It was found that the model performance of all water quality variables was better in the fine-grid model, as revealed by higher correlation coefficients and lower root mean squared errors, and that DIN and TSS were among the variables with a large deviation between the two models (Figure 4 and Table 3). Given that model resolution impacted simulating circulation [31], the discrepancy in these two variables with a strong axial gradient along the bay was probably attributable to the along-bay transport processes, which was substantiated subsequently.

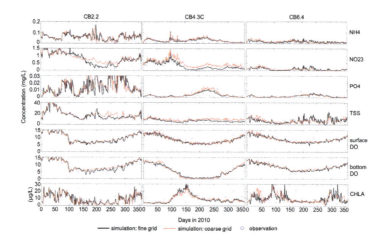

Figure 3. Time series of observed (open dots) and simulated (black solid line, fine-grid results; red dash line, coarse-grid results) water quality and phytoplankton state variables at three sampling sites in Chesapeake Bay (Figure 1) in 2010: NH4 (ammonia), NO23 (nitrite and nitrate), PO4 (phosphate), TSS (total suspended solids), DO (dissolved oxygen) and CHLA (chlorophyll-a).

Table 3. Model observation statistics with two sets of model grids in 2010.

Grid	Variable	n	*CC*	p	*RMSE*
	DIN	105	0.895	<0.001	0.141
	DIP	105	0.410	<0.001	0.016
Fine	TSS	105	0.801	<0.001	2.209
	DO	210	0.892	<0.001	1.525
	CHLA	104	0.480	<0.001	7.516
	DIN	105	0.765	<0.001	0.259
	DIP	105	0.400	<0.001	0.016
Coarse	TSS	105	0.610	<0.001	3.686
	DO	210	0.872	<0.001	1.700
	CHLA	104	0.455	<0.001	7.548

Note: n: sample size; *CC* and p: correlation coefficient and its p-value; *RMSE*: root mean squared error.

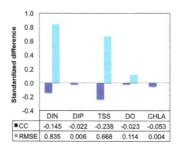

	DIN	DIP	TSS	DO	CHLA
■CC	-0.145	-0.022	-0.238	-0.023	-0.053
▨RMSE	0.835	0.006	0.668	0.114	0.004

Figure 4. Standardized difference of *CC* and *RMSE* in the coarse-grid model compared to the fine-grid model. Standardized score are calculated as follows: $Z_{CC} = (CC_{coarse} - CC_{fine})/CC_{fine}$, $Z_{RMSE} = (RMSE_{coasrse} - RMSE_{fine})/RMSE_{fine}$. *CC* and *RMSE* denote the correlation coefficient and root mean squared error between the model simulation and the observation, respectively. The raw data of *CC* and *RMSE* are shown in Table 3. The five variables are DIN (dissolved inorganic nitrogen, including ammonia, nitrite and nitrate), DIP (dissolved inorganic phosphorus), TSS (total suspended solids), DO (dissolved oxygen) and CHLA (chlorophyll-a).

Thus, we calculated the freshwater delivery (Equation (7)) across transects at the upper, middle, and lower bay, which, not influenced by the biological processes, represented the downstream transport capacity of the riverine source at these portions of the estuary.

$$Q_{fv} = \iint v \frac{\Delta S}{S_0} dA \qquad (7)$$

In the equation, v is the southward velocity, S_0 is the density of ambient water, ΔS is the density difference with the ambient water and A is the cross-sectional area. Time series of the freshwater transport at the upper bay resembled that of nitrate and TSS (Figures 1, 3 and 5), which supported our conclusion that circulation was responsible for improved water quality simulation in the high-resolution model. During the relatively dry summer, the freshwater transport of the coarse-grid model was higher across the upper-bay transect than the fine-grid model, but slightly lower across the mid-bay transect (Figures 1 and 5). That is, more riverine nutrients and TSS were retained between these two transects (e.g., the station CB4.3C), which further supported the relationship between the physical transport and water quality simulation. In addition, the freshwater transport through the lower-bay section calculated in the coarse-grid model fell short of that in the refined model (Figures 1 and 5), and as a result, the nitrate and TSS, whose major sources were the upstream riverine inputs, were lower at the lower-bay station CB6.4 in the low-resolution model (Figure 3).

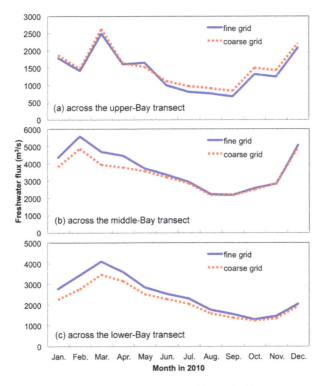

Figure 5. Freshwater transport across the (**a**) upper-, (**b**) middle-, and (**c**) lower-Bay transects (Figure 1) in the fine-gird (blue solid line) and coarse-grid (red dash line) models.

Therefore, the refinement of spatial resolution improved the simulation of axial material transport along CB and the corresponding water quality variability. Using the high-resolution model, the CCs of DIN and TSS could increase by 10%–25%, and the *RMSEs* decrease by over 60% (Figure 4), so we adopted the refined model to conduct the following sensitivity tests.

Even though not quantified, the previous findings [14,45] were similar pertaining to model resolution. Namely, more realistic physical processes were resolved in higher-resolution model, which will in turn improve the model performance of water quality variables in both freshwater and coastal systems [14,46]. When a finer model grid is necessary, a structured-grid model usually requires increasing the spatial resolution of the whole domain or applying the sometimes problematic model nesting methods [24]. Thereby, the extensive application of high-resolution unstructured grid water quality models is highly recommended given their flexibility in regional model refinement at relatively low computational cost. However, many other factors should be taken into consideration when refining the regional mesh size; for example, high resolution may lead to errors in sub-grid-scale processes, alteration of parameterization [45] and declined computational efficiency (e.g., the computational time decreased ~28% when the coarse grid was used).

3.1.2. Sensitivity to Vertical Resolution

We applied six, 11 and 21 sigma levels to examine the response of water quality variables to vertical resolution. The sensitivity of vertical resolution was not as high as that of the horizontal resolution, and DIP and CHLA are among the most sensitive variables in comparison with the observational data. For example, at the productive mid-bay station CB4.3C, the model with six sigma levels underestimated the phosphate concentration by up to 0.005 mg/L in summer (Figure 6a) and overestimated the peak CHLA by up to 10 µg/L during the spring bloom compared to the model with 11 sigma levels (Figure 6b); in contrast, the difference between models with 11 and 21 sigma levels was not as significant (Figure 6c,d). The model with 21 sigma levels has the highest model-observation agreement for DIP (*CC* = 0.642 and *RMSE* = 0.014), while the model performance of CHLA simulation was highest in the 11-sigma-level model (*CC* = 0.480 and *RMSE* = 7.516).

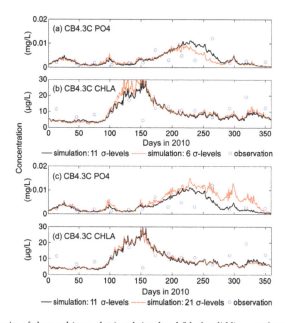

Figure 6. Time series of observed (open dots) and simulated (black solid line, results of 11 sigma levels; black dash line, results of six (**a,b**) or 21 (**c,d**) sigma levels) phosphate (**a,c**) and CHLA (**b,d**) at Station CB4.3C in Chesapeake Bay (Figure 1) in 2010.

The simulated hydrodynamic and water quality differences between the 11-sigma-level and 21-sigma-level model were quantified along and across the bay. The difference of salinity in the highly-productive May was mostly within one; the DIN discrepancy was maximized on the western flank and was mostly within 0.2 mg/L; phytoplankton biomass with 21 sigma levels exceeded that of the 11-sigma-level model by up to 0.1 mg/L, especially in the lower bay and on the eastern flank; the DO difference was around 0.4 mg/L throughout the water column (Figure 7). Thus, the overall model results of 11 sigma levels were similar to that of 21 sigma levels, while the difference from the six-sigma-level model was relatively large, which was also found in the CB hydrodynamic simulation [31]. In addition, the computational time of the models with six and 21 sigma levels was 54.6% and 194.0% that of the 11-sigma-level model, respectively. In consideration of the above results and the relative computational efficiency, we applied 11 sigma levels for further analyses.

When determining the vertical resolution in water quality models, it is essential to consider, but not be confined to, the overall depth, vertical circulation of the system, purpose of study and the acceptable computational expense. For instance, ten sigma layers were sufficient to simulate the seasonal nutrient cycle in Puget Sound whose maximum depth was over 200 m [21]. Conducting sensitivity tests on sigma levels could help detect the potential problems of low resolution and save the unnecessary computational time running high-resolution models.

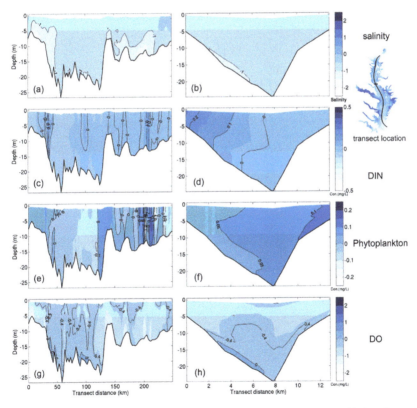

Figure 7. Difference in simulated (**a**) along-bay and (**b**) across-bay salinity in May; (**c**) along-bay and (**d**) across-bay dissolved inorganic nitrogen in May; (**e**) along-bay and (**f**) across-bay phytoplankton biomass in May and (**g**) along-bay and (**h**) across-bay dissolved oxygen in July between the 11-sigma-level and 21-sigma-level models. The along-bay and across-bay transects are shown on the rightmost panel.

3.2. Uncertainties Associated with the Hydrodynamic Simulation

3.2.1. Sensitivity to Different Wind Datasets

Two main sources of winds over the study area are the NARR and observed data, which were applied to several studies of DO simulation [12,15,47,48]. Scully [48] claimed that the usage of measured wind displayed asymmetry in strength (strongest from the south and weakest from the west) in summer. The wind rose diagrams from May–August in 2010 revealed that both winds showed the aforementioned asymmetry, while the southerly wind was more frequent in the NARR simulation (Figure 8). The model performance of DO simulation under the observed winds (*CC* = 0.823 and *RMSE* = 1.957) was close, but inferior to that driven by the NARR winds (*CC* = 0.892 and *RMSE* = 1.525, Table 3).

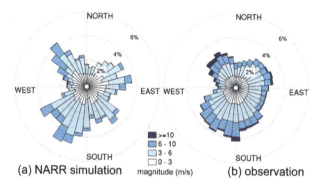

Figure 8. Wind rose plot in the hypoxia season (from May–August) in 2010: (**a**) spatially-averaged NARR data; and (**b**) observation from National Data Buoy Center and National Centers for Environmental Information.

At the upper- and mid-bay stations CB2.2 and CB4.3C, simulations forced by both winds exhibited similar DO reproduction, except that the DO concentration under the observed winds was slightly overestimated, particularly at the surface (Figure 9). In addition, the scenario under the observed wind underestimated DO by 2–3 mg/L in spring and fall at CB4.3C (Figure 9d). In the scenario with the mixing process driven by the observed winds and the reaeration process driven by the NARR winds, DO time series at both stations were similar to that under the observed winds (Figure 9), which indicated that the difference of two wind sources was primarily attributable to the mixing process instead of the wind-driven reaeration. Namely, the lower vertical mixing due to less frequent southerly winds accounted for the overestimation of surface DO in summer and the lower overall model skill of DO simulation. Thus, we adopted the NARR wind data for the 10-year simulation and sensitivity tests.

Winds can exert a substantial control on the onset, development and elimination of summer hypoxia in CB, and wind-driven lateral circulation and mixing may induce the ventilation of the bottom waters [49]. In other systems, wind could modulate the DO advection by direct entrainment [17,18]. Increasing the spatial resolution of observed winds and reducing data gaps might improve the DO simulation in water quality models.

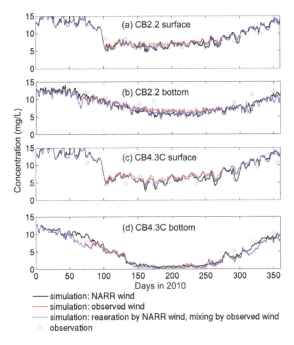

Figure 9. Time series of observed (open dots) and simulated (black solid line, results driven by the NARR wind data; black dashed line, results driven by the observed wind data (Table 2); blue dashed line, results using NARR wind-driven mixing and observed wind-driven reaeration) dissolved oxygen at two sampling sites in Chesapeake Bay (Figure 1) in 2010: Station CB2.2 at (**a**) the surface and (**b**) the bottom; Station CB4.3C at (**a**) the surface and (**b**) the bottom.

3.2.2. Sensitivity to Vertical Eddy Viscosity

Since FVCOM-ICM used the turbulence closure process from the hydrodynamic model, vertical eddy viscosity was a key coupling parameter between hydrodynamic and water quality models [24]. In our sensitivity experiments, we adjusted the vertical eddy viscosity by altering the Prandtl number. The baseline scenario was from the calibrated hydrodynamic model [31], and four other scenarios showed roughly 25%, 50%, 200% and 400% of the eddy viscosity in the baseline case (Table 2 and Figure 10a).

With enhanced mixing, the vertical DO difference in summer steadily declined at the inner bay, indicating an enhanced vertical exchange of oxygen (Figure 10b). When turbulent mixing was reduced from the baseline case, i.e., under the az1 and az2 scenarios (Table 2), the vertical difference was more sensitive to eddy viscosity, as revealed by a larger DO difference, than the two other scenarios (Figure 10b). Of all of the cases, the baseline scenario rendered the highest correlation with the observed DO and lowest deviation (Figure 10d). Therefore, the appropriate representation of turbulent mixing could improve the simulation of DO vertical exchange, as also suggested by Irby et al. [23].

Besides vertical ventilation of oxygen, the surface phytoplankton biomass was positively related to the eddy viscosity in summer (Figure 10c), which implied that the algal growth was limited by the amount of regenerated nutrients delivered to the surface. The nutrient cycling should be largely influenced by the extent of turbulent mixing, and this finding was consistent with the field study by Malone et al. [35]. Similarly to DO results, the baseline scenario exhibited the best model performance of CHLA simulation; CHLA responded even more sensitively than DO in terms of CCs and *RMSEs* (Figure 10e). According to previous studies, turbulence intensity and nutrient availability are dominant environmental factors controlling phytoplankton patchiness [50,51]; our results indicated that simulation of eddy mixing in physically-complex estuaries like CB was crucial to modeling the spatial heterogeneity of phytoplankton, especially during summer when most primary production was supported by the remineralized nutrient. Adjusting mixing parameters with caution is recommended, and field investigations of turbulent mixing in CB are necessary to validate the model performance, as well as to decipher its interplay with phytoplankton distribution.

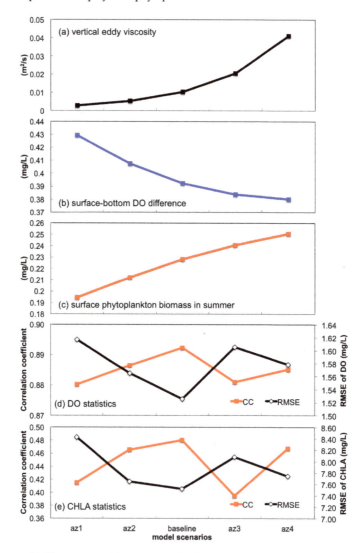

Figure 10. (a) The average eddy viscosity; (b) the surface-to-bottom difference of dissolved oxygen in the hypoxia season (from May–August); (c) surface phytoplankton biomass in summer (from June–August); *CC* and *RMSE* of (d) dissolved oxygen and (e) chlorophyll-a in 2010 in the five scenarios of varying eddy viscosity (az1, az2, baseline, az3 and az4 in Table 2). *CC* and *RMSE* denote the correlation coefficient and root mean squared error between the model simulation and the observation, respectively.

3.2.3. Sensitivity to Bottom Roughness Length Scale

Another uncertainty originating from the hydrodynamic simulation was the bottom stress, and the input of the spatially-non-uniform bottom roughness length scale regulated the drag coefficient and the bottom friction. Compared to the calibrated model [31], the bottom roughness length scale was scaled to 25%, 50%, 200% and 300% to investigate its impacts on nutrient transport and DO variation (Table 2).

Along the gradient of bottom roughness, the vertical eddy viscosity did not vary much among these scenarios (Figure 11a). Moreover, the differences in CCs and *RMSEs* of DIN in these five scenarios were below 0.005 and 0.004 (mg/L), respectively (Figure 11b). The minimal variation among the nitrogen simulation from these scenarios indicated that bottom roughness was hardly a main uncertainty source for nitrogen simulation. In contrast, the discrepancy in DO simulation was slightly larger than that in DIN, and the range of differences in CCs and *RMSEs* among cases could exceed 0.01 and 0.07 (mg/L), respectively (Figure 11c). This phenomenon was likely related to the horizontal oxygen exchange near the bottom since the vertical mixing was not prominently affected (Figure 11a). The baseline case achieved the highest correlation with the DO observation and the lowest error, even though it did not perform the best in DIN simulation (Figure 11b,c). Based on the model skills of DIN and DO, the two variables responded relatively strongly to bottom roughness compared with the others.

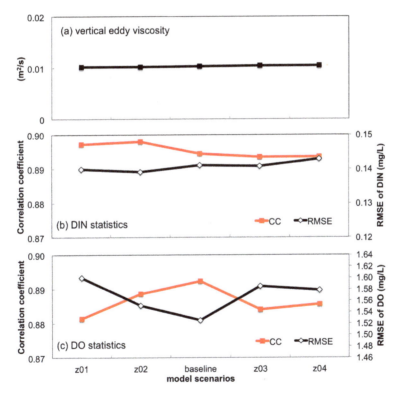

Figure 11. (**a**) The average eddy viscosity; *CC* and *RMSE* of (**b**) dissolved inorganic nitrogen and (**c**) dissolved oxygen in 2010 in five scenarios of varying bottom roughness length scale (z01, z02, baseline, z03 and z04 in Table 2). *CC* and *RMSE* denote the correlation coefficient and root mean squared error between the model simulation and the observation, respectively.

3.3. Uncertainties Associated with the Model Inputs

3.3.1. Sensitivity to Boundary Nutrient Loading

Boundary nutrient loading has been rated as an important driver in water quality models, and the accuracy of nutrient loading from riverine, benthic and other sources in a water quality model is fundamental to guide and advise the nutrient reduction plan [28]. It is essential to test how the variations in nutrient loading act on the water quality modeling results in the modeling framework. As many previous studies concentrated on the effect of nutrient loading on hypoxia in CB [3,4], we placed an emphasis on the response of phytoplankton production to complement previous studies.

The riverine nitrogen, phosphorus and silicon loading were scaled at the same time by 25%, 50%, 75%, 80%, 90%, 95%, 105%, 110% and 120% in order to maintain the stoichiometry in nutrient sources (Table 2), and the freshwater discharge was not adjusted to avoid changes in the physical environment (e.g., stratification field). We examined the surface DIN concentration and phytoplankton biomass in May, the period of peak spring bloom in 2010. With nutrient enrichment, the surface DIN concentration and phytoplankton biomass displayed a near linear increase (Figure 12). Based on our estimation, the 5%, 10% and 20% variation in nutrient loading could result in 2.9%–3.4%, 5.9%–6.8% and 11.2%–14.0% fluctuation in inner-bay nutrient concentration and phytoplankton biomass. In comparison, the benthic nutrient loading from the sediment diagenesis sub-model had a less significant control on the nutrient concentration and phytoplankton biomass in the water column, since up to 20% variation in benthic nutrient inputs could cause only 2.4%–2.9% alteration in surface DIN concentration and 4.2%–5.0% changes in surface phytoplankton biomass (Figure 12). Our model responded insensitively to the nutrient concentration at the open boundary, where nutrients and phytoplankton are flushed out of the model domain (Figure 1), since up to a 100% alteration in open boundary nutrient concentration led to a negligible (0.7%–0.9%) decrease of inner-bay nutrient concentration and phytoplankton biomass (Figure 12).

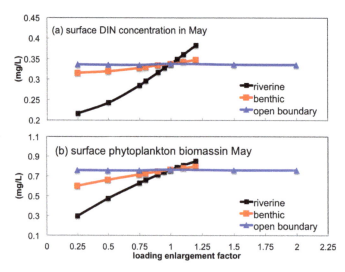

Figure 12. The relationship between the enlargement factor of riverine, benthic and open boundary nutrient loading (see Table 2) and the (**a**) surface dissolved inorganic nitrogen concentration and (**b**) phytoplankton biomass in May 2010.

Therefore, the riverine nutrient loading or nutrients from the watershed accounted for the largest uncertainty in the water quality simulation among all of the loading sources. The little contribution of open boundary loading was probably due to the low nutrient concentration on the continental shelf compared to in the estuary [52]. These results are similar to those in the CBEMP [53]. Thus, the loading estimation in the watershed model was critical to the biogeochemical simulation in the estuary, and the anthropogenic nutrient reduction in the CB watershed is the most effective way of alleviating eutrophication in the water column.

3.3.2. Sensitivity of Predation Terms to Phytoplankton Simulation

There are two major predation sources of phytoplankton in the model, zooplankton and suspension feeders (e.g., *Corbicula fluminea*, *Rangia cuneata* and *Crassostrea virginica*). We switched off these two modules to examine their controls on the phytoplankton biomass. When the zooplankton predation was eliminated, the surface phytoplankton biomass in May increased by 3.8%. When we turned off the filtration on the benthos, the surface phytoplankton biomass in May increased by 1.6%. That is, zooplankton predation on phytoplankton was more significant than suspension feeding; however, neither of them could result in a large (>5%) biomass loss during the peak spring bloom in CB, and their sensitivity was not as high as the nutrient loading. Extensive observation of the suspension feeder density and zooplankton spatial distribution is still necessary because they could exert a large influence on the spatial heterogeneity of algal distribution [45].

4. Model Calibration and Validation

4.1. A 10-Year (2003–2012) Model Simulation

To further validate the model settings, we ran the model in a 10-year (2003–2012) period and evaluated the overall model performance using the CBP mooring data. During this period, modeled DIN, DIP, DO, TSS and CHLA showed significant correlations with observational data ($p < 0.001$), and their *RMSEs* were relatively small (Figure 13). Robson [54] reviewed that most reliable aquatic water quality models could simulate nutrients and phytoplankton with *CC* of 0.632–0.775 and relative error of ~40%. In comparison, our model showed even higher agreement of DIN (*CC* = 0.925) and DO (*CC* = 0.922) with empirical data than the above criteria, while the correlations with observed DIP (*CC* = 0.705) and TSS (*CC* = 0.684) were within the average range of typical water quality models (Figure 13). However, the CHLA (*CC* = 0.477) simulated by our model tended to overestimate in low-production periods and was below the criteria (Figure 13).

The desirable modeling confidence of DO and CHLA, two principal water quality criteria for CB [28,55], for the purpose of water quality management was primarily as follows: *CC*, 0.707 for DO and 0.447 for CHLA; standard deviation, 50% for DO and 300% for CHLA [56]. The *RMSEs* of both DO and CHLA in our model, whose values were close to the corresponding standard deviation, were less than these criteria; the corresponding correlation coefficients of DO and CHLA also exceeded those in the criteria (Figure 13). Therefore, this modeling package generated reasonably well the representation of the main water quality variables in the 10-year simulation, and the model skill ensured the confidence in utilizing this model in assisting water quality management and studying the complex biophysical interactions driving the CB biogeochemical cycles.

In terms of model calibration to the empirical data, another noteworthy fact is that this modeling system exhibited the best performance in surface CHLA and the second best in bottom CHLA among the five current complex eutrophication models for CB [23], although the simulation skill of CHLA was not as good as other simulated variables in our model (Figure 13). In order to further corroborate the spatial CHLA distribution and figure out the challenges underlying in modeling phytoplankton, we then compared our simulated surface CHLA to that measured by remote sensing in the following subsection.

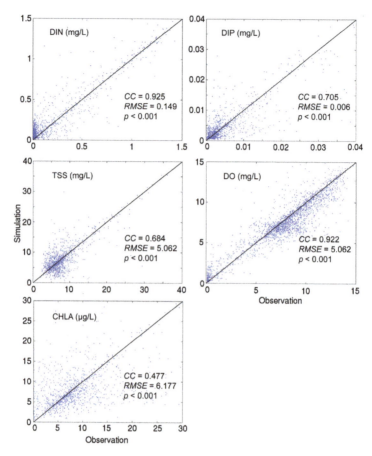

Figure 13. Comparison between modeled and observed dissolved inorganic nitrogen (DIN) and phosphorus (DIP), dissolved oxygen (DO), total suspended solids (TSS) and chlorophyll-a (CHLA) from 2003–2012. CC and *p* denote the correlation coefficient and its *p*-value, and *RMSE* is the root mean squared error.

4.2. Comparison of Simulated CHLA with Remote Sensing Images

During the spring bloom (usually peaking in May), the lower-bay and mid-bay areas in both modeled and remote sensing images were characterized by a high CHLA concentration (Figure 14a,b), in which diatoms dominated [6]. In a wet year (e.g., 2011), the magnitude and extent of the spring bloom were greater than other years (Figure 14b). In summer, the entire phytoplankton biomass, with dinoflagellates and cyanobacteria the dominant groups [6], became lower than that in spring, and the chlorophyll maxima were generally shifted northwards due to reduced stream flow (Figure 14c) or even disappeared for lack of nutrient input (Figure 14d). These results were consistent with many previous field observations in CB [5,6,10,26,57,58], which suggested that our model followed the general seasonal and inter-annual patterns of phytoplankton distribution.

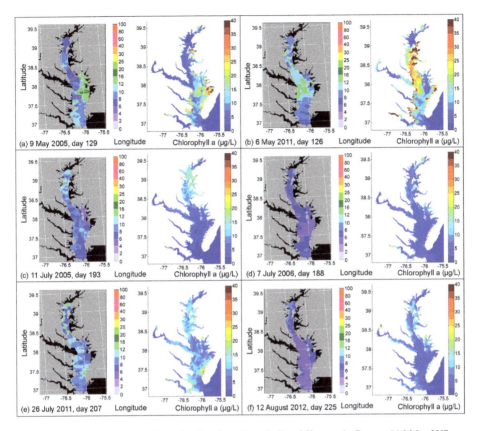

Figure 14. Remote sensing and simulated surface chlorophyll-a of Chesapeake Bay on: (**a**) 9 May 2005; (**b**) 6 May 2011; (**c**) 11 July 2005; (**d**) 7 July 2006; (**e**) 26 July 2011; and (**f**) 12 August 2012. Remote sensing data source: Chesapeake Bay Remote Sensing Program.

Except for the major seasonal pattern, phytoplankton usually appeared in patches (Figure 14a,e,f). These "hot spots" of chlorophyll generally included the eastern embayment (Figure 14a,f), littoral zones (Figure 14e), areas near the Patapsco River (Figures 1 and 14f) and specific mid-bay regions (Figure 14e). Spatial heterogeneity of phytoplankton, probably regulated by the regional nutrient enrichment, grazing, advection, stratification and the balance of various biophysical mechanisms, was a phenomenon frequently observed, but far from well understood [45,59,60]. Our model was capable of capturing most of the realistic CHLA patches, but might slightly deviate in location, extent or magnitude (Figure 14), which partially accounted for the low model skills of CHLA relative to other variables.

The difficulty in accurately simulating the localized and sporadic phytoplankton bloom was one major source of error in CHLA simulation, and it was also noticed in other models [45]. One possible explanation for the inaccuracy in primary production simulation was that phytoplankton growth, an unsteady state, accumulated the errors from processes, such as hydrodynamic conditions, nutrient transport, light attenuation, interspecific competition and predator-prey interaction [60]. Pertaining to our modeling effort, the potential improvement in CHLA simulation desired both field observation and model development from at least the following aspects: investigating vertical migration of phytoplankton, formulating the heterotrophic capability of dinoflagellates, considering sufficient phytoplankton groups and quantifying the grazing pressure by herbivores besides zooplankton.

5. Conclusions

A three-dimensional unstructured grid biophysical model (FVCOM-ICM) was applied to CB and its adjacent coastal ocean to investigate the biophysical controls on the main water quality variables. In the process of model calibration, a series of sensitivity experiments was conducted on major sources of uncertainties. The model showed reasonable agreement with observed water quality variables, such as DIN, DIP, TSS, DO and CHLA during a 10-year simulation period (2003–2012), and the simulated surface CHLA could represent the seasonal and spatial distribution patterns revealed by remote sensing images. The main conclusions based on the sensitivity tests are summarized below.

(1) Grid refinement improved the model performance of most variables, particularly for DIN and TSS. The finer grid favored modeling the realistic material transport from the Susquehanna River to the bay mouth, especially in the mid-bay portion. Eleven sigma levels were applied in consideration of the balance between computational accuracy and efficiency. The unstructured grid-based water quality models made it feasible to reach high resolution in biologically-active regions (e.g., littoral zones and the main channel) without significantly adding to the overall computational burden.

(2) The effects of wind source on DO simulation were compared between the NARR modeled and observed winds. Both winds represented directional asymmetry in summer (southerly winds strongest and westerly weakest), while the observed winds showed lower frequency in southerly winds. The DO simulation forced by these two wind sources had good agreement with empirical data, except that the surface DO was overestimated under the observed winds. Due to stronger mixing from the more frequent southerly winds, the NARR winds were preferred in our water quality model.

(3) Turbulent mixing and bottom stress were two potential sources of uncertainties in water quality simulation. Appropriate representation of vertical eddy viscosity was propitious to model the vertical oxygen ventilation and the new primary production fueled with recycled nutrients. Bottom friction exerted a moderate impact only on the horizontal oxygen mixing. In terms of water quality simulation, the vertical mixing process was more influential than bottom roughness.

(4) Uncertainties in the riverine source could exert a relatively larger influence on the inner-bay nutrient concentration and phytoplankton biomass during the spring bloom than those in benthic nutrient flux and open boundary loading. Zooplankton predation on phytoplankton was more significant than that of the filtration of suspension feeders.

As a simplification of the real-world systems, all water quality models rely on assumptions and have limitations, including ours. For instance, in addition to those mentioned in Section 4.2, we did not consider the tidal marshes surrounding CB. However, our calibration efforts and sensitivity tests have displayed the feasibility and reliability of such a holistic modeling approach in simulating the main environmental indicators in CB and discerning complex internal biophysical interactions on the lower estuarine-coastal food web. Our biophysical approach will be further utilized to decipher the potential response of water quality cycles in the context of climate change and investigate the estuarine-shelf nutrient exchange.

Acknowledgments: This project is partially supported by the Delmarva Land Grant Institution Cooperative Seed Grant Program. L. Jiang was partially supported by a Department Teaching Assistantship.

Author Contributions: Meng Xia put forward the scientific ideas; design the modeling experiments and organizes the manuscript. Long Jiang calibrated the water quality model and ran the numerical experiments under the supervision of Meng Xia. Both authors contributed to the study.

Conflicts of Interest: The authors declare no conflict of interest.

J. Mar. Sci. Eng. **2016**, *4*, 52

References

1. Gillmore, J.; Glendening, P.; Ridge, T.; Williams, A.; Browner, C.; Bolling, B. *Chesapeake 2000 Agreement*; United States Environmental Protection Agency Chesapeake Bay Program: Annapolis, MD, USA, 2000.

2. Kemp, W.M.; Boynton, W.R.; Adolf, J.E.; Boesch, D.F.; Boicourt, W.C.; Brush, G.; Cornwell, J.C.; Fisher, T.R.; Glibert, P.M.; Hagy, J.D.; et al. Eutrophication of Chesapeake Bay: Historical trends and ecological interactions. *Mar. Ecol. Prog. Ser.* **2005**, *303*, 1–29. [CrossRef]

3. Hagy, J.D.; Boynton, W.R.; Keefe, C.W.; Wood, K.V. Hypoxia in Chesapeake Bay, 1950–2001: Long-term change in relation to nutrient loading and river flow. *Estuaries* **2004**, *27*, 634–658. [CrossRef]

4. Murphy, R.R.; Kemp, W.M.; Ball, W.P. Long-term trends in Chesapeake Bay seasonal hypoxia, stratification, and nutrient loading. *Estuar. Coasts* **2011**, *34*, 1293–1309. [CrossRef]

5. Harding, L.W.; Mallonee, M.E.; Perry, E.S. Toward a predictive understanding of primary productivity in a temperate, partially stratified estuary. *Estuar. Coast. Shelf Sci.* **2002**, *55*, 437–463. [CrossRef]

6. Marshall, H.G.; Lane, M.F.; Nesius, K.K.; Burchardt, L. Assessment and significance of phytoplankton species composition within Chesapeake Bay and Virginia tributaries through a long-term monitoring program. *Environ. Monit. Assess.* **2009**, *150*, 143–155. [CrossRef] [PubMed]

7. Smith, E.M.; Kemp, W.M. Seasonal and regional variations in plankton community production and respiration for Chesapeake Bay. *Mar. Ecol. Prog. Ser.* **1995**, *116*, 217–231. [CrossRef]

8. Harding, L.W. Long-term trends in the distribution of phytoplankton in Chesapeake Bay: Roles of light, nutrients and streamflow. *Mar. Ecol. Prog. Ser.* **1994**, *104*, 267. [CrossRef]

9. Prasad, M.B.K.; Sapiano, M.R.; Anderson, C.R.; Long, W.; Murtugudde, R. Long-term variability of nutrients and chlorophyll in the Chesapeake Bay: A retrospective analysis, 1985–2008. *Estuar. Coasts* **2010**, *33*, 1128–1143. [CrossRef]

10. Son, S.; Wang, M.; Harding, L.W. Satellite-measured net primary production in the Chesapeake Bay. *Remote Sens. Environ.* **2014**, *144*, 109–119. [CrossRef]

11. Cerco, C.F.; Kim, C.-S.; Noel, M.R. *The 2010 Chesapeake Bay Eutrophication Model*; U.S. Army Corps of Engineers Waterways Experiment Station: Vicksburg, MS, USA, 2010.

12. Feng, Y.; Friedrichs, M.A.; Wilkin, J.; Tian, H.; Yang, Q.; Hofmann, E.E.; Wiggert, J.D.; Hood, R.R. Chesapeake Bay nitrogen fluxes derived from a land-estuarine ocean biogeochemical modeling system: Model description, evaluation and nitrogen budgets. *J. Geophys. Res. Biogeosci.* **2015**, *120*, 1666–1695. [CrossRef]

13. Pennock, J.R. Chlorophyll distributions in the Delaware estuary: Regulation by light-limitation. *Estuar. Coast. Shelf Sci.* **1985**, *21*, 711–725. [CrossRef]

14. Jiang, L.; Xia, M.; Ludsin, S.A.; Rutherford, E.S.; Mason, D.M.; Jarrin, J.M.; Pangle, K.L. Biophysical modeling assessment of the drivers for plankton dynamics in dreissenid-colonized western Lake Erie. *Ecol. Model.* **2015**, *308*, 18–33. [CrossRef]

15. Testa, J.M.; Li, Y.; Lee, Y.J.; Li, M.; Brady, D.C.; di Toro, D.M.; Kemp, W.M.; Fitzpatrick, J.J. Quantifying the effects of nutrient loading on dissolved O_2 cycling and hypoxia in Chesapeake Bay using a coupled hydrodynamic-biogeochemical model. *J. Mar. Syst.* **2014**, *139*, 139–158. [CrossRef]

16. Xia, M.; Craig, P.M.; Schaeffer, B.; Stoddard, A.; Liu, Z.; Peng, M.; Zhang, H.; Wallen, C.M.; Bailey, N.; Mandrup-Poulsen, J. Influence of physical forcing on bottom-water dissolved oxygen within Caloosahatchee River Estuary, Florida. *J. Environ. Eng.* **2010**, *136*, 1032–1044. [CrossRef]

17. Xia, M.; Craig, P.M.; Wallen, C.M.; Stoddard, A.; Mandrup-Poulsen, J.; Peng, M.; Schaeffer, B.; Liu, Z. Numerical simulation of salinity and dissolved oxygen at Perdido Bay and adjacent coastal ocean. *J. Coast. Res.* **2011**, *27*, 73–86. [CrossRef]

18. Xia, M.; Jiang, L. Influence of wind and river discharge on the hypoxia in a shallow bay. *Ocean Dyn.* **2015**, *65*, 665–678. [CrossRef]

19. Fitzpatrick, J.J. Assessing skill of estuarine and coastal eutrophication models for water quality managers. *J. Mar. Syst.* **2009**, *76*, 195–211. [CrossRef]

20. Ganju, N.K.; Brush, M.J.; Rashleigh, B.; Aretxabaleta, A.L.; del Barrio, P.; Grear, J.S.; Harris, L.A.; Lake, S.J.; McCardell, G.; O'Donnell, J.; et al. Progress and challenges in coupled hydrodynamic-ecological estuarine modeling. *Estuar. Coasts* **2015**, *39*, 311–332. [CrossRef]

21. Khangaonkar, T.; Sackmann, B.; Long, W.; Mohamedali, T.; Roberts, M. Simulation of annual biogeochemical cycles of nutrient balance, phytoplankton bloom(s), and DO in Puget Sound using an unstructured grid model. *Ocean Dyn.* **2012**, *62*, 1353–1379. [CrossRef]

22. Ganju, N.K.; Sherwood, C.R. Effect of roughness formulation on the performance of a coupled wave, hydrodynamic, and sediment transport model. *Ocean Model.* **2010**, *33*, 299–313. [CrossRef]

23. Irby, I.D.; Friedrichs, M.A.M.; Friedrichs, C.T.; Bever, A.J.; Hood, R.R.; Lanerolle, L.W.J.; Scully, M.E.; Sellner, K.; Shen, J.; Testa, J.; et al. Challenges associated with modeling low-oxygen waters in Chesapeake Bay: A multiple model comparison. *Biogeosciences* **2016**, *13*, 2011–2028. [CrossRef]

24. Kim, T.; Khangaonkar, T. An offline unstructured biogeochemical model (UBM) for complex estuarine and coastal environments. *Environ. Model. Softw.* **2012**, *31*, 47–63. [CrossRef]

25. Shen, J.; Wang, H.V. Determining the age of water and long-term transport timescale of the Chesapeake Bay. *Estuar. Coast. Shelf Sci.* **2007**, *74*, 585–598. [CrossRef]

26. Fisher, T.R.; Harding, L.W.; Stanley, D.W.; Ward, L.G. Phytoplankton, nutrients, and turbidity in the Chesapeake, Delaware, and Hudson estuaries. *Estuar. Coast. Shelf Sci.* **1988**, *27*, 61–93. [CrossRef]

27. Wang, D.-P. Wind-driven circulation in the Chesapeake Bay, winter 1975. *J. Phys. Oceanogr.* **1979**, *9*, 564–572. [CrossRef]

28. U.S. Environmental Protection Agency. *Chesapeake Bay Total Maximum Daily Load for Nitrogen, Phosphorus, and Sediment*; Chesapeake Bay Program Office: Annapolis, MD, USA, 2010.

29. Testa, J.M.; Kemp, W.M. Hypoxia-induced shifts in nitrogen and phosphorus cycling in Chesapeake Bay. *Limnol. Oceanogr.* **2012**, *57*, 835–850. [CrossRef]

30. Li, J.; Glibert, P.M.; Gao, Y. Temporal and spatial changes in Chesapeake Bay water quality and relationships to *Prorocentrum minimum*, *Karlodinium veneficum*, and CyanoHAB events, 1991–2008. *Harmful Algae* **2015**, *42*, 1–14. [CrossRef]

31. Jiang, L.; Xia, M. Dynamics of the Chesapeake Bay outflow plume: Realistic plume simulation and its seasonal and interannual variability. *J. Geophys. Res. Oceans* **2016**, *121*, 1424–1445. [CrossRef]

32. Di Toro, D.M.; Fitzpatrick, J.J. *Chesapeake Bay Sediment Flux Model*; HydroQual, Inc.: Mahwah, NJ, USA, 1993.

33. Meyers, M.B.; di Toro, D.M.; Lowe, S.A. Coupling suspension feeders to the Chesapeake Bay Eutrophication Model. *Water Qual. Ecosyst. Model.* **2000**, *1*, 123–140. [CrossRef]

34. Cerco, C.F.; Cole, T. *User's Guide to the CE-QUAL-ICM Three-Dimensional Eutrophication Model: Release*; version 1.0 Report; US Army Engineer Waterways Experiment Station: Vicksburg, MS, USA, 1995.

35. Malone, T.C.; Crocker, L.H.; Pike, S.E.; Wendler, B.W. Influences of river flow on the dynamics of phytoplankton production in a partially stratified estuary. *Mar. Ecol. Prog. Ser.* **1988**, *48*, 235–249. [CrossRef]

36. U.S. Environmental Protection Agency. Chesapeake Bay Program water quality data. Available online: http://www.chesapeakebay.net/data (accessed on 18 August 2016).

37. National Atmospheric Deposition Program data. Available online: http://nadp.sws.uiuc.edu/data/ (accessed on 18 August 2016).

38. World Ocean Atlas 2005 data. Available online: http://www.nodc.noaa.gov/OC5/WOA05/pr_woa05.html (accessed on 18 August 2016).

39. National Center for Environmental Prediction. North America Regional Reanalysis data. Available online: http://www.esrl.noaa.gov/psd/data/gridded/data.narr.html (accessed on 18 August 2016).

40. Chesapeake Bay Remote Sensing Program data. Available online: http://www.cbrsp.org/index.html (accessed on 18 August 2016).

41. U.S. Geological Survey data. Available online: http://md.water.usgs.gov/waterdata/chesinflow/wy/ (accessed on 18 August 2016).

42. National Data Buoy Center data. Available online: http://www.ndbc.noaa.gov (accessed on 18 August 2016).

43. National Centers for Environmental Information data. Available online: http://www.ncdc.noaa.gov (accessed on 18 August 2016).

44. Boynton, W.R.; Garber, J.H.; Summers, R.; Kemp, W.M. Inputs, transformations, and transport of nitrogen and phosphorus in Chesapeake Bay and selected tributaries. *Estuaries* **1995**, *18*, 285–314. [CrossRef]

45. Cerco, C.F.; Noel, M.R. Incremental improvements in Chesapeake Bay environmental model package. *J. Environ. Eng.* **2005**, *131*, 745–754. [CrossRef]

46. Chenillat, F.; Franks, P.J.; Rivière, P.; Capet, X.; Grima, N.; Blanke, B. Plankton dynamics in a cyclonic eddy in the Southern California Current System. *J. Geophys. Res. Oceans* **2015**, *120*, 5566–5588. [CrossRef]

47. Du, J.; Shen, J. Decoupling the influence of biological and physical processes on the dissolved oxygen in the Chesapeake Bay. *J. Geophys. Res. Oceans* **2015**, *120*, 78–93. [CrossRef]
48. Scully, M.E. Physical controls on hypoxia in Chesapeake Bay: A numerical modeling study. *J. Geophys. Res. Oceans* **2013**, *118*, 1239–1256. [CrossRef]
49. Scully, M.E. Wind modulation of dissolved oxygen in Chesapeake Bay. *Estuar. Coasts* **2010**, *33*, 1164–1175. [CrossRef]
50. Belyaev, V.I. Modelling the influence of turbulence on phytoplankton photosynthesis. *Ecol. Model.* **1992**, *60*, 11–29. [CrossRef]
51. Estrada, M.; Berdalet, E. Phytoplankton in a turbulent world. *Sci. Mar.* **1998**, *61* (Suppl. 1), 125–140.
52. Filippino, K.C.; Bernhardt, P.W.; Mulholland, M.R. Chesapeake Bay plume morphology and the effects on nutrient dynamics and primary productivity in the coastal zone. *Estuar. Coasts* **2009**, *32*, 410–424. [CrossRef]
53. Cerco, C.F.; Noel, M.R. *The 2002 Chesapeake Bay Eutrophication Model*; U.S. Army Corps of Engineers, Waterways Experiment Station: Vicksburg, MS, USA, 2004.
54. Robson, B.J. State of the art in modelling of phosphorus in aquatic systems: Review, criticisms and commentary. *Environ. Model. Softw.* **2014**, *61*, 339–359. [CrossRef]
55. Harding, L.W.; Batiuk, R.A.; Fisher, T.R.; Gallegos, C.L.; Malone, T.C.; Miller, W.D.; Mulholland, M.R.; Paerl, H.W.; Perry, E.S.; Tango, P. Scientific bases for numerical chlorophyll criteria in Chesapeake Bay. *Estuar. Coasts* **2014**, *37*, 134–148. [CrossRef]
56. Linker, L.C.; Shenk, G.W.; Wang, P.; Cerco, C.F.; Butt, A.J.; Tango, P.J.; Savidge, R.W. *A Comparison of the Chesapeake Bay Estuary Model Calibration with 1985–1994 Observed Data and Method of Application to Water Quality Criteria*; Modeling Subcommittee of the Chesapeake Bay Program: Annapolis, MD, USA, 2002.
57. Adolf, J.E.; Yeager, C.L.; Miller, W.D.; Mallonee, M.E.; Harding, L.W. Environmental forcing of phytoplankton floral composition, biomass, and primary productivity in Chesapeake Bay, USA. *Estuar. Coast. Shelf Sci.* **2006**, *67*, 108–122. [CrossRef]
58. Harding, L.W.; Meeson, B.W.; Fisher, T.R. Phytoplankton production in two east coast estuaries: Photosynthesis-light functions and patterns of carbon assimilation in Chesapeake and Delaware Bays. *Estuar. Coast. Shelf Sci.* **1986**, *23*, 773–806. [CrossRef]
59. Bronk, D.A.; Glibert, P.M.; Malone, T.C.; Banahan, S.; Sahlsten, E. Inorganic and organic nitrogen cycling in Chesapeake Bay: Autotrophic versus heterotrophic processes and relationships to carbon flux. *Aquat. Microb. Ecol.* **1998**, *15*, 177–189. [CrossRef]
60. Roman, M.; Zhang, X.; McGilliard, C.; Boicourt, W. Seasonal and annual variability in the spatial patterns of plankton biomass in Chesapeake Bay. *Limnol. Oceanogr.* **2005**, *50*, 480–492. [CrossRef]

Journal of
Marine Science and Engineering

Article

Effects of Harbor Shape on the Induced Sedimentation; L-Type Basin

Rozita Kian [1,*,†], Deniz Velioglu [2,‡], Ahmet Cevdet Yalciner [2,‡] and Andrey Zaytsev [3,‡]

[1] Ocean Engineering Department, University of Rhode Island, Narragansett, RI 02882, USA
[2] Civil Engineering Department, Middle East Technical University, Ankara 06800, Turkey;
    denizcivil@gmail.com (D.V.); yalciner@metu.edu.tr (A.C.Y.)
[3] Special Research Bureau for Automation of Marine Researches, Far Eastern Branch of Russian Academy of
    Sciences, Uzhno-Sakhalinsk 693013, Russia; aizaytsev@mail.ru
*   Correspondence: rozita_kian@uri.edu; Tel.: +1-401-874-61-39
†   Current address: Department of Ocean Engineering, University of Rhode Island, Narragansett,
    RI 02882, USA.
‡   These authors contributed equally to this work.

Academic Editor: Richard P. Signell
Received: 18 July 2016; Accepted: 24 August 2016; Published: 2 September 2016

Abstract: Tsunamis in shallow water zones lead to sea water level rise and fall, strong currents, forces (drag, impact, uplift, etc.), morphological changes (erosion, deposition), dynamic water pressure, as well as resonant oscillations. As a result, ground materials under the tsunami motion move, and scour/erosion/deposition patterns can be observed in the region. Ports and harbors as enclosed basins are the main examples of coastal structures that usually encounter natural hazards with small or huge damaging scales. Morphological changes are one of the important phenomena in the basins under short and long wave attack. Tsunamis as long waves lead to sedimentation in the basins, and therefore, in this study, the relation to the current pattern is noticed to determine sedimentation modes. Accordingly, we present a methodology based on the computation of the instantaneous Rouse number to investigate the tsunami motion and to calculate the respective sedimentation. This study aims to investigate the effects of the incident wave period on an L-type harbor sedimentation with a flat bathymetry using a numerical tool, NAMI DANCE, which solves non-linear shallow water equations. The results showed that the corner points on the bending part of the basin are always the critical points where water surface elevation and current velocity amplify in the exterior and interior corners, respectively.

Keywords: numerical modeling; amplification; L-type basin; Rouse number

1. Introduction

Ocean waves cannot generate enough energy to affect open coasts by resonance amplification, yet they can cause hazardous oscillations as they enter the enclosed or semi-enclosed basins and harbors. Tsunamis are known to be a very destructive phenomenon in shallow water, leading to sea water level rise and fall, strong currents, scour and morphological changes (erosion, deposition), resonant oscillations and seiches [1,2]. Wave radiation via the semi-enclosed basins is an important factor in decaying energy. Nonetheless, making the harbor entrance narrower results in the amplification of arriving wave. In fact, both harbor resonance period and harbor damage parameters can be related by harbor structures' design determining the harbor geometry [3]. Generally, wave disturbance is a major factor in harbor design assumptions [4]. Breakwaters are capable of protecting the harbors against short waves [5], but the ability of long waves (with 25–300-s periods) in entering the harbors makes it often beyond control and causes oscillation problems [6–8]. Periods of oscillations can be in the range of a few seconds to a few minutes depending on the harbor geometry [9,10]. Several regular-shaped basins have been simulated to determine the first and the second mode of free oscillations of the basins, such as the L-type basin in [11]. The current study investigates the effect of wave period on the estimation of tsunami evolution, propagation and amplification, as well as tsunami currents and morphology changes in L-type basins with flat bathymetry. Here, a methodology is presented based on the computation of the instantaneous Rouse number [12] during tsunami simulation to investigate the tsunami motion and to determine the mode of the sediment transport. This is by computing the spatial and temporal change of the Rouse number under tsunami inundation according to the approach given in [13]. Accordingly, the numerical model NAMI DANCE [14] is employed to study the oscillations and amplification of waves and currents, as well as sediment motions in a harbor of the L shape with a flat bathymetry. This numerical tool has been developed by the C++ programming language using the leap-frog scheme numerical solution procedure. It utilizes the finite difference computational method to solve linear and nonlinear forms of depth-averaged shallow water equations in long wave problems. Since some natural harbors can be in the L shape after smoothing, here we investigate the current amplification and sediment movement in L-type basins for several free oscillation periods. It is observed that the corner points in the bending part of L-type basins are the critical points where the wave amplitude and current velocity amplify in basin free oscillation wave periods. Furthermore, the exposed sediment motion can be categorized according to the Rouse number values.

2. Materials and Methods

2.1. Rouse Number

The sediment motion can be observed by monitoring the spatial and temporal changes of the Rouse number. The Rouse number is a dimensionless number for classifying the modes of sediment transport [13]. It is defined as the ratio of particle settling velocity to the shear velocity:

$$R_0 = \frac{w_s}{\beta \kappa u_*} \tag{1}$$

where u_* is the shear velocity, β denotes the ratio of sediment diffusion to momentum diffusion coefficients (approximately equal to 1), κ is the von Karman constant (equal to 0.4) and settling velocity w_s is given by [13]:

$$w_s = \frac{8\nu}{d} \left(\sqrt{1 + \frac{(s-1)gd^3}{72\nu^2}} - 1 \right) \tag{2}$$

where s is the density of sand in water, i.e., the ratio of sediment density to water density (ρ_s/ρ), d represents the mean grain size, g is gravitational acceleration, ν denotes kinematic viscosity and u_* is the shear velocity and can be written according to Equation (3) [13].

$$u_* = u\sqrt{\frac{f}{8}} \tag{3}$$

where f is the Darcy friction factor in the range of (0.006–0.039), and it is generally assumed to be equal to 0.01 in tsunami cases [13]. The mean grain size (d) for the entire domain is assumed 0.3 mm, which is a close value to the real cases (i.e., Belek area [15,16]). The values for the constants required for settling velocity and shear velocity calculations are listed in Table 1.

Table 1. Typical constants.

ν, Kinematic Viscosity	1.0×10^{-6} m^2/s
g, Gravitational Acceleration	9.81 m/s^2
ρ, Density of Water	1025 kg/m^3
ρ_s, Density of Sediment Particles	2650 kg/m^3

Modes of the sediment transport can be determined according to the Rouse number values. Sediment transport modes are in the form of bed load, suspended load and wash load (Table 2). Rouse number values greater than 2.5 represent the bed load form of sediment motion, while a value less than 0.8 is the mode of wash load sediment motion fully supported by the flow. Large values of the Rouse number indicate slower sediment motion and less severe erosion or deposition. On the other hand, smaller values of the Rouse number show more severe erosion in the topography.

Table 2. Modes of transport according to the Rouse number [13].

Mode of Transport	Rouse Number
Initiation of Motion (Deposition)	$R_0 > 7$
Bed Load	$2.5 < R_0 < 7.5$
Suspended Load: (50% Suspended), Density of Water	$1.2 < R_0 < 2.5$
Suspended Load: (100% Suspended)	$0.8 < R_0 < 1.2$
Wash Load	$R_0 < 0.8$

2.2. Numerical Model

The effect of wave period on tsunami-induced sedimentation in the L-type basins is investigated using NAMI DANCE code. The governing equations of NAMI DANCE are the nonlinear form of shallow water equations. The schematic form of the basin in the simulations and 10 selected gauge points is illustrated in Figure 1. Depicted in Figure 1a are the metric dimensions of the basin, while Figure 1b shows the dimensions in the geographical outline (longitude-latitude) used in NAMI DANCE simulations. Initially, 100 gauge points are selected out of which 10 points are presented here. The bathymetry is flat, and the water depth is 20 m. LA in Figure 1a is the vertical dimension, and LB is the horizontal dimension of the basin. In half of the simulations, LA and LB are both used as 1000 m and another half of LA is 800 m (by placing the input source 200 m from the border), while LB is kept constant as 1000 m. The bending side is used as 400 m, and the grid size (Δx) and time step (Δt) are selected as 2 m and 0.005 s, respectively in all simulations. The input waves are in the form of several sinusoidal functions. They are sinusoidal crest lines entering parallel to the horizontal side (B side) from the basin entrance (400 m opening in the A side). The input waves are considered to have a 1-m amplitude with several random periods (16 s, 46 s, 90 s, 146 s and 328 s). Among those, 328 s, 146 s and 90 s are the second, fourth and seventh modes of the basin free oscillations [17], respectively. The differences of harbor modes for LA/LB = 0.8 and LA/LB = 1 are negligible (less than 5 s), and hence, they are only presented for the L-type basin with LA/LB = 1 dimensions in [17]. The boundaries are set with a 20-m wall; therefore, they perform as reflective, where their effects are considered in the next waves during the simulations after the first wave reaches the boundaries. It is worth mentioning that all simulations are performed for 40 min.

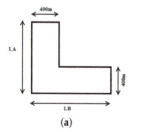

(a)

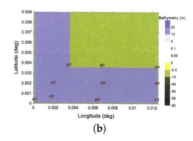

(b)

Figure 1. L-type basin used in the simulations. (**a**) LA is the vertical dimension and LB the horizontal dimension of the L-type basin. (**b**) Dimensions are in the geographical outline. Red stars represent the gauge points.

3. Results

3.1. Free Surface Elevation

The spatial distribution of maximum water elevation, maximum current velocity and the minimum Rouse number are computed at each grid in the domain during the 40-min simulations. Shown in Figure 2 is the maximum water surface elevation for a sinusoidal line crest long wave pertaining to a 1-m wave amplitude LA/LB = 0.8 in the left column and LA/LB = 1 in the right column. The time history of the free surface elevations in two corner points of the basin, Gauge 57 (g57, interior corner) and Gauge 63 (g63, exterior corner), is also shown for the first 30 min in Figure 3.

The results of the maximum water surface elevation in Figure 2 show that the corner points on the bending part of the basin are always the critical points where water surface elevation amplifies in the exterior corner (Gauge 63). Therefore, the time series of free surface elevations are also represented in Figure 3 to evaluate their behavior during the simulation. The seventh mode of the basin free oscillation period (90 s) is a very critical wave period, and there are approximate wave and current amplifications in the entire basin.

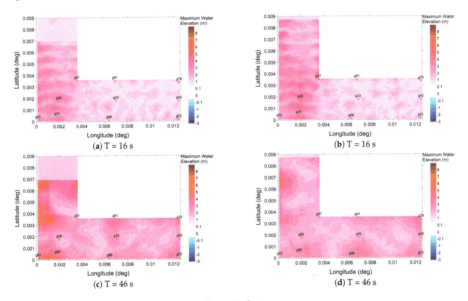

Figure 2. *Cont.*

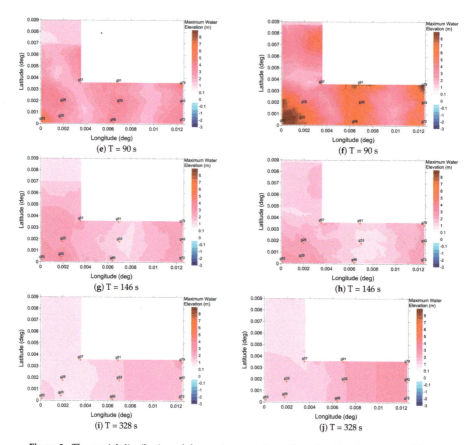

Figure 2. The spatial distribution of the maximum water surface elevation (m) computed by the simulation of the sinusoidal line crest long wave with a 1-m wave amplitude with T = 16 s, T = 46 s, T = 90 s, T = 146 s, T = 328 s for LA/LB = 0.8 in the left column and LA/LB = 1 in the right column.

3.2. Current Velocity

The maximum current velocities for the sinusoidal line crest long wave are shown in Figure 4. The results pertain to a 1-m wave amplitude where the conditions with LA/LB = 0.8 and LA/LB = 1 are depicted in the left and the right columns, respectively. The time history of the current velocity in two corner points of the basin, Gauge 57 and Gauge 63, are shown in Figure 5.

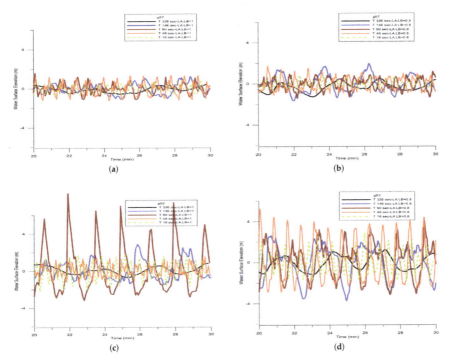

Figure 3. Time history of water surface elevation computed by the simulation of the sinusoidal line crest long wave with a 1-m wave amplitude with T = 16 s, T = 46 s, T = 90 s, T = 146 s, T = 328 s for LA/LB = 1 (left column), for LA/LB = 0.8 (right column) in Gauge 57 (**a,b**) and Gauge 63 (**c,d**).

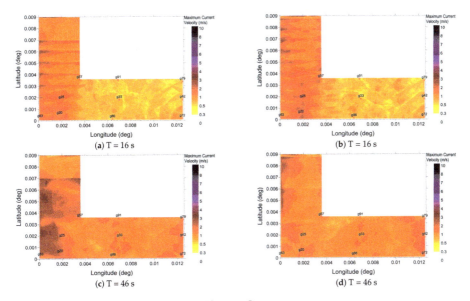

Figure 4. *Cont.*

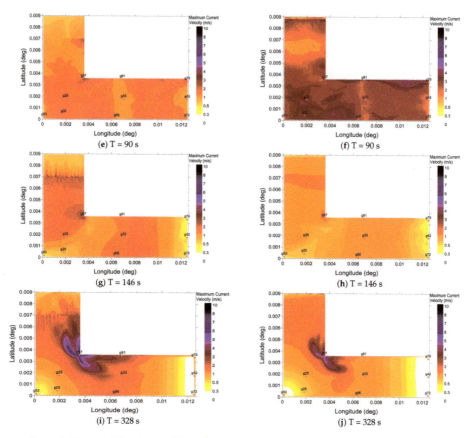

Figure 4. The spatial distribution of the maximum current velocity (m/s) computed by the simulation of the sinusoidal line crest long wave with a 1-m wave amplitude with T = 16 s, T = 46 s, T = 90 s, T = 146 s, T = 328 s for LA/LB = 0.8 in the left column and LA/LB = 1 in the right column (**a–j**).

The results presented in Figure 4 demonstrate that the corner points on the bending part of the basin are always the critical points where current velocity amplifies in the interior corners (Gauge 57). Therefore, similar to the previous case, the time series of the current velocity are also represented in Figure 5 to see their behavior during the simulation. Briefly, Gauge 63 in the exterior corner of the L-type basin is the location in which the water surface elevation amplifies extremely, but there is no current amplification. Furthermore, the current velocity amplifies extremely in Gauge 57 in the interior corner of the L-type basin, however with no wave amplification.

Comparing Figure 2 and Figure 4, it can be inferred that in shorter wave periods, the vertical side of the basin (A side) is more exposed to the wave and current amplifications, but in larger wave periods, the maximum values occur in the horizontal side of the L (B side).

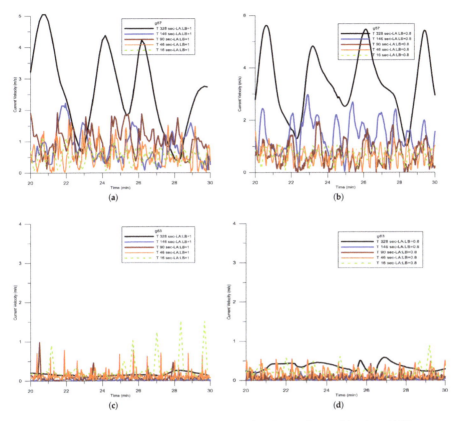

Figure 5. Time history of the current velocity computed by the simulation of the sinusoidal line crest long wave with a 1-m wave amplitude with T = 16 s, T = 46 s, T = 90 s, T = 146 s, T = 328 s for LA/LB = 1 (left column), for LA/LB = 0.8 (right column) in Gauge 57 (**a,b**) and Gauge 63 (**c,d**).

3.3. Rouse Number

The minimum Rouse number distribution, as well as the maximum velocity vectors are shown in Figure 6. According to the range of the Rouse number values, the sediment motion in the exterior corner (Gauge 63) is in bed load mode for larger wave periods (T 146 s and 328 s). In the end side of the basin, sediments move in the form of bed load in larger wave periods, as well. This indicates that these areas in the basin have high potential to be exposed by the material deposition.

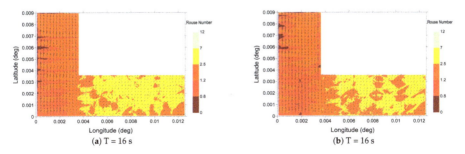

Figure 6. *Cont.*

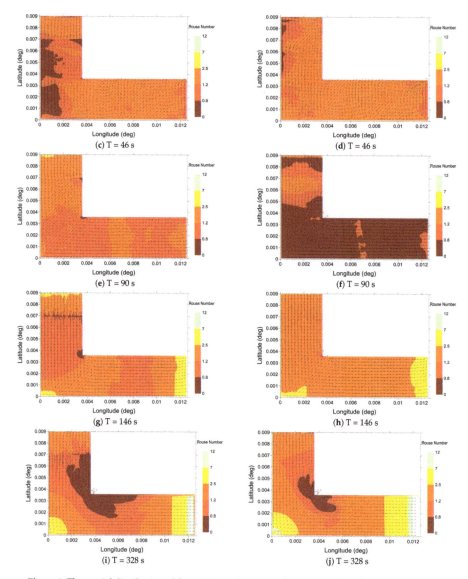

Figure 6. The spatial distribution of the minimum Rouse number computed by the simulation of the sinusoidal line crest long wave with a 1-m wave amplitude with T = 16 s, T = 46 s, T = 90 s, T = 146 s, T = 328 s for LA/LB = 0.8 in the left column and LA/LB = 1 in the right column (**a–j**), respectively. The maximum velocity vectors are also shown for each case.

4. Discussion

The behavior of an L-type basin with a flat depth is studied for wave and current amplification. Furthermore, the sediment motion as a morphological change pattern is investigated via 10 selected gauge points. The results of the maximum water surface elevation, maximum current velocity and minimum Rouse number show that the corner points on the bending side of the basin are always the critical points where water surface elevation and current velocity amplify in the exterior corner point (Gauge 57) and interior corner point (Gauge 63), respectively. Therefore, the time series of free surface elevation and current velocity are also examined to see their behavior during the simulation. According to the time history results of the water surface elevation and current velocity, it is evident that when the vertical side is shorter (LA/LB = 0.8), the amplification magnitude of the free surface elevation and current velocity in the interior corner point of the basin (Gauge 57) is larger than the case with the longer side (LA/LB = 1); however, the opposite holds for the exterior corner point (Gauge 63). Besides, the simulation results show that in the same L-type basin, in shorter wave periods, the wave and current amplifications mostly occur in the vertical side of the basin (A side), where the input source wave begins to propagate. Nevertheless, in larger wave periods, the amplifications take place in the horizontal side of the L-type basin (B side). Therefore, we can conclude that the dimensions of the L-type basin do not affect the occurrence region of the critical points for maximum water surface elevation and maximum current velocity. In all gauge points (except corner points), the wave and current amplify simultaneously if the wave period meets the free oscillation period in the basin. However, it is noticeable that in the interior (smaller) side of L-type basins, the amplification is higher than the exterior (larger) side of it. Furthermore, large periods affect the end parts of the basin more than the smaller wave periods. This phenomenon is more obvious in wave amplification. Comparing the maximum current velocity results with the minimum Rouse number results, one can conclude that the pattern of sediment motion in the mentioned two critical corner points and in the whole basin depends on both the current pattern and magnitude. In large wave periods, the sediment motion in the exterior corner (Gauge 63) is often in the bed load form, while in the interior corner (Gauge 57) in the wash load form. This indicates that, in higher periods, the interior and exterior corners can be exposed to the sediment erosion and deposition, respectively. However, sediment motion in long wave conditions needs further analysis in closed basins, where it becomes a prominent problem for harbors and ports. Further studies on sediment motion seem necessary to determine the performance and validity of NLSWEwhen the volume of the transmitted sediments needs to be measured under the current behavior of the long waves. Furthermore, more investigations should be performed to analyze the behavior of L-type basins with varying depths and then applied to real harbors of this type.

Acknowledgments: Support by 603839 ASTARTE Project of EU, UDAP C-12-14 project of AFAD, Turkey, Russia Turkey Joint Research grant project No. 213M534 of TUBITAK Turkey, grant MK-4315.2015.5 and grants of RFBR 14-05-00092, 15-55-45053 are acknowledged.

Author Contributions: R.K. started with the preliminary simulations and test, developed the necessary database and input wave data, conveyed all simulations, interpreted, compared and discussed the results and prepared the paper. D.V. contributed to the quality and analysis of the data. A.C.Y. and A.Z. took part in the development and insertion of the new module to the numerical tool NAMI DANCE and reviewed the results and discussions.

Conflicts of Interest: The authors declare no conflict of interest.

References

1. Keshtpoor, M.; Puleo, J.A.; Gebert, J.; Plant, N.G. Numerical simulation of nearshore hydrodynamics and sediment transport downdrift of a tidal inlet. *J. Waterw. Port Coast. Ocean Eng.* **2014**, *141*, 0414035.
2. Keshtpoor, M.; Puleo, J.A.; Shi, F. Downdrift beach erosion adjacent to the Indian River inlet, Delaware, USA. *Shore Beach* **2014**, *82*, 31–41.
3. Kian, R.; Yalciner, A.C.; Aytore, B.; Zaytsev, A. Wave amplification and resonance in enclosed basins; A case study in Haydarpasa Port of Istanbul. In Proceedings of the Currents, Waves and Turbulence Measurement (CWTM) 2015 IEEE/OES, St. Petersburg, FL, USA, 2–6 March 2015; Volume 11, pp. 1–7.
4. Sawaragi, T.; Kubo, M. The motion of a moored ship in a harbour basin. In *Coastal Engineering*; American Society of Civil Engineers: New York, NY, USA, 1982; pp. 2743–2762.
5. Van der Molen, W.; Monárdez Santander, P.; Van Dongeren, A.R. Modeling of Infragravity Waves and Moored Ship Motions in Tomakomai Port. In Proceedings of the Harbor Long Wave Conference, Yokosuka, Japan, July 2004 .
6. Kioka, W.R. Long period oscillations in a harbour caused by typhoon. In *Coastal Engineering*; American Society of Civil Engineers: New York, NY, USA, 1996; pp. 1491–1502.

7. Jeong, W.M.; Chae, J.W.; Park, W.S.; Jung, K.T. Field measurements and numerical modelling of harbour oscillations during storm waves. In *Coastal Engineering*; American Society of Civil Engineers: New York, NY, USA, 1996; pp. 1268–1279.

8. Bellotti, G.; Franco, L. Measurement of long waves at the harbor of Marina di Carrara, Italy. *Ocean Dyn.* **2011**, *61*, 2051–2059.

9. Rabinovich, A.B. Seiches and Harbor Oscillations. In *Handbook of Coastal and Ocean Engineering*; World Scientific Publishing Co.: Singapore, 2009; pp. 193–236.

10. Thotagamuwage, D.T.P. Harbour Oscillations: Generation and Minimisation of Their Impacts. Ph.D. Dissertation, The University of Western Australia, Perth, Western Australia, 2014.

11. Kakinuma, T.; Toyofuku, T.; Inoue, T. Numerical Analysis of Harbor Oscillation in Harbors of Various Shapes. Available online: https://icce-ojs-tamu.tdl.org/icce/index.php/icce/article/view/6840/pdf (accessed on 1 September 2016).

12. Kian, R.; Pamuk, A.; Yalciner, A.C.; Zaytsev, A. Effects of tsunami parameters on the sedimentation. In Proceedings of the Coastal Sediments Conference (CS15), San Diego, CA, USA, 13–15 May 2015; Volume 8, pp. 67–74.

13. Yeh, H.; Li, W. Tsunami scour and sedimentation. In Proceedings of the 4nd International Conference on Scour and Erosion, American Geophysical Union, San Francisco, CA, USA, December 2008; pp. 95–106.

14. NAMI DANCE Manual. Zaytsev, C., Yalciner, P.K., (Eds.); Tsunami Simulation/Visualization Code NAMI DANCE versions 4.9. 2010. Available online: http://www.namidance.ce.metu.edu.tr (accessed on 3 July 2014).

15. Ergin, M.; Keskin, S.; Dogan, A.U.; Kadıoglu, Y.K.; Karakas, Z. Grain size and heavy mineral distribution as related to hinterland and environmental conditions for modern beach sediments from the Gulfs of Antalya and Finike, eastern Mediterranean. *Mar Geol.* **2007**, *240*, 185–196.

16. Pamuk, A. Assessment of Inland Tsunami Parameters and Their Effects on Morphology. Master's Thesis, Middle East Technical University, Ankara, Turkey, 2014.

17. Kian, R. Tsunami Induced Wave and Current Amplification and Sedimentation in Closed Basins. Ph.D. Dissertation, Middle East Technical University, Ankara, Turkey, 2015.

Journal of
Marine Science and Engineering

Review

An Exploration of Wind Stress Calculation Techniques in Hurricane Storm Surge Modeling

Kyra M. Bryant [1] and Muhammad Akbar [2,*]

[1]   Department of Civil and Environmental Engineering, Tennessee State University, Nashville, TN 37209, USA; kmb5482@yahoo.com

[2]   Department of Mechanical and Manufacturing Engineering, Tennessee State University, Nashville, TN 37209, USA

*   Correspondence: makbar@tnstate.edu; Tel.: +1-615-963-5392

Academic Editor: Richard P. Signell
Received: 18 July 2016; Accepted: 30 August 2016; Published: 13 September 2016

Abstract: As hurricanes continue to threaten coastal communities, accurate storm surge forecasting remains a global priority. Achieving a reliable storm surge prediction necessitates accurate hurricane intensity and wind field information. The wind field must be converted to wind stress, which represents the air-sea momentum flux component required in storm surge and other oceanic models. This conversion requires a multiplicative drag coefficient for the air density and wind speed to represent the air-sea momentum exchange at a given location. Air density is a known parameter and wind speed is a forecasted variable, whereas the drag coefficient is calculated using an empirical correlation. The correlation's accuracy has brewed a controversy of its own for more than half a century. This review paper examines the lineage of drag coefficient correlations and their acceptance among scientists.

Keywords: drag coefficient; wind stress; storm surge; estuarine and coastal modeling; hydrodynamic modeling; wave modeling; air-sea interaction; air-sea momentum flux; hurricane intensity; tropical cyclone

---

1. Introduction

Hurricanes, also referred to as tropical cyclones or typhoons, transfer vast amounts of heat from tropical areas to cooler climates, while bringing rain to dry lands, to maintain global atmospheric balance [1–7]. Along the way, they can be exceedingly destructive, and at times turn into very expensive natural disasters. In many unfortunate cases, fatalities have occurred through storm surges and flooding that follow the hurricane's landfall. In 1970, a cyclone in the Bay of Bengal claimed approximately 300,000 lives [8–10]. In 2005, Hurricane Katrina in the Gulf of Mexico claimed an estimated 1833 lives [11,12] and cost over $100 billion in damages [13–16]. The magnitude of these catastrophes is driven by hurricane wind, which serves a vital role in the development and behavior of associated storm surge and wave propagation. As evidence points to a future of more intense storms due to an increasing sea surface temperature [4,17–20], the need for a high-performing forecasting model is now a global priority. Hurricane track forecasting has improved significantly over the years, but forecasting hurricane intensity remains fraught with uncertainty [21].

Hurricane wind interacts with the ocean to create air-sea momentum fluxes or wind stress. This wind stress drives oceanic circulation and serves as a vital surface forcing for waves and storm surges, which lead to flooding once a hurricane makes landfall [22–27]. The momentum transfer between the atmosphere and sea interface is described as the air–sea momentum exchange. Modeling reliable surface wave fields and oceanic circulation requires an accurate estimate of the momentum exchange for wind stress formulation [26,28].

Since 1916, wind stress has traditionally been calculated from the product of air density, a drag coefficient, and the quantity wind speed squared [29]. Unlike wind density and speed, which are measurable quantities, the drag coefficient must be approximated as a function of speed, offering ample room for flexibility. This flexibility has baffled scientists since its inception, stimulating decades of debate [24,30–32]. Since hurricane wind data was limited in earlier decades due to insufficient technology [33], investigators were often forced to extrapolate drag coefficients from lower wind speeds to higher wind speeds, typically from 25 m/s to extreme high winds [24,25]. As technology progressed, data eventually revealed a significant difference in the drag coefficients between low and high wind speeds. Observations indicated a reduced drag coefficient for wind speeds above 33 m/s [26]. Yet, some prediction models to-date still utilize the outdated correlations [28,34–36], while others have incorporated ad hoc modifications, such as capping [37].

This review study chronologically explores the evolution of various drag coefficient correlations. It provides their derivations and unravels historic origins rarely discussed in open literature. Drag coefficient correlations from 1959 to 2015 are examined. In addition, the breakthrough of dropwindsondes in the late 1990s is examined along with its effect on the drag coefficient.

2. Historical Theory: Early Wind Stress Formulations (1687–1955)

2.1. Newton (1687)–Bermoulli, d'Alembert, Euler, Navier (1700s)–Cauchy, Poisson, Saint-Venant, Stokes (1800s)–Prandtl (1904)

Wind stress signifies the shear stress exerted by the wind on the surface of the earth and ocean. The concept of fluid flow and shear stress was first postulated by Sir Isaac Newton in 1687 [38]. In his second book of the *Principia*, in Section IX, "The circular motion of fluids", he published an extraordinary hypothesis in Latin. The hypothesis was translated into English by Andrew Motte in 1729 as, "The resistance arising from the want of lubricity in the parts of a fluid, is, other things being equal, proportional to the velocity with which the parts of the fluid are separated from one other." Here, the resistance is the shear stress (τ), the lubricity in the parts of a fluid is the viscosity, (μ), and the velocity with which the parts of the fluid are separated from one another is the velocity gradient $\left(\frac{du}{dy}\right)$ [39]. After Newton, the Swiss mathematician and physicist Daniel Bernouilli published his famous work *Hydrodynamica* in 1738 about the conservation of energy [40]. In 1752, French mathematician Jean le Rond d'Alembert proved that for incompressible and inviscid potential flow, the drag force is zero on a body moving with a constant velocity relative to the fluid [41]. In 1757, the famous Swiss mathematician Leonhard Euler published an important set of equations for inviscid flow called the Euler equations [42]. To account for viscosity, the equations of motion were developed independently by four Frenchmen—Navier in 1822, Cauchy in 1823, Poisson in 1829, and Saint-Venant in 1837, and one Irishman—Stokes in 1845. The well-known Navier-Stokes equations became a universal basis for fluid mechanics analysis [43]. In August 1904, Ludwig Prandtl, a 29-year-old professor from the Technische Hochschule in Hanover, Germany, gave a ten minute presentation [38], introducing the boundary layer theory to explain the flow of a slightly viscous fluid near a solid surface. He showed that the flow past a body can be divided into two regions: a very thin layer, where the viscosity is important, and the remaining region outside this layer, where the viscosity can be neglected. This theory turned out to be exceptionally useful [44,45]. The skin-friction drag force next to the surface negated previous beliefs that viscosity in water and air was negligible [46]. He also introduced the shear (friction) velocity to explain the boundary layer phenomena [45,47]:

$$U_* = \sqrt{\frac{\tau_b}{\rho}} \tag{1}$$

where U_* is the shear velocity, τ_b, is the shear stress at the boundary layer, and ρ is the air density.

2.2. Ekman (1905)

It is worth mentioning that while studying the slope of the Baltic sea during a storm in 1872, Ekman produced a relation that is strikingly similar to the traditional wind stress formula developed a decade later (presented in the next sub-section). Around 1905, he combined his results with the field measurements of Colding (1876) and obtained the following formula for wind stress at the water surface [48,49]:

$$\tau_b = 2.6 \times 10^{-3} \rho W^2 \tag{2}$$

where W and ρ are wind the wind speed and density, respectively.

2.3. Taylor (1915)

After wind observations conducted in 1915, British physicist G.I. Taylor theorized the presence of a nondimensional skin friction coefficient to characterize the drag exerted from a solid surface onto a passing flow [29]. He proposed the following equation to depict this skin friction on the earth's surface:

$$\tau_b = \rho C U_s^2 \tag{3a}$$

where U_s is the velocity near the surface and C is a constant skin friction coefficient with an approximate value between 0.002 and 0.003 for the ground at Salisbury Plain, where the wind observations were made [29,50]. These approximations match Ekman's formula, given as Equation (2).

To resolve the disparity between field and laboratory results, the surface wind stress formula eventually evolved to be [51]:

$$\tau = \rho C_d U^2 \tag{3b}$$

where τ is wind stress, C_d is the drag coefficient, and U is the mean wind speed most often denoted as U_{10} for the neutral-stability wind speed at 10 m height [52]. This equation became the general practice for estimating the interfacial stress with a wind-speed dependent drag coefficient [53]. By comparing Equations (1) and (3b), one can deduce

$$U_*^2 = C_d U_{10}^2 \tag{4}$$

Last of all, Taylor also introduced the mixing length concept [54], though Prandtl is traditionally credited for it since he fully used the concept.

2.4. Prandtl (1925)

By 1925, Prandtl merged theory and experimental data, which previously showed great discrepancies [55]. One such achievement is the mixing length model, which resulted from his attempt to convey eddy viscosity, previously introduced by Boussinesq, in terms of flow conditions. The model theorized turbulent flow by accounting for the variability of turbulent mixing [56,57]. In terms of the mixing length, l, he is translated as stating it "may be considered as the diameter of the masses of fluid moving as a whole in each individual case; or again, as the distance traversed by a mass of this type before it becomes blended in with neighboring masses..." and this is "only a rough approximation" [58–61]. In simple terms, it is the distance a fluid element or eddy retains its identity as it strays from the mean streamline. This concept led to Prandtl's mixing length formula for turbulent shear stress [62],

$$\tau = \rho l^2 \left| \frac{d\overline{U}}{dz} \right| \frac{d\overline{U}}{dz} \tag{5}$$

where $\overline{U}$ and z are the mean velocity and distance from the wall, respectively. The Mixing Length Theory became a successful method for calculating turbulent flow, leading to one of the greatest oceanographic applications [49].

2.5. Von Kármán (1930) and Prandtl (1932)

Five years later, Prandtl's doctoral student from the University of Göttingen in Germany, Theodore von Kármán, studied the behavior of turbulence close to a boundary, or wall. Prandtl assumed that l is proportional to the distance, z, ($l \propto z$), such that

$$l = kz \tag{6}$$

where k is a constant [62–65]. This simple proportionality suggests that turbulent fluctuations must vanish at $z = 0$, making $l = 0$. Inversely, l must increase with z [64]. Substituting Equations (1) and (6) into Equation (5) yields

$$\frac{d\bar{U}}{dz} = \frac{U_*}{k}\frac{1}{z} \tag{7}$$

Integrating Equation (7) once with respect to z reduces to the following:

$$U(z) = \frac{U_*}{k}\ln(z) + C \tag{8}$$

When solved, Equation (8) results into the von Kármán-Prandtl logarithmic velocity profile law for a neutrally stratified atmosphere [65],

$$U = \frac{U_*}{k}\ln\left(\frac{z}{z_0}\right) \tag{9}$$

where z_0 is the surface roughness length. Von Kármán published Equation (9) as the Law of the Wall in 1930 [66], while Prandtl published it in 1932 [67]. Laboratory studies have since found k to be between 0.40 and 0.41, and it is often referred to as the von Kármán constant.

For neutral atmospheric stability [68], this equation became the usual law for wind profiles, which suggests that wind speed increases logarithmically with height [69,70]. From Equations (4) and (9), a relationship of z_0 and C_d can be derived as

$$kC_d^{-\frac{1}{2}} = \ln\left(\frac{z_{10}}{z_0}\right) \tag{10}$$

2.6. Charnock (1955)

In 1955, Charnock exercised Equation (9) while conducting a laboratory experiment over a 1.6-km × 1-km reservoir [69]. He used anemometers to measure the mean wind speed in the lowest 8 m over the reservoir. Wind profiles were created using $\frac{U_*}{k}$ as slope and z_0 as the intercept from Equation (9) for comparison with profiles from other researchers. The comparisons resulted in a better agreement than expected and confirmed z_0's dependence on U_*. He characterized their relationship using the following equation:

$$\alpha = \frac{gz_0}{U_*^2} \tag{11}$$

where α is the proportionality constant and g is gravitational acceleration. Charnock originally proposed 0.012 as the value for α.

Charnock's discovery of the proportionality constant became a turning point in wind stress dialogue. The drag coefficient, C_d, can be obtained using Equations (4), (10), and (11). If z_0 is mainly dependent on U_* and wind velocity follows a logarithmic profile, then the drag coefficient must also increase with the wind velocity. Charnock's constant has long been used as a basis for many forthcoming studies. However, the proportionality constant does not account for the sea state, which may refer to wind wave fields or swell systems [71], limiting its accuracy and usability [68,72,73].

3. Historical Correlations: Early Drag Coefficient Formulations (1959–1997)

3.1. Wilson (1959, 1960)

During a severe storm in the northern Atlantic Ocean of 15–18 December 1959, numerous weather ships reported very high seas [51]. The threat of storm tides developing in the New York Bay from hurricanes moving through the Atlantic Ocean stimulated an urgent need for a dependable surface wind stress value. In return, investigators hoped to predict such hurricane storm tides. Wilson summarized 47 previous studies as having the following 10-m neutral values for the drag coefficient, C_{10}, and wind speed [51,73]:

$$C_{10} \times 10^3 = \begin{cases} 1.49, 1\frac{m}{s} < U_{10} < 10\frac{m}{s}, \\ 2.37, \quad U_{10} > 10\frac{m}{s}. \end{cases} \tag{12}$$

Wilson denoted wind speeds above 10 m/s as high winds. While both, laboratory and field studies, were considered, this era depended on limited data at hurricane wind speeds and premature technology. Meteorological observations for remote and inaccessible ocean areas were simply nonexistent [33].

3.2. Wu (1967)

In 1967, Wu collected 12 laboratory and 30 oceanic observations, concluding that the drag coefficient reached a saturated value and remained constant for wind speeds greater than 15 m/s [73]. This claim supported the speculation that waves cannot grow forever with wind velocity, as Charnock's relation implies. The following formulae were his original proposed methods for finding the drag coefficient:

$$C_{10} \times 10^3 = \begin{cases} 0.5 \times U_{10}^{\frac{1}{2}}, 1\frac{m}{s} < U_{10} < 15\frac{m}{s}, \\ 2.6, \quad U_{10} > 15\frac{m}{s}. \end{cases} \tag{13}$$

This parameterization leaves a noticeable gap at $U_{10} = 15$ m/s. For $U_{10} = 14.9$ m/s, $C_{10} \times 10^3 = 1.9$. For $U_{10} = 15.1$ m/s, $C_{10} \times 10^3 = 2.6$. Wu attributes this discontinuity to the intersection of wind velocity and phase velocity. He states that for wind velocities below 15 m/s, waves pull the air mass. Conversely, the air mass pushes waves for wind velocities above 15 m/s. He noted $U_{10} = 15$ m/s as the critical wind velocity.

Wu would later alter his perspective of a constant drag coefficient at high winds, but this early work displays significance as it is one of the earliest published studies to doubt the idea of an increasing drag coefficient by proposing a saturated drag coefficient for *strong winds*. Of course, merely increasing critical wind speeds from 10 m/s to 15 m/s does not account for even the weakest Category I hurricane, but like Wilson, Wu was forced to rely on narrow datasets.

3.3. Garratt (1967)

A decade later, Garratt addressed the following four major methods used to measure wind stress: surface water tilting, geostrophic flow departure, wind profile, and eddy correlation (Reynolds flux) [50]. He explained each technique and included their individual limitations. He then compiled data from 1967 to 1975 (Dataset 1), which were collected using the wind profile and eddy correlation methods. Wind speeds varied from 2 m/s to 21 m/s. Additionally, he assembled hurricane data from 1957 to 1975 (Dataset 2), which had been inferred using the geostrophic flow departure method with wind speeds ranging from 7.5 to 52 m/s. Garratt attributed data scatter among Dataset 1 as a result of insufficiently long averaging periods and calibration uncertainties from the field technology over the sea.

After analyzing the data collections, Garratt proposed two options for calculating the neutral drag coefficient. They consisted of a power law relation

$$C_{10} \times 10^3 = 0.51 U_{10}^{0.46}, \quad 4\frac{m}{s} < U_{10} < 21\frac{m}{s} \tag{14}$$

and a linear relation

$$C_{10} \times 10^3 = 0.75 + 0.067 U_{10}, \quad 4\frac{m}{s} < U_{10} < 21\frac{m}{s} \tag{15}$$

Equation (14) closely resembles Wu's Equation (13), but Garratt opposed Wu's proposal of a constant drag coefficient above 15 m/s. He validated Charnock's relation with the data collections, producing a Charnock constant, α, of 0.0144 and a von Kármán constant, k, of 0.41 ± 0.025.

Garratt's results have been published in a multitude of textbooks, and his review analysis influenced numerous other investigators. Modified and unmodified versions of Garratt's linear law for the drag coefficient, Equation (15), are used in the ADvanced CIRCulation (ADCIRC) storm surge model [37], CALifornia METeorological model (CALMET) [74], Curvilinear Hydrodynamics in Three-Dimensions-Waterways Experiment Station (CH3D-WES) [75], NOAA's Hurricane Research Division Wind Analysis System (H*WIND)/Interactive Objective Kinematic Analysis (IOKA) [76], and presumably more.

3.4. Smith (1980)

According to Smith, the sea state is determined by fetch, duration, water depth, and surface slick conditions [32] from natural oils and impurities, which reduce the surface roughness [77]. He anticipated higher drag coefficients at short fetches, due to growing waves absorbing momentum from the wind. Smith applied the eddy correlation method to analyze direct measurements collected offshore, onshore, and alongshore from thrust, Gill, and Aerovane anemometers on an offshore platform. He notes that the Smith and Banke [78] portion of data was potentially affected by breaking waves due to shoaling and being collected at limited fetch, which falsely represents the open ocean. He observed that as Charnock predicted, the drag coefficient measured for long fetch increased with increasing wind speeds up to 22 m/s as follows:

$$C_{10} \times 10^3 = 0.61 + 0.063 U_{10}, \quad 6\frac{m}{s} < U_{10} < 22\frac{m}{s} \tag{16}$$

This correlation is slightly lower than those proposed by Smith and Banke [78] and Garratt [50]. During periods of alongshore winds, he was surprised to find the drag coefficient to be much lower than during offshore or onshore winds. Smith speculated oil from numerous sources along the shoreline as a possible reason. This would affect the surface slick conditions and reduce the surface roughness, but observing slicks was not included in the experiment. He also concluded that a stronger correlation existed between the drag coefficient and wind speed rather than wave height.

3.5. Wu (1980, 1982)

In 1980, Wu revisited the drag coefficient debate, arguing that Charnock's relation, which most studies revolved around, offered a basic correlation between the drag coefficient and wind velocity and fetch, but Charnock constant values continued to be scattered [79]. More specifically, the relation tended to work well in the laboratory but was inconsistent in the field. Even though the logarithmic wind profile and Charnock relation had generally been accepted, he questioned whether or not the drag coefficient depended exclusively on wind velocity, while its dependency on fetch had sparsely been explored. Wu (1) reasoned that the drag coefficient increases with wind velocity and decreases with fetch; (2) offered a refined Charnock relation including surface tension and viscosity; and (3) generated a single, linear law empirical formula for estimating oceanic drag coefficients at all wind velocities to replace his previous correlation from Equation (13).

He used his previous laboratory and oceanic data to verify Equation (10) at exceptionally diverse fetches. The value of the Charnock constant, α, was chosen to be 0.0156 to provide the best correlation between laboratory and oceanic data, which fell in the typical range of other studies, 0.012–0.035. After exploring different Charnock constants and wind velocities at 10-m heights and fetches at $U_{10} = 10\frac{m}{s}$, Wu found that short fetches yield greater drag coefficients. This study of fetch verified Wu's claim that the drag coefficient decreases with fetch.

Wu reasoned that scattered Charnock values found in various studies were due to how the roughness length was defined, how the drag coefficient was calculated, and how the Charnock values were obtained through curve fitting. He suggested that the roughness length increased with wind friction velocity at a faster rate than the Charnock relation implies. To remedy these errors, he offered a refined Charnock relation which included roughness length, wind-friction velocity, gravity, surface tension, and viscosity. While viscosity and surface tension are minor parameters, Wu disputed they were far from negligible. He recommended future studies to consider other parameters, such as, wind gustiness, swells, currents, and sea spray at high wind velocities.

Lastly, Wu realized that his 1967 study failed to consider data collection methods used to measure wind stress. Nine data sets were collected using the surface tilting method, a technique found to be grossly affected by wave setup and susceptible to errors from horizontal temperature gradients [50], tidal and seiche movements, and near-shore wave effects [80]. In contrast, the wind profile method faces limitations only at low heights of 1-m and low winds of 3 m/s, while the eddy correlation method requires a fixed and stable platform. Therefore, these sets were eliminated and replaced with 12 newer data sets collected by wind profile and eddy correlation methods, similar to the remaining original data sets. Upon closer examination, the following linear formula resulted in a better fit of the modified data than his previously proposed correlation, Equation (13):

$$C_{10} \times 10^3 = 0.8 + 0.065 U_{10}, \qquad U_{10} > 1\frac{m}{s} \tag{17}$$

This equation closely resembles Garratt's Equation (15). Two years later, he proclaimed this empirical formula to be applicable in hurricane wind speeds as well [81]. This well-known linear parameterization can be seen in the source code of the third generation wave model, Simulating WAves Nearshore (SWAN) [82].

3.6. Large & Pond (1981, 1982)

During this time, Large and Pond introduced the dissipation method for measuring wind stress [83]. While the eddy correlation method provided the most direct measurement, it worked best on stable platforms, making its application during storms, in remote ocean areas, unfeasible due to instrument sensitivity. The dissipation method, on the other hand, was capable of operating on moving platforms. Between September 1976 and April 1977, measurements were taken on a 59-m deep water stable tower off the harbor of Halifax, Nova Scotia. Using a modified Gill propeller-vane anemometer, 196 runs were completed using the eddy correlation method to measure velocity. The results were nearly identical to measurements taken by the Bedford Institute of Oceanography. During the eddy correlation runs, 192 dissipation runs were recorded almost concurrently, totaling 1086 h worth of momentum flux data. For wind speed under 20 m/s, each method produced similar results. Between July 1977 and April 1978, 505 h of measurements were taken from the CCGS Quadra in more open sea conditions with higher wind speeds using the dissipation method. Their analysis revealed that the hourly averaged C_{10} is constant for wind speed between 4 and 10 m/s, but linear for wind speeds between 10 and 26 m/s, as follows:

$$C_{10} \times 10^3 = \begin{cases} 1.14, & 4\frac{m}{s} < U_{10} \leq 10\frac{m}{s}, \\ 0.49 + 0.065 U_{10}, & 10\frac{m}{s} < U_{10} < 26\frac{m}{s}. \end{cases} \tag{18}$$

The duo continued their study for the following two years. Recognizing that extrapolated parameterization from near-shore observations to high wind speeds in the ocean were insufficient, and direct measurements were too arduous and expensive at the time, they resumed their experimental dissipation program. The investigators deeply explored the concept of a bulk aerodynamic method intended for larger scale studies over long periods of oceanic and atmospheric circulation [84]. The concept originates from the hypothesis that the drag coefficient, Stanton number (dimensionless heat transfer coefficient), and Dalton number (dimensionless moisture transfer coefficient), referred to as the bulk aerodynamic (exchange) coefficients [85], are approximately equal [70]. This method yields heat flux estimations based on the bulk transfer coefficients of momentum, sensible heat, and water vapor [86]. When parameterizing the kinematic fluxes in bulk quantity, Large and Pond calculated the drag coefficient using Equation (10) [87]. Overall, their work is heavily cited in textbooks [88] and almost always included when comparing multiple linear drag formulas.

The studies presented above are among the most notable drag coefficient formulae from 1948 to 1997. However, there are many more formulae available in the open literature. Table 1 depicts a cumulative synopsis of the most popular published drag coefficient correlations of this era.

Table 1. Early Drag Coefficient Formulations (1948–1997).

Date	Author	Drag Coefficient Formula
1948 *	Neumann [73]	$C_{10} \times 10^3 = 0.9 \times U_{10}^{-\frac{1}{2}}$, $1\frac{m}{s} < U_{10} < 30\frac{m}{s}$.
1951 *	Francis [73,89]	$C_{10} \times 10^3 = 1.3 U_{10}$, $1\frac{m}{s} < U_{10} < 25\frac{m}{s}$.
1958 *	Sheppard [73,90]	$C_{10} \times 10^3 = 0.8 + 0.114 U_{10}$, $1\frac{m}{s} < U_{10} < 20\frac{m}{s}$.
1960	Wilson [51,73]	$C_{10} \times 10^3 = \begin{cases} 1.49, 1\frac{m}{s} < U_{10} < 10\frac{m}{s}, \\ 2.37, U_{10} > 10\frac{m}{s}. \end{cases}$ (12)
1962 *	Deacon & Webb [73,91]	$C_{10} \times 10^3 = 1.0 + 0.07 U_{10}$, $1\frac{m}{s} < U_{10} < 14\frac{m}{s}$.
1967	Wu [73]	$C_{10} \times 10^3 = \begin{cases} 0.5 \times U_{10}^{\frac{1}{2}}, 1\frac{m}{s} < U_{10} < 15\frac{m}{s}. \\ 2.6, U_{10} > 15\frac{m}{s}. \end{cases}$ (13)
1975 *	Smith & Banke [78]	$C_{10} \times 10^3 = 0.61 + 0.075 U_{10}$, $6\frac{m}{s} < U_{10} < 21\frac{m}{s}$.
1977	Garratt [50]	$C_{10} \times 10^3 = 0.51 U_{10}^{0.46}$. $4\frac{m}{s} < U_{10} < 21\frac{m}{s}$, (14) $C_{10} \times 10^3 = 0.75 + 0.067 U_{10}$. $4\frac{m}{s} < U_{10} < 21\frac{m}{s}$. (15)
1980	Smith [32]	$C_{10} \times 10^3 = 0.61 + 0.063 U_{10}$, $6\frac{m}{s} < U_{10} < 22\frac{m}{s}$. (16)
1980, 1982	Wu [79,81]	$C_{10} \times 10^3 = 0.8 + 0.065 U_{10}$, $U_{10} > 1 \frac{m}{s}$. (17)
1981	Large & Pond [83]	$C_{10} \times 10^3 = \begin{cases} 1.14, 4\frac{m}{s} < U_{10} \leq 10\frac{m}{s}, \\ 0.49 + 0.065 U_{10}, 10\frac{m}{s} < U_{10} < 26\frac{m}{s}. \end{cases}$ (18)
1992 *	Anderson [92]	$C_{10} \times 10^3 = 0.49 + 0.071 U_{10}$, $4.5\frac{m}{s} < U_{10} < 21\frac{m}{s}$.
1995 *	Yelland & Taylor [93]	$C_{10} \times 10^3 = 0.60 + 0.070 U_{10}$, $6\frac{m}{s} < U_{10} < 26\frac{m}{s}$.
1997 *	Yelland et al. [27]	$C_{10} \times 10^3 = 0.50 + 0.071 U_{10}$, $6\frac{m}{s} < U_{10} < 26\frac{m}{s}$.

* Popular parameterizations not discussed in detail here.

4. Saturated Drag Coefficient

4.1. GPS Dropwindsondes

From the late 1960s through the 1990s, investigators felt confident that a positive linear relationship between the drag coefficient and wind speed existed. Multiple studies, mentioned previously, verified this logic, although it only held true for wind speeds under 26 m/s. As for higher wind speeds, data had been unavailable at the time, especially in regions over the deep ocean.

In the early 1970s, the National Center for Atmospheric Research's (NCAR's) Atmospheric Technology Division developed the first Omega-based dropwindsonde [94]. Nearly 26 years later, NCAR developed the Airborne Vertical Atmospheric Profiling System and began testing by fall [95]. Simultaneously, the National Oceanic and Atmospheric Administration's (NOAA's) Aircraft Operation Center acquired the Gulfstream IV-SP (G-IV) for weather reconnaissance research missions to foster meteorological data from impending hurricanes. In 1997, the Tropical Prediction Center, currently the U.S. National Hurricane Center (NHC), released almost 200 of NCAR's enhanced Global Positioning System-based dropwindsondes (GPS sondes) from the G-IV in the vicinity of three hurricanes (Figure 1).

(a)   (b)

Figure 1. (**a**) Gulfstream IV-SP (G-IV) [96]; (**b**) GPS Sonde and Launch [97].

The square-coned parachuted GPS sonde weighed 400-g. As it fell 10–15 m/s, it measured vertical profiles of ambient temperature, pressure, humidity, wind speed, and wind direction every half second from altitudes up to 24 km. The GPS receiver could derive winds, providing ±0.5 m/s wind accuracies with a 0.1 m/s resolution [97].

Ten to fifteen missions were anticipated for its inaugural year, but only three were completed in the Atlantic and two in the east Pacific during 1997 due to minimal hurricane activity. In addition, only one mission attained complete data samples in all quadrants. Undeterred by the debut's undersized activity (22 of 200 sondes), mean track forecasts improved 32% and intensity forecasts improved 20%, which was equivalent to the previous 20–25 years of accumulated progress [98]. By 1999, 331 high resolution wind profile measurements existed near hurricane eyewalls. GPS sondes, alongside mooring systems, extended data collection beyond gale force winds into extreme conditions, while embarking into locations previously considered unfeasible.

4.2. Powell et al. (2003)

In 2003, the 331 wind profiles from the 1997–1999 GPS sondes data collection were analyzed [26]. The mean boundary layer analysis consisted of the following five groups below 500 m: 30–39 m/s (72 profiles), 40–49 m/s (105 profiles), 50–59 m/s (55 profiles), 60–69 m/s (61 profiles), and 70–85 m/s (38 profiles). The lowest 100–150 m of each group was fitted by a least squares line to determine the intercept on a natural log height scale. The strongest wind speed group contained insufficient low-level samples. Rearranging Equation (9) yields

$$\ln(z) = \frac{k}{U_*} U + \ln(z_0) \tag{9a}$$

Thus, the slope is $\frac{k}{U_*}$ and the intercept is z_0 on a natural log height scale. Since $k = 0.4$, shear velocity, U_*, can be determined with the slope value. Substituting the shear velocity into Equation (1) along with density yields the wind stress, τ. Finally, the drag coefficient can be found by substituting the wind stress, density, and wind speed at 10-m into Equation (3b). Other estimates of shear velocity, the surface roughness length, and the drag coefficient were calculated using the eddy correlation method and dissipation method.

Their results exposed a much lower surface momentum flux above hurricane force ($U_{10} > 33$ m/s). Rather than incessant escalation, it leveled off. C_d and z_0 increased until $U_{10} = 33$ m/s. At $U_{10} > 33$ m/s, C_d decreased, and at $U_{10} > 40$ m/s, z_0 leveled off. Friction velocity also increased until $U_{10} = 40$ m/s and leveled off. The most notable discovery was the decline in C_d and z_0 from 40 to 51 m/s. This was the first observational data collected at such wind speeds, and it contradicted the previous proposition that velocity and the drag coefficient increase linearly endlessly. The team hypothetically attributed the reduction to sea foam, spray, and bubbles resulting from steep wave faces breaking and forming a slip surface. In conclusion, they suggested more GPS sonde studies to examine the effects of shallow water shoaling, azimuth-dependent sea state and wind-shear-induced asymmetries, and heat and moisture transfer.

4.3. Donelan et al. (2004)

The following year in 2004, the analyzed results from the GPS sonde data collection was corroborated with an experiment at the Air–Sea Interaction Facility at the University of Miami [53]. Using a 15-m × 1-m × 1-m tank divided between air and water, the stress was measured by hot-film anemometry, and the water surface elevation was measured by digital particle image velocimetry and laser/line scan cameras. When using hot-film anemometry at high wind speeds with a direct stress measurement, such as eddy correlation or Reynolds, spray droplets landing on the film alters the measurements. Therefore, an x-film anemometer was used to measure the Reynolds stress for 0–26 m/s wind speeds and corrected at the surface with the measured horizontal pressure gradient. The surface stress at high wind speeds was measured using a momentum budget of tank sections, called the surface slope method. All-in-all, three data sets from the facility were used consisting of the eddy correlation method, profile method, and surface slope method. A fourth set of data from Ocampo-Torres et al. (1994) [99], obtained using the profile method, was also used for comparison.

Wind speed measurements at 30-cm were extrapolated to 10-m, and all four data set results were congruent. This confirmed the surface slope method as a valid technique for stress measurements at high wind speeds. The drag coefficient increased with wind speeds between 3 and 33 m/s, similar to previously mentioned correlations. Yet, the results were lower than those of Large and Pond (1981) [83], although the general trend was the same. In accordance with Powell et al. (2003) [26], Donelan and his team observed a saturated drag coefficient for speeds above 33 m/s. The investigators concluded that beyond wind speeds of 33 m/s, the aerodynamic roughness reaches its limit. As the open ocean moves from gale to hurricane force, continuous intense wave-breaking occurs and high wind speeds blow away crests. This fills the air with sea spray and the surface with spume, altering its frictional and roughness characteristics.

As technology upgrades ensued, progress in obtaining measurements at high wind speeds followed. A general consensus had been established regarding the drag coefficient's nature at low to moderate wind speeds (<26 m/s). Vis-à-vis high wind speeds, a study analyzing field measurements and a study examining laboratory data both concluded the drag coefficient ceases to increase after 33 m/s and instead, saturates. This would require a significant shift in wind stress calculations for high wind speeds. What was previously believed would need to be unlearned and rediscovered.

5. Latest Drag Coefficient Formulations (2006–2015)

5.1. Powell (2006)

Beginning in 2005, Powell analyzed 2664 GPS sonde profiles from 1997 to 2005 [100] captured in the Northern hemisphere. The dataset included 2003 Hurricanes Fabian and Isabel from the Coupled Boundary Layer Air-Sea Transfer (CBLAST) experiment (explored further in Section 5.4), 2004 Hurricanes Frances, Ivan, and Jeanne, and 2005 Hurricanes Katrina, Rita, and Wilma.

The composite group was narrowed down to 1270 profiles within 2–200-km of each hurricane's center with wind speeds greater than 20 m/s. Using the profile method, Powell observed that C_d linearly increases with U_{10} to a maximum value of 0.002 at 41 m/s. As U_{10} approached 61 m/s, C_d decreased to a minimum of 0.0006. However, this increasing-decreasing behavior of C_d was restricted to the front left sector of the storm and for a radial distance more than 30-km from the center. Profiles less than 30-km from the storm's center resulted in drag coefficients around 0.001 with minimal disparity, which supports Donelan's continuous wave-breaking hypothesis [53].

Powell explored the drag coefficients azimuthal dependence. A previous study used radar altimeter wave data, in conjunction with a wind analysis of Hurricane Bonnie (1998), to create three sectors of the storm [101,102]. Assuming the storm is moving towards $0°$, the right sector is $21°–150°$ clockwise, the rear sector is $151°–240°$ clockwise, and the front left sector is $241°–020°$ clockwise (see Black et al. 2007 [102] and Holthuijsen et al. 2012 [103] for a more detailed account). For the right sector in regions beyond 30 km of the storm's center, C_d was observed to be nearly constant until $U_{10} = 45$ m/s, in which it began to increase linearly. For the rear sector, C_d was also nearly constant until $U_{10} = 34$ m/s, in which it began to decrease. For the front left sector, C_d increased linearly up to values as high as 0.0047 for $U_{10} = 36$ m/s. For higher wind speeds, C_d steadily and quickly decreased.

The initial GPS sonde analysis [26] contained insufficient samples for extreme wind speeds. In contrast, this study reviewed an ample amount of profiles to conclude that C_d decreases in extreme winds. Powell's study argues that radial distance and storm relative azimuth carry weight in C_d calculations. As a result, ADCIRC offers a formulation based on Powell's findings as an alternative to Garratt's correlation [50] for tropical cyclones. This formulation divides the storm into the three sectors and calculates C_d accordingly [37].

$$\text{Right Sector}: C_d = \begin{cases} (0.75 + 0.067U_{10}) \times 10^{-3}, & U_{10} \leq 35\frac{m}{s}, \\ 0.0020 + \frac{(0.0030 - 0.0020)}{(45.0 - 35.0)}(U_{10} - 35.0), & 35\frac{m}{s} \leq U_{10} \leq 45\frac{m}{s}, \\ 0.0030, & U_{10} > 45\frac{m}{s}. \end{cases} \tag{19a}$$

$$\text{Rear Sector}: C_d = \begin{cases} (0.75 + 0.067U_{10}) \times 10^{-3}, & U_{10} \leq 35\frac{m}{s}, \\ 0.0020 + \frac{(0.0010 - 0.0020)}{(45.0 - 35.0)}(U_{10} - 35.0), & 35\frac{m}{s} \leq U_{10} \leq 45\frac{m}{s}, \\ 0.0010, & U_{10} > 45\frac{m}{s}. \end{cases} \tag{19b}$$

$$\text{Left Front Sector}: C_d = \begin{cases} 0.0018, & U_{10} \leq 25\frac{m}{s}, \\ 0.0018 + \frac{(0.0045 - 0.0018)}{(30.0 - 25.0)}(U_{10} - 25.0), & 25\frac{m}{s} \leq U_{10} \leq 30\frac{m}{s}, \\ 0.0045 + \frac{(0.0010 - 0.0045)}{(45.0 - 30.0)}(U_{10} - 35.0), & 30\frac{m}{s} \leq U_{10} \leq 45\frac{m}{s}, \\ 0.0010, & U_{10} > 45\frac{m}{s}. \end{cases} \tag{19c}$$

Powell encourages the modeling community to further experiment with radial distance and storm relative azimuth when calculating C_d.

5.2. Moon et al. (2006)

In 2004, 10 Atlantic Ocean hurricanes from 1998 to 2003, simulated from a coupled wave-wind (CWW) model, were post-processed. At low wind speeds, typically $U_{10} \leq 12.5$ m/s, the bulk parameterization used in NHC's Geophysical Fluid Dynamics Laboratory (GFDL) hurricane model matches with the observational data. However, the same could not be claimed for z_0 at

$U_{10} > 12.5$ m/s [24,104]. Therefore, the authors derived new parameterizations for $U_{10} > 12.5$ m/s. The following empirical relationship between z_0 and U_{10} was established in 2006 [104]:

$$z_0 = \frac{0.0185}{g} \left(0.001 U_{10}^2 + 0.028 U_{10}\right)^2, \quad U_{10} \le 12.5 \frac{m}{s}, \tag{20a}$$

using polynomial fitting, and

$$z_0 = (0.085 U_{10} - 0.58) \times 10^{-3}, \quad U_{10} > 12.5 \frac{m}{s}. \tag{20b}$$

using a linear fitting regression of the CWW results, with a 0.87 regression coefficient. Substituting Equation (20b) into Equation (9) using polynomial fitting, with a regression coefficient of 0.99, yields U_{10} as a function of U_* as follows:

$$U_{10} = -0.56 U_*^2 + 20.255 U_* + 2.458 \tag{20c}$$

Combining Equation (20a–c) yields

$$z_0 = \begin{cases} \frac{0.0185}{g} U_*^2, & U_{10} \le 12.5 \frac{m}{s}, \\ \left[0.085 \left(-0.56 U_*^2 + 20.255 U_* + 2.458\right) - 0.58\right] \times 10^{-3}, & U_{10} > 12.5 \frac{m}{s}. \end{cases} \tag{20d}$$

This physics-based parameterization can be used in combination with Equation (10) to estimate the drag coefficient. Here, the drag coefficient levels off between $0.002 \le C_d \le 0.003$ from high wind speeds between 20 and 77 m/s.

A previous study indicated that the operational GFDL hurricane prediction model tends to under-predict the surface wind speeds for strong hurricanes [105]. Thus, this proposed parameterization was tested on five Atlantic Ocean hurricanes in 11 forecasts using the GFDL hurricane prediction model. The results showed an increase in maximum wind speed prediction and no substantial change in central pressure prediction, improving pressure-wind relationship predictions for strong hurricanes. Yet the investigators noted that other numerical prediction models may not underpredict maximum wind speeds, warranting simulations with various models for validation. In conclusion, the authors noted intentions of further exploring the theory of sea state affecting the air-sea momentum flux, in addition to wind speed [106,107], since a hurricane storm's center greatly affects the sea state in various areas [24,108].

5.3. Jarosz et al. (2007)

The following year, an entirely different method for estimating the drag coefficient was introduced by Jarosz et al. [28]. The investigators revealed that all previous techniques are based on measurements from the atmospheric side of the air-sea interface, which they coined as "top down". This practice produces tainted results near the ocean surface due to intense wave-breaking and sea spray [53]. Instead, they recommend a "bottom up" technique, which uses ocean currents from the full water-column to determine the air-sea momentum exchange. It requires measurements to be taken from the ocean side of the interface with full water-column ocean current observations. The observed data is utilized in the momentum equation to calculate the drag coefficient. They argue that using the ocean-side of the air-sea interface generates a reliable and accurate determination of the air–sea momentum exchange.

To calculate this momentum transfer in terms of the drag coefficient, they substitute their variation of Equation (3b) into the along-shelf momentum equation as follows:

$$\tau = \rho C_d |W| W_x \tag{3c}$$

$$\frac{\partial U}{\partial t} - fV = \frac{\tau}{\rho_r H} - \frac{rU}{H} \tag{21a}$$

$$C_d = \frac{\rho_r H}{\rho \, |W| \, W_x} \left(\frac{\partial U}{\partial t} - fV + \frac{rU}{H} \right) \tag{21b}$$

where $|W|$ is the wind velocity magnitude at 10 m, W_x is the along-shelf velocity component, U is the depth-integrated along-shelf velocity component, f is the Coriolis parameter $(0.71 \times 10^{-4} \cdot \text{s}^{-1})$, V is the depth-integrated cross-shelf velocity component, ρ_r is the reference density $(1025 \, kg \cdot m^{-3})$, H is the water depth, and r is the resistance coefficient constant at the sea floor. The authors parametrically used r-values between 0.001 and 0.1 cm/s.

Six gauge moorings measured the ocean current and wave/tide during Hurricane Ivan (2004) as the storm passed directly over them on the outer continental shelf in the northeastern Gulf of Mexico. The data was analyzed using Equation (21b). Results below 30 m/s were scattered, but their study illustrated that the drag coefficient reaches a peak wind speed of 32 m/s and then decreases as wind speed increases. While the results above 32 m/s matched previous studies [26,53], the technique renders a few limitations. The authors pointed out that a bottom-up approach imposes the almost impossible requirement of deploying the sensors in the ocean under the highly unpredictable path of a hurricane. Moreover, the sensors must survive the enormous forces of the hurricane.

5.4. Black et al. (2007)

From 2000 to 2005, the Office of Naval Research funded 17 investigators from a number of academic and government laboratories to undergo the CBLAST hurricane experiment [102]. The project's primary purpose was to advance comprehension of the physical processes at the air–sea interface to improve hurricane intensity forecasting. To accomplish this, airborne remote, in situ, and expendable probe sensors were combined with air-deployed ocean platforms to increase understanding of high-wind air-sea fluxes by expanding the observation range of the exchange coefficients to hurricane-force winds and above. The Air Force Reserve Command's 53rd Weather Reconnaissance Squadron assisted in the air deployment.

In 2003, a total of 12 flights, including 12 stepped-descent patterns, were flown on 6 days in Hurricane Fabian and Isabela. An additional 10 flights and three surveillance flights were flown during that period. An array of 16 drifting buoys and six floats were deployed. In 2004, CBLAST flights were flown in Hurricane Frances on 4 days, Ivan on 5 days, and Jeanne on 3 days. The key success in that year was the air deployment of 38 drifting buoys and 14 floats ahead of Hurricane Frances on August 31. All drifters and floats deployed were successful.

The deployments and experiments developed an extensive dataset, resulting in a huge success for air–sea flux measurements during actual hurricanes. They concluded that the drag coefficient levels off at 22–23 m/s, which is appreciably lower than the threshold value previous studies reported to be at 33 m/s [26,28,53]. The drag coefficient value in hurricane conditions above 33 m/s was found to be under 0.002, which is slightly lower than reported values from earlier studies. The study was stated to be ongoing, utilizing and investing in the most recent advancements in airborne technology to advance coupled models. Their overall goal continues to strive for improvements in hurricane intensity and track prediction.

5.5. Moon et al. (2009)

In 2009, three wind stress formulations were tested for Typhoon Maemi [25]. Three C_d parameterizations at high winds speeds were tested in this surge simulation as follows: (Case 1) the linear relationship by Wu [81], (Case 2) the fast-increasing C_d by the Wavewatch III (WW3) model [109], and (Case 3) the leveling-off C_d by Moon et al. (2004) [110], which is based on the CWW model. Case 1 revisited Equation (17). Case 2 was an internal C_d parameterization of the WW3 using the following:

$$C_d \times 10^3 = \left(0.021 + \frac{10.4}{R^{1.23} + 1.85} \right) \tag{22}$$

$$R = \ln \left(\frac{10g}{x\sqrt{\propto U_{e10}^2}} \right) \tag{23}$$

$$\alpha = 0.57 \left(\frac{c_p}{U_*} \right)^{-\frac{3}{2}} \tag{24}$$

where U_e is the effective wind speed at high frequencies and c_p is the wave phase speed at peak frequency. Case 3 was a leveling-off C_d from CWW, incorporating the WW3 spectrum combined with the spectral tail, which calculates a wave-induced stress vector, a mean wind profile, and c_p. The results showed that for a high resolution model, Case 1 overestimated the drag coefficient at high winds, Case 2 overestimated it even more, and Case 3 matched closest to the GPS sonde data analysis [26]. The trend was reversed for a model with coarse resolution. A higher resolution mesh produced a higher surge if other conditions were the same. The authors argued this was attributed to the higher resolution surge model averaging the surge height over a smaller area, and the fact that the coastal geography and topography were better resolved. According to these results, incorporating wave parameters with the drag coefficient, along with a high resolution storm surge model, yields better results.

5.6. Foreman & Emeis (2010)

In an attempt to address the enigma surrounding C_d, Foreman and Emeis chose to return to the fundamental definition of the neutral drag coefficient [111]. The authors indicate that the traditional drag coefficient definition, as shown in Equation (4), implies that U_* is directly proportional to U_{10}. According to Equation (4), the square root of C_d is the slope of U_* vs. U_{10}. Yet, when the authors plot the data collected from several studies between 1975 and 2009, the C_d illustrated is not constant.

In order to properly describe the data, the investigators theorize a constant must be included in the definition as follow:

$$U_* = C_m (U_{10} - U_0) + b \tag{25}$$

where C_m is the revised drag coefficient and b is a constant. According to the large compilation of data collected in other studies, $C_m = 0.051$, $U_0 = 8$ m/s, and $b = -0.14$ m/s for $U_{10} \geq 8$ m/s and $U_* \geq 0.27$ m/s. The authors suggest that U_* and U_{10} are proportional but not directly proportional due to the transition to rough flow at low wind speeds, necessitating a constant. This new drag coefficient definition is said to be applicable for a range of locations including the open ocean, limited-fetch cases, and even lakes. This new definition is particularly useful at high wind speeds. However, it is expected to be less valid in limited water depth areas.

5.7. Andreas et al. (2012)

Inspired by the new definition presented by Foreman and Emeis (2010) [111], Andreas and his team decided to test its validity. By including the definition, they deduced the following transformation of Equation (4) [52]:

$$C_{10} = \left(\frac{U_*}{U_{10}} \right)^2 = C_m^2 \left(1 + \frac{b}{C_m U_{10}} \right)^2 \tag{26}$$

According to this parameterization, C_{10} increases monotonically with increasing wind speeds, then rolls off and asymptotes at C_m^2 in high wind speeds, creating a natural limit. To test its soundness, the authors used 778 measurements from over the sea with wind speeds up to 21.8 m/s. For Equation (26), they found $C_m = 0.0581$ and $b = -0.214$ m/s for $U_{10} \geq 9$ m/s, with a correlation coefficient of 0.929.

For further validation, the authors added ~6858 additional near-surface eddy-covariance flux measurements collected from low-flying aircrafts with a 1-m to 49-m altitude range, with wind speeds up 27 m/s. Due to the rough flow at low wind speeds, the investigators chose to use only data for

$U_{10} \geq 9$ m/s. For Equation (26), they concluded $C_m = 0.0583$ and $b = -0.243$ m/s for wind speeds between 9 and 24 m/s, and corroborated the theory that U_* increases linearly with U_{10} although the slopes and intercepts are different at different wind speeds. Andreas and his team concluded by offering the following unified drag parameterization for weak-to-strong winds:

$$U_* = 0.239 + 0.0433\{(U_{10} - 8.271) + [0.120(U_{10} - 8.271)^2 + 0.181]^{1/2}\} \tag{27}$$

This equation can be incorporated into Equation (4) to obtain the neutral drag coefficient. In 2014, Equation (27) was incorporated into a fast bulk flux algorithm, which the authors named Version 4.0 [112].

5.8. Zijlema et al. (2012)

In 2012, the JOint North Sea WAve Project (JONSWAP) formulation for bottom friction for spectral wave models was re-examined [113]. They noticed that lower wind drag and lower bottom friction provide essentially the same hindcast results in a storm. Therefore, they reviewed a large number of published C_d observations. The C_d values from nine authoritative studies were analyzed [26,28,50,78,81,83,100,102,114–116]. Analysis of these studies revealed (1) an almost linear increase in C_d with wind speeds up to 20 m/s; (2) a leveling off of C_d at wind speeds of 35 m/s; and (3) very low C_d values by 60 m/s.

The investigators provide the following alternative parameterization for the wind drag coefficient:

$$C_{10} \times 10^3 = \left(0.55 + 2.97\tilde{U} - 1.49\tilde{U}^2\right) \tag{28a}$$

$$\tilde{U} = \frac{U_{10}}{U_{ref}} \tag{28b}$$

$$U_{ref} = 31.5 \, \frac{m}{s} \tag{28c}$$

This parameterization was found by fitting a 2nd order polynomial to the data with the number of independent observations in each data set as a weight, adding emphasis to [50,83,116]. When possible, duplicate datasets were removed from newer studies if they were previously included in an older study. The reference wind, U_{ref}, is the wind speed where the drag coefficient is highest in Equation (26).

Using Equation (28a) results in 10%–30% lower C_d values for high winds (15 m/s $\leq U_{10} \leq$ 32.6 m/s) and more than 30% lower C_d values for hurricane winds ($U_{10} \geq$ 32.6 m/s) when compared to Equation (17). The investigators state that the leveling off and decrease seen in their analysis is supported by field data [73,117], lab observations [53], inverse modeling of hurricane wave hindcasts [118], and theory [35,119–123]. With the exception of [28], they indicated that airside observation of energy transfer to waves underestimates wave growth [124,125]. This is important as it nullifies wave growth scaling with a C_d-based friction velocity. It was noted that this discovery must be addressed in a future study. This new drag equation, Equation (28a), replaced the original parameterization of Wu (1982) [81] in SWAN [82]. However, since the new parameterization estimates a lower drag coefficient, accurate wave and storm surge estimates require using a lower bottom friction coefficient of 0.038 m^2/s^3 than the original value of 0.067 m^2/s^3. SWAN has incorporated Equation (28a) as an alternative to Equation (17) since version 41.01. Their recommended bottom friction was also integrated into SWAN [82].

5.9. Holthuijsen et al. (2012)

Holthuijsen and his collaborators mixed vintage data with modern data to investigate the effects of white caps and streaks on the drag coefficient [103]. The data consisted of unique aerial reconnaissance films from a collection of hurricanes between 1966 and 1980. Frames of these storms were originally captured from the nadir point of aerial cameras during low-level flights, as opposed to typical oblique images. The authors noted that such low-level flights are dangerous and have been terminated due to safety concerns. Additionally, 1149 high-resolution wind profiles were used from NOAA's 1998–2005 GPS sonde collection over the Atlantic. They compared their drag coefficient results to those from eight authoritative studies [26,28,50,78,81,83,102,116].

Their study indicated that the wind speed dependence of the drag coefficient varies spatially due to the wind-swell sea state. The authors defined three distinct swell conditions near the radius-to-maximum-wind (i.e., near field)—following swell occurs in the right-front sector, cross swell occurs in the left-front sector, and opposing swell occurs in the rear sector. This general pattern coincides with the azimuthal sectors observed in Hurricane Bonnie (1998) [100–102]. For lower wind speeds in the far field, cross swell dominates everywhere except to the right of the eye.

The frames from the film illustrate the ocean's surface spotted with white caps and streaks. As wind speed increases, the white caps, streaks, and sea spray progressively multiply and join together to create a white out or slip layer, and surface roughness begins to decrease. This results in low drag coefficient values to the right and rear sectors near the eye. Yet the region to the left of the eye and far rear of the eye produce very high drag coefficient values. These characteristics disprove the idea of a uniform drag coefficient and increasing roughness for high winds. In their study, the drag coefficient leveled off to approximately 0.002 for wind speeds between 30 and 35 m/s for following and opposing swell conditions. On the other hand, the drag coefficient peaked near 0.005 for cross swell conditions before decreasing, based on 38 wind profiles. This implies that cross swell delays the drag reduction, perhaps by delaying the foam-spray slip layer production. For wind speeds between 60 and 79 m/s, at a radial distance less than 30-km from the center, the drag coefficient was as low as 0.0007, indicating a smooth surface in the most extreme winds. This might be attributed to foam generated near the eye wall from continuous wave-breaking [53] and fetch-limited waves.

The following equation is not a formal fit of the data, but rather presented by the authors as a preliminary assessment of the data to approximate the drag coefficient with and without cross swell:

$$C_d \times 10^3 = min \left\{ \left[a + b \left(\frac{U_{10}}{U_{ref,1}} \right)^c \right], d \left[1 - \left(\frac{U_{10}}{U_{ref,2}} \right)^e \right] \right\} \tag{29}$$

where $U_{ref,1}$ is 27.5 m/s and $U_{ref,2}$ is 54 m/s. For no swell, opposing swell, and following swell, the authors listed $a = 1.05$, $b = 1.25$, $c = 1.4$, $d = 2.3$, and $e = 10$. For cross well, $a = 0.7$, $b = 1.1$, $c = 6$, $d = 8.2$, and $e = 2.5$. The lower limit is $C_d = 0.7 \times 10^{-3}$.

5.10. Edson et al. (2013)

In 1996, Fairall and his colleagues had developed a drag coefficient algorithm for low to moderate winds [126] for the Tropical Ocean Global Atmosphere (TOGA) Coupled Ocean-Atmosphere Response Experiment (COARE) [127]. By 2002, this popular bulk parameterization was upgraded to include winds between 0 and 20 m/s and named COARE 3.0 [128]. The modifications were based on 2777 1-h direct flux measurements and approximately 100-h of wind speed data above 10 m/s. Unlike other parameterizations, the COARE drag coefficient is a function of surface roughness, atmospheric stability, and gustiness [129].

In 2013, Edson and his team worked to improve the surface roughness and drag coefficient of COARE 3.0 using four different oceanic datasets. Three of the datasets contained wind profiles, and all four had direct covariance estimates of momentum flux. Using the direct covariance method, the surface stress is calculated as

$$\tau = -\rho \overline{uw} = \rho C_d U_r^2 \tag{3d}$$

where U_r is the wind speed relative to the water. The effect of surface waves on momentum exchange through surface roughness was investigated and the drag coefficient is calculated using Equation (10). However, the COARE algorithm calculates the surface roughness as $z_0 = z_0^{smooth} + z_0^{rough}$, to distinguish between aerodynamically smooth roughness and roughness elements from wind stress in surface gravity waves. The smooth component is calculated as $\gamma\frac{v}{u_*}$, where γ is the roughness Reynolds number for smooth flow (0.11–determined from experiments) and v is kinematic viscosity. The rough component is typically found from the scaling proposed by Charnock given in Equation (11), $\alpha\frac{u_*^2}{g}$. For this study [129], they determined that COARE 3.0 overestimated the drag at the lowest wind speeds and underestimated it at the highest wind speeds. In addition, it overestimated surface stress and Charnock values at low winds and underestimated them at high winds. To remedy this problem, the average data between 7 and 18 m/s was fit using $\alpha = mU_{10} + b$, where m is 0.017 m/s and b is -0.005. As a result, COARE 3.5 was created which eradicated these flaws.

The resulting drag coefficients for high winds were larger than previous studies in the literature. To avoid flow distortion which results from direct covariance and mean wind measurements taken from shipboard observations, the investigators used data from fixed towers and low-profile platforms. While data above 22 m/s was limited, the increasing drag coefficient rate slowed above 19 m/s. For Equation (26), they found $C_m = 0.062$ and $b = -0.28$ m/s for $U_{10} \geq 8.5$ m/s, which is relatively close to the values reported by Andreas et al. (2012) [52]. Their function naturally asymptotes at 0.0038, whereas the value was 0.0034 for Andreas et al. (2012). The team admitted the formula was inappropriate for tropical cyclones, but their results advocate a slower rate of increase for the drag coefficient between 20 and 25 m/s.

Wave age- and wave slope-dependent parameterizations were additionally investigated for surface roughness, but the resulting COARE 3.5 wind speed-dependent formula, which withheld wave information, was in agreement with the wide range of data consisting of wind speeds up to 25 m/s and a variety of wave conditions. They concluded that there is a linear relationship between wind speed and inverse wave age for wind speeds up to 25 m/s in long-fetch conditions, and the wave age data would not further improve COARE 3.5 wind speed-dependent drag coefficient calculation. They pointed out that this linear relationship between wind speed and inverse wave age breaks down in the fetch-limited and shallow water environments.

5.11. Zachary et al. (2013)

During Hurricane Ike (2008), Texas Tech University deployed a portable surface weather observing station, called a StickNet platform, created by their Wind Science and Engineering Research Center [130]. The device collected onshore wind measurements on the Bolivar Peninsula near Galveston, Texas, 90-m from the 3-km Houston ship channel, allowing researchers to estimate C_d values near the coastal shore [131]. The team used the coupled wave and circulation model, SWAN+ADCIRC, to simulate a hindcast representing the wave and surge conditions.

The model used Equations (19a–c) to estimate C_d and found the value to increase to a maximum value of 0.0022 at $U_{10} = 28$ m/s. After wind speed correction, they observed C_d level off at $U_{10} = 22$ m/s. The investigators reported substantial differences in C_d values in the deep ocean versus alongshore at slow wind speeds. Their study resulted in higher C_d values than those reported in any of the comparison deep water studies at slower wind speeds. This is potentially attributed to the complex bathymetry and wave conditions due to sea spray and skimming flow within the channel. They fear storm surge models may underestimate the surge if using a deep water wind speed-dependent C_d for shallow water coastal regions and commented that additional forcing parameterizations are needed in such complex roughness situations.

5.12. Vickers et al. (2013)

From 1992 to 2008, four aircraft datasets from 11 experiments resulted in 5800 eddy-covariance turbulence flux measurements [132]. Vickers and his team examined the sensitivity of the neutral drag coefficient to six different bin averaging analysis methods. Bin averaging the 10-m neutral drag coefficient, C_{10}, in weak winds led to overestimation of the coefficient. They stated the error stemmed from the conversion of random flux sampling errors into systematic errors.

A major development in the study was the classification of four discrete wind regimes. Weak winds, under 4 m/s, were ill-posed, as they were highly sensitive to the method of analysis. Moderate winds between 4 and 10 m/s held a constant C_{10}. Strong winds between 10 and 20 m/s had a linearly increasing C_{10} with wind speed. Very strong winds, greater than 20 m/s, had a decreasing C_{10} with increasing wind speed. The onset of enhanced drag at $C_{10} = 10$ m/s is most likely due to wave breaking and transition to fully aerodynamically rough flow. The authors disclosed that the very strong wind regime was developed from only one experiment, and more data is needed to confirm those results.

5.13. Peng & Li (2015)

After an extensive review of constant, linear, and non-linear C_d parameterizations, Peng and Li hypothesized that C_d is a parabolic function in 2015 [133]. They assert C_d is underestimated in intermediate wind speeds using a linearly-increasing formula and overestimated in very high wind speeds using non-decreasing formulae. They proposed that a parabolic C_d for intermediate to high wind speeds could alleviate these flaws.

Using a 4-Dimensional Variational Data Assimilation (4DVAR) technique, the investigators determined C_d values for the South China Sea by assimilating the observed water levels into a storm surge model. Employing [26,28] as a basis, which deduces the maximum C_d to occur at 32–33 m/s, they propose the following parabolic parameterization of C_d:

$$C_d = -a\,(U_{10} - 33)^2 + c \qquad (30)$$

where a and c are initially set at $(a_0, c_0) = (2.0 \times 10^{-6}, 2.34 \times 10^{-3})$. Eighteen relatively strong typhoons, which passed through the South China Sea from 2006 to 2011, with a minimum 0.2-m storm surge, were utilized to define and validate Equation (30). Values a and c were optimized for 10 of the typhoons by improving the disparity between the modeled and observed storm surges. This resulted in the mean values of $a = 0.00215$ and $c = 2.797$. Both values were inserted in Equation (30) and utilized in a storm surge model for the remaining eight typhoons.

Overall, their parabolic parameterization improved the storm surge simulations and lowered the root-mean-squared-errors when compared to the results simulated using seven other authoritative correlations [53,83,128,134–136]. The authors noted that the values found are specific to the South China Sea region. While the model is valid in other regions, the values of a and c must be established in a similar manner using observations for that particular area.

5.14. Zhao et al. (2015)

In 2015, Zhao and his team of investigators explored C_d's behavior in the South China Sea. They studied typhoon measurements, collected from wind propeller anemometers stationed on a coastal observation tower, to observe the effect of water depth on C_d [137]. The coastal observation tower stands 6.5-km from the shore in 14-m deep water anchored by concrete tanks. One minute mean wind profiles for Typhoons Hagupit (2008) and Chanthu (2010) were examined, and 289 of the 1441 nearshore samples were used.

The team concluded that water depth unequivocally affects the drag coefficient when compared to deep open ocean results. Although the C_d against wind speed plot is similar to that of open ocean conditions, the curve shifts towards a regime of lower wind speed. In other words, the C_d maximum occurs approximately at 24 m/s, which is 5–15 m/s lower than that of the open sea. This is prospectively due to shoaling and wave conditions pertaining to the shallow water. They proposed a C_d formulation as a function of wind speed and water depth. Their numerical tests showed that the proposed C_d improves the prediction of the typhoon track, U_{10}, and central pressure results. Their results indicated that coastal wave, sea spray, hurricane, and storm surge models may need to consider the sea state in the drag coefficient calculation to improve predictions.

5.15. Bi et al. (2015)

Bi and her team investigated C_d from seven typhoons in the South China Sea from 2008 to 2014 [138]. Data collected from two towers in varying water depths along the shore were examined. One tower was positioned 6.5-km from the coastline on a platform in 15-m of water over the South China Sea. The second tower was located on a 90-m × 40-m island, 10-m above mean sea level. Anemometers and sensors collected data from the east side of the towers, facing the sea.

This group found that C_d first decreases as wind speed increases to 10 m/s. After that, C_d increases to 0.002 until wind speeds reach 18 m/s. Between 18 and 27 m/s wind speeds, the drag coefficient decreases. When compared between the two towers, the drag coefficient was higher in shallow water by 40% for $U_{10} < 10$ m/s. The drag coefficient difference disappears between the two towers at wind speeds higher than 10 m/s. This was possibly due to the wave conditions and local bathymetry along the shore in shallow water. The investigators declared no C_d-dependence on the typhoon quadrant. Last, they verified that the eddy covariance and inertial dissipation methods for estimating the momentum fluxes produced similar results. In contrast, the momentum flux values derived from the flux profile method are larger over the sea than those from the other two methods. They urge other investigators to practice prudence when using this method on a heterogeneous surface.

Table 2 offers a list of drag coefficient parameterizations following the development of GPS sondes. Figure 2 illustrates many of the drag coefficient correlations from 1958 to 2015.

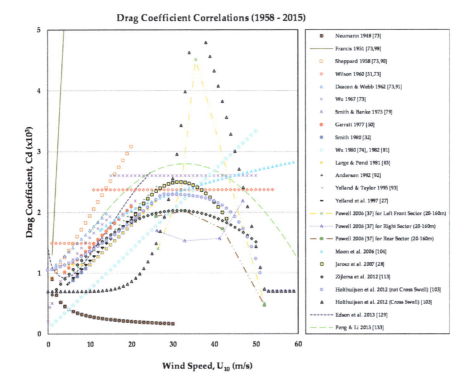

Figure 2. Drag Coefficient Correlations (1958–2015).

Table 2. Drag Coefficient Formulations following the Development of GPS Sondes (2006–2015).

Date	Author	Drag Coefficient Formula
2006	ADCIRC, adapted from Powell [37]	Right Sector: $C_d = \begin{cases} (0.75+0.067U_{10})\times10^{-3}, & U_{10}\leq35\frac{m}{s}, \\ 0.0020+\frac{(0.0030-0.0020)}{(45.0-35.0)}(U_{10}-35.0), & 35\frac{m}{s}\leq U_{10}\leq45\frac{m}{s}, \quad\text{(19a)} \\ 0.0030, & U_{10}>45\frac{m}{s}. \end{cases}$ Rear Sector: $\begin{cases} (0.75+0.067U_{10})\times10^{-3}, & U_{10}\leq35\frac{m}{s}, \\ 0.0020+\frac{(0.0010-0.0020)}{(45.0-35.0)}(U_{10}-35.0), & 35\frac{m}{s}\leq U_{10}\leq45\frac{m}{s}, \quad\text{(19b)} \\ 0.0010, & U_{10}>45\frac{m}{s}. \end{cases}$ Left Front Sector: $C_d = \begin{cases} 0.0018, & U_{10}\leq25\frac{m}{s}, \\ 0.0018+\frac{(0.0045-0.0018)}{(30.0-25.0)}(U_{10}-25.0), & 25\frac{m}{s}\leq U_{10}\leq30\frac{m}{s}, \\ 0.0045+\frac{(0.0010-0.0045)}{(45.0-30.0)}(U_{10}-35.0), & 30\frac{m}{s}\leq U_{10}\leq45\frac{m}{s}, \\ 0.0010, & U_{10}>45\frac{m}{s}. \end{cases}$ (19c)
2006	Moon et al. [104]	$z_0 = \begin{cases} \frac{0.0185}{g}U_*^2, & U_{10}\leq12.5\frac{m}{s}, \\ [0.085(-0.56U_*^2+20.255U_*+2.458)-0.58]\times10^{-3}, & U_{10}>12.5\frac{m}{s}. \end{cases}$ (20d)
2007	Jarosz et al. [28]	$\tau=\rho C_d |W|W_x$, (3c) $\frac{\partial U}{\partial t}-fV=\frac{\tau}{\rho_r H}-\frac{rU}{H}$, (21a) $C_d=\frac{\rho H}{\rho|W|W_x}(\frac{\partial U}{\partial t}-fV+\frac{rU}{H})$. (21b)
2010	Foreman & Emeis [111]	$U_*=C_m(U_{10}-U_0)+b$. (25)
2012	Andreas et al. [52]	$u_*=0.239+0.0433\left\{(U_{10}-8.271)+[0.120(U_{10}-8.271)^2+0.181]^{1/2}\right\}$. (27)
2012	Zijlema et al. [113]	$C_{10}\times10^3=(0.55+2.97\tilde{U}-1.49\tilde{U}^2)$, (28a) $\tilde{U}=\frac{U_{10}}{U_{ref}}$. (28b) $U_{ref}=31.5\frac{m}{s}$. (28c)
2012	Holthuijsen et al. [103]	$C_d\times10^3=min\left\{[a+b(\frac{U_{10}}{U_{ref,1}})^C], d[1-(\frac{U_{10}}{U_{ref,2}})^e]\right\}$, (29)
2013	Edson et al. [129]	$\tau=-\rho\overline{uw}=\rho C_d U_r$. (3d)
2015	Peng & Li [133]	$C_d=-a(U_{10}-33)^2+C$. (30)

6. Concluding Remarks

As hurricane storm surges became a recognizable threat to coastal communities, investigators grew anxious to estimate the surface wind stress correctly. The classical wind stress calculation requires an appropriate representation of the drag coefficient, which depends on the air and sea conditions at a given time and place. Charnock's proportionality constant was the turning point in approximating the drag coefficient, which implies that as wind speed increases, the drag coefficient must increase. Contemporary researchers performed laboratory and oceanic observations to relate the drag coefficient with the measured wind speed. Some proposed constant drag coefficients, especially at high wind velocities. Others proposed linearly varying drag coefficients for a range of wind speeds. Some even suggested there are other sea conditions, such as fetch, air–sea surface tension, viscosity, etc. that must be considered to estimate the drag coefficient correctly. However, the notion of 'high' wind speeds was too limited, not even reaching the range of Category I hurricane values. With the limited technology available at that time, researchers were able to exhaust four methods of determining wind stress, two of which are still prevalent today (wind profile and eddy correlation). Yet, as long as data observation in extreme conditions remained impossible, examiners approached a stalemate and were forced to extrapolate their positive linear correlation to strong hurricane winds. As the computer age approached, hurricane and oceanic forecasting models quickly followed. By default, modelers accepted linear drag coefficient correlations with no other obvious options available.

By the late 1990s, the GPS sonde emerged, allowing storm hunters to do something once believed impossible: collect data in and around the eye of a hurricane. Just as the scientific community accepted a linear drag coefficient, evidence gave investigators no choice but to accept a lower drag coefficient at extreme high winds. On the other hand, literature argues that some forecasting models continue to use a linear drag coefficient, which is apt to overestimate the value in very high winds. One simple modification to remedy a modeling program consisting of a linear drag coefficient is to embed a cap whenever it exceeds a specific value. Yet, some studies indicate a leveling-off of C_d at 32–33 m/s, while others state it happens even sooner at 22–23 m/s.

Despite the influx of progressive technology, hurricane intensity forecasting remains a dawdling advancement, as opposed to hurricane track forecasting. Historically, C_d has been calculated as a function of wind speed. New information suggests other factors, such as wave-breaking, sea spray, and sea foam might contribute to the reduction of C_d. Research already shows C_d values near shore vary far more than its value offshore due to shoaling, local bathymetry, and water depth. Additionally, C_d is potentially related to the sea state of the ocean, relative to a storm's center. All of these aspects must be taken into account, which leaves future investigators with an ambitious agenda. The sooner advancements are achieved in forecasting hurricane intensity, regardless of the avenue, the faster authorities can better serve coastal communities in danger.

Acknowledgments: This study was supported by an HBCU-UP Research Initiation Award (HRD-1401062) granted from the National Science Foundation to Muhammad Akbar. The authors are grateful to M.A. Donelan for his valuable suggestions in improving the content of the paper.

Author Contributions: K.B. performed the literature review and wrote the draft. M.A. conceived the critical review and modified the manuscript.

Conflicts of Interest: The authors declare sole responsibility of the research results. Authors and programs mentioned and the founding sponsors had no role in the design of the study; in the collection, analyses, or interpretation of data; in the writing of data; in the writing of the manuscript, and in the decision to publish the results. The authors recognize the abundance of research surrounding this topic and were incapable of including all available studies.

References

1. Barry, R.G.; Chorley, R.J. *Atmosphere, Weather, and Climate*; Routledge: London, UK, 2003.
2. Caso, M.; González-Abraham, C.; Ezcurra, E. Divergent ecological effects of oceanographic anomalies on terrestrial ecosystems of the Mexican Pacific coast. *Proc. Natl. Acad. Sic. USA* **2007**, *104*, 10530–10535. [CrossRef] [PubMed]
3. Emanuel, K. The contribution of tropical cyclones to the oceans' meridional heat transport. *J. Geophys. Res. Atmos.* **2001**, *106*, 14771–14782. [CrossRef]
4. Emanuel, K. Tropical Cyclones. *Annu. Rev. Earth Planet. Sci.* **2003**, *31*, 75–104. [CrossRef]
5. Neely, W. *The Great Bahamian Hurricanes of 1899 and 1932: The Story of Two of the Greatest and Deadliest Hurricanes to Impact the Bahamas*; iUniverse Inc.: Bloomington, IN, USA, 2012.
6. Nicholson, S.E. *Dryland Climatology*; Cambridge University Press: New York, NY, USA, 2011.
7. Saha, P. *Modern Climatology*; Allied Publishers Pvt. Ltd.: New Delhi, India, 2012.
8. Murty, T.S.; Flather, R.A.; Henry, R.F. The storm surge problem in the bay of Bengal. *Prog. Oceanogr.* **1986**, *16*, 195–233. [CrossRef]
9. Shamsuddoha, M.; Chowdhury, R.K. *Climate Change Impact and Disaster Vunerablities in the Coastal Areas of Bangladesh*; Coastal Association for Social Transformation Trust (COAST Trust): Dhaka, Bangladesh, 2007.
10. Shultz, J.M.; Russell, J.; Espinel, Z. Epidemiology of tropical cyclones: The dynamics of disaster, disease, and development. *Epidemiol. Rev.* **2005**, *27*, 21–35. [CrossRef] [PubMed]
11. Beven, J.L.; Avila, L.A.; Blake, E.S.; Brown, D.P.; Franklin, J.L.; Knabb, R.D.; Pasch, R.J.; Rhome, J.R.; Stewart, S.R. Atlantic Hurricane Season of 2005. *Mon. Weather Rev.* **2008**, *136*, 1109–1173. [CrossRef]
12. Knabb, R.D.; Rhome, J.R.; Brown, D.P. Tropical Cyclone Report for Hurricane Katrina. Available online: http://www.nhc.noaa.gov/data/tcr/AL122005_Katrina.pdf (accessed on 1 September 2016).

13. Baade, R.A.; Baumann, R.; Matheson, V. Estimating the Economic Impact of Natural and Social Disasters, with an Application to Hurricane Katrina. *Urban Stud.* **2007**, *44*, 2061–2076. [CrossRef]

14. Burton, M.; Hicks, M. *Hurricane Katrina: Preliminary Estimates of Commercial and Public Sector Damages*; Marshall University Center Business and Economy Reseach: Huntington, WV, USA, 2005; pp. 1–13.

15. Curry, J.A.; Webster, P.J.; Holland, G.J. Mixing politics and science in testing the hypothesis that greenhouse warming is causing a global increase in hurricane intensity. *Bull. Am. Meteorol. Soc.* **2006**, *87*, 1025–1037. [CrossRef]

16. Lott, N.; Ross, T. *Tracking and Evaluating US Billion Dollar Weather Disasters, 1980–2005*; NOAA National Climatic Data Center: Asheville, NC, USA, 2015.

17. Emanuel, K. Increasing destructiveness of tropical cyclones over the past 30 years. *Nature* **2005**, *436*, 686–688. [CrossRef] [PubMed]

18. Knutson, T.R.; Tuleya, R.E. Impact of CO_2-induced warming on simulated hurricane intensity and precipitation: Sensitivity to the choice of climate model and convective parameterization. *J. Clim.* **2004**, *17*, 3477–3495. [CrossRef]

19. Trenberth, K. Uncertainty in Hurricanes and Global Warming. *Science* **2005**, *308*, 1753–1754. [CrossRef] [PubMed]

20. Webster, P.J.; Holland, G.J.; Curry, J.A.; Chang, H.-R. Changes in tropical cyclone number, duration, and intensity in a warming environment. *Science* **2005**, *309*, 1844–1846. [CrossRef] [PubMed]

21. Willoughby, H.E. Hurricane heat engines. *Nature* **1999**, *401*, 649–650. [CrossRef]

22. Donelan, M.A.; Drennan, W.M.; Katsaros, K.B. The Air–Sea Momentum Flux in Conditions of Wind Sea and Swell. *J. Phys. Oceanogr.* **1997**, *27*, 2087–2099. [CrossRef]

23. Fan, Y.; Ginis, I.; Hara, T. The Effect of Wind-Wave-Current Interaction on Air–Sea Momentum Fluxes and Ocean Response in Tropical Cyclones. *J. Phys. Oceanogr.* **2009**, *39*, 1019–1034. [CrossRef]

24. Moon, I.-J.; Ginis, I.; Hara, T. Effect of Surface Waves on Air–Sea Momentum Exchange. Part II: Behavior of Drag Coefficient under Tropical Cyclones. *J. Atmos. Sci.* **2004**, *61*, 2334–2348. [CrossRef]

25. Moon, I.-J.; Kwon, J.-I.; Lee, J.-C.; Shim, J.-S.; Kang, S.K.; Oh, I.S.; Kwon, S.J. Effect of the surface wind stress parameterization on the storm surge modeling. *Ocean Model.* **2009**, *29*, 115–127. [CrossRef]

26. Powell, M.D.; Vickery, P.J.; Reinhold, T.A. Reduced drag coefficient for high wind speeds in tropical cyclones. *Nature* **2003**, *422*, 279–283. [CrossRef] [PubMed]

27. Yelland, M.J.; Moat, B.I.; Taylor, P.K.; Pascal, R.W.; Hutchings, J.; Cornell, V.C. Wind Stress Measurements from the Open Ocean Corrected for Airflow Distortion by the Ship. *J. Phys. Oceanogr.* **1998**, *28*, 1511–1526. [CrossRef]

28. Jarosz, E.; Mitchell, D.A.; Wang, D.W.; Teague, W.J. Major Tropical Cyclone. **2007**, *557*, 2005–2007.

29. Taylor, G.I. Skin friction of the wind on the earth's surface. *Proc. R. Soc. Lond. Ser. A* **1916**, *92*, 196–199. [CrossRef]

30. Masuda, T.; Kusaba, A. On the local equilibrium of winds and wind-waves in relation to surface drag. *J. Oceanogr. Soc. Jpn.* **1987**, *43*, 28–36. [CrossRef]

31. Mellor, G.L. *Users Guide for a Three Dimensional, Primitive Equation, Numberical Ocean Model*; Program in Atmospheric and Ocean Sciences, Princeton University: Princeton, NJ, USA, 1998.

32. Smith, S.D. Wind stress and heat flux over the ocean in gale force winds. *J. Phys. Oceanogr.* **1980**, *10*, 709–726. [CrossRef]

33. Govind, P.K. Omega windfinding systems. *J. Appl. Meteorol.* **1975**, *14*, 1503–1511. [CrossRef]

34. Chen, X.; Yu, Y. Enhancement of wind stress evaluation method under storm conditions. *Clim. Dyn.* **2016**. [CrossRef]

35. Makin, V.K. A note on the drag of the sea surface at hurricane winds. *Bound. Layer Meteorol.* **2005**, *115*, 169–176. [CrossRef]

36. Peng, S.; Li, Y.; Xie, L. Adjusting the wind stress drag coefficient in storm surge forecasting using an adjoint technique. *J. Atmos. Ocean. Technol.* **2013**, *30*, 590–608. [CrossRef]

37. Luettich, R.; Westerink, J. *ADCIRC: A (Parallel) ADvanced CIRCulation Model for Oceanic, Coastal and Estuarine Waters*; ADCIRC: Morehead, NC, USA, 2015.

38. Anderson, J.D. Ludwig Prandtl's Boundary Layer. *Phys. Today* **2005**, *58*, 42–48. [CrossRef]

39. Franco, J.M.; Partal, P. RHEOLOGY—The Newtonian Fluid. *Eolss* **2000**, *I*, 74–77.

40. Ball, W.W.R. *A Short Account of The History of Mathematics*; Dover Publications, Inc.: Queens County, NY, USA, 1960.

41. Grimberg, G.; Pauls, W.; Frisch, U. Genesis of d'Alembert's paradox and analytical elaboration of the drag problem. *Phys. D Nonlinear Phenom.* **2008**, *237*, 1878–1886. [CrossRef]

42. Frisch, U. Translation of Leonhard Euler's: General Principles of the Motion of Fluids. Available online: https://arxiv.org/abs/0802.2383 (accessed on 2 September 2016).

43. Darrigol, O. Between Hydrodynamics and Elasticity Theory: The First Five Births of the Navier-Stokes Equation. *Arch. Hist. Exact Sci.* **2016**, *56*, 95–150. [CrossRef]

44. Tani, I. History of Boundary Layer Theory. *Annu. Rev. Fluid Mech.* **1977**, *9*, 87–111. [CrossRef]

45. Schlichting, H.; Gersten, K. *Boundary Layer Theory*; Springer: New York, NY, USA, 1999.

46. Arakeri, F.; Shankar, P. Ludwig Prandtl and Boundary Layers in Fluid Flow How a Small Viscosity can Cause Large Effects. *Resonance* **2000**, *5*, 48–63. [CrossRef]

47. Weber, R.O. Remarks on the Definition and Estimation of Friction Velocity. *Bound. Layer Meteorol.* **1999**, *93*, 197–209. [CrossRef]

48. Ekman, V.W. On the influence of the earth's rotation on ocean currents. *Ark. Mat. Astron. Fys.* **1905**, *2*, 1–53.

49. Sverdrup, H.U.; Johnson, M.W.; Fleming, R.H. *The Oceans: Their Physics, Chemistry, and General Biology*; Prentice-Hall, Inc.: Upper Saddle River, NJ, USA, 1942.

50. Garratt, J.R. Review of Drag Coefficients over Oceans and Continents. *Mon. Weather Rev.* **1977**, *105*, 915–929. [CrossRef]

51. Wilson, B.W. Note on surface wind stress over water at low and high wind speeds. *J. Geophys. Res.* **1960**, *65*, 3377–3382. [CrossRef]

52. Andreas, E.L.; Mahrt, L.; Vickers, D. A New Drag Relation for Aerodynamically Rough Flow over the Ocean. *J. Atmos. Sci.* **2012**, *69*, 2520–2537. [CrossRef]

53. Donelan, M.A.; Haus, B.K.; Reul, N.; Plant, W.J.; Stiassnie, M.; Graber, H.C.; Brown, O.B.; Saltzman, E.S. On the limiting aerodynamic roughness of the ocean in very strong winds. *Geophys. Res. Lett.* **2004**, *31*, 1–5. [CrossRef]

54. Kundu, P.K.; Cohen, I.M.; Dowling, D.R. *Fluid Mechanics*; Academic Press: New York, NY, USA, 2012.

55. Schlichting, H.; Gersten, K. *Boundary-Layer Theory*; Springer Science & Business Media: Berlin, Germany, 2003.

56. McDonough, J.M. Introductory Lectures on Turbulence: Physics, Mathematics and Modeling. 2007. Avaliable online: https://www.engr.uky.edu/~acfd/lctr-notes634.pdf (accessed on 1 September 2016).

57. Ting, D. *Basics of Engineering Turbulence*; Academic Press: New York, NY, USA, 2016.

58. Bradshaw, P. Possible origin of Prandt's mixing-length theory. *Nature* **1974**, *249*, 135–136. [CrossRef]

59. Prandtl, L. Über die ausgebildete Turbulenz. In Proceedings of the 2nd International Congress Applied Mechanics, Zurich, Switzerland, 12–17 September 1926; pp. 62–74.

60. Tollmien, W.; Schlichting, H.; Görtler, H.; Riegels, F.W. Chronologische Folge der Veröffentilchungen. In *Ludwig Prandtl Gesammelte Abhandlungen*; Springer-Verlag: Berlin-Heidelberg, Germany, 1961; pp. 1–9.

61. Vos, R.; Farokhi, S. *Introduction to Transonic Aerodynamics*; Springer Netherlands: Dordrecht, The Netherlands, 2015.

62. Schlichting, H. *Lecture Series 'Boundary Layer Theory' Part II—Turbulent Flows*; National Advisory Committee for Aeronautics (NACA): Washington, DC, USA, 1949.

63. Fowler, A. *Mathematical Geoscience*; Springer Science & Business Media: London, UK, 2011.

64. Furbish, D.J. *Fluid Physics in Geology: An Introduction to Fluid Motions on Earth's Surface and within Its Crust*; Oxford University Press: Oxford, UK, 1996.

65. Pye, K.; Tsoar, H. *Aeolian Sand and sand Dunes*; Springer-Verlag: Berlin, Germany, 2008.

66. Von Kármán, T. Mechanische änlichkeit und turbulenz. *Nachrichten von der Gesellschaft der Wissenschaften zu Göttingen, Math. Klasse* **1930**, *1930*, 58–76.

67. Kantha, L.H.; Clayson, C.A. *Small Scale Processes in Geophysical Fluid Flows*; Academic Press: New York, NY, USA, 2000.

68. Guan, C.; Xie, L. On the Linear Parameterization of Drag Coefficient over Sea Surface. *J. Phys. Oceanogr.* **2004**, *34*, 2847–2851. [CrossRef]

69. Charnock, H. Wind stress on a water surface. *Q. J. R. Meteorol. Soc.* **1955**, *81*, 639–640. [CrossRef]

70. Roll, H. *Physics of the Marine Atmosphere*; Academic Press: New York, NY, USA, 1965.

71. Mansour, A.E.; Ertekin, R.C. *Proceedings of the 15th International Ship and Offshore Structures Congress: 3-Volume Set*; Elsevier: Amsterdam, The Netherlands, 2003; p. 23.

72. Takagaki, N.; Komori, S.; Suzuki, N.; Iwano, K.; Kuramoto, T.; Shimada, S.; Kurose, R.; Takahashi, K. Strong correlation between the drag coefficient and the shape of the wind sea spectrum over a broad range of wind speeds. *Geophys. Res. Lett.* **2012**, *39*, 1–6. [CrossRef]

73. Wu, J. *Wind Stress and Surface Roughness at Air-Sea Interface*; HYRDRONAUTICS, Inc.: Laurel, MD, USA, 1967.

74. Scire, J.S.; Robe, F.R.; Fernau, M.; Yamartino, R.J. *A User's Guide for the CALMET Meteorological Model*; Earth Tech. Inc.: Land O Lakes, FL, USA, 2000.

75. Johnson, B.H.; Heath, R.E.; Hsieh, B.B.; Kim, K.W.; Butler, L. *User's Guide for a Three-Dimensional Numerical Hydrodynamic, Salinity, and Temperature Model of Chesapeake Bay (No. WES/TR/HL-91-20)*; US Army Engineer Waterways Experiment Station: Vicksburg, MS, USA, 1991.

76. Dietrich, J.C.; Bunya, S.; Westerink, J.J.; Ebersole, B.A.; Smith, J.M.; Atkinson, J.H.; Jensen, R.; Resio, D.T.; Luettich, R.A.; Dawson, C.; et al. A high-resolution coupled riverine flow, tide, wind, wind wave, and storm surge model for southern louisiana and mississippi. Part II: Synoptic description and analysis of hurricanes katrina and rita. *Mon. Weather Rev.* **2010**, *138*, 378–404. [CrossRef]

77. Wright, L.D. Beaches and coastal geology: Sea slick. *Encycl. Earth Sci.* **1982**. [CrossRef]

78. Smith, S.D.; Banke, E.G. Variation of the sea surface drag coefficient with wind speed. *Q. J. R. Meteorol. Soc.* **1975**, *101*, 665–673. [CrossRef]

79. Wu, J. Wind-Stress coefficients over Sea surface near Neutral Conditions—A Revisit. *J. Phys. Oceanogr.* **1980**, *10*, 727–740. [CrossRef]

80. Roll, H.U. *Physics of the Marine Atmosphere: International Geophysics Series Volume 7*; Academic Press: New York, NY, USA, 2016.

81. Wu, J. Wind stress coefficients over sea surface from breeze to hurricane. *J. Geophys. Res. Oceans* **1982**, *87*, 9704–9706. [CrossRef]

82. SWAN: Scientific and Technical Documentation. Available online: http://swanmodel.sourceforge.net/download/zip/swantech.pdf (accessed on 2 September 2016).

83. Large, W.G.; Pond, S. Open Ocean Momentum Flux Measurements in Moderate to Strong Winds. *J. Phys. Oceanogr.* **1981**, *11*, 324–336. [CrossRef]

84. Pond, S.; Fissel, B.; Paulson, C.A. A note no bulk aerodynamic coefficients for sensible heat and moisture fluxes. *Bound. Layer Meteorol.* **1974**, *6*, 333–339. [CrossRef]

85. Friehe, C.A.; Schmitt, K.F. Parameterization of Air-Sea Interface Fluxes of Sensible Heat and Moisture by the Bulk Aerodynamic Formulas. *J. Phys. Oceanogr.* **1976**, *6*, 801–809. [CrossRef]

86. Kondo, J. Air-sea bulk transfer coefficients in diabatic conditions. *Bound. Layer Meteorol.* **1975**, *9*, 91–112. [CrossRef]

87. Large, W.G.; Pond, S. Sensible and latent heat flux measurements over the ocean. *J. Phys. Oceanogr.* **1982**, *12*, 464–482. [CrossRef]

88. Liss, P.S.; Duce, R.A. *The Sea Surface and Global Change*; Cambridge University Press: Cambridge, UK, 2005.

89. Francis, J.R. The aerodynamic drag of a free water surface. *Proc. R. Soc. Lond. A Math. Phys. Eng. Sci.* **1951**, *206*, 387–406. [CrossRef]

90. Sheppard, P.A. Transfer across the earth's surface and through the air above. *Q. J. R. Meteorol. Soc.* **1958**, *84*, 205–224. [CrossRef]

91. Deacon, E.L.; Webb, E.K. *Physical Oceanography: II. Interchange of Properties between Sea and Air*; Commonwealth Scientific and Industrial Research Organization: Perth, Australia, 1962.

92. Anderson, R.J. A Study of Wind Stress and Heat Flux over the Open Ocean by the Inertial-Dissipation Method. *J. Phys. Oceanogr.* **1993**, *23*, 2153–2161. [CrossRef]

93. Yelland, M.; Taylor, P.K. Wind stress measurements from the open ocean. *Am. Meteorol. Soc.* **1996**, *26*, 541–558. [CrossRef]

94. Cole, H.L.; Rossby, S.; Govind, P.K. The NCAR windfinding dropsonde. *Atmos. Technol.* **1973**, *2*, 19–24.

95. Hock, T.F.; Franklin, J.L. The NCAR GPS Dropwindsonde. *Bull. Am. Meteorol. Soc.* **1999**, *80*, 407–420. [CrossRef]

96. NOAA. Aircraft operation center. Gulfstream IV-SP (G-IV). Available online: https://upload.wikimedia.org/wikipedia/commons/archive/2/2a/20151001222423%21G4-1_%28Gulfstream%29.jpg (accessed on 5 September 2016).

97. NCAR. NCAR UCAR EOL: AVAPS dropsonde. Available online: https://www.eol.ucar.edu/content/gallery-2 (accessed on 5 September 2016).

98. Aberson, S.D.; Franklin, J.L. Impact on hurricane track and intensity forecasts of GPS dropwindsonde observations from the first-season flights of the NOAA Gulfstream-IV jet aircraft. *Bull. Am. Meteorol. Soc.* **1999**, *80*, 421–427. [CrossRef]

99. Ocampo-Torres, F.J.; Donelan, M.A. Laboratory measurements of mass transfer of carbon dioxide and water vapour for smooth and rough flow conditions. *Tellus* **1994**, *46*, 16–32. [CrossRef]

100. Powell, M.D. *Final Report on the NOAA Joint Hurricane Testbed: Drag Coefficient Distribution and Wind Speed Dependence in Tropical Cyclones*; NOAA/AOML: Miami, FL, USA, 2007.

101. Wright, C.W.; Walsh, E.J.; Vandemark, D.; Krabill, W.B.; Garcia, A.W.; Houston, S.H.; Powell, M.D.; Black, P.G.; Marks, F.D. Hurricane Directional Wave Spectrum Spatial Variation in the Open Ocean. *J. Phys. Oceanogr.* **2001**, *31*, 2472–2488. [CrossRef]

102. Black, P.G.; D'Asaro, E.A.; Drennan, W.M.; French, J.R.; Niller, P.P.; Sanford, T.B.; Terrill, E.J.; Walsh, E.J.; Zhang, J.A. Air–sea exchange in hurricanes: synthesis of observations from the coupled boundary layer air–sea transfer experiment. *Am. Meteorol. Soc.* **2007**, *88*, 359–374. [CrossRef]

103. Holthuijsen, L.H.; Powell, M.D.; Pietrzak, J.D. Wind and waves in extreme hurricanes. *J. Geophys. Res. Oceans* **2012**, *117*. [CrossRef]

104. Moon, I.-J.; Ginis, I.; Hara, T.; Thomas, B. A physics-based parameterization of air–sea momentum flux at high wind speeds and its impact on hurricane intensity predictions. *Mon. Weather Rev.* **2007**, *135*, 2869–2878. [CrossRef]

105. Ginis, I.; Khain, A.P.; Morozovsky, E. Effects of large eddies on the structure of the marine boundary layer under strong wind conditions. *J. Atmos. Sci.* **2004**, *72*, 3049–3063. [CrossRef]

106. Smith, S.D.; Anderson, R.J.; Oost, W.A.; Kraan, C.; Maat, N.; de Cosmo, J.; Katsaros, K.B.; Davidson, K.L.; Bumke, K.; Hasse, L.; et al. Sea surface wind stress and drag coefficients: The HEXOS results. *Bound. Layer Meteorol.* **1992**, *60*, 109–142. [CrossRef]

107. Toba, Y.; Iida, N.; Kawamura, H.; Ebuchi, N.; Jones, I.S. Wave dependence of sea-surface wind stress. *J. Phys. Oceanogr.* **1990**, *20*, 705–721. [CrossRef]

108. Moon, I.-J.; Ginis, I.; Hara, T.; Tolman, H.; Wright, C.W.; Walsh, E.J. Numerical simulation of sea surface directional wave spectra under hurricane wind forcing. *J. Phys. Oceanogr.* **2003**, *33*, 1680–1706. [CrossRef]

109. Tolman, H.L. User Manual and System Documentation of WAVEWATCH-IIITM Version 3.14. Available online: http://nopp.ncep.noaa.gov/mmab/papers/tn276/MMAB_276.pdf (accessed on 2 September 2016).

110. Moon, I.-J.; Hara, T.; Ginis, I.; Belcher, S.E.; Tolman, H.L. Effect of surface waves on air sea momentum exchange. Part I: Effect of mature and growing seas. *J. Atmos. Sci.* **2004**, *61*, 2321–2333. [CrossRef]

111. Foreman, R.J.; Emeis, S. Revisiting the definition of the drag coefficient in the marine atmospheric boundary layer. *J. Phys. Oceanogr.* **2010**, *40*, 2325–2332. [CrossRef]

112. Andreas, E.L.; Mahrt, L.; Vickers, D. An improved bulk air-sea surface flux algorithm, including spray-mediated transfer. *Q. J. R. Meteorol. Soc.* **2015**, *141*, 642–654. [CrossRef]

113. Zijlema, M.; van Vledder, G.P.; Holthuijsen, L.H. Bottom friction and wind drag for wave models. *Coast. Eng.* **2012**, *65*, 19–26. [CrossRef]

114. Powell, M.D. New findings on hurricane intensity, wind field extent and surface drag coefficient behavior. In Proceedings of the Tenth International Workshop on Wave Hindcasting and Forecasting and Coastal Hazard Symposium, Oahu, HI, USA, 11–16 November 2007.

115. Powell, M.D. New findings on Cd behavior in tropical cyclones. In Proceedings of the 28th Conference on Hurricanes and Tropical Meteorology, Orlando, FL, USA, 28 April 2008.

116. Petersen, G.N.; Renfrew, I.A. Aircraft-based observations of air–sea fluxes over Denmark Strait and the Irminger Sea during high wind speed conditions. *Q. J. R. Meteorol. Soc.* **2009**, *135*, 2030–2045. [CrossRef]

117. Amorocho, J.; DeVries, J.J. A new evaluation of the wind stress coefficient over water surfaces. *J. Geophys. Res. Oceans* **1980**, *85*, 433–442. [CrossRef]

118. Yokota, M.; Hashimoto, N.; Kawaguchi, K.; Kawai, H. Development of an inverse estimation method of sea surface drag coefficient under strong wind conditions. *Coast. Eng.* **2009**, *65*, 181–185. [CrossRef]

119. Bye, J.A.T.; Jenkins, A.D. Drag coefficient reduction at very high wind speeds. *J. Geophys. Res.* **2006**, *111*, 1–9. [CrossRef]

120. Bye, J.A.; Wolff, J.-O. Charnock dynamics: A model for the velocity structure in the wave boundary layer of the air–sea interface. *Ocean Dyn.* **2008**, *58*, 31–42. [CrossRef]

121. Kudryavtsev, V.N. On the effect of sea drops on the atmospheric boundary layer. *J. Geophys. Res. Oceans* **2006**, *111*, 1–18. [CrossRef]

122. Kudryavtsev, V.N.; Makin, V.K. Aerodynamic roughness of the sea surface at high winds. *Bound. Layer Meteorol.* **2007**, *125*, 289–303. [CrossRef]

123. Soloviev, A.; Lukas, R. Effects of bubbles and sea spray on air–sea exchange in hurricane conditions. *Bound. Layer Meteorol.* **2010**, *136*, 365–376. [CrossRef]

124. Belcher, S.E.; Hunt, J.C.R. Turbulent flow over hills and waves. *Annu. Rev. Fluid Mech.* **1998**, *30*, 507–538. [CrossRef]

125. Peirson, W.L.; Garcia, A.W. On the wind-induced growth of slow water waves of finite steepness. *J. Fluid Mech.* **2008**, *608*, 243–274. [CrossRef]

126. Fairall, C.W.; Bradley, E.F.; Rogers, D.P.; Edson, J.B.; Young, G.S. Bulk parameterization of air-sea fluxes for Tropical Ocean-Global Atmosphere Coupled-Ocean Atmosphere Response Experiment. *J. Geophys. Res.* **1996**, *101*, 3747–3764. [CrossRef]

127. Webster, P.; Lukas, R. TOGA COARE: The coupled ocean-atmosphere response experiment. *Bull. Am. Meteorol. Soc.* **1992**, *73*, 1377–1416. [CrossRef]

128. Fairall, C.W.; Bradley, E.F.; Hare, J.E.; Grachev, A.A.; Edson, J.B. Bulk parameterization of air–sea fluxes: Updates and verification for the COARE algorithm. *J. Clim.* **2003**, *16*, 571–591. [CrossRef]

129. Edson, J.B.; Jampana, V.; Weller, R.A.; Bigorre, S.P.; Plueddemann, A.J.; Fairall, C.W.; Miller, S.D.; Mahrt, L.; Vickers, D.; Hersbach, H. On the exchange of momentum over the open ocean. *J. Phys. Oceanogr.* **2013**, *43*, 1589–1610. [CrossRef]

130. Weiss, C.C.; Schroeder, J.L. StickNet: A new portable, rapidly deployable surface observation system. *Bull. Am. Meteorol. Soc.* **2008**, *89*, 1502–1503.

131. Zachry, B.C.; Schroeder, J.L.; Kennedy, A.B.; Westerink, J.J.; Letchford, C.W.; Hope, M.E. A case study of nearshore drag coefficient behavior during hurricane ike (2008). *J. Appl. Meteorol. Climatol.* **2013**, *52*, 2139–2146. [CrossRef]

132. Vickers, D.; Mahrt, L.; Andreas, E.L. Estimates of the 10-m neutral sea surface drag coefficient from aircraft eddy-covariance measurements. *J. Phys. Oceanogr.* **2013**, *43*, 301–310. [CrossRef]

133. Peng, S.; Li, Y. A parabolic model of drag coefficient for storm surge simulation in the South China Sea. *Sci. Rep.* **2015**, *5*. [CrossRef] [PubMed]

134. Large, W.G.; Yeager, S.G. The global climatology of an interannually varying air-sea flux data set. *Clim. Dyn. Dyn.* **2008**, *33*, 341–364. [CrossRef]

135. Mueller, J.A.; Veron, F. Nonlinear formulation of the bulk surface stress over breaking waves: Feedback mechanisms from air-flow separation. *Bound. Layer Meteorol.* **2009**, *130*, 117–134. [CrossRef]

136. Hersbach, H. Sea-surface roughness and drag coefficient as function of neutral wind speed. *J. Phys. Oceanogr.* **2011**, *41*, 247–251. [CrossRef]

137. Zhao, W.; Liu, Z.; Dai, C.; Song, G.; Lv, Q. Typhoon air-sea drag coefficient in coastal regions. *J. Geophys. Res. Oceans* **2015**, *120*, 716–727. [CrossRef]

138. Bi, X.; Gao, Z.; Liu, Y.; Liu, F.; Song, Q.; Huang, J.; Huang, H.; Mao, W.; Liu, C. Observed drag coefficients in high winds in the near offshore of the South China Sea. *J. Geophys. Res. Atmos.* **2015**, *120*, 6444–6459. [CrossRef]

Article

Influence of Wind Strength and Duration on Relative Hypoxia Reductions by Opposite Wind Directions in an Estuary with an Asymmetric Channel

Ping Wang [1,*], Harry Wang [2], Lewis Linker [3] and Kyle Hinson [4]

[1]   Virginia Institute of Marine Science, Chesapeake Bay Office, 410 Severn Avenue, Annapolis, MD 21403, USA
[2]   Virginia Institute of Marine Science, P.O. Box 1346, Gloucester Point, VA 23062, USA; wang@vims.edu
[3]   USEPA Chesapeake Bay Program Office, 410 Severn Avenue, Annapolis, MD 21403, USA;
      linker.lewis@epa.gov
[4]   Chesapeake Research Consortium, 645 Contees Wharf Road, Edgewater, MD 21037, USA;
      khinson@chesapeakebay.net
*   Correspondence: pwang@chesapeakebay.net; Tel.: +1-410-267-5744

Academic Editor: Richard P. Signell
Received: 8 July 2016; Accepted: 9 September 2016; Published: 19 September 2016

Abstract: Computer model experiments are applied to analyze hypoxia reductions for opposing wind directions under various speeds and durations in the north–south oriented, two-layer-circulated Chesapeake estuary. Wind's role in destratification is the main mechanism in short-term reduction of hypoxia. Hypoxia can also be reduced by wind-enhanced estuarine circulation associated with winds that have down-estuary straining components that promote bottom-returned oxygen-rich seawater intrusion. The up-bay-ward along-channel component of straining by the southerly or easterly wind induces greater destratification than the down-bay-ward straining by the opposite wind direction, i.e., northerly or westerly winds. While under the modulation of the west-skewed asymmetric cross-channel bathymetry in the Bay's hypoxic zone, the westward cross-channel straining by easterly or northerly winds causes greater destratification than its opposite wind direction. The wind-induced cross-channel circulation can be completed much more rapidly than the wind-induced along-channel circulation, and the former is usually more effective than the latter in destratification and hypoxia reduction in an early wind period. The relative importance of cross-channel versus along-channel circulation for a particular wind direction can change with wind speed and duration. The existence of month-long prevailing unidirectional winds in the Chesapeake is explored, and the relative hypoxia reductions among different prevailing directions are analyzed. Scenarios of wind with intermittent calm or reversing directions on an hourly scale are also simulated and compared.

Keywords: summer hypoxia/anoxia; wind speeds and directions; prolonged unidirectional wind

1. Introduction

Excessive nutrient and organic matter loads from the watershed and nutrient-driven algal blooms in the spring and summer are the main drivers of summer hypoxia and anoxia in the Chesapeake Bay estuary [1,2]. On the other hand, destratification by wind can increase dissolved oxygen (DO) in deep water and reduce hypoxia [3–5]. With the north-south oriented (Bay head to mouth) Chesapeake Bay main channel, different wind directions cause different degrees of destratification and associated reduction in hypoxia [6–10]. Hypoxia describes a condition of depressed dissolved oxygen, defined as concentrations less than 2 mg/L [11,12], and is a primary concern for Chesapeake water quality management [13]. The lower bound of hypoxia (DO $\leq$ 0.2 mg/L) is referred to as anoxia. This study uses anoxic volume (the volume of water with DO levels $\leq$ 0.2 mg/L) to measure the extent of the hypoxic condition and provide a reference for relative hypoxia reductions between opposite wind directions when wind speed or duration changes.

There are three ways by which wind can effect destratification and mixing [6]: (a) direct wind mixing; (b) along channel straining; and (c) cross channel straining. *Direct wind mixing* agitates the water surface and transmits energy downwards to disturb lower layers and effect stratification. Destratification is stronger in southerly (S) and northerly (N) winds than in easterly (E) and westerly (W) winds in most locations in the Chesapeake Bay, because the northerly and southerly winds have longer fetches along the main channel's orientation [6]. *Cross channel straining* by westward or eastward components of the wind-induced flow generates counterclockwise or clockwise (looking to the north) circulation and disturbs the stratified layers. The cross-channel bathymetry along the Bay's hypoxic/anoxic zone in the northerly Bay is dominant with a steeper and narrower slope on the eastern shoal (Figure 1). Such a bathymetry shown from a vertical cross-channel Profile in the Northern Bay is abbreviated the PN-type bathymetry or cross section. The asymmetric bathymetry modifies wind-induced cross-channel circulation differently among varying wind directions. In the strongly stratified summer in the Chesapeake Bay, circulation by easterly winds promotes greater destratification and hypoxia reduction than that caused by westerly winds [10,14]. *Along-channel straining* by the up-Bay-ward southerly winds pushes surface water to the Bay head, whereby water levels are elevated and downwelling is induced. This then creates a return down-Bay-ward bottom current, generating along-channel circulation. In the exact opposite manner, down-Bay-ward northerly winds push surface water to the Bay mouth, generating along-channel circulation via a return up-Bay-ward bottom current, in a reverse spin-direction to that produced by the southerly wind. Southerly winds blow against the net direction of surface flow and can reduce stratification significantly. Although along-channel straining by northerly winds point in the same direction as net surface flow, which could promote stratification, wind-induced cross-channel circulation and direct wind mixing can still cause significant mixing and destratification at speeds greater than 4 m/s [6,10].

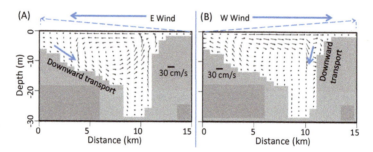

Figure 1. Flow velocity and lateral circulation pattern at a PN-type cross section in two opposite wind directions: (**A**) Easterly wind; and (**B**) westerly wind (after Wang et al. [10]). Note: The velocities were averaged from the first 12 h of the wind event of 8 m/s. The long dashed arrow indicates the tilt of the free surface when surface water is flushed from the upwind site to the downwind site. The dark arrow along the slope shows the direction of downwelling due to elevated water level.

Due to the Coriolis effect, the wind-induced surface water flow by all four idealized wind directions have both along-channel and cross-channel components (Table 1). The wind-induced along-channel circulation by the northerly and southerly winds is much stronger than the wind-induced cross-channel circulation by the easterly and westerly winds, because of the longer fetches associated with northerly and southerly winds. Indeed, the east- or west- components of the northerly and southerly winds are as strong as the east- or west-components of easterly and westerly winds at the same speeds, and are even greater in narrow channels.

Table 1. Directions of along-channel and cross-channel components of wind-induced surface flow in the Chesapeake Bay main channel [1].

Wind direction	Direction of surface flux of along-channel circulation	Direction of surface flux of cross-channel circulation
Northerly	To S (down-Bay-ward), principal	To W, secondary
Southerly	To N, (up-Bay-ward), principal	To E, secondary
Easterly	To N, secondary	To W, principal
Westerly	To S, secondary	To E, principal

[1] After Table 2 of Wang et al. [10].

Model experiments of 2–3 day winds at 6–8 m/s in the Chesapeake Bay indicated that the southerly wind reduced more hypoxic volume than the northerly wind during their respective periods of peak hypoxia reduction [7,14], illustrated in Figure 2. This is due to greater destratification by the along-channel straining in the southerly wind. After analyzing time-series development of stratification and bottom DO, Wang et al. [10] found that, under the modulation of asymmetric cross-channel bathymetry on wind-induced cross-channel circulation, northerly winds caused greater destratification and hypoxia reduction than southerly winds in the early wind period (i.e., before Hour 24 of an 8 m/s wind event) when the wind-induced along-channel circulation does not strongly influence the Bay's hypoxic/anoxic center.

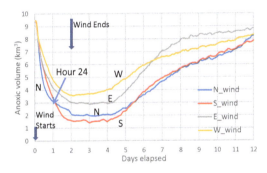

Figure 2. Time series of predicted anoxic volume (defined as the volume of water with DO ≤ 0.2 mg/L) in the mainstem Bay for 4 idealized wind directions at 8 m/s for 2 days. From Wang et al. [14].

Destratification by wind promotes the mixing of bottom and surface waters thereby oxygenating lower layers and reducing hypoxia, which has been studied extensively [4,7,15–17]. Besides the destratification-related hypoxia reduction, there is another mechanism that reduces hypoxia by wind, which is related to an enhanced estuarine circulation. This is mainly influenced by the wind directions that induce a down-Bay-ward component of surface-flow, e.g., the northerly or westerly wind. Down-Bay-ward along-channel straining generates a returned up-Bay-ward force at the bottom, thereby enhancing estuarine circulation. The promoted seawater intrusion along the lower layer can bring in oxygen-rich water to the Bay's hypoxic zone and reduce hypoxia, and this effect could be more prominent under a prolonged period of northerly wind [14].

The *overall destratification* by wind direction is dependent on the aforementioned three types of mixing processes. The *overall hypoxia reduction* is dependent on the amount of oxygen-rich water intruding into the lower level of the hypoxic zone, where destratification plays an important role, and potentially enhanced bottom seawater intrusion. The two processes can also differ as to which wind direction produces a greater hypoxia reduction, and the strengths of the effects can vary with wind speed and duration. Thus, complicated phenomena can occur in winds of different durations and speeds. Most studies of relative influences on destratification or hypoxia reduction by two opposite wind directions were based on relatively short duration wind events, equal to or less than three days [6–8,10]. The relative hypoxia reductions among wind directions could differ among prolonged, e.g., months long, unidirectional winds compared to short period wind events (hours to three days). This paper explores such a range of model experiments, including various wind speeds and durations, and analyses the temporal development of anoxic volume to better assess wind's influence on hypoxia and anoxia. The hydrodynamics and mechanisms that explain the differential destratification and hypoxia reduction by different wind directions have been described previously [6,8,10] and this analysis will primarily focus on model simulated anoxic volumes.

Because wind direction can change frequently this work also conducted model experiments on winds with directions changing hourly or four-hourly, with or without intermittent periods of no wind velocity, to compare against unidirectional winds of constant speed. Despite frequent changes in wind direction, the phenomena of unidirectional prevailing winds in some seasons have been observed in the Chesapeake. It is therefore of interest to study how anoxia is affected by different month-long prevailing unidirectional winds. This work will establish additional model scenarios involving both the observed and modified wind fields that have prevailing directions in certain months to analyze the impacts on anoxia and hypoxia. Because the surface flow direction could change with tidal stages, the influence of tides is also briefly studied.

2. Methods

The coupled CH3D hydrodynamic model and CE-QUAL-ICM water quality model, which compose the Chesapeake Bay Water Quality and Sediment Transport Model (WQSTM) [18], is used. The WQSTM is peer reviewed and was applied in the development of the Chesapeake Total Maximum Daily Load (TMDL) [13]. The hydrodynamic module simulates estuarine circulation considering factors of wind, freshwater inputs, tides, and Coriolis effects [19]. The water quality module simulates 36 state variables including various species of nutrients, 3 types of phytoplankton, and related biochemical processes. The errors of estimated DO in the mainstem are 0.3 mg/L and -0.45 mg/L at depths of 6.7–12.8 m and depths greater than 12.8 m, respectively [18]. Hourly anoxic volume of the Bay is calculated by adding volumes of the model cells that have hourly DO $\leq$ 0.2 mg/L. Several sets of model scenarios were designed to analyze the effects of wind speed, direction, and duration. Appendix A further describes the model.

2.1. Scenario Sets of Winds at a Fixed Speed and Fixed Direction

In this category of scenarios at fixed speed and fixed direction, three scenario sets were designed. Scenario Sets A, B, and C model wind durations of two days, 1 h, and 20 days, respectively. Within a scenario set, an individual scenario has either no speed or a fixed wind speed and direction from the north (N), south (S), east (E), or west (W). All wind events began (labeled as Hour 0) at 4:00 a.m. on Day 222 of Year 1996 after a spin-up of 221 days under a no-wind condition. The wind speed was also set to zero after the wind event. Daily nutrient inputs comparable to those observed in 1996 were estimated from a watershed model [20]. The scenario of no-wind throughout year 1996 is used as a reference to quantify the extent of anoxia reduction. Year 1996 had high winter-spring nutrient load that yielded higher summer anoxia compared to most other years.

A subset of Scenario Set A (Scenario Set A_8) of 8 m/s winds over two days is defined as the Core Scenario Set, and is used as a baseline to compare to other scenarios. This is because the mechanisms leading to differences in destratification and changes in bottom DO for opposite wind directions, including the cross-channel versus along-channel circulation and the effect of cross-channel bathymetry, have been analyzed comprehensively [10].

2.2. Scenario Set D: Fixed Wind Direction with Intermittent No-Wind at Every Odd Hour

Similar to the Core Scenario Set, Scenario Set D lasts for two days in a fixed direction with speeds of 8 m/s. However, wind speeds of 8 m/s occur only at even hours, and there is no wind speed at odd hours. The scenarios are labeled d_0_d, where d will be substituted by N, S, E, or W to indicate the central direction from which the wind blows (at 8 m/s) and 0 implies the intermittent no-wind condition.

2.3. Scenario Set E: Reversing Direction at Every Even Hour, and No-Wind at Every Odd Hour

Scenario Set E is a modification of Scenario Set D wherein there are no wind speeds at odd hours and speeds of 8 m/s during even hours. However, the direction of the 8 m/s winds reverses every even hour, switching between S and N, or E and W. A scenario would be labeled, for example, S_0_N if the direction of the wind switches between southerly and northerly.

2.4. Scenario Set F: Reversing Wind Direction Every One Hour

Scenario Set F is similar to the Core Scenario Set; speeds are constant at 8 m/s, but direction reverses every hour, switching between S and N, or E and W and are labeled S_N or E_W.

2.5. Scenario Set G: Wind Direction Rotates ± 90 Degrees Every 4 h from a Central Direction

Most wind conditions in Scenario Set G are the same as those in the Core Scenario Set, i.e., wind speeds of 8 m/s lasting approximately 2 days starting at 4:00 a.m. on Day 222 of 1996, with difference being a rotation of ± 90 degrees about a central wind direction (N, S, E, or W) every 4 h (Table 2). The scenarios are labeled d ± 90, where d represents the central wind direction. A fifth scenario, S_360, rotates 8 m/s winds clockwise every 4 h, starting from the south.

Table 2. Scenario Set G: Direction rotates ± 90 degree every 4 h from a central direction [1].

Hour		Wind direction at hours since wind starts										Prevail direction
		0–4	4	8	12	16	20	24	28	32	36	40	
Scenario name	S ± 90	S	W	S	E	S	W	S	E	S	W	W	S
	N ± 90	N	E	N	W	N	E	N	W	N	E	E	N
	E ± 90	E	N	E	S	E	N	E	S	E	N	N	E
	W ± 90	W	S	W	N	W	S	W	N	W	S	S	W
	S_360 [2]	S	W	N	E	S	W	N	E	S	W	W	Non

[1] Wind speed = 8 m/s throughout the wind event. [2] There is no central direction for Scenario S_360, which begins with southerly winds.

2.6. Scenario Set H: Year-Long Winds at a Fixed Direction

This set of scenarios preserved observed 1996 wind speeds, but the directions were fixed to only N, S, E, or W. The fixed unidirectional wind began at Day 1 of 1996 after a five-year (1991–1995) spin-up using observed wind conditions. Daily freshwater and nutrient inputs were based on the calibrated watershed model. The scenario set is labeled Y96_d (Table 3), where d specifies the wind direction. Two other scenarios are also conducted for reference. Scenario Y96_0 has no-wind in 1996, and Scenario Y96_obs uses the observed wind direction and speed.

Table 3. Scenario Set H: Using observed wind speeds in 1996, but are fixed to one direction for a year.

Scenario name	Wind speeds	Wind direction	Watershed inputs	Note
Y96_N	1996 obs	Northerly	1996 obs	
Y96_S	1996 obs	Southerly	1996 obs	Wind directions are modified
Y96_E	1996 obs	Easterly	1996 obs	starting on 1 January for the
Y96_W	1996 obs	Westerly	1996 obs	entire year
Y96_0	0 m/s	N/A	1996 obs	
Y96_obs	1996 obs	1996 obs	1996 obs	Equals 1996 calibration run

2.7. Scenario Set I: Rotating Direction Based on Observed Wind

June 1996 and July 2004 had especially dominant southerly winds (Figure 3). In Scenario Set I, the observed wind directions are rotated clockwise 90, 180, or 270 degrees (Table 4). They are labeled as Yyy_cw90, Yyy_cw180, and Yyy_cw270, respectively, where yy represents either 1996 or 2004 to indicate the year of base-data for wind and watershed inputs. Only the winds in a specified summer month, i.e., June 1996 or July 2004, were rotated. The prevailing directions of these scenarios are listed in Table 4. The scenario without rotation is labeled Yyy_cw00, which is also labeled Yyy_obs, as a non-rotation scenario is equivalent to the observed wind condition.

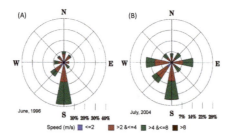

Figure 3. Wind roses of: (**A**) June 1996; and (**B**) July 2004.

Table 4. Scenarios Set I: Rotating wind directions from the observed wind fields that had a month-long prevailing direction.

Scenario names for modification on		Angles of wind dir rotated	Prevailing wind dir after rotate
1996, June wind	2004, July wind		
Y96_obs	Y04_obs	No rotate	S
Y96_cw90	Y04_cw90	90° c.w.	W
Y96_cw180	Y04_cw180	180° c.w.	N
Y96_cw270	Y04_cw270	270° c.w.	E

Table 5 summarizes the above nine scenario sets. Note: The scenario labeled Y96_obs in all scenarios sets (Tables 3 and 4) is identical in each.

Table 5. Summary of scenario sets.

	Wind direction	Speed (m/s)	Duration	Notes	Symbol for Scenario *
A	Fixed, (blowing from N, S, E, W)	Constant (e.g., at 8, 4, 2, etc., m/s)	2 days		A_8 is specifically for speed = 8 m/s
B	Fixed	Constant (e.g., at 8, 4, 2, etc., m/s)	1 h	Start at 4:00 a.m. 8 August 1996, with 7-month spin up.	
C	Fixed	Constant (e.g., at 8, 4, 2, etc. m/s)	20 days		
D	Fixed	8 m/s at even hours, 0 at odd hours	~2 days		d_0_d
E	Reverse at every even hour	8 m/s at even hours, 0 at odd hours	~2 days		S_0_N or E_0_W
F	Reverse every 1-h	Constant 8 m/s	~2 days		S_N or E_W
G	Rotating ± 90° every 4 h from a central direction.	Constant 8 m/s	~2 days		d ± 90. See Table 2.
H	Fixed	Observed	Year-long	1996	Y96_d. See Table 3.
I	Rotating 90°, 180°, and 270° from the observed direction	Observed	June or July	1996, 2004	See Table 4

* Note: d is to be substituted with N, S, E or W to represent the central wind direction. 0 indicates intermittent no wind.

3. Results and Discussions

The analyses are based on model simulated anoxic volumes, mainly the reduction of anoxic volume from the no-wind scenario. The anoxic volumes are only compared at or before the peak reduction, while the post-peak recovery of anoxic volume is not covered in this paper.

3.1. Relative Anoxia Reduction by Wind Directions in Two-Day Wind Events

The core scenario A_8 (wind speeds of 8 m/s for two days, Figure 4D) is the same as the key scenario used in Wang et al. [10]. Here it is used as a reference to compare the results from other scenarios. Thus, it is useful to review the key findings by Wang et al. [10]. The minimum point of the curves in Figure 4D represents the maximum anoxic volume reduction. The dominant PN-type cross-channel bathymetry in the Bay's anoxic center provides a favorable condition for the easterly wind to have a greater destratification than the westerly wind under the wind-induced cross-channel circulation [10]. Thus, the easterly wind reduces more anoxia than the westerly wind. The direction of the southerly and northerly wind travel, respectively, against and along with the net transport direction of the surface fresher water, resulting in stronger destratification and greater reduction of anoxia by the southerly wind [6,7]. Notably, before Hour 24 of the wind event, northerly winds reduced anoxia more than southerly winds, also due to the effects of the PN-type bathymetry that modulates the wind-induced cross-channel circulation [10]. The northerly wind has westward straining component as the easterly wind, and the southerly wind has eastward straining component as the westerly wind. Thus, under the modulation of the PN-type bathymetry on the wind-induced cross-channel circulation, the northerly wind promotes greater destratification. Cross-channel circulation under the simulated wind speeds could be completed in a couple of hours, while a timeline of 1–2 days is necessary for the wind-induced along-channel circulation to effectively influence the anoxic center [21]. Before Hour 24, the northerly wind reduces more anoxic volume than the southerly wind, when the wind-induced cross-channel circulation plays a more important role. Following this period, however, the southerly wind-induced along-channel circulation (via downwelling from the Bay head) influences a wider area of the anoxic zone, leading to an overall greater anoxia reduction. The rest of this section will discuss anoxia reduction by winds at speeds different than the Core Scenario.

Northerly versus southerly wind. At a speed of 10 m/s, the transition point of greater anoxia reduction from northerly winds to southerly winds occurs one hour earlier (at Hour 23, Figure 4E) than the Core Scenario (Figure 4D), because the influence of the wind-induced along-channel circulation by the southerly wind is greater at higher speeds.

At speeds of 6 m/s, the maximum anoxic volume reduction by northerly winds becomes closer to that produced by southerly winds, and the transition to greater anoxia reduction by southerly winds is delayed to Hour 32 (Figure 4C). This is due to a slower influence exercised upon the anoxic center by the wind-induced along-channel circulation at lower wind speeds.

At 2 or 4 m/s wind speeds, destratification is weak and the influence of wind-induced along-channel circulation by southerly winds is weak and slow. The aforementioned transition does not occur, and northerly winds reduce anoxia more than southerly winds across the entire time period (Figure 4A,B). Again, this is primarily controlled by the wind-induced cross-channel circulation under the modulation of the PN-type cross-channel bathymetry.

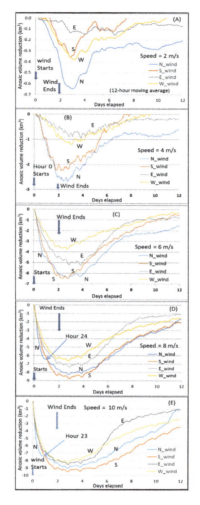

Figure 4. Hourly anoxic volume reduction in the mainstem Bay compared to the no-wind condition forfour idealized wind directions in Scenario Set A (two-day duration) at five speed settings: (**A**) 2 m/s; (**B**) 4 m/s; (**C**) 6 m/s; (**D**) 8 m/s; and (**E**) 10 m/s. The initial anoxic volume was approximately 10 km^3 before the wind event, which began at 4:00 a.m. of 10 August 1996 (i.e., Hour 0), and is the origin (i.e., 0) of the x-axis.

It should also be noted that the promoted up-Bay-ward bottom seawater intrusion promoted by northerly winds also plays a certain role, which can be seen in DO contours of along-channel sections in Figures 5 and 6. Figure 5 represents Hour 24 of the two-day wind scenario at 8 m/s, while Figure 6 shows Hour 48 of a two-day wind scenario at 2 m/s. The symbol X by the x-axis marks the southern end of the 0 mg/L DO isopleths that intersect with the bottom bathymetry. Compared to the no-wind scenarios in Figures 5A and 6A, the X retreats northwards for northerly winds (Figures 5B and 6B) and extends further south in southerly winds (Figures 5C and 6C). The role of the enhanced bottom seawater intrusion in anoxia reduction is difficult to quantitatively separate from other mechanisms. In 8 m/s wind velocities, the bulk anoxia reduction are mainly controlled by wind's mixing and destratification, while the contribution of oxygenation by enhanced bottom seawater intrusion from northerly (or westerly) winds is relatively small (Figure 5). In 2 m/s wind velocities, mixing or destratification is weak, the initial stratification is well maintained, and the DO isopleths in the four winds are similar to those in the no-wind condition (Figure 6), exhibiting virtually no difference. The intrusion of oxygen-rich seawater via enhanced estuarine circulation by northerly winds caused the 0 mg/L DO isopleths to shrink and reduced overall anoxic volume. This can be further seen in Figure 7 where bottom DO concentrations are plotted, northerly winds produce higher bottom DO than southerly winds, consistent with the anoxic volume reduction by northerly versus southerly winds shown in Figure 4A.

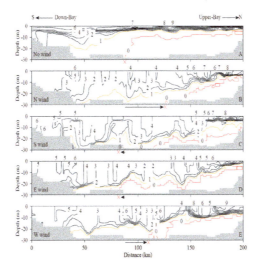

Figure 5. Contours of DO concentration (mg/L) along the main channel from mid lower Bay (south) to mid upper Bay (north) at Hour 24 of a two-day wind scenario at 8 m/s.

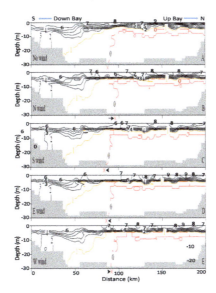

Figure 6. Contours of DO concentration (mg/L) along the main channel from mid lower Bay (south) to mid upper Bay (north) at Hour 48 of a two-day wind scenario at 2 m/s.

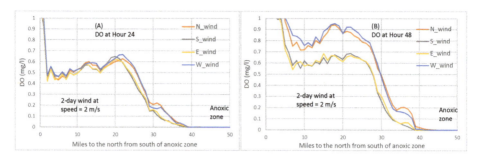

Figure 7. Bottom DO concentrations (mg/L) along the main channel near the south boundary of the anoxic zone for the two-day scenario at 2 m/s. The traverse is approximate at the locations from 50 km to 100 km in Figure 5 or Figure 6: (**A**) Hour 24 of the wind event; and (**B**) Hour 48 of the wind event.

Easterly versus westerly winds. In easterly and westerly winds, the wind-induced cross-channel circulation is the dominant component that causes mixing and anoxia reduction. The PN-type cross-channel bathymetry provides favorable conditions for easterly winds over westerly winds to effect destratification by cross-channel circulation to a greater extent. Additionally, easterly winds have an up-Bay-ward component of along-channel straining, like southerly winds. Thus, at speeds of 6 m/s and greater in the two-day winds, easterly winds reduced more anoxia than westerly winds throughout the entire two-day wind event (Figure 4C–E).

At wind speeds of 2 or 4 m/s, destratification induced by easterly and westerly winds was weak and the enhanced estuarine circulation due to westerly winds became relatively important in reducing anoxia, especially in the late wind period. Before Day 1, the hypoxia reduction was mainly controlled by the bathymetry-modulated wind-induced cross-channel circulation; therefore, easterly winds had a greater anoxia reduction than westerly winds. After about 24 h, westerly winds had a greater anoxia reduction than easterly winds, including the point of peak anoxia reduction (Figure 4A,B), which is mainly due to the enhanced estuarine circulation by the westerly wind. The influence of bottom seawater intrusion on anoxia by westerly versus easterly winds can also be seen in Figure 6 by the direction in which the symbol X moves. At wind speeds of 2 m/s, westerly winds caused the 0 mg/L DO isopleths to retreat northwards, reducing anoxia (Figure 6E), and westerly winds produced higher bottom DO than easterly winds (Figure 7). During most times after Hour 24 in the scenarios of wind speeds equal to 2 or 4 m/s, westerly winds reduced anoxia to a greater extent than easterly winds (Figure 4A,B). Before Hour 24, easterly winds reduced more anoxic volume because this period was still primarily controlled by the bathymetry-modulated cross-channel circulation, while the enhanced estuarine circulation effected by westerly winds had not yet reached the anoxic center to a significant extent.

The above processes help to explain the summary figure (Figure 8) of maximum anoxia reduction among wind directions at different speeds of the two-day winds, as seen in Figure 4.

Assessing the influence of tide. The stages of tide (ebb versus flood) at the moment when the wind event starts can also influence the responses of destratification to wind's longitudinal straining [22,23]. Figure 9b shows simulated hourly anoxic volume on 10 and 11 August 1996 from a no-wind scenario. The average daily anoxic volume increased from Day 1 to Day 2 due to strong oxygen consumption in early August. The two peaks and two valleys of anoxic volume in one day (Figure 9b) were associated with the M2 tide (Figure 9a). The peaks of the anoxic volume (lower DO) were associated with the stage of low-water after ebb tide, and the valleys of the anoxic volume (higher DO) were associated with the stage of high-water after flood tide. The flood tide brought oxygen-rich seawater to the anoxic zone and reduced anoxic volume. The influence of tides on the fluctuation of anoxic volume reached approximately 0.3 km^3 in this simulated high anoxic period.

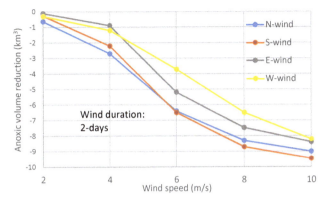

Figure 8. Peak anoxic volume reduction in the mainstem Bay from the no-wind condition by four wind directions in Scenario Set A (i.e., two-day duration) at five speed settings. Greater negative values correspond to greater anoxia reductions.

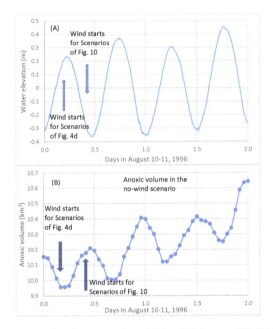

Figure 9. Tidal stage and simulated annoxic volume in 10 and 11 August 1996: (**A**) Water elevation at the Bay mouth; and (**B**) simulated anoxic volume in the no wind scenario. The M2 tide contributes significantly to the fluctuation of anoxic volume.

The first arrow in Figure 9A,B indicates the wind starting time in scenario set A_8 (Figure 4d). It started at 4:00 a.m. on 10 August 1996, near high-tide as ebbing began at the Bay mouth. The second arrow indicates the wind's starting time for another scenario set of 8 m/s winds, but the wind event began 6 hours later, at 10:00 a.m., near low-tide when flooding began at the Bay mouth. Figure 10 plots the simulated anoxic volume reductions by the latter scenario set of 8 m/s winds.

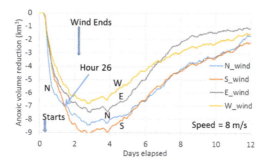

Figure 10. Hourly anoxic volume reduction in the mainstem Bay from four idealized wind directions (compared to no wind) over a two-day duration at 8 m/s that began 6 hours later at a different tidal stage than that in Scenario Set A-8. The initial anoxic volume was about 10 km^3 before the wind event started. To better compare Figure 4d in temporal development, the origin of the x-axis in both Figures 10 and 4d is at 4:00 a.m. on 10 August 1996. Here, Hour 0 (wind starts) lies at 10:00 a.m., 6 hours past the origin point.

For a better comparison of Figures 10 and 4d in temporal development, the origin of the x-axis in both figures is set to 4:00 a.m. on 10 August 1996. The wind events for the scenarios in Figure 10 began 6 hours later, delineated in the graph. There is no significant difference in relative anoxia reduction among wind directions between Figures 10 and 4d. In Figure 10, the northerly wind reduced slightly more anoxia, and the time transitioning from greater anoxia reductions between northerly winds and southerly winds was delayed 2 hours, to Hour 26 of the wind event. Northerly winds can have certain advantages in destratification/anoxia reduction in flood tide versus ebb tide. It is difficult to determine a reference location for tidal stages that relate to wind-induced destratification in the anoxic center, because the time difference of the co-tidal lines is approximately 6–8 hours between the Bay mouth and the anoxic center in the mid-Bay and approximately 12 hours between the Bay mouth and the Bay head [24]. The Bay mouth is used as reference location for tidal stages where the tidal changes are forced. Further analysis of this point lies beyond the scope of this work. The model experiments presented in Figures 10 and 4d indicate that greater anoxia reduction by northerly winds than southerly winds before Hour 24 is not due to tidal stages during the wind events, and both experiments confirmed the argument of Wang et al. [10] regarding the modulation of wind-induced cross-channel circulation by the PN-type bathymetry.

3.2. Relative Anoxia Reduction by Wind Directions in One-Hour Wind Events

Although there rarely exists a continuous calm period for a few days with only one hour of wind, it is worthwhile to conduct model experiments to assess the response of anoxia to one-hour wind events. In the model experiments of one-hour winds, the post-wind recovery of anoxia appeared soon after the wind event stopped. The peak anoxia reduction occurred about 4–5 h after the end of the wind event for wind speeds at 4–8 m/s, and occurred sooner at lower wind speeds. The maximum reduction of anoxic volume was less than 0.3 km^3 at wind speeds of 6 m/s or lower (Figure 11), near the same magnitude of the tidal influence on anoxic volume (Figure 9). The differences in anoxia reduction among wind directions in wind speeds less than 4 m/s were not prominent, most are less than 0.1 km^3.

The wind-induced along-channel circulation in one-hour wind events did not significantly influence the center of anoxia, while the cross-channel circulation became more important in reducing the peak anoxic volume (Figure 11). The modulation of the PN-type bathymetry caused easterly winds to reduce more anoxia than westerly winds, and northerly winds to reduce more anoxia than southerly winds.

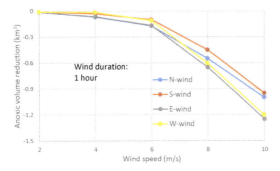

Figure 11. Peak anoxic volume reduction in the mainstem Bay compared to a no-wind condition by four wind directions in Scenario Set B (i.e., one-hour duration) at five speed settings. Greater negative values correspond to greater anoxia reductions.

In two-day wind events, northerly and southerly winds reduced more anoxia than easterly and westerly winds, but in most cases of one-hour winds easterly (or westerly) winds reduced more anoxia than northerly (or southerly) winds, as explained in the following using Figure 12. In Figure 12, the dashed arrow approximates the returned flow along the bed from the downwind shore. The wind-induced cross-channel circulation can complete its cycle in an hour, and the deepest bottom was influenced to a certain degree, to a greater extent by easterly winds than by northerly winds, because the travel distance of the returned bottom current was shorter in easterly winds. Thus, in the one-hour wind events easterly winds had greater anoxia reduction than northerly winds. However, if the wind event continued for several hours, the wind-induced cross-channel circulation by northerly and easterly winds would involve several cycles. Because the bottom was constantly influenced by the wind-induced circulation, and not by travel distances, the anoxia reduction by wind-induced cross-channel circulation by northerly and easterly winds became similar. The northerly wind had stronger direct wind mixing (due to a longer fetch) and stronger longitudinal straining than the easterly wind, and the influence of longitudinal straining was stronger later in the wind period than the first hour of the wind event. Overall, northerly winds caused greater destratification and anoxia reduction than easterly winds in the later period of two-day wind events. Similarly, westerly winds reduced more anoxia than southerly winds if the wind event only lasted for one hour. This phenomenon is more prominent for greater wind speeds (8 or 10 m/s).

In summary, the peak anoxia reductions between opposite wind directions in the one-hour wind events (Figure 11) are comparable to the anoxia reduction in the first 2–6 h of two-day wind events (Figure 4) that are mainly controlled by wind-induced cross-channel circulation and wind induced direct mixing. These are different from the peak anoxia reductions in two-day wind scenarios (Figure 8), since the latter generates more influence by wind-induced along-channel circulation. Generally, in one-hour wind events, the northerly winds effected a greater anoxia reduction than southerly winds, easterly winds had greater anoxia reduction than westerly winds (Figure 11), and easterly (or westerly) winds had greater anoxia reduction than northerly (or southerly) winds.

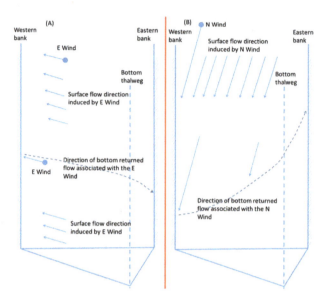

Figure 12. Schematic flow directions of the bottom returned current by winds: (**A**) easterly wind; and (**B**) northerly wind.

3.3. Relative Anoxia Reduction among Wind Directions during Prolonged Unidirectional Winds

3.3.1. Anoxia Reduction by Wind Directions in 20-Day Wind Events

When a unidirectional wind event is extended to 20 days, the peak anoxia reduction occurs at a later time, between Day 21 and 23 or 1–3 days after the end of the wind event (Figure 13). As the wind event continues past two days, the roles of wind-induced along-channel circulation can play a greater role in destratification and anoxia reduction. In addition, the enhanced estuarine circulation in the northerly or westerly winds would contribute more to anoxia reduction. The combination of wind-induced along and cross-channel circulation would be expected to produce more complicated phenomena related to anoxia reduction.

At wind speeds of 2 m/s, the influence of anoxia reduction by wind-induced along-channel circulation is insignificant and occurs later than winds of greater speeds, while the bathymetry-modulated wind-induced cross-channel circulation becomes more important, which favors greater destratification by northerly over southerly winds. On the other hand, the enhanced estuarine circulation by northerly winds also plays a role in hypoxia reduction. Thus, northerly winds reduce more anoxia than southerly winds during the entire wind period for both the two-day (Figure 4a) and 20-day (Figure 13a) wind events. For easterly versus westerly winds in both two-day and 20-day wind events, prior to the end of Day 1, the easterly wind reduced more anoxic volume than the westerly wind. This is because during the early part of the wind event, the returned bottom current by wind-induced longitudinal circulation had not influenced the Bay center, while the wind-induced cross-channel circulation was dominant. With the modulation of the cross-channel bathymetry, easterly winds caused a greater hypoxia reduction than westerly winds. From Day 2 onwards, westerly winds caused greater hypoxia reduction than easterly winds in both the two-day (Figure 4a) and 20-day (Figure 13a) wind events due to enhanced estuarine circulation by westerly winds.

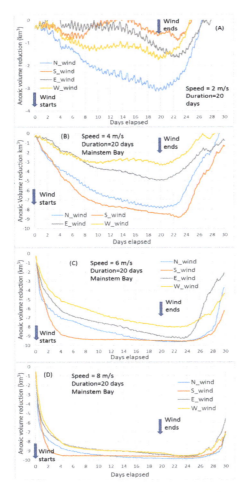

Figure 13. Model simulated anoxic volume reduction in the mainstem Bay compared to a no-wind condition by four idealized wind directions in Scenario Set C (i.e., 20-day duration) at four wind speed settings: (**A**) 2 m/s; (**B**) 4 m/s; (**C**) 6 m/s; and (**D**) 8 m/s. The initial anoxic volume was approximately 10 km³ prior to the wind event.

At wind speeds of 4 m/s (Figure 13B), wind's destratification began to play a greater role in anoxia reduction. After Day 3, southerly winds reduced more anoxia than northerly winds because of a greater influence by wind-induced along-channel circulation. This transition was not observed in the two-day wind event (Figure 4B) since wind stopped prior to Day 3. On easterly versus westerly winds, in both the 20-day wind and two-day wind events there was a transition from more anoxia reduction by easterly winds to westerly winds at approximate the end of Day 1 (Figures 13B and 4B). Prior to the end of Day 1, the bathymetry-modulated wind-induced cross-channel circulation played a greater role in anoxia reduction; after Day 1, the enhanced estuarine circulation by the westerly wind began to play a greater role. The returned bottom currents by wind's along-channel straining are due to downwelling at the Bay head or mouth region. Since this response is a Bay-wide process, it could take an extended period, e.g., 8–31 h to influence the bottom of the mid-Bay [25]. Extended travel time is needed for the down-bay-ward returned bottom current induced by southerly or easterly winds, because the current direction is against the seawater intrusion. It was estimated to be about

0.5–1 day for the returned bottom current in 8 m/s southerly winds to effectively influence the anoxic center in the mid Bay [10]. Compared to northerly or southerly winds, under the same wind speeds in easterly or westerly winds, there was much weaker along-channel straining. For 4 m/s easterly winds, it was estimated to take more than five days for the returned bottom current (from the Bay head) to show an effective influence on the anoxic center. Figure 13B shows that a 20-day wind event at 4 m/s, the easterly wind begins to reduce more anoxic volume than the westerly wind on Day 7.5. This is potentially due to the returned bottom current, because at this time the returned bottom current associated with the easterly wind gradually plays its role. The overall response of DO is a combined effect of bathymetry modulated cross-channel circulation and the returned bottom flow that favors easterly winds a greater anoxia reduction over westerly winds after Day 7.5, although the influence of enhanced estuarine circulation by westerly winds can be more effective as the unidirectional wind prolonged. In the 20-day wind scenarios, the second transition to greater anoxia reduction from westerly to easterly winds modeled at speed of 4 m/s (Figure 13B) did not exist at speeds of 2 m/s (Figure 13A) because of weak destratification that reduced easterly winds' effectiveness. This transition is also absent from the scenarios of two-day wind at speeds of 4 m/s (Figure 4B), because wind stopped after Day 2.

At wind speed of 8 m/s, wind's destratification was strong, and was the main factor in reducing anoxia. Similar to a two-day wind event at the same speed (Figure 4D), after Day 1 in the 20 day wind scenario, southerly winds reduced more anoxia than northerly winds (Figure 13D) as wind-induced along-channel circulation outweighed the effects of wind-induced cross-channel circulation. As winds continued after Day 2, relative anoxia reductions between opposite wind directions changed. In this prolonged unidirectional wind event northerly winds' addition of oxygen-rich seawater by enhanced estuarine circulation factored more heavily. After Day 4, the rate of anoxia reduction (by referring to the slope of the curves, Figure 13D) was greater by northerly winds than by southerly winds, and the two curves intersected on Day 11.5. From this point onwards, northerly winds reduced anoxia more than southerly winds. Of the two transitions seen in Figure 13D, only the first at Hour 24 from northerly to southerly winds was present in the two day wind event.

In the 8 m/s two-day wind scenarios, easterly winds had greater maximum anoxia reduction than westerly winds (Figure 4D) throughout the entire period. In 20-day wind scenarios, easterly winds still had greater maximum anoxia reduction than westerly winds (Figure 13D), but underwent two transitions (at Day 4 and Day 14) in relative anoxia reduction between the two wind directions. In the first few hours, the PN-type bathymetry modulated cross-channel circulation caused easterly winds to reduce more anoxia than westerly winds. This was controlled by the destratification-related anoxia reduction, in which easterly winds caused a greater destratification than westerly winds. After Day 2, the rate of anoxia reduction was greater for westerly than easterly winds (referring to the slope of the curves, Figure 13D), again mainly due to enhanced estuarine circulation, but the anoxic volume was still lower in the easterly winds. At Day 5, westerly winds began to yield lower anoxic volume, but the rate of anoxia reduction began to slow down to a point that yielded similar amount anoxic volume as the easterly winds did. During this time following the transition, the up-Bay-ward component of longitudinal straining by easterly winds induced downwelling at the Bay head and a return down-Bay-ward bottom current bringing fresher water to the Bay's anoxic area. Combined with PN-type bathymetry modulated cross-channel circulation, on Day 16, easterly winds then began to exercise greater anoxia reduction. These were controlled by multiple mechanisms including wind's along-channel straining, cross-channel straining, the modulation of bathymetry, the supply of oxygen-rich water by returned bottom flow from the Bay mouth or head, the influence of tide, etc. A detailed hydrodynamic analysis and quantification of these multiple effects are needed to explain the detailed phenomena, but they are beyond the scope of this work. Besides destratification, the up-Bay-ward along-channel straining by southerly or easterly winds can cause downwelling of oxygen-rich freshwater at the Bay head and be transported down-Bay-ward by the bottom return force.

Since the direction goes against the bottom current of the estuarine circulation, its influence could be less significant compared to other factors influencing anoxia.

At wind speeds of 6 m/s, the wind-induced destratification among all wind directions and wind-enhanced estuarine circulation by northerly and westerly winds are moderately strong in 20-day wind events. The differential responses of anoxia reduction among wind directions (Figure 13C) are in between the scenarios with velocities of 4 and 8 m/s (Figure 13B,D).

3.3.2. Anoxia Reduction by Wind Directions in Year-Long Unidirectional Winds

Figure 14 plots simulated daily anoxic volumes from Scenario Set H, which models year-long unidirectional winds. Here, the wind speeds were the same as the observed in all scenarios except zero for Scenario Y96_0. Southerly and northerly winds resulted in lower anoxic volume than easterly and westerly winds (Figure 14) because of the longer fetch and greater potential for destratification. The anoxic volume simulated using the observed wind (obs wind) lies in between the northerly-southerly winds and the easterly-westerly winds (Figure 14), as the observed wind directions varied with time. The sum of anoxic volume-day over the year (487 km³) was less than that affected by northerly-southerly winds, and greater than that affected by easterly-westerly winds. The no-wind scenario yielded the highest anoxic volume, two times greater than that observed.

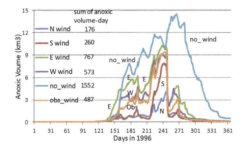

Figure 14. Scenario Set H: Daily anoxic volume for year-long unidirectional wind events. Note: Lower anoxic volume corresponds to a greater reduction of anoxia compared to the no-wind condition.

In two-day wind scenarios at 8 m/s, southerly winds reduced more anoxia than northerly winds (Figure 4D). This relationship was reversed for year-long winds, in which northerly winds had a lesser anoxic volume (Figure 14). For the short two-day wind period, the promoted bottom seawater intrusion in the northerly wind was insignificant, while the stronger destratification by the southerly wind could effectively influence the Bay's anoxic center and increase bottom DO. Under longer periods of unidirectional wind, promoted seawater intrusion by northerly winds became prominent, reducing anoxia significantly.

The relative strengths of anoxia reduction by easterly and westerly winds for the two scenario sets of contrasting durations (Figures 4D and 14) were also opposite. The PN-type bathymetry in the anoxic center provided favorable conditions for greater destratification by easterly winds [10]. In short wind events, easterly winds caused greater destratification and reduced more anoxia. However, under a prolonged westerly wind, its southward component of straining promoted the intrusion of oxygen-rich seawater. During year-long unidirectional winds westerly winds' anoxia reduction could supersede the easterly winds' destratification-related anoxia reduction.

The relatively weak winds in 1996 could be another factor. The winds in the summer of 1996 were relatively weak, mostly (>80%) below 4 m/s, with wind velocities only exceeding 8 m/s for a few hours (≤5%). Therefore, the mechanisms of anoxia reduction in the 20-day winds of 2 or 4 m/s (Figure 13A,B) can be more useful to explain the simulated phenomena in the year-long wind scenarios. In weak winds, the destratification-related anoxia reduction by southerly or easterly winds becomes less significant, while enhanced seawater intrusion under prolonged unidirectional northerly or westerly winds becomes more important in reducing anoxia.

The Bay mouth lies at the south of the Bay, facing east. A prolonged southerly wind could extend the estuarine residence time, which could promote eutrophication process. The easterly wind has westward and northward straining components on the surface water movement, and could also extend the residence time. Notably for easterly winds, anoxia occurred earlier and produced greater anoxic volume than the no-wind condition in the late spring and early summer (Figure 14). This was mainly due to the trapping of nutrients in the Bay and weaker destratification than southerly or northerly winds. Although westerly winds caused even weaker destratification than easterly winds, prolonged westerly winds effected more seawater intrusion and shorter residence times yielding lower anoxic volumes. The unidirectional wind event began on 1 January in this set of scenarios and the retarded residence times could significantly affect the biochemical processes in the spring and oxygen consumption in the summer. Because the two-day wind scenarios began in August and only lasted for a short period, the differential hypoxia reduction between wind directions was mainly controlled by wind's mixing and estuarine circulation, while the differences in biological processes' associated residence times were negligible.

3.4. Intermittent Hourly Winds: Scenario Set D

In contrast with the Core Scenario set of constant wind speeds, in Scenario Set D the wind intermittently stopped for every odd-hour and blew at 8 m/s during even hours. Scenario Set D yielded a 1.5–2 km^3 smaller reduction in anoxic volume than the counterpart wind directions of the Core Scenario (Figure 15). Still, the anoxia reductions by Scenario Set D were greater than their counterpart wind directions at constant speeds of 6 m/s (Figure 8), suggesting that intermittent winds can still strongly reduce anoxia as long as the speed reaches a certain threshold that causes destratification.

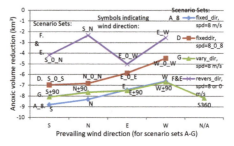

Figure 15. Peak anoxic volume reduction by dominant wind direcitons in scenario sets of two-day winds with speeds = 8 m/s or interlayered with no wind. Greater negative values correspond to greater anoxia reductions.

3.5. Winds of Hourly Reversing Directions: Scenario Sets F and E

Scenario S_N of Scenario Set F switches between southerly and northerly wind directions every hour, and is used to compare the southerly and northerly winds of Scenario A_8 (Figure 15). Similarly, Scenario E_W is used to compare the easterly and westerly winds of Scenario A_8. All have speeds of 8 m/s over a two-day period. The frequent switching seemed to negate the effects of the preceding wind direction. The anoxia reduction by Scenario E_W was 4–5 km^3 less than the reduction by constant westerly or easterly winds, and the anoxia reduction by Scenario S_N was 6–7 km^3 less than the reduction by constant northerly or southerly winds (Figure 15). With intermittent no wind between reversing wind directions (e.g., Scenario S_0_N or E_0_W) the reduction of anoxic volume was approximately 2 km^3 more than the S_N or E_W scenarios. Nevertheless, Scenario S_0_N and

E_0_W still had a reduction in anoxic volume of 3–4 km^3 less than the constant unidirectional southerly or northerly winds and easterly or westerly winds, respectively.

The anoxic volume reduction by Scenario E_0_W lies in between reductions modeled in Scenarios E_0_E and W_0_W. Scenario E_0_E had more frequent easterly winds than the other two scenarios, and yielded more anoxia reduction. The intermittent no wind between switching directions in Scenario E_0_W weakened the cancellation of anoxia reduction processes by the two switching wind directions, therefore, still had a greater anoxia reduction than Scenario W_0_W. Cross-channel circulation was important in destratification by easterly and westerly winds. The widths of cross channel around the anoxic center were narrow. The wind's effect could be effectively realized within the one-hour period of calm. The next phase of wind in opposite direction generated the next round of reduction. Because of more frequencies in easterly wind, Scenario E_0_W had a greater anoxia reduction than Scenario W_0_W. While, Scenario E_W had no calm period between changing directions, significantly reducing destratification.

Compared to Scenario N_0_N and S_0_S, Scenario S_0_N had an approximately 3 km^3 lesser reduction of anoxic volume. The wind-induced circulation of along-channel transport by northerly or southerly winds could not be completed within a single hour. Reversing wind directions weakened the actions of the preceding wind direction. Therefore, Scenario S_0_N had weaker anoxia reduction than both Scenarios S_0_S and N_0_N. Scenario S_N switched wind directions between southerly and northerly each hour without a calm period, and yielded even weaker anoxia reduction. This model experiment confirms that wind-induced along-channel circulation affects the anoxic center much more slowly than wind-induced cross-channel circulation.

3.6. Winds with Rotating Directions at Fixed Speeds of 8 m/s: Scenario G

A comparison of anoxia reduction among scenarios with ± 90 degrees rotation about a central direction every 4 h (Scenario Set G) and the Core Scenario was also completed. For a scenario rotating about a southerly or northerly central direction (S ± 90 or N ± 90), the anoxic volume reduction was about 0.6 km^3 less than that caused by the winds of fixed southerly or northerly direction (Figure 15). This can be attributed to the addition of easterly and westerly winds (Table 2), which had shorter fetch and generated weaker destratification than southerly or northerly winds. For scenarios rotating about an easterly or westerly central direction (i.e., E ± 90 or W ± 90), anoxia reductions were slightly increased than the corresponding easterly (E) wind or westerly (W) wind of Core Scenario A_8, because of the inclusion of southerly and northerly winds.

Scenario S_360 had a decreased reduction in anoxia than the wind in a constant southerly direction did, as expected. Surprisingly, it also reduced more anoxia than Scenario S ± 90 did, and the causes are unclear. It is hypothesized that a continuous rotating direction is more effective in destratification and anoxia reduction than a rotation backwards along an already traversed path that could weaken the anoxia reduction effects of a prior wind direction.

These scenarios indicate that turbulence induced by winds of gradual changing directions at a similar speed generally can continue to weaken stratification. In many cases, directional change of 90 degrees does not significantly cancel out wind induced circulations. It is more likely that conditions in the Chesapeake Bay often lie somewhere in between scenarios G and D. For time scales of a few days, in most cases a prevailing southerly wind would cause greater anoxia reduction than a prevailing northerly wind, and would also hold true for prevailing easterly versus westerly winds. However, for month-long prevailing unidirectional wind the relative anoxia reductions between opposite wind directions can exhibit different anoxia reduction patterns, which will be discussed in the next section.

3.7. Scenarios Based on Naturally Occurred Month-Long Prevailing Winds: Scenario I

June 1996 and July 2004 both had observed prevailing southerly winds, although other directions were included intermittently (Figure 3). Southerly prevailing winds in Scenario Y96_obs were flipped in Scenario Y96_cw180 (Table 6) becoming northerly prevailing winds, which yielded lower anoxic volume than Scenario Y96_obs. Scenario Y96_cw90's prevailing westerly winds yielded lower anoxic volume than the scenario of prevailing easterly winds (Y96_cw270). Scenarios with prevailing northerly or southerly wind also yielded lower anoxic volumes than either the scenario of prevailing easterly or westerly wind. The results are comparable to the relative anoxia reductions by scenarios with low wind speeds (e.g., 2 or 4 m/s) of two-day winds (Figure 4A,B), and year-long unidirectional wind scenarios (i.e., Scenario Set H, Figure 14).

Table 6. Anoxic volume in June 1996 and July 2004 for Scenario Set I (rotating wind direction).

Wind field modified	1996 nutrient load and June Wind			2004 nutrient load and July Wind		
	Scenario name	Dominate wind dir	June AV	Scenario name	Dominate wind dir	July AV
No-rotation	Y96_obs	S	1.504	Y04_obs	S + some W	1.336
90° c rotate	Y96_cw90	W	1.899	Y04_cw90	W + some N	1.249
180° c rotate	Y96_cw180	N	1.018	Y04_cw180	N + some E	0.828
270° c rotate	Y96_cw270	E	2.052	Y04_cw270	E + some S	1.709

Similar phenomena were also found from scenarios of rotating wind direction in July 2004. The same patterns held in this instance, although westerly prevailing winds (Y04_cw90) also yielded slightly lower model estimated anoxic volume than southerly prevailing winds (Y04_obs). This was due to a greater frequency of westerly (and easterly) winds with the prevalent southerly winds in the July 2004 condition (Figure 3B) than in the June 1996 condition (Figure 3A). When rotating 90 degrees to prevail westerly in scenario Y04_cw90, there were considerable frequencies in northerly (and southerly) winds. Superposed by the influence of northerly winds to the promoted saline water intrusion by the month-long westerly prevailing winds, slightly lower simulated anoxia was generated, in contrast with the original prevailing southerly wind field.

Besides the prevailing wind directions, the wind-rose (Figure 3) also shows relative frequency of other wind directions in June 1996 and July 2004. However, it cannot determine whether the prevailing wind events were frequently interlayered by events of other wind directions, or whether the events of prevailing direction and the other directions were aggregated separately in two periods. The impact on anoxia reduction could differ between the two cases. The initial anoxia intensities and wind speeds and directions prior to the time period of model analysis could affect. These questions can be studied further through more model experimentation, but are beyond the scope of this work.

4. Conclusions

The model experiments in this work analyzed the impact of wind speed and duration on relative hypoxia reductions for opposite wind directions within the north-south oriented Chesapeake Bay. Besides presenting the reduction of summer hypoxia by wind's mixing and destratification-related processes, this study further explores another process of hypoxia reduction by wind; this process is primarily associated with enhanced estuarine circulation bringing oxygen-rich seawater to the Bay via winds with down-estuary straining components, i.e., northerly and westerly winds. In strong wind events equal to or greater than 6 m/s, model experiments showed that destratification processes are the main mechanisms by which wind can reduce anoxia. At low wind speeds (e.g., 2 m/s) or in prolonged unidirectional wind events, an enhanced estuarine circulation-related process plays a greater role in hypoxia reduction.

For two-day wind events of speeds equal to 8 m/s, easterly winds cause greater hypoxia reduction than westerly winds because of greater destratification (Wang et al., 2016) [10]. This is primarily due to the modulation of the PN-type bathymetry to wind-induced cross-channel circulation, where the easterly wind causes a greater destratification and hypoxia reduction than the westerly wind in the strongly stratified Chesapeake summer. The second reason is that easterly winds have an up-Bay-ward component of straining that cause greater destratification than westerly winds. However, at low wind speeds, e.g., 2 m/s, when stratification is well preserved or in prolonged unidirectional wind events, westerly winds yield a greater reduction of hypoxia because enhanced estuarine circulation brings oxygen-rich seawater to the hypoxic zone.

In the first 24 hours of a two-day wind event at speeds of 8 m/s, the PN-type bathymetry causes northerly winds to reduce more hypoxia than southerly winds because of greater destratification by wind-induced cross-channel circulation. In later wind periods, i.e., after Hour 24, southerly winds cause a greater hypoxia reduction because the influence of wind-induced along-channel circulation becomes dominant in the Bay's hypoxic zone [10]. If the unidirectional wind events continue for more than 12 days, there is a second transition, and northerly winds begin to reduce hypoxia further once more, as the enhanced estuarine circulation begins to play a significant role in reducing hypoxia. This study shows that the timing of these transitions varies with wind speeds, and that there is no second transition if the wind event is short. In weaker wind events (e.g., wind speeds of 2 m/s), wind's destratification is weak and the enhanced estuarine circulation by northerly winds becomes an important factor in reducing hypoxia. Therefore, at all of the times of the simulated 2-day or 20-day wind events, northerly winds reduce more hypoxia than southerly winds.

Most natural wind events are episodic and are subject to frequent changes in wind direction. The relative influences on hypoxia by wind directions might then be characterized by short-period wind events. On the other hand, it is also unlikely that wind events will occur for only one hour over a period of a few days. Thus, the model experiments of two-day wind as well as their modified scenarios can be more useful in analyzing relative hypoxia reduction among observed wind directions. The model experiments demonstrated that if an 8 m/s hourly intermittent wind maintains the same direction, and then it can still strongly reduce hypoxia approximately equal to 75% of the anoxia reductions by nonstop winds over two days. Reductions in hypoxia by winds that reverse directions hourly are largely negated by the previous phase of wind direction. If there is an intermittent calm period between reversing directions, the cancellation effect is lessened, and the hypoxia reduction is approximately 50% of the reduction produced by constant winds. If the wind direction rotates up to $\pm$ 90 degrees about a central direction, it can still yield high hypoxia reduction, equivalent to approximately 90%–100% of the reduction induced by constant winds. These results were derived from model simulations under specific initial stratification and hypoxia conditions, and the percent anoxia/hypoxia reductions should be expected to differ under altered conditions. This paper describes differences in hypoxia reduction for wind directions. In general, change of wind speeds could have more influence on hypoxia than the change of wind directions. Indicated from Figures 8 and 11, in the model experimental setting of speeds at 4 to 10 m/s over short time periods, e.g., one hour or two days, a change in speed of 10%–20% results in a greater hypoxic volume change than switching wind direction.

Month-long unidirectional prevailing winds can exist, during which period the relative influences on hypoxia reduction by wind directions could be differ from the model experiments of short-period wind events.

Relative effectiveness of destratification in the hypoxic zone between opposite wind directions varies with wind speed and duration, as do the subsequent relative reductions of hypoxia. These responses are associated with changes in relative destratification by wind-induced cross-channel circulation and along-channel circulation, as well as enhanced estuarine circulation for different wind speeds and durations. The model experiments in this work provide additional supportive evidence on the modulation of PN-type bathymetry that provide favorable conditions for greater destratification by easterly winds compared to westerly winds, and northerly winds compared to southerly winds [10,14]. The strengths of initial stratification, tidal stages, and some other factors can also affect these results, and further detailed analyses are needed to obtain a more complete picture. Note that the above conclusions were drawn from model experiments. Although this model can simulate reasonable responses of anoxic volume to altered wind strengths and directions, care should be taken when applied to management analysis.

J. Mar. Sci. Eng. **2016**, *4*, 62

Acknowledgments: The writers appreciate the professional input and support to this research from Richard Batiuk, the Associate Director for Science at USEPA Chesapeake Bay Program Office. This project is supported by USEPA Grant CB963060-01.

Author Contributions: P. Wang and L. Linker conceived and designed the experiments; H. Wang, K. Hinson and P. Wang performed the experiments; P. Wang and H. Wang analyzed the data; and P. Wang, K. Hinson and L. Linker wrote the paper.

Appendix A. Description of Computer Model That Is Used in the Study

The Chesapeake Bay Water Quality and Sediment Transport Model (WQSTM) is a coupled CH3D hydrodynamic model and ICM water quality model [18]. The CH3D model was first developed for the US Army Engineer Waterways Experiment Station [25] and has been extensively modified since [19]. The model computes numerical solutions for the basic equations of continuity, motion, and mass conservation. It simulates physical processes controlling Bay-wide circulation and mixing, such as tides, wind, temperature and density effects, freshwater inflows, turbulence, and the effect of the earth's rotation. The vertical diffusivity is computed by a turbulent kinetic energy (t-k-ε) closure model [26,27]. Details of the solution scheme are provided by Johnson et al. [19]. The horizontal resolution of model cells is approximately 1 km × 1 km, and are reduced to 0.5 km at the deep channel area. The physical transport of materials, for example, the salinity (Sa) fields, are computed thusly:

$$\frac{\partial(Sa)}{\partial t} = -R_O \left(\frac{\partial(uSa)}{\partial x} + \frac{\partial(vSa)}{\partial y} + \frac{\partial(wSa)}{\partial z} \right) + \frac{Ek_H}{Pr_H} \left(\frac{\partial(K_H \partial(Sa)/\partial x)}{\partial x} + \frac{\partial(K_H \partial(Sa)/\partial y)}{\partial y} \right) + \frac{Ek_V}{Pr_V} \frac{\partial(K_V \partial Sa/\partial z)}{\partial z} \tag{A1}$$

where, u, v, and w represent the x (W->E), y (S->N), and z (down->up) velocity components, respectively; t = time; R_o = Rossby number; K = turbulent eddy coefficients; Ek = Ekman number; Pr = Prandtl number; and the subscript H (horizontal) or V (vertical) for the K, Ek and Pr variables indicates their horizontal or vertical component, respectively. The model was calibrated for 10 years using a 1991–2000 hydrology. In the mainstem Bay, compared against the observed data on the same date, the mean difference and the relative difference of the model for salinity are −0.01 ppt and 10%, respectively.

The ICM water quality model simulates 36 state variables including various forms of nitrogen, phosphorus and carbon, three generalized groups of algae, dissolved oxygen, sediment diagenesis and other state variables relevant to Chesapeake water quality. The time rate change of a state variable (C) within a control volume is:

$$F(C) = \iiint \frac{\partial C}{\partial t} dV \tag{A2}$$

where V is a control volume.

For each control volume, i, and for each state variable, transport and kinetics are calculated based on the mass-conservation equation:

$$\frac{\delta V_i \cdot C_i}{\delta t} = \sum_{k=1}^{n} Q_k C_k + \sum_{k=1}^{n} A_k D_k \frac{\delta C_k}{\delta x_k} + S_i \tag{A3}$$

where, V_i = volume of ith control volume (m³); C_i = concentration in ith control volume (g·m⁻³); t, x = temporal and spatial coordinates; n = number of flow faces attached to ith control volume; Q_k = volumetric flow across flow face k of ith control volume (m³·s⁻¹); C_k = concentration in flow across face k (g·m⁻³); A_k = area of flow face k (m²); D_k = diffusion coefficient at flow face k (m²·s⁻¹); and S_i = sum of external loads and kinetic sources and sinks in ith control volume (g·s⁻¹).

The WQSTM simulates nutrient transport and dynamics in the estuary in variable time steps of approximately 2–5 minutes. The oxygen kinetics consists of an air-sea exchange, algal photosynthesis and respiration, heterotrophic respiration, and various oxidation and reduction reactions of the simulated substances, with a full carbon based DO simulation. The model was calibrated with observed data for 10 years (1991–2000). In the mainstem DO estimates, at depths less than 6.7 meters, the model mean error (ME) and relative error (RE) are 0.14 g/m^3 and 11.2%; at depths between 6.7–12.8 meters, the ME and RE are 0.30 g/m^3 and 19.4%; and at depths greater than 12.8 meters, the ME and RE are −0.45 g/m^3 and 28.7% [18], respectively.

Figure A1 presents an example of multi-year model calibration in salinity and bottom DO in a deep monitoring station, CB4.1C. Although model simulated dissolved oxygen can have an approximate 30% deviation from observed values, generally the model performed well in producing proportional responses of anoxic volume to changes in wind, and had much lower relative errors (less than 10%) among scenarios in regards to proportional changes in wind strength.

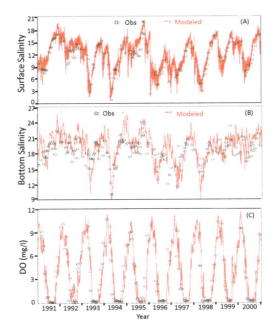

Figure A1. Model simulated versus observed for year 1991−2000: (**A**) surface salinity; (**B**) bottom salinity; and (**C**) bottom dissolved oxygen at Chesapeake Bay monitoring station CB4.1C (from Wang et al. [10]).

References

1. Officer, C.B.; Biggs, R.B.; Taft, J.L.; Cronin, L.E.; Tyler, M.A.; Boynton, W. R. Chesapeake Bay anoxia: Origin, development and significance. *Science* **1984**, *233*, 22–27. [CrossRef] [PubMed]
2. Harding, L.W.; Leffler, M.; Mackiernan, G.B. *Dissolved Oxygen in The Chesapeake Bay: A Scientific Consensus*; Maryland Sea College: College Park, MD, USA, 1992; p. 18.
3. Kato, H.; Phillips, O.M. On the penetration of a turbulent layer into a stratified fluid. *J. Fluid Mech.* **1969**, *37*, 643–655. [CrossRef]
4. Malone, T.C.; Kemp, W.M.; Ducklow, H.W.; Boynton, W.R.; Tuttle, J.H.; Jonas, R.B. Lateral variation in the production and fate of phytoplankton in a partially stratified estuary. *Mar. Ecol. Prog. Ser.* **1986**, *32*, 149–160. [CrossRef]
5. O'Donnell, J.; Dam, H.G.; Bohlen, W.F.; Fitzgerald, W.; Gay, P.S.; Houk, A.E.; Cohen, D.C.; Howard-Strobel, M.M. Intermittent ventilation in the hypoxic zone of western Long Island Sound during the summer of 2004. *J. Geophys. Res.* **2008**, *v113*, C09025. [CrossRef]
6. Chen, S.N.; Sanford, L.P. Axial wind effects on stratification and longitudinal salt transport in an idealized, partially mixed estuary. *J. Phys. Oceanogr.* **2009**, *39*, 1905–1920. [CrossRef]

7. Scully, M.E. Wind modulation of dissolved oxygen in Chesapeake Bay. *Estuar. Coasts* **2010**, *33*, 1164–1175. [CrossRef]

8. Li, Y.; Li, M. Effects of winds on stratification and circulation in a partially mixed estuary. *J Geophys. Res.* **2011**, *v116*, C12012. [CrossRef]

9. Scully, M.E. Physical controls on hypoxia in Chesapeake Bay: A numerical modeling study. *J. Geophys. Res.* **2013**, *118*, 1239–1256. [CrossRef]

10. Wang, P.; Wang, H.; Linker, L.; Tian, R. Effects of cross-channel bathymetry and wind direction on destratification and hypoxia reduction in the Chesapeake Bay. *Estuar. Coast. Shelf Sci.* **2016**. [CrossRef]

11. Diaz, R.J.; Rosenberg, R. Marine benthic hypoxia: a review of its ecological effects and the behavioural responses of benthic macrofauna. *Oceanogr. Mar. Biol. Annu. Rev.* **1995**, *33*, 245–303.

12. Hagy, J.D.; Boynton, W.R.; Keefe, C.W.; Wood, K.V. Hypoxia in Chesapeake Bay, 1950–2001: Long-term changes in relation to nutrient loading and river flow. *Estuaries* **2004**, *27*, 634–658. [CrossRef]

13. USEPA (U.S. Environmental Protection Agency). Chesapeake Bay Total Maximum Daily Load for Nitrogen, Phosphorus and Sediment. Available online: https://www.epa.gov/sites/production/files/2014-12/documents/cbay_final_tmdl_exec_sum_section_1_through_3_final_0.pdf (accessed on 12 September 2016).

14. Wang, P.; Wang, H. The Wind Effect on Chesapeake Bay Destratification and Hypoxia. In Proceedings of the July 2012 Modeling Subcommittee Quarterly Meeting, Annapolis, MD, USA, 11 July 2012.

15. Wang, P.; Wang, H.; Linker, L. Relative importance of nutrient load and wind on regulating interannual summer hypoxia in the Chesapeake Bay. *Estuar. Coasts* **2015**, *38*, 1048–1061. [CrossRef]

16. Kemp, W.M.; Boynton, W.R.; Adolf, J.E.; Boesch, D.F.; Boicourt, W.C.; Brush, G.; Cornwell, J.C.; Fisher, T.R.; Glibert, P.M.; Hagy, J.D.; et al. Eutrophication of Chesapeake Bay: Historical trends and ecological interactions. *Mar. Ecol. Prog. Ser.* **2005**, *303*, 1–29. [CrossRef]

17. Murphy, R.R.; Kemp, W.M.; Ball, V.P. Long-term trends in Chesapeake Bay seasonal hypoxia, stratification, and nutrient loading. *Estuar. Coasts* **2011**, *34*, 1293–1309.

18. Cerco, C.F.; Kim, S.C.; Noel, M. *The 2010 Chesapeake Bay Eutrophication Model: A Report to USEPA Chesapeake Bay Program*; US Army Engineer Research and Development Center: Vicksburg, MS, USA, 2010.

19. Johnson, B.; Heath, R.; Hsieh, B.; Kim, K.; Butler, L. *User's Guide for a Three-Dimensional Numerical Hydrodynamic, Salinity, and Temperature Model of Chesapeake Bay*; Technical Report HL-91-20; Department of the Army Waterways Experiment Station: Vicksburg, MS, USA, 1991.

20. Shenk, G.W.; Linker, L.C. Development and Application of the 2010 Chesapeake TMDL Watershed Model. *J. Am. Water Resour. Assoc.* **2013**. [CrossRef]

21. Pritchard, D.W.; Vieira, M.E.C. Vertical variations in residual current response to meteorological forcing in the mid-Chesapeake Bay. In *The Estuary as A Filter*; Kennedy, V.S., Ed.; Academic Press: Orlando, FL, USA, 1984; pp. 27–65.

22. Breitburg, D.L. Nearshore hypoxia in Chesapeake Bay: Patterns and relationships among physical factors. *Estuar. Coast. Shelf Sci.* **1990**, *30*, 593–609. [CrossRef]

23. Jay, D.A.; Musiak, J.D. Internal tidal asymmetry in channel flows: Rigins and consequence. *Coast. Estuar. Stud.* **1996**, *50*, 211–249.

24. Fisher, C.W. Tidal Circulation in Chesapeake Bay. Ph.D. Thesis, Old Dominion University, Norfolk, UK, 1986; p. 255.

25. Sheng, Y.P. *A Three-Dimensional Model of Coastal, Estuarine and Lake Currents Using a Boundary-Fitted Grid*; Titan Systems New Jersey Inc.: Princeton, NJ, USA, 1986.

26. Rodi, W. *Turbulence Models and Their Application in Hydraulics—A State of The Art Review*; IAHR (International Association of Hydraulic Research): Delft, Netherlands, 1993.

27. Bloss, S.; Lehfeldt, R.; Patterson, R. Modeling turbulent transport in stratified estuary. *J. Hydraul. Eng.* **1988**, *114*, 1115–1133. [CrossRef]

Journal of
*Marine Science
and Engineering*

Article

Statistical Interpolation of Tidal Datums and Computation of Its Associated Spatially Varying Uncertainty

Lei Shi [1,2,*] and Edward Myers [1]

1   Coast Survey Development Laboratory, NOAA, Silver Spring, MD 20910, USA; edward.myers@noaa.gov
2   Earth Resources Technology, Laurel, MD 20707, USA
*   Correspondence: l.shi@noaa.gov; Tel.: +1-301-713-2809

Academic Editor: Richard P. Signell
Received: 15 July 2016; Accepted: 19 September 2016; Published: 22 September 2016

Abstract: Tidal datums are key components in NOAA's Vertical Datum transformation project (VDatum). In this paper, we propose a statistical interpolation method, derived from the variational principle, to calculate tidal datums by blending the modeled and the observed tidal datums. Through the implementation of this statistical interpolation method in the Chesapeake and Delaware Bays, we conclude that the statistical interpolation method for tidal datums has great advantages over the currently used deterministic interpolation method. The foremost, and inherent, advantage of the statistical interpolation is its capability to integrate data from different sources and with different accuracies without concern for their relative spatial locations. The second advantage is that it provides a spatially varying uncertainty for the entire domain in which data is being integrated. The latter is especially helpful for the decision-making process of where new instruments would be most effectively placed. Lastly, the test case results show that the statistical interpolation reduced the bias, maximum absolute error, mean absolute error, and root mean square error in comparison to the current deterministic approach.

Keywords: tides; tidal datum; uncertainty; VDatum; variational method; statistical interpolation; optimal interpolation; Chesapeake Bay; Delaware Bay

1. Introduction

A vertical datum is a base elevation used as a reference from which to reckon heights or depths. It is called a tidal datum when defined in terms of a certain phase of the tide. For marine applications, tidal datums are the reference planes from which measurements of height and depth are made [1] and from which marine boundaries are determined. To determine the tidal datum as the reference plane is a challenge. Tidal datum data derived from observed tidal elevation time series are only available in limited locations, where there are at least two to three months or longer of water level time series records. Practically, various deterministic spatial interpolations [2,3] can be used to generate a spatially continuous tidal datum distribution over the water. If a hydrodynamic tidal model exists in that region, tidal datums derived from the tidal model can be used as the first estimate field, which is subsequently corrected by adding the correction field interpolated from observation and model discrepancies at the stations.

NOAA's National Ocean Service (NOS) has developed a software tool called VDatum that provides vertical datum transformations between tidal, orthometric and ellipsoid-based vertical datums [4]. Over the years, customers and developers of VDatum have raised questions about the uncertainty associated with the VDatum conversions between different vertical datums. Initial efforts were made to quantify uncertainty in both datum transformations and the datums themselves, leading to estimates that could be used for each geographic region represented in VDatum. However, the approach presented here to estimate uncertainties in the tidal datums will provide a path forward in VDatum to eventually be able to provide a more continuous, spatially varying estimate of the uncertainty.

An important part of VDatum's vertical datum transformations is that the values returned by the VDatum software need to be equivalent to values determined through observations at tide gauge locations. The NOAA/NOS' Center for Operational Oceanographic Products and Services (CO-OPS) is commissioned to set up the national tidal station network for water level measurements, as well as the establishment of the tidal datum bench marks. The measured tidal datum values at 19 year National Tidal Datum Epoch (NTDE) stations are published in CO-OPS publications and on their website. For consistency, the vertical datum relationships in VDatum need to match the published tidal datum values at the CO-OPS NTDE stations. It is also desirable that the analysis field be close to observed data at CO-OPS non-NTDE stations. This requirement has been one of the guiding principles in the development of the statistical interpolation presented here.

As mentioned, the current tidal datums in the VDatum transformation are computed by integrating modeled and observed tidal datums through a prediction and correction procedure, the latter of which uses a deterministic spatial interpolation method. A solver based on Laplace's equation is currently used for the spatial interpolation of modeled tidal datum and observed tidal datum discrepancies over the water. The inherent drawback of this spatial interpolation approach is the apparent lack of any physical or statistical principle governing the tidal datums [3]. Laplace's interpolation is a low-order interpolation scheme, and the interpolated surface becomes singular at the data points. As a deterministic interpolation method, it is also unable to provide spatially varying uncertainty estimates of the tidal datum product. One alternative for estimating the uncertainty in the tidal datums is to use the delete-one jackknifing method [3,5]. Jackknifing has a tendency to overestimate the error and is more appropriate in providing a single-value average estimate of the uncertainty over the whole domain [3]. The delete-one jackknifing method can provide a good estimate of the uncertainty of the tidal datum product over a large domain, under the condition that the sample size is very large and samples are randomly distributed spatially. However, these conditions are rarely met. As VDatum currently provides single-value uncertainty estimates in the tidal datums for each regional application, the next goal to improve the uncertainty estimates is to provide a spatially varying uncertainty field for each tidal datum. We propose here a statistical interpolation and uncertainty estimation methodology that would provide such a product with spatially varying uncertainty. The interpolation method is derived from the variational principle in data assimilation [6,7] by minimizing a cost function, similar to the three-dimensional variational method (3DVAR). The construction of the cost function is such that the discrepancy between (1) the analysis solution that minimizes the cost function and (2) the CO-OPS' observation values at the observation stations satisfies the constraint that is prescribed by the user. This is achieved by introducing a diagonal weight matrix that regulates the weight of the observed tidal datum error of a particular station in the cost function, therefore also regulating the analysis results. In Section 2, we will first review the mathematical formulation of the statistical interpolation method and its uncertainty calculation, followed by a description of input matrices in our test case region and the calculation of the error covariance matrices. Results from the test case are presented in Section 3, followed by a discussion in Section 4 and the conclusions and recommendations in Section 5.

2. Method and Data Input

2.1. Method and Mathematical Formulation

Assume that we have a size $n \times 1$ discrete modeled tidal datum field f_m at model mesh nodes and a size $m \times 1$ observed tidal datum data set f_o at CO-OPS station locations. Both f_m and f_o follow a normal distribution, and $Var(f_m) = P$, $Var(f_o) = R$ respectively. How do we determine a new $n \times 1$ tidal datum analysis field f at the model mesh nodes by blending f_m and f_o using a certain criterion?

In line with the conventional variational method, we first define a cost function $J(f)$, and then solve f by minimizing the cost function $J(f)$. The cost function $J(f)$ is defined as

$$J(f) = \frac{1}{2}(f - f_m)^T P^{-1}(f - f_m) + \frac{1}{2}(f_o - Hf)^T (W^{-\frac{1}{2}})^T R^{-1} W^{-\frac{1}{2}}(f_o - Hf) \tag{1}$$

where H (size $m \times n$) is the interpolation matrix projecting the modeled field to the observed data locations, W (size $m \times m$) is a diagonal weight matrix that adjusts how much the final product f differs from the observed values at the station locations. It is assumed the model and observation fields are unbiased. The analysis field f that minimizes the cost function $J(f)$ is

$$f = f_m + G(f_o - Hf_m) \tag{2}$$

where $G = PH^T[W^{\frac{1}{2}}R(W^{\frac{1}{2}})^T + HPH^T]^{-1}$ is called the gain matrix; f is the unbiased estimate of the true tidal datum field, and the posterior error covariance matrix P_a is given by

$$P_a = Var(f) = (I - GH)P(I - GH)^T + GRG^T \tag{3}$$

where I is the identity matrix.

The weight matrix W provides flexibility and an option if we want the analysis field f to match or be close to the observed values at the observation locations. For a uniform weight distribution $W = I$, the method is identical to the optimal interpolation (OI) method. The analysis field f at the observed locations can be different from the observed values. If a diagonal element $W(i,i) = 0$ ($i \in [1, 2, ..., m]$), then the interpolated values f are forced to match the observed values at the station i, independent of the observed error covariance matrix R.

2.2. Test Case and Input Data

The Chesapeake Bay, Delaware Bay and adjacent coastal ocean (Figure 1) are used as our test domain to apply the statistical interpolation method to calculate the the Mean Higher High Water (MHHW) tidal datum field and its associated uncertainty field. The Mean High Water (MHW), Mean Low Water (MLW) and Mean Lower Low Water (MLLW) tidal datums are also calculated similarly, but the results will not be presented in this paper. The hydrodynamic tidal model had been developed for the area by Yang et al. [8] in a previous VDatum tidal model development project. In this section, we will give a detailed description of input matrices in our test case, and the calculation of the error covariance matrices.

2.2.1. Observed Tidal Datums f_o and Determination of the Observed Error Covariance R

The observed tidal datums f_o are derived from water level time series collected at the CO-OPS' tidal gauges. NOS has a standard method to process the time series and calculate the tidal datums [9]. The observed error covariance matrix R is a size $m \times m$ diagonal matrix. The individual diagonal element of R is the variance, or the square of the standard deviation, of the observed tidal datum errors. Both the observed tidal datums and the error standard deviations are provided by CO-OPS [10,11] following Swanson [12] and Bodnar's [13] formulation.

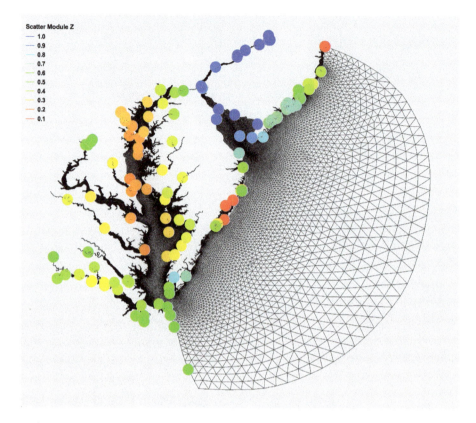

Figure 1. Hydrodynamic tidal model domain (Yang et al. (2008)) and observed tidal datum MHHW (m) shown in color-coded dots at tidal station locations.

2.2.2. Tidal Datums Derived from the Hydrodynamic Model Time Series f_m

If we have a hydrodynamic tidal model, then the tidal datums can be derived from the modeled water level time series using the same process as that used for the observed water level time series [9]. The biggest advantage of the tidal model is that it provides continuous spatial coverage for coastal and estuarine waters where the navigational safety is mostly of concern. It provides a perfect background tidal datum field (Figure 2) for model-observation data integration. The hydrodynamic model employed in the tidal simulation to compute the tidal datums here is the ADvanced CIRCulation (ADCIRC) finite element model [14,15] in its barotropic two-dimensional depth-integrated (2DDI) mode. The bias of all station model errors is relatively small at 0.41 cm, the maximum absolute error (MAXE) for MHHW is 25.37 cm, the mean absolute error (MAE) is 4.48 cm, and the root mean square error (RMSE) is 6.33 cm (Table 1).

Table 1. Error statistics (cm) for the model, Laplace's interpolation, and statistical interpolation of the tidal datum MHHW.

Data Field	Bias	MAXE	MAE	RMSE
Model	0.41	25.37	4.48	6.33
Laplace's	−0.22	12.31	2.06	2.94
Statistical	−0.12	10.68	1.62	2.51

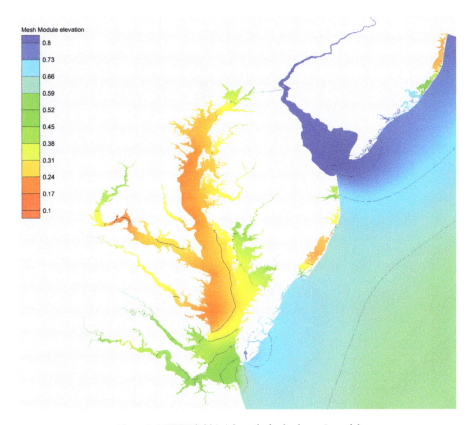

Figure 2. MHHW field (m) from the hydrodynamic model.

2.2.3. Model Error Covariance Matrix P

The model error covariance matrix is defined as $P_{ij} = \mathrm{var}(f_{n1}f_{n2}) = \sigma_{n1}\sigma_{n2}\mathrm{corr}(f_{n1}f_{n2})$, $(1 \leq i, j \leq n$, unit: m^{-2}), σ_{n1}, σ_{n2} are standard deviations of the model errors at nodes n_1 and n_2. The correlation between two points is calculated using a three-day moving average tidal datum time series. The underlying assumption is that the magnitude of the error signal in the tidal datum time series is proportional to the tidal datum signal. Here we give a constant value to σ_{n1} and σ_{n2}, calculated by comparing observed and modeled tidal datum discrepancies over the model domain (Figure 3). For the Chesapeake and Delaware Bays model, the model error standard deviation is 6.33 cm. The covariance matrix is not related to the distance between node points n_1 and n_2. In an idealized case, it may be true, but in reality the model is not perfect. To limit observation stations far away from the station of interest from interfering with the results, the covariance is adjusted and decreases exponentially over the distance between nodes n_1 and n_2. The relaxation spatial scale for this is 200 km in our application.

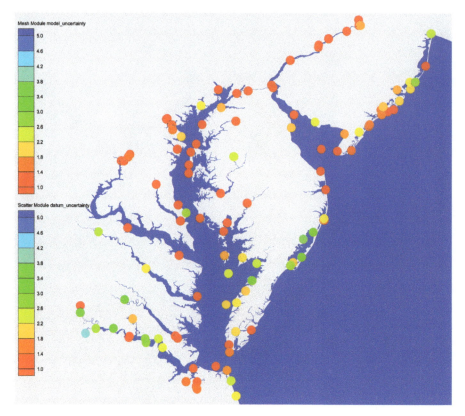

Figure 3. Observed tidal datum MHHW uncertainties from CO-OPS in standard deviation (cm) at station locations (colored dots) and modeled tidal datum MHHW uncertainty expressed as error standard deviation (background) before the interpolation.

2.2.4. Interpolation Matrix, H

The interpolation matrix H is a size $m \times n$ matrix projecting the modeled field to the observed data locations; h_{ij} ($1 \leq i \leq m$, $1 \leq j \leq n$, unit: non-dimensional) is the weight of the model nodes j in determining model values at the observation locations i. In our application, we use a linear triangular interpolation to project the model value to the observation location. H is solely determined by the spatial location of the model mesh nodes and observation locations.

2.2.5. Weight Matrix, W

The weight matrix W is a size $m \times m$ diagonal matrix determining the weight of R in the computation of the analysis field f. The diagonal element w_{ii} ($0 \leq w_{ii} \leq 1$, $1 \leq i \leq m$) is the weight of the observation error variance r_{ii} at station i in the determination of analysis field f. If $w_{ii} = 0$, the analysis results will be independent of the observation error at station i. Analysis field f will be the same as the observed value at that station, and the uncertainty will be the same as the CO-OPS assigned value. If $w_{ii} = 1$, then the analysis field will take full account of the error covariance R at station i. The analysis field f will be the local optimal combination of the model results and observations that minimizes the cost function. The posterior uncertainty/error at the station will be reduced, less than both the CO-OPS assigned error and the background model error.

2.2.6. Constraint and Determination of Weight Matrix, *W*

The constraint that the VDatum technical team adopted for statistical interpolation is simple: the discrepancy between the analysis field and the observations at all subordinate stations should be equal to or less than 1 cm or the CO-OPS's uncertainty value, whichever is less. The weight matrix *W* will be determined through iteration following this predetermined constraint.

3. Results

While Equations (2) and (3) provide the general framework of the statistical interpolation, the results can vary depending on the estimation of the observation and model error covariance matrices, as well as on the weight matrix (and constraint) that decides the impact of observed error covariance on the final tidal datum product.

Tidal Datum Analysis Field

The statistical interpolation produces the spatially distributed properties, in this case, MHHW (Figure 4). The interpolation adjusts the background model values over the whole domain. It corrects apparent discrepancies between observations and model results for MHHW (Figure 2) at the observation locations by statistically blending the observations and model results. Unless the observed value is 100% accurate (e.g., zero error), the adjusted values will be different from the observed values. The results indicate that the adjustments to MHHW at the stations are very small. The average magnitude of an adjustment is 1 cm, and the maximum adjustment is around 5 cm.

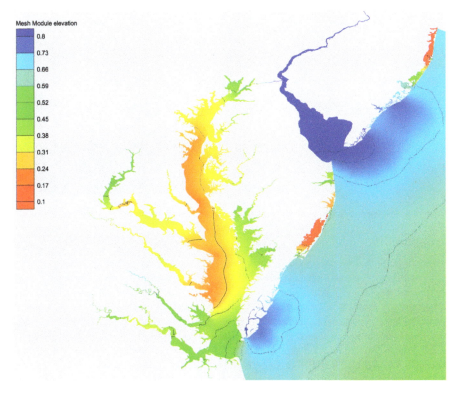

Figure 4. Tidal datum MHHW (m) after statistical interpolation.

The error statistics, shown in Table 1, indicate that the statistically interpolated tidal datum MHHW consistently improved all the error measures (bias, MAXE, MAE, and RMSE) in comparison with the modeled and Laplace's interpolated MHHW.

The statistical interpolation not only provides us with the product, but it also produces uncertainty estimates (Figure 5). The background model uncertainty had been improved dramatically in comparison with the model uncertainty (Figure 3). The statistical interpolation reduces the uncertainty of the tidal datum product in Chesapeake Bay (which is indicated from the color change under the same color bar), Delaware Bay and the associated coastal areas, and to a lesser extent in the offshore area in the southeast corner of the domain away from the coast where tidal gauge stations are located (Figure 5).

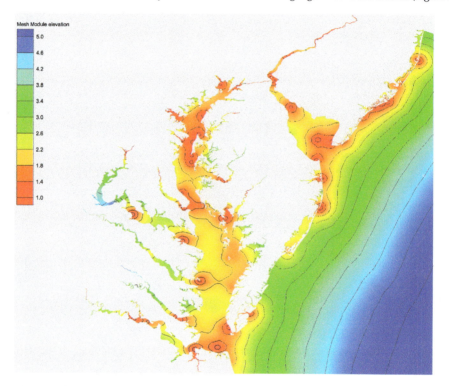

Figure 5. The posterior uncertainty (cm) of the interpolated tidal datum product (MHHW, Figure 4).

4. Discussion

The constraint that we adopted is a compromise between an analysis field that matches ($W = 0$) CO-OPS' observed values and a statistically optimal analysis field ($W = I$, statistically optimal implies a lowest overall uncertainty). When we force the analysis field to match all of the observations ($W = 0$), the uncertainty at 24 out of 117 total observed data locations is at its highest within the vicinity of those stations (local maxima). That raises a question of whether the inclusion of one particular station into the data assimilation improves the overall results by reducing the uncertainty. The difference between the inclusion and non-inclusion of one particular station into the data assimilation under all matching ($W = 0$) and OI cases ($W = I$) can be best illustrated by a simple numerical test to evaluate the differences in the uncertainty fields before and after removing one station in the data assimilation. Here we present the test results for Cove Point (Figures 6 and 7), where the CO-OPS' tidal datum uncertainty is 2.74 cm. Cove Point is one of 24 locations (out of 117) for which the uncertainty at the observed point is at its highest within its vicinity for all matching cases ($W = 0$).

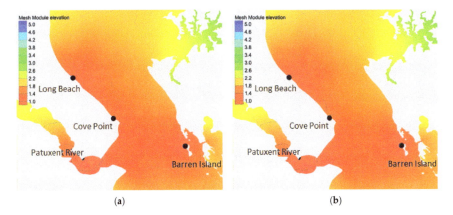

Figure 6. Comparison of spatially varying uncertainty (cm) of the interpolated tidal datums with and without Cove Point data in the OI case. (**a**) Interpolation with the Cove Point observed data; (**b**) interpolation without the Cove Point observed data.

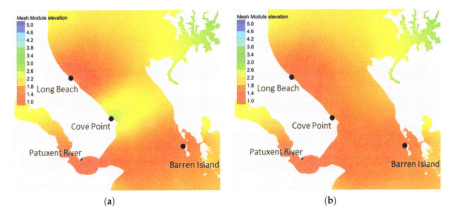

Figure 7. Comparison of spatially varying uncertainty (cm) of the interpolated tidal datums with and without Cove Point data in the matching case. (**a**) Interpolation with the observed data; (**b**) interpolation without the observed data.

Table 2 shows the results from this simple test. For the OI case (Figure 6), the uncertainty by assimilating the Cove Point data is 1.21 cm, much better than the CO-OPS 2.47 cm uncertainty from the observations (Figure 6a). Without assimilation, the uncertainty is 1.39 cm (Figure 6b). For the matching case with the Cove Point data assimilated, the uncertainty at the observed location of Cove Point is given by CO-OPS as 2.47 cm, which is relatively high if compared with its neighboring stations Long Beach and Barren Island (Figure 7a). Without assimilating the Cove Point data, the uncertainty at that location is 1.40 cm (Figure 7b). The uncertainty also decreases in the vicinity of Cove Point. Excluding the Cove Point data from assimilation/interpolation is the best option for the matching case. Mathematically/statistically speaking, for the OI case, it can be shown that any data is good data to reduce the uncertainty as long as we know its quality. For the matching case, it is sometimes better to discard a bad data point (although it is still valuable using OI) without assimilation if a neighboring observation is close and good enough to bridge the gap and produce a better result (as shown in the Cove Point case, Figure 7a,b). If all points match except Cove Point, but Cove Point is still assimilated with ($0 \leq w_{ii} \leq 1$), the uncertainty is 1.32 cm. This is lower than the uncertainty (1.40 cm) when Cove Point is not assimilated, and much lower than the CO-OPS uncertainty from the observations (2.74 cm).

Table 2. Uncertainty (cm) at the observation station (Cove Point, Chesapeake Bay) with and without assimilation of the data in the OI and matching cases. Also presented is the uncertainty in a case where all stations are forced to match except Cove Point, which is assimilated but not forced to match.

Data Field	Observed Data Assimilated	Observed Data Not Assimilated
OI ($W = I$)	1.21	1.39
Matching ($W = 0$)	2.47	1.40
Matching, except Cove Point	1.32	1.40

The results from further tests of all CO-OPS stations are very clear. For OI, any inclusion of an additional data point will reduce the uncertainty. For the matching case, while for the majority of the data locations the inclusion of data reduces the uncertainty, some do not. The current constraint for statistical interpolation is the compromise reached to minimize the discrepancy between the final tidal datum product and the CO-OPS values. It also provides flexibility in producing a better uncertainty estimate even though it is no longer optimal.

5. Conclusions

In this paper, we propose a generalized statistical interpolation method to integrate modeled tidal datums and observed tidal datums. The interpolation method is derived from the variational method by minimizing a cost function, similar to 3D variational data assimilation. A diagonal weight matrix is introduced to regulate the weight of the observed tidal datum error of a particular station in the cost function, and therefore also in the analysis results. The mathematical formulation of the method derived is more general than Optimal Interpolation (OI) or 3D variational method (3DVAR), but follows very closely the framework of OI and 3DVAR, which is widely used in meteorological and oceanographic applications for model and observation data integration. In a special case, when the weight matrix is an identity matrix, the results are statistically optimal, and the method is identical to OI.

In this application, the setting of the weight matrix follows the constraint that the discrepancy at all stations is less than 1 cm or the CO-OPS' uncertainty value, whichever is less, and is calculated through an iterative process. The obvious advantage of the statistical interpolation is that the method provides a spatially varying uncertainty of the tidal datum products. Considering that the tidal datum itself is a statistical result from data processing of a long time series, the statistical property calculated from the modeled time series for interpolation is more plausible than any deterministic interpolation. The spatially varying uncertainty can pinpoint regions with low uncertainty levels and help with decision-making on the number and locations of new tidal gauge installations in a geographic area.

From a data assimilation point of view, the statistical interpolation is capable of incorporating all kinds of observed or modeled data with different degrees of uncertainty. The ingestion of additional data will improve the quality and reduce the uncertainty of the product/results.

Our proposed method satisfies our goal to have the tidal datum products be as close to the CO-OPS observations as possible. While it is statistically sub-optimal, it will generally allow the inclusion of any data that will reduce the uncertainty. In our application in the Chesapeake and Delaware Bays, the statistical interpolation in comparison with the raw model output and Laplace's interpolation reduces the bias, MAXE, MAE, and RMSE. We would strongly recommend statistical interpolation under constraint for tidal datum interpolation in VDatum production. NOAA's VDatum team has approved this recommendation and accepted the method as the standard procedure for future tidal datum product development.

In the future, the capability of data integration from various sources is probably the most important feature of the statistical interpolation. We expect a steady accumulation of data from various sources (third party observations, different model results). The statistical interpolation or data assimilation provides a perfect framework for data integration. Overall, the statistical interpolation is a better data processing and management tool, and it produces a better tidal datum product with lower uncertainty.

Acknowledgments: Authors would like to thank the NOAA/NOS' NGS, CO-OPS and OCS VDatum project tri-office management and technical teams' support of the project. We would also like to thank many experts in and outside of NOAA for going through the project report review process and providing valuable comments and advice to improve the technical report and manuscript.

Author Contributions: L.S. and E.M. conceived and designed the experiments; L.S. performed the experiments and data analysis; L.S. and E.M. drafted the manuscript. Both authors read and approved the final manuscript.

Conflicts of Interest: The authors declare no conflict of interest.

References

1. Hicks, S.D. Tidal Datums and Their Uses—A Summary. *Shore Beach* **1985**, *53*, 27–32.
2. Hess, K.W. Spatial Interpolation of Tidal Data in Irregularly-Shaped Coastal Regions by Numerical Solution of Laplace's Equation. *Estuar. Coast. Shelf Sci.* **2002**, *54*, 175–192. [CrossRef]
3. Shi, L.; Hess, K.; Myers, E. Spatial Interpolation of Tidal Data Using a Multiple-Order Harmonic Equation for Unstructured Grids. *Int. J. Geosci.* **2013**, *4*, 1425–1437. [CrossRef]
4. Hess, K.W.; Kenny, M.; Myers, E. *Standard Procedures to Develop and Support NOAA's Vertical Datum Transformation Tool, VDATUM*; NOAA NOS Technical Report; NOAA: Silver Spring, MD, USA, 2012.
5. Emery, W.J.; Thomson, R.E. *Data Analysis Methods in Physical Oceanography*; Elsevier Science: Amsterdam, The Netherlands, 2001.
6. Ide, K.; Courtier, P.; Ghil, M.; Lorenc, A. Unified notation for data assimilation: Operational, sequential and variational. *J. Meteor. Soc. Jpn.* **1997**, *75*, 181–189.
7. Lorenc, A.C. Development of an operational variational assimilation scheme. *J. Meteor. Soc. Jpn.* **1997**, *75*, 339–346.
8. Yang, Z.; Myers, E.P.; Wong, A.M.; White, S.A. VDatum for Chesapeake Bay, Delaware Bay, and Adjacent Coastal Water Areas: Tidal Datums and Sea Surface Topography. Available online: http://vdatum.noaa.gov/download/publications/TM_NOS-CS15_FY08_26_Yang_VDatumCHES-DEL.pdf (accessed on 19 September 2016).
9. Scherer, W.; Stoney, W.M.; Mero, T.N.; O'Hargan, M.; Gibson, W.M.; Hubbard, J.R.; Weiss, M.I.; Varmer, O.; Via, B.; Frilot, D.M.; et al. *Tidal Datums and Their Applications*; Gill, S.K., Schultz, J.R., Eds.; NOAA Special Publication: Rockville, MD, USA, 2001.
10. Gill, S.K.; Fisher, K.M. A Network Gaps Analysis for the National Water Level Observation Network. Available online: http://tidesandcurrents.noaa.gov/publications/Technical_Memorandum_NOS_COOPS_0048.pdf (accessed on 19 September 2016).
11. Michalski, M. *USA_MD_Report: Tide Station, Tidal Datum and Geodetic Datum Assessment for VDatum Project*; NOAA: Silver Spring, MD, USA, 2011.
12. Swanson, R.L. *Variability of Tidal Datums and Accuracy in Determining Datums from Short Series of Observations*; U.S. Department of Commerce, NOAA, NOS: Rockville, MD, USA, 1974.
13. Bodnar, A.N. Estimating accuracies of tidal datums from short term observations. Available online: https://tidesandcurrents.noaa.gov/publications/NOAA_Technical_Report_NOS_COOPS_077.pdf (accessed on 19 September 2016).
14. Luettich, R.A.; Westerink, J.J.; Scheffner, N.W. ADCIRC: An Advanced Three-Dimensional Circulation Model of Shelves, Coasts, and Estuaries, Report 1: Theory and methodology of ADCIRC-2DDI and ADCIRC-3DL. Available online: http://citeseerx.ist.psu.edu/viewdoc/download?doi=10.1.1.472.429&rep=rep1&type=pdf (accessed on 19 September 2016).
15. Luettich, R.A.; Westerink, J.J. Formulation and Numerical Implementation of the 2D/3D ADCIRC Finite Element Model version 44.XX. Available online: http://citeseerx.ist.psu.edu/viewdoc/download?doi=10.1.1.675.3043&rep=rep1&type=pdf (accessed on 19 September 2016).

Journal of
*Marine Science
and Engineering*

Article

Long-Term Morphological Modeling of Barrier Island Tidal Inlets

Richard Styles [1,*], Mitchell E. Brown [1], Katherine E. Brutsché [1], Honghai Li [1], Tanya M. Beck [1] and Alejandro Sánchez [2]

[1] U.S. Army Engineer Research and Development Center, Coastal and Hydraulics Laboratory,
     3909 Halls Ferry Road, Vicksburg, MS 39180, USA; mitchell.e.brown@usace.army.mil (M.E.B.);
     katherine.e.brutsche@usace.army.mil (K.E.B.); honghai.li@usace.army.mil (H.L.);
     tanya.m.beck@usace.army.mil (T.M.B.)
[2] Institute for Water Resources, Hydrologic Engineering Center, 609 Second Street, Davis, CA 95616, USA;
     alejandro.sanchez@usace.army.mil
*   Correspondence: richard.styles@usace.army.mil; Tel.: +1-601-634-4065

Academic Editors: Richard P. Signell and Dong-Sheng Jeng
Received: 25 July 2016; Accepted: 15 September 2016; Published: 23 September 2016

Abstract: The primary focus of this study is to apply a two-dimensional (2-D) coupled flow-wave-sediment modeling system to simulate the development and growth of idealized barrier island tidal inlets. The idealized systems are drawn from nine U.S. coastal inlets representing Pacific Coast, Gulf Coast and Atlantic Coast geographical and climatological environments. A morphological factor is used to effectively model 100 years of inlet evolution and the resulting morphological state is gauged in terms of the driving hydrodynamic processes. Overall, the model performs within the range of established theoretically predicted inlet cross-sectional area. The model compares favorably to theoretical models of maximum inlet currents, which serve as a measure of inlet stability. Major morphological differences are linked to inlet geometry and tidal forcing. Narrower inlets develop channels that are more aligned with the inlet axis while wider inlets develop channels that appear as immature braided channel networks similar to tidal flats in regions with abundant sediment supply. Ebb shoals with strong tidal forcing extend further from shore and spread laterally, promoting multi-lobe development bisected by ebb shoal channels. Ebb shoals with moderate tidal forcing form crescent bars bracketing a single shore-normal channel. Longshore transport contributes to ebb shoal asymmetry and provides bed material to help maintain the sediment balance in the bay.

Keywords: hydrodynamic modeling; tidal inlets; long-term morphological change; sediment transport; morphodynamic modeling; coastal inlet evolution

---

1. Introduction

Tidal inlets are some of the most dynamically active systems in coastal zones [1]. Inlets connect the continents to the sea and are primary pathways for terrestrial sediments to the ocean. Coastline evolution and stability are tied to inlet processes, as inlets function as both sources and sinks of sediment and can disrupt longshore transport pathways modulating the growth, migration and erosion of adjacent shorelines. The processes governing inlet behavior present complex engineering challenges that affect the global economy and quality of life for coastal communities.

Long-term behavior of tidal inlets in barrier island systems is controlled by a number of dynamically complex and competing physical processes [1,2]. Tidal currents concentrated in the inlet throat mobilize sediment and maintain an open connection between the coastal ocean and bay. Longshore transport introduces sediment into the system that modulates the mass balance by contributing to the development of the ebb shoal delta and bypassing to the down-drift beach [2].

Within this conceptual framework, sediments are continually reworked through complex interactions between local waves, ebb shoal morphology and reversing tidal currents.

Numerical models produce quantitative predictions and have been widely used to study the morphodynamics of tidal inlet systems on long time scales. Cayocca [3] used a two-dimensional (2-D) coupled wave, hydrodynamic, and sediment transport model to investigate the stability and potential evolution of the Arcachon Lagoon on the French Atlantic coast. In addition to simulating the lagoon with present-day bathymetry, Cayocca [3] conducted idealized simulations with an initial constant bathymetry to study long-term bay and inlet evolution. The results were consistent with historical observations and provided evidence that the lagoon was likely a stable feature under the present wave and tidal regime.

Using a 2-D morphodynamic model, Dissanayake et al. [4] set up an idealized inlet system with dimensions similar to the Ameland Inlet in the Dutch Wadden Sea to simulate inlet evolution for periods of 50, 100, and 300 years. The model did not include wave forcing or Coriolis force, as the primary focus was to investigate inlet-cross-section growth rates and ebb shoal delta evolution. The results showed rapid ebb shoal growth and inlet channel deepening during the first 20 years followed by a longer period of weaker development, eventually stabilizing to an equilibrium asymptote. The ebb shoal lobe and main channel orientation were rotated from a shore-normal direction in agreement with the long-shore tidal circulation patterns in the area.

Yu et al. [5] used a 2-D hydrodynamic and sediment transport model to predict inlet and bay evolution over a 60-year timeframe. Their domain consisted of nine idealized multiple-inlet barrier island configurations on a rectilinear grid with an initially uniform bathymetry in the bay and inlet. Each configuration had different spatial scales but with similar tidal forcing and non-cohesive sediments with a common grain size. They did not consider winds, waves or Coriolis force on the assumption that tides were the primary factors contributing to bay area development and inlet cross-sectional area growth. They derived theoretically a power law relating inlet cross-sectional area to total bay area, which was confirmed by the numerical simulations.

Van der Wegen and Roelvink [6] conducted idealized 2-D simulations to investigate the long-term (8000 years) evolution of an idealized rectangular basin (2.5 km by 80 km) to understand pattern formation in an elongated bay. They noted rapid morphological development in the first few decades followed by moderate deepening of the bay over the remaining timeframe.

Nahon et al. [7] used a 2-D morphodynamic model to examine the effects of varying tide and wave regimes on tidal inlet evolution. The model comprised a single idealized lagoon/inlet system without Coriolis force and was driven by a single M2 tidal constituent. The simulations included nine wave and hydrodynamic scenarios encompassing the range of energy conditions as classified by Hayes [2]. Model performance was measured in terms of goodness of fit between the model results and tidal prism relationship with the data of Jarrett [8].

In addition to long-term evolution of the system as a whole, other studies have focused on the evolution of the ebb shoal. Van Leeuwen et al. [9] developed a 2-D hydrodynamic model to investigate morphological characteristics of ebb tidal deltas. The model was driven by tidal forcing only and was first set up for an inlet/bay system with substantial inlet and alongshore tidal flow. They noted that residual currents and tidal asymmetry were the two major mechanisms controlling sediment transport. The process of ebb shoal evolution led to two asymmetric channels that were skewed in the downdrift direction owing to strong longshore tidal currents. In addition to the idealized model runs, they conducted long-term (500 years) simulations of the Frisian Inlet in the Dutch Wadden Sea. During the first 100 years, the channel deepened rapidly, producing two asymmetric ebb shoals on the eastern and western side offshore of the wide inlet throat. Ebb shoal growth proceeded more slowly after about 200 years but remained asymmetric. Channel deepening continued, yet slowed during the last 100 years of the simulation indicating that the system had not reached equilibrium. They noted that the general characteristics including the two ebb shoals were similar to the present configuration of the Frisian Inlet.

Van Der Vegt et al. [10] investigated the mechanisms responsible for creating symmetric ebb tidal deltas. To simplify the analysis they restricted their model domain to parallel depth contours and drove the model with symmetric forcing. The inlet axis was oriented normal to the coastline and the system was forced with a shore-normal wave field and no directly forced along-shore flow or Coriolis force. The resulting morphological evolution led to an ebb channel centered in the inlet that branched offshore producing two symmetric channels. Flow divergence led to shoaling at the end of the ebb channel producing an ebb shoal. Sensitivity studies under varying tidal prism, inlet width, wave height, and sediment transport formulations did not produce any significant qualitative changes. Model results were used to evaluate existing power law formulas relating shoal volume to tidal prism and correctly predicted the slope when scaled against previous measurements. The model underestimated the total sand volume, which may be a function of the sediment transport or wave transformation formulations.

These previous studies focused on the morphodynamics of both existing and idealized inlets with and without wave forcing or Coriolis force for varying simulation timeframes (decades to centuries). Robust numerical models are needed to investigate long-term climatological impacts to tidal inlet systems in a regime of global sea level change. This study aims to explore how idealized immature inlets develop and evolve toward a long-term (100 years) equilibrium or quasi-equilibrium state. To place the results in the context of real-world systems and to assess model confidence, the forcing conditions are derived from nine U.S. inlets representing a range of wave and tidal climates. Model performance is gauged in terms of established empirical methodologies that describe the equilibrium and stability characteristics of barrier island tidal inlets. The results focus on inlet morphology, hydrodynamics and equilibrium characteristics. The discussion addresses the varying morphological patterns and how they relate to the forcing conditions.

2. Materials and Methods

2.1. Numerical Model

The Coastal Modeling System (CMS) is an integrated suite of numerical models for simulating water surface elevation, current, waves, sediment transport, and morphology change [11]. The system includes relevant nearshore processes, such as wave-current interactions, wetting/drying, sediment avalanching, and wind stresses. The CMS consists of a hydrodynamic and sediment transport model, CMS-Flow, and a spectral wave model, CMS-Wave.

CMS-Flow is a 2-D finite-volume model that solves the depth-integrated mass conservation and shallow-water momentum equations on a non-uniform Cartesian grid. The wave radiation stress and wave field information calculated by CMS-Wave are supplied to CMS-Flow for the flow and sediment transport calculations. Currents, water level, and morphology changes are fed into CMS-Wave to increase the accuracy of the wave transformation predictions [12–14].

CMS-Wave is a two-dimensional finite-difference spectral wave transformation model that solves the steady-state wave-action balance and diffraction equation on a non-uniform Cartesian grid [15,16]. The model can simulate important nearshore wave processes including diffraction, refraction, reflection, wave breaking and dissipation mechanisms, wave-wave and wave-current interactions, and wave generation and growth. It is a full-plane model with primary waves propagating from open boundaries toward the inner domain. Additional model features include a grid nesting capability, wave run-up on the beach face, wave transmission through structures, wave overtopping, and storm wave generation.

The CMS modeling system has been developed specifically for coastal applications for both long and short term studies [12]. The modeling system has been validated for the hydrodynamics, waves and sediment transport with analytical solutions, laboratory data and field measurements [11,17,18]. Previous applications relevant to the present study include navigation, tidal inlets, coastal erosion, shoreline change, and sediment budgets.

2.2. Morphology Acceleration Factor

Using a process-based morphodynamic model to conduct long-term simulations requires intensive computational time. Considering the difference in time scales between hydrodynamic and transport processes and morphological changes, a morphological acceleration factor (MAF) is used for CMS simulations, in which the morphological time step is a constant multiplier of a morphological factor and a much smaller hydrodynamic time step to simulate morphology change at an accelerated rate [19]. For example, a simulation of 5 years and an acceleration factor of 20 would produce 100 years of effective sediment transport and morphology change with the computational time associated with only 5 years of simulation time. The MAF is applied after all hydrodynamic and sediment transport processes have been computed for that time step. The calculated changes are then multiplied by the selected MAF and updates to the grid bathymetry are made. This approach is repeated at each time step.

Sensitivity testing was conducted on one of the model setups to determine the largest MAF which produced qualitatively comparable results to using no acceleration. Test cases were simulated for an effective ten-year period depending on the assigned MAF values of 1, 2, 5, 10, and 20. For example, for a MAF value of one, the test case was run for ten years and for a MAF value of 10, the test case was run for one year. A comparison for MAF values of 1, 10 and 20 is shown in Figure 1. Examining the morphology at the end of each run and comparing with the initial case with no acceleration, it was determined that a MAF value of 20 was an acceptable value. Since the MAF value would be applied to all nine model setups, a more conservative MAF value of 10 was selected.

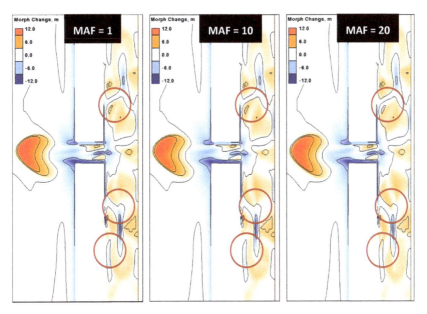

Figure 1. Comparison of morphologic change for Morphology Acceleration Factor (MAF) values of 1, 10, and 20. Blue and red colors represent morphology change over the morphology change contours (black lines) from MAF value of 1, and red ovals indicate areas of observed qualitative change.

2.3. Inlet Geometry

Nine idealized inlet geometries are chosen using characteristic basin dimensions derived from coastal inlets along the U.S. Pacific, Atlantic and Gulf coasts (Table 1). Three inlet types are chosen from each of the three coastal regions in order to obtain a representation of natural inlet types and to define input parameter values and boundary conditions using realistic tide and wave forcing. The three coasts represent different energy regimes in terms of wave and tidal energy flux with the Pacific Coast denoted as 'highly exposed', the Atlantic Coast as 'moderately exposed' and the Gulf Coast as 'mildly exposed' [20]. For clarity and to distinguish the different model results, the idealized inlets are referred to by the names of their real inlet counterparts, which are shown in Figure 2. It should be noted that other than the initial and boundary conditions specified here, the idealized simulations are not intended to represent the morphology of the real inlets. Rather, the inlet characteristics are used to represent a range of possible isolated barrier island tidal inlets that could exist.

Figure 2. Map of the nine selected inlets modeled in this study.

The bay area is rectangular with the width and length chosen to approximate its natural inlet counterpart. Cusps, spits, headlands and other morphologic characteristics cause natural bays to differ from a simple rectangular shape. However, the degree to which the model is producing results consistent with the long-term evolution of tidal inlets is gauged in terms of the O'Brien relationship and the Escoffier analysis. These simplified approaches assume a featureless bay with simplified dimensions, so the detailed geometry is less important than the volume capacity of the system. Idealized inlets have simplified boundary conditions making it easier to evaluate the effects of varying wave, tide and basin geometry on inlet evolution [7]. However, bay storage is critical to the hydraulics and the idealized systems are constructed with the same area and thus storage capacity as their natural inlet counterparts.

Table 1. Geometric characteristics and selected model parameter settings for the 9 simulated inlets.

	West Coast			Gulf Coast			East Coast		
	Grays Harbor	MCR *	Humboldt	East Pass	Johns Pass	Galveston	Oregon Inlet	Shinnecock	Newburyport
Inlet Length (m)	2000	5700	6600	700	600	7500	1500	680	1500
Inlet Width (m)	550	2200	3600	500	190	2800	1100	310	500
Inlet Depth (m)	11.9	15.6	13.5	3.5	5.3	3.5	2.5	7.7	7.0
Bay Length (km)	22	15	10	47	5	30	80	13	6
Bay Width (km)	3	15	38	7.4	3	42	38	3.2	3
Initial Bay Depth (m)	3.4	3.4	5.6	3.5	1.8	3.5	2.5	2.2	1.8
Offshore Length (km)	12	32	44	15	6	50	36	13	12
Offshore Width (km)	6	15	19	7	4	24	12	5	5
Grain Size (mm)	0.20	0.35	0.35	0.35	0.20	0.14	0.35	0.25	0.30
Grid Cells (Active)	17876 (16936)	17948 (17128)	25788 (24842)	25246 (24236)	19482 (18636)	16960 (16108)	29068 (28078)	19714 (18864)	16678 (15878)
Avg. Latitude (degrees)	40.7	46.9	46.2	30.4	27.7	29.5	35.8	40.8	42.8
Run Time	5 days, 5 h	4 days, 12 h	7 days, 20 h	7 days, 12 h	6 days, 15 h	3 days, 20 h	11 days, 12 h	6 days, 10 h	5 days, 6 h

* Mouth of the Columbia River.

The initial bathymetry is uniform within the bay and inlet throat and deepens offshore following an equilibrium beach profile [21]. A single sediment grain size is used in each model domain. Initial depths and grain sizes are characteristic of their associated natural inlet. Bay metrics including ebb shoal volume, inlet length, inlet width, and tidal prism are derived from the inlet morphological database maintained at the Coastal and Hydraulics Laboratory (http://cirp.usace.army.mil). The model includes a constant Coriolis parameter, which is chosen as the average latitude of the corresponding inlet.

2.4. Model Input and Boundary Conditions

Amplitude and phase of tidal constituents are extracted from the National Oceanic and Atmospheric Administration tide database for the nine inlet areas. A total of thirteen tidal constituents are used to reconstruct the tidal time series for each region (Table 2). Tidal characteristics vary widely between study sites in amplitude, phase and dominant constituents. The thirteen constituents represent some of the largest tidal amplitudes for each given inlet area. The water surface elevation time series generated from these constituents does not include the 18.6 year lunar nodal cycle, which produces an average 4% change in mean tidal range and can affect velocities in an inlet throat as the larger tidal range increases tidal prism [22]. The 100-year simulation timeframe exceeds the nodal frequency so the potentially larger tidal prism is regarded as a finite perturbation and is not expected to significantly affect the results. Furthermore, the initial bathymetry is comprised of a flat featureless bottom, which evolves into deep channels separated by shoals, so the net morphological change is very large compared to perturbations potentially induced by nodal tide fluctuations.

Table 2. Tidal Constituents.

		West Coast			Gulf Coast			East Coast		
		Grays Harbor	MCR *	Humboldt	Galveston	East Pass	Johns Pass	Oregon Inlet	Shinnecock	Newburyport
M2	Amp	0.985	0.929	0.700	0.116	0.032	0.246	0.138	0.440	1.169
	Phase	240.7	250.6	215.1	282.1	90.3	123.1	16.2	353.6	115.7
S2	Amp	0.270	0.249	0.175	0.029	0.016	0.096	0.023	0.090	0.165
	Phase	271.3	278.5	236.6	297.5	97.3	141.0	37.1	22.7	153.0
N2	Amp	0.203	0.188	0.148	0.032	0.006	0.046	0.030	0.099	0.239
	Phase	217.9	226.8	190.5	257.7	105.6	120.3	358.5	338.9	85.6
K1	Amp	0.425	0.415	0.401	0.142	0.142	0.158	0.030	0.065	0.130
	Phase	244.0	248.4	233.4	37.3	19.1	12.4	188.7	172.0	211.2
M4	Amp	0.026	0.015	0.012	0.003	0.0	0.009	0.0	0.0	0.010
	Phase	210.0	245.9	200.6	277.0	318.1	76.0	344.8	46.0	133.0
O1	Amp	0.259	0.260	0.249	0.128	0.137	0.151	0.018	0.039	0.104
	Phase	228.4	232.5	217.2	36.9	10.7	3.6	193.3	174.7	194.2
NU2	Amp	0.041	0.032	0.029	0.006	0.001	0.010	0.006	0.019	0.046
	Phase	218.6	230.0	194.5	260.9	103.5	121.6	8.1	340.9	89.6
SSA	Amp	0.000	0.052	0.038	0.086	0.050	0.037	0.026	0.028	0.018
	Phase	0.0	184.1	264.1	55.6	70.1	48.2	10.5	42.9	89.8
SA	Amp	0.126	0.111	0.065	0.066	0.095	0.091	0.046	0.067	0.032
	Phase	289.6	307.2	255.0	155.7	160.1	151.9	158.9	129.1	126.3
Q1	Amp	0.045	0.044	0.044	0.025	0.030	0.032	0.007	0.007	0.020
	Phase	222.4	225.0	211.3	36.7	357.8	348.0	200.4	175.6	185.8
P1	Amp	0.131	0.124	0.126	0.047	0.045	0.053	0.013	0.021	0.043
	Phase	239.9	246.8	231.2	37.3	20.0	12.5	216.6	172.2	209.9
L2	Amp	0.030	0.027	0.016	0.003	0.001	0.007	0.005	0.012	0.033
	Phase	243.1	267.5	225.2	306.5	75.0	143.1	35.6	8.3	145.9
K2	Amp	0.072	0.070	0.047	0.008	0.004	0.027	0.005	0.025	0.045
	Phase	264.3	271.2	228.3	298.7	97.2	134.6	33.5	25.0	156.1

* Mouth of the Columbia River.

Wave data are derived from the Wave Information Studies (WIS) database maintained by the Coastal and Hydraulics Laboratory (CHL), U.S. Army Corps of Engineers [23]. The WIS data are comprised of a network of virtual buoys located along all U.S. coasts, the Great Lakes and other U.S. island territories. The program maintains long-term (~35 years) hindcast model predictions of wave conditions including directional spectra, significant wave height, peak period, average period and direction.

Without 100 years of data to force CMS-Wave, a representative sub-sample is chosen that characterizes the long-term wave climate but does not require wave data from a specific timeframe. Given that the purpose of this study is to investigate the morphological evolution of tidal inlets, it is more important for the model to capture the average sediment transport processes as opposed to the details of long-term, variable wave conditions. As such, the WIS data are used to drive a longshore sediment transport model and the wave conditions that produce the average long-term transport rate are used to drive CMS-Wave.

Longshore sediment transport rate (Q) is predicted using the CERC formula:

$$Q = k \left(\frac{\rho \sqrt{g}}{16 \sqrt{\gamma} \left(\rho_s - \rho\right) \left(1 - p'_m\right)} \right) H_{br}^{2.5} \sin\left(2\theta_{br}\right) \tag{1}$$

where k is a constant (=0.39), γ is the breaker index (=0.78), ρ is fluid density, ρ_s is sediment density, g is acceleration due to gravity, H_{br} is the wave height at breaking, and θ_{br} is the wave angle at breaking [24]. The transport rate is computed using hourly WIS hindcast wave height and direction hindcasts between 1 January, 1980 and 31 December, 2011 (32 years). The average yearly transport rate that is in closest agreement with the transport rate for the full record is used in the CMS-Wave simulations. In this way, the CMS-Wave model can be run by repeating only a single year wave time series, which reduces the input file size yet produces an average longshore transport rate that is consistent with the 32-year record.

Wave roses depicting the average directional wave conditions from the WIS record are depicted in Figure 3. The Pacific Coast inlets (Grays Harbor, Mouth of the Columbia River, and Humboldt) have the highest average wave conditions. The integrated half-plane spectra subdivided into 10 degree bins indicate that the largest waves approach from the west and northwest with maximum heights exceeding 8 m at MCR and Greys Harbor. The Atlantic Coast inlets (Oregon, Shinnecock and Newburyport) show medium wave height conditions and greater directional spreading. Waves are primarily from the southeast at all stations with maximum wave heights around 6 m at Oregon Inlet. The Gulf Coast inlets (Galveston, East Pass and Johns Pass) have the lowest average wave heights. Wave direction varies between sites owing to the difference in shore orientation, limited fetch, and other factors. At Galveston and East Pass, waves are generally from the southeast and south, respectively, with greater spreading at East Pass. Wave direction at Johns Pass is skewed towards the shore parallel direction and average wave height is lower. Many extra-tropical storms are centered well north of the Gulf of Mexico. These "nor'easters" are typically preceded by strong southerly pre-frontal wind, and following the passage of the front, the winds switch to the north-northeast leading to the observed pattern.

Open boundary conditions are prescribed along the three offshore boundaries and closed boundary conditions along the shoreline, inlet and bay. All three of the offshore boundaries are forced by water surface elevation derived from the tidal constituents. The offshore water surface elevation is adjusted to account for wave forcing [13]. The waves are applied on a separate grid with identical spatial coverage as the flow grid. The wave directional spectra characteristics are prescribed at the offshore boundary and generate a wave field across the entire offshore boundary for each time step. The closed boundaries are rigid and do not deform during the simulation. The interior region includes wetting and drying so that shoals can become exposed during low tide. Morphological patterns that develop adjacent to the closed boundaries are influenced by the zero flux condition normal to the boundaries. The degree to which the closed boundaries produce morphological features that are more an artifact of the boundary conditions as opposed to the dynamics of the system are addressed where appropriate.

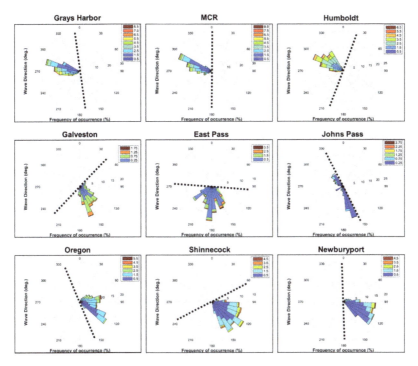

Figure 3. Wave conditions at the nine inlets. Dashed line denotes shoreline orientation and wave height is in meters.

2.5. Model Validation

Long-term wave, current and inlet morphological evolution data are not available, so model calibration is conducted using established empirical formulations that describe the long-term equilibrium and stability characteristics of barrier island tidal inlets. The simulations are designed to predict inlet stability including equilibrium inlet cross-sectional area, so one of the factors used to assess model performance is the tidal prism relationship, originally theorized by O'Brien [25],

$$A = CP^n \tag{2}$$

where A is the inlet cross-sectional area, P is tidal prism, and C and n are the empirically derived constants. The scarcity of field data at that time encouraged later studies that included a greater number of inlets with more accurate tide measurements [26]. The collective results confirm the basic tidal prism relationship with C and n showing some sensitivity to wave energy, bay area, tidal regime, and the presence of jetties [8,26,27]. Empirically derived values for C and n vary between 4.0×10^{-5} to 2.0×10^{-6} and 0.85 to 1.1, respectively.

Inlet stability is determined by the redistribution of sediment by tidal and wave forces. Escoffier [28] theorized that stable inlets form when the maximum flow equals an equilibrium value resulting in a stable cross-sectional area (A) due to sediment transport processes. If the maximum flow in the inlet (U) exceeds the equilibrium value then A increases. If the maximum flow is less than the equilibrium value the inlet will contract and may eventually close. Escoffier [28,29] constructed a theoretical framework to quantify the equilibrium approach using simplified momentum and continuity arguments for single inlet systems. His approach is used to construct maximum velocity curves as a function of A for the idealized inlets and compare the results to the model.

The tidal prism relationship and Escoffier analysis can be used to evaluate inlet equilibrium and stability, but they do not provide metrics to gauge the sediment transport processes and associated morphological evolution. Walton and Adams [20] theorized that the tidal prism is a measure of the water volume flux through the inlet and should correlate with the ebb shoal storage capacity. Using data from 44 U.S. inlets, they developed an empirical relationship for ebb shoal volume with a similar functional form as the tidal prism relationship:

$$V_s = aP^b \tag{3}$$

where V_s is the shoal volume and a and b are the empirically derived constants. Equations (2) and (3) are used to gauge the degree to which model predictions adhere to the equilibrium tidal inlet theory.

3. Results

3.1. Morphology

The final morphology for the nine inlets is depicted in Figure 4. In all cases, the bed features are indicative of barrier island systems including well developed ebb shoal deltas, deepening and channelization of the inlet throat, and development of dendritic channel networks in the bay (for some cases).

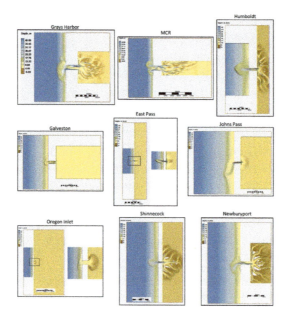

Figure 4. Final bed morphology. The top three inlets are along the West Coast of the United States, the middle three inlets are along the Gulf Coast, and the bottom three inlets are along the Eastern Coast. White areas shown inside the bays denote areas that were considered dry (above the water level) at the end of the simulation. For clarity, color scale and map legend vary between inlets.

The ebb shoal morphological characteristics vary between the different coastal settings. In some cases (Johns Pass and Newburyport), the terminal lobe is skewed and elongated in the alongshore direction. In other cases (Humboldt, East Pass, Shinnecock), the lobe is more symmetrical with respect to the inlet axis, with an ebb shoal channel that terminates at a crescent bar. For these cases, marginal flood channels form on either side of the lobe separating the ebb shoal from the adjacent beaches.

The two largest ebb shoals (Grays Harbor and MCR) have more complex morphology including multiple lobes with varying degrees of width and offshore extent. The lobes are dissected by ebb channels that are in proportion to the width and length of the associated bars. Galveston and Oregon have shoals that extend laterally similar to Grays Harbor but the lobes are less pronounced and the overall scale is smaller.

There are two major inlet types based on inlet width. The three inlets (Grays Harbor, MCR and Galveston) with widths >2000 m show a complex channel structure within the inlet throat. These systems tend to form alternating scour depressions on opposite ends of the inlet separated by a shallower region in the middle. The deepest sections are near the inlet edges as opposed to the centerline. This has the effect of producing a sinuous thalweg that is not only deeper on either end but meanders as it traverses the inlet throat. Inlets with widths <2000 m tend to form more pronounced channels that are nearer to the centerline of the inlet throat. Shallow banks form on the sides of the inlet separated by a deeper mid-section. There is some lateral displacement of the thalweg from the centerline especially at the inlet entrance for cases with relatively strong longshore transport (Johns Pass and Newburyport) as implied by the orientation of the ebb shoal channel.

The bays likewise have developed into two distinct geomorphological types. Bays with strong tidal forcing evolve into a series of incised channels distributed into random patterns of elongated fingers. Initially, the channels form near the landward end of the inlet as the alternating tidal currents erode sediment forming depressions. Once an initial scour depression has formed, the tidal flow concentrates along the depression parallel to the inlet axis. This, in turn, widens and lengthens the depression into a series of dendritic channels that extend deep into the bay. The degree of lateral spreading is more pronounced in bays that are elongated in the shore parallel direction. Overall, the channels resemble tidal creek networks, which are common to barrier island systems with abundant sediment supply. The Gulf Coast inlets and Oregon Inlet on the Atlantic Coast do not show a pronounced channel network system. Tidal forcing at the Gulf Coast inlets is weak so there is less likelihood of channel network development. However, channel network formation in the bay is apparent for East Pass and Johns Pass. At Oregon Inlet, the bay is very large and tidal currents decay rapidly upon entering the bay. The weak currents are insufficient to erode sediment to the point where scour depressions, and ultimately channels, could develop in the 100 year timeframe of this study. Instead, the bay forms a wide shallow depression that spreads radially from the inlet terminating at a crescent flood shoal.

The net sediment volume change in the bay, inlet and ebb shoal is depicted in Figure 5. In all cases except Galveston, ebb shoal volume increases more rapidly at first but then at a reduced rate for the remainder of the simulation. The inlet shows an inverse trend in which the ebb shoal volume increases at a faster rate at the beginning of the simulation and then the rate of growth increases more gradually. The bay volume decreases for all cases except Humboldt Bay and the three Atlantic Coast inlets. The results indicate that all inlets are approaching an equilibrium configuration, at which point the temporal change in sediment volume would vanish. Treating the three locations as a semi-closed sedimentary system, the total increase in ebb shoal volume nearly balances bay and inlet losses for Grays Harbor, MCR, Galveston and East Pass. The mass balance for Johns Pass suggests the ebb shoal accumulation exceeds inlet and bay losses. For the three Atlantic Coast inlets and Humboldt Bay, the ebb shoal and bay show net gains that exceed inlet losses suggesting sediment supply from littoral transport.

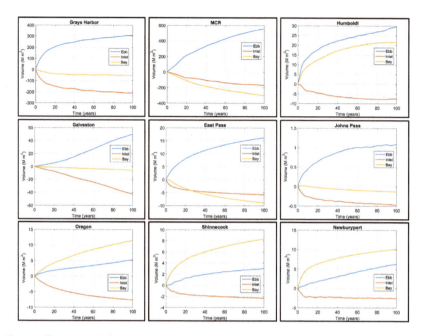

Figure 5. Change in sediment volume during the 100-year simulation. Units are millions of cubic meters.

3.2. Longshore Sediment Transport

Longshore transport is computed by defining ten equally spaced shore-normal transects bracketing the centerline of the inlet axis and integrating the transport vector from the shoreline to two km offshore (Figure 6). Each group of five transects below (negative *y*-axis) and above (positive *y*-axis) the origin is averaged over the full record giving the net longshore transport across the inlet entrance. The locations are expressed in terms of the Cartesian coordinate system as opposed to earth coordinates since the orientation of the real inlets varies between coasts. The convention is that positive values denote transport in the positive *y*-direction. Net longshore transport is negative at all inlets except Humboldt, East Pass and Shinnecock (Figure 7). Transport direction at Humboldt and Shinnecock is convergent, meaning the longshore transport on both sides of the inlet entrance is directed towards the inlet. Transport at East Pass is positive on both sides of the inlet. Transport is greatest for the Pacific Coast, followed by the Atlantic Coast and then the Gulf Coast (except Galveston) in general agreement with the wave conditions for each coastal type. The gross and net longshore sediment transport magnitudes were not quantitatively analyzed in this study, yet they do provide a qualitative assessment of the volume of material that is entering the inlet system in addition to inlet/bay equilibrium adjustments.

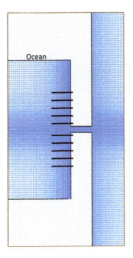

Figure 6. Humboldt model grid illustrating the location of the cross-shore transect placements. Similar transects were defined on all nine model grids to computer long-shore transport values.

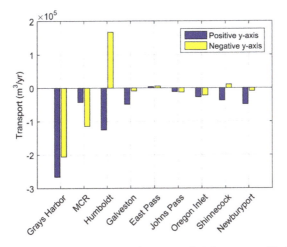

Figure 7. Average longshore sediment transport bracketing the inlet entrance. The legend signifies the location where the transport is computed, i.e., positive-y axis is above or on the upside of the inlet entrance referenced to plan view (Figure 4).

3.3. Hydrodynamics

The maximum flood currents near the end of the 100-year simulation are depicted in Figure 8. Flood currents enter radially and strengthen in the inlet throat with the largest flows in the deeper sections. Maximum flows in the three widest inlets (Grays Harbor, MCR, Galveston) are not uniform along the inlet nor are they oriented along the centerline but occur in the deeper areas. In fact, the strongest currents at Galveston occur along the side of the inlet. Within the bay, currents align with the channels or spread radially for systems without well-defined channel networks. Maximum tidal currents are lowest for the three Gulf Coast inlets as a result of the lower tidal range and associated weaker forcing.

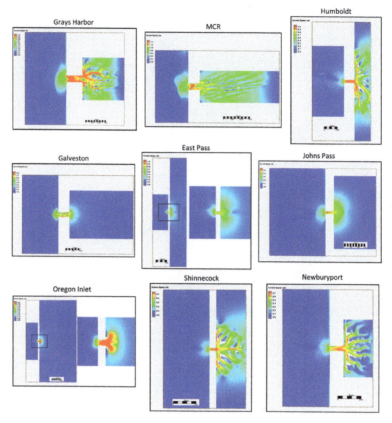

Figure 8. Maximum flood currents near the end of the simulation. For clarity, the color scale varies between inlets. White areas shown inside the bays denote areas that were considered dry (above the water level) at the time chosen for the plot.

The maximum ebb currents near the end of the 100-year simulation are depicted in Figure 9. All inlets show an ebb flow jet that extends offshore. The three widest inlets (Grays Harbor, MCR and Galveston) show more lateral spreading indicating greater dispersion of tidal energy. Currents are highest in the inlet throat and the spatial distribution varies such that higher speeds coincide with the deeper sections. Ebb currents in the bay follow established channels and accelerate upon approach to the inlet. Gulf Coast bays without well-defined channel networks show radial ebb currents.

Time series of depth averaged currents extracted from the inlet throat midway between the ocean and bay are depicted in Figure 10. The figure also includes individual plots depicting the last year of the simulation to elucidate tidal current asymmetry. Except for Galveston, in which the current amplitude increases slightly during the first half of the simulation, the tidal current envelope shows a decrease in amplitude during the simulation. The rate of contraction varies between inlets, but generally is faster near the beginning of the simulation and then more gradual. With the exception of Oregon Inlet and the three Gulf Coast inlets, peak currents are on the order of 1 m/s at 100 years. Maximum ebb currents at Grays Harbor, MCR and the three Gulf Coast inlets are higher than maximum flood currents indicating ebb dominated conditions. All the other inlets have higher flood currents and, therefore, are flood dominated.

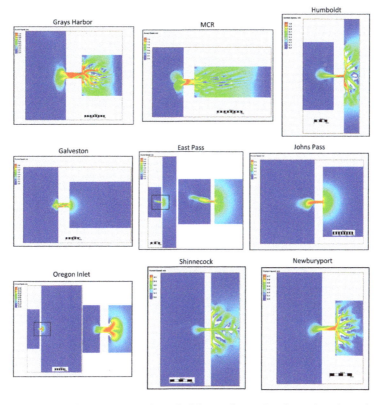

Figure 9. Maximum ebb currents near the end of the simulation. For clarity, the color scale varies between inlets. White areas shown inside the bays denote areas that were considered dry (above the water level) at the time chosen for the plot.

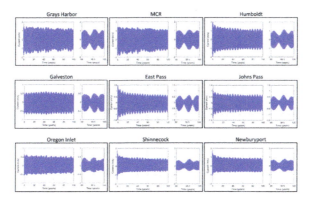

Figure 10. Time series of along-channel currents in the inlet throat.

3.4. Comparison to Empirical Formulas

The tidal prism relationship (Equation (2)) expresses the cross-sectional area as a function of tidal prism and is an intrinsic metric used to characterize the morphology of quasi-stable inlet systems. In practice, the tidal prism is associated with spring tide conditions when the currents have the potential to mobilize the greatest volume of sediment. In order to gauge the numerical simulations in terms of equilibrium inlet theory, the tidal prism is calculated at the end of the simulation along with the associated cross-sectional area. The resulting tidal prism is input into the tidal prism relationship to predict the theoretical cross-sectional area, which is compared to the model prediction. Because several authors have reported different values for the fitting parameters (C, n) that define the tidal prism relationship the results present the maximum and minimum bounds. These are further subdivided between maximum and minimum reported for the three different coasts as referenced above. Shoal volume is compared to the Walton and Adams formula, with the fitting parameters further subdivided based on their classification for the three different coastal areas.

Cross-sectional area as a function of tidal prism for the nine idealized inlets tends to fall within the theoretical range previously reported (Figure 11). The model overpredicts Johns Pass and generally lies closer to either the middle range or the minimum for the other inlets. As sediment transport is associated with the strongest currents the empirical predicted shoal volume is theorized to correlate with the spring tides at equilibrium. The model tends to underpredict shoal volume compared to the Walton and Adams empirical relationship (Figure 12).

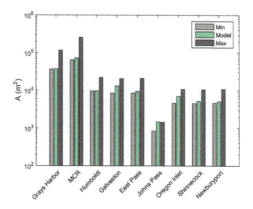

Figure 11. Model predicted cross-sectional area at the end of the simulation. Minimum and maximum denote the empirical tidal prism relationship [8].

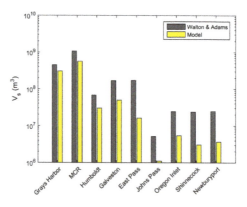

Figure 12. Shoal volume at the end of the simulation derived from the model and the empirical formula of Walton and Adams.

The Escoffier analysis provides criteria to gauge inlet stability. The solid curves (Figure 13) denote the theoretically predicted maximum tidal current as a function of cross-sectional area. The input parameters (e.g., bay area, inlet dimensions, water surface elevation) are derived from the model. Points that lie to the right of the peak denote stable inlet conditions. The minimal cross sectional area for the real inlet counterparts are also noted for comparison. The model results are based on the minimal inlet cross-sectional area and maximum flow speed over a tidal cycle. The record is low-pass filtered using a 30-day window to delineate the overall trend. The model results reveal inlet area growth and a net reduction in the maximum current that trends with the theoretical predictions. As the simulation progresses the change in cross-sectional area and associated maximum flow speed diminishes, leading to the grouping of data points for the larger cross-sections.

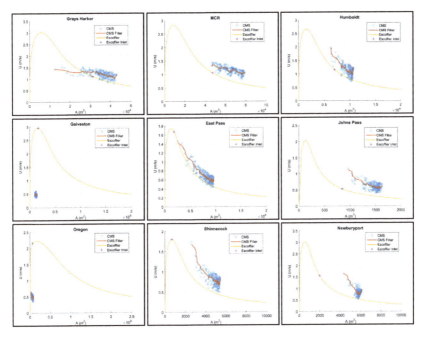

Figure 13. Escoffier curve for the idealized inlets. CMS denotes model estimates and plus symbols denote the cross-sectional area of the real inlets. Open circles are the model predicted maximum flow versus inlet cross-sectional area.

4. Discussion

4.1. Morphology

In all cases morphological evolution of an initial featureless system includes channel formation in the inlet, and ebb shoal formation offshore of the entrance. Well defined channel networks form in bays with stronger tidal flows, in particular the Pacific and two Atlantic Coast cases. In systems with weaker tidal flows, the bays do not develop channel networks but rather form flood deltas and truncated depressions adjacent to the inlet. Longshore transport, in some cases, shifts the terminal lobe and ebb channel in the direction of net transport.

4.1.1. Inlet Morphology

Morphological evolution in the inlet consists of two primary types. The first type is characterized by rapid channel growth in the first 20 to 40 years followed by slower deepening for the remainder of the simulation and in some cases migration of the thalweg from the centerline. Shoal formation along the sides of the inlet near the entrance and exit results from flow separation around the 90°

corners as the tidal current converges. This inlet type is associated with smaller bays and smaller inlet cross-sections. The narrower width constricts the flow allowing the inlet to develop a single deeper channel.

The second type includes multiple channel formation in the inlet with widely varying morphological patterns. This inlet type consists of deeper channels forming on the sides of the inlet near the entrance and exit separated by a shallower section in the middle. The deepest sections occur off center of the inlet axis, such that the thalweg crosses from one side of the inlet near the entrance to the other side near the bay. The channel is wider and shallower in the middle section. This inlet type is associated with inlets wider than 2000 m and larger bays (MCR, Grays Harbor and Galveston). The pattern is indicative of an immature channel network typical of tidal flats and low lying coastal wetlands such as salt marshes [30]. Variations in depth along the thalweg also occur in unmanaged natural inlets and some of this variability is linked to sediment transport processes [31].

The wider inlet permits the development of instabilities in the flow field and sediment transport conditions that lead to bifurcated networks. Confinement due to the finite inlet width prohibits channel network lateral expansion. Instead, the channel forms incised sections along the sides to compensate for the restrictive lateral boundary. Overall, the wider inlets exhibit morphological patterns similar to coastal wetlands, which are defined by random channel networks similar to terrestrial watersheds [32].

4.1.2. Bay Morphology

Bay morphology includes dendritic channel network formation for systems with strong tidal flow. Bay channels form in random bifurcated networks that decrease in depth and width as a function of distance from the inlet. For systems in which the shore parallel bay length is greater than the shore normal length, channels tend to align with the bay upon exiting the inlet and then branch into smaller and shallower secondary channels that extend in the cross-shore direction. The channels are separated by shoals that in some instances are exposed during low tide indicating that the model is producing bars. The pattern is very typical of coastal plain salt marshes and other tidal flat areas with an abundant sediment supply [30].

Systems characterized by weak tidal flow do not form channel networks and the majority of channel deepening is confined near the inlet. In these cases the bay may accumulate sediment over the course of the simulation resulting in sedimentation, e.g., flood shoal development in the form of a crescent bar in the case of Johns Pass. The absence of channel network development is tied to the weak forcing, which is further reduced through the inlet and in the expansion zone as the flow enters the bay. Channels formed in the inlet end abruptly at the edge of the bay signifying the reduction in current speed and associated weak sediment mobilization capacity.

For real systems, weak tidal flows may prohibit expansive tidal flat formation or at least confine it to the back side of the barrier island near the inlet where the scouring capacity of tidal currents to produce and grow channels is greatest. Creek network expansion would be slow for a stable inlet system, but could be more active in systems with inlet migration [33].

Inlets showing ebb dominance include the three Gulf Coast inlets, MCR and Grays Harbor. Bay sediment volume decreases throughout the simulation indicating net erosion and export of sediment. Ebb dominance is associated with generally lower tidal range [34] as is the case for the three Gulf Coast inlets. Grays Harbor and MCR have relatively large tidal ranges but their actual inlet counterparts are located on an active continental margin and are not classified as barrier island systems, but rather as river mouth estuaries [35]. Therefore, the bay dimensions are less controlled by local sediment redistribution and more by the underlying geology. Long-term deepening of the bay changes the hypsometry and can increase exchange via flow routing through deeper channels. This, in turn, can increase the capacity of the bay and associated tidal prism [36]. Channel deepening without similar sediment loss on the tidal flats reduces the tidal phase speed difference between flood and ebb and can favor ebb dominance [30].

4.1.3. Ebb Shoal Morphology

Ebb shoals develop into different patterns as a function of tide and wave forcing. For Humboldt, East Pass and Shinnecock the channel is fairly symmetric with respect to the inlet axis and extends offshore forming a crescent bar. The ebb shoal is bisected by the ebb channel, which helps transport sediment further offshore, thereby extending the shoal. The shoal is detached from the adjacent beach by near-symmetric, yet much narrower, marginal flood channels. These attributes are associated with tide-dominated inlets, which can form large crescent shoals and associated marginal flood channels [37]. The longshore sediment transport at Humboldt and Shinnecock is convergent delivering sediment to the inlet from both the updrift and downdrift littoral zones. This aids in maintaining the quasi-symmetric bar by supplying sediment that can be reworked by cross-shore tidal forcing at the inlet entrance. Transport at East Pass is positive and non-convergent at the inlet. However, the longshore transport is weakest of all inlets and the slight rotation of the crescent bar is in agreement with the positive longshore transport.

For cases with significant longshore transport, the channel forms an acute angle to the shoreline rotated in the down-drift direction and the shoal consists of a series of elongated bars. Up- and down-drift bars attached to the shoreline are separated by bypassing bars that form the outer cusp of the ebb shoal. This is most pronounced for Johns Pass and Newburyport, which show clear up- and down-drift bars bracketing the ebb channel. In both cases, the longshore transport is negative in agreement with the angle of the bars and ebb channel. Down-drift rotation of the ebb channel and a mature bar complex are associated with wave-dominant or mixed-energy inlets [37], such as the Gulf Coast and central New England [38], respectively.

Grays Harbor and MCR, which have the strongest tidal forcing, develop large ebb delta complexes with multiple lobes each dissected by respective ebb shoal channels. These ebb shoals form under the action of strong tidal forcing that redistributes sediment offshore and laterally to produce the broad bifurcated ebb delta pattern. The larger inlet width produces a wider exiting jet that can develop instabilities producing lateral shear patterns that favor multiple flow pathways [9]. In turn, sediment transport varies laterally across the inlet to effect the development of multi-lobe deltas as characterized by Grays Harbor and MCR. Longshore transport is negative at both inlets, but varies in terms of longshore convergence, i.e., Grays Harbor receives more sediment from the updrift side compared to losses at the downdrift side while MCR is the opposite. The largest lobe at Grays Harbor is slightly skewed downdrift while the opposite is true for MCR. Galveston and Oregon show similar longshore transport patterns as Grays Harbor but reduced in magnitude, and also possess similarly skewed downdrift ebb shoals.

Similar patterns as seen at MCR in which the orientation of the ebb shoal is opposite to the longshore drift has been attributed to the interaction of nearshore tidal currents and inlet tidal currents [39]. However in the present case, the increased transport downdrift of the inlet leads to greater erosion of MCR's ebb shoal. As the net longshore sediment transport delivers sediment to the shoal from the updrift side, the greater loss on the downdrift side produces asymmetric erosion and the associated skewed delta morphology.

4.1.4. Sediment Budget

In all cases, the ebb shoal and the inlet initially increase and decrease in volume, respectively. The bay either increases or decreases due to hydrodynamic conditions and the dominant sediment transport. In cases with flood dominance, the bay accumulates sediment forming flood shoals with varying degrees of channel development. In some cases, ebb shoal accumulation approximately balances inlet and bay losses suggesting that sediment is redistributed locally and longshore transport primarily bypasses the system [40]. For the cases in which the bay accumulates sediment (Humboldt Bay, Oregon, Newburyport, and Shinnecock), bay and ebb shoal gains far exceed inlet losses implying that the majority of sediment supply is derived from coastal transport. For the case of Humboldt Bay and Shinnecock sediment transport converges at the inlet, which can be redistributed by tidal currents to supply the bay. For Oregon and Newburyport, the transport is directed in the negative *y*-direction but the net transport at the inlet throat is convergent (i.e., larger flux on the updrift side and smaller flux on the downdrift side). The net flux towards the inlet can likewise be carried by the tidal currents to the bay.

These systems are initially sediment starved and rely on an abundant sediment supply derived from the littoral zone to establish long-term equilibrium. The majority of the longshore transport is primarily due to waves as the tidal currents decay rapidly away from the inlet entrance. As waves deliver sediment to the inlet via longshore transport, the tidal currents then redistribute it to the ebb shoal and bay. Without the wave contribution, the ebb shoal and bay would remain sediment starved and would likely not approach equilibrium as suggested by the asymptotic relaxation of the sediment volume curves near the end of the simulation. Insufficient sediment supply can have a destabilizing effect such that the inlet, bay, and ebb shoal are unable to obey established stability theory [36].

4.2. Inlet Stability

The dominant flow is driven by tides and includes semi-diurnal, diurnal, and fortnightly components as representative of tidal conditions at the nine inlets. Tidal currents at the beginning of the simulations are generally largest and then decay as the inlet cross-section expands. Usually after about 20 years, the tidal current envelope becomes more uniform with the exception of spring/neap and seasonal variations. As such, the currents that occur during spring tide, which are responsible for the greatest sediment transport, become fairly uniform through the remainder of the simulation. Near the end of the simulation, spring tidal current speeds for the Pacific and Atlantic Coast inlets are ~1 m/s and lower for the Gulf Coast inlets (~0.5 m/s).

Escoffier [29] theorized that the equilibrium cross-sectional area occurs at the point where the Escoffier curve intersects an equilibrium velocity, which he assumed is constant. Without direct measurements he and others [41] speculated this to be about 1 m/s, based on the depth averaged flow required to mobilize newly deposited sediment but unable to erode the channel bed further. With the exception of Oregon and Galveston inlets, the modeled currents at the beginning of the simulation are >1 m/s and asymptotically approach, or at a minimum follow the curvature of, the Escoffier solution (Figure 13). The initial velocity for Oregon and Galveston is <1 m/s and fall well below the theoretical curve.

These are the two largest bays and according to the Escoffier theory should have equilibrium velocities that are greater than those calculated. The predicted cross-sectional area lies to the left of the peak in the Escoffier curve signifying unstable conditions. If the velocity predicted by the model near the end of the simulation (about 0.5 m/s for Galveston and Oregon) is projected to intersect with the Escoffier solution, then the equilibrium cross-sectional areas would be 2.0×10^5 m^2 for Galveston and 2.5×10^5 m^2 for Oregon. This is more than ten times the cross-sectional area produced by the model. For the same tidal forcing, a much larger cross-sectional area will produce smaller velocities to preserve continuity. Weaker flows will reduce sediment transport capacity and be unable to maintain a large inlet cross-section. The relatively weak initial forcing is sufficient to deepen the channel but insufficient to establish equilibrium within the simulated 100 years.

One of the underlying assumptions in Escoffier's theory is that the water surface elevation in the bay remains horizontal such that the bay oscillates uniformly [29]. The phase lag between the entrance and furthest reaches of long shallow bays combined with friction can lead to nonlinearities that modulate volume flux and water surface elevations through the system [42,43]. In these cases, the dynamics are inherently more complex and the basic Escoffier theory is less applicable because co-oscillations and other factors distort the phase lag between ocean and bay. While all inlets show some degree of variable surface elevation, the assumptions imposed by Escoffier are strained the most for Oregon and Galveston. Using the phase speed for shallow-water waves, $C_T = \sqrt{gh}$, where g is the acceleration due to gravity and h is the average depth in the bay, it takes 4 (Oregon) and 2 (Galveston) hours for the tide to propagate to the furthest reaches of the bay. With the exception of East Pass, this is greater than the other inlets by a factor of two illustrating the larger phase lag, and associated water surface elevation difference, between the furthest reaches of the bay and the inlet. However, East Pass's bay area is three times smaller than Galveston and nine times smaller than Oregon so bay filling is faster through continuity. Straining the limits of the Escoffier assumptions is likely a contributing factor to the lack of agreement between model predictions and the Escoffier theory for these larger shallow bays.

4.3. Long-Term Model Predictions

The results are compared to the tidal prism relationship and the empirical formulas for ebb shoal volume. All of the inlets fall within the empirical range of the tidal prism relationship from previous studies with the exception of Johns Pass, which overpredicts the cross-sectional area. Galveston and Oregon are near the middle of the empirically derived range and the others are closer to the lower limit. However, all of the inlets are still deepening after 100 years so the cross-sectional areas would increase somewhat before reaching equilibrium.

The model tends to under-predict the ebb shoal volume compared to the Walton and Adams [21] empirical formula. In most cases, the ebb shoal volume is still growing at the end of the simulation so the comparison would likely improve if the simulations are run longer. It is possible that the shoal is underpredicted because the modeled offshore slope is steeper in the vicinity of the inlet. In this case, shoal growth may be incomplete as the strong ebb jet seen at some inlets has the capacity to transport sediment further from shore into deeper regions [44], where it cannot be recovered by tide and wave-riven transport to supply the ebb shoal. Walton and Adams [20] noted smaller ebb shoals with increasing wave energy. The increased wave power prohibits the maintenance of shoals that otherwise would be in equilibrium with the tidal forcing [39]. The waves used in the study show high angles to the shoreline for most cases. The high angle may increase erosion leading to smaller ebb shoals than would be expected based on empirical models that are formulated using only the tidal prism. Because of the power law dependence on tidal prism to predict ebb shoal volume, the empirical solutions are very sensitive to changes in the exponent. As such, small changes in the fitting parameters can result in large differences in predicted shoal volume. More field data could help refine the exponent and coefficient values for specific coastal regions and improve shoal volume predictions.

The maximum inlet velocity decays over time in agreement with the Escoffier solution in which $U \sim 1/A$ for stable inlets [45]. The modeled maximum velocity is less than predicted by the Escoffier formula signifying that the modeled inlets are within the equilibrium regime and that further simulation will reduce the maximum current to the threshold for the initiation of sediment motion and prohibit further cross-sectional area growth. Oregon and Galveston are notable exceptions and potential reasons for the lack of agreement with the theory are discussed above. In most cases, the predicted cross-sectional area is greater than the corresponding inlet; however, given that the inlets are idealized direct comparisons serve only as a guide to gauge overall model performance and deviations are conceivable. Even so, there are a few specific explanations why idealized inlet modeling studies may overpredict channel deepening. Previous work has shown that a single grain size class can lead to over-deepening due to misrepresentation of bed composition by excluding larger particles that require greater bed stress for mobilization [3]. MCR showed the greatest erosion rate and sensitivity studies to grain size were conducted including increasing the grain size from 0.35 to 0.80 mm. The erosion rate was slower initially but the final depth did not change. Natural tidal inlets consist of varying degrees of cross-bedding and mixed sediments that contribute to armoring, which are not captured in the model leading to greater erosion of the simulated channel [46]. In addition, the idealized inlets have fixed boundaries and constrict the flow so that the tendency is to generate faster currents that deepen the inlet as opposed to wider inlets with slower currents.

J. Mar. Sci. Eng. **2016**, *4*, 65

5. Conclusions

This study focused on the long-term morphological evolution of idealized barrier island tidal inlets. The study was motivated by the need to develop tools that could be used to investigate long-term change in support of engineering projects focused on environmental and other issues affected by sea level rise. The numerical modeling system (CMS) included coupled wave-flow-sediment transport models that were applied to nine idealized inlet/bay systems typical of the U.S. Pacific, Gulf and Atlantic coasts. Starting with a featureless surface, the model generated the major morphological characteristics typical of barrier island inlets for simulations spanning 100 years. In all cases morphological evolution included channel formation in the inlet, and ebb shoal formation offshore of the entrance.

Well defined channel networks similar to salt marshes and other tidal flat areas formed in bays with stronger tidal flows. In systems with weaker tidal flows, the bays did not develop channel networks but rather formed flood deltas and truncated depressions adjacent to the inlet. In the inlet throat, channel formation and morphology were linked to inlet width. Inlets with widths <2000 m tended to form more pronounced channels that were nearer to the centerline. Inlets with widths >2000 m were more complex and formed depressions and scour holes similar to immature channel networks associated with salt marshes or deltas. Ebb delta formation included large multi-lobe shoals for the larger inlets with strong tidal forcing and crescent bars bracketing well-defined ebb channels for smaller inlets with weaker tidal forcing. Longshore transport contributed to ebb shoal asymmetry by shifting the main lobe in the direction of net transport. The degree of ebb shoal asymmetry was controlled by the relative longshore transport both in magnitude and convergence near the inlet.

Modeled inlet cross-sectional area was in general agreement with the tidal prism relationship. Shoal volume did not show as good agreement and was underpredicted. Other factors such as incident wave angle, local beach slope, fixed lateral boundaries, and sensitivity to the fitting parameters for the empirical shoal volume formula were not as well constrained and may contribute to the bias towards smaller shoals predicted by the model.

Acknowledgments: This work was funded by the Coastal Inlets Research Program and the Center for Directed Research, U.S. Army Engineer Research and Development Center.

Author Contributions: T.M.B., A.S. and R.S. conceived and designed the project; M.E.B., A.S., K.E.B. and H.L. setup and performed the model runs; R.S., M.E.B., A.S. and H.L. analyzed the data; R.S., M.E.B. and H.L. wrote the paper.

Conflicts of Interest: The authors declare no conflict of interest. The founding sponsors had no role in the design of the study; in the collection, analyses, or interpretation of data; in the writing of the manuscript, and in the decision to publish the results.

References

1. Komar, P.D. Tidal-inlet processes and morphology related to the transport of sediments. *J. Coast. Res.* **1996**, *23*, 23–45.
2. Hayes, M.O. General morphology and sediment patterns in tidal inlets. *Sediment. Geol.* **1980**, *26*, 139–156. [CrossRef]
3. Cayocca, F. Long-term morphological modeling of a tidal inlet: The Arcachon Basin, France. *Coast. Eng.* **2001**, *42*, 115–142. [CrossRef]
4. Dissanayake, D.; Roelvink, J.; Van der Wegen, M. Modelled channel patterns in a schematized tidal inlet. *Coast. Eng.* **2009**, *56*, 1069–1083. [CrossRef]
5. Yu, Q.; Wang, Y.; Flemming, B.; Gao, S. Scale-dependent characteristics of equilibrium morphology of tidal basins along the dutch-german north sea coast. *Mar. Geol.* **2014**, *348*, 63–72. [CrossRef]
6. Van der Wegen, M.; Roelvink, J.A. Long-term morphodynamic evolution of a tidal embayment using a two-dimensional, process-based model. *J. Geophys. Res. Oceans* **2008**, *113*. [CrossRef]
7. Nahon, A.; Bertin, X.; Fortunato, A.B.; Oliveira, A. Process-based 2dh morphodynamic modeling of tidal inlets: A comparison with empirical classifications and theories. *Mar. Geol.* **2012**, *291*, 1–11. [CrossRef]

8. Jarrett, J.T. *Tidal Prism-Inlet Area Relationships*; U.S. Army Engineer Waterways Experiment Station: Vicksburg, MS, USA, 1976.
9. Van Leeuwen, S.; Van der Vegt, M.; De Swart, H. Morphodynamics of ebb-tidal deltas: A model approach. *Estuar. Coast. Shelf Sci.* **2003**, *57*, 899–907. [CrossRef]
10. Van der Vegt, M.; Schuttelaars, H.; De Swart, H. Modeling the equilibrium of tide-dominated ebb-tidal deltas. *J. Geophys. Res. Earth Surf.* **2006**. [CrossRef]
11. Sanchez, A.; Wu, W.; Beck, T.; Li, H.; Rosati, J., III; Thomas, R.; Rosati, J.; Demirbilek, Z.; Brown, M.; Reed, C. *Verification and Validation of The Coastal Modeling System, Report 3: Hydrodynamics*; Coastal and Hydraulics Laboratory Technical Report ERDC-CHL-TR-11-10; U.S. Army Engineer Research and Development Center: Vicksburg, MS, USA, 2011.
12. Reed, C.W.; Brown, M.E.; Sánchez, A.; Wu, W.; Buttolph, A.M. The Coastal Modeling System flow model (CMS-Flow): Past and present. *J. Coast. Res.* **2011**. [CrossRef]
13. Sánchez, A.; Wu, W. A non-equilibrium sediment transport model for coastal inlets and navigation channels. *J. Coast. Res.* **2011**. [CrossRef]
14. Sánchez, A.; Wu, W.; Li, H.; Brown, M.; Reed, C.; Rosati, J.D.; Demirbilek, Z. *Coastal Modeling System: Mathematical Formulations and Numerical Methods*; U.S. Army Engineer Research and Development Center, Coastal and Hydraulics Laboratory: Vicksburg, MS, USA, 2014.
15. Lin, L.; Demirbilek, Z.; Mase, H.; Zheng, J.; Yamada, F. *Cms-Wave: A Nearshore Spectral Wave Processes Model For Coastal Inlets and Navigation Projects*; U.S. Army Engineer Research and Development Center: Vicksburg, MS, USA, 2008.
16. Lin, L.; Demirbilek, Z.; Mase, H. Recent capabilities of CMS-Wave: A coastal wave model for inlets and navigation projects. *J. Coast. Res.* **2011**. [CrossRef]
17. Lin, L.; Demirbilek, Z.; Thomas, R.; Rosati, J., III. *Verification and Validation of the Coastal Modeling System, Report 2: CMS-Wave*; U.S. Army Engineer Research and Development Center: Vicksburg, MS, USA, 2011.
18. Sanchez, A.; Wu, W.; Beck, T.; Li, H.; Rosati, J.; Demirbilek, Z.; Brown, M. *Verification and Validation of the Coastal Modeling System, Report 4, CMS-Flow: Sediment Transport and Morphology Change*; CHL-TR-11-10; U.S. Army Engineer Research and Development Center: Vicksburg, MS, USA, 2011.
19. Lesser, G.; Roelvink, J.; Van Kester, J.; Stelling, G. Development and validation of a three-dimensional morphological model. *Coast. Eng.* **2004**, *51*, 883–915. [CrossRef]
20. Walton, T.L.; Adams, W.D. Capacity of inlet outer bars to store sand. *Coast. Eng. Proc.* **1976**, *1*, 1919–1937.
21. Robert, G.D. Equilibrium beach profiles: Characteristics and applications. *J. Coast. Res.* **1991**, *7*, 53–84.
22. Wang, Z.; Townend, I. Influence of the nodal tide on the morphological response of estuaries. *Mar. Geol.* **2012**, *291*, 73–82. [CrossRef]
23. Hubertz, J. *The Wave Information Studies Wave Model, Version 2.0 (User's Guide)*; Coastal Engineering Research Center: Vicksburg, MS, USA, 1992.
24. Rosati, J.D.; Walton, T.L.; Bodge, K. Longshore sediment transport. *Coast. Eng. Man. III* **2002**, *2*, 113.
25. O'Brien, M.P. Estuary tidal prism related to entrance areas. *Civ. Eng.* **1939**, *1*, 738–739.
26. Kraus, N.C. Inlet cross-sectional area calculated by process-based model. *Coast. Eng. Proc.* **1998**, *1*, 3265–3278.
27. O'Brien, M.P. Equilibrium flow areas of inlets on sandy coasts. *J. Waterw. Harb. Div.* **1969**, *95*, 43–52.
28. Escoffier, F.F. The stability of tidal inlets. *Shore Beach* **1940**, *8*, 114–115.
29. Escoffier, F.F. *Hydraulics and Stability of Tidal Inlets*; U.S. Army Coastal Engineering Research Center: Vicksburg, MS, USA, 1977; p. 72.
30. Fagherazzi, S.; Furbish, D.J. On the shape and widening of salt marsh creeks. *J. Geophys. Res. Oceans* **2001**, *106*, 991–1003. [CrossRef]
31. Wargo, C.A.; Styles, R. Along channel flow and sediment dynamics at north inlet, south carolina. *Estuar. Coast. Shelf Sci.* **2007**, *71*, 669–682. [CrossRef]
32. Novakowski, K.I.; Torres, R.; Gardner, L.R.; Voulgaris, G. Geomorphic analysis of tidal creek networks. *Water Resour. Res.* **2004**, *40*. [CrossRef]
33. Roman, C.T.; Peck, J.A.; Allen, J.R.; King, J.W.; Appleby, P.G. Accretion of a new england (USA) salt marsh in response to inlet migration, storms, and sea-level rise. *Estuar. Coast. Shelf Sci.* **1997**, *45*, 717–727. [CrossRef]
34. Friedrichs, C.T.; Perry, J.E. Tidal salt marsh morphodynamics: A synthesis. *J. Coast. Res.* **2001**, *SI27*, 7–37.
35. Hume, T.M.; Herdendorf, C.E. On the use of empirical stability relationships for characterising estuaries. *J. Coast. Res.* **1993**, *9*, 413–422.

36. FitzGerald, D.M. Geomorphic variability and morphologic and sedimentologic controls on tidal inlets. *J. Coast. Res.* **1996**, *SI23*, 47–71.

37. Kraus, N.C. *Engineering of Tidal Inlets and Morphologic Consequences*; U.S. Army Engineer Research and Development Center: Vicksburg, MS, USA, 2008.

38. FitzGerald, D.; Buynevich, I.; Davis, R.; Fenster, M. New england tidal inlets with special reference to riverine-associated inlet systems. *Geomorphology* **2002**, *48*, 179–208. [CrossRef]

39. Sha, L.; Van den Berg, J. Variation in ebb-tidal delta geometry along the coast of the netherlands and the german bight. *J. Coast. Res.* **1993**, *9*, 730–746.

40. Kraus, N.C. Reservoir model of ebb-tidal shoal evolution and sand bypassing. *J. Waterw. Port Coast. Ocean Eng.* **2000**, *126*, 305–313. [CrossRef]

41. Seabergh, W.C.; Kraus, N.C. *PC Program for Coastal Inlet Stability Analysis*; US Army Engineer Waterways Experiment Station: Vicksburg, MS, USA, 1997; p. 7.

42. Speer, P.; Aubrey, D. A study of non-linear tidal propagation in shallow inlet/estuarine systems part II: Theory. *Estuar. Coast. Shelf Sci.* **1985**, *21*, 207–224. [CrossRef]

43. Lanzoni, S.; Seminara, G. Long-term evolution and morphodynamic equilibrium of tidal channels. *J. Geophys. Res. Oceans* **2002**, *107*. [CrossRef]

44. Özsoy, E. Ebb-tidal jets: A model of suspended sediment and mass transport at tidal inlets. *Estuar. Coast. Shelf Sci.* **1986**, *22*, 45–62. [CrossRef]

45. De Swart, H.; Zimmerman, J. Morphodynamics of tidal inlet systems. *Annu. Rev. Fluid Mech.* **2009**, *41*, 203–229. [CrossRef]

46. Dastgheib, A.; Roelvink, J.; Wang, Z. Long-term process-based morphological modeling of the marsdiep tidal basin. *Mar. Geol.* **2008**, *256*, 90–100. [CrossRef]

Journal of
Marine Science and Engineering

Article

Assessment of Damage and Adaptation Strategies for Structures and Infrastructure from Storm Surge and Sea Level Rise for a Coastal Community in Rhode Island, United States

Christopher Small [1], Tyler Blanpied [1], Alicia Kauffman [1], Conor O'Neil [1], Nicholas Proulx [1], Mathew Rajacich [1], Hailey Simpson [1], Jeffrey White [1], Malcolm L. Spaulding [1], Christopher D.P. Baxter [2,*] and J. Craig Swanson [3]

[1] Department of Ocean Engineering, University of Rhode Island, Narragansett, RI 02882, USA; csmall42@my.uri.edu (C.S.); tyblanpied@my.uri.edu (T.B.); a.kauffman86@gmail.com (A.K.); oneil216@my.uri.edu (C.O.); nicholas_proulx@my.uri.edu (N.P.); mrajacich@my.uri.edu (M.R.); hsimpson94@my.uri.edu (H.S.); jeffrey_white@my.uri.edu (J.W.); spaulding@egr.uri.edu (M.L.S.)
[2] Departments of Ocean/Civil and Environmental Engineering, University of Rhode Island, Narragansett, RI 02882, USA
[3] Swanson Environmental Associates LLC, Saunderstown, RI 02874, USA; Craig.Swanson@swansonenvironmental.com
* Correspondence: cbaxter@uri.edu; Tel.: +1-401-874-6575

Academic Editor: Richard Signell
Received: 11 August 2016; Accepted: 14 October 2016; Published: 20 October 2016

Abstract: This paper presents an evaluation of inundation, erosion, and wave damage for a coastal community in Rhode Island, USA. A methodology called the Coastal Environmental Risk Index (CERI) was used that incorporates levels of inundation including sea level rise, wave heights using STWAVE, and detailed information about individual structures from an E911 database. This information was input into damage functions developed by the U.S. Army Corps of Engineers following Hurricane Sandy. Damage from erosion was evaluated separately from local published erosion rates. Using CERI, two different adaptation strategies were evaluated that included a combination of dune restoration, protective berms, and a tide gate. A total of 151 out of 708 structures were estimated to be protected from inundation and wave action by the combined measures. More importantly, the use of CERI allowed for the assessment of the impact of different adaptation strategies on both individual structures and an entire community in a Geographical Information Systems (GIS) environment. This tool shows promise for use by coastal managers to assess damage and mitigate risk to coastal communities.

Keywords: inundation damage; wave damage; sea level rise; damage functions; coastal resilience

1. Introduction

Matunuck, Rhode Island is a coastal community in the northeast United States that is vulnerable to the effects of storm surge, sea level rise, and erosion. As such, it is representative of many small communities that are facing these challenges without the resources of large urban cities. The Matunuck Beach community (Figure 1) has only one evacuation route, which is a coastal road that runs parallel to the shore and is highly susceptible to flooding. Erosion rates in this area are among the highest in Rhode Island [1], ranging from 0.8 to 3.5 ft/year (Figure 2). Figure 3 shows photographs of a local restaurant in the study area taken in the 1950s and 2012, clearly showing the loss of shoreline [2]. The evacuation route for the community can be seen in Figures 1 and 2 directly behind the restaurant.

Sea level is also increasing at this site, and estimates of sea level rise by 2100 range from 0.5 ft assuming a linear increase from historical records to almost 7 ft using the National Oceanic and Atmospheric Administration's (NOAA) most conservative projections (Figure 4) [3]. The Rhode Island Coastal Resources Management Council (RI CRMC), which is the state agency responsible for preservation, protection, and development of the coast, has adopted NOAA's most conservative projections of sea level rise (1 ft by 2025, 2 ft by 2050, and 7 ft by 2100) in their regulatory guidelines.

Given these challenges facing the Matunuck Beach community, the objectives of this study were the following:

- Estimate the inundation, wave attack, and erosion damage to the existing structures and infrastructure caused by a 100-year storm event, with and without 7 ft of sea level rise, and estimate the total damage;
- Identify adaptation strategies to reduce the damage from inundation, wave attack, and erosion; and
- Determine the impact associated with each adaptation strategy.

Figure 1. Site map of the coastal community of Matunuck, Rhode Island that was chosen for this study.

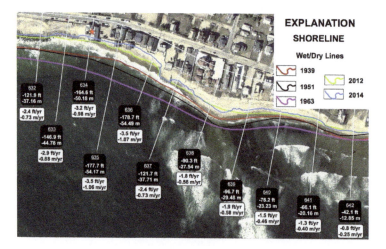

Figure 2. Shoreline change rates for the study area [1].

This was accomplished using a Geographical Information Systems (GIS) tool called the Coastal Environmental Risk Index (CERI) [4]. CERI is designed as an objective, quantitative tool to assess the risk that structures and infrastructure face from storm surges, including flooding and the associated wave environment, in the presence of sea level rise (SLR), and shoreline erosion/accretion. Additional details on CERI are provided in [4] including information on other assessment and index tools designed for this purpose. CERI can readily be extended to include hydrological flooding (e.g., rivers and streams). This feature was not, however, implemented in the present analysis since there are no substantial hydrological sources of flooding in the study area.

Figure 3. Photographs of a local restaurant in the study area from: (**a**) the 1950s; and (**b**) 2012, showing the loss of shoreline due to erosion [2].

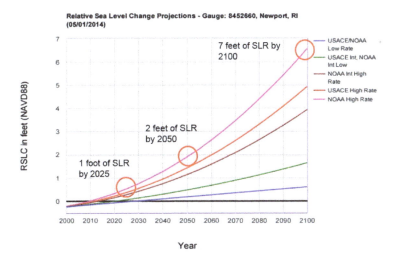

Figure 4. Sea level change projections for the southern coast of Rhode Island [3]. USACE, US Army Corps of Engineers; NOAA, National Oceanic and Atmospheric Administration.

2. Methods

Figure 5 shows a flow chart of the organization of CERI. Inputs into CERI include detailed information about the structures within the study area, topography and bathymetry, and levels of inundation, wave heights, and erosion for different storm events. The level of damage for each structure was estimated using damage functions developed by the U.S. Army Corps of Engineers as part of the North Atlantic Coast Comprehensive Study (NACCS) [5]. The results were presented in terms of probability and cumulative distribution functions and graphically in a GIS. Based on these estimates of damage, different adaptation strategies were evaluated based on the reduction in damage to structures for different storm events with and without sea level rise.

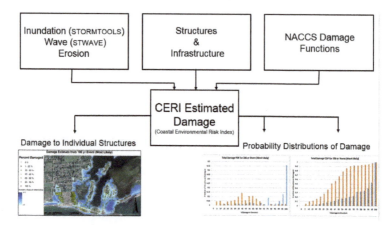

Figure 5. Flow chart showing the methodology used to estimate damage from storm surge and sea level rise in this study (See [3]). CERI, Coastal Environmental Risk Index; NACCS, North Atlantic Coast Comprehensive Study.

A Digital Elevation Model (DEM) of the study area was obtained from a combination of NOAA bathymetry and a 2011 Light Detection And Ranging (LIDAR) topographic survey [6]. All elevations are referenced to the North American Vertical Datum of 1988 (NAVD 88). The accuracy of the DEM was evaluated using three approaches. In the first approach, values from the DEM at selected locations in Charlestown and South Kingstown, Rhode Island (adjacent to the study area) were compared to publically available Letters of Mapping Amendment (LOMAs), which document the lowest grade elevation at a particular structure. Elevations from fifteen LOMAs were used for the comparison. The second approach involved a comparison of elevations from three LIDAR control points near the study area with the corresponding values from the DEM. The third approach involved a comparison of elevations reported on building plans for several properties in South Kingstown with values from the DEM. Values of root mean square error for these three approaches were 0.78 ft, 0.04 ft, and 0.67 ft, respectively, which were considered to be reasonable.

2.1. Classification of Structures

As part of the NACCS, the U.S. Army Corps of Engineers created a classification system of coastal infrastructure to be able to differentiate damage from inundation and wave attack between different structures. Seven structural prototypes were presented: (1) apartments; (2) and (3) commercial; (4) high rise; (5) single and two story residences with no basement; (6) single and two-story residences with basements; and (7) elevated or stilted buildings on pile foundations. In some cases prototypes were further sub-divided; for example, prototype 5A is a single story residence with no basement and 5B is a two story residence with no basement.

The study area consisted of 359 single story residences without basements (5A), 104 two story residences without basements (5B), 83 single story residences with basements (6A), 139 two story residences with basements (6B), 7 open stilted structures, and 16 enclosed stilted structures (7B). There was a total of 708 structures in the study area, and their distribution is shown in Figure 6. The structures in the study area were classified visually during visits to the site.

Figure 6. Distribution of structure type (i.e., prototypes) within the study area.

The NACCS damage functions require information about both the type of structure being impacted and the Furnished Floor Elevation (FFE), as the majority of damage occurs when inundation and waves exceeds the FFE. Values of FFE were obtained during site visits, and Figure 7 shows the values of FFE above grade for each structure. Included in the figure is the topography referenced to NAVD 88. Of particular interest in Figure 7 is the southwest corner of the study area, which shows both the main road (and evacuation route) and a collection of mobile homes at the ground surface (FFE < 1 ft) at very low elevations (< 5 ft above NAVD 88).

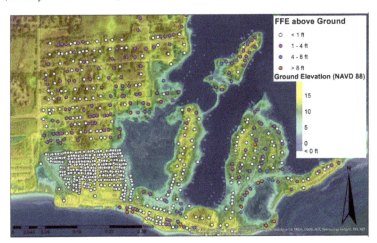

Figure 7. Values of Furnished Floor Elevation (FFE) for each structure and topography within the study area.

2.2. Inundation, Waves, and Erosion

Figure 8 illustrates how the U.S. Federal Emergency Management Agency (FEMA) defines the coastal zone in terms of flooding from both inundation and wave action. Inundation from storm surge is defined by a still water elevation (SWEL), and the impact of waves is added to the SWEL to define a Base Flood Elevation (BFE).

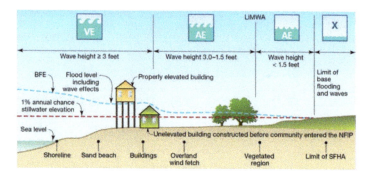

Figure 8. The U.S. Federal Emergency Management Agency's (FEMA) designation of Special Flood Hazard Areas (SFHA) showing the base flood elevation (BFE) as the sum of the still water elevation from storm surge inundation and wave action [7].

Levels of inundation were estimated using an on-line tool developed for Rhode Island called STORMTOOLS [4,8]. Water levels for events of various return periods were obtained from NOAA's gauge station in Newport, RI. The values were scaled based on storm models from the NACCS study [9] to obtain levels of inundation for 25, 50, and 100 year storm events that included 1, 3 and 7 feet of sea level rise, respectively. The NACCS water levels were derived from their surge plus tide (96 random tides) simulation case at the upper 95% confidence limit. This confidence interval was selected to account for uncertainties in the analysis. The results also included wave induced set up since the simulations were based on a fully coupled surge-wave model system. Values of inundation within the study area were provided on a 1 m grid, and Figure 9 shows the estimated inundation of the study area from a 100-year storm event [10].

Figure 9. Extent of inundation within the study area from a 100-year storm event using the online tool STORMTOOLS [9].

Significant offshore wave heights (H_{mo}) were obtained using two approaches from the US Army Corps of Engineers (USACE): the Coastal Storm Modeling System (CSTORM-MS) and the Wave Information Studies (WIS) dataset. CSTORM-MS is a suite of modeling tools that includes a deep water wave model (WAM), a nearshore wave model (STWAVE), and an advanced circulation model (ADCIRC). As part of the NACCS, 1030 separate synthetic tropical storms were modeled. Using these synthetic storms along with extratropical storms modeled from 100 historical storms, wave heights and wind and water levels were estimated for the northeast U.S. The second approach involved the Wave Information Studies (WIS), which provide modeled wave estimates from hindcast data (1980 to 2010) at discrete locations offshore.

Different probability distributions from both data sets were used to identify the significant wave height with a probability of exceedance of 1%. Values ranged from 30 to 33 ft (9 to 10 m) and 30 ft (9 m) was used as the input to nearshore wave modeling. Nearshore wave heights were modeled using the 2-D wave modeling program STeady State Spectral WAVE (STWAVE). Inputs included the DEM, bottom friction, and offshore significant wave height. STWAVE includes refraction, shoaling, and both depth-induced and steepness-induced breaking. Importantly, wave run-up is not included since it is not allowed in the USACE damage assessment methodology.

The NACCS uses controlling wave crest heights above FFE to determine wave damage at each structure. Values of significant wave height from STWAVE were multiplied by 1.12 to convert them to a controlling wave crest height.

Erosion within the study area was estimated using shoreline change maps as shown in Figure 2. Based on the historical position of the shoreline from 1938 to 2014 [1], future erosion rates were projected using the historical rates and also two exponentially increasing erosion rates (an upper and lower estimate) that account qualitatively for the effects of increasing sea level rise. Figure 10 shows estimates of the shoreline position within the study area in 100 years. The projected shoreline erosion would clearly impact a number of structures, ranging from 59 for the historical rates up to 349 using the more conservative exponentially increasing rate.

Figure 10. Estimated positions of the shoreline in the study area after 100 years using the historical erosion rate and two exponentially increasing erosion rates.

2.3. NACCS Damage Functions

The NACCS was conducted in the wake of Superstorm Sandy by the US Army Corps of Engineers (USACE) North Atlantic Division. The overall goal of the study was to develop a framework for managing risk in coastal communities. A tiered approach was proposed including characterizing environmental conditions, analyzing risk and vulnerability, and identifying and comparing possible solutions [10]. A key part of the study was the Physical Depth Damage Function Report [5], in which relationships between amounts of damage from inundation, wave action, and erosion for different coastal structures were proposed. Water level measurements at specific locations were measured following Superstorm Sandy and compared to the amount of damage caused to structures at those locations. A panel of coastal experts was convened to review the available data and damage functions were developed to estimate the minimum, most likely, and maximum damage to a structure based on the structure type and water level (from inundation and waves) at the structure. It was recommended [5] to evaluate each damage function separately and use the function that yields the largest estimate of damage as the measure of total damage from the storm.

Figure 11 shows examples of damage functions from the NACCS. Figure 11a,b show the relationship between the percent damage and elevation from inundation and wave attack for a single story residence with no basement (prototype 5A). The flood depth relative to FFE is used in the inundation damage function and the controlling wave crest height relative to FFE is used for the wave damage function. Figure 11c shows the inundation damage function for a single story structure with a basement (prototype 6A). This function reflects the damage that can occur from inundation of basements even if the flood depth is below the FFE.

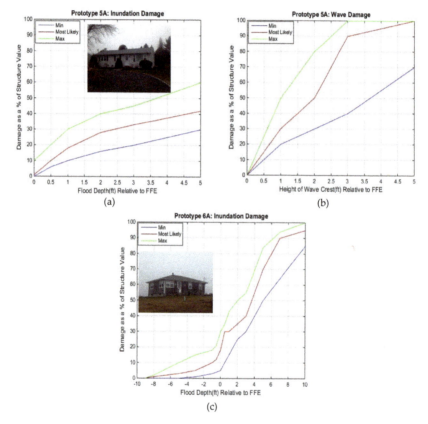

Figure 11. Examples of damage functions proposed by the NACCS: (**a**) inundation damage to single story residences with no basement (prototype 5A); (**b**) wave damage to single story residences with no basement (5A); and (**c**) inundation damage to single story residences with a basement (6A). Inset photographs show 5A and 6A structures within the study area.

3. Results and Discussion

3.1. Assessment of Damage from Inundation and Waves

The estimated water levels from inundation and wave action were combined with the FFE at each structure and input into the appropriate damage functions for each prototype. Water levels were determined for two storm scenarios, a 100 year event, with and without 7 feet of sea level rise. As described above, the damage was calculated separately for inundation and waves and the larger of the two was used as the total damage. Damage from erosion was assessed directly from local erosion rates rather than from damage functions.

Figure 12 shows the estimated inundation damage for the study area from a 100 year event with no sea level rise using the "most likely" damage curves. The main sources of damage (>20%) occur in the low lying area in the southwest corner of the study area where the coastal road turns inland, a low barrier beach in the southeast corner of the study area, and from the wetlands within the coastal pond due to back flooding.

Figure 13 shows the estimated wave damage from a 100 year storm with no sea level rise. Maximum estimated wave heights along the coastline were 6.5–10 ft (2–3 m), however, most of the wave heights were <1 m. A comparison of Figures 12 and 13 suggests that waves are present at locations where there is no inundation. This is the result of different resolutions of the wave and inundation estimates; the STWAVE results had a resolution of 10 m while the results from STORMTOOLS had a resolution of 1 m. This was resolved by setting the wave heights to zero wherever there was no inundation.

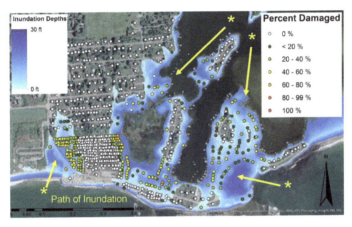

Figure 12. Estimated inundation damage to each structure from a 100 year storm event with no sea level rise using the "most likely" damage curves. Inundation depths from STORMTOOLS are also shown.

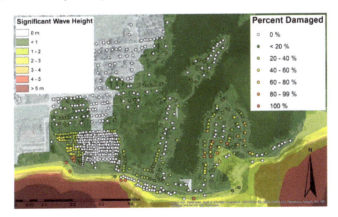

Figure 13. Estimated wave damage to each structure from a 100 year storm event with no sea level rise using the "most likely" damage curves. Wave height estimates from STWAVE are also shown.

Figure 14 shows the total damage estimated for each structure within the study area. Close inspection of these figures shows that, as expected, wave damage dominates along the coastline and transitions to inundation damage dominating further inland and along the coastal pond. For this storm event, 253 of the 708 structures were estimated to have suffered some amount of damage.

Figure 15 shows the total damage from inundation and waves for a 100 year storm event with 7 feet of sea level rise (SLR). The extent of inundation is included, which clearly shows the increase in flooded areas. With sea level rise, the entire coastal road parallel to the shore is flooded. The estimated damage for the majority of the structures along the coastal road ranged from 80% to 100%, and wave damage dominated for most of these structures. In this case 578 of the 708 structures were estimated to have damage, which was 324 more than from the 100 year storm event with no sea level rise.

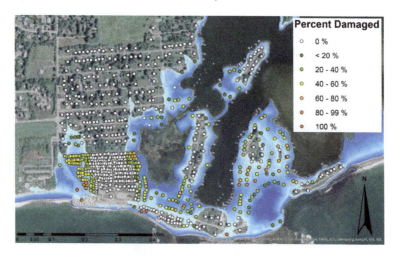

Figure 14. Total estimated damage to each structure from a 100 year storm event with no sea level rise. The extent of inundation is also shown.

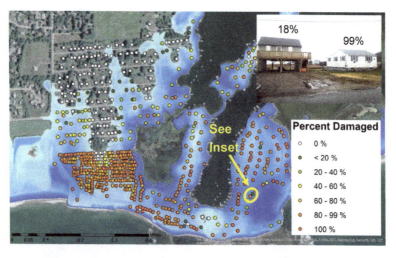

Figure 15. Total estimated damage to each structure from a 100 year storm event with 7 feet of sea level rise. The extent of inundation is also shown.

Two adjacent structures at the eastern end of the study area (shown in the yellow circle and the inset photograph in Figure 15) illustrate the obvious importance of elevation in mitigating inundation and wave damage. Damage to the elevated structure (Prototype 7A) is estimated to be 18% for a 100 year storm event with 7 feet of sea level rise while the adjacent single story home with a basement (Prototype 5B) is completely destroyed.

Table 1 summarizes the results in terms of both the number and percentage of structures that are damaged for each prototype. Columns (a) and (c) (in green) summarize the results from a 100 year storm event and columns (b) and (d) (in blue) show the results from a 100 year storm event with 7 feet of sea level rise. Approximately 35% of the one and two story structures (prototypes 5A, 5B, 6A, and 6B) are expected to be damaged from a 100 year storm event with no sea level rise. However, only 12% of these structures are estimated to be damaged more than 50%. It should be noted that 50% damage is a critical threshold for the RI CRMC, the states principal coastal regulatory agency; above this amount homeowners must rebuild to current building codes (i.e., increased loads, elevation of FFE, etc.). For the 100 year storm event with 7 feet of sea level rise, 75% of one and two story structures are expected to suffer some damage, and almost 60% of the structures would suffer more than 50% damage.

The performance of the elevated structures (prototypes 7A and 7B) is markedly different (in orange). Of the 23 elevated structures, approximately 60% (14 structures) are expected to suffer some damage during a 100 year storm event, however 13% have more than 50% damage. For a 100 year storm event with 7 feet of sea level rise, the percentage of elevated structures with more than 50% damage increased to approximately 52%. This suggests that at least half of the structures in the study area that are currently elevated on piles may still be vulnerable to damage when the effects of sea level rise are considered.

Table 1. Summary of the total damage estimates by prototype for a 100 year storm event with and without 7 feet of sea level rise.

Prototype (Number of Structures)	Structures with Damage (Number/%)		Structures with >50% Damage (Number/%)	
	(a) 100 Year Storm with No SLR	(b) 100 Year Storm with 7′ SLR [1]	(c) 100 Year Storm with No SLR	(d) 100 Year Storm with 7′ SLR
5A, Single story with no basement (359 Structures)	128 (36%)	336 (94%)	48 (13%)	314 (87%)
5B, Two story with no basement (104 Structures)	33 (32%)	79 (76%)	7 (7%)	56 (54%)
6A, Single story with basement (83 Structures)	31 (37%)	56 (67%)	12 (15%)	43 (52%)
6B, Two story with basement (139 Structures)	48 (35%)	89 (64%)	13 (9%)	68 (49%)
7A, Elevated building with open pile foundation (7 Structures)	6 (86%)	7 (100%)	2 (29%)	5 (71%)
7B, Elevated building with enclosed pile foundation (16 Structures)	8 (50%)	11 (69%)	1 (6%)	7 (44%)
Total Number of Structures (708)	254 (36%)	578 (82%)	83 (12%)	493 (70%)

[1] SLR = Sea Level Rise

3.2. Evaluation of Adaptation Strategies

After using CERI to analyze damage from inundation and waves within the study area, two adaptation measures were evaluated. Although these measures are in the conceptual design stage, they can be evaluated based on the estimated reduction in damage to structures and infrastructure. As such, CERI can be used as a tool to aid planners, local governments, and emergency managers in evaluating different strategies to mitigate damage from storm events.

The two adaptation measures that were evaluated are shown in Figure 16. The first involved restoration of a dune and a coastal pond/wetland in the southwest corner of the study area. The primary function of this measure is to protect a collection of low-lying single story homes (see Figure 14) and the coastal road/evacuation route. The second adaptation measure is a combination of berms, a tide gate, and a restored dune along the eastern end of the study area, with the primary function of mitigating back flooding from the coastal pond.

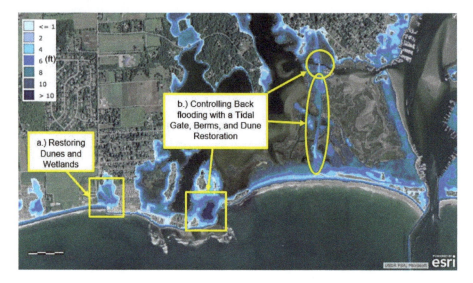

Figure 16. Two adaptation measures proposed and analyzed for the study area.

3.2.1. Dune Restoration

Figure 17a shows a series of photographs of the southwest corner of the study area from 2004 to 2015. Over the past 11 years there has been significant erosion at this location which has impacted the coastal pond and is currently (2016) encroaching on the coastal road. This area is the path of inundation for up to a 100 year storm event without sea level rise (Figure 17b) and is therefore a good location for a coastal protection system. Figure 18 shows a cross section across which a restored dune is proposed. At this location approximately 9000 ft^3 of fill would be required to raise the elevation to above the level of inundation from a 100 year event.

One potential solution would be to design and build a reinforced dune with a core of geotextile sand containers (GSC), such as the recently completed Montauk Stabilization Project in Long Island, New York [11]. Potential advantages of using reinforced dunes included the added stability over dunes without GSCs (particularly during the first five years while dune grass plantings are maturing) and reduced costs and permitting restrictions relative to hardened structures. Additionally, "soft" solutions such as reinforced dunes are typically designed for events with lower return periods than 100 years (e.g., 25 or 50 years), and as such they can provide a cost-effective solution that gives decision makers more time to assess the actual impacts of sea level rise on coastal communities.

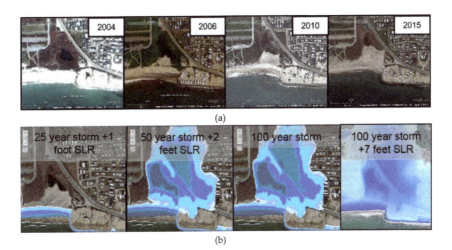

(a)

(b)

Figure 17. (**a**) Photographs showing significant erosion in the southwest corner of the study area since 2004; and (**b**) estimates of inundation for different storm events and levels of sea level rise.

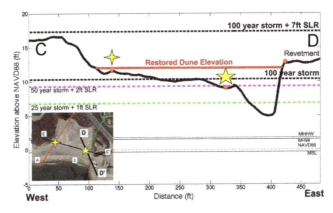

Figure 18. Cross section of southwest corner of the study area where a reinforced dune is proposed to mitigate damage from a 100 year storm event.

It is estimated that construction of a reinforced dune at this location would protect 81 structures (Table 2) and would also protect the coastal road and evacuation route from storm surge and wave action up to a 100 year event (without sea level rise).

3.2.2. Mitigation of Back Flooding

Much of the inundation in the study area comes from back flooding of the coastal pond north of the Matunuck Beach community. Mitigation of this flooding requires a combination of measures in the southeast corner and east of the study area. These include a tidal gate at the inlet of the pond (Figure 16), berms along sections of a shore-perpendicular road, and a restored dune in the southeast corner of the study area. A review of inundation levels with STORMTOOLS indicated that, even with these measures, storm events with 25 year return periods would still flood the coastal pond through numerous low-lying areas east of the study area. Therefore, only a 25 year storm event was evaluated for possible mitigation. Table 2 shows that, using these measures, mitigation of flooding of the coastal pond from a 25 year storm event would protect 70 structures from damage.

Table 2. Effects of different adaptation measures in terms of structures protected for a given storm event.

	(a) Restoration of Dunes and Coastal Pond/Wetland	(b) Mitigation of Back Flooding
Design Event	100 year storm event	25 year storm event
Number of Structures Protected	81	70
Additional Impacts of Adaptation	Also protects evacuation route for community	Protects inland structures outside the study area

3.3. Benefits and Limitations of CERI

The ability to assess damage from inundation and wave action is a powerful tool for coastal planners, state agencies, and emergency managers. It is particularly useful for identifying structures and infrastructure that are most vulnerable from storm events and can be used to evaluate the impact or benefits of adaptation measures. This approach is also flexible enough to incorporate different storm scenarios and levels of sea level rise into the analysis. Wave run up and wind damage are currently not included, however, these could be addressed in the future using more advanced models (e.g., FUNWAVE) and additional damage functions.

4. Conclusions

Matunuck is a coastal village in South Kingstown, RI that has one of the highest erosion rates in the state, and the structures and infrastructure are at risk from inundation and wave damage from storms. The only evacuation route for much of the community is highly susceptible to flooding. Sea level rise is predicted by NOAA to be as high as 7 feet by 2100. Given these issues, the objective of this paper was to estimate inundation, wave, and erosion damage to the existing structures and infrastructure in this community caused by a 100 year storm with and without 7 feet of sea level rise. Adaptation strategies were identified to reduce the damage from inundation, wave, and erosion due to both storm scenarios and the reduction of damage associated with each adaptation strategy was determined.

A methodology called the Coastal Environmental Risk Index (CERI) was used to estimate the amount of damage relative to the first floor elevation of every structure in the study area. This can be generalized for any coastal community and it is unique because it gives information on damage to individual structures in a particular area. In order to create this tool, a GIS environment was utilized with STORMTOOLS inundation layers to find the estimated inundation depths, and Steady State Spectral Wave Model (STWAVE) modeling was used to find the estimated wave heights for the area of interest. This information was input into damage functions proposed by the U.S. Army Corps of Engineers' NACCS. The total damage to each structure was considered to be the maximum of the estimated inundation and wave damage.

The level of estimated damage was heavily dependent on the local topography and structure type. Approximately 35% of the one and two story structures (prototypes 5A, 5B, 6A, and 6B) are expected to be damaged from a 100 year storm event with no sea level rise. However, only 12% of these structures are estimated to be damaged more than 50%. This is notable, as 50% damage represents a critical threshold for the RICRMC; above this amount homeowners must rebuild to current building codes. In Rhode Island, this includes elevation of the rebuilt structure above the BFE +1 ft., maintenance of a 50 ft. setback from the shoreline (or movement of the structure in the case of significant erosion), and compliance with the American Society of Civil Engineers' standard ASCE 24-05 Flood Resistant Design and Construction. For the 100 year storm event with 7 feet of sea level rise, 75% of one and two story structures are expected to suffer some damage, and almost 60% of the structures would suffer more than 50% damage.

Shoreline erosion within the study area was estimated using local rates developed from historical positions of the shoreline and extrapolated while incorporating sea level rise and local effects. It is estimated that, by 2100, 59 to 349 structures within the study area will be impacted by erosion.

J. Mar. Sci. Eng. **2016**, *4*, 67

Two adaptation measures were evaluated: restoration of a dune in the southwest corner of the study area, and a combination of berms, a tidal gate, and a restored dune along the eastern end of the study area. A total of 151 of 708 structures are estimated to be protected from inundation and wave action using these measures.

Most importantly, this paper illustrates the benefits of using CERI to evaluate damage on a structure-by-structure basis and for its evaluation of different storm scenarios and adaptation measures. As such, this tool shows promise for use by coastal managers to manage risk to coastal communities.

Acknowledgments: This study was performed as part of a senior design class for Ocean Engineering undergraduates at the University of Rhode Island. Funding for participation in the 14th Estuarine and Coastal Modeling Conference and for publishing costs were provided by the Rhode Island Sea Grant. This support is gratefully appreciated.

Author Contributions: The students taking the class performed the study and prepared a final report and presentation of the work. The students included Christopher Small, Tyler Blanpied, Alicia Kauffman, Connor O'Neil, Nicholas Proulx, Mathew Rajacich, Hailey Simpson, and Jeffrey White. Malcolm L. Spaulding was the architect of CERI and served as a course advisor. Christopher D.P. Baxter was the course instructor and prepared this paper on behalf of the students. J. Craig Swanson served as an external advisor to the course.

Conflicts of Interest: The authors declare no conflict of interest.

References

1. Boothroyd, J.C.; Hollis, R.J.; Oakley, B.A.; Henderson, R.E. 2016, Shoreline Change from 1939–2014, Washington County, Rhode Island. 1:2,000 scale. Rhode Island Geological Survey. 45 maps. Available online: http://www.crmc.ri.gov/maps/maps_shorechange.html (accessed on 17 October 2016).
2. Boyd, J. (University of Michigan, Ann Arbor, MI, USA). Personal communication, 2015.
3. NOAA Sea Level Rise Viewer. Available online: https://coast.noaa.gov/digitalcoast/tools/slr (accessed on 17 October 2016).
4. Spaulding, M.L.; Grilli, A.; Damon, C.; Crean, T.; Fugate, G.; Oakley, B.A.; Stempel, P. STORMTOOLS: Coastal Environmental Risk Index (CERI). *J. Mar. Sci. Eng.* **2016**, *4*, 54. [CrossRef]
5. U.S. Army Corps of Engineers. Physical Depth Damage Function Summary Report, North Atlantic Comprehensive Coastal Study: Resilient Adaptation to Increasing Risk. Available online: http://www.nad.usace.army.mil/Portals/40/docs/NACCS/10A_PhysicalDepthDmgFxSummary_26Jan2015.pdf (accessed on 17 October 2016).
6. Rhode Island Geographical Information System. Available online: http://www.rigis.org/data/topo (accessed on 14 July 2016).
7. Coastal Mapping Basics. Available online: http://www.region2coastal.com/resources/coastal-mapping-basics/ (accessed on 6 April 2015).
8. Spaulding, M.L.; Isaji, T.; Damon, C.; Fugate, G. Application of STORMTOOLS's simplified flood inundation model, with and without sea level rise, to RI coastal waters. In Proceedings of the ASCE Solutions to Coastal Disasters Conference, Boston, MA, USA, September 2015.
9. U.S. Army Corps of Engineers. Main Report, North Atlantic Coast Comprehensive Study: Resilient Adaptation to Increasing Risk. Available online: http://www.nad.usace.army.mil/Portals/40/docs/NACCS/NACCS_main_report.pdf (accessed on 17 October 2016).
10. RI CRMC Shoreline Change Special Area Management Plan. Available online: http://www.beachsamp.org/resources/stormtools/ (accessed on 10 August 2016).
11. U.S. Army Corps of Engineers. Main Report, Downtown Montauk Stabilization Project. 2014. Available online: http://www.nan.usace.army.mil/Portals/37/docs/civilworks/projects/ny/coast/fimp/DM_files/HSLRR/App_E_Public%20Access%20Plan%20Oct2014.pdf (accessed on 17 October 2016).

Article

Dynamic Reusable Workflows for Ocean Science

Richard P. Signell [1,*], Filipe Fernandes [2] and Kyle Wilcox [3]

1   U.S. Geological Survey, Woods Hole, MA 02543, USA
2   Southeast Coastal Ocean Observing Regional Association, Charleston, SC 29422, USA; ocefpaf@gmail.com
3   Axiom Data Science, Wickford, RI 02852, USA; kyle@axiomdatascience.com
*   Correspondence: rsignell@usgs.gov; Tel.: +1-508-457-2229

Academic Editor: Dong-Sheng Jeng
Received: 8 September 2016; Accepted: 19 October 2016; Published: 25 October 2016

Abstract: Digital catalogs of ocean data have been available for decades, but advances in standardized services and software for catalog searches and data access now make it possible to create catalog-driven workflows that automate—end-to-end—data search, analysis, and visualization of data from multiple distributed sources. Further, these workflows may be shared, reused, and adapted with ease. Here we describe a workflow developed within the US Integrated Ocean Observing System (IOOS) which automates the skill assessment of water temperature forecasts from multiple ocean forecast models, allowing improved forecast products to be delivered for an open water swim event. A series of Jupyter Notebooks are used to capture and document the end-to-end workflow using a collection of Python tools that facilitate working with standardized catalog and data services. The workflow first searches a catalog of metadata using the Open Geospatial Consortium (OGC) Catalog Service for the Web (CSW), then accesses data service endpoints found in the metadata records using the OGC Sensor Observation Service (SOS) for in situ sensor data and OPeNDAP services for remotely-sensed and model data. Skill metrics are computed and time series comparisons of forecast model and observed data are displayed interactively, leveraging the capabilities of modern web browsers. The resulting workflow not only solves a challenging specific problem, but highlights the benefits of dynamic, reusable workflows in general. These workflows adapt as new data enter the data system, facilitate reproducible science, provide templates from which new scientific workflows can be developed, and encourage data providers to use standardized services. As applied to the ocean swim event, the workflow exposed problems with two of the ocean forecast products which led to improved regional forecasts once errors were corrected. While the example is specific, the approach is general, and we hope to see increased use of dynamic notebooks across geoscience domains.

Keywords: numerical modeling; reproducibility; catalog services; data services; web services; metadata; ocean forecasting; ocean modeling; data management; data system; interoperability; OPeNDAP; THREDDS; CSW; Jupyter Notebooks

1. Introduction

1.1. Motivation

When tackling a scientific or engineering problem that requires integrating information from a large number of data providers, a challenging issue can be simply finding and acquiring the data. While digital systems for cataloging scientific data have existed for decades (e.g., NASA GCMD [1] and GEOSS Portal [2]) these systems have typically been used to conduct geospatial, temporal, and keyword searches that return links to web sites or documents containing data in a variety of forms and formats, requiring significant work on the part of the would-be user to determine how to access, download, and decode the data they require.

However, with the increasing availability of standardized, varied, and powerful web-based data services, users can now employ catalog services to not only find data across multiple providers, but then to acquire these data in a programmatic way, so that both search and access are automated.

This approach is being supported by organizations worldwide (for example, the national catalogs data.gov, data.gov.uk, data.gov.au, geodata.gov.gr). Here we describe support and use within the US Integrated Ocean Observing system (IOOS) [3,4], a partnership between 17 federal agencies and 11 regional associations (Figure 1). IOOS partners use a wide range of different sensors and models, but are required to supply data using approved web services: for example, OGC-SOS [5] and/or ERDDAP [6] for sensor data, OPeNDAP [7] with CF-Conventions [8] for model data. They are also required to provide ISO 19115-2 metadata [9] for each dataset. The use of both standardized web services and standardized metadata enables a high degree of interoperability [10,11].

Figure 1. IOOS is a NOAA-led partnership between 11 Regional Associations (shown here) and 17 federal agencies with a wide range of observed and modeled data products distributed via a system of web service providers and a centralized catalog of metadata.

Demonstrating how to effectively use these catalogs and data services can be challenging. Fortunately, with the rise of interactive, scientific notebooks that use modern browsers as a client to communicate with back-end servers, end-to-end workflows for scientific data discovery, access, analysis, and visualization can be constructed that embed code, descriptions, and results into documents that can be shared, reused, and adapted by others [12].

We demonstrate here a specific application of this approach to assessing the predictive skills of water temperature forecasts from multiple ocean models within the US Integrated Ocean Observing System (US-IOOS).

1.2. The Boston Light Swim Problem

The Boston Light Swim ("Granddaddy of American Open Water Swims") is an eight-mile swim that has been held every August since 1907. With a no-wet-suit requirement and water temperatures as low as 58 degrees F, swimmers are monitored carefully and pulled from the water if they do not make specified waypoints in required times (swimmers must finish the entire race within 5 h). Since water temperatures can fluctuate substantially with wind events, such as upwelling, race organizers are interested in forecast water temperatures so they can inform swimmers and their support teams of how hazardous conditions are likely to be.

On 13 August 2015, two days before the race, swim organizers expressed concern that the highest-resolution IOOS forecast model was predicting very cold temperatures for race day (Figure 2) and they inquired about the degree they should believe the model. To address this issue, we realized we could simply reuse an existing workflow developed for the IOOS System Test [13], which automated the assessment of predicted water levels at coastal tide gauge locations. What if we just deployed the same notebook to assess the quality of predicted water temperatures, but changed the search criteria to look for water temperatures rather than water levels? This simple modification was successful and allowed us to respond to the swimmers' issue with improved forecast products, demonstrating the power of the dynamic, reusable workflow approach.

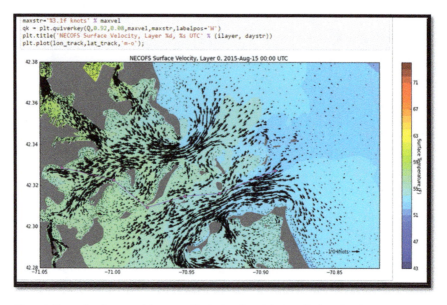

Figure 2. Screenshot from a web browser, displaying the original prediction of surface currents and forecast water temperatures in the Boston Harbor region from the IOOS NECOFS-MassBay model. This snapshot is at 00:00 UTC on the day of the Boston Light Swim, and is shown as embedded in a Jupyter Notebook given to the swim organizers. The magenta line indicates the eight-mile race route. The swimmers start offshore in colder water, and swim into the harbor following the incoming tide. The model is predicting 52–53 °F water temperatures at the race start, dangerously cold for a no-wet suit swim.

2. Methods

2.1. Approach

We constructed the workflow as a series of Jupyter Notebooks (Supplementary Materials), web applications that combine live code, equations, visualizations, and explanatory text [14]. Although the workflow could have been constructed as a single notebook, we split the tasks into three notebooks to allow users to more easily re-run certain sections of the workflow. The first notebook performs queries on a catalog service (or services), then retrieves data using discovered data services and saves the results to disk. The second notebook loads the retrieved data and creates skill assessment products, writing those products to disk. The third notebook loads the products and displays them on an interactive map in the browser. In the following sections, we describe the components that make this workflow possible, and then describe the function of each notebook in more detail.

2.2. Standard Web Services

As previously mentioned, data providers in IOOS are required to provide web data services from an approved list of international and community standards. For sensor data, one of the most commonly-supported services is OGC-SOS and for model output, OPeNDAP with CF Conventions. These services are designed to allow time series and model output from diverse sensors and modeling systems to be treated in a common way, without model- or sensor-specific code required for access and use. Typically in IOOS these services are provided by the Unidata THREDDS Data Server (TDS) [15], free open-source software which allows collections of NetCDF [16] files to be virtually aggregated and supplemented with metadata via NcML [17] (Figure 3). For more information on the benefits of the TDS approach and how data providers can establish standard services, see [18–22].

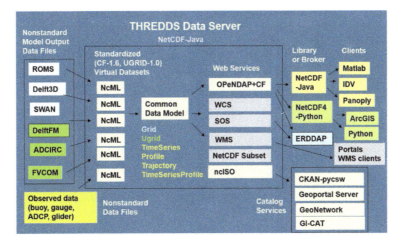

Figure 3. IOOS data interoperability approach using the Unidata THREDDS Data Server. Collections of non-CF compliant NetCDF, GRIB, and HDF files can be aggregated and made CF compliant via the NetCDF Markup Language (NCML). This allows datasets to be represented using a common data model, which then may be delivered via a variety of standardized web services, and consumed by a variety of clients and applications. In this paper we focus on accessing web services using Python.

In addition to requiring standardized data services, IOOS also requires that standardized ISO metadata (ISO 19115-2) be created for each dataset. This is easily generated using the ncISO software [23], which automatically converts attributes from NetCDF, NcML, and the TDS into ISO metadata documents. Each region of IOOS maintains a web-accessible folder of ISO metadata that is harvested daily into a centralized database, which can then be searched using a GUI or programmatically using the OGC-CSW service. These capabilities are provided by the free open-source CKAN [24] and pycsw [25] software packages.

With these services in place, we used a series of Jupyter Notebooks to (1) search and acquire data; (2) compute skill assessment metrics; and (3) show the skill assessment results on an interactive map. The Jupyter Notebooks combine the ability to document the workflow, show actual code used for search, access, analysis, and visualization, as well as the results, in a single reproducible document format. Although Jupyter Notebooks can be constructed using many languages, including MATLAB, R, and Julia, here we use Python due to the availability of packages that facilitate working with the web services used in IOOS.

2.3. Fetch Data Notebook

This notebook searches for data by querying a CSW service to extract metadata records from the IOOS that meet the user-specified criteria, then extracts data from the SOS and OPeNDAP+CF data service endpoints discovered in the returned records. First, data are extracted from sensor datasets using SOS, then the time series from the model dataset are interpolated to the sensor locations using OPeNDAP.

The user (someone who knows how to run a Notebook, but who does not necessarily know Python) specifies the following information:

- One or more CSW catalog service endpoints [URL1, URL2, ...];
- A geographic bounding box [lon_min, lat_min, lon_max, lat_max];
- A time extent [time_min, time_max]; and
- Variable of interest [identified by one or more standard names].

The specific example used in the Boston Light Swim is shown in Figure 4.

The notebook uses this information and the *OWSLib* package [26] to construct the CSW query and parse the CSW responses. The CSW query used here is quite sophisticated: we search records that contain any of our list of CF standard names, eliminate records that contain the string *Averages*, and then select only those records that contain data within the bounding box and time extent window (Figure 5).

From these records we then search for OPeNDAP and SOS service URLs, since our workflow knows how to extract data from these two data service endpoints. Then using the IOOS-developed *pyoos* package [27], observed data are extracted from the SOS data URLs using high level routines from both NOAA NDBC and NOAA CO-OPS SOS services. The data are then interpolated onto a common hourly time base to facilitate comparison.

With the observed data extracted, we loop through the OPeNDAP URLs, opening the URLs using the British Met Office-developed *iris* package [28], which uses the CF conventions to allow model-independent extraction of simulation data together with corresponding temporal and geospatial coordinate information. This allows model-independent extraction of simulated time series at the grid cell closest to the observed data. The extracted model time series is then interpolated onto the same one-hour time base to facilitate model-data comparison. The observed and modeled time series data are then saved to disk, ready to be loaded into the Skill Score notebook.

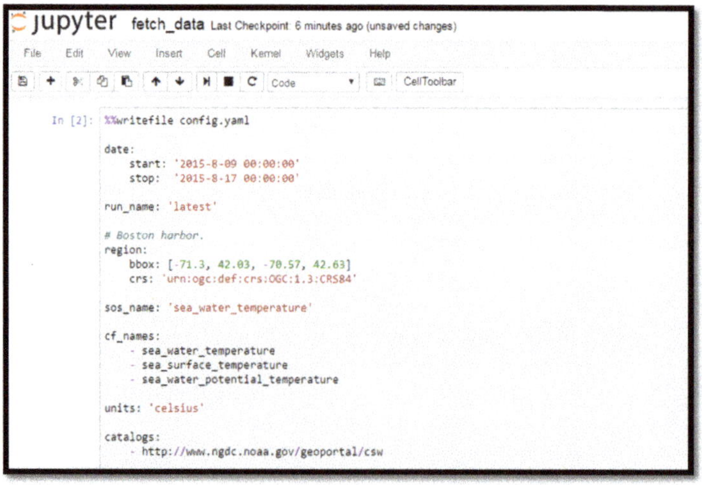

Figure 4. Screenshot from the beginning of the Fetch Data notebook, where the user specifies the date range, region, parameter of interest, and CSW catalog endpoint to search for data.

```
In [ ]: def make_filter(config):
            from owslib import fes
            from ioos_tools.ioos import fes_date_filter
            kw = dict(wildCard='*', escapeChar='\\',
                      singleChar='?', propertyname='apiso:AnyText')

            or_filt = fes.Or([fes.PropertyIsLike(literal=('*%s*' % val), **kw)
                              for val in config['cf_names']])

            # Exclude ROMS Averages files.
            not_filt = fes.Not([fes.PropertyIsLike(literal='*Averages*', **kw)])

            begin, end = fes_date_filter(config['date']['start'],
                                         config['date']['stop'])

            bbox_crs = fes.BBox(config['region']['bbox'],
                                crs=config['region']['crs'])

            return [fes.And([bbox_crs, begin, end, or_filt, not_filt])]

        filter_list = make_filter(config)

In [ ]: csw = CatalogueServiceWeb(endpoint, timeout=120)
        csw.getrecords2(constraints=filter_list, esn='full')
```

Figure 5. Screenshot from a section of the Fetch Data notebook, illustrating the complex construction of filters used to search only for datasets with specific variable names, bounding box, and temporal extent. Here we additionally exclude datasets that contain the text "Averages" because previous query attempts returned ROMS Averages files that turned out to be versions of ROMS History files that had the tide filtered out. This illustrates the type of customization that many dynamic workflows may require, as catalogs can contain extraneous or duplicate datasets that need be filtered out to effectively use a given workflow.

2.4. Skill Score Notebook

This notebook loads the time series data from observations and models from the Fetch Data notebook and computes a variety of skill metrics, including model bias, central root mean squared error, and correlation (Figure 6). It makes use of the *scikit-learn* package [29] for skill metrics, and the *pandas* [30] package for reading and manipulating time series and data frames. The skill metrics are stored on disk for use in the Map Display notebook.

jupyter skill_score Last Checkpoint: a day ago (unsaved changes)

File Edit View Insert Cell Kernel Widgets Help

Code CellToolbar

```
In [17]: from ioos_tools.ioos import to_html, save_html, load_ncs
         from ioos_tools.skill_score import mean_bias, apply_skill

         dfs = load_ncs(config)

         df = apply_skill(dfs, mean_bias, remove_mean=False, filter_tides=False)
         skill_score = dict(mean_bias=df.to_dict())

         # Filter out stations with no valid comparison.
         df.dropna(how='all', axis=1, inplace=True)
         df = df.applymap('{:.2f}'.format).replace('nan', '--')
         df
```

Out[17]:

	16 NM East of Boston, MA	Buoy A0102, Mass Bay	Boston, MA
G1_SST_GLOBAL	0.56	0.93	0.47
NECOFS_FVCOM_OCEAN_MASSBAY_FORECAST	8.16	9.13	3.84
NECOFS_GOM3_FORECAST	0.60	0.77	0.92
coawst_4_use_best	0.78	0.75	5.68
global	1.74	1.35	--

Figure 6. Screenshot from a section of the Skill Score notebook, illustrating the computation of skill score metrics using *pandas* data frames. Here we see the mean bias calculation, with the results showing significant bias in the NECOFS MassBay Forecast at all locations, and in the COAWST model forecast in Boston Harbor.

2.5. Map Display Notebook

This notebook loads the previously-saved time series data and skill metrics and displays them on an interactive map (Figure 7). The *bokeh* package [31] is used to automatically create JavaScript plots that are embedded in the notebook, allowing the user to see data locations on a map and click on them to see interactive plots of the time series comparison, along with certain skill metrics. The user can also see the locations of the nearest model grid cells where the time series were extracted to compare with data.

Figure 7. Screenshot from a section of the Map Display notebook, showing the region searched, the observational station locations, and the number of model datasets found at each station location. Clicking on the plot icon at each station location displays an interactive time series plot of the type shown in Figures 8 and 9.

3. Results

The workflow executed with the 2015 Boston Light Swim input parameters discovered in situ temperature data from NOAA NDBC buoys and University of Maine buoys offshore in Massachusetts Bay, and from NOAA CO-OPS tide stations inshore in Boston Harbor (Figure 7). The workflow also discovered temperature data from a remotely-sensed dataset and from four different forecast models that cover the region.

The remotely-sensed data was a daily global product derived from multiple sensors and gap-filled via interpolation over cloudy regions (G1_SST_GLOBAL), while the forecast products discovered were:

- The HYCOM global model run by NCEP, a regular grid model with 9.25 km resolution that assimilates temperature data (HYCOM);
- The COAWST East and Gulf Coast model run by the U.S. Geological Survey, a regular grid model with 5 km resolution that does not directly assimilate data, but indirectly assimilates data by nudging the temperature field toward the HYCOM model (COAWST);
- The NECOFS Gulf of Maine model run by UMASS Dartmouth, a triangular mesh model with variable resolution from 1500 m offshore in Massachusetts Bay to 500 m in Boston Harbor, that assimilates temperature data (NECOFS-GOM)

- The NECOFS Massachusetts Bay model run by UMASS Dartmouth, a triangular mesh model with variable resolution from 1500 m offshore in Massachusetts Bay to 100 m in Boston Harbor, that does not assimilate temperature data (NECOFS-MassBay)

The results showed that two models had significant biases with respect to the data. The COAWST model was too warm in Boston Harbor by about 6 °C (Figure 8), and the highest resolution NECOFS-MassBay model was too cold at all three locations—nearly 8 °C off at the Boston Buoy (Figure 9) and at the NERACOOS Buoy A (not shown, as similar to the Boston Buoy). The lowest resolution HYCOM model and the NECOFS-GOM model were relatively close at all three locations, with average biases less than 2 °C.

To further investigate the issues with the COAWST and NECOFS-MassBay models, we extracted the simulated temperature fields over the entire domain from both models.

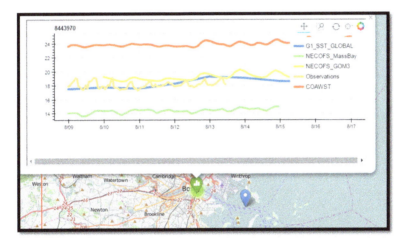

Figure 8. Screenshot from the Map Display notebook, showing the NECOFS_MassBay model about 4 °C colder than observations, and the COAWST model 6 °C warmer than observations. The NECOFS_GOM3 model is within a degree of the in situ observations (as is the G1_SST_GLOBAL global SST product derived from remote sensing).

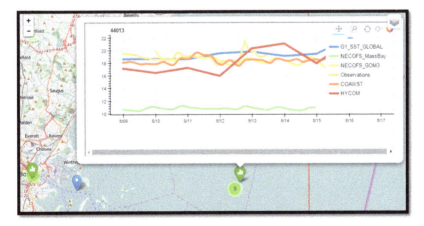

Figure 9. Screenshot from the Map Display notebook, showing the NECOFS_MassBay model about 8 °C colder than observations, and the COAWST model is now within a degree of observations. The global HYCOM model appears here also, and is within a few degrees of the observations.

The COAWST temperature field showed multiple hot spots along the coast, including Boston Harbor (not shown). Further investigation with the COAWST forecast modelers revealed that these hot spots were regions outside the domain of the HYCOM model from which temperatures were being nudged. Within these regions, temperatures were getting assigned to 25 °C, instead of using the nearest HYCOM values. This issue was promptly corrected by the modelers.

The NECOFS-MassBay temperature field showed uniformly cold temperatures throughout the domain, with the exception of a thin band of water along the open boundary (not shown). Further investigation with the NECOFS-MassBay modelers revealed that the NECOFS-MassBay model temperature field is forced by the NECOFS-GOM model along the open boundary, and that the atmospheric model used to drive both the NECOFS-GOM and NECOFS-MassBay model has too many clouds, and therefore underrepresents, the amount of short-wave radiation into the ocean. In the NECOFS-GOM model, this problem is masked because the model assimilates remotely-sensed SST data, but in the NECOFS-MassBay model, the modelers assumed the domain was small enough that the NECOFS-GOM forcing along the boundary would be sufficient to control the temperature field and, therefore, no temperature data was assimilated. The findings here showed this assumption needs reevaluation.

With confidence that the bias in the NECOFS-MassBay model was consistent over the region of the Boston Light Swim, we provided the swimmers with bias-corrected forecast maps from the NECOFS-MassBay model for each hour of the race. The swimmers reported that these corrected maps were very useful and were within 1–2 °C of temperatures observed during the swim.

4. Discussion

The use of dynamic, reusable workflows has a number of technological and scientific benefits. The use of the catalog allows data to be discovered dynamically, and the reproducible workflow means the results can be verified by others and used to create entirely new workflows. In fact, the set of sea surface temperature skill-assessment notebooks used here was derived from a set of water level skill-assessment notebooks developed for the IOOS System Test [13]. We simply changed the CF Standard Names from specifying sea surface height to specifying sea water temperature.

The fact that the notebook is driven by a catalog search means that it dynamically discovers new data that are available (and drops data that are no longer available!). When one of the authors (R.S.) was testing the notebook before a presentation, he was surprised (and delighted) to find a new model appearing in the skill assessment plot because another modeling group had registered their data with the catalog service. It is also not necessary to limit the search to one catalog service endpoint. Although we only used the IOOS CSW service for this 2015 Boston Light Swim example, a list of endpoints can be used, and we now include the data.gov CSW service as well.

To reproduce the workflow, the notebook must be shared, but also the environment necessary to run the notebook must be shared. This has traditionally been challenging, as sets of notebooks, like the one discussed here, depend on many packages, some with binary dependencies that can be tricky to build on all major platforms. Luckily, with the rise of technologies like GitHub [32], docker [33], Anaconda Python [34], conda [35], and conda-forge [36], services like binder [37] can now allow users to view a rendered notebook on GitHub, complete with embedded code, output, and graphics, and then click a button that starts up a notebook server on the Cloud, provisioned with the appropriate environment to run that notebook. Users can just click "run all" to execute the workflow, without installing anything locally, and without leaving their web browser.

Making it easy to conduct automated skill assessments has a number of other benefits as well. For modelers, it means they can spend more time on science, and less time performing mundane data tasks. For users, it means they can conduct their own skill assessment of existing models, instead of relying only on the modelers themselves. This is particularly important now that there are realistic regional and global simulations that are far beyond the ability of the modelers to test for all possible uses.

The success of this dynamic, reusable workflow shows what can happen when a community agrees on a common set of web services and a common vocabulary. In this case the participants did not already have an established vocabulary or established custom services, so IOOS provided best-practice suggestions for both software and service configuration to enable their approved services. IOOS data providers who wish to have their data plugged into the system can either follow the procedures described in [22] or see if one of the regional associations or Federal backbone partners can host their data and provide services. To enable workflows like this across communities with a variety of established services and vocabularies, brokering approaches for web services [38] and semantic approaches [39] will be necessary.

This workflow demonstrates the power of the dynamic, reusable workflow approach, but there are caveats and room for future improvements:

- Notebooks allow rich documentation, but it is still up to the developer to describe the workflow, use clear variable names and produce well-structured, readable code.
- While the software in dynamic workflows is always reproducible, the results of a specific workflow may not be reproducible if the data sources no longer exist or have changed.
- Workflow developers cannot expect standardized services and metadata to solve all data-wrangling problems. Some time and expertise is typically still needed to adapt discovered data sources to a specific workflow.
- Tools for standardized catalog and data service access need to be developed beyond Python, to support other major scientific analysis languages and environments used by scientists and developers (e.g., MATLAB, R, JavaScript, Julia, ArcGIS).
- Better documentation and support is needed to document how users can take advantage of workflows like this, and also for providers to connect their data to standardized services
- As data and catalog services become more heavily used, the software supporting these services needs to be made more robust and scalable. Requests to the THREDDS Data Server, for example, are single-threaded, and many simultaneous requests can overwhelm the server.
- The examples in this paper used nearest-neighbor lookup to extract time series from models. For more sophisticated interpolation schemes, tools that work with the topology of unstructured and staggered grid model output are required, taking advantage of the UGRID [40] and SGRID [41] conventions the community has developed.
- While it is possible to run the notebooks without understanding the details of the coding, it currently does require understanding of how to run a notebook (e.g., launch the binder service, navigate to the notebook, click on "run all" under the "cell" drop-down menu). Tools for deploying notebooks as simple web apps that hide this complexity from users are in development by the Jupyter team.

5. Conclusions

There are a number of benefits to developing dynamic, reusable workflows. Through catalog searches and use of interoperable web services they enable more effective assessment of large, distributed collections of data, such as numerical model results. More eyes on the model results means more feedback to modelers, resulting in better models. Complex data analysis from a variety of sources can be automated and dynamically respond as new data enter (or leave) the system. The notebook approach allows rich documentation of the workflow, and automatic generation of software environments allow users to easily run specific notebooks on local computers, on remote machines, or in the Cloud. The workflows also serve as training by example for potential users of standardized catalogs and data services, as well as demonstrating the type of custom workflow elements typically required for success. The workflows can also be easily modified to form the basis for new scientific applications. Often a new application will highlight issues that need fixing before it can function. Sometimes these are minor metadata or service issues that can easily be fixed by providers, and sometimes these are more major issues that require further research and development of standards, services, or tools. Regardless of the issue, fixing it for a specific workflow not only enables success for that workflow, but for an entire class of workflows and, thus, the larger geoscience community. With their numerous benefits demonstrated here, we anticipate dynamic, reusable workflows will become more common and expanded to more applications, services, and geoscience domains.

To reproduce the Boston Light Swim notebooks, visit IOOS Notebooks Demos on GitHub [42] and follow the instructions to install and run locally, or click the run "launch binder" button to run remotely on the Cloud.

Supplementary Materials: The Jupyter Notebooks described here are available online at: https://github.com/ioos/notebooks_demos.

Acknowledgments: F.F. and K.W. would like to acknowledge support from SECOORA and the IOOS Program Office. R.S. thanks Tom Kralidis with guidance on using CSW services and for his development of the *pycsw* and *OWSLib* python packages used here. Thanks to the Unidata Program Center for producing effective community-driven tools like *netcdf* and the *THREDDS Data Server*. Thanks also to the *Jupyter* team for creating the notebook approach. Any use of trade, firm, or product names is for descriptive purposes only and does not imply endorsement by the U.S. Government.

Author Contributions: Richard P. Signell conceived and led the project. Richard P. Signell wrote the paper. Filipe Fernandes developed most of the notebook code and played a major role in making the software environment reproducible. Kyle Wilcox developed and contributed to several of the key software packages used in the workflow.

Conflicts of Interest: The authors declare no conflict of interest.

References

1. Global Change Master Directory. Available online: http://gcmd.nasa.gov (accessed on 2 September 2016).
2. GEOSS Portal. Available online: http://www.geoportal.org (accessed on 2 September 2016).
3. Zdenka, W.; Manley, J. Ocean Observing: Delivering the Benefits. *Mar. Technol. Soc. J.* **2010**, *44*, 4–5. [CrossRef]
4. Robert, B.; Beard, R.; Burnett, W.; Crout, R.; Griffith, B.; Jensen, R.; Signell, R. Implementing the National Integrated Ocean Observing System (IOOS®)—From the Federal Agency Perspective. *Mar. Technol. Soc. J.* **2010**, *44*, 32–41. [CrossRef]
5. OGC Sensor Observation Service. Available online: http://www.opengeospatial.org/standards/sos (accessed on 7 September 2016).
6. ERDDAP. Available online: http://coastwatch.pfel.noaa.gov/erddap/index.html (accessed on 7 September 2016).
7. OPeNDAP. Available online: https://www.opendap.org (accessed on 7 September 2016).
8. Climate and Forecast Metadata Conventions. Available online: http://cfconventions.org (accessed on 7 September 2016).
9. ISO 19115-2 Metadata. Available online: http://www.iso.org/iso/home/store/catalogue_tc/catalogue_detail.htm?csnumber=67039 (accessed on 7 September 2016).
10. De La Beaujardière, J.; Beegle-Krause, C.J.; Bermudez, L.; Hankin, S.; Hazard, L.; Howlett, E.; Le, S.; Proctor, R.; Signell, R.P.; Snowden, D.; et al. Ocean and Coastal Data Management. *Eur. Space Agency* **2010**, 226–236. [CrossRef]
11. Hankin, S.; Bermudez, L.; Blower, J.D.; Blumenthal, B.; Casey, K.S.; Fornwall, M.; Graybeal, J.; Guralnick, R.P.; Habermann, T.; Howlett, E.; et al. NetCDF-CF-OPeNDAP: Standards for Ocean Data Interoperability and Object Lessons for Community Data Standards Processes. *Eur. Space Agency* **2010**, 450–458. [CrossRef]
12. Helen, S. Interactive Notebooks: Sharing the Code. *Nature* **2014**, *515*, 151–152.
13. IOOS System Test Wiki. Available online: https://github.com/ioos/system-test/wiki (accessed on 2 September 2016).
14. Jupyter Project. Available online: http://jupyter.org (accessed on 7 September 2016).
15. THREDDS Data Server. Available online: http://www.unidata.ucar.edu/software/thredds/current/tds/ (accessed on 7 September 2016).
16. Network Common Data Form. Available online: http://www.unidata.ucar.edu/software/netcdf/ (accessed on 7 September 2016).

17. NetCDF Markup Language. Available online: http://www.unidata.ucar.edu/software/thredds/current/netcdf-java/ncml/ (accessed on 7 September 2016).

18. Signell, R.P.; Carniel, S.; Chiggiato, J.; Janekovic, I.; Pullen, J.; Sherwood, C.R. Collaboration Tools and Techniques for Large Model Datasets. *J. Mar. Syst.* **2008**, *69*, 154–161. [CrossRef]

19. Signell, R.P. Model Data Interoperability for the United States Integrated Ocean Observing System (IOOS). *Am. Soc. Civ. Eng.* **2010**, 221–238. [CrossRef]

20. Bergamasco, A.; Benetazzo, A.; Carniel, S.; Falcieri, F.M.; Minuzzo, T.; Signell, R.P.; Sclavo, M. Knowledge Discovery in Large Model Datasets in the Marine Environment: The THREDDS Data Server Example. *Adv. Oceanogr. Limnol.* **2012**, *3*, 41–50. [CrossRef]

21. Signell, R.P.; Snowden, D.P. Advances in a Distributed Approach for Ocean Model Data Interoperability. *J. Mar. Sci. Eng.* **2014**, *2*, 194–208. [CrossRef]

22. Signell, R.P.; Camossi, E. Technical Note: Harmonising Metocean Model Data via Standard Web Services within Small Research Groups. *Ocean Sci.* **2016**, *12*, 633–645. [CrossRef]

23. ncISO. Available online: http://www.ngdc.noaa.gov/eds/tds/ (accessed on 7 September 2016).

24. CKAN. Available online: http://ckan.org (accessed on 7 September 2016).

25. pycsw. Available online: http://pycsw.org (accessed on 7 September 2016).

26. OWSLib. Available online: https://geopython.github.io/OWSLib (accessed on 7 September 2016).

27. pyoos. Available online: https://github.com/ioos/pyoos (accessed on 7 September 2016).

28. iris. Available online: http://scitools.org.uk/iris/ (accessed on 7 September 2016).

29. pandas. Available online: http://pandas.pydata.org (accessed on 7 September 2016).

30. scikit-learn. Available online: http://scikit-learn.org (accessed on 8 September 2016).

31. bokeh. Available online: http://bokeh.pydata.org (accessed on 7 September 2016).

32. GitHub. Available online: http://github.com (accessed on 7 September 2016).

33. Docker. Available online: http://www.docker.com (accessed on 7 September 2016).

34. Anaconda Python. Available online: https://docs.continuum.io/anaconda/ (accessed on 7 September 2016).

35. conda. Available online: http://conda.pydata.org/docs/index.html (accessed on 7 September 2016).

36. conda-forge. Available online: https://conda-forge.github.io (accessed on 7 September 2016).

37. Binder. Available online: http://mybinder.org/ (accessed on 7 September 2016).

38. Nativi, S.; Craglia, M.; Pearlman, J. Earth Science Infrastructures Interoperability: The Brokering Approach. *IEEE J. Sel. Top. Appl. Earth Obs. Remote Sens.* **2013**, *6*, 1118–1129. [CrossRef]

39. Fox, P.; McGuinness, D.; Middleton, D.; Cinquini, L.; Darnell, J.A.; Garcia, J.; West, P.; Benedict, J.; Solomon, S. Semantically-Enabled Large-Scale Science Data Repositories. In *The Semantic Web—ISWC 2006*; Cruz, I., Decker, S., Allemang, D., Preist, C., Schwabe, D., Mika, P., Uschold, M., Aroyo, L.M., Eds.; Springer: Heidelberg/Berlin, Germany, 2006; Volume 4273, pp. 792–805. Available online: http://link.springer.com/10.1007/11926078_57 (accessed on 7 September 2016).

40. UGRID Conventions. Available online: http://ugrid-conventions.github.io/ugrid-conventions (accessed on 2 September 2016).

41. SGRID Conventions. Available online: http://sgrid.github.io/sgrid (accessed on 2 September 2016).

42. IOOS Notebook Demos. Available online: https://github.com/ioos/notebooks_demos (accessed on 2 September 2016).

Article

Combining Inverse and Transport Modeling to Estimate Bacterial Loading and Transport in a Tidal Embayment

Mac Sisson [1,*], Jian Shen [1] and Anne Schlegel [2]

1   Virginia Institute of Marine Science, College of William & Mary, Gloucester Point, VA 23062, USA;
    shen@vims.edu
2   Virginia Department of Environmental Quality, Central Office, 629 East Main Street, Richmond, VA 23218,
    USA; Anne.Schlegel@deq.virginia.gov
*   Correspondence: sisson@vims.edu; Tel.: +1-804-684-7209

Academic Editor: Rich Signell
Received: 2 August 2016; Accepted: 9 October 2016; Published: 2 November 2016

Abstract: Poquoson River is a tidal coastal embayment located along the Western Shore of the Chesapeake Bay about 4 km south of the York River mouth in the City of Poquoson and in York County, Virginia. Its drainage area has diversified land uses, including high densities of residence, agricultural, salt marsh land uses, as well as a National Wildlife Refuge. This embayment experiences elevated bacterial concentration due to excess bacterial inputs from storm water runoff, nonpoint sources, and wash off from marshes due to tide and wind-induced set-up and set-down. Bacteria can also grow in the marsh and small tributaries. It is difficult to use a traditional watershed model to simulate bacterial loading, especially in this low-lying marsh area with abundant wildlife, while runoff is not solely driven by precipitation. An inverse approach is introduced to estimate loading from unknown sources based on observations in the embayment. The estimated loadings were combined with loadings estimated from different sources (human, wildlife, agriculture, pets, etc.) and input to the watershed model. The watershed model simulated long-term flow and bacterial loading and discharged to a three-dimensional transport model driven by tide, wind, and freshwater discharge. The transport model efficiently simulates the transport and fate of the bacterial concentration in the embayment and is capable of determining the loading reduction needed to improve the water quality condition of the embayment. Combining inverse, watershed, and transport models is a sound approach for simulating bacterial transport correctly in the coastal embayment with complex unknown bacterial sources, which are not solely driven by precipitation.

Keywords: transport modeling; inverse modeling; bacterial loading estimation; traditional watershed modeling

1. Introduction

Fecal pathogens of lakes, rivers, and estuaries are hazardous to public health through water contact recreation, and ingestion of contaminated fish and shellfish. Bacterial levels are elevated in many Virginia waters and hundreds of waterbodies are listed as contaminated bacterially. To provide the basis for States to establish water quality-based pollution control, the development of fecal coliform total maximum daily loads (TMDLs) has been mandated to establish the allowable loading for the pollutant that a waterbody can receive without exceeding water quality standards.

Deterministic models have been widely used to simulate bacterial transport. These models are linked to watershed models that provide bacterial loadings discharged to estuaries and lakes [1–4]. For a relatively small coastal embayment, the tidal prism model has often been used for simulating bacterial transport and fate [3,5,6]. The accuracy of the model simulation depends highly on the correct estimation of daily bacterial loading from the watershed. The watershed models, such as HSPF [7], SWAT [8,9], and LSPC [10], simulate nonpoint source freshwater flow and its associated nonpoint source pollutants. The bacterial loading inputs to the watershed are estimated based on land-use categories and bacterial source distribution including livestock, bio-solids application, wildlife, failing of septic systems, and pets. The advantage of using a watershed model is that it can directly link watershed bacterial sources to the bacterial concentration in the estuaries. It will be extremely useful for understanding the contribution of each bacterial source and to design a management plan to control bacterial loadings. One of the difficulties of using a watershed model is providing bacterial loading to the watershed. These loadings are determined based on the estimation of annual mean results such as wildlife density with consideration of seasonal variation. Because of large variations of watershed land uses and land-use practices, the accurate estimation of bacterial loading is difficult. There are several approaches that have been applied to improve the estimation of bacterial sources based on inverse modeling [11–14]. However, these applications are for estimating an annual mean loading. It is difficult to use them for estimating long-term seasonal and daily loadings. In this study, we propose to use a combined watershed and inverse modeling approach to simulate bacterial loading in the watershed. For those familiar with agricultural bacterial sources, such as bio-solid application and livestock, the watershed model provides a good estimation of sources. For these sources with large variations or unknown sources, such as wildlife and migration birds, the inverse model can be used to estimate seasonal loading and can be used to adjust the bacterial loading for the watershed to improve the watershed model simulations.

The Poquoson River watershed has diversified land uses, including high-density residential, agricultural, and salt marsh land uses, as well as a National Wildlife Refuge. This embayment experiences elevated bacterial concentration due to excess bacterial inputs from stormwater runoff, nonpoint sources, and wash off from marsh areas due to tide and wind-induced set-up and set-down. The bacteria can also grow in the marshes and small tributaries. It is difficult to use a traditional watershed model to simulate bacterial loading, especially in this low-lying marsh area with abundant wildlife, while runoff is not solely driven by precipitation. We combine inverse modeling, watershed modeling (HSPC), and transport modeling (EFDC) to simulate the bacterial transport, which provides a sound approach for simulating bacterial transport correctly in the coastal embayment with complex unknown bacterial sources.

2. Study Area

The Poquoson River watershed is located along the Western Shore of the Chesapeake Bay about 4 km south of the York River mouth (Figure 1). The Poquoson River drains northeast to the main stem of the Bay. The tide range of the embayment is about 0.71 m and mean water depth is about 2 m. A total of 12 segments of the Poquoson River are listed on the 2006 Virginia 305(b)/303(d) Water Quality Assessment Integrated Report [15] as impaired waterbodies due to violations of the State's water quality standards for fecal coliform and enterococcus.

The Poquoson River watershed has diversified land uses, including high densities of residential, agricultural, and salt marshes, as well as a National Wildlife Refuge. The land-use characterization for the entire Poquoson River watershed was based on land cover 2006 data from the NOAA Coastal Change Analysis Program (C-CAP) (http://www.csc.noaa.gov/digitalcoast/data/ccapregional/). Dominant land uses in the watershed were found to be forest (32%), wetlands (31%), and urban and open space (30%), which account for 93% of the total area in the watershed. For the adjacent Back Creek, the dominant land uses are wetland (48%), forest (19%), and urban (16%). A large portion of the watershed is either tidal wetlands or marshes. The surface water runs off from the watershed and discharges to the embayment through stormwater and point sources. The Virginia Division of Health, Department of Shellfish Sanitation (VDH-DSS) is a state agency that has occupied 64 fecal coliform measurement stations (Figure 2) in the Poquoson River during the period 1990–2012. Routine measurements are conducted monthly. Figure 3 shows the annual mean fecal coliform concentration from 1990 to 2012. It can be seen that fecal coliform concentrations varied from year to year. High concentrations often occurred in wet hydrological years of 1998, 1999, and 2004, but not always following the precipitation variation. Monthly bacterial distribution is also shown in Figure 3 for the years 1990–2012.

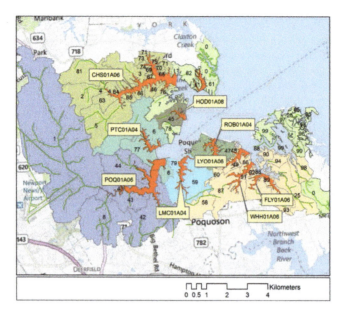

Figure 1. A map of Poquoson River and listed impairment segments (original color).

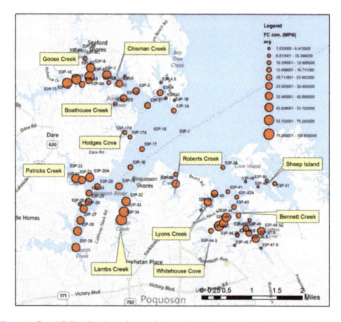

Figure 2. Spatial distribution of mean bacterial concentrations at VDH-DSS stations.

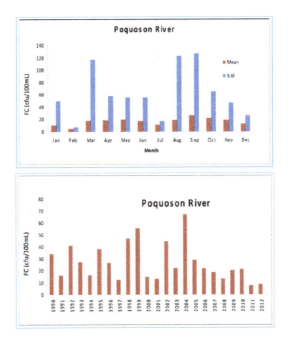

Figure 3. Mean and standard deviation of monthly bacteria distribution (**upper panel**) and annual mean concentration of fecal bacteria (**lower panel**) (1990–2012).

Mean daily high concentrations occur in spring (March to May) and fall (August to November). Large variations occur in March, August, and September. The bacteria can also grow in the marsh and small tributaries and be washed off due to tide and wind-induced set-up and set-down. A distribution of average fecal bacterial concentration is shown in Figure 3. It shows that high concentrations are located in the upstream of the tributaries and concentrations decrease gradually toward the downstream due to tidal flushing and decay.

3. Modeling Approach

3.1. Watershed Model

There are many watershed models that have been used for simulating watershed processes, which include the Hydrologic Simulation Program in FORTRAN (HSPF) [7] and the Soil and Water Assessment Tool (SWART) [8,9]. The watershed model LSPC and hydrodynamics models are used for this study. The LSPC model is a stand-alone, personal computer-based watershed modeling program developed in Microsoft C^{++} [10]. It includes selected HSPF algorithms for simulating hydrology, sediment, and general water quality on land, as well as a simplified stream transport model [7,10,16,17]. Like other watershed models, LSPC is a precipitation-driven model and requires necessary meteorological data as model input. The watershed is segmented into 56 hydrologically connected subwatersheds (Figure 1). The land-use input to the model for characterization for the entire Poquoson River watershed was based on land cover 2006 data from the NOAA Coastal Change Analysis Program (C-CAP) (http://www.csc.noaa.gov/digitalcoast/data/ccapregional/). The classification matches part of the National Land Cover Database (NLCD) with more detailed land use for wetlands. The uniqueness of this land use is that it has more detailed land use for wetlands. For modeling purposes, the land uses are grouped by urban pervious and impervious, forest, cropland, wetland, and open space. The pervious and impervious forms of urban land use are obtained from high and median intensity residential land uses. The model input to drive the model simulation of runoff is hourly precipitation. The nonpoint source simulation uses a traditional buildup and wash-off approach. Pollutants from various sources (livestock, wildlife, septic systems, bio-solids application, stormwater, etc.) accumulate on the land surface and are subject to runoff during rain events. Different land uses are associated with various anthropogenic and natural processes that determine the potential pollutant load [3]. The human impact is estimated based on failure of septic systems, human population and pets, and point sources. The wildlife population is estimated based on statistical values of the wildlife density for different habitats in this region as shown in Table 1. The pollutants that are contributed by interflow and groundwater are also modeled in LSPC for each land use category. Pollutant loadings from surface runoff, interflow, and groundwater outflow are combined to form the final loading output from LSPC.

Table 1. Typical Wildlife Densities and Wildlife Habitat.

Wildlife Type	Population Density	Habitat Requirements
Deer	0.094 animals/acre	Entire watershed, except open water and urban development
Raccoon	0.078 animals/acre	Forest and Wetland within 600 feet of streams and ponds
Raccoon	0.016 animals/acre	Upland Forest
Muskrat	50/mile	Streams and Rivers
Nutria	18.5/mile	Streams and Rivers
Duck/birds	1.53 animals/acre *	Entire Watershed

* 0.77 animals/acre is applied to Plum Tree Island National Wildlife Refuge and 25% of this density is applied to the rest of the Poquoson River watershed based on tidal prism model.

3.2. Three-Dimensional Transport Model

The Environmental Fluid Dynamics Code (EFDC) model is selected to simulate hydrodynamics. EFDC is a general purpose modeling package for simulating 1D, 2D, and 3D flow and transport in surface water systems including: rivers, lakes, estuaries, reservoirs, wetlands, and oceanic coastal regions. It was originally developed at the Virginia Institute of Marine Science for estuarine and coastal applications and is considered public domain software [18,19]. The EFDC model has been integrated into the EPA's TMDL Modeling Toolbox for supporting TMDL development (http://www.epa.gov/athens/wwqtsc/html/hydrodynamic_models.html). The model grid includes 1593 water cells that cover many tributaries and small embayments (Figure 4). Three layers were used in the vertical for this shallow system, which can simulate stratification in this shallow estuary adequately. The model was forced by hourly tide and salinity at the mouth. The inputs are based on a large Chesapeake Bay model simulation [20]. The surface wind is obtained at Gloucester Point. Temperature is not simulated. A constant decay of 1.0 per day was used for the bacterial loss in the stream [13,21–23]. Numerical model calibration of fecal coliform was conducted for the period of 2008–2012. Daily flow and loading from watershed model simulation is discharged to the 3D model to the grid cells adjacent to the watershed or small creeks of the adjacent watershed. For a watershed that connects to more than one 3D model grid cell, the flow and loading are evenly distributed to the 3D model grids. Because the flow from Harwood Mills Reservoir mainly overflows from the spillway and bacterial concentration inside the reservoir meets the water quality standard, it has a minor influence on the downstream. Therefore, the loading from the watershed of Harwood Mills Reservoir was estimated based on the observation flow and mean bacterial concentration of measurements instead of using output from the watershed model. The 3D model is calibrated for surface elevation and salinity. As there are no NOAA tide observations, the model is calibrated to the predicted tide. A constant roughness height of 0.3 cm is used for the model. The timestep for the model simulation is 30 s.

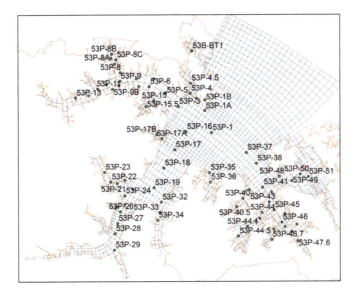

Figure 4. Locations of observation stations and the EFDC numerical model grid.

3.3. Inverse Tidal Prism Model

In order to estimate unknown bacterial sources, we used the tidal prism model approach to estimate loading based on observation. Using monthly observations data, the seasonal variation of unknown sources can be estimated. The tidal prism model has been used for the coastal embayment [5,6]. In the model, the governing mass-balance equation expressed in the change of mass in a model segment over one tidal cycle, Δm, is:

$$\Delta m = [\text{mass in}] - [\text{mass out}] + [\text{sources}] + [\text{kinetics}] \tag{1}$$

where [mass in] and [mass out] account for the mass transport due to the water movement (referred to as "physical transport processes"), [sources] includes point and nonpoint source inputs over one tidal cycle, and [kinetics] represents the biogeochemical kinetic processes (referred to as "kinetic processes"), which may cause an increase or a decrease of a particular substance within a segment of the water body. Without any loss of generality, three-connection segments including a side tributary segment can be illustrated as shown in Figure 5. The mass balance can be written as:

$$\frac{d\left(V_{i,j}C_{i,j}\right)}{dt} = Q_{(i+1,j),(i,j)}C_{i+1,j} - Q_{(i,j),(i+1,j)}C_{i,j} + Q_{(i-1,j),(i,j)}C_{i-1,j} - Q_{(i,j),(i-1,j)}C_{i,j} +$$
$$Q_{(i,j+1),(i,j)}C_{i,j+1} - Q_{(i,j),(i,j+1)}C_{i,j} - k_{ij}VC_{i,j} + L_{i,j} \tag{2}$$

where $C_{i,j}$ is the bacterial concentration at segment (i,j), $Q_{(i,j),(m,n)}$ is the flux from segment (i,j) to segment (m,n), $V_{i,j}$ is the volume, $R_{i,j}$ is the freshwater upstream of segment of segment (i,j) that includes discharge to segment (i,j), and $k_{i,j}$ is the decay rate. $Q_{(i,j),(m,n)}$ can be computed based on the tidal prism method. For example, the flood flux $Q_{(i,j),(i-1,j)}$ is the tidal prism upstream of the segment $(I-1,j)$, which equals $(1-\alpha)T_{i-1,j}$. Where $T_{i-1,j}$ is the tidal prism upstream of the segment (including) of $(I-1,j)$, that is the volume between high tide and low tide in a tidal cycle. α is the return ratio. Since water brought into the basin on flood tide mixes with the water inside, a portion of the pollutant mass in the basin is flushed out on the following ebb tide. A portion of clean water will flood into the estuary during the next flood tide. The returning ratio ranges from 0 to 1, and is used to represent the fraction of water volume that leaves the basin at falling tide and returns at the following rising tide [5,6]. If α exceeds zero, this indicates that a portion equal to $(1 - \alpha)$ of the flood water is clean water from downstream. The ebb tide volume $Q_{(i-1,j),(i,j)} = Q_{(i,j),(i-1,j)} + R_{i-1,j}$ is the inflow during the flood phase of tide plus the revised discharge. For Poquoson, the value $\alpha = 0.45$ was applied [6].

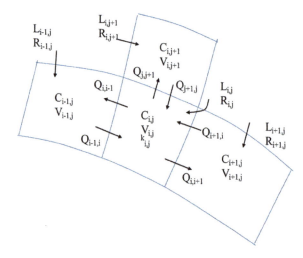

Figure 5. A diagram of tidal model segments.

If we assume that the transport reaches steady state during the measurement period and also assume that all the concentration $C_{i,j}$ and a decay constant are known, the loading $L_{i,j}$ can conveniently be computed from this set of algebraic equations based on Equation (2). The decay rate ranges from 0.7 to 3.0 per day in saltwater [21,22]. A constant decay rate of 1.0/day is used as a conservative approach. The return ratio can be estimated based on the salinity. An average value of 0.4 was applied, which is suitable for Virginia estuaries based on previous study [6]. The segmentation of the tidal prism model is shown in Figure 6. There are 51 segments for the estuary.

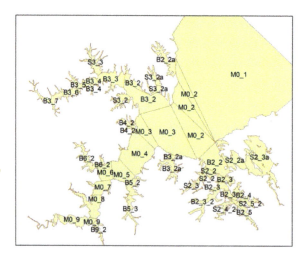

Figure 6. Segmentation and tidal prism model of Poquoson River.

4. Model Results and Discussion

4.1. Watershed Model

The hourly precipitation at Gloucester Point is used to drive the model. The calibration process involved adjustment of the model parameters used to represent the hydrologic processes until acceptable agreement between simulated flows and field measurements was achieved. Since there is no USGS gage or any other continuous flow data available in the Poquoson River watershed, a reference watershed was used for calibration. The USGS Gage 01670000 in Beaverdam Swamp near Ark, VA, located approximately 20 miles north of the Poquoson River watershed, is used to calibrate the model parameters for hydrology simulation. This is the only gauge station in this region. The observation period was from 1980 to 1989. The land uses of forest and wetland and soil types are similar to those of the Poquoson River watershed, but it has less urban land. The USGS flow is used mainly for calibration of non-urban land. The US-EPA conducted a watershed simulation for the tidal water region. The EPA model results are also used for the model calibration as the LSPC and the EPA models are similar watershed models. Figure 7 shows the time series comparison of daily stream flow for years 1985 and 1987 for the watershed of Beaverdam Swamp using USGS data and a selected urban subwatershed in the Poquoson River watershed using EPA data. It can be seen that model results match the EPA model results very well as the precipitation data used for this watershed are similar. Based on this comparison, it can be seen that the LSPC model has reasonably reproduced the observations. The key model parameters for the hydrological simulation are listed in Table 2.

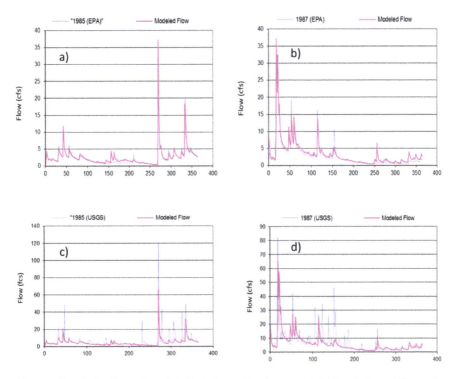

Figure 7. Time Series Comparison of the Daily Stream Flow between Model Simulation and Observed Data from USGS Stream Gage 01670000 in 1985 and 1987 (panels (**a**,**b**) show unit acreage flow, panels (**c**,**d**) show comparisons to USGS gage).

Table 2. Key parameters used for hydrological simulation.

Name	Units	Possible Range *	Calibrated Value	Note
LZSN	in	2.0–15	6.93	lower zone nominal soil moisture storage
INFILT	in/h	0.001–0.50	0.036–0.09	index to the infiltration capacity of the soil
KVARY	1/in	0.85–0.999	1	variable groundwater recession
AGWRC		0.0–0.5	0.97	base groundwater recession
BASETP		0.0–0.2	0.02	fraction of remaining potential e–t that can be satisfied from base flow
INFTW		1.0–10.0	8	interflow inflow parameter
IRC	1/day	0.3–0.85	0.6	nterflow recession parameter
NON-INTERCEPT	in	0.01–0.40	0.058–0.165	interception storage capacity
MON-UZSB	in	0.05–2.0	0.35–0.90	upper zone nominal storage
MON-LZETP		0.1–0.9	0.10–0.60	lower zone evapotranspiration parameter

* http://pubs.usgs.gov/sir/2005/5099/.

4.2. Tidal Prism Model

Because a large portion of the watershed is tidal wetlands and marshes, both migratory birds and local residence birds are dominant. The watershed model is set up based on the estimated annual bird population and seasonal variation. However, accurate population and seasonal variations are unknown. The bacteria can also grow in the wetland and marsh areas. To better simulate the loading, the inverse tidal prism model is applied. The estuary was segmented into 51 tidal segments including tributaries. Monthly observation data are averaged for each segment if more than one observation station were found to be located inside the segment. The linear interpolation of bacteria concentration was obtained for the segment without observations. The decay constant used for the tidal prism model is 1.0 per day. Figure 8 shows a comparison of the model simulation of the inverse tidal prism model and the watershed model for four segments in the tidal marsh area. It can be seen that the watershed model under-predicted the loading by one to two orders of magnitude. The average difference of the watershed model prediction of loading and that of the tidal prism model is shown in Figure 9. Large differences often occurred in the marsh and wetland areas. For some urban land uses, the large differences are due to estimations of stormwater. For example, although we can estimate the pet population, it is difficult to estimate the distribution of pet wastes. With the use of loading estimated by the watershed model, we are able to correct the watershed loading input seasonally. We only use a multi-year seasonal average value to correct the watershed loading. Because wildlife is the dominant source, we compute the ratio of the TP model and watershed model and use the ratio to correct the wildlife for forest, wetland, and marsh land-use areas. For urban land use, the correction ratio is also applied to pets. With the use of corrected loading for the watershed, the watershed model was used to simulate the daily flow and bacterial loading. The computed loading for each watershed is fed to the 3D model.

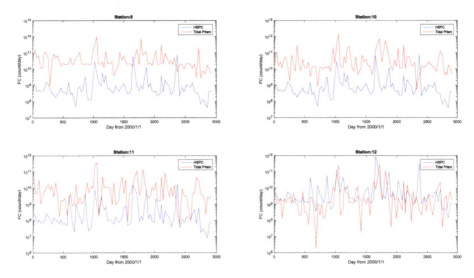

Figure 8. Comparison of bacterial loading simulation between the watershed model and the inverse tidal prism model.

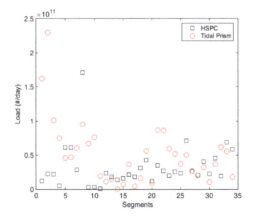

Figure 9. Comparison of model mean loading from 2008 to 2013 between the watershed model (HSPC) and the inverse tidal prism model.

4.3. Simulation of Bacterial Transport

The 3D model simulation is conducted from 2008 to 2012. Model results at four selected stations (one in each major region) are shown in Figures 10 and 11, respectively, for the bacterial concentration at stations located at the upstream of Poquoson River, the tributary of Chisman Creek, the tidal marsh area, and the middle of the Poquoson River. It can be seen that the model simulated the observed data quite well. As bacterial concentrations in the River are highly driven by events, i.e., SSOs and boating activities, as well as the direct access of wildlife, some discrepancies can be expected. In particular, the model can miss some observations of high concentration, as the causes of these events are unknown. Overall, model simulations are satisfactory.

It can be seen that the model simulates well for bacterial variation in the estuary. Because many random events are unknown, the model calibration focuses on matching the general seasonal variation rather than matching individual events. Another method of comparison of the model results and observations is to view the accumulative fecal coliform concentrations at all observation stations to ensure that the 90th percentile concentration is correctly modeled. Figure 12 shows the comparison of the cumulative distributions of modeled and observed concentrations. It can be seen that the model matches observations very well. These results suggest that there is good agreement between observed data and simulated data during the calibration period, indicating that the model has the ability to simulate bacteria in the Poquoson River and can be applied in the development of the TMDL. Bacteria variations over an eight-year period are consistent.

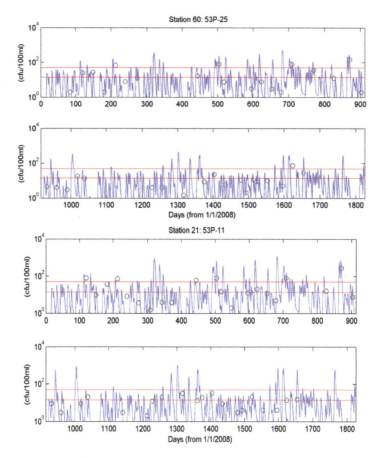

Figure 10. Comparison of model simulation of bacterial concentration and observation for the upstream of Poquoson River and Chisman Creek.

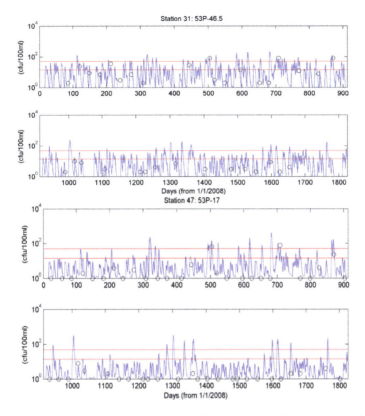

Figure 11. Comparison of model simulation of bacterial concentrations and observations in the tidal marsh area and the middle of the Poquoson River.

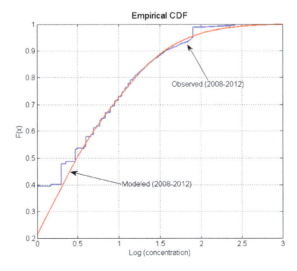

Figure 12. Comparison of cumulative distribution of modeled and observed fecal coliform concentrations at all stations from 2008 to 2012.

5. Conclusions

An approach using a combined watershed model, inverse tidal prism model, and 3D estuary transport model to simulate bacterial concentration in the Poquoson is presented. We introduce the inverse tidal prism model to estimate seasonal bacterial loading. Because the tidal prism model is very efficient in terms of computation, it is feasible to estimate loading, although the spatial resolution is not high enough. The estimated loadings are used to correct the loading input to the watershed model, which is based on the statistical estimation of bacterial loadings for difference bacterial sources, including human, wildlife, agriculture, pets, etc. The watershed model simulates long-term flow and bacterial loading and discharged to a three-dimensional transport model driven by tide, wind, and freshwater discharge. The transport model efficiently simulates the transport and fate of the bacterial concentration in the embayment and is capable of determining the loading reduction needed to improve the water quality condition of the embayment. With the use of inverse modeling, the bacterial loading simulated by the watershed model can be adequately adjusted, which improves both the loading simulation and the 3D model simulation of bacterial transport.

Acknowledgments: The funding of this research project is supported by Virginia Department of Environmental Quality. We thank Daniel Powell of the Department of Health, Division of Shellfish Sanitation (VDH-DSS) and Jennifer Howell of the Department of Environmental Quality, Tidewater Regional Office (DEQ-TRO) for their suggestions.

Author Contributions: Mac Sisson and Jian Shen worked closely on the model development and simulation. Anne Schlegel provided guidance for the TMDL project and approach and reviewed the paper.

Conflicts of Interest: The authors declare no conflict of interest.

References

1. Im, S.; Brannan, K.M.; Mostaghimi, S.; Cho, J. Simulating fecal coliform bacteria loading from an urbanizing watershed. *J. Environ. Sci. Health Part A* **2004**, *39*, 663–679. [CrossRef]
2. Sai, S.; Lung, W.S. Modeling sediment impact on the transport of fecal bacteria. *Water Res.* **2005**, *39*, 5232–5240.
3. Shen, J.; Sun, S.; Wang, T. Development of the fecal coliform total maximum daily load using loading simulation program C++ and tidal prism model in estuary shellfish growing areas: A case study in the Nassawadox Coastal Embayment, Virginia. *J. Environ. Sci. Health Part A* **2005**, *40*, 1791–1807. [CrossRef]
4. Steets, B.M.; Holden, P.A. A mechanistic model of runoff-associated fecal coliform fate and transport through a coastal lagoon. *Water Res.* **2003**, *37*, 589–608. [CrossRef]
5. Kuo, A.Y.; Neilson, B.J. A modified tidal prism model for water quality in small coastal embayments. *Water Sci. Technol.* **1988**, *20*, 133–142.
6. Kuo, A.; Park, K.; Kim, S.; Lin, J. A tidal prism water quality model for small coastal basins. *Coast. Manag.* **2005**, *33*, 101–117. [CrossRef]
7. Bicknell, B.R.; Imhoff, J.C.; Kittle, J.; Donigian, A.S.; Johansen, R.C. *Hydrological Simulation Program—FORTRAN, User's Manual for Release 11*; United States Environmental Protection Agency, Environmental Research Laboratory: Athens, GA, USA, 1996.
8. Arnold, J.G.; Moriasi, D.N.; Gassman, P.W.; Abbaspour, K.C.; White, M.J.; Srinvasan, R.; Santhi, C.; Harmel, R.D.; van Griensven, A.; van Liew, M.W.; et al. SWAT: Model use, calibration, and validation. *Trans. ASABE* **2012**, *55*, 1491–1508. [CrossRef]
9. Neitsch, S.L.; Arnold, J.G.; Kiniry, J.R.; Williams, J.R. *Soil and Water Assessment Tool Theoretical Document*; Grassland, Soil and Water Research Laboratory, Agricultural Research Service: Temple, TX, USA, 2005.
10. Shen, J.; Parker, P.; Riverson, J. A new approach for a windows-based watershed modeling system based on a database-supporting architecture. *Environ. Model. Softw.* **2005**, *20*, 1127–1138. [CrossRef]
11. Shen, J. Optimal estimation of parameters for an estuarine eutrophication model. *Ecol. Model.* **2006**, *191*, 521–537. [CrossRef]
12. Shen, J.; Jia, J.; Sisson, M. Inverse estimation of nonpoint sources of fecal coliform for establishing allowable load for Wye River, Maryland. *Water Res.* **2006**, *40*, 3333–3342. [CrossRef] [PubMed]
13. Shen, J.; Zhao, Y. Combined Bayesian statistics and load duration curve method for bacteria nonpoint source loading estimation. *Water Res.* **2010**, *44*, 77–84. [CrossRef] [PubMed]

14. Shen, J.; Zhao, Y. A Bayesian approach for estimating bacterial nonpoint source loading in an estuary with limited observations. *J. Environ. Sci. Health Part A* **2009**, *44*, 1574–1584. [CrossRef] [PubMed]

15. VA-DEQ (Virginia Department of Environmental Quality). *Total Maximum Daily Load (TMDL) Report for Shellfish Areas Listed due to Bacterial Contamination: Poquoson River and Back Creek*; Virginia Institute of Marine Science: Gloucester Point, VA, USA, 2006.

16. USEPA (United States Environmental Protection Agency). *Total Maximum Daily Load for Pathogens, Flint Creek Watershed*; USEPA: Morgan County, AL, USA, 2001.

17. USEPA (United States Environmental Protection Agency). *Total Maximum Daily Load (TMDL) for Metals, Pathogens and Turbidity in the Hurricane Creek Watershed, Tuscaloosa County, Alabama*; USEPA: Atlanta, GA, USA, 2001.

18. Hamrick, J.M. *A Three-Dimensional Environmental Fluid Dynamics Computer Code: Theoretical and Computational Aspects*; Special Report in Applied Marine Science and Ocean Engineering, No. 317; Virginia Institute of Marine Science (VIMS), the College of William and Mary: Gloucester Point, VA, USA, 1992; p. 63.

19. Hamrick, J.M. Estuarine environmental impact assessment using a three-dimensional circulation and transport model. In Proceedings of the 2nd International Conference on Estuarine and Coastal Modeling, Tampa, FL, USA, 13–15 November 1992; ASCE: New York, NY, USA, 1992; pp. 293–303.

20. Hong, B.; Shen, J. Response of estuarine salinity and transport processes to potential future sea-level rise in the Chesapeake Bay. *Estuar. Coast. Shelf Sci.* **2012**, *104*, 33–45. [CrossRef]

21. Mancini, J.L. Numerical estimates of coliform mortality rates under various conditions. *J. WPCF* **1978**, *50*, 2477–2484.

22. Thomann, R.V.; Mueller, J.A. *Principles of Surface Water Quality Modeling and Control*; Harper and Row: New York, NY, USA, 1987.

23. VA-DGIF (Virginia Department of Game and Inland Fisheries). Available online: http://www.dgif.virginia.gov/wp-content/uploads/virginia_deer-management-plan.pdf (accessed on 13 October 2016).

Journal of
Marine Science and Engineering

Article

Improvements for the Western North Atlantic, Caribbean and Gulf of Mexico ADCIRC Tidal Database (EC2015)

Christine Szpilka [1,*], Kendra Dresback [1], Randall Kolar [1], Jesse Feyen [2] and Jindong Wang [3,4]

[1] School of Civil Engineering and Environmental Science, University of Oklahoma, 202 W. Boyd Room 334, Norman, OK 73019, USA; dresback@ou.edu (K.D.); kolar@ou.edu (R.K.)
[2] NOAA/Great Lakes Environmental Research Laboratory, 4840 South State Road, Ann Arbor, MI 48108, USA; Jesse.Feyen@noaa.gov
[3] NOAA/National Ocean Service/Coast Survey Development Laboratory, 1315 East-West Highway, Silver Spring, MD 20910, USA; jindong.wang@gmail.com
[4] Earth Resources Technology, Inc., 14401 Sweitzer Lane, Suite 300, Laurel, MD 20707, USA
* Correspondence: cmszpilka@ou.edu; Tel.: +1-405-325-5911

Academic Editor: Richard P. Signell
Received: 17 July 2016; Accepted: 1 November 2016; Published: 8 November 2016

Abstract: This research details the development and validation of an updated constituent tidal database for the Western North Atlantic, Caribbean and Gulf of Mexico (WNAT) region, referred to as the EC2015 database. Regional databases, such as EC2015, provide much higher resolution than global databases allowing users to more accurately define the tidal forcing on smaller sub-region domains. The database last underwent major updates in 2001 and was developed using the two-dimensional, depth-integrated form of the coastal hydrodynamic model, ADvanced CIRCulation (ADCIRC), which solves the shallow-water equations in the generalized wave continuity equation form. Six main areas of improvement are examined: (1) placement of the open ocean boundary; (2) higher coastal resolution using Vertical Datum (VDatum) models; (3) updated bathymetry from global databases; (4) updated boundary forcing compared using two global tidal databases; (5) updated bottom friction formulations; and (6) improved model physics by incorporating the advective terms in ADCIRC. The skill of the improved database is compared to that of its predecessor and is calculated using harmonic data from the National Oceanic and Atmospheric Administration Center for Operational Oceanographic Products and Services (NOAA CO-OPS) stations and historic International Hydrographic Organization (IHO) data. Overall, the EC2015 database significantly reduces errors realized in the EC2001 database and improves the quality of coastal tidal constituents available for smaller sub-regional models in the Western North Atlantic, Caribbean and Gulf of Mexico (WNAT) region.

Keywords: tidal constituent database; WNAT region; ADCIRC

---

1. Introduction

Small-scale regional hydrodynamic models are widely used to study many varied physical processes such as sediment transport [1–3]; storm surge inundation [4–6]; real-time surge forecast systems [7–10]; sea level rise [11–14]; passive fish and larval transport, as well as coupled ecological behavior [15–17]; combined hydrologic and hydrodynamic processes [9,18]; passive transport of oil spills [19] and coupled hydrodynamic-marsh interactions with biological feedback [20]. Each of these complex applications requires reliable tidal boundary forcing in order to provide accurate results. In particular, many coastal ocean models utilize tidal databases in order to specify the tidal boundary conditions in these regional studies. When no other data is available, the boundary conditions are often selected from global tidal databases. However, while global tidal databases are highly accurate in the deep ocean, they often lack the resolution over continental shelves and in the shallower near-shore regions to adequately resolve the astronomical and associated nonlinear tides in the immediate coastal regions [21]. Therefore, it is necessary to create smaller-scale tidal databases that are able to resolve the near-shore environment. Over the past 25 years, three such databases have been developed for the eastern coast of the United States [22–24]. These regional databases use the finite element ADvanced CIRCulation model (ADCIRC) forced with a global tidal database at the open ocean boundary to develop the tidal profile within the domain.

Historically, the eastern (and gulf) coast of the United States has been modeled with a large domain that encompasses the entire Western North Atlantic, Gulf of Mexico and Caribbean Sea, herein referred to as the WNAT domain, and has traditionally had the open ocean boundary located at the 60° W meridian [22,25,26]. This larger domain provides easier forcing as the boundary lies mostly in the deeper Atlantic Ocean and includes only a small portion of the continental shelves near the coastline.

The first tidal database for the WNAT region, EC1991, was state of the art for its time and had 19,858 nodes and 36,653 elements with elements ranging from 7 km at the coastline to about 140 km in the deeper ocean. The bathymetry was extracted from the Earth Topography 5 min gridded resolution (ETOPO5) global bathymetric database. The EC1991 database included elevation and velocity harmonics for the O_1, K_1, Q_1, M_2, S_2, N_2 and K_2 constituents [22].

An updated version, EC1995, was created in order to take advantage of the National Ocean Service (NOS) hydrographic survey database for nearshore bathymetry, which has since been digitized [27]. The NOS bathymetric database includes raw sounding tracks from ship surveys and typically covers coastal areas out to the continental shelf in U.S. coastal waters. This updated version had 31,435 nodes and 58,369 elements and a minimum element size of 750 m in Perdido Bay between Alabama and Florida and a maximum element size of 105 km. The average coastal element size was about 5 km with regions of the Florida peninsula and the Gulf Coast west of the Mississippi River typically having 10 km resolution. The EC1995 database included elevation and velocity harmonics for the steady, O_1, K_1, M_2, S_2, N_2, M_4 and M_6 constituents.

The next generation, EC2001, database utilized a grid with 254,565 nodes and 492,179 elements and had a minimum element size of 200 m in the Mississippi River Delta region and a maximum element size of 29 km. The New Orleans area was the most highly resolved with average element sizes of 1 km and some areas of finer 500 m resolution. However, the remainder of the domain had typical coastal element sizes closer to 2–3 km. The original EC2001 database included elevation and velocity harmonics for the O_1, K_1, Q_1, M_2, S_2, N_2 and K_2 constituents [23]. As an intermediate update, a longer run of 410 days with additional P_1 tidal boundary forcing was recomputed in 2008, ec2001_v2e [24], to provide the NOS suite of 37 tidal constituents [28] for both species.

In comparison, the latest version, EC2015, database has 2,066,216 nodes and 3,770,720 elements with a minimum element size of 13 m in the Puerto Rico and Long Island Sound regions (as well as some small Florida channels) and a maximum element size of 46 km near the open boundary. With a few exceptions, the entire WNAT coastline (United States water only) has typical resolutions of 250–500 m with even more detail in inland channels and inlets. As per the 2008 update to the EC2001 database, the EC2015 database provides the computed amplitude and phase of elevation and velocity for the 37 standard NOS tidal constituents. Table 1 summarizes the grid features of the WNAT domain tidal databases.

Table 1. Summary of grid features for Western North Atlantic, Caribbean and Gulf of Mexico (WNAT) domain ADvanced CIRCulation model (ADCIRC) tidal databases.

Database Name	# of Mesh Nodes	# of Mesh Elements	Avg. Coastal Resolution (km)	Min. Coastal Resolution (m)	Max. Deep Ocean Resolution (km)
EC1991	19,858	36,653	7	1000	140
EC1995	31,435	58,369	5	750	105
EC2001	254,565	492,179	1 to 3	200	29
EC2015	2,066,216	3,770,720	0.25 to 0.5	13	46

In the next sections, we present the improvements that have been incorporated into this latest generation tidal database and the remaining challenges. We summarize the development of the EC2015 tidal constituent database; present a skill assessment for global, regional and site specific locations; and discuss how the database can and should be used. Limitations of the database are also discussed. In the interest of brevity, we will only present the skill assessment for these 8 primary constituents: M_2, S_2, N_2, K_2, O_1, K_1, P_1 and Q_1.

2. Materials and Methods

2.1. ADCIRC Computational Model

2.1.1. General Model Details

As mentioned before, the enhancements to this database will employ the ADCIRC regional hydrodynamic model. ADCIRC utilizes the full non-linear St. Venant (shallow water) equations, using the traditional hydrostatic pressure and Boussinesq approximations. The depth-averaged generalized wave continuity equation is used to solve for the free surface elevation, along with the non-conservative form of the momentum equation for the velocity components. The equations are discretized horizontally in space using continuous Galerkin, linear finite elements with equal-order interpolating functions (linear C^0), while time is discretized using an efficient, split-step, Crank-Nicholson algorithm with the nonlinear terms evaluated explicitly. There have been many papers written about the development and usage of the ADCIRC computational model, but basic details for the equations of ADCIRC can be found in [29–31].

One of the advances within ADCIRC since the East Coast database was last updated in 2001 is the addition of Manning's n friction representations. Users are able to specify specific quadratic friction coefficients, Chezy friction coefficients or Manning's n values throughout the domain [32]. For the Manning's n implementation, the n values are converted to an equivalent quadratic friction coefficient within ADCIRC before the bottom stress is calculated [30]. This equivalent quadratic friction coefficient is calculated for each node at every time step as

$$CF(t) = \frac{gn^2}{\sqrt[3]{depth + eta(t)}} \tag{1}$$

where g is the gravitational constant (9.81 m/s^2), n is the Manning's coefficient, *depth* is bathymetric depth (m) and *eta(t)* is the water surface elevation at time t (m). Note that the computed quadratic friction coefficient, $CF(t)$, can also be limited on the lower end by specifying the minimum CF value in the input file. Otherwise, the values can become quite small as the depth becomes large.

2.1.2. Model Input Parameters

Unless otherwise noted in the appropriate methods and results subsections, all of the ADCIRC model runs used the parameters in the following descriptions. The EC2015 tidal database was developed from a 410-day simulation run in order to capture the long-period non-linear tides. A smooth hyperbolic tangent ramp function is applied to both the boundary forcing and the tidal potential forcing functions for the first 25 days. Then the model is allowed to run for another 20 days before the internal ADCIRC harmonic analysis is started for the final 365 days of the simulation. A one-minute interval is used for the internal harmonic decomposition. Tidal potential forcing is applied to the interior of the domain for the O_1, K_1, Q_1 and P_1 diurnal constituents and the M_2, N_2, S_2 and K_2 semidiurnal constituents. In addition to these eight constituents, the open ocean boundary is also forced with the Mm, Mf, M_4, MN_4 and MS_4 constituents. Nodal factors and equilibrium arguments were set for a 410-day run starting on November 17, 1991; this translates to the harmonic analysis occurring over the entire year of 1992, which is the middle of the current National Tidal Datum Epoch from 1983 to 2001. Unless otherwise noted, tidal forcing was extracted from the TPXO7.2 global tidal database [33].

A time-step of 1.0 s was used yielding a maximum Courant number of 0.76 in the U.S. Virgin Islands and of 0.3 along the Atlantic and Gulf coasts. The time weighting factors for the three-level implicit scheme in the GWCE form of the momentum equation are 0.35, 0.30 and 0.35 for the future, present and past time levels respectively. A two-level Crank-Nicholson scheme is used for the momentum equations. The lateral eddy viscosity coefficient was set equal to 5.0 m^2/s and a non-linear quadratic bottom friction scheme with a constant value of 0.0025 was used for all runs except for the variable bottom-friction comparisons. Specific friction settings for the Manning's n formulation and the variable CF runs are detailed in Section 2.2.5 below; for all variable friction tests, a lower limit of 0.0025 was used. A spatially variable but temporally constant GWCE, G or τ_0, parameter was used such that G is dependent upon the local depth and is set as follows: if the depth is ≥ 10, G is set to 0.005, if the depth is <10, G is set to 0.020.

Due to the large overall mesh domain, variable Coriolis forces were enabled. The non-linear finite amplitude option was utilized with wetting and drying enabled. With the newly expanded open ocean boundary, it was possible to enable the advective terms, as detailed in Section 2.2.6 below.

2.2. Improvements for the ADCIRC Tidal Database

The WNAT domain has been improved upon bit by bit over the past 25 years. As technology has progressed in that time, larger computational domains have been possible. Additionally, with advances in remote data collection methods, more accurate and plentiful data is now available for the bathymetric profile of the world's oceans and the location of coastlines. For the latest generation East Coast tidal database, six areas of improvement were examined:

1. Move the open ocean boundary out away from the Lesser Antilles
2. Improve the coastal resolution using the NOAA VDATUM product grids
3. Update the deep water bathymetry
4. Use the latest global tidal database products for forcing on the open ocean boundary
5. Compare three bottom friction schemes for improved accuracy
6. Improve the model physics by enabling the advective terms within ADCIRC

In the following subsections, we detail the methods used for each of these areas. Improvements realized in the harmonic constituent accuracy, as compared with CO-OPS and IHO field measurements, will be presented in the results section.

2.2.1. Open Ocean Boundary Placement

The open ocean boundary has been moved out from the traditional 60° W meridian that has been used for the past 25 years. Figure 1 shows the new extended model domain with the traditional boundary shown in red as a vertical line near the new boundary. The purpose of this expanded domain was to improve model stability by moving the open ocean boundary further away from the complexities of the Lesser Antilles island chain that separates the Caribbean Sea from the Atlantic Ocean. The traditional EC2001 domain becomes unstable near these islands when the quarter-diurnal constituents (M_4, MS_4, and MN_4) are included in the boundary forcing. The EC2001_extended mesh was created at NOAA and has the same coastline and bathymetry in the interior as the EC2001 domain, but with a different boundary location.

There were two guiding principles for choosing this new open ocean boundary location: (1) to avoid any nearby amphidromic regions of the principal tidal constituents—M_2, S_2, N_2, K_1 and O_1; and (2) to create a smooth boundary with gradually changing element size. For elements closer to the coast, the element size was chosen to be smaller and then to gradually increase in size away from the coast. The new boundary curves to the west near Nova Scotia in order to create a smooth transition, without sharp corners, from the ocean boundary to the land boundary. It also prevents the introduction of the Gulf of St. Lawrence into the model domain. One other important design feature was to avoid having too small of elements across shelf breaks, particularly in the southern part of the boundary near the Lesser Antilles.

After a suitable boundary location was found, a one-year fully non-linear tidal simulation was performed to confirm the stability and robustness of the new boundary location. All thirteen of the TPXO7.2 global tidal model constituents were used to force the open boundary (M_2, S_2, N_2, K_2, K_1, O_1, P_1, Q_1, Mf, Mm, M_4, MS_4, and MN_4) during this stability test.

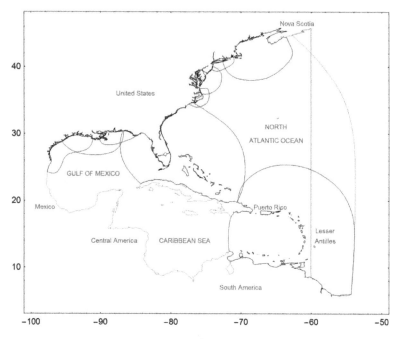

Figure 1. Location of new EC2001_extended model domain (shown in gray) compared to the traditional EC2001 boundary at the 60° W meridian (shown in red—remainder of shoreline is same as gray); and location of the nine VDatum domains (shown in black) used to update the coastal resolution and bathymetry in the EC2015 model. Note that the coarser gray shoreline is not visible underneath the black.

2.2.2. Increased Coastal Resolution

Each of the WNAT predecessors has gradually added more resolution along the coastline as data and computation capabilities were more readily available. However, this version marks a substantially increased level of coastal resolution for such a large study region. Recall from Table 1 that there are nearly 8 times the number of nodes in the EC2015 mesh when compared to the EC2001 mesh.

Over the past 15 plus years, NOAA has undertaken an ambitious study of the United States coastline to create a tool for transformation between different vertical datums. The VDatum (Vertical Datum) tool provides a single source for accurately and easily transforming geospatial data among different tidal, orthometric and ellipsoidal vertical datums along the United States coast. It allows the user to combine data from different horizontal and vertical reference systems into a common system in order to create integrated digital elevation models. The interested reader is referred to the VDatum website for more general information about the VDatum tool and for regional publications [34].

In order to create accurate tidal datum fields for the coastal regions, a series of highly resolved coastal grids were developed for each region of the East and Gulf Coast for the United States, as well as Puerto Rico and the U.S. Virgin Islands. Figure 1 shows the boundaries of the nine VDatum grids that are presently available in the WNAT domain, with the remainder of the EC2001_extended boundary shown to clearly illustrate the regions where VDatum meshes were used. Individual reports [35–43] for each of these domains are available on the VDatum website.

Notice that there are several areas of overlap between these regional VDatum subdomains. For each of these overlaps, the individual grids were carefully pieced together in such a way as to preserve the source grid with the highest coastal resolution. For the shelf regions within these overlaps, a transitional mesh was created at an appropriate distance from the shoreline that smoothly blended the triangulations of the two VDatum meshes. Finally, the bathymetry from the highest resolution source was reapplied onto the new triangulation. This process was repeated for each of the overlapping areas. A comparison of the East Coast of the United States from North Carolina to Maine in the EC2015 model and the previous EC2001 model is shown in Figure 2. Notice the inclusion of more inland channels, rivers and islands; as well as a more detailed shoreline.

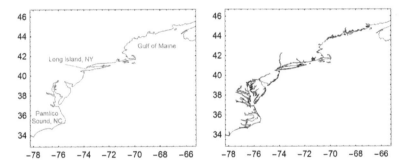

Figure 2. Comparison of coastal resolution in the EC2001 (**left**) and EC2015 (**right**) models from North Carolina to Maine.

It is important to note that the high-resolution meshes created for the VDatum project are in a Model Zero (MZ) vertical datum. The interested reader is referred to the VDatum Standard Operating Procedure manual [44]; but the basic idea is that small corrections are added/subtracted from the original charted bathymetry in an iterative manner until the simulation converges to a solution. The converged solution is verified against harmonic constituent data available within the region. This was necessary since the original bathymetric sources were all in different tidal datums and no tool existed to transform them into a unified vertical datum. The resulting vertical datum of the high resolution coastline is MZ. Although, model zero is not necessarily the same as mean sea level (MSL) due to non-linear dynamic effects, for our purposes, we have to assume that the VDatum coastline is approximately relative to MSL.

The next step was to replace the coastline of the newly created EC2001_extended mesh with this higher resolved coastline. During this step, we also compared localized truncation error analysis

(LTEA) meshes of various resolution for the Florida South Atlantic Bight region as we transitioned from the VDatum coastline into the deeper waters [45]. While exploring the various options, it was discovered that several smaller channels along the Georgia and Carolina coasts had not been included in the original VDatum mesh. We decided not to pursue the LTEA meshing at this time, due to the large grid size and time involved to process the size functions. Instead, any hydrologically significant channels were added using NOAA National Ocean Service (NOS) charts and sounding data. However, because these areas were outside of the original VDatum "wet" area, the proper conversion from the NOS sounding datum (usually MLLW or MLW) to the common MSL datum was estimated from the nearest wet conversion points output from the VDatum tool, typically at the mouth of the channel. In order to extrapolate the conversions up the length of the new channels, the slope of the surrounding channel topography was examined and average slope values (for each stream reach) were used to "march" the sounding datum to MSL conversions upstream from the channel mouth. At points in the channel where the surrounding topographic slope changed, a new reach slope value was used to continue marching upstream.

2.2.3. Updated Global Bathymetry

Once the improved coastline was merged into the EC2001_extended model, the next task was to update the bathymetry of all the non-coastal U.S. waters, which had last been updated in 2001. Two different global bathymetry sources were examined: the ETOPO$_1$ Global Relief Model from the National Geophysical Data Center and the SRTM30_PLUS model from the Scripps Institute of Oceanography.

The ETOPO$_1$ product is a 1 arc-minute global relief model of the Earth's surface. It integrates land topography and ocean bathymetry and was built from numerous regional and global data sets. Older two arc-minute and 5 arc-minute products are still available, although they have been deprecated by the latest model. The horizontal datum of ETOPO$_1$ is WGS84 geographic and the vertical datum is sea level. "More specific vertical datums, such as mean sea level, mean high water, and mean low water, differ by less than the vertical accuracy of ETOPO$_1$ (~10 m at best), and are therefore effectively equivalent" [46]. Various methods are available for obtaining the ETOPO$_1$ product from their website [47].

The SRTM30_PLUS product is a 30 arc-second global relief model of the Earth's surface, also derived from a wide variety of sources. However, rather than only being a compilation of existing bathymetric data sources, it also uses these data sources to modify global satellite bathymetry based on the latest altimeter-derived gravity models [48,49]. Depths are reported in meters and negative values indicate data points that are below sea level. Additionally, catalogs of the data sources and estimated errors in the depth and navigation for each point are available. Various methods of obtaining the data are available at their website [50].

After data was downloaded for each of these sources, the procedure was to create a bounding polygon of all water that was included in the various VDatum regional grids and only update the water that was outside of that polygon, see Figure 1 (all regions that are within the gray boundary but outside of the black boundaries were updated). This meant that most of the Gulf of Mexico and Caribbean coastline, including the southern coast of Cuba, Haiti and Jamaica had to be updated with global sources that were not necessarily meant to be used in shallow coastal regions. We compared both of the global sources and noticed that the ETOPO$_1$ product resulted in a great deal of oscillations in shallower regions (checkerboard type pattern from one point to the next), particularly along the southern coast of Cuba. In comparison, the SRTM30_PLUS product did not suffer as much with this issue, although it did exhibit occasional oscillations in shallower regions. In general, both products were developed for deeper water not coastal areas and the resolution and depth accuracy is not high enough to adequately resolve shallow coastal waters—with average errors in the 10 m range, all depths below 10 m are suspect. Overall, it was decided to use a single source for the updated bathymetry and the SRTM30_PLUS database was used as it exhibited fewer oscillations in the shallower, near-shore regions. However, after interpolation of the global data set, there were nodes within the grid that were suspect—e.g., sharp change in bathymetry relative to surrounding nodes. The bathymetry at these suspect grid nodes was then hand-cleaned by interpolating from surrounding values in the mesh itself instead of directly from the global source. This removed most sharp oscillations along the non-US coastlines between topographic and bathymetric values, however, further inspection may reveal that some errors still exist.

2.2.4. Updated Open Ocean Forcing

Once an updated physical model had been developed for the entire WNAT region, it was necessary to extract tidal forcing information from available global tidal models at the open-ocean boundary. Since the last version of the East Coast ADCIRC tidal database in 2001, significant improvements have been made in the global tidal modeling community as well. Therefore, we compared two different choices for the boundary conditions: the TPXO7.2 model obtained from the Oregon State University Tidal Inversion Software (OTIS) and the Finite Element Solution FES2012 model from the French Tidal Group [33,51].

OTIS implements an efficient representer scheme for the general inversion calculation for tidal processing of TOPEX/Poseidon altimeter data going back to 2002. TPXO7.2 is a more recent version of a global model of ocean tides obtained from OTIS. The solution best fits, in a least-squares sense, the Laplace Tidal Equations and along-track averaged altimetry data [52,53]. TPXO products are updated as more altimetry and bathymetry data becomes available; since the beginning of the EC2001 project, they have since updated to TPXO8, but for consistency we wanted all of the model runs to have the same forcing so we continued to use TPXO7.2. Tides are provided as complex amplitudes of earth-relative sea-surface elevation for 13 constituents at a 1/4 degree resolution for the global ocean; software and accompanying data can be downloaded from their website [33].

Similarly, the French Tidal Group utilizes a global unstructured grid to model the tidal barotropic equations in a spectral configuration and then employs representer data assimilation from long-term satellite altimetry data to correct the tidal signals. FES products are provided on a 1/16 degree resolution for 32 tidal constituents over the global ocean. The most recent version is FES2012, which was produced by Noveltis, Legos and CLS Space Oceanography Division and is distributed by Aviso [51,54].

After extracting the tidal constituent information from each of these databases, a visual comparison was made of the amplitude and phase information that would be used as input into the ADCIRC model. Since the TPXO products only have information for 13 constituents, it was decided to use these same thirteen harmonic constituents to force the ocean boundary (diurnal—O_1 K_1 P_1 Q_1; semi-diurnal—M_2 S_2 N_2 K_2; quarter-diurnal—M_4 MS_4 MN_4; and long term—Mf Mm) in order to maintain a comparable forcing suite. In general, there were very few visual differences between these two models, particularly for the diurnal, semi-diurnal and long term constituents. What differences did exist were typically concentrated at the northern boundary near Nova Scotia (refer to Figure 1 for geographic locations within the WNAT domain). Similarly, among the quarter-diurnal constituents, most of the amplitude differences were focused along the boundary as it approached the coast of Nova Scotia. However, the phasing of the quarter-diurnal constituents was significantly different all along the boundary; note that the amplitudes of these constituents are often on the order of 10^{-3} to 10^{-2} m. Additionally, the phasing of the Q_1 constituent in each of the global products departed rapidly from each other as the boundary neared the Nova Scotia coast. A more quantitative comparison was made by calculating the maximum absolute difference in amplitude and phase over all 187 open ocean boundary nodes; these results are given in Table 2.

Table 2. Maximum absolute differences along the entire EC2015 boundary between the TPXO7.2 and FES2012 global tidal database products.

Constituent	Amplitude (cm)	Phase (Degrees)
O_1	1.28	20.20
K_1	2.26	10.95
P_1	1.25	34.62
Q_1	0.55	122.14
M_2	2.03	1.10
N_2	0.44	6.39
S_2	1.31	7.95
K_2	1.00	10.01
M_4	0.86	34.49
MS_4	0.95	58.66
MN_4	0.11	16.22
Mf	0.21	39.85
Mm	0.06	6.67

While interesting, this was not enough information to determine if one global model was better than the other. In the results section, we will present the actual ADCIRC harmonic differences due to the boundary forcing.

2.2.5. Bottom Friction Assignment

Finally, we examined three variations of the quadratic friction formulation for the EC2015 database: a constant *CF* version and two variable friction formulations. For the variable formulations, we used a merged combination of the *CF* values that had been developed for each of the VDatum regions and we also used the collaborative United States Geological Survey (USGS) usSEABED [55] database of core samples to assign appropriate Manning's *n* friction values.

Of the nine VDatum grids that fall within the EC2015 model domain, five had a variable quadratic bottom friction scheme. It was not necessary to be as rigorous in combining these friction values, as the areas of grid overlap did not have any conflicting friction values. Therefore, each VDatum region was simply mapped onto the EC2015 model and then combined canonically.

The usSEABED database contains three files for each region: "EXT—numeric data extracted from lab-based investigations, PRS—numeric data parsed from word-based data and CLC—numeric data calculated from the application of models or empirical relationship files" [55]. Each of these datasets has limitations and describes the data in different ways; they can be combined to create a more extensive coverage of the seafloor characteristics. For the EC2015 study, we had to limit the richness of the dataset in order to make it tractable for such a large study area. Therefore a relatively simple approach wherein the grain distributions within the "Gravel", "Sand", "Mud" and "Clay" columns of the original usSEABEDS data were aggregated into a single description based upon percentages in each class. This created a verbal distinction only between gravel, sand and silt that did not worry about actual grainsize distributions. Each larger coastal area was then assigned a descriptive designation with an associated shelf Manning's *n* value: muddy/silty: $n = 0.015$, sandy: $n = 0.022$ (upon visual examination, there were no large areas that were entirely gravel, just independent data points so no gravel appropriate Manning's *n* values were assigned in this stage). After a region was classified by bed type, depth-dependent linear interpolation was used to assign Manning's *n* values over each section of the coastal/shelf. For water depths between 5 m and 200 m, the shelf value was assigned; for depths greater than 200 m the post-Ike "deep ocean" value of 0.012 was assigned; finally, for depths less than 5 m, values were linearly interpolated from a value of 0.025 at zero depth to the shelf value at 5 m depth. This slightly larger zero-depth Manning's *n* value is meant to take into account the impeded flow characteristics due to extremely shallow water. After this process was completed, smaller sub-regions were assigned estuary specific "shelf" values and very coarse sub-grids were defined over the sub-regions, then these sub-grids went through the linear depth interpolation process again with these new values. Only a few estuaries were assigned values different than their surrounding shelves. Table 3 provides the rough geographical shelf regions and specific estuaries that were used in this process, as well as the assigned shelf Manning's *n* values.

Table 3. Geographic regions used for Manning's *n* assignment from usSEABEDS data.

Geographic Region	Bed Description	Assigned Shelf Value
Louisiana/Texas	muddy/silty	0.015
Florida	sandy	0.022
Mexico/South America/Caribbean [1]	sandy	0.022
Atlantic Coast	sandy	0.022
Delaware/Chesapeake Bays	silty	0.015
Westernmost New York Sound	silty	0.015

[1] No data was available for these regions, so a general assumption was made.

This is a very simplified approach to assigning friction values given the rich dataset available. However, in the time available for the project, it was impossible to interpolate between each of the usSEABEDS data points and "smooth" the ensuing profile since there could be distances on the order of kilometers from a boulder site that was surrounded by sand. Without knowing the physical extents of the boulders, it is a judgement call how to transition from the one or two boulder indicated grainsizes to the surrounding sand bed. An area of future work would be an efficient interpolation scheme for such a diverse and scattered data set. Depending upon the water depth at an area of interest, it may not be as important as one might think however. If we look again at Equation (1) and note that initially $eta(t) = 0$, then we can compute the equivalent quadratic friction coefficient, as ADCIRC does internally. This allows a visual comparison between the Manning's *n* friction representation and the assigned VDatum friction representation. Figures 3 and 4 show regional views for the Gulf of Maine/New York Sound area and the Mississippi River delta area. For both Figures, panel (a) shows the bathymetric depth profile, panel (b) shows the assigned VDatum quadratic friction coefficients, panel (c) shows the simplified Manning's *n* assignment, and panel (d) shows the computed equivalent quadratic friction coefficient associated with (a) and (c).

Note that in both figures, the scales for panels (b) through (d) are the same. However, owing to the difference in regional bathymetry, the bathymetry scales for panel (a) in each figure are different. For the deeper Atlantic coast region, notice that although there is some variation in the Manning's *n* profile itself, the computed quadratic friction values do not show as much detail due to the overall deep bathymetry. Meanwhile, for the Louisiana region, the bathymetry scale is more abbreviated (from 0 m to 500 m with more detail in the first hundred meters) and there is more detail to the coastal *CF* values due to the shallower nature of that region.

Due to the inherent simplifications in the Manning's *n* assignments, a sensitivity study of the computed harmonic constituents to the assigned Manning's *n* values was conducted. The originally assigned Manning's *n* values were multiplied by factors of 90% and 110% and the resulting harmonic responses were compared. More details of this sensitivity study are given in the results section.

2.2.6. Inclusion of ADCIRC Non-linear Advective Terms

The final effort was to include the non-linear advective terms in the ADCIRC formulation; the interested reader is referred to [56] for details about the development of these terms and equations. In practice, these terms enter in by activating two flags in the input file. In past versions of the East Coast tidal database, the location of the open ocean boundary near the Lesser Antilles island chain caused instabilities if these terms were activated. Therefore, until the boundary was moved as part of this study, it was not possible to include fully non-linear advection and compare how the tidal response varied due to these terms.

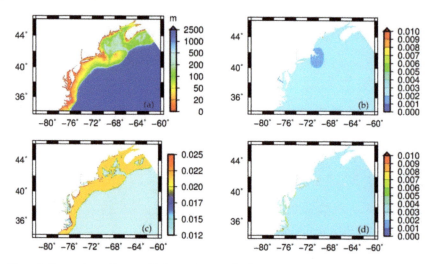

Figure 3. Comparison of bottom friction assignment for the Atlantic coastline from North Carolina to Maine: (**a**) bathymetry—scale from 0 m to 2500 m, (**b**) assigned Vertical Datum (VDatum) friction coefficient (*CF*) values, (**c**) assigned Manning's *n* values and (**d**) computed *CF* values from bathymetry and assigned Manning's *n* values.

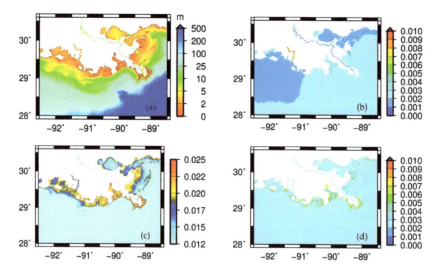

Figure 4. Comparison of bottom friction assignment for the Louisiana coastline: (**a**) bathymetry—scale from 0 m to 500 m, (**b**) assigned VDatum *CF* values, (**c**) assigned Manning's *n* values and (**d**) computed equivalent *CF* values from bathymetry and assigned Manning's *n* values.

2.2.7. Summary of Tidal Database Improvements

Six different areas of improvement have been presented for the EC2015 tidal database. Where possible, each model improvement was isolated to determine the accuracy improvement that was due only to that component of the project. However, the improved coastal resolution and updated bathymetry were lumped into the final EC2015 release and were not studied individually. Table 4 provides a summary of the simulations that were completed for this study; including the run designation, description, mesh domain, inclusion of the advection terms, friction scheme and boundary forcing. For the boundary forcing, the textual label indicates which global tidal database was used and the number indicates how many constituents were used (e.g., TPXO-10 indicates that the TPXO7.2 global database was used with only 10 constituents—recall that the quarter-diurnal constituents create instability in the EC2001 domain for long-term simulations). For clarity, when reporting results, labeling figures and during the discussion, the results will be referred to by their run designation.

Table 4. Summary of model parameters for the model simulations completed in this study.

Run Designation	Description	Grid	Advection	Friction Scheme	Boundary Forcing [1]
EC2001	EC2001 extracted	EC2001	Off	0.0025	TPXO-10
EC2001-ext	EC2001 extended mesh	EC2001_ext	Off	0.0025	TPXO-10
FES1	FES 2012	EC2015	On	0.0025	FES-13
OTIS1	TPXO 7.2	EC2015	On	0.0025	TPXO-13
OTIS3	EC2015 release version	EC2015	On	VDatum	TPXO-13
OTIS3noadv	EC2015 advection off	EC2015	Off	VDatum	TPXO-13
OTIS4	Manning n	EC2015	On	Manning's n	TPXO-13
OTIS5	90% Manning n	EC2015	On	90% Manning	TPXO-13
OTIS6	110% Manning n	EC2015	On	110% Manning	TPXO-13

[1] The textual part of the label indicates which global tidal database was used, while the number indicates how many constituents were included.

The EC2001 tidal database was rerun with the most recent version of ADCIRC to ensure that we could expect a fair comparison with the EC2015 results. Error analysis confirmed that the new version of ADCIRC was recreating the harmonic constituents from the 2008 updated tidal database [23]. In subsequent sections, all reference to the EC2001 model indicate that constituents were directly extracted from the previous version of the database at the same locations as the recent improvements. In order to test the affects due solely to the boundary location, a new input file that mimicked the 2008 update, but used the new expanded boundary, was created; this run designation is given by EC2001-ext. The only difference in the input file is that boundary forcing was extracted from the TPXO7.2 global tidal database at the new boundary node locations.

A series of runs using the final EC2015 model domain (boundary placement, updated bathymetry and improved coastal resolution all lumped together) were conducted; all seven of these used the full thirteen-constituent suite of boundary forcing and six of them include the advective terms. The OTIS1 and FES1 simulations differ only in whether the TPXO7.2 or FES 2012 global tidal databases were used for the boundary conditions; a constant bottom friction was utilized in order to isolate the boundary forcing. Additionally, four variable bottom friction runs were conducted to compare the harmonic response to various friction schemes; OTIS3 used the merged VDatum friction, OTIS4 used the original Manning's n assignments, OTIS5 used the OTIS4 Manning's n values scaled by 90%, and OTIS6 scaled these by 110%. Finally, in order to test the advective terms, the OTIS3noadv simulation mimics the OTIS3 simulation but with the advective terms turned off.

2.3. Validation of the Improved ADCIRC Tidal Database

Two sources of harmonic constituent data were used to validate the new EC2015 tidal database. The analysis techniques used to compute model errors are also discussed in this section.

2.3.1. Validation Data

The Center for Operational Oceanographic Products and Services (CO-OPS) keeps a record of tidal benchmarks and harmonic data at stations throughout the United States [57]. Tidal harmonic data was available at 404 such stations in the EC2015 domain. Additionally, historical data from the International Hydrographic Organization (IHO) was used to provide wider coverage, specifically in the deeper regions beyond the continental shelves [58]. There is a higher measure of uncertainty in the IHO data, as information about the source of the constituents (e.g., length of analysis and data records) is not available; furthermore, the three-decimal digits precision of longitude and latitude coordinates used to locate the stations are sometimes insufficient to determine the physical location of the data collection. At the request of some of the participating countries, the bank was removed from public distribution in about 2002 [59]. Of the about 4190 IHO stations available worldwide, 277 fall within the EC2015 domain. For skill assessment purposes, all 681 stations (404 from CO-OPS and 277 from IHO) were classified by regional location (Atlantic, Gulf of Mexico, Caribbean Sea), as well as coastal proximity versus deep ocean.

The overall locations of the available 681 data stations are shown in Figure 5a; while Figure 5b,c and Figure 6 show zoomed views of the various regions. In all of these figures, the gray boundary depicts the new EC2015 model domain while the green boundary depicts the old EC2001 model domain; the data locations from CO-OPS are shown in blue while IHO data locations are shown in red; data locations shown with a cyan circle surrounding them are not wet in the EC2001 domain and are excluded from any error comparisons that specifically say that only wet stations were used; finally, sample regional scatter plots are provided in Appendix B for the 10 stations that are shown with a black X and indicated by station number.

Of these 681 stations, only 367 were considered wet in the EC2001 model, where by wet we mean that they are either within the domain itself (280) or were near enough to the boundary in the main water bodies that nearest neighbor data extraction (87) was valid. Stations that were far inland or within small channels are not extracted from the EC2001 database as they were not physically represented in the older database. All stations shown in Figures 5 and 6 without a cyan circle denote the location of these 367 stations where harmonics were extracted from the EC2001 database for comparison with the new EC2015 database. Appendix A provides a list of all 681 stations with the CO-OPS station designation (when applicable), lon/lat location, station name and assigned region (Table A1). Station numbers indicated with a single * are close enough to the boundary to use nearest element approximations within the EC2001 model, while those with a double ** are not located within the extents of the EC2001 model and are not used for statistics or station scatter plots when comparing results. Actual longitude and latitude coordinates were not shifted when extracting from the EC2001 database, as the nearest element is most likely where the station would have been manually shifted anyway.

2.3.2. Validation Methods

In order to determine which model best captured the tidal harmonic data at the available data stations, we looked at a variety of error measures. For each station, we examined scatter plots of measured and computed amplitude and phase for the eight primary tidal constituents (M_2, S_2, N_2, K_2, O_1, K_1, P_1 and Q_1). Ideally, the computed and measured values would have a one-to-one correspondence. Scatter plots were also made that included all 681 stations for each of these eight constituents and a least-squares linear regression was computed. Additionally, comparison scatters showing both the EC2001 and EC2015 models for these eight constituents were created using the 367 wet stations in the EC2001 tidal database.

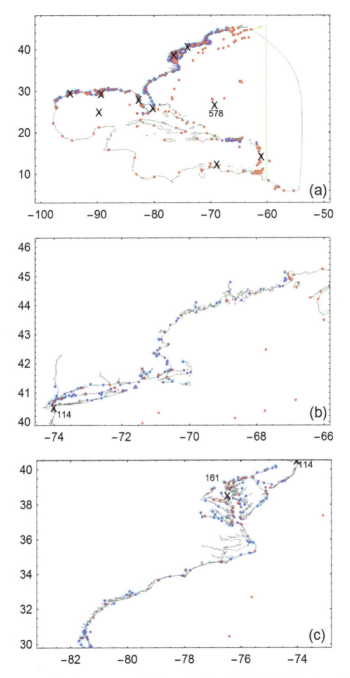

Figure 5. Locations for the stations available for validating the WNAT tidal databases: (a) global; (b) New York and Maine coast; and (c) Delaware down to Georgia. Blue points are from NOAA, red points are from IHO, cyan circles indicate stations that are in EC2015 (gray boundaries) but are not wet in EC2001 (green boundaries). Scatterplots are shown in Appendix B for points shown by an X.

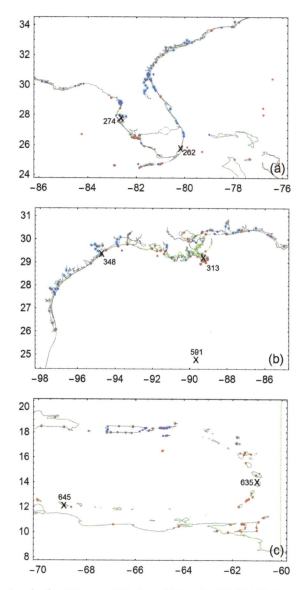

Figure 6. Locations for the stations available for validating the WNAT tidal databases: (a) Florida, (b) Gulf of Mexico and (c) Caribbean Sea. Blue points are from NOAA, red points are from IHO, cyan circles indicate stations that are in EC2015 (gray boundaries) but are not wet in EC2001 (green boundaries). Scatterplots are shown in Appendix B for points shown by an X.

In addition to these qualitative measures, three different error measures were calculated to quantify the skill of each model. For the phase, the mean absolute error was computed as

$$MAE = \frac{1}{8np} \sum_{e=1}^{np} \sum_{k=1}^{8} \left| \text{data}_{e,k} - \text{model}_{e,k} \right| \tag{2}$$

where errors are summed over the number of data points for a particular region (e) as well as the number of constituents (k). To calculate the mean errors for an individual constituent, the second sum would only be computed for $k = 1$ and the 8 is removed from the denominator.

Due to some constituents having very small amplitudes, the mean relative error was computed for amplitudes only as

$$MRE = \frac{1}{8np} \sum_{e=1}^{np} \sum_{k=1}^{8} \frac{|data_{e,k} - model_{e,k}|}{data_{e,k}} \tag{3}$$

where the same summation rules apply. Note that if the errors are on the same order of magnitude as the data, the relative errors will be close to 100%. Additionally, a composite root mean square (RMS) error, combining the phase and amplitude error for each constituent into a single error metric, was calculated at each station as

$$A_E = \sqrt{0.5\left(A_m^2 + A_o^2\right) - A_m A_o \cos\left(\pi\left(h_m - h_o\right)/180\right)} \tag{4}$$

where A_m is the modeled amplitude in meters, A_o is the observed amplitude in meters, h_m is the modeled phase (degrees GMT) and h_o is the observed phase (degrees GMT). As before, the mean errors are calculated by summing over the number of data points for any particular region as well as the number of constituents,

$$MeanRMSE = \frac{1}{8np} \sum_{e=1}^{np} \sum_{k=1}^{8} \left(A_E\right)_{e,k} \tag{5}$$

In order to compare the skill of the new EC2015 model versus the previous EC2001 database, harmonic constituents were extracted from the 2001 database (2008 updated) at the stations that were within (or close enough to) the bounds of the EC2001 model. Mean errors were then computed for both databases at those 367 locations. However, mean errors were also calculated at all 681 stations for the new EC2015 database. Table 5 provides the total number of stations in each region that were used for statistics for each model; parenthetical numbers include only the stations that were physically within the EC2001 domain, not the nearest neighbors.

Table 5. Total number of validation stations available in each region for the most recent East Coast models.

Model	Atlantic Ocean	Deep Stations [2]	Gulf of Mexico	Caribbean	Global
EC2001	204 (151) [1]	31	90 (74)	73 (55)	367 (280)
EC2015	414	31	178	89	681

[1] Numbers in parentheses indicate how many were actually within the EC2001 domain while the first number includes those stations approximated with nearest neighbors. [2] The deep stations are also included in the Atlantic and Gulf of Mexico regional numbers.

3. Results

3.1. Results for the Various Improvements

In this section some of the model improvements are examined independently to determine how effective they are at increasing the tidal constituent accuracy. For brevity, only the regional mean RMS error comparisons are provided here. Full error analysis, as described in Section 2.3.2, will be provided in Section 3.2 when the EC2001 model is compared to the final release EC2015 model. Figure 7 presents the regional mean RMS errors for all nine simulations that were previously presented in Table 4. These mean errors were computed using only the 367 wet stations that are common to all model domains.

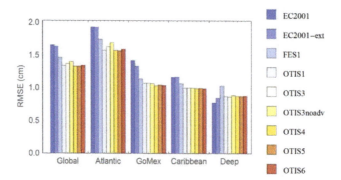

Figure 7. Comparison of regional root mean square (RMS) errors using the 367 wet stations for all nine study simulations summarized in Table 4.

3.1.1. Boundary Placement

As described in Section 2.2.1, the open ocean boundary has been moved out away from the Lesser Antilles Islands and the historical 60° W meridian that has been used for over 25 years. In order to test how much of an affect the new boundary placement has on the extracted harmonic constituents, the new EC2001_extended model was run with an identical input file as was used for the 2008 updates to the EC2001 tidal database, ec2001_v2e, [23]: a larger time step of 5.0 s is possible with these coarser meshes, the non-linear advective terms were turned off and only 10 forcing frequencies were used on the open boundary—the three quarter-diurnal constituents were not used in order to match the EC2001 simulation. All other parameters are as described in Section 2.1.2.

Concentrating only on the EC2001 and EC2001-ext results in Figure 7, we note that simply moving the boundary out away from the Lesser Antilles does not significantly improve the overall accuracy, although it does help the stability of the model. The Atlantic and Caribbean regional errors are unchanged, while the global errors are only slightly reduced. A moderate error reduction is realized in the Gulf of Mexico region and the deep stations actually have slightly higher mean errors.

3.1.2. Comparison of Open Ocean Boundary Forcing

Two different global tidal databases have been examined as input to the EC2015 model: FES12 and TPXO7.2. Looking at the FES1 and OTIS1 bars in Figure 7, we note that for all regions the OTIS1 simulation has less error than the FES1 simulation; these error reductions are most significant in the Atlantic region and deep water stations. Although the differences are rather small, it is obvious that the TPXO global database is providing more accurate results than the FES12 database.

3.1.3. Comparison of Bottom Friction Schemes

In this study, three different bottom friction schemes are compared: constant $CF = 0.0025$, VDatum quadratic friction coefficients and Manning's n formulation with n values estimated using the USGS usSEABEDS data. Due to the simplified assignment of the Manning's n values, sensitivity to the actual Manning's n specification was also examined.

Looking at the mean RMS errors for the OTIS1 through OTIS6 simulations (ignoring OTIS3noadv) in Figure 7, we note that there is actually very little difference in the mean errors for the Gulf of Mexico, Caribbean and Deep stations for any of the five friction simulations. Furthermore, we see that there is also little difference in the three Manning's n simulations (OTIS4 through OTIS6) in any of the regions. This is encouraging as it means that there is very little to no model sensitivity to small perturbations in the Manning's n values. Although a rather simplified approach for assigning these values was used, we should not be too concerned with the approach, assuming that representative values for each region were chosen carefully. Finally, we note that the VDatum friction scheme (OTIS3) has slightly higher mean errors in the Atlantic region.

Examination of the individual constituents indicate that there is very little difference in the mean errors for the various friction simulations. The exception is the M_2 constituent which has slightly higher errors of about 0.3 cm for the OTIS3 simulation than all of the others. If one were to look at scatter plots of individual stations, then more substantial differences could be detected; however, on average, most constituents are insensitive to small changes in the bottom friction. Given the simplifications of the Manning's n assignments and the prior validation of the VDatum CF values during the VDatum model development, for this release (EC2015) we have chosen to implement the VDatum friction values.

3.1.4. Inclusion of Advective Terms

Finally, when examining the OTIS3 and OTIS3noadv error bars, we note that very little difference can be seen between the errors in the Gulf of Mexico and Caribbean regions. However, there are noticeable differences in the Atlantic Ocean and Deep stations, with the OTIS3noadv bars having slightly higher error than their counterpart. From this, we conclude that the addition of the advective terms does reduce the mean errors in the tidal constituent harmonics, particularly in the Atlantic coastal regions. While not shown here, it is noteworthy that these differences are more significant when all 681 stations are used to calculate the mean errors; this is due to the higher percentage of stations in the shallower coastal regions and narrow channels where the advective processes are more dominant.

3.2. Comparison of EC2015 and EC2001

For the EC2015 tidal database release, the VDatum friction formulation and TPXO7.2 boundary forcing with all 13 constituents was used; all other model input parameters are as given above in Section 2.1.2. For results and discussion, when we refer to EC2001 we mean the updated 2008 version [24]. Scatter plots of computed versus measured amplitudes and phases (and their linear best-fit) for the EC2001 and EC2015 databases are shown in Figure 8 for the dominant diurnal and semi-diurnal tidal signals: K_1 and M_2. Additionally, Table 6 provides the best fit statistics for all eight primary constituents at the 367 validation stations that are common to both databases.

Table 6. Summary of best-fit linear statistics for the 367 common validation stations in the EC2001 and EC2015 tidal databases.

				Harmonic Amplitudes					
Model	**Best-fit**	O_1	K_1	P_1	Q_1	M_2	S_2	N_2	K_2
EC2001	Slope	1.082	1.053	0.989	1.065	1.025	0.938	0.916	1.013
	R^2	0.973	0.964	0.956	0.959	0.989	0.959	0.971	0.943
EC2015	Slope	1.054	1.024	1.014	1.106	1.010	0.946	0.911	1.027
	R^2	0.984	0.978	0.964	0.960	0.996	0.975	0.980	0.964
				Harmonic Phases					
Model	**Best-fit**	O_1	K_1	P_1	Q_1	M_2	S_2	N_2	K_2
EC2001	Slope	0.988	0.995	0.981	0.967	0.980	0.959	0.976	0.960
	R^2	0.994	0.995	0.995	0.992	0.972	0.963	0.979	0.946
EC2015	Slope	0.983	0.975	0.988	0.955	0.986	0.951	0.986	0.964
	R^2	0.997	0.997	0.997	0.993	0.984	0.974	0.987	0.962

For a perfect fit of the validation data, both the slope and R^2 values would have a value of unity. Notice that although the slope may not be improved for all eight constituents, the R^2 value is closer to unity for all of them, indicating a tighter distribution. The larger apparent scatter in the diurnal amplitudes is due to their much smaller magnitudes, while the scatter in the semi-diurnal phases resides mostly in the Caribbean and Gulf of Mexico stations where the predominant constituents are diurnal. Additionally, many of the CO-OPS validation stations on Puerto Rico have data records that are significantly less than one year.

Similarly, if we look at scatter plots of individual stations, we can compare how each of the databases performs for that point. Since there are 681 validation stations, only a few representative stations are provided herein. Figures B1–B5 in Appendix B provide plots for the 10 stations that were shown by a black X in Figures 6 and 7; plots are grouped together by region: Atlantic coast, Florida coast, Gulf of Mexico, Caribbean Sea and deep ocean stations. In order to illustrate the station differences due to the friction formulation, results for both the VDatum and Manning's n friction formulations are shown in these plots. Other than the bottom friction itself, all other ADCIRC parameters are the same for these two data sets. First, note that the different friction formulations typically affect the amplitude response of the model more than the phase (with the exception of station 313 at Pilottown, LA and station 645 at Curacao Willemstad). Recall that there are no river boundary conditions in these simulations, they are purely tidally driven. Therefore, stations such as Pilottown, LA that are located on a major river will not exhibit the proper harmonic response as they do not include the effects of riverine flow. Generally, the new EC2015 model is within the 5%–10% error bars for amplitudes and 10°–20° error bars for phase. For stations that are not, such as station 348 at Galveston Bay Entrance, where some constituents are overestimated while others are underestimated, a thorough examination of the nearby bathymetry may be warranted. While every effort was made to use the most recent bathymetry data available by incorporating the VDatum models, for some regions the only available NOS charts can be around 100 years old.

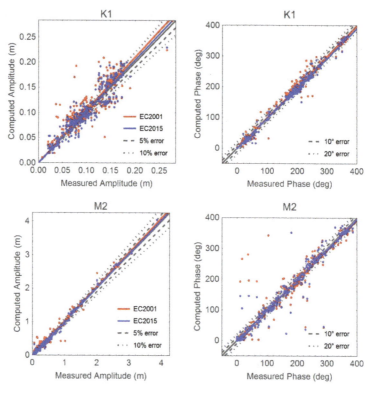

Figure 8. Comparison of scatter plots for the dominant constituents (K_1, M_2) for the EC2001 and EC2015 tidal databases using the 367 common validation data stations.

It is also instructive to see if there are sub-regional patterns in the errors (at the individual water body scale), which can help to guide future efforts at improving the tidal database. Plots of relative amplitude and absolute phase errors for the EC2015 model at each of the 681 stations are provided in Figures C1–C7 in Appendix C for the M_2 and K_1 constituents (same zoom views given in Figures 5 and 6). Plots are only provided for the dominant constituent in the sub regions: Gulf of Maine, Atlantic coast and Florida–M_2 and Gulf of Mexico and Caribbean Sea—K_1. Points shown in blue are underestimating the amplitudes (or exhibit a phase lag), while points shown in red are overestimating (exhibit a phase lead). The symbol shapes indicate to what degree the model is over/under estimating; we would like to see amplitude errors less than 10% and phase errors less than 20°. Several general trends can be gleaned from these plots:

- The M_2 amplitudes in the Gulf of Maine are slightly overestimated (generally less than 5% but a few as high as 20%) while those at the east end of Long Island Sound are overestimated about 10%–20%. Meanwhile stations along the remainder of the Atlantic coast down through Florida are underestimated by 5%–10% on average, with a few isolated stations overestimating. The Chesapeake Bay and Florida Key regions have several stations that are underestimated by more than 10%. For the 681 stations, 309 or roughly 45% of them have relative amplitude errors above the desired 10% threshold; most of these lie within the Gulf Coast and Caribbean regions where the semi-diurnal amplitudes are small and the remaining are fairly evenly distributed throughout the domain.

- The M_2 phases are generally lagged for the entire Atlantic coast and Florida region, with the exception of the Gulf of Maine (which exhibits slight 0%–5% phase leads). The most severe phase lags are often in the upper reaches of the estuaries, embayments and rivers. Of the 404 stations, only 111 (or 16%) have absolute phase errors greater than the desired 20°; most of these lie within the Chesapeake Bay, Gulf Coast and Caribbean regions.

- The amplitudes for the diurnal K_1 constituent are generally overestimated along the Gulf coasts and the Caribbean, although there are a few stations that are underestimated. While many of the Gulf of Mexico stations are outside of the desired 10% range, the majority of the Caribbean Sea stations are below this threshold. A higher number of the 681 stations (57%) fall outside of the desired 10% relative amplitude error range—of these stations, 60% are along the Atlantic coast where the semi-diurnal tides usually dominate and 30% are in the Gulf of Mexico with the remainder in the Caribbean Sea.

- Meanwhile, the phases for the K_1 constituent generally exhibit a phase lag in the Gulf of Mexico and Caribbean Sea basins and are typically more accurate. However, the stations along the northern Texas coast often exhibit phase leads. Only 8% fall outside of the desired 20° error range and two-thirds of those are along the Atlantic coast.

Finally, mean RMS errors for regions are shown in Figure 9, while mean absolute phase errors and mean relative amplitude errors are provided in Table 7. Looking primarily at the 367 validation stations that are common to both databases (blue diamonds for EC2001 and red circles for EC2015), we can draw several general conclusions.

- Globally, the greatest overall RMS improvement is realized in the M2 constituent (1.1 cm reduction). All of the constituents (except Q1) exhibit 2°–4° reductions in mean absolute phase error and 1%–7% reductions in mean relative amplitude errors. Overall, there is a 4% reduction in amplitude errors and about 2° in phase errors.

- For the Atlantic region, RMS error reductions of about 0.3 cm are gained in the O_1, K_1 and N_2 constituents and 1.4 cm for the M_2 constituent. In general, all of the constituents have 2°–3° reductions in mean absolute phase errors. However, the Q_1 and K_2 constituents actually have higher errors in the 2°–3° range. Additionally, with the exception of Q_1 which is roughly unchanged, the diurnal constituents exhibit 1 to 8% reductions in relative amplitude errors while the semi-diurnal have 3%–8% reductions in error.

- For the Gulf of Mexico, the greatest RMS error improvements are in the O_1 and K_1 (0.5 cm), M_2 (1.0 cm) and S_2 (0.3 cm) constituents. Mean absolute phase errors are improved by 1°–3° for the diurnal constituents and 3°–11° for the semi-diurnal (with the exception of S_2 which exhibits little change). Meanwhile, mean relative amplitude errors are reduced by 2%–6% for the diurnal constituents and by 8%–13% for the semi-diurnal (with the exception of Q_1 and M_2 which exhibit error increases of 2%–3%).

- For the Caribbean region, there are minor RMS error improvements of about 0.2 cm in the O_1, K_1 and S_2 constituents and 0.4 cm for M_2 while most of the other constituents are reduced by less than 0.1 cm. Mean absolute phase errors increase by 1°–2° for the diurnal constituents and decrease by 2°–9° for the semi-diurnal constituents. Mean relative amplitude errors decrease by 2%–11% for the diurnal constituents and 2% for M_2; while N_2 and K_2 increase by about 1%. Given these erratic trends, it is instructive to note that the data records used at CO-OPS to generate the harmonic constituent data in the U.S. Virgin Islands and Puerto Rico are often as small as 29 days.

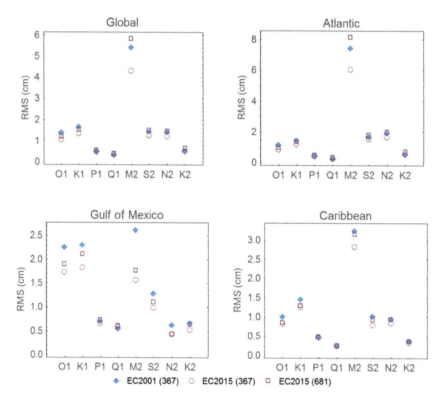

Figure 9. Mean RMS errors (cm) in harmonic constituents for the EC2001 and EC2015 ADCIRC tidal databases for each region of the WNAT model domain.

Table 7. Comparison of mean relative amplitude and mean absolute phase errors by region for each of the eight primary harmonic constituents and summed over all eight constituents for the EC2001 and EC2015 tidal databases: only common 367 wet validation stations used in the summations.

	Mean Relative Amplitude Errors (%)							
Constituent	Entire Domain		Atlantic Ocean		Gulf of Mexico		Caribbean Sea	
	EC2001	EC2015	EC2001	EC2015	EC2001	EC2015	EC2001	EC2015
O_1	18.99	12.12	18.68	10.35	18.11	15.59	20.91	12.74
K_1	19.51	14.02	18.93	12.96	18.42	15.97	22.45	14.56
P_1	18.46	17.27	17.04	16.19	18.25	17.42	22.83	20.23
Q_1	21.79	21.00	19.89	20.34	21.26	24.56	28.86	17.50
M_2	23.39	20.65	13.39	8.50	38.31	39.81	32.95	30.98
S_2	23.77	18.08	17.01	12.76	37.83	24.54	25.33	25.06
N_2	22.57	19.20	14.76	11.97	39.76	31.60	23.66	24.72
K_2	31.40	25.06	20.01	11.78	61.82	54.28	33.73	34.71
All 8	22.40	18.29	17.42	12.98	30.90	27.23	26.16	22.49
	Mean Absolute Phase Errors (deg)							
Constituent	Entire Domain		Atlantic Ocean		Gulf of Mexico		Caribbean Sea	
	EC2001	EC2015	EC2001	EC2015	EC2001	EC2015	EC2001	EC2015
O_1	10.37	8.49	11.02	9.41	9.30	6.53	9.87	8.34
K_1	8.87	7.47	9.21	7.73	8.44	6.27	8.49	8.25
P_1	9.59	7.66	9.52	7.55	8.90	6.71	10.69	9.17
Q_1	13.70	14.22	15.22	17.03	9.85	8.20	14.83	14.58
M_2	15.49	12.19	9.53	7.24	23.53	19.05	22.21	17.55
S_2	16.24	14.35	9.40	8.53	26.62	22.81	22.64	20.27
N_2	17.16	12.98	10.40	7.53	27.45	17.94	23.95	22.72
K_2	19.11	19.57	12.06	15.72	30.19	25.05	29.17	25.67
All 8	13.76	12.00	10.72	9.97	17.72	13.79	17.60	15.65

4. Discussion

Table 8 provides a summary of the global RMS errors for the eight primary constituents, as well as the mean regional errors summed over these constituents, for each of the nine model simulations done as part of this study (statistics computed using only the 367 common validation data points).

Table 8. Summary of RMS errors (cm) for the 367 common validation stations: global means for the eight primary constituents and regional means summed over all eight primary harmonic constituents.

	Mean Global Constituent RMS Errors (cm)							
Run Designation	O_1	K_1	P_1	Q_1	M_2	S_2	N_2	K_2
EC2001	1.411	1.678	0.537	0.354	5.445	1.468	1.440	0.558
EC2001-ext	1.231	1.617	0.574	0.393	5.350	1.488	1.488	0.603
FES1	1.188	1.495	0.684	0.379	4.003	1.878	1.321	0.487
OTIS1	1.109	1.401	0.519	0.377	4.022	1.264	1.282	0.510
OTIS3	1.079	1.381	0.508	0.379	4.330	1.272	1.230	0.545
OTIS3noadv	1.048	1.366	0.504	0.378	4.653	1.266	1.208	0.534
OTIS4	1.108	1.375	0.517	0.373	3.980	1.263	1.282	0.503
OTIS5	1.104	1.382	0.516	0.374	3.972	1.264	1.275	0.506
OTIS6	1.118	1.372	0.521	0.372	4.028	1.264	1.296	0.500
	Mean Regional RMS Errors (cm)				
Run Designation	Global	Atlantic Ocean	Gulf of Mexico	Caribbean Sea	Deep Ocean
EC2001	1.655	1.928	1.419	1.161	0.774
EC2001-ext	1.634	1.925	1.334	1.167	0.848
FES1	1.466	1.744	1.139	1.067	1.035
OTIS1	1.343	1.575	1.076	1.002	0.874
OTIS3	1.374	1.632	1.074	1.001	0.867
OTIS3noadv	1.405	1.691	1.066	1.000	0.888
OTIS4	1.332	1.577	1.035	0.995	0.875
OTIS5	1.331	1.569	1.046	0.999	0.873
OTIS6	1.341	1.593	1.038	0.991	0.878

Notice that the placement of the boundary did not significantly change either the individual constituents (greatest change was a less than 0.2 cm reduction for O_1) or the regional means, where the greatest difference was less than 0.1 cm. Recall from Section 2.2.1 that this improvement was included primarily to increase the model stability for the long-term simulations of 410 days that were necessary for this study. While the slight model improvement is appreciated, it was not expected or required.

Meanwhile, the inclusion of the advective terms did not significantly affect the mean errors either. The largest difference was in the M_2 constituent, which exhibited 0.3 cm reductions of error when the advective terms were included in the simulation, and the largest regional change was for the Atlantic stations (less than 0.05 cm difference). While these are not significant error reductions, it is important to include as much of the model physics as possible. Furthermore, examination of scatter plots for individual stations shows that the inclusion of the advective terms can have significant influence on certain types of stations (rivers, channels, shallower estuaries, etc.) where we would expect the hydrodynamics to be more dominated by advection.

Turning now to the open ocean boundary forcing, we note that the simulation with TPXO 7.2 forcing is on average more accurate than the FES2012 forcing. The most significant difference is for the S_2 constituent, which exhibits 0.6 cm less error when the TPXO 7.2 product is used as the boundary condition, with the only other noticeable improvement being in the P_1 constituent (about 0.15 cm). Regionally, the reductions are about 0.15 cm for the deep and Atlantic stations. Interestingly, neither of these constituents has the highest phase or amplitude errors in Table 2. Visual examination of P_1 amplitudes and phases along the open boundary indicate that the FES2012 product has a considerable phase lag, compared to TPXO 7.2, for this constituent along the entire length and a noticeable departure for the amplitudes near the coast of Nova Scotia. However, there are no significant differences visible for the S_2 constituent. From this we infer that the non-linear interactions between the tides can indeed be very complex. Additionally, this highlights the need for accurate boundary conditions at any modeling level.

Finally, comparison of the various bottom friction schemes indicates that the bottom friction does not noticeably affect the overall statistical errors; there are very few differences across the OTIS1, OTIS3 and OTIS4 through OTIS6 simulations for constituents or regions. The exception to this is that the OTIS3 simulation is about 0.3 cm higher than all of the others for the M_2 constituent, with most of these errors occurring (on average) in the Atlantic region. However, as shown in Appendix B, individual stations can be significantly affected when the bottom friction is varied, from which we infer that overall statistical improvement could be gained by optimizing the friction scheme in each coastal embayment and estuary.

5. Conclusions

The results indicate that most of the reduction in harmonic constituent errors are due to the increased coastal resolution and updated coastal bathymetry. On average, very little overall improvement was realized solely from the bottom friction representation, inclusion of advective terms or new open ocean boundary location. However, these do contribute to the overall stability and robustness of the model, as well as having localized effects on the harmonic accuracy.

To put the errors in context, we also computed the mean RMS error (for all eight primary constituents) between the CO-OPS station data and the IHO data for the 63 stations that were available in both data sets. The mean error for all 63 stations was 0.72 cm, while the minimum and maximum error over all stations were 0.19 cm and 2.94 cm, respectively. On average, one could expect the data itself to be in error by about 0.7 cm at a given station, which is about half of the global RMS errors reported in Table 8. The measured to computed error measures reported throughout the paper include these errors in the data; thus, a significant portion of the reported errors stem from the uncertainty in the data itself.

Future improvements to the WNAT tidal database could include better bottom friction representations in individual water bodies that have not been optimized (e.g., the upper reaches of Chesapeake Bay, marshy areas along the Florida coast and other regions indicated by the figures in Appendix C) and updated bathymetry for inlets and other important conveyances (e.g., Pamlico Sound inlets) as the VDatum models themselves are updated with more recent sounding data.

It is recommended that users of the EC2015 tidal database follow two basic guidelines: (1) choose your regional open ocean boundary location to be well outside of estuaries and bays and (2) make sure that your regional model bathymetry matches the database bathymetry at your boundary. Additionally, while harmonic information is available for 37 constituents, use caution when applying larger suites as only eight have been validated. Further guidelines and limitations are provided in Appendix D for the interested reader. The EC2015 tidal database is available on the ADCIRC website [24].

Acknowledgments: Funding for the project was provided by the National Oceanic and Atmospheric Administration. Additional resources were provided by the University of Oklahoma. The computing for this project was performed at the OU Supercomputing Center for Education & Research (OSCER) at the University of Oklahoma (OU). Any opinions, conclusions, or findings are those of the authors and are not necessarily endorsed by the funding agencies. We also thank the reviewers for their insightful and constructive comments during the review process.

Author Contributions: R.K, K.D. and J.F. conceived the project and decided upon the six areas of improvement; J.W. created and validated the new EC2001_extended model domain and provided VDatum model grids and the most recent approved CO-OPS tidal constituent data; C.S. created the new EC2015 model domain, performed all of the ADCIRC model simulations to test the various improvements and analyzed the model results; K.D. modified the ADCIRC source code to allow internal harmonic analysis for large grids and the full suite of 37 constituents; C.S. wrote the paper.

Conflicts of Interest: The authors declare no conflict of interest. J.F. as a representative of the funding sponsor, was involved in designing the study. The funding sponsors had no role in the analyses or interpretation of data; in the writing of the manuscript, or in the decision to publish the results.

Appendix A

The locations, names and regional classification of all 681 validation stations are given herein; the last 277 stations are marked with IHO in the CO-OPS ID column to indicate that they are from the IHO bank of tidal constituents. Stations marked with a single asterisk are considered "wet" in the EC2001 model even though they are approximated by their nearest neighbor. Meanwhile, those marked with a double asterisk are not included in scatter plots or statistical error metrics for the EC2001 database since they are well outside the domain of the boundary or are in channels and other features that are not represented in the EC2001 model. Abbreviations for the region designations are as follows: Atlantic Ocean—A, Gulf of Mexico—G, Caribbean Sea—C, Deep water—D.

Table A1. Geographic location, name and regional classification for available validation stations.

ID	CO-OPS	Longitude	Latitude	Station Name	Region
1	2695540	−64.70331	32.37339	Bermuda Esso Pier, St. Georges Island	A
2	8410140	−66.98290	44.90460	Eastport, Passamaquoddy Bay	A
3 **	8410714	−67.10840	44.87045	Coffin Point, Coffin Neck	A
4 **	8410715	−67.13000	44.92330	Garnet Point, Hersey Neck	A
5 **	8410834	−67.14375	45.12889	Pettegrove Point, Dochet Island	A
6 **	8410864	−67.15167	44.82333	Gravelly Pt., Whiting Bay	A
7	8411060	−67.20917	44.65637	Cutler Farris Wharf, Little River	A
8	8411250	−67.29670	44.64170	Cutler Naval Base, Machias Bay	A
9 **	8412581	−67.87500	44.54000	Milbridge, Narraguagus River	A
10 **	8413320	−68.20500	44.39170	Bar Harbor, Frenchman Bay	A
11	8413825	−68.43500	44.17000	Mackerel Cove, Swans Island	A
12	8414249	−68.62093	44.19231	Oceanville, Deer Island	A
13 **	8414612	−68.77190	44.78765	Bangor, Penobscot River	A
14	8414721	−68.81330	44.47170	Fort Point, Penobscot River	A
15	8414888	−68.88840	44.16080	Pulpit Harbor, Penobscot Bay	A
16 **	8415490	−69.10170	44.10500	Rockland	A
17 **	8415709	−69.18170	44.07136	Thomaston, St George River	A
18	8417177	−69.78500	43.75500	Hunniwell Point, Kennebec River	A
19 **	8417208	−69.79708	44.08721	Richmond, Kennebec River	A
20 **	8417227	−69.80880	43.92500	Bath, Kennebec River	A
21 **	8418150	−70.24601	43.65608	Portland, Casco Bay	A
22 *	8418445	−70.33330	43.54000	Pine Point, Scarborough River	A
23 *	8418606	−70.38170	43.46170	Camp Ellis, Saco River	A
24 *	8419317	−70.56303	43.31966	Wells, Webhannet River	A
25 **	8419870	−70.74170	43.08000	Seavey Island, Portsmouth Harbor	A
26 **	8423898	−70.71167	43.07179	Fort Point, Newcastle Island	A
27 **	8440273	−70.90800	42.83600	Salisbury Point, Merrimack River	A
28 *	8440452	−70.82000	42.81670	Plum Island, Merrimack River Ent.	A
29 **	8440466	−70.87330	42.81500	Newburyport, Merrimack River	A
30 *	8441551	−70.61507	42.66033	Rockport Harbor	A
31 **	8442645	−70.87649	42.52295	Salem, Salem Harbor	A
32 **	8443187	−70.94330	42.45830	Lynn, Lynn Harbor	A
33 **	8443970	−71.04720	42.35750	Boston, Boston Harbor	A
34	8444162	−70.89170	42.32830	Boston Light, Boston Harbor	A
35 **	8444525	−70.95330	42.28000	Nut Island, Quincy Bay	A
36 **	8444788	−70.96670	42.24830	Shipyard Point, Weymouth Fore River	A
37	8445138	−70.72476	42.20099	Scituate, Scituate Harbor	A
38	8446009	−70.63873	42.08330	Brant Rock, Green Harbor River	A
39 **	8446121	−70.18216	42.04959	Provincetown, Cape Cod	A
40 **	8446166	−70.66789	42.03830	Duxbury, Duxbury Harbor	A
41 *	8446493	−70.66170	41.96000	Plymouth, Plymouth Harbor	A
42 **	8447173	−70.53500	41.77500	Sagamore, Cape Cod Canal	A
43 **	8447191	−70.56170	41.77000	Bournedale, Cape Cod Canal	A
44 *	8447241	−70.15550	41.75600	Sesuit Harbor, East Dennis	A
45 **	8447259	−70.59342	41.74585	Bourne Bridge, Cape Cod Canal	A
46 **	8447270	−70.61670	41.74170	Buzzards Bay, Cape Cod Canal	A
47 **	8447295	−70.62425	41.73500	Gray Gables, Buzzards Bay	A
48	8447368	−70.71500	41.71170	Great Hill	A
49 **	8447386	−71.16550	41.70580	Fall River, Hope Bay	A
50	8447416	−70.71941	41.69578	Piney Point, Wings Cove	A
51 *	8447435	−69.94887	41.68847	Chatham, Lydia Cove	A
52	8447495	−70.05670	41.66478	Saquatucket Harbor	A
53	8447712	−70.89981	41.59292	New Bedford, Clarks Point	A
54	8447842	−70.92830	41.53830	Round Hill Point	A
55	8447930	−70.67170	41.52330	Woods Hole, Buzzards Bay	A
56 **	8448157	−70.59870	41.45830	Vineyard Haven, Vineyard Hvn Hbr	A
57 **	8448558	−70.51150	41.38822	Edgartown, Martha's Vineyard	A

Table A1. *Cont.*

ID	CO-OPS	Longitude	Latitude	Station Name	Region
58 *	8448725	−70.76795	41.35461	Menemsha Harbor	A
59 **	8449130	−70.09438	41.28503	Nantucket Island, Nantucket Sound	A
60 *	8451552	−71.25500	41.63670	Bristol Ferry	A
61	8452660	−71.32670	41.50500	Newport, Narragansett Bay	A
62	8452944	−71.34330	41.71670	Conimicut Light, Narragansett Bay	A
63	8453742	−71.38670	41.49670	West Jamestown	A
64 **	8454000	−71.39978	41.80786	Providence, Providence River	A
65 *	8454049	−71.41100	41.58680	Quonset Point	A
66 **	8454538	−71.44346	41.57384	Wickford, Narragansett Bay	A
67	8455083	−71.49000	41.36330	Point Judith, Harbor Of Refuge	A
68	8458022	−71.76170	41.32830	Weekapaug Point, Block Island Sound	A
69	8459338	−71.55621	41.17404	Block Island Harbor, Old Harbor	A
70	8459479	−71.58000	41.22830	Sandy Point, Block Island Sound	A
71	8459681	−71.61064	41.16330	Block Island, Block Island Sound	A
72 **	8461490	−72.08975	41.36105	New London, Thames River	A
73 **	8463701	−72.53170	41.26830	Clinton, Clinton Harbor	A
74 **	8465705	−72.90830	41.28330	New Haven, New Haven Harbor	A
75 **	8467150	−73.18170	41.17330	Bridgeport, Bridgeport Harbor	A
76 *	8467373	−73.21330	41.15670	Black Rock Harbor, Cedar Creek	A
77 **	8467726	−73.28286	41.13249	Southport, Southport Harbor	A
78	8468799	−73.48000	41.03830	Long Neck Point, Long Island Sound	A
79	8510321	−71.85586	41.07199	Montauk Point Light	A
80 *	8510448	−71.93500	41.07330	Lake Montauk (U.S.C.G.)	A
81 **	8510560	−71.96000	41.04830	Montauk, Fort Pond Bay	A
82	8510719	−72.03191	41.25792	Silver Eel Pond, Fishers Island	A
83 *	8511171	−72.19000	41.03500	Threemile Harbor Entrance	A
84	8511236	−72.20521	41.17125	Plum Island Plum Gut Harbor	A
85	8511671	−72.30670	41.13670	Orient, Orient Harbor	A
86	8512668	−72.56170	41.01500	Mattituck Inlet, Long Island	A
87 **	8512735	−72.58170	40.93470	South Jamesport, Great Peconic	A
88 **	8512769	−72.58667	40.81830	Shinnecock Yacht Club, Penn. Creek	A
89 *	8512987	−72.64500	40.98170	Northville Fuel Dock, Long Island	A
90	8513825	−72.86830	40.73830	Smith Point Bridge, Narrow Bay	A
91 *	8514322	−73.00000	40.74780	Patchogue, Patchogue River	A
92 *	8514422	−73.04330	40.96500	Cedar Beach	A
93 **	8515586	−73.35330	40.90000	Northport, Northport Bay	A
94	8515786	−73.40000	40.95330	Eatons Neck, Huntington Bay	A
95 **	8515921	−73.43170	40.91000	Lloyd Harbor Lighthouse	A
96 **	8516061	−73.47000	40.87330	Cold Springs Harbor	A
97 **	8516299	−73.55000	40.90330	Bayville Bridge, Oyster Bay	A
98 **	8516614	−73.65500	40.86330	Glen Cove Yacht Club, Long Island	A
99 **	8516761	−73.70330	40.83170	Port Washington, Manhassset Bay	A
100 *	8516945	−73.76490	40.81030	Kings Point, Long Island Sound	A
101 **	8516990	−73.78170	40.79330	Willets Point, Little Bay, East River	A
102 **	8517276	−73.85670	40.78330	College Pt, Ft. Of 110Th St	A
103 **	8517847	−73.99517	40.70374	Brooklyn Bridge, East River	A
104	8518091	−73.67170	40.96170	Rye Beach, Amusement Park	A
105 **	8518639	−73.90625	40.80133	Port Morris, East 138Th St.	A
106 **	8518668	−73.94170	40.77670	Horns Hook, E. 90Th St. Hell Gate	A
107 **	8518687	−73.95830	40.75830	Queensboro Bridge, East River	A
108 **	8518699	−73.96956	40.71170	Williamsburg Bridge	A
109 **	8518750	−74.01436	40.70020	The Battery, New York Harbor	A
110 **	8518903	−73.92500	40.87830	Spuyten Duyvil Ck, Ent., Hudson R.	A
111 **	8518905	−73.91670	40.90330	Riverdale, Hudson River	A
112 **	8518924	−73.96330	41.21830	Haverstraw Bay	A
113 **	8519483	−74.14230	40.63980	Bergen Point West, Kill Van Kull	A

Table A1. *Cont.*

ID	CO-OPS	Longitude	Latitude	Station Name	Region
114 *	8531680	−74.00940	40.46690	Sandy Hook	A
115	8534720	−74.41830	39.35500	Atlantic City, Atlantic Ocean	A
116	8534770	−74.47670	39.33500	Ventnor City, Fishing Pier	A
117 *	8534836	−74.53330	39.30830	Longport, Risely Channel	A
118 *	8536110	−74.96000	38.96833	Cape May Canal, Delaware Bay	A
119 *	8536581	−74.89170	39.12830	Bidwell Creek Entrance, Del. Bay	A
120 *	8536931	−75.17500	39.23830	Fortescue Creek	A
121	8537121	−75.37500	39.30500	Ship John Shoal, Delaware River	A
122 **	8538886	−75.04300	40.01194	Tacony-Palmyra Bridge	A
123 **	8539094	−74.86970	40.08170	Burlington, Delaware River	A
124 **	8539487	−74.73670	40.13670	Fieldsboro, Delaware River	A
125 **	8539993	−74.75500	40.18830	Trenton Marine Terminal	A
126 **	8540433	−75.41000	39.81170	Marcus Hook	A
127 **	8545240	−75.14091	39.93333	Philadelphia (U.S.C.G.), Del. River	A
128 **	8545530	−75.13830	39.95330	Philadelphia (Pier 11 North), Del. R	A
129 **	8548989	−74.75170	40.13670	Newbold, Delaware River	A
130 **	8551762	−75.58830	39.58170	Delaware City, Delaware River	A
131 **	8551910	−75.57331	39.55870	Reedy Point, C&D Canal	A
132 *	8554399	−75.40000	39.18500	Mahon River Entrance, Del. Bay	A
133	8555889	−75.11333	38.98667	Brandywine Shoal Light, Del. Bay	A
134 *	8557380	−75.12000	38.78200	Lewes, Ft. Miles	A
135 *	8558690	−75.07000	38.61000	Indian River Inlet	A
136	8570280	−75.08330	38.32670	Ocean City, Fishing Pier	A
137 **	8570283	−75.09167	38.32833	Ocean City Inlet	A
138 **	8570536	−75.18909	38.21516	South Point, Chincoteague Bay	A
139 **	8570649	−75.28500	38.14830	Public Landing, Chincoteague Bay	A
140 **	8571091	−75.86330	37.97670	Crisfield	A
141	8571117	−76.02895	37.99826	Ewell, Smith Island	A
142	8571421	−76.03830	38.22000	Bishops Head, Hoopers Strait	A
143 **	8571559	−76.00500	38.30000	Mccreadys Creek, Fishing Bay	A
144 *	8571579	−76.26500	38.34170	Barren Island, Chesapeake Bay	A
145 **	8571773	−75.81930	38.48396	Vienna, Nanicoke River	A
146 **	8571892	−76.06818	38.57354	Cambridge, Choptank River	A
147 *	8572467	−76.37330	38.83670	Kent Point, Chesapeake Bay	A
148 **	8572669	−75.94500	38.91670	Hillsboro, Tuckahoe Creek	A
149 *	8572770	−76.35500	38.95670	Matapeake	A
150	8572955	−76.30110	39.03170	Love Point Pier, Kent Island	A
151 **	8573349	−75.92500	39.24500	Crumpton, Chester River	A
152 *	8573364	−76.24577	39.21333	Tolchester Beach, Chesapeake Bay	A
153 *	8573704	−76.06330	39.37170	Betterton, Sassafras River	A
154 **	8573903	−75.91670	39.50330	Town Point Wharf	A
155 **	8573927	−75.81000	39.52766	Chesapeake City	A
156 **	8574070	−76.09000	39.53670	Havre De Grace, Chesapeake Bay	A
157 **	8574459	−76.25500	39.38830	Pond Point, Bush River	A
158 **	8574680	−76.57833	39.26667	Baltimore (Fort McHenry)	A
159 **	8574683	−76.58500	39.26170	Fort McHenry Marsh, Patapsco R	A
160 **	8575512	−76.48099	38.98441	U.S. Naval Academy, Severn River	A
161	8577004	−76.47261	38.46579	Long Beach, Chesapeake Bay	A
162 *	8577188	−76.39640	38.39340	Cove Point	A
163 **	8577330	−76.45167	38.31667	Solomons Island, Patuxent River	A
164 **	8579542	−76.68333	38.65500	Lower Marlboro, Patuxent River	A
165 **	8579997	−76.93923	38.93240	Bladensburg, Anacostia River	A
166 **	8594900	−77.02167	38.87333	Washington, Potomac River	A
167 **	8630308	−75.40516	37.90701	Chincoteague Channel, South End	A
168	8632200	−75.98844	37.16519	Kiptopeke, Chesapeake Bay	A
169 *	8632366	−76.02450	37.26330	Cape Charles Harbor (U.S.C.G.)	A
170	8632837	−76.01500	37.53830	Rappahannock Light	A

Table A1. *Cont.*

ID	CO-OPS	Longitude	Latitude	Station Name	Region
171 **	8632869	−75.91670	37.55670	Gaskins Pt., Occohannock Creek	A
172	8633532	−75.99288	37.82926	Tangier Island, Chesapeake Bay	A
173	8635150	−76.96000	38.25170	Colonial Beach, Potomac River	A
174 **	8635257	−77.24297	38.21330	Rappahannock Bend	A
175 **	8635750	−76.46444	37.99590	Lewisetta, Potomac River	A
176 **	8635985	−76.78330	37.87330	Wares Wharf, Rappahannock R	A
177 *	8636580	−76.29000	37.61442	Windmill Point, Rappahannock R	A
178 **	8636653	−76.98996	37.58327	Lester Manor	A
179 *	8637289	−76.27330	37.34670	New Point	A
180	8637590	−76.22170	37.25670	New Point, Comfort Shoal	A
181 **	8637624	−76.50000	37.24670	Gloucester Point, York River	A
182 **	8637689	−76.47833	37.22667	Yorktown U.S.C.G. Training Center	A
183 **	8638339	−76.39911	36.82322	Western Branch	A
184 **	8638421	−76.66830	37.05670	Burwell Bay, James River	A
185 **	8638424	−76.66330	37.22000	Kingsmill, James River	A
186 **	8638433	−76.78330	37.18500	Scotland, James River	A
187 **	8638445	−76.91170	37.40330	Lanexa, Chicahominy River	A
188 **	8638450	−76.94330	37.23988	Tettington, James River	A
189 **	8638489	−77.37338	37.26686	Puddledock, Appomattox River	A
190 **	8638495	−77.42060	37.52451	Richmond River Locks, James River	A
191 *	8638610	−76.33000	36.94667	Sewells Point, Hampton Roads	A
192 **	8638660	−76.29202	36.82168	Norfolk Naval Shipyard	A
193	8638863	−76.11333	36.96667	Chesapeake Bay Bridge Tunnel	A
194	8639207	−75.96984	36.83180	Inside Channel, Rudee Inlet	A
195 **	8639348	−76.30172	36.77804	Money Point, S. Br. Elizabeth River	A
196	8651370	−75.74669	36.18331	Duck, Frf Pier	A
197 **	8652247	−75.76890	35.90370	Manns Harbor, Croatan Sound	A
198 **	8652437	−75.65645	35.84482	Oyster Creek, Croatan Sound	A
199 **	8652547	−75.70000	35.81170	Roanoke Marshes Light, Croatan S	A
200 **	8652587	−75.54936	35.79429	Oregon Inlet Marina, Pamlico S	A
201	8654400	−75.63500	35.22330	Cape Hatteras Fishing Pier	A
202 **	8654467	−75.70417	35.20950	U.S.C.G. Hatteras, Pamlico S	A
203 **	8654792	−75.98945	35.11564	Ocracoke Island	A
204 **	8655875	−76.34330	34.87500	Sea Level, Core Sound	A
205 **	8656483	−76.67000	34.72000	Beaufort, Duke Marine Lab	A
206	8656590	−76.71170	34.69330	Atlantic Beach Triple S Pier	A
207 **	8658120	−77.95330	34.22670	Wilmington, Cape Fear River	A
208	8658163	−77.78566	34.21330	Wrightsville Beach	A
209 **	8659084	−78.01830	33.91500	Southport	A
210	8659182	−78.08170	33.90170	Oak Island, Atlantic Ocean	A
211 *	8659897	−78.50670	33.86500	Sunset Beach Pier, Atlantic Ocean	A
212	8661070	−78.91830	33.65500	Springmaid Pier, Atlantic Ocean	A
213 **	8664022	−79.92138	33.00880	Gen. Dynamics Pier, Cooper R.	A
214 **	8664545	−79.83000	32.92670	Cainhoy, Wando River	A
215 **	8664941	−79.70670	32.85670	South Capers Island, Capers Creek	A
216 **	8665099	−80.02170	32.83670	I-526 Bridge, Ashley River	A
217 **	8665530	−79.92378	32.78170	Charleston, Cooper River Entrance	A
218 **	8667633	−80.78410	32.50250	Clarendon Plantation, Whale Br.	A
219 **	8668498	−80.46500	32.34000	Hunting Island Pier, Fripps Inlet	A
220	8668918	−80.73670	32.26670	Ribaut Island, Skull Creek	A
221 **	8670870	−80.90170	32.03373	Fort Pulaski, Savannah River	A
222 **	8677344	−81.39670	31.13170	St Simons Lighthouse	A
223 **	8679511	−81.51323	30.79781	Kings Bay	A
224 **	8679758	−81.47170	30.76330	Dungeness, Seacamp Dock	A
225 **	8679964	−81.54830	30.72000	St. Marys, St. Marys River	A
226 **	8720011	−81.46500	30.70830	Cut 1N, St Marys River Entr	A
227	8720012	−81.30170	30.71670	Cut 2N, St Marys River Entr	A

Table A1. *Cont.*

ID	CO-OPS	Longitude	Latitude	Station Name	Region
228 **	8720030	−81.46539	30.67171	Fernandina Beach, Amelia River	A
229 **	8720051	−81.52330	30.64330	Lanceford Creek, Lofton	A
230 **	8720098	−81.51500	30.56830	Nassauville, Nassau River East	A
231 **	8720211	−81.41330	30.40000	Mayport (Naval Sta.) St Johns R	A
232 **	8720218	−81.43000	30.39670	Bar Pilots Dock, St Johns River	A
233 **	8720219	−81.55830	30.38670	Dames Point, St. Johns River	A
234 **	8720220	−81.43170	30.39330	Mayport (Ferry) Saint Johns R	A
235 **	8720225	−81.63408	30.38337	Phoenix Park	A
236 **	8720242	−81.62000	30.36000	Longbranch, St Johns River	A
237 *	8720291	−81.38670	30.28330	Jacksonville Beach	A
238 **	8720357	−81.69164	30.19170	I-295 Bridge, West End, St Johns R	A
239 **	8720503	−81.62830	29.97830	Red Bay Point, St Johns River	A
240 **	8720554	−81.30000	29.91670	Vilano Beach (ICWW)	A
241 **	8720582	−81.30670	29.86670	State Road 312, Matanzas River	A
242	8720587	−81.26330	29.85670	St. Augustine Beach, Atlantic	A
243 **	8720625	−81.54832	29.80165	Racy Point, St Johns River	A
244 **	8720651	−81.25830	29.76830	Crescent Beach, Matanzas River	A
245 **	8720692	−81.22786	29.70453	State Road A1A Bridge	A
246 **	8720757	−81.20500	29.61500	Bings Landing, Matanzas River	A
247 **	8720767	−81.68170	29.59500	Buffalo Bluff, St. Johns River	A
248 **	8720774	−81.63170	29.64328	Palatka, St. Johns River	A
249 **	8720832	−81.67520	29.47675	Welaka, St. Johns River	A
250 *	8721020	−81.00500	29.22830	Daytona Beach (Ocean)	A
251 **	8721604	−80.59350	28.41580	Trident Pier, Port Canaveral	A
252 **	8721608	−80.60152	28.40871	Canaveral Harbor Entrance	A
253 **	8722125	−80.37170	27.63170	Vero Beach, Indian River	A
254 **	8722208	−80.32500	27.47170	North Beach Causeway, Indian R	A
255 **	8722548	−80.06670	26.84330	Pga Boulevard Bridge, Palm Beach	A
256 **	8722588	−80.05096	26.77000	Port Of W. Palm Beach, Lake Worth	A
257 **	8722669	−80.04670	26.61330	Lake Worth (ICWW)	A
258	8722670	−80.03330	26.61170	Lake Worth Pier, Atlantic Ocean	A
259 *	8723080	−80.12000	25.90330	Haulover Pier, N. Miami Beach	A
260	8723170	−80.13154	25.76830	Miami Beach (City Pier)	A
261	8723178	−80.13000	25.76330	Miami Beach, Government Cut	A
262	8723214	−80.16180	25.73140	Virginia Key, Biscayne Bay	A
263 *	8723962	−81.01670	24.71830	Key Colony Beach	G
264 *	8723970	−81.10500	24.71170	Vaca Key, Florida Bay	G
265 *	8724580	−81.80790	24.55570	Key West	G
266	8724635	−81.87830	24.45330	Sand Key Lighthouse	G
267	8724671	−81.92153	24.71828	Smith Shoal Light, Fl	G
268	8724698	−82.92000	24.63170	Loggerhead Key, Dry Tortugas	G
269 *	8725110	−81.80750	26.13170	Naples, Gulf Of Mexico	G
270 **	8725520	−81.87120	26.64770	Fort Myers, Caloosahatchee River	G
271	8726347	−82.76000	27.60170	Egmont Key, Tampa Bay	G
272	8726364	−82.72670	27.61500	Mullet Key, Tampa Bay	G
273	8726384	−82.56210	27.63870	Port Manatee, Tampa Bay	G
274	8726520	−82.62690	27.76060	St. Petersburg, Tampa Bay	G
275 *	8726607	−82.55376	27.85778	Port Tampa, Old Tampa Bay	G
276 **	8726667	−82.42500	27.91333	Csx Rockport, Mckay Bay Entrance	G
277	8726724	−82.83170	27.97830	Clearwater Beach, Gulf Of Mexico	G
278 **	8726738	−82.68500	27.98830	Safety Harbor, Old Tampa Bay	G
279 **	8727235	−82.63830	28.69170	Johns Island, Chassahowitzka Bay	G
280 **	8727274	−82.63830	28.76170	Mason Creek, Homosassa Bay	G
281 **	8727277	−82.69540	28.77170	Tuckers Island, Homosassa River	G
282 **	8727293	−82.60330	28.80063	Halls River Bridge, Halls River	G
283 **	8727306	−82.65830	28.82500	Ozello	G
284 **	8727328	−82.66670	28.86330	Ozello North	G

Table A1. *Cont.*

ID	CO-OPS	Longitude	Latitude	Station Name	Region
285	8727333	−82.72330	28.87000	Mangrove Point, Crystal Bay	G
286 **	8727336	−82.63500	28.88170	Dixie Bay	G
287 **	8727348	−82.63829	28.90505	Twin Rivers Marina, Crystal River	G
288 **	8727359	−82.69170	28.92330	Shell Island, Crystal River	G
289	8727520	−83.03170	29.13500	Cedar Key, Gulf Of Mexico	G
290 *	8728229	−84.29000	30.05870	Shell Point, Walker Creek	G
291 *	8728360	−84.51170	29.91500	Turkey Point	G
292 **	8728690	−84.98138	29.72670	Apalachicola, Apalachicola River	G
293 **	8729108	−85.66694	30.15228	Panama City, St. Andrew Bay	G
294	8729210	−85.87830	30.21330	Panama City Beach, Gulf Of Mexico	G
295 **	8729501	−86.49330	30.50330	Valpariso, Boggy Bayou	G
296	8729678	−86.86500	30.37670	Navarre Beach	G
297 **	8729905	−87.35670	30.41860	Millview, Perdido Bay	G
298 **	8729941	−87.42881	30.38694	Blue Angels Park, Perdido Bay	G
299 **	8731439	−87.68428	30.27982	Gulf Shores, Icww	G
300 *	8733821	−87.93453	30.48664	Point Clear, Mobile Bay	G
301	8735180	−88.07500	30.25000	Dauphin Island, Mobile Bay	G
302 **	8735391	−88.08800	30.56517	SH 163 Bridge, Dog River	G
303 **	8737048	−88.04010	30.70830	Mobile State Docks, Mobile River	G
304	8741196	−88.53330	30.34000	Pascagoula Point, Miss. Sound	G
305 *	8742221	−88.66670	30.23830	Horn Island, Mississippi Sound	G
306 **	8743281	−88.79830	30.39170	Ocean Springs	G
307 **	8744117	−88.90330	30.41175	Biloxi, Bay Of Biloxi	G
308	8745557	−89.08170	30.36000	Gulfport Harbor, Mississippi Sound	G
309	8747437	−89.32578	30.32639	Bay Waveland Yacht, Bay St. Louis	G
310	8747766	−89.36670	30.28170	Waveland, Mississippi Sound	G
311	8760417	−89.04447	29.20075	Devon Energy Facility, North Pass	G
312	8760551	−89.14000	28.99000	South Pass	G
313	8760721	−89.25830	29.17830	Pilottown	G
314	8760849	−89.35120	29.27330	Venice, Grand Pass	G
315	8760922	−89.40750	28.93220	Pilot Station East, SW Pass	G
316	8760943	−89.41830	28.92500	Pilot Station, SW Pass	G
317 *	8761305	−89.67325	29.86811	Shell Beach, Lake Borgne	G
318 *	8761529	−89.83500	29.94500	Martello Castle, Lake Borgne	G
319	8761819	−90.03830	29.40170	Texaco Dock, Hackberry Bay	G
320 *	8761927	−90.11342	30.02717	U.S.C.G. New Canal, Lake Pont.	G
321 **	8762075	−90.20860	29.11430	Port Fourchon, Belle Pass	G
322	8763535	−90.97600	29.17390	Texas Gas Platform, Caillou Bay	G
323 **	8764025	−91.23000	29.74330	Stouts Pass At Six Mile Lake	G
324 **	8764044	−91.23750	29.66750	Berwick, Atchafalaya River, La	G
325	8764227	−91.33810	29.45500	Lawma, Amerada Pass	G
326	8764311	−91.38500	29.37170	Eugene Island	G
327	8765251	−91.88000	29.71336	Cypremort Point	G
328 *	8767816	−93.22167	30.22364	Lake Charles, Calcasieu River	G
329	8767961	−93.30069	30.19031	Bulk Terminal #1	G
330	8768094	−93.34289	29.76817	Calcasieu Pass, East Jetty	G
331 **	8770475	−93.93130	29.86670	Port Arthur, Sabine Naches Canal	G
332 **	8770520	−93.88170	29.98000	Rainbow Bridge, Neches River	G
333 **	8770539	−93.89500	29.76670	Mesquite Point	G
334 **	8770559	−94.69040	29.71330	Round Point, Trinity Bay	G
335 **	8770570	−93.87010	29.72840	Sabine Pass North	G
336 **	8770597	−93.72170	30.09830	Orange (Old Navy Base)	G
337 **	8770613	−94.98500	29.68170	Morgans Point, Barbours Cut	G
338 **	8770625	−94.86830	29.68000	Umbrella Point, Trinity Bay	G
339 **	8770733	−95.07830	29.76500	Lynchburg Landing, San Jacinto R	G
340 **	8770743	−95.09000	29.75670	Battleship Texas, Houston Ship Ch	G

Table A1. *Cont.*

ID	CO-OPS	Longitude	Latitude	Station Name	Region
341 **	8770777	−95.26580	29.72580	Manchester, Houston Ship Ch	G
342	8770822	−93.83694	29.67806	Texas Point, Sabine Pass	G
343 **	8770933	−95.06670	29.56330	Clear Lake	G
344 **	8770971	−94.51330	29.51500	Rollover Pass	G
345 **	8771013	−94.91830	29.48000	Eagle Point, Galveston Bay	G
346	8771081	−93.64000	29.49830	Sabine Offshore	G
347 **	8771328	−94.78000	29.36500	Port Bolivar, Bolivar Roads	G
348	8771341	−94.72483	29.35733	Galveston Bay Ent North Jetty	G
349 **	8771450	−94.79330	29.31000	Galveston Pier 21	G
350	8771510	−94.78940	29.28530	Galveston Pleasure Pier, GoMex	G
351 **	8772440	−95.30830	28.94830	Freeport, Dow Barge Canal	G
352 **	8772447	−95.30250	28.94310	U.S.C.G. Freeport, Entr Channel	G
353 **	8773037	−96.71170	28.40800	Seadrift, San Antonio Bay	G
354 **	8773259	−96.59500	28.64000	Port Lavaca, Lavaca Causeway	G
355 **	8773701	−96.38830	28.45170	Port O'Connor, Matagorda Bay	G
356 **	8774513	−97.02170	28.11830	Copano Bay State Fishing Pier	G
357 **	8774770	−97.04670	28.02170	Rockport, Aransas Bay	G
358 **	8775188	−97.47500	27.85830	White Point Bay	G
359 **	8775237	−97.07330	27.83890	Port Aransas	G
360	8775270	−97.05000	27.82670	Port Aransas, H. Caldwell Pier	G
361 **	8775283	−97.20330	27.82130	Port Ingleside, Corpus Christi Bay	G
362 **	8775296	−97.39000	27.81170	Texas State Aquarium, Corpus	G
363 **	8775421	−97.28000	27.70500	Corpus Christi Naval Air Station	G
364 **	8775792	−97.23670	27.63330	Packery Channel	G
365	8775870	−97.21670	27.58000	Corpus Christi, Gulf Of Mexico	G
366 **	8779748	−97.17670	26.07670	South Padre Island (U.S.C.G)	G
367	8779750	−97.15670	26.06830	Padre Island, Brazos Santiago Pass	G
368 **	8779770	−97.21500	26.06000	Port Isabel, Laguna Madre	G
369	9500966	−97.78050	22.26200	Madero, Tampico Harbor, Mexico	G
370	9650593	−87.87000	15.89300	Puerto Cortes	C
371	9710441	−78.99700	26.71000	Settlement Point, Grand Bahamas	C
372	9751309	−64.72100	18.36800	Leinster Point (Bay), St. John	C
373 *	9751364	−64.70500	17.75000	Christiansted, St. Croix Island	C
374 **	9751373	−64.71480	18.34560	St John'S Island, Coral Harbor	C
375 **	9751381	−64.72400	18.31800	Lameshur Bay, St. John	C
376	9751401	−64.75410	17.69500	Lime Tree Bay, St Croix	C
377	9751467	−64.80400	18.36090	Lovango Cay, St John	C
378	9751494	−64.81800	18.29700	Dog Island, St Thomas	C
379 **	9751567	−64.86905	18.31870	Benner Bay	C
380	9751583	−64.86400	18.34870	Water Bay, Saint Thomas	C
381 *	9751584	−64.88400	17.71300	Frederiksted, St. Croix Island	C
382 **	9751639	−64.92030	18.33570	Charlotte Amalie, St. Thomas	C
383 *	9751768	−64.96270	18.37110	Ruy Point, St Thomas	C
384 *	9751774	−65.03500	18.36300	Botany Bay, St Thomas	C
385	9752235	−65.30200	18.30100	Culebra	C
386	9752619	−65.44400	18.15300	Isabel Segunda, Vieques Island	C
387 *	9752695	−65.47100	18.09395	Esperanza, Vieques Island	C
388	9752962	−65.57000	18.34500	Isla Palominos	C
389 *	9753216	−65.63100	18.33500	Playa De Fajardo	C
390 *	9753641	−65.71102	18.18700	Naguabo	C
391 *	9754228	−65.83300	18.05500	Yabucoa Harbor	C
392 **	9755371	−66.11600	18.45900	San Juan, La Puntilla, San Juan Bay	C
393	9755679	−66.15800	17.92800	Las Mareas	C
394 *	9756639	−66.40700	17.95390	Santa Isabel	C
395	9757809	−66.70210	18.48140	Arecibo, Puerto Rico	C
396	9758053	−66.76200	17.97300	Penuelas, Punta Guayanilla	C

Table A1. *Cont.*

ID	CO-OPS	Longitude	Latitude	Station Name	Region
397 **	9759110	−67.04603	17.97000	Magueyes Island	C
398 **	9759189	−67.18900	18.07500	Puerto Real	C
399 **	9759197	−67.19700	17.95100	Bahia Salinas	C
400 *	9759394	−67.16080	18.21790	Mayaguez, Puerto Rico	C
401	9759412	−67.16500	18.45700	Aguadilla, Crashboat Beach	C
402	9759421	−67.18530	18.16500	Punta Guanajabo, Mayagues	C
403	9759938	−67.93900	18.09000	Mona Island	C
404 *	9761115	−61.82100	17.59040	Barbuda	C
405	IHO	−66.05000	45.23330	Partridge Island	A
406	IHO	−67.04999	45.06667	St Andrews	A
407	IHO	−66.86667	45.04583	Back Bay	A
408	IHO	−65.06665	45.05000	Margretsville	A
409	IHO	−67.01711	44.96622	Fairhaven	A
410	IHO	−66.98333	44.90000	Eastport	A
411	IHO	−66.95354	44.88334	Welshpool	A
412	IHO	−62.75896	44.77344	Murphy Cove	A
413 **	IHO	−66.75010	44.76557	North Head	A
414	IHO	−65.83334	44.66667	Deep Cove	A
415	IHO	−63.56712	44.64378	Halifax	A
416	IHO	−66.79999	44.60000	Outer Wood Island	A
417	IHO	−63.95001	44.49900	Indian Harbour	A
418 **	IHO	−66.10001	44.46390	Sandy Cove	A
419 **	IHO	−68.20001	44.40000	Bar Harbour	A
420	IHO	−68.01666	44.40000	Prospect Harbour	A
421	IHO	−66.39999	44.25000	Lighthouse Cove	A
422	IHO	−66.16666	44.20000	Meteghan	A
423	IHO	−68.88333	44.14642	Pulpit Harbour	A
424	IHO	−64.66210	43.98320	Liverpool	A
425	IHO	−65.10420	43.66480	Lockeport	A
426 **	IHO	−70.24667	43.65667	Portland	A
427	IHO	−65.74290	43.52580	Woods Harbour	A
428	IHO	−66.00000	43.50000	Flat Island	A
429	IHO	−66.00000	43.48333	Seal Island	A
430 **	IHO	−70.74167	43.08000	Portsmouth (Navy Yard)	A
431	IHO	−63.20001	42.81667	Fundy 1	A/D
432	IHO	−63.98334	42.78333	SB2	A/D
433	IHO	−64.36667	42.61666	Fundy 21	A/D
434	IHO	−67.71667	42.46667	Fundy 6	A/D
435 **	IHO	−71.03326	42.35078	Boston (Commonwealth Piers)	A
436	IHO	−65.50000	42.11666	Fundy 22a	A/D
437	IHO	−65.63333	42.05000	Fundy 22b	A/D
438 **	IHO	−71.39694	41.80080	Providence	A
439 *	IHO	−70.50000	41.77482	E Cape Cod Canal	A
440 **	IHO	−70.61667	41.74072	WCape Cod Canal	A
441 **	IHO	−70.62512	41.73333	Buzzards Bay	A
442	IHO	−65.79999	41.73333	Fundy 3	A/D
443 *	IHO	−70.89999	41.60000	New Bedford	A
444	IHO	−71.33334	41.50000	Newport	A
445	IHO	−70.67143	41.52422	Woods Hole (Ocean Inst)	A
446 **	IHO	−72.09900	41.34903	New London	A
447	IHO	−72.35001	41.26667	Connecticut River Ent	A
448 *	IHO	−73.16666	41.16667	Bridgeport	A
449	IHO	−72.20001	41.16521	Plum Island	A
450 *	IHO	−71.96667	41.05000	montauk	A
451 **	IHO	−73.06728	40.95027	Port Jefferson	A
452 *	IHO	−73.78333	40.80000	Willets Point	A
453 **	IHO	−73.85006	40.78285	College Point	A

Table A1. *Cont.*

ID	CO-OPS	Longitude	Latitude	Station Name	Region
454	IHO	−66.83334	40.73333	Fundy 4	A/D
455 **	IHO	−73.23280	40.71533	Bayshore Long Island	A
456 **	IHO	−74.01666	40.70000	New York: Battery	A
457 **	IHO	−74.01666	40.68333	New York: Governor's Island	A
458	IHO	−74.03333	40.60000	New York: Fort Hamilton	A
459	IHO	−74.01666	40.46833	Sandy Hook	A
460	IHO	−67.75000	40.36666	Fundy 23	A/D
461	IHO	−70.89999	40.30000	IAPSO: 30-1.2.32	A/D
462	IHO	−68.63333	40.11667	IAPSO: 30-1.2.1	A/D
463 **	IHO	−75.13333	39.95000	Philadelphia	A
464	IHO	−71.38333	39.95000	IAPSO: 30-1.2.2	A/D
465 **	IHO	−75.58334	39.58333	Delaware City	A
466 **	IHO	−75.56665	39.55000	Reedy Point	A
467 **	IHO	−75.81665	39.53140	Chesapeake City	A
468 **	IHO	−75.88333	39.51667	Court House Point	A
469 **	IHO	−75.98419	39.43576	Elk River Entrance	A
470	IHO	−76.26666	39.28333	Pooles Island Light	A
471 **	IHO	−76.58070	39.26940	Baltimore	A
472	IHO	−72.16666	39.21667	IAPSO: 30-1.2.17	A/D
473	IHO	−71.36667	39.16667	IAPSO: 30-1.2.19	A/D
474	IHO	−76.41666	39.15000	Seven Foot Knoll Light	A
475	IHO	−76.30221	39.04201	Love Point Light	A
476 **	IHO	−76.48191	38.98550	Annapolis	A
477 *	IHO	−74.96000	38.96833	Cape May Ferry Terminal	A
478	IHO	−76.43335	38.90000	Thomas Point Shoal Light	A
479 **	IHO	−77.01725	38.86094	Washington D.C.	A
480 **	IHO	−75.10220	38.78790	Breakwater Harbour	A
481 **	IHO	−75.07045	38.60092	Indian River Inlet	A
482 **	IHO	−76.06341	38.57254	Cambridge	A
483 **	IHO	−76.45001	38.31667	Solomons Island	A
484 **	IHO	−76.41666	38.31667	Drum Point Light	A
485	IHO	−76.95001	38.25000	Colonial Beach	A
486	IHO	−76.75000	38.21667	Colton Point	A
487	IHO	−76.53333	38.13334	Piney Point	A
488	IHO	−76.10001	38.06667	Holland Island Bar Light	A
489	IHO	−76.26666	37.80000	Great Wicomico Light	A
490	IHO	−76.26666	37.56667	Stingray Point Light	A
491	IHO	−73.08334	37.36666	IAPSO: 30-1.2.16	A/D
492 **	IHO	−77.26666	37.31667	City Point Hopewell	A
493 **	IHO	−76.02449	37.26667	Cape Charles	A
494 **	IHO	−76.49882	37.24811	Gloucester Point	A
495	IHO	−76.29999	37.00000	Old Point Comfort	A
496 **	IHO	−76.33334	36.95000	Hampton Roads (Sewall Pt.)	A
497	IHO	−75.96667	36.83333	Virginia Beach	A
498	IHO	−75.50000	35.33333	Avon	A
499 *	IHO	−76.68335	34.71667	Morehead City	A
500 **	IHO	−77.95001	34.23333	Wilmington	A
501 *	IHO	−78.01667	33.91500	Southport	A
502	IHO	−78.89999	33.66667	Myrtle Beach	A
503 **	IHO	−79.91666	32.78333	Charleston	A
504	IHO	−75.61667	32.68333	IAPSO: 30-1.2.3	A/D
505	IHO	−64.64999	32.36666	St. Davids Island	A
506 **	IHO	−80.78279	32.31757	Port Royal Sound	A
507	IHO	−64.83334	32.31667	Ireland Island	A
508 **	IHO	−80.89995	32.03360	Savannah River Entrance	A
509	IHO	−64.43335	32.01667	IAPSO: 30-1.2.18	A/D
510 **	IHO	−81.20050	31.53659	Sapelo Sound	A

Table A1. *Cont.*

ID	CO-OPS	Longitude	Latitude	Station Name	Region
511 **	IHO	−88.04010	30.70830	Mobile	G
512	IHO	−76.41666	30.43333	IAPSO: 30-1.2.11	A/D
513 **	IHO	−88.90330	30.41175	Biloxi	G
514 **	IHO	−87.21667	30.40000	Pensacola	G
515 *	IHO	−81.43259	30.39928	Mayport	A
516 **	IHO	−87.26428	30.34872	Warrington Navy Yard	G
517 **	IHO	−81.61667	30.35000	Jacksonville Dredger Dept.	A
518	IHO	−90.29999	30.29805	Pass Nanchac Light	G
519	IHO	−89.33334	30.30000	Bay St Louis	G
520	IHO	−89.16666	30.23333	Cat Island	G
521 **	IHO	−88.01666	30.23333	Mobile Point Light	G
522 **	IHO	−85.74736	30.16939	Alligator Bayou	G
523	IHO	−84.18335	30.06667	St Marks Light	G
524	IHO	−90.11667	30.02376	West End	G
525 **	IHO	−90.06803	29.91999	New Orleans	G
526	IHO	−93.34736	29.78333	Calcasieu Pass Light	G
527 **	IHO	−94.69040	29.71333	Round Point	G
528	IHO	−84.98334	29.71667	Apalachicola	G
529	IHO	−93.85001	29.70000	Sabine	G
530 **	IHO	−94.98334	29.68333	Morgan Point	G
531 *	IHO	−94.49038	29.51828	Gilchrist	G
532	IHO	−92.03492	29.57862	Lighthouse Point	G
533 **	IHO	−91.54999	29.51667	Point Chevreuil	G
534	IHO	−91.76710	29.48820	South Point	G
535	IHO	−89.16666	29.48333	Breton Island	G
536 **	IHO	−91.27077	29.51204	Shell Island	G
537	IHO	−91.59734	29.50966	Rabbit Island Pass	G
538	IHO	−91.38500	29.37170	Eugene Island	G
539 **	IHO	−89.33334	29.36667	Jack Bay	G
540	IHO	−94.70001	29.33333	Galveston Bay Entrance	G
541	IHO	−91.75000	29.28667	Point au Fer	G
542 **	IHO	−94.78333	29.31667	Galveston	G
543 **	IHO	−89.96667	29.26667	Bayou Rigaud	G
544	IHO	−89.60001	29.25000	Empire Jetty	G
545	IHO	−81.00000	29.23333	Daytona Beach	A
546 **	IHO	−95.00000	29.21667	Carancahua Reef	G
547	IHO	−89.04999	29.21667	Lonesome Bayou	G
548 **	IHO	−81.00000	29.21667	Daytona Beach	A
549	IHO	−83.03167	29.13333	Cedar Kay	G
550	IHO	−89.03333	29.11667	Southeast Pass	G
551	IHO	−89.26666	29.05000	Joseph Bayou	G
552	IHO	−89.16666	29.01667	Port Eads	G
553	IHO	−89.13333	28.98333	South Pass	G
554	IHO	−95.29999	28.93333	Freeport	G
555	IHO	−89.42833	28.93167	Southwest Pass	G
556 *	IHO	−82.66874	28.45132	Indian Bay	G
557	IHO	−76.79999	28.45000	IAPSO: 30-1.2.15	A/D
558	IHO	−67.53333	28.23333	IAPSO: 30-1.2.5	A/D
559	IHO	−69.75000	28.13333	IAPSO: 30-1.2.4	A/D
560 **	IHO	−97.04999	28.01667	Rockport	G
561	IHO	−76.78333	28.01667	IAPSO: 30-1.2.14	A/D
562	IHO	−69.66666	27.98333	IAPSO: 30-1.2.8	A/D
563	IHO	−69.66666	27.96667	IAPSO: 30-1.2.7	A/D
564 **	IHO	−97.39999	27.81493	Nueces Bay	G
565	IHO	−82.61667	27.76667	St Petersburg	G
566 *	IHO	−82.73295	27.53391	Anna Maria	G
567 **	IHO	−82.25000	26.71667	South Boca Grande	G
568	IHO	−84.25000	26.70000	IAPSO: 30-1.2.13	G/D

Table A1. *Cont.*

ID	CO-OPS	Longitude	Latitude	Station Name	Region
569 **	IHO	−81.86667	26.65000	Fort Myers	G
570 **	IHO	−82.06665	26.63333	Matlacha Pass	G
571 **	IHO	−82.08081	26.55000	Tropical Homesites	G
572 **	IHO	−82.18335	26.51667	Captiva Island	G
573 **	IHO	−82.08334	26.48333	St James City	G
574 **	IHO	−82.01666	26.48333	Punta Rassa	G
575	IHO	−69.33334	26.46667	IAPSO: 30-1.2.13	A/D
576 **	IHO	−81.95001	26.45511	Matanzas Pass	G
577 **	IHO	−81.93335	26.45000	Hurricane Bay San Carlos	G
578	IHO	−69.31665	26.45000	IAPSO: 30-1.2.9	A/D
579 **	IHO	−81.90951	26.43333	Estero Island Estero Bay	G
580 **	IHO	−81.85938	26.43120	Mound Key Estero Bay	G
581 **	IHO	−81.89248	26.41690	Ostego Bay	G
582 **	IHO	−81.88324	26.40748	Carlos Point Estero Bay	G
583 **	IHO	−97.35001	26.35000	North Point	G
584 **	IHO	−97.21500	26.06000	Port Isabel	G
585	IHO	−97.14999	26.06667	South Padre Island	G
586	IHO	−79.89999	25.85000	IAPSO: 30-1.2.12	A/D
587	IHO	−79.28333	25.55000	Cat Cay	A
588	IHO	−77.35001	25.08333	Nassau	A
589	IHO	−77.96208	25.04691	Anros Island	A
590	IHO	−76.15000	24.76667	Eleuthera	A
591	IHO	−89.64999	24.76667	IAPSO: 30-1.2.6	G/D
592	IHO	−80.93335	24.76667	Grassy Key	A
593 **	IHO	−81.01666	24.71667	Marathon Shores	A
594	IHO	−82.88333	24.63333	Tortugas	G
595	IHO	−81.79994	24.54559	Key West	G
596	IHO	−75.96631	23.66719	Steventon Great Exuma	A
597	IHO	−82.33334	23.17150	Habana	G
598	IHO	−74.95001	23.00000	Long Island	A
599	IHO	−73.04999	22.33333	Start Point Mayaguana	A
600	IHO	−97.76990	22.25000	Tampico	G
601	IHO	−74.29999	22.16667	Datum Bay	A
602	IHO	−79.97908	21.72682	Casilda	C
603	IHO	−82.91677	21.44490	Carapachibey	C
604	IHO	−71.14999	21.43333	Grand Turk	A
605	IHO	−89.65000	21.30000	Progreso	G
606	IHO	−76.10860	21.11580	Gibara	A
607	IHO	−74.49380	20.36023	Baracoa	A
608	IHO	−75.14999	19.89300	Guantanamo Bay	C
609	IHO	−90.55310	19.85580	Campeche	G
610	IHO	−70.65910	19.78300	Puerto Plata	A
611 **	IHO	−69.31665	19.19590	Samana	A
612	IHO	−96.11160	19.18333	Vera Cruz	G
613 **	IHO	−64.38333	18.72501	Anegada	A
614	IHO	−72.35384	18.55022	Port au Prince	C
615 **	IHO	−69.88333	18.46527	Ciudad Trujillo	C
616 **	IHO	−66.11600	18.45900	San Juan	A
617 **	IHO	−64.61667	18.42723	Tortola	C
618 **	IHO	−68.95001	18.41036	La Romana	C
619 *	IHO	−64.93335	18.33333	St Thomas	C
620	IHO	−65.28333	18.30000	Great Harbor	C
621	IHO	−78.13333	18.20000	Savanna la Mar	C
622	IHO	−94.41666	18.15805	Coatzacoalcos	G
623 **	IHO	−67.04603	17.97000	Magueyes Island	C
624 **	IHO	−61.85111	17.12284	St Johns	C
625	IHO	−64.88333	16.53333	IAPSO: 30-1.3.2	C/D
626	IHO	−64.91666	16.50000	IAPSO: 30-1.3.1	C/D

Table A1. *Cont.*

ID	CO-OPS	Longitude	Latitude	Station Name	Region
627 **	IHO	−61.50000	16.38333	Petit Canal	C
628 *	IHO	−61.69943	16.33476	Sainte Rose	C
629	IHO	−61.26666	16.25000	Saint Francois	C
630	IHO	−61.53702	16.23290	Pointe a Pitre	C
631	IHO	−87.95001	15.83333	Puerto Cortes	C
632 *	IHO	−61.46667	15.56667	Portsmouth	C
633	IHO	−61.04999	14.58333	Fort de France	C
634	IHO	−83.36667	14.01667	Puerto Cabezas	C
635	IHO	−61.00110	14.02240	Castries	C
636	IHO	−61.23334	13.13333	Kingstown St Vincent	C
637 **	IHO	−59.61454	13.08616	Carlisle Bay	A
638	IHO	−61.18335	12.83333	Mustique Grand Bay	C
639	IHO	−61.33334	12.70329	Charlestown Bay	C
640	IHO	−61.35001	12.63333	Tobago Cays	C
641	IHO	−70.05290	12.60000	Aruba Malmok Bay	C
642	IHO	−61.41778	12.59252	Clifton Harbour	C
643	IHO	−70.03554	12.51347	Aruba Oranjestad	C
644	IHO	−61.45709	12.48783	Hillsborough Bay	C
645	IHO	−68.93335	12.10000	Curacao Willemstad	C
646 *	IHO	−61.75652	12.05000	St Georges	C
647	IHO	−68.64999	12.00000	Klein Curacao n.w. Coast	C
648 *	IHO	−70.21667	11.75000	Amuay	C
649 *	IHO	−60.73360	11.16920	Scarborough	A
650	IHO	−71.64651	11.02353	Zaparita	C
651	IHO	−71.58334	11.00000	Malecon	C
652	IHO	−71.56665	10.96667	Zapara Island	C
653	IHO	−71.61667	10.88333	Tablazo	C
654	IHO	−60.93335	10.83689	Toco	A
655	IHO	−71.63333	10.81667	Punta Palmas	C
656 **	IHO	−61.60001	10.68333	Carenage Bay	C
657	IHO	−61.64999	10.66667	Gaspar Grande	C
658 *	IHO	−61.51692	10.64955	Port of Spain	C
659	IHO	−66.93335	10.61667	La Guaira	C
660	IHO	−62.08334	10.61667	Puerto de Hierro	C
661	IHO	−64.20470	10.45000	Cumana	C
662	IHO	−61.01932	10.40000	Nariva River	A
663	IHO	−75.57640	10.38333	Cartagena	C
664	IHO	−61.48334	10.36667	Point Lisas	C
665	IHO	−61.70001	10.18333	Point Fortin	C
666 **	IHO	−62.64310	10.12410	Punta Gorda	C
667 *	IHO	−61.01666	10.15000	Guayaguayare Bay	A
668 *	IHO	−61.64999	10.06667	Erin Bay	C
669	IHO	−62.20001	10.01667	Rio Pedernales	C
670	IHO	−83.03333	10.00267	Puerto Limon	C
671	IHO	−79.91666	9.36667	Colon	C
672	IHO	−79.91666	9.35000	Cristobal (Canal Zone)	C
673 **	IHO	−59.79999	8.41667	Waini Point	A
674 **	IHO	−58.25000	6.95000	Bluejacket Beacon	A
675 **	IHO	−58.04999	6.95000	Demerara Beacon	A
676 **	IHO	−58.41666	6.86667	Parika	A
677 *	IHO	−58.16666	6.83333	Georgetown	A
678 **	IHO	−57.95001	6.78333	Belfield	A
679 **	IHO	−58.61667	6.40000	Bartica	A
680 *	IHO	−57.01666	5.96667	Nickerie River Mouth	A
681 **	IHO	−55.21667	5.98630	Surinam River Entrance Light	A

* Station is approximated by nearest neighbor for harmonic extraction since it is not within the actual bounds of the EC2001 model domain but is near the edge of the domain; ** Station is not included in EC2001 error measures or scatter plots as it is not physically within the EC2001 model domain and is far removed from the domain.

Appendix B

Scatter plots for the 10 stations shown by a black X in Figures 5 and 6 are provided herein. Both the EC2015 Manning's *n* and VDatum friction models are compared to the EC2001 model. Note that other than the Pilottown, LA station (313) and Curacoa, Willemstad (645) stations, the different friction formulations generally create more of a difference in the amplitude response than they do in the phase response. Plots are grouped according to region.

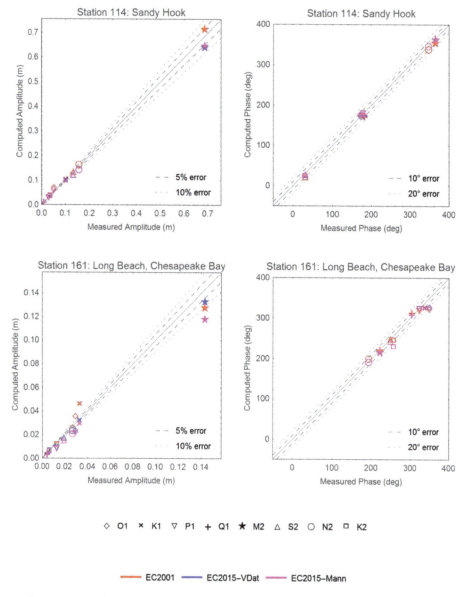

Figure B1. Scatterplots of computed versus measured harmonic data for representative stations along the Atlantic coast.

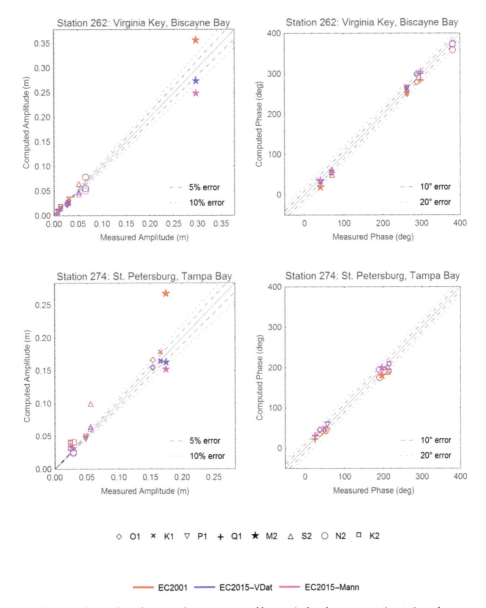

Figure B2. Scatterplots of computed versus measured harmonic data for representative stations along the Florida coast.

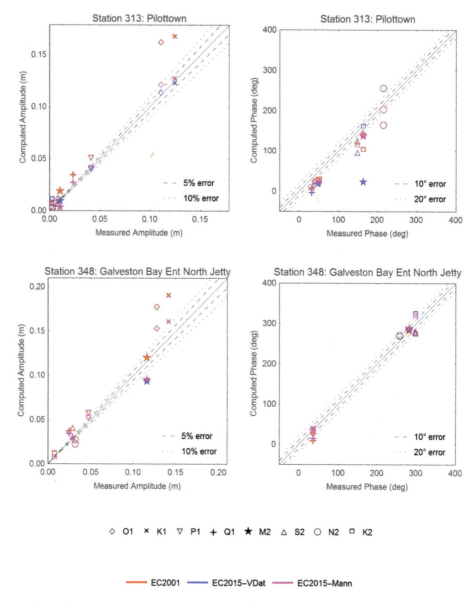

Figure B3. Scatterplots of computed versus measured harmonic data for representative stations along the Gulf of Mexico coast.

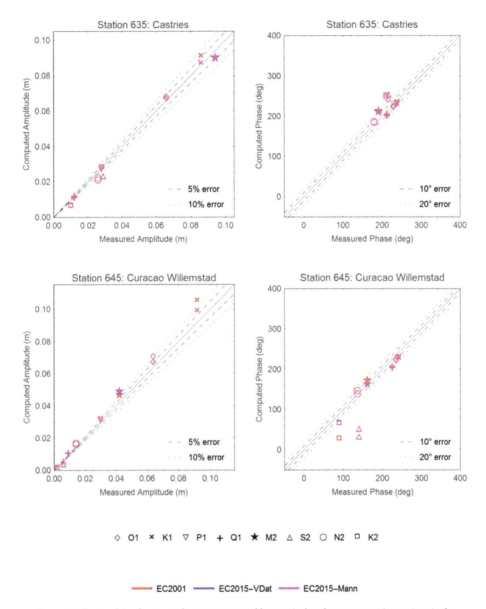

Figure B4. Scatterplots of computed versus measured harmonic data for representative stations in the Caribbean Sea.

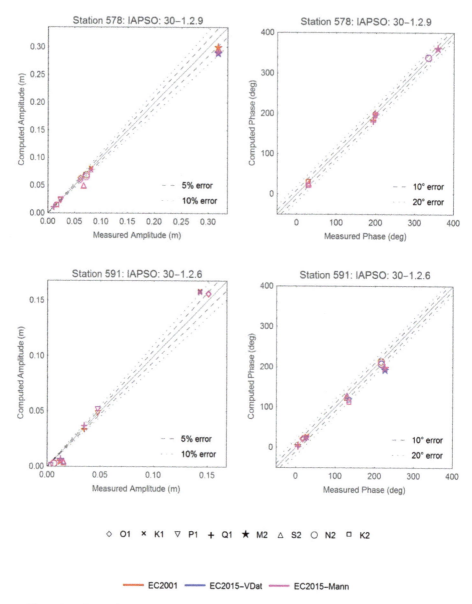

Figure B5. Scatterplots of computed versus measured harmonic data for representative deep IHO stations.

Appendix C

The actual geographic distribution of errors for the K_1 and M_2 constituents are provided at all 681 validation stations in the following seven figures. Although the same regional views given in Figures 5 and 6 are used herein, only the dominant constituent is shown in each subregion: Gulf of Maine, Atlantic Coast and Florida Coast—M_2, Gulf of Mexico and Caribbean Sea—K_1. Symbol shapes denote the magnitude of the errors while the colors represent whether the EC2015 model is over (red) or underestimating (blue) the amplitudes. Similarly, blue symbols denote locations where the model exhibits a phase lag while red symbols denote a phase lead.

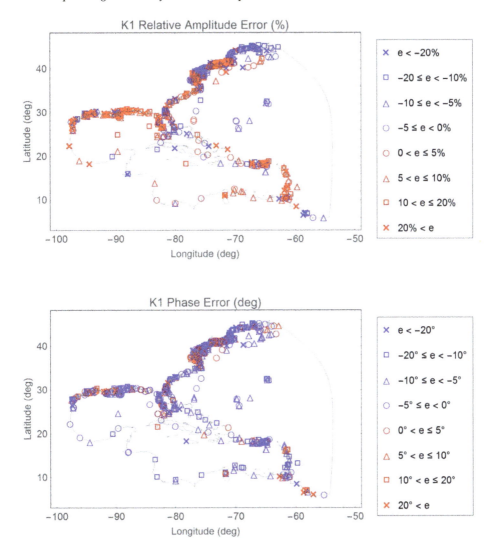

Figure C1. Distribution of relative amplitude and absolute phase errors for the K_1 constituent: global view.

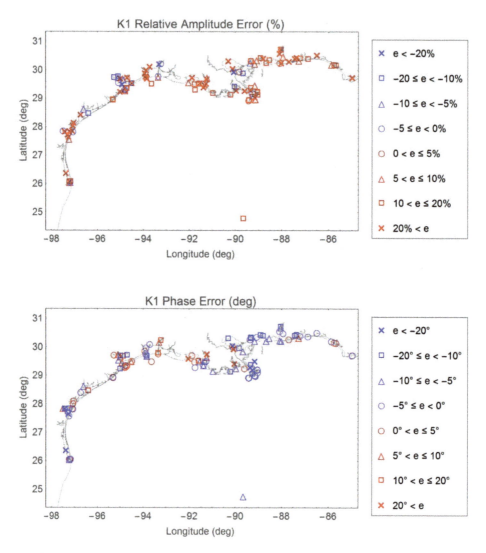

Figure C2. Distribution of relative amplitude and absolute phase errors for the K_1 constituent: Gulf of Mexico.

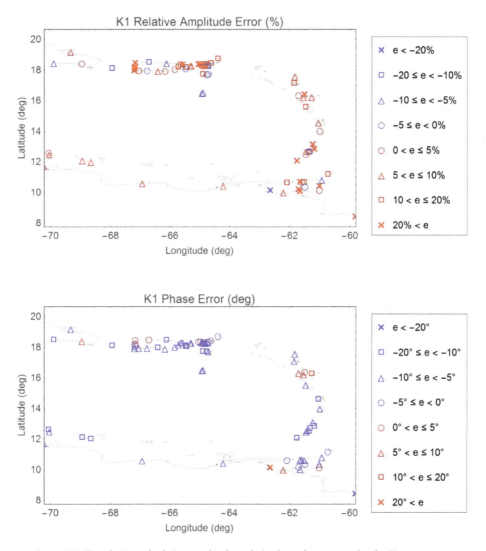

Figure C3. Distribution of relative amplitude and absolute phase errors for the K_1 constituent: Caribbean Sea.

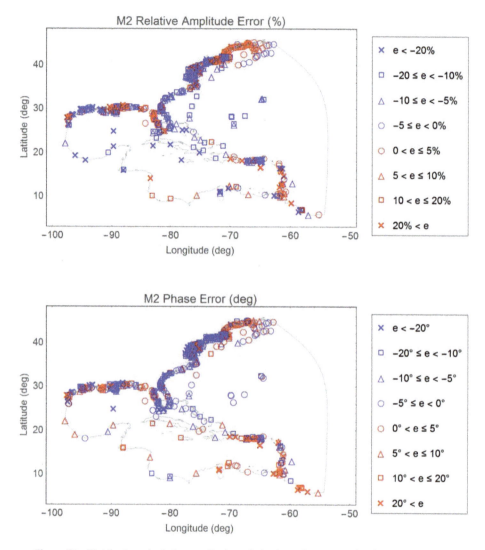

Figure C4. Distribution of relative amplitude and absolute phase errors for the M$_2$ constituent: global view.

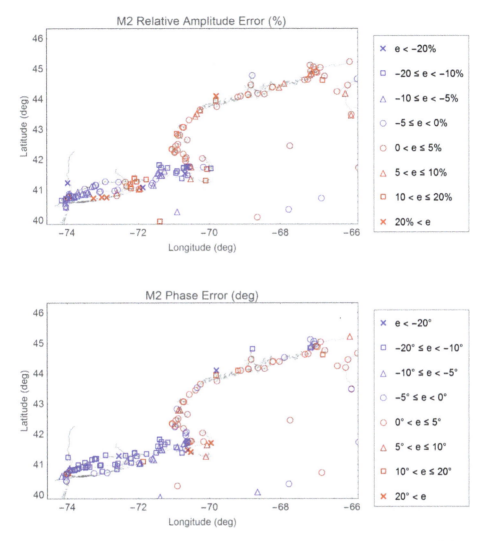

Figure C5. Distribution of relative amplitude and absolute phase errors for the M_2 constituent: Gulf of Maine and New York Bight.

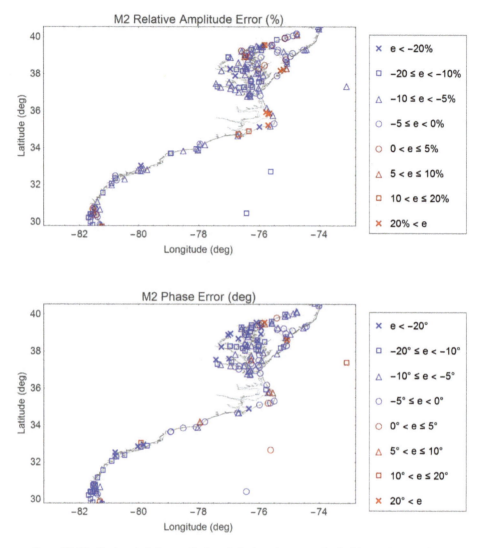

Figure C6. Distribution of relative amplitude and absolute phase errors for the M_2 constituent: Atlantic coast from Delaware to Georgia.

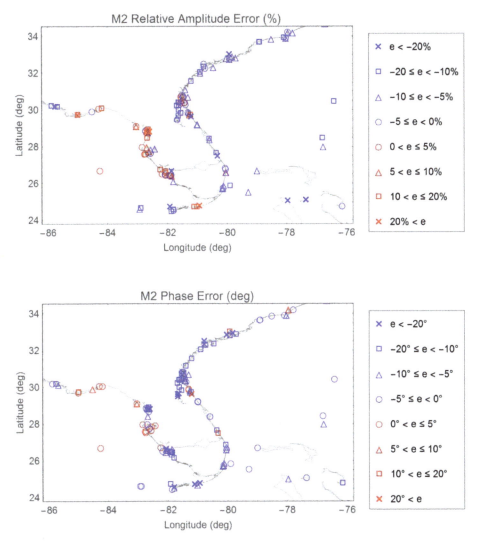

Figure C7. Distribution of relative amplitude and absolute phase errors for the M_2 constituent: Florida coast.

Appendix D

Herein we provide general applicability and usage guidelines for the EC205 tidal database. It is recommended that users read through these sections to understand the limitations of the database before they apply it to their own regions of interest.

Appendix D.1. Applicability Guidelines for the EC2015 Tidal Database

The EC2015 tidal database provides elevation amplitudes and phases throughout the WNAT domain for all 37 constituents frequently used by NOS. Although data for all 37 constituents are included in the database, care should be taken when deciding how many of these constituents are important for the user's intended application. Often, accurate results can be obtained when using only the primary astronomic tides, particularly if the boundary of interest is in deeper water, far removed from the coastline.

This database does not provide information regarding responses associated with density effects, riverine driven circulation, wind and atmospheric pressure driven events and/or oceanic currents. Vertical and horizontal variations in density can set up steric level differences in sea surface elevation, can drive significant horizontal circulation patterns, and can cause variation in the vertical structure of the currents. These effects tend to be important in estuarine or delta systems with significant freshwater riverine inflows. Furthermore the seasonal heating of the upper layers of the ocean's surface directly drives the expansion in the upper layer water volume that is associated with a seasonal fluctuation of water level. This can be especially significant in the Gulf of Mexico and the Caribbean Sea. It is noted that published tidal constituent data includes these seasonal sea surface expansions as long-term tidal constituents such as the Sa Solar annual and the Ssa Solar semiannual constituents. From a tidal hydrodynamics perspective these long-term constituents (with periods of a year and half a year respectively) are of astronomical origin and should appear as weak tides. They may also be generated through nonlinear interactions that lead to extremely weak responses. Nonetheless, in harmonically-decomposed measured field data, these constituents can appear as significant constituents since the driving radiational heating process is also an annual event. In the Gulf of Mexico, the Sa and Ssa elevation constituents can be almost as large as the dominant diurnal tides while current responses are much smaller due to the long-term period associated with these constituents. Thus it is emphasized that the EC2015 computations are entirely barotropic and do not include any of these density effects.

Rivers were not included in the EC2015 tidal database calculations. The barotropic pressure gradient and mass input effects of the river will be important in the immediate vicinity of the river outlet and will diminish away from the river outlet. Wind driven and/or atmospheric pressure driven effects such as coastal setup and storm surge and any basinwide modes that may be set up by these processes are also not included in the database. These effects can be significant on the shelf as well as within bays and estuaries. Major oceanic circulation patterns such as the Gulf Stream and the associated loop currents and other eddies, which are shed from it, are not included in the database. These currents tend to reside off the shelf in deep ocean waters but can be associated with fast flows in the 1 to 2 m/s range.

Finally the local accuracy of the EC2015 tidal computations will be affected by the accuracy of the geometry and bathymetry locally defined in the WNAT-based EC2015 grid. Geometric and bathymetric inaccuracies in the grid will especially affect the accuracy of the currents. Obviously a missing estuary or island or inaccurate bathymetry will greatly influence the database computations.

Appendix D.2. Usage Guidelines for the EC2015 Tidal Database

The EC2015 tidal constituent database can be applied anywhere within the defined WNAT domain. However, the prevailing hydrodynamics in a specific region will determine how accurately the currents will be predicted. If the surface elevation response and currents are indeed dominated by astronomical tides, then the database will provide an excellent prediction of the response. A good estimate of the accuracy of the EC2015 tides can be obtained by examining the regional error estimates given in Tables 7 and 8, or by examining the error plots provided for the dominant constituents in Appendix C; although plots are only provided for the M_2 and K_1 constituents, in general, all four of the semi-diurnal constituents follow the same regional trends, as do the diurnal constituents. Furthermore how accurately the EC2015 grid and bathymetry describe the region of specific interest influences the accuracy and appropriateness of applying database values.

For locations that are tidally dominated and for which the EC2015 grid accurately describes both local geometry and bathymetry, the database can be directly applied to extract tidal elevations and currents. Because the thirty-seven constituents are computed at every node and are defined within the framework of a finite element grid, values at any point within the domain can be readily interpolated from the nodal values within which the point lies.

An extraction program, ADCIRC_db_extract.F90, together with the EC2015 finite element grid file, ec2012_v3d_chk.grd, accompany the tidal database. The user must supply an input file that provides the number of extraction points desired followed by the list of coordinates for those points. The extraction program will prompt the user for this input files as well as the name of the grid used to create the database. The program will also prompt the user whether they would like to produce the harmonic constituent output for elevations, velocities or both and then will produce the harmonic extraction output for amplitude and phase at the specified location(s) according to the user's request. Elevation output is stored in elev_hc.out while velocity output is stored in vel_hc.out. Additionally, diagnostic output is written to tides.dia and provides the location of each extraction point in the global mesh as well as the interpolation weights used to calculate the harmonic constituents. The KDTREE2 search algorithms have been incorporated into the new extraction program to facilitate a speedier search response. Finally, the program takes advantage of dynamic allocation in order to avoid the old hardcoded array limitations found in previous extraction routines. The ADCIRC_db_extract.F90 program will work with any old ADCIRC databases that utilized the individual fort.53 and fort.54 file formats.

A time-history of response can be readily Fourier synthesized using the outputs in the elev_hc.out and vel_hc.out files. For example a time-history of water-surface elevation can be computed as

$$\zeta(x,y,t) = \sum A_i(x,y) f_i(t_0) \cos\left[\sigma_i(t-t_0) + V_i(t_0) - h_i(x,y)\right] \tag{D1}$$

where $A_i(x,y)$ and $h_i(x,y)$ are the amplitude and phase, respectively, at the location (x,y) of interest for constituent i, which are provided by the EC2015 tidal database, and the frequency $\sigma_i = 2\pi/T_i$. The frequencies σ_i in rad/sec and periods T_i in hours for each of the 37 constituents included in the database are presented in Table D1. It is important to specify frequencies precisely, at least to eight significant figures. The nodal factor $f_i(t_0)$ and the equilibrium argument, $V_i(t_0)$, relative to reference time t_0 can be computed using program tide_fac.f, which is available as a utility program on the ADCIRC website [60].

Table D1. Frequencies and periods for EC2015 harmonic constituents.

Constituent	Frequency (Rad/s)	Period (h)
M(2)	0.0001405189	12.42
N(2)	0.0001378797	12.66
S(2)	0.0001454441	12.00
O(1)	0.0000675977	25.82
K(1)	0.0000729212	23.93
K(2)	0.0001458423	11.97
L(2)	0.0001431581	12.19
2N(2)	0.0001352405	12.91
R(2)	0.0001456432	11.98
T(2)	0.0001452450	12.02
Lambda(2)	0.0001428049	12.22
Mu(2)	0.0001355937	12.87
Nu(2)	0.0001382329	12.63
J(1)	0.0000755604	23.10
M(1)	0.0000702820	24.83
OO(1)	0.0000782446	22.31
P(1)	0.0000725229	24.07
Q(1)	0.0000649585	26.87

Table D1. *Cont.*

Constituent	Frequency (Rad/s)	Period (h)
2Q(1)	0.0000623193	28.01
Rho(1)	0.0000653117	26.72
M(4)	0.0002810378	6.21
M(6)	0.0004215567	4.14
M(8)	0.0005620756	3.11
S(4)	0.0002908882	6.00
S(6)	0.0004363323	4.00
M(3)	0.0002107784	8.28
S(1)	0.0000727221	24.00
MK(3)	0.0002134401	8.18
2MK(3)	0.0002081166	8.39
MN(4)	0.0002783986	6.27
MS(4)	0.0002859630	6.10
2SM(2)	0.0001503693	11.61
Mf	0.0000053234	327.86
Msf	0.0000049252	354.37
Mm	0.0000026392	661.31
Sa	0.0000001991	8765.82
Ssa	0.0000003982	4382.91

In locations and/or at times where the hydrodynamics is not tidally dominated and/or the EC2015 grid does not provide sufficient geometric and/or bathymetric detail, a regional model that interfaces with the EC2015 model will lead to a better representation of regional flows. Some examples of cases where this may be appropriate include: (a) bays or estuaries not included in the grid; (b) shallow nonlinearly-dominated inlets or estuaries; (c) coastal and/or estuarine regions barotropically and/or baroclinically influenced by a significant riverine discharge; (d) combined wind- and tidally-driven circulation on a shelf. The basic idea is to construct a domain/grid that extends onto or beyond the shelf within the EC2015 domain. The open ocean boundary is then forced using the tidal constituent data from the EC2015 tidal data base. The defined domain may also include additional regional detail in geometric and bathymetric definition, may include additional forcing functions on select boundaries or within the domain, and/or may include additional terms in the governing equations.

The regional model open ocean boundary should be placed away from the region of immediate interest, and its exact position and shape depends on the application. In no case should the boundary be placed at the mouth or entrance to an embayment of interest. The tidal constituents on the open ocean boundary nodes of the regional model are extracted in the same way as a simple point location. It may be necessary to add an additional forcing component to the boundary elevation and/or radiation forcing function to account for additional interior domain processes and forces. In the development of a regional model it is also recommended that the bathymetry along the open boundary match the bathymetry of the EC2015 grid. This will help ensure that the boundary condition extracted from the EC2015 database is physically consistent with the regional model. Failure to match bathymetries along the regional model open boundary can lead to unrealistic gyre formation and/or instabilities in the regional model computations. The bathymetry can depart from that comprising the EC2015 grid away from the open boundary area.

The EC2015 tidal database is available on the ADCIRC website as two separate compressed files: EC2015_elev-only_tidaldatabase.tar, which contains all of the extraction programs, grids, and sample notes but only has the fort.53 elevation harmonics; and EC2015_tidaldatabase.tar, which has everything given in the previous file with the addition of the fort.54 velocity harmonics [24]. You will only need to download one of the files depending upon whether you wish to have access to the velocity data as well.

In addition to the ADCIRC_db_extract.F90 extraction program, the database also includes another utility for "cutting" a portion of the global database out for visualization within SMS (or other tools). The HarmonicResultScope.f90 program works much the same way as ResultScope.f90, for those who are familiar with that ADCIRC utility program. Additional notes about the usage of each of these programs, as well as sample input and output files for each, are included in the TidalExtract/ directory within the database tar file.

References

1. Pandoe, W.; Edge, B. Case Study for a Cohesive Sediment Transport Model for Matagorda Bay, Texas, with Coupled ADCIRC 2D-Transport and SWAN Wave Models. *J. Hydraul. Eng.* **2008**, *134*, 303–314. [CrossRef]
2. Grzegorzewski, A.S.; Johnson, B.D.; Wamsley, T.V.; Rosati, J.D. Sediment transport and morphology modeling of Ship Island, Mississippi, USA, during storm events. In Proceedings of Coastal Dynamics 2013, Arcachon Convention Centre, Arcachon, France, 24–28 June 2013; pp. 1505–1516.
3. Miles, T.; Seroka, G.; Kohut, J.; Schofield, O.; Glenn, S. Glider observations and modeling of sediment transport in Hurricane Sandy. *J. Geophys. Res. Oceans* **2015**, *120*, 1771–1791. [CrossRef]
4. Dietsche, D.; Hagen, S.C.; Bacopoulos, P. Storm Surge Simulations for Hurricane Hugo (1989): On the Significance of Inundation Areas. *J. Waterw. Port Coast. Ocean Eng.* **2007**, *133*, 183–191. [CrossRef]
5. Irish, J.L.; Resio, D.T.; Ratcliff, J.J. The influence of storm size on hurricane surge. *J. Phys. Oceanogr.* **2008**, *38*, 2003–2013. [CrossRef]
6. Kerr, P.C.; Donahue, A.S.; Westerink, J.J.; Luettich, R.A., Jr.; Zheng, L.Y.; Weisberg, R.H.; Huang, Y.; Wang, H.V.; Teng, Y.; Forrest, D.R.; et al. U.S. IOOS coastal and ocean modeling testbed: Inter-model evaluation of tides, waves, and hurricane surge in the Gulf of Mexico. *J. Geophys. Res. Oceans* **2013**, *118*, 5129–5172. [CrossRef]
7. Mattocks, C.; Forbes, C. A real-time, event-triggered storm surge forecasting system for the state of North Carolina. *Ocean Model.* **2008**, *25*, 95–119. [CrossRef]
8. Fleming, J.G.; Fulcher, C.W.; Luettich, R.A.; Estrade, B.D.; Allen, G.D.; Winer, S.H. A Real Time Storm Surge Forecasting System Using ADCIRC. In Proceedings of International Conference on Estuarine and Coastal Modeling 2007, Newport, RI, USA, 5–7 November 2007; Spaulding, M.L., Ed.; ASCE: Reston, VA, USA, 2008; pp. 893–912.
9. Dresback, K.M.; Fleming, J.G.; Blanton, B.O.; Kaiser, C.; Gourley, J.J.; Tromble, E.M.; Luettich, R.A., Jr.; Kolar, R.L.; Hong, Y.; van Cooten, S.; et al. Skill Assessment of a Real-Time Forecast System Utilizing a Coupled Hydrologic and Coastal Hydrodynamic Modeling During Hurricane Irene (2011). *Cont. Shelf Res.* **2013**, *71*, 78–94. [CrossRef]
10. Dietrich, J.C.; Dawson, C.N.; Proft, J.M.; Howard, M.T.; Wells, G.; Fleming, J.G.; Luettich, R.A., Jr.; Westerink, J.J.; Cobell, Z.; Vitse, M.; et al. Real-Time Forecasting and Visualization of Hurricane Waves and Storm Surge Using SWAN + ADCIRC and FigureGen. *Comput. Chall. Geosci.* **2013**, *156*, 49–70.
11. Feyen, J.; Hess, K.; Spargo, E.; Wong, A.; White, S.; Sellars, J.; Gill, S. Development of a continuous bathymetric/topographic unstructured coastal flooding model to study sea level rise in North Carolina. In Proceedings of International Conference on Estuarine and Coastal Modeling 2005, Charleston, SC, USA, 31 October–2 November 2005; Spaulding, M.L., Ed.; ASCE: Reston, VA, USA, 2006; pp. 338–356.
12. Atkinson, J.; McKee Smith, J.; Bender, C. Sea-Level Rise Effects on Storm Surge and Nearshore Waves on the Texas Coast: Influence of Landscape and Storm Characteristics. *J. Waterw. Port Coast. Ocean Eng.* **2013**, *139*, 98–117. [CrossRef]
13. Bilskie, M.V.; Hagen, S.C.; Medeiros, S.C.; Passeri, D.L. Dynamics of sea level rise and coastal flooding on a changing landscape. *Geophys. Res. Lett.* **2014**, *41*, 927–934. [CrossRef]
14. Cheng, T.K.; Hill, D.F.; Beamer, J.; García-Medina, G. Climate change impacts on wave and surge processes in a Pacific Northwest (USA) estuary. *J. Geophys. Res. Oceans* **2015**, *120*, 182–200. [CrossRef]
15. Carr, S.D.; Hench, J.L.; Luettich, R.A.; Forward, R.B.; Tankersley, R.A. Spatial patterns in the ovigerous Callinectes sapidus spawning migration: Results from a coupled behavioral-physical model. *Mar. Ecol. Prog. Ser.* **2005**, *294*, 213–226. [CrossRef]

16. Oliveira, A.; Fortunato, A.B.; Pinto, L. Modeling the hydrodynamics and the fate of passive and active tracers in the Guadiana estuary. *Estuar. Coast. Shelf Sci.* **2006**, *70*, 76–84. [CrossRef]

17. Reyns, N.B.; Eggleston, D.B.; Luettich, R.A. Secondary dispersal of early juvenile blue crabs within a wind-driven estuary. *Limnol. Oceanogr.* **2006**, *51*, 1982–1995. [CrossRef]

18. Tromble, E.; Kolar, R.; Dresback, K.; Luettich, R. River Flux Boundary Conditions in a Coupled Hydrologic-Hydrodynamic Modeling System. In Proceedings of International Conference on Estuarine and Coastal Modeling 2011, St. Augustine, FL, USA, 7–9 November 2011; Spaulding, M.L., Ed.; ASCE: Reston, VA, USA, 2013; pp. 510–527.

19. Dietrich, J.C.; Trahan, C.J.; Howard, M.T.; Fleming, J.G.; Weaver, R.J.; Tanaka, S.; Yu, L.; Luettich, R.A., Jr.; Dawson, C.N.; Westerink, J.J.; et al. Surface Trajectories of Oil Transport along the Northern Coastline of the Gulf of Mexico. *Cont. Shelf Res.* **2012**, *41*, 17–47. [CrossRef]

20. Alizad, K.; Hagen, S.C.; Morris, J.T.; Bacopoulos, P.; Bilskie, M.V.; Weishampel, J.F.; Medeiros, S.C. A coupled two-dimensional hydrodynamic-marsh model with biological feedback. *Ecol. Model.* **2016**, *327*, 29–43. [CrossRef]

21. Lyard, F.; Lefevre, F.; Letellier, T.; Francis, O. Modelling the Global Ocean Tides: Modern Insights from FES2004. *Ocean Dyn.* **2006**, *56*, 394–415. [CrossRef]

22. Westerink, J.J.; Luettich, R.A.; Scheffner, N.W. *ADCIRC: An Advanced Three-Dimensional Circulation Model for Shelves, Coasts, and Estuaries, Report 3: Development of a Tidal Constituent Database for the Western North Atlantic and Gulf of Mexico*; Technical Report DRP 92-6; U.S. Army Engineer Research and Development Center, Coastal and Hydraulics Laboratory: Vicksburg, MS, USA, 1993. Available online: http://www.unc.edu/ims/adcirc/publications/1993/1993_Westerink02.pdf (accessed on 27 June 2016).

23. Mukai, A.Y.; Westerink, J.J.; Luettich, R.A.; Mark, D. *Eastcoast 2001: A Tidal Constituent Database for the Western North Atlantic, Gulf of Mexico and Caribbean Sea*; Technical Report ERDC/CHL TR-02-24; U.S. Army Engineer Research and Development Center, Coastal and Hydraulics Laboratory: Vicksburg, MS, USA, 2002; p. 201. Available online: http://www.unc.edu/ims/adcirc/publications/2002/2002_Mukai01.pdf (accessed on 27 June 2016).

24. ADCIRC Tidal Databases—ADCIRC. Available online: http://adcirc.org/products/adcirc-tidal-databases/ (accessed on 1 July 2016).

25. Westerink, J.J.; Luettich, R.A.; Muccino, J.C. Modelling tides in the western North Atlantic using unstructured graded grids. *Tellus A* **1994**, *46*, 178–199. [CrossRef]

26. Blain, C.A.; Westerink, J.J.; Luettich, R.A. The influence of domain size on the response characteristics of a hurricane storm surge model. *J. Geophys. Res.* **1994**, *99*, 18467–18479. [CrossRef]

27. Bathymetric Data Viewer. Available online: http://maps.ngdc.noaa.gov/viewers/bathymetry/ (accessed on 8 September 2016).

28. Schureman, P. *Manual of Harmonic Analysis and Prediction of Tides*; Special Publication 98, Coast and Geodetic Survey; U.S. Department of Commerce: Washington, DC, USA, 1958; p. 317.

29. Kinnmark, I.P.E. *The Shallow Water Wave Equations: Formulations, Analysis and Application*; Springer: Berlin, Germany, 1986.

30. Luettich, R.A.; Westerink, J.J.; Scheffner, N.W. *ADCIRC: An Advanced Three-Dimensional Circulation Model for Shelves, Coasts, and Estuaries; Report 1: Theory and Methodology of ADCIRC-2DDI and ADCIRC-3DL*; Technical Report CERC-TR-DRP-92-6; U.S. Army Corps of Engineers, U.S. Department of the Army: Washington, DC, USA, 1992.

31. Kolar, R.L.; Gray, W.G.; Westerink, J.J.; Luettich, R.A. Shallow Water Modeling in Spherical Coordinates: Equation Formulation, Numerical Implementation and Application. *J. Hydraul. Res.* **1994**, *32*, 3–24. [CrossRef]

32. Bunya, S.; Dietrich, J.C.; Westerink, J.J.; Ebersole, B.A.; Smith, J.M.; Atkinson, J.H.; Jensen, R.; Resio, D.T.; Luettich, R.A.; Dawson, C.; et al. A High-Resolution Coupled Riverine Flow, Tide, Wind, Wind Wave, and Storm Surge Model for Southern Louisiana and Mississippi. Part 1: Model Development and Validation. *Mon. Weather Rev.* **2010**, *138*, 345–377. [CrossRef]

33. OSU Tidal Data Inversion. Available online: http://volkov.oce.orst.edu/tides/global.html (accessed on 27 June 2016).

34. NOAA/NOS's VDatum 3.6: Vertical Datums Transformation. Available online: http://vdatum.noaa.gov/welcome.html (accessed on 27 June 2016).

35. Hess, K.; Spargo, E.; Wong, A.; White, S.; Gill, S. *VDatum for Central Coastal North Carolina: Tidal Datums, Marine Grids, and Sea Surface Topography*; NOAA Technical Report NOS CS 21; U.S. Department of Commerce: Silver Spring, MD, USA, 2005. Available online: http://vdatum.noaa.gov/download/publications/2005_TechReport_CS21.pdf (accessed on 16 June 2016).

36. Spargo, E.; White, S.; Hess, K. *VDatum for the Northeast Gulf of Mexico from Mobile Bay, Alabama, to Cape San Blas, Florida: Tidal Datum Modeling and Population of the Marine Grids*; NOAA Technical Report NOS CS 14; U.S. Department of Commerce: Silver Spring, MD, USA, 2008. Available online: http://vdatum.noaa.gov/download/publications/TM_NOS-CS14_FY08_28_EmilyHess_NEGulfOfMexico.pdf (accessed on 16 June 2016).

37. Yang, Z.; Myers, E.; Wong, A.; White, S. *VDatum for Chesapeake Bay, Delaware Bay and Adjacent Coastal Water Areas: Tidal Datums and Sea Surface Topography*; NOAA Technical Report NOS CS 15; U.S. Department of Commerce: Silver Spring, MD, USA, 2008. Available online: http://vdatum.noaa.gov/download/publications/TM_NOS-CS15_FY08_26_Yang_VDatumCHES-DEL.pdf (accessed on 16 June 2016).

38. Yang, Z.; Myers, E.; White, S. *VDatum for Eastern Louisiana and Mississippi Coastal Waters: Tidal Datums, Marine Grids, and Sea Surface Topography*; NOAA Technical Memorandum NOS CS 19; U.S. Department of Commerce: Silver Spring, MD, USA, 2010. Available online: https://vdatum.noaa.gov/download/publications/CS_19_FY09_26_Zizang_VDatum_NewOrleans_techMemor.pdf (accessed on 16 June 2016).

39. Yang, Z.; Myers, E.; White, S. *VDatum for Great South Bay, New York Bight and New York Harbor: Tidal Datums, Marine Grids, and Sea Surface Topography*; NOAA Technical Memorandum NOS CS 21; U.S. Department of Commerce: Silver Spring, MD, USA, 2010. Available online: https://vdatum.noaa.gov/download/publications/CS_21_FY09_25_Zizang_VDatum_GreatSouthBay_techMemor.pdf (accessed on 16 June 2016).

40. Yang, Z.; Myers, E.; Jeong, I.; White, S. *VDatum for Coastal Waters from the Florida Shelf to the South Atlantic Bight: Tidal Datums, Marine Grids, and Sea Surface Topography*; NOAA Technical Memorandum NOS CS 27; U.S. Department of Commerce: Silver Spring, MD, USA, 2012. Available online: https://vdatum.noaa.gov/download/publications/TM_NOS-CS27_FY12-14_VDatum_FL_SA_zyang.pdf (accessed on 16 June 2016).

41. Xu, J.; Myers, E.; Jeong, I.; White, S. *VDatum for Coastal Waters of Texas and Western Louisiana: Tidal Datums and Topography of the Sea Surface*; NOAA Technical Memorandum NOS CS 29; U.S. Department of Commerce: Silver Spring, MD, USA, 2013. Available online: https://vdatum.noaa.gov/download/publications/TM_NOS-CS29_FY13_Xu_TexasWesternLouisiana.pdf (accessed on 16 June 2016).

42. Yang, Z.; Myers, E.; Jeong, I.; White, S. *VDatum for the Gulf of Maine: Tidal Datums and Topography of the Sea Surface*; NOAA Technical Memorandum NOS CS 31; U.S. Department of Commerce: Silver Spring, MD, USA, 2013. Available online: http://vdatum.noaa.gov/download/publications/TM_NOS_CS_31_FY13_04_Yang_VDatumGulfOfMaine.pdf (accessed on 16 June 2016).

43. Wang, J.; Myers, E.; Jeong, I.; White, S. *VDatum for the Coastal Waters of Puerto Rico and the U. S. Virgin Islands: Tidal Datums, Marine Grid, and Sea Surface Topography*; NOAA Technical Memorandum NOS CS 33; U.S. Department of Commerce: Silver Spring, MD, USA, 2013. Available online: https://vdatum.noaa.gov/download/publications/TM_NOS_CS33_FY14_02_JWang_VDatumPuertoRico.pdf (accessed on 16 June 2016).

44. VDatum Manual for Development and Support of NOAA's Vertical Datum Transformation Tool, VDatum. Version 1.01. 2012. Available online: http://www.nauticalcharts.noaa.gov/csdl/publications/Manual_2012.06.26.doc (accessed on 27 June 2016).

45. Bacopoulos, P.; Parrish, D.M.; Hagen, S.C. Unstructured mesh assessment for tidal model of the South Atlantic Bight and its estuaries. *J. Hydraul. Res.* **2011**, *49*, 487–502. [CrossRef]

46. Amante, C.; Eakins, B.W. *ETOPO1 1 Arc-Minute Global Relief Model: Procedures, Data Sources and Analysis*; NOAA Technical Memorandum NESDIS NGDC-24; National Geophysical Data Center, NOAA: Boulder, CO, USA, 2009. Available online: https://www.ngdc.noaa.gov/mgg/global/relief/ETOPO1/docs/ETOPO1.pdf (accessed on 2 November 2012).

47. ETOPO1 Global Relief. Available online: http://www.ngdc.noaa.gov/mgg/global/global.html (accessed on 27 June 2016).

48. Becker, J.J.; Sandwell, D.T.; Smith, W.H.F.; Braud, J.; Binder, B.; Depner, J.; Fabre, D.; Factor, J.; Ingalls, S.; Kim, S.-H.; et al. Global Bathymetry and Elevation Data at 30 Arc Seconds Resolution: SRTM30_PLUS. *Mar. Geod.* **2009**, *32*, 355–371. [CrossRef]

49. Sandwell, D.T.; Müller, R.D.; Smith, W.H.F.; Garcia, E.; Francis, R. New global marine gravity model from CryoSat-2 and Jason-1 reveals buried tectonic structure. *Science* **2014**, *346*, 65–67. [CrossRef]

50. Satellite Geodesy, IGPP, SIO, UCSD | Global Topography | SRTM30, Multibeam and Predicted. Available online: http://topex.ucsd.edu/WWW_html/srtm30_plus.html (accessed on 27 June 2016).

51. Global Tide - FES: Aviso+. Available online: http://www.aviso.altimetry.fr/en/data/products/auxiliary-products/global-tide-fes.html (accessed on 27 June 2016).

52. Egbert, G.D.; Bennett, A.F.; Foreman, M.G.G. TOPEX/POSEIDON tides estimated using a global inverse model. *J. Geophys. Res.* **1994**, *99*, 24821–24852. [CrossRef]

53. Egbert, G.D.; Erofeeva, S.Y. Efficient inverse modeling of barotropic ocean tides. *J. Atmos. Oceanic Technol.* **2002**, *19*, 183–204. [CrossRef]

54. Carrère, L.; Lyard, F.; Cancet, M.; Roblou, L.; Guillot, A. FES2012: A new global tidal model taking advantage of nearly 20 years of altimetry measurements. In Proceedings of meeting "20 Years of Progress in Radar Altimetry Symposium", Venice, Italy, 24–29 September 2012.

55. USGS Coastal and Marine Geology—usSEABED. Available online: http://walrus.wr.usgs.gov/usseabed/index.html (accessed on 29 June 2016).

56. Kolar, R.L.; Westerink, J.J.; Cantekin, M.E.; Blain, C.A. Aspects of nonlinear simulations using shallow-water models based on the wave continuity equation. *Comput. Fluids* **1993**, *23*, 523–538. [CrossRef]

57. NOAA Tides and Currents. Available online: http://tidesandcurrents.noaa.gov/ (accessed on 8 September 2016).

58. *IHO Tidal Constituent Bank: Station Catalogue*; Department of Fisheries and Oceans: Ottawa, ON, Canada, 1979.

59. Qi, S. Use of International Hydrographic Organization Tidal Data for Improved Tidal Prediction. Master's Thesis, Portland State University, Portland, OR, USA, December 2012.

60. ADCIRC Utility Programs—ADCIRC. Available online: http://adcirc.org/home/related-software/adcirc-utility-programs/ (accessed on July 2016).

Journal of
*Marine Science
and Engineering*

Article

Application of the Forward Sensitivity Method to a GWCE-Based Shallow Water Model

Evan M. Tromble [1,†,‡], Sivaramakrishnan Lakshmivarahan [2,‡], Randall L. Kolar [1,‡] and Kendra M. Dresback [1,*,‡]

[1]   School of Civil Engineering and Environmental Science, University of Oklahoma, Norman, OK 73019, USA; etromble@gmail.com (E.M.T.); kolar@ou.edu (R.L.K.)
[2]   School of Computer Science, University of Oklahoma, Norman, OK 73019, USA; varahan@ou.edu
*   Correspondence: dresback@ou.edu; Tel.: +1-405-325-8529
†   Current address: Garver, Norman, OK 73069, USA.
‡   These authors contributed equally to this work.

Academic Editor: Richard Signell
Received: 23 September 2016; Accepted: 1 November 2016; Published: 10 November 2016

Abstract: The Forward Sensitivity Method (FSM) is applied to a GWCE-based shallow water model to analyze the sensitivity to the numerical parameter, G, that determines the balance between the wave and primitive forms of the continuity equation. Results show that the sensitivity to G calculated in the sensitivity evolution portion of the FSM is consistent with the actual sensitivity to G computed from multiple simulations using finite differences. The data assimilation step in the FSM is shown to be effective in selecting G that minimizes an objective function, in this case model errors based on sensitivities. Additionally, the FSM sensitivity results show $2\Delta x$ oscillations in the elevation and velocity fields develop when G is increased too high, suggesting the FSM may be an effective tool for determining the upper limit of G for real-world applications.

Keywords: shallow water equations; GWCE; forward sensitivity method; data assimilation

1. Introduction

The Generalized Wave Continuity Equation (GWCE) [1] is an extension of the Wave Continuity Equation (WCE) [2], which was introduced to eliminate the spurious oscillations that plagued finite element solutions of the primitive Shallow Water Equations (SWE). The GWCE contains a numerical parameter, G, that determines whether the GWCE tends towards a wave equation form (low G) or the primitive continuity equation (high G). It has undergone rigorous analytical studies, which have shown that the GWCE is consistent with the primitive continuity as long as the initial conditions satisfy continuity [1]. However, Kinnmark went on to show that even if that condition is not satisfied exactly, then the solution remains robust as long as the numerical parameter, G, satisfies some minimal conditions, e.g., $G > 0$. Many other studies have shown the superior wave propagation characteristics of the GWCE, including non-aliased solutions for short waves (e.g., [3]) and low-dissipation for physical waves (e.g., [4]). In that G is a numerical parameter, akin to a penalty parameter commonly found in classic finite element methods, there have been numerous studies that sought to identify an "optimum" value of G (e.g., [5–7]). Additionally, it should go without saying that all numerical algorithms introduce conceptual errors (e.g., missing physics) and truncation errors into the solution; a goal of modeling is to minimize the adverse impact of those errors. A big contribution of the current manuscript is that it goes a step further than previous analyses because the methodology can be applied to nonlinear problems and because it opens the door for data assimilation, which is a widely-accepted practice of "tuning" a model to account for missing physics (e.g., subgrid scale processes). However, in the end, real-world applications over the last 30 years provide the truest test of the GWCE. For example, the resulting algorithm is employed in the production version of the widely-used ADCIRC code ([8–10]), which has a long history of providing accurate, robust results in a wide variety of applications, including tide- and wind-driven circulation, hurricane storm surge and inundation, baroclinic transport, sediment transport and coastal dredging feasibility, and larval and oil spill conveyance settings ([11–17]).

The WCE was first introduced by Lynch and Gray in 1979 [2]; in 1986, Kinnmark generalized the WCE to the GWCE by introducing a weighting factor, G, that is distinct from the bottom friction parameter, τ [1]. Kolar et al. [5] found that G has a large effect on model results and that a value $G > \tau$ is necessary to minimize errors. Atkinson et al. [7] analyzed the wave propagation characteristics of the GWCE-based SWE, and they found that the GWCE-based system is nearly identical to the primitive SWE, with a quasi-bubble velocity approximation [18], for a specific G parameterization. The dispersion analysis results of [7] have guided the recent selection of G (cf. [11,16]), where spatially-variable parameter selection has been employed for diverse applications. However, specification of a value (or parameterization) for G is an on-going issue.

In general, techniques applied to analyze the GWCE-based system have been limited to linear analysis (or analysis of the linearized equations), e.g., dispersion and Fourier analysis. These classic techniques are also limited to constant bathymetry domains and interior nodes. Herein, the Forward Sensitivity Method (FSM) [19] is applied to analyze the 1D, GWCE-based SWE. In this analysis, both constant and non-constant bathymetry cases are analyzed. As mentioned in [19], the FSM builds on sensitivity function analysis (e.g., [20]) and includes an optimization component that allows observations to be used to correct the model. The FSM is a deterministic data assimilation strategy for correcting forecast errors when a deterministic model is used in the analysis. Forecast error is defined by the difference between the model solution and the given (noisy) observation that the model is supposed to capture in the first place. A model can be either perfect or imperfect. Recall that a solution of a dynamic model depends on: (a) initial conditions; (b) the values of parameters; and (c) the boundary conditions. Since these three factors control the evolution of the model solution, these are collectively called "control". The goal of FSM is to find corrections to the control so as to drive the forecast errors as close to zero as possible in the least squares sense. FSM was first reported in Lakshmivarahan and Lewis [19] and is closely related to the now classic adjoint sensitivity-based 4D VAR method [21]. The FSM-based approach is quite general and can handle both linear and nonlinear models and can be used to correct the forecast errors due to all three components: initial conditions, boundary conditions and parameters. A comprehensive account of FSM and varied applications is given in Lakshmivarahan et al. [22]. The method is applied to analyze a differential equation describing the air/sea interaction in [19]. In contrast to dispersion analysis, which is limited in applicability (e.g., linear equations, interior nodes, constant bathymetry), the FSM can be applied to analyze the non-linear equations at all nodal locations within the domain. The FSM has the added capability of accounting for boundary conditions, whereas other methods look only at interior points.

While FSM is applicable to non-linear systems, the analysis in this manuscript is limited to the linear system, with the intent being to present the exploration of a new analysis tool for shallow water equation models. Application to the non-linear GWCE-based shallow water equations has been performed [23], and the results will be presented in a subsequent paper. As presented first, derivation of the equations for the evolution of the sensitivity functions follows [19]. Then, the FSM sensitivities are analyzed for two domains, which is followed by a validation of the FSM sensitivities with a numerical analog sensitivity approach. Section 3 begins with the presentation of the methodology, based on [19], for computing parameter corrections, and concludes with applications for the linear sloping domain. Section 4 contains the results of a proof-of-concept sequential optimization. Subsequently, a comparison between FSM and dispersion analysis is presented in Section 5. Finally, conclusions are made based on the analysis herein.

2. Sensitivity Function Evolution

2.1. Derivation of Sensitivity Equations

The 1D linear inviscid GWCE and momentum equation are given by Equations (1) and (2), respectively,

$$\zeta_{tt} + G\zeta_t + (G - \tau)hu_x - gh\zeta_{xx} = 0 \tag{1}$$

$$u_t + \tau u + g\zeta_x = 0 \tag{2}$$

where ζ is the water surface elevation, G is the weighting parameter in the GWCE, τ is the bottom friction term, h is bathymetry, u is depth-averaged velocity and g is the gravitational acceleration. Additionally, the subscripts denote partial derivatives, i.e., ζ_{tt} is the second partial derivative of ζ with respect to time.

Application of the continuous Galerkin finite element method, using constant grid spacing, and a finite difference time discretization results in Equations (3) and (4) for the GWCE and momentum equation, respectively,

$$\frac{1}{\Delta t^2}\mathbf{M}_{i,j}(\zeta_j^{k+1} - 2\zeta_j^k + \zeta_j^{k-1}) + \frac{G}{2\Delta t}\mathbf{M}_{i,j}(\zeta_j^{k+1} - \zeta_j^{k-1})$$
$$-(G - \tau)h_j\mathbf{B}_{i,j}u_j^k + g\bar{h}\mathbf{S}_{i,j}(\alpha_1\zeta_j^{k+1} + \alpha_2\zeta_j^k + \alpha_3\zeta_j^{k-1}) = 0 \tag{3}$$

$$\frac{1}{\Delta t}\mathbf{M}_{i,j}^L(u_j^{k+1} - u_j^k) + \frac{\tau}{2}\mathbf{M}_{i,j}^L(u_j^{k+1} + u_j^k) + \frac{g}{2}\mathbf{B}_{i,j}^T(\zeta_j^{k+1} + \zeta_j^k) = 0 \tag{4}$$

where, on an element basis, $\mathbf{M}_{i,j} = \frac{\Delta x}{6}\left(\begin{smallmatrix} 2 & 1 \\ 1 & 2 \end{smallmatrix}\right)$, h_j indicates a nodal bathymetry value, $\mathbf{B}_{i,j} = \frac{1}{2}\left(\begin{smallmatrix} -1 & -1 \\ 1 & 1 \end{smallmatrix}\right)$, $\bar{h}$ is an elemental average bathymetry value, $\mathbf{S}_{i,j} = \frac{1}{\Delta x}\left(\begin{smallmatrix} 1 & -1 \\ -1 & 1 \end{smallmatrix}\right)$, $\mathbf{M}_{i,j}^L = \frac{\Delta x}{2}\left(\begin{smallmatrix} 1 & 0 \\ 0 & 1 \end{smallmatrix}\right)$, $\mathbf{B}_{i,j}^T = \frac{1}{2}\left(\begin{smallmatrix} -1 & 1 \\ -1 & 1 \end{smallmatrix}\right)$. The α_i's are time-weight parameters subject to $\alpha_1 + \alpha_2 + \alpha_3 = 1.0$.

The system can be written symbolically, as:

$$\mathbf{A}(G)\mathbf{c}^{k+1} = \mathbf{B}(G)\mathbf{c}^k + \mathbf{C}(G)\mathbf{c}^{k-1} + \mathbf{f}_{bc}^{k+1} \tag{5}$$

where the coefficient matrices $\mathbf{A}(G), \mathbf{B}(G), \mathbf{C}(G) \in \mathbf{R}^{2n \times 2n}$ are square matrices with dimensions of twice the number of nodes, n, for each of the three time levels; the vectors of variables are $\mathbf{c}^{k+1}, \mathbf{c}^k, \mathbf{c}^{k-1} \in \mathbf{R}^{2n}$; and the forcing vector is $\mathbf{f}_{bc}^{k+1} \in \mathbf{R}^n$.

The FSM allows calculation of the sensitivity to different aspects of the control, which includes initial and boundary conditions, as well as physical, empirical and numerical parameters. Herein, the focus is on the numerical parameter G. The sensitivity to G is the rate of change of the solution due to a change in G. Given the system described in Equation (5), the sensitivity is found by taking the derivative with respect to G, as shown in Equation (6).

$$\frac{\partial}{\partial G}[\mathbf{A}(G)\mathbf{c}^{k+1}] = \frac{\partial}{\partial G}[\mathbf{B}(G)\mathbf{c}^k + \mathbf{C}(G)\mathbf{c}^{k-1} + \mathbf{f}_{bc}^{k+1}] \tag{6}$$

Application of the product rule, the definition of the sensitivity of the solution to G at a given time as $\mathbf{w}^k = \partial \mathbf{c}^k / \partial G$, and rearrangement yields:

$$\mathbf{A}(G)\mathbf{w}^{k+1} = -\frac{\partial \mathbf{A}(G)}{\partial G}\mathbf{c}^{k+1} + \frac{\partial \mathbf{B}(G)}{\partial G}\mathbf{c}^k + \frac{\partial \mathbf{C}(G)}{\partial G}\mathbf{c}^{k-1} + \mathbf{B}(G)\mathbf{w}^k + \mathbf{C}(G)\mathbf{w}^{k-1} \tag{7}$$

Note that the forcing vector is considered to be independent of G. According to Equation (7), the unknown sensitivity vector can be computed from the previous sensitivities and elevation and velocity fields, although $\mathbf{c}^{k+1}$ must be calculated before $\mathbf{w}^{k+1}$. The three time-level scheme requires sets of sensitivity values at times k and $k - 1$. Results herein have cold start initial conditions, where the initial elevation and velocity fields are zero throughout the domain. As such, the initial conditions do not depend on G, and the initial conditions for the sensitivity to G are $\mathbf{w}^{-1} = \mathbf{w}^0 = [0, \ldots, 0]^T \in \mathbf{R}^{2n}$.

2.2. Sensitivity Results for Tidal Problem on the Linear Sloping Domain

The parameters for the test case on the linear sloping domain are given in Table 1. The number of nodes (and, thus, the grid spacing) was varied, with 11, 21, 41 and 81 nodes, constant Δx grids being employed. Additionally, the simulation duration and time step were variable. Finally, both explicit ($\alpha_1 = 0, \alpha_2 = \alpha_3 = 1/2$) and implicit ($\alpha_1 = \alpha_2 = \alpha_3 = 1/3$) versions of the code were assessed. The differences between the results from the explicit and implicit models (both flow variables and sensitivities to G) were immaterial over the stable range of G values, although the implicit α specification allows stability at lower G values than the explicit version (for this test case, the implicit model was stable at G values two orders of magnitude smaller than the lowest stable value using the explicit version).

Table 1. Parameters for the linear sloping domain test case.

Parameter	Value
Bathymetry at open boundary	20.0 m
Bottom slope	1.25×10^{-4} m/m
Domain length	40.0 km
τ	0.001 s^{-1}
Tidal forcing amplitude	1.0 m
Tidal forcing period	44,714.8 s
Ramp duration	1.0 days

Simulations with each grid, using a G value of 0.001 s^{-1} were performed for a period of 3.0 days, with output recorded every 5.0 min for the last day. For the three coarsest grids, $\Delta t = 1.0$ s, while a time step of 0.5 s was used for the 81-node grid. Nodal elevation and elevation sensitivity to G results at select locations in the domain are shown in Figure 1. The node number listed on each panel corresponds to the node number for the location in the 21-node grid. The first panel, labeled "Node 1", shows the specified (i.e., Dirichlet) elevation boundary time series. On each panel, there are four solid lines. Each line shows the temporal evolution of the water surface elevation at the specified location for a particular domain, corresponding to the 11-, 21-, 41- and 81-node domains. The four solid lines are overlain on one another because the time series at the boundary are equivalent. Additionally, each panel has four dashed lines, corresponding to the same grids as for the solid lines. The dashed lines for Node 1 (along the line $y = 0$) show that the elevation sensitivity to G is zero, which is due to the elevation boundary condition being independent of G.

The second panel, labeled "Node 3," shows results 4.0 km into the domain. For this test case, the elevation time series is independent of Δx, as is evident by the indistinguishable solid lines. However, the magnitude of the elevation sensitivity to G is dependent on grid resolution, with the magnitude decreasing substantially with increased resolution. The reduction in sensitivity to G with increased grid resolution (i.e., smaller Δx) suggests that a solution with only a limited dependence on G can be obtained for this domain if sufficient resolution is utilized. Additionally, the timing of the sensitivity is consistent for the different grids, with co-located zero sensitivity values, which are approximately 90 degrees out-of-phase from the zero elevation values.

Similar general trends hold for elevation and elevation sensitivity to G time series in the middle ("Node 11") and on the right side ("Node 21") of the domain. Again, the elevation time series are indistinguishable. However, the magnitude of the sensitivity to G is highly-dependent on Δx. Additionally, the magnitude of the sensitivity to G, as well as the amount the elevation and elevation sensitivity time series are out-of-phase depend on the location in the domain, with the magnitude and the phase difference increasing with distance from the ocean boundary.

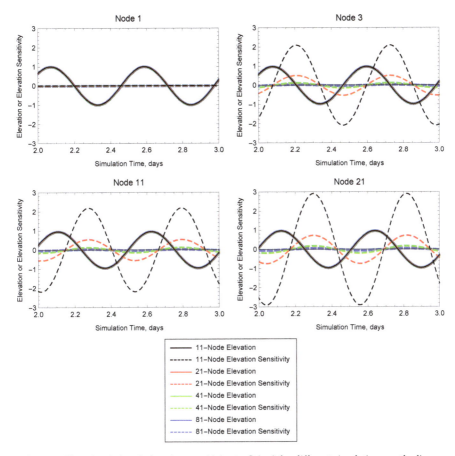

Figure 1. Elevation (m) and elevation sensitivity to G (ms) for different simulations on the linear sloping domain, with each simulation using a different resolution grid (11-node, black; 21-node, red; 41-node, green; and 81-node, blue). The solid lines depict the elevation results, while the dashed lines show the temporal evolution of the sensitivity of the elevation to G. The node number listed in the title for each panel is the node number in the 21-node grid associated with a given location.

Figure 2 shows the velocity equivalents to the elevation results shown in Figure 1. At the ocean boundary, the velocity results are slightly dependent on Δx. Additionally, it is noteworthy that there is a relatively large sensitivity to G at this location. The elevation value is specified at the boundary, so changes to velocity resulting from changes to G result in changes to the amount of mass entering and exiting the domain at the open boundary throughout the simulation. For the other locations in the domain, the velocity time series overlay one another. The velocity sensitivity to G at the ocean boundary shows that, regardless of grid resolution, the velocity is highly dependent on the choice of G, which has significant implications on global mass balance, as noted in [5]. Throughout most of the domain, the phase shift of the velocity sensitivity to G is independent of Δx, as was the case with the elevation results in Figure 1; the location denoted by "Node 3" is the aberration, as there is a phase shift for the velocity sensitivity for different grid resolutions. Furthermore, as with the elevations, the magnitude of the sensitivity to G decreases with increasing grid resolution, and the sensitivity is lower in magnitude the closer to the land boundary where velocity is specified.

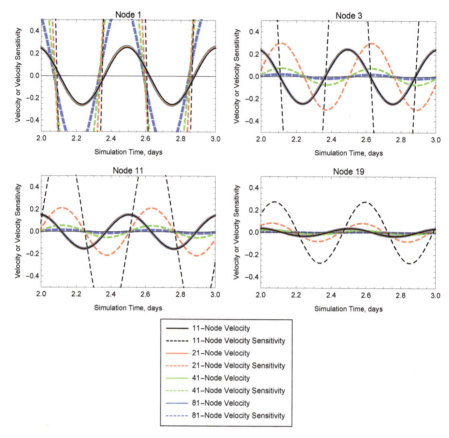

Figure 2. Velocity (m/s) and velocity sensitivity to G (m) for different simulations on the linear sloping domain, with each simulation using a different resolution grid (11-node, black; 21-node, red; 41-node, green; and 81-node, blue). The solid lines depict the velocity results, while the dashed lines show the temporal evolution of the sensitivity of the velocity to G. The node number listed in the title for each panel is the node number in the 21-node grid associated with a given location.

In order to assess the impact of different G values on the sensitivity of the solution to G, the implicit version of the code was used, with a Δt of 5.0 s, for simulations with G values of 0.00001, 0.0001, 0.001, 0.01 and 0.1 s^{-1}. Additionally, the simulations were 10.0 days in duration. The sensitivity values over the last two days of the simulation, for Nodes 2–7, are shown in Figure 3. The gaps in Figure 3 correspond to times when the sensitivity value is below the minimum ordinate value (which is just greater than zero) on the plot, although generally, these instances correspond to times when the sensitivity is negative for the current set of simulations.

Increasing G results in a decrease in the magnitude of the peak sensitivity. To a lesser extent, increasing G changes the timing of the sensitivity. Specifically, when G is increased from 0.00001 to 0.0001 s^{-1}, there is a small decrease in the magnitude of the peak sensitivity and a shift in the timing, so the peak sensitivity occurs earlier. For the even-numbered nodes, these trends continue for subsequent increases in G, although the decrease in sensitivity magnitude is more prevalent than the shift in timing of the peak. In contrast to the results for the even-numbered nodes, the sensitivity results for the three highest G values at the odd-numbered nodes are not coincident in time. Specifically, at Node 3, the results for G values of 0.01 and 0.1 s^{-1} show a phase shift compared to the G value of 0.001 s^{-1}.

For the same set of simulations (varying G value), the velocity sensitivity to G follows the same general trends as the elevation sensitivity.

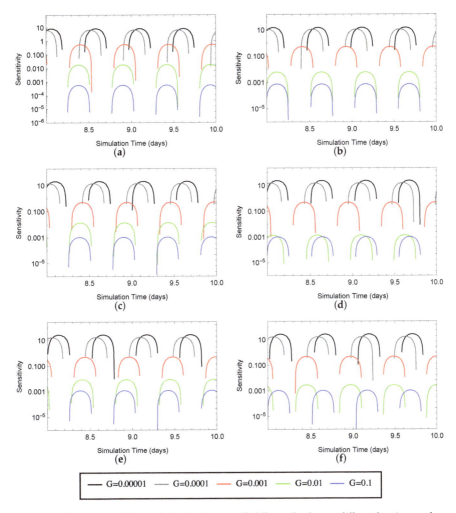

Figure 3. Elevation sensitivity to G, for simulations with different G values, at different locations on the 21-node linear sloping domain. The five different lines on each plot correspond to the five simulations, each with a different value of G as indicated in the legend below the figures. (**a**) Node 2; (**b**) Node 3; (**c**) Node 4; (**d**) Node 5; (**e**) Node 6; (**f**) Node 7.

The GWCE was introduced for CG finite element modeling to control spurious $2\Delta x$ oscillations present in solutions of the shallow water equations using the primitive continuity equation. Increasing G shifts the GWCE towards the primitive continuity equation. The elevation sensitivity results show $2\Delta x$ oscillations in the sensitivity to G for values of the numerical parameter of 0.01 s^{-1} and larger for this application on the linear sloping domain, suggesting those values result in the GWCE becoming "too primitive" for this test case. The decrease in the magnitude of the sensitivity to G as G increases is consistent with the formulation of the equations. Introduction of non-zero G values results in the primitive continuity portion of the GWCE contributing. Eventually, as G values are increased, the primitive continuity term becomes dominant, and further increases in G will have only minimal impacts on the solution.

2.3. Sensitivity Results for Tidal Problem over a Seamount

The simulation parameters for this second test case, using a seamount domain, are listed in Table 2; the values are similar to those used for the case in Section 2.2. The base, 31-node, seamount domain is shown in Figure 4. The length of the simulations was 5.0 days, and the time step was 5.0 s.

Table 2. Parameters for the seamount domain test case.

Parameter	Value
Bathymetry at open boundary	50.0 m
Domain length	60.0 km
τ	0.001 s^{-1}
Tidal forcing amplitude	1.0 m
Tidal forcing period	44,714.8 s
Ramp duration	1.0 days

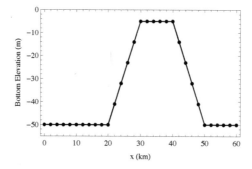

Figure 4. Bathymetry and node locations for the seamount domain.

The elevation sensitivity results (not shown), indicate that the general trends present from the linear sloping domain test case also apply for the seamount domain. Specifically, the magnitude of the sensitivity decreases with increasing G, and the peak sensitivities occur earlier in time for higher G values. Furthermore, node-to-node oscillations in the sensitivities occur for the higher G values in the set, with the $2\Delta x$ oscillations readily apparent for the highest G value, 0.1 s^{-1}.

The elevation sensitivity results from the four simulations with different G values are summarized by the left panel of Figure 5, which shows the peak elevation sensitivity to G, over the last day of the simulation, for each node in the domain for simulations with different G values (0.0001, 0.001, 0.01, 0.1 s^{-1}). The general trend is for the peak elevation sensitivity to increase with distance from the ocean boundary. The results with $G = 0.01$ s^{-1} show $2\Delta x$ oscillations in the magnitude of the peak sensitivity for a substantial portion of the domain, which is indicative of the GWCE becoming "too primitive", even though the sign of the sensitivity does not follow the traditional $2\Delta x$ oscillation pattern that occurs for the highest G values.

The right panel of Figure 5 shows the peak velocity sensitivity to G over the last day of the simulation for each node in the seamount domain for the four simulations with different G values. The sensitivity is zero at the land boundary (Node 31); the peak velocity sensitivity increases from a minimum at the land boundary to a maximum over the seamount (Nodes 16–21), then decreases oceanward of the seamount. The results with a G value of 0.01 s^{-1} show short wavelength oscillations in the peak velocity sensitivity for the majority of the domain. In contrast, the results for the highest G value, 0.1 s^{-1}, do not show prevalent oscillations in the peak velocity sensitivity landward of the start of the rise of the seamount (Node 11). However, a smooth set of peak velocity sensitivity points is not a sufficient condition to conclude that the G value is below the "too primitive" threshold. Time series analysis of the velocity sensitivities for the highest G value reveals the node-to-node switching of signs on the sensitivities, i.e., the positive peak sensitivities for the odd-numbered nodes correspond to the same times as the maximum negative sensitivities for the even-numbered nodes, and vice versa.

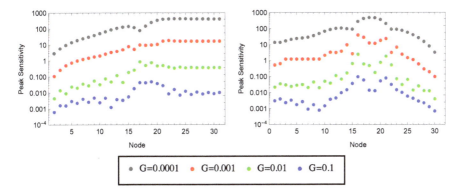

Figure 5. Peak elevation (**left panel**) and velocity (**right panel**) sensitivity to G for implicit runs on the seamount domain. Each dot denotes the peak elevation sensitivity value, for a given node, over the last day of a five day simulation. The color of the dot is based on the G value shown in the legend.

2.4. Comparison of FSM and Numerical Analog Sensitivities

The FSM sensitivity results presented previously predict the changes in the solution (elevations or velocities) that result from a change in the numerical parameter, G. To verify the procedure for computing the FSM sensitivity, the FSM sensitivity is compared to a numerical analog sensitivity. The numerical analog sensitivity is computed using finite differences. In particular, by comparing the results from two simulations with different G values, finite difference approximation of the sensitivity to G can be calculated using Equation (8),

$$\frac{\partial \zeta}{\partial G} \approx \frac{\Delta \zeta}{\Delta G} = \frac{(\zeta_j^k)_2 - (\zeta_j^k)_1}{G_2 - G_1} \tag{8}$$

where the subscripts 1 and 2 refer to the two different simulations.

A comparison of the FSM and numerical analog elevation sensitivities to G for Node 11 in the linear sloping domain is shown in Figure 6. The left panel in Figure 6 is a comparison of the FSM sensitivity to G (black line), for a simulation with a G value of 0.001 s^{-1}, to the numerical analog sensitivity (red line) calculated using results from simulations with G values of 0.001 and 0.003 s^{-1} ($\Delta G = 0.002$). The evolutions of the sensitivities have the same shape, although the magnitude of numerical analog is significantly lower than the FSM sensitivity. The right panel of Figure 6 is a comparison of the FSM sensitivity to G to the forward numerical analog with a smaller difference in G values, $\Delta G = 0.0001$ s^{-1}. It is readily apparent that decreasing the difference in G used to compute the numerical analog reduces the difference between the FSM and numerical analog sensitivities, although the numerical analog sensitivity is still smaller in magnitude than the FSM sensitivity.

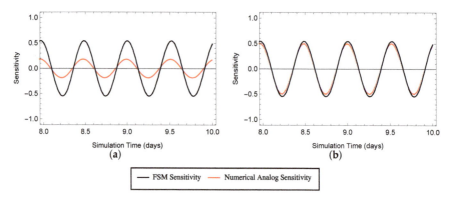

Figure 6. Comparison of forward sensitivity method and numerical analog elevation sensitivity results for the last two days of an explicit model simulation on the linear sloping domain. In each panel, the black line depicts the temporal evolution to the FSM elevation sensitivity to G for a simulation with $G = 0.001$ s^{-1}. The red line shows the time series of the numerical analog sensitivities. In the left panel, the two G values used for the simulations were 0.001 and 0.003 s^{-1}, while G values of 0.001 and 0.0011 s^{-1} were used to generate the numerical analog for the right panel. (a) $\Delta G = 0.002$ s^{-1}; (b) $\Delta G = 0.0001$ s^{-1}.

However, this underprediction by the numerical analog is directly related to the choice of G values used to compute the numerical analog. In this case, the second value of G used to generate the numerical analog is larger than the value of G for which the sensitivity is desired, which will be referred to as a forward numerical analog (because $G_2 > G_1$, meaning ΔG is positive). The sensitivity to G decreases with increasing G (c.f., Figure 3), so the forward numerical analog to G is generally lower than the FSM sensitivity for a simulation with $G = G_1$. Furthermore, for forward numerical analogs, increasing ΔG increases the underprediction. In contrast, use of a similar backward numerical analog would show that the numerical analog sensitivity is slightly greater in magnitude than the FSM sensitivity.

The results presented above show that the sensitivities computed using the FSM are consistent with the sensitivities calculated using the numerical analog as ΔG goes to zero, and the comparison confirms that the behavior predicted by the FSM actually occurs in the solution as G varies. As such, the FSM presents an opportunity to perform data assimilation, explored in Section 3, based on errors between observations and results from a simulation with a given value of G, although one could alternatively use a numerical analog approach to compute sensitivities for use in the data assimilation step. The equivalence of the FSM and numerical analog sensitivities gives rise to the following question: what is the benefit of FSM over a reasonably simple and straightforward numerical finite difference calculation? In the case of the constant G simulations presented herein, the two methods would require similar computational effort. However, for multi-parameter estimation, as is required for spatially- and temporally-variable G specification, where sensitivities to p variables is necessary, $p+1$ ADCIRC simulations would be necessary to compute the p numerical analog sensitivities (with one base run and p simulations with a small change in each parameter), whereas the FSM sensitivities to p parameters can be computed during an individual simulation.

3. Data Assimilation Using Forward Sensitivities

3.1. Data Assimilation Approach

The second component of the FSM is the data assimilation step to correct G using the sensitivities and computed model errors. As presented in [19], using a first-order approach, where only the first term in the Taylor series expansion is retained, the error is equal to the product of the sensitivity and the correction, as given by Equation (9),

$$\mathbf{e}(x, t, G) = \mathbf{z}(x, t) - \mathbf{c}(x, t, G) \approx (\Delta G)\mathbf{w}(x, t, G) \tag{9}$$

where for spatial location x, time t and numerical parameter value G, $\mathbf{e}(x, t, G)$ is the simulation error, $\mathbf{z}(x, t)$ is the observation value, $\mathbf{c}(x, t, G)$ is the model result, ΔG is the correction to the numerical parameter and $\mathbf{w}(x, t, G)$ is the sensitivity to G.

The correction can be computed in a variety of ways. The simplest correction uses an observation at one point in space, x_j, at one time, t_k, along with the model results for the same location in space and time. The correction, ΔG, to the value used for the simulation, G_0, based on this one observation is shown in Equation (10).

$$\Delta G(G_0) = \frac{e(x_j, t_k, G_0)}{w(x_j, t_k, G_0)} \tag{10}$$

Least-squares minimization is a more sophisticated approach that allows for the use of multiple observations in space or time. For the results herein, least-squares minimization will be applied on a nodal basis. In other words, the observations and model results for a given point in space, over a range of time, will be used to compute a least-squares correction to G. This is analogous to the real-world situation where a buoy collects a time series of water surface elevation data at a fixed location in the domain. Conversely, least-squares minimization could be applied on a temporal basis where errors throughout the domain, at a given time, are used to generate a correction to G.

The least-squares correction, based on results and observations for node j using *nrecs* values in time, requires the vector of sensitivities $\mathbf{H}_j$ and the error vector $\mathbf{e}_j$.

$$\mathbf{H}_j = \{w_j^1, w_j^2, ..., w_j^{nrecs}\}^T \tag{11}$$

$$\mathbf{e}_j = \{z_j^1 - c_j^1, z_j^2 - c_j^2, ..., z_j^{nrecs} - c_j^{nrecs}\}^T \tag{12}$$

The optimal least-squares correction, adapted from [19] for a scalar parameter, is given by Equation (13).

$$(\Delta G)_j = \frac{\mathbf{H}_j^T \mathbf{e}_j}{\mathbf{H}_j^T \mathbf{H}_j} \tag{13}$$

The optimal least-squares correction is a standard result that is presented in [21], which provides additional detail about the origins of the analysis technique.

3.2. Correction to CG Results on the Linear Sloping Domain

In this section, "observations" will be taken from model results generated using the 2D CG version of ADCIRC on a rectangular grid that is uniform in the y-direction. The 2D code was run implicitly with the same parameters as the 1D code, and the 2D domain consists of 11 nodes in the y-direction for each of the 21 nodes in the x-direction for the linear sloping domain. Results for the sixth line of nodes (the centerline) from a simulation with a constant G value of 0.001 s^{-1} are used as the observations. Furthermore, the x-component of the velocity from the 2D model is used as the velocity observation; the y-component of the velocity is ignored, but is generally several orders of magnitude less than the x-component (and close to zero).

The purpose of the data assimilation step in the FSM is to reduce model error. Therefore, before delving into the calculations of the corrections, it is informative to analyze model error for a range of G values. The error metric is the temporal mean of the root mean square error in space, denoted as $\overline{RMSE_x}$. The equation for the temporal mean of the root mean square elevation error in space is shown in Equation (14).

$$\overline{RMSE_x(\zeta)} = \frac{1}{nrecs} \sum_{k=1}^{nrecs} (RMSE_x(\zeta))^k \tag{14}$$

The elevation error results are shown in the left panel of Figure 7, while the velocity error results are shown in the right panel.

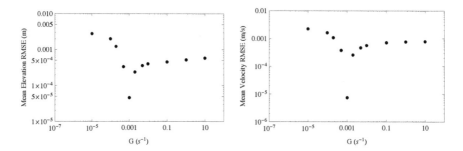

Figure 7. $\overline{RMSE_x(\zeta)}$ (**left panel**) and $\overline{RMSE_x(u)}$ (**right panel**) results, over the last two days of 10.0-day simulation, for simulations with different values of G on the linear sloping domain, using observations from the 2D CG ADCIRC model with $G = 0.001$ s^{-1}.

For the G values used in the implicit 1D simulations, the minimum elevation and velocity errors are achieved when approximately the same G value is used in the 1D model as was used in the 2D model (to create the observations). The value of G that minimizes the error (i.e., $G \approx 0.001$ s^{-1}) is the value of G that should be revealed using the data assimilation step of the FSM. When available, elevation data are often in the form of time series at discrete location. Thus, herein, a time series of elevation observations will be used to calculate errors, and the correction will be computed using those errors and the corresponding time series of sensitivity values for a given node, as per Equation (13).

The correction varies for a given run depend on which node is used to calculate the correction. For example, the corrections based on the results from the simulation with $G = 0.0001$ s^{-1} are shown in Figure 8. The error and the sensitivity of the elevation results to G are both zero at the left boundary node, so the correction is not computed at that location (Node 1); rather, the correction is set to zero for plotting purposes. The correction can be calculated for each of the other nodes in the domain, and Figure 8 shows the correction to be just slightly greater than 0.0001 s^{-1} for each of the nodes. However, we know the optimal correction is close to 0.0009 s^{-1}, based on the values of G used for the runs to generate the model and observation results. The discrepancy between the computed least-squares correction and the optimal correction (which would result in the new value of G being the one that minimizes the model error) is a result of the variation in the sensitivity with G, as well as the fact that only the first order terms are kept in the Taylor series development of the correction equation. The sensitivity to G is much greater when $G = 0.0001$ s^{-1} than when $G = 0.001$ s^{-1}. Because the correction varies inversely with the sensitivity, the correction calculated using the sensitivity from the run with $G = 0.0001$ s^{-1} is, expectedly, low.

In order to show how the correction varies with G, the maximum, minimum and mean of the nodal corrections were calculated. Referring back to Figure 8, which shows a set of nodal least-squares corrections for the simulation with $G = 0.0001$ s^{-1}, the maximum correction is from Node 2, $\Delta G = 0.000168$ s^{-1}, while the minimum comes from Node 9 ($\Delta G = 0.000107$ s^{-1}). The mean correction is the arithmetic mean of the nodal corrections for Nodes 2–21. The results are shown in Figure 9.

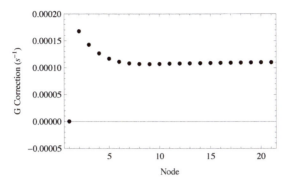

Figure 8. Nodal least-squares corrections, ΔG, for each node based on results for an implicit simulation with $G = 0.0001$ s^{-1} using output from the last two days of the 10.0-day simulation on the linear sloping domain. Observations are from the 2D CG ADCIRC code with $G = 0.001$ s^{-1}.

As seen in Figure 9, for a given simulation, the maximum, minimum and mean corrections are similar for simulations with G values less than 0.005 s^{-1}. Thus, regardless of location in the domain, the correction is similar, as was the case for the set of corrections shown in Figure 8. Interestingly, for the simulations with G values less than 0.001 s^{-1}, the corrections are larger for the simulations with G values closer to the target value, which seems counterintuitive. However, as mentioned previously, the large variation in sensitivity with G causes under-corrections for simulations with low G values.

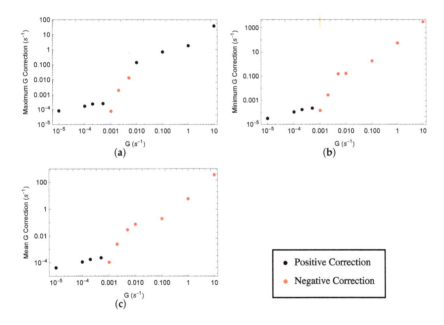

Figure 9. Maximum, minimum and mean nodal least-squares correction, ΔG, for simulations over a range of G values, using output from the last two days of the 10.0-day simulation on the linear sloping domain. The magnitude of the correction is shown as the ordinate, while the color of the dot corresponds to the sign of the correction: positive corrections are shown in black, and negative corrections are shown in red. Observations are from the 2D CG ADCIRC code with $G = 0.001$ s^{-1}. (**a**) Maximum; (**b**) minimum; (**c**) mean.

For the simulations with G values of 0.002 and 0.005 s^{-1}, the corrections are consistent and negative, as expected. However, the mean correction is larger in magnitude than the value of G used for the simulation. For example, the mean correction for the simulation with $G = 0.005$ s^{-1} is $\Delta G = -0.289$ s^{-1}. In contrast to the corrections from simulations with G values less than the optimal value, simulations with G values greater than the optimal value have corrections that are too large in magnitude.

Furthermore, for G values of 0.01 s^{-1} and above, some of the corrections are positive (indicated by the black dots on the top left panel in Figure 9), which is opposite in sign from the mean corrections. The presence of positive and negative corrections for the same simulation is a result of the GWCE becoming "too primitive". The initial appearance (lowest G value that experiences oscillations) corresponds to the G threshold above which spurious oscillations are generated. When the solution becomes "too primitive", the sensitivities start to become irregular. Rather than being similar from one node to the next, the sensitivities for successive nodes are opposite in sign or have varying magnitudes of the same sign. This transition from a normal pattern of sensitivities to an irregular one produces the aberrant correction results.

The difference in results for two model simulations is given by Equation (15).

$$\Delta \zeta = \int_{G}^{G+\Delta G} w(x, t, G) \, \partial G \tag{15}$$

For G values just greater than $G = 0.001$ s^{-1}, the sensitivities are similar from node to node. Therefore, the errors for model simulations with small deviations from the target value used in these studies will be similar between nodes, as long as G is not increased too much. When $G = 0.01$ s^{-1}, there are $2\Delta x$ oscillations in the sensitivities. Thus, at some G value between 0.001 and 0.01 s^{-1}, $2\Delta x$ oscillations begin to develop in the error values as a result of the oscillations in the sensitivities.

By computing the numerical analog using the target value as one of the G values for the simulation, the result is the average sensitivity over the span of G values. This average sensitivity can be compared to the FSM sensitivity, which gives the instantaneous sensitivity value. Figure 10 is a comparison of the numerical analog sensitivity between G values of 0.001 and 0.1 s^{-1} and FSM sensitivity for $G = 0.1$ s^{-1} for the 11th and 12th nodes in the linear sloping domain. It is readily apparent that the FSM sensitivity results are opposite in sign for the two nodes. However, the numerical analog sensitivity results are similar for the two nodes. The notable difference is the magnitude of the numerical analog sensitivities is larger for Node 12 than Node 11, which implies there is more error for results at Node 12 than Node 11. In this case, the ΔG value used to compute the numerical analog is -0.099 s^{-1}. Therefore, when the numerical analog sensitivity is positive, the error is negative, and vice versa. It should also be noted that the FSM sensitivities are, generally, in-phase with the numerical analog sensitivities for Node 12, whereas the two sets of sensitivities are out-of-phase for Node 11. Therefore, an additional increase in G away from $G = 0.001$ s^{-1} will cause increases in the magnitude of the error at Node 12 and decreases in the magnitude of the error at Node 11.

As mentioned previously, the occurrences of positive numerical analog sensitivities in Figure 10 (e.g., the peak values occurring approximately 8.0, 8.5, 9.0, 9.5 and 10.0 days into the simulation) correspond to times of negative model error (compared to the simulation with $G = 0.001$ s^{-1}), and vice versa. Therefore, 9.0 days into the simulation, the error is negative at Nodes 11 and 12. For Node 11, the numerical analog and FSM sensitivities are out-of-phase, which means that, generally, when the FSM sensitivity is positive/negative, the error is positive/negative (numerical analog sensitivity is negative/positive). Subsequently, the correction to G will be positive, which is the wrong direction. In contrast, the numerical analog and FSM sensitivities are generally in-phase at Node 12, which results in the correction to G being negative, because the product of the error and sensitivity vectors is negative. The corrections to G for each of the nodes are shown in Figure 11. As expected, based on Figure 10, the correction produced using results for Node 11 is positive, while the correction generated using results for Node 12 is negative.

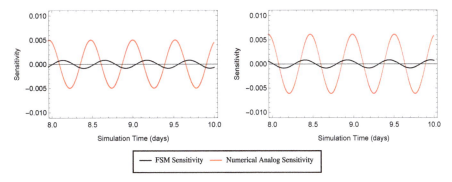

Figure 10. Numerical analog sensitivity (red) between implicit 1D results with G= 0.001 s^{-1} and $G = 0.1$ s^{-1} and FSM sensitivity (black) for $G = 0.1$ s^{-1} for the 11th (**left panel**) and 12th (**right panel**) nodes in the linear sloping domain.

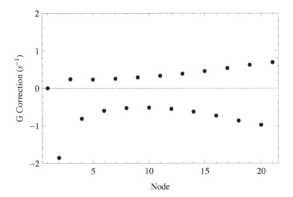

Figure 11. Nodal least-squares corrections, ΔG, for each node based on results for an implicit simulation with $G = 0.1$ s^{-1} using output from the last two days of the 10.0-day simulation on the linear sloping domain. Observations are from the 2D CG ADCIRC code with $G = 0.001$ s^{-1}.

4. Sequential Optimization

In the previous section, corrections to G were calculated based on model errors and sensitivities to G. In this section, the correction, ΔG, is added to the previous G value to determine the next G value. This process is continued until the new correction is below a certain threshold, which signifies that the optimization process has converged at the target value.

The linear sloping domain is used for this proof-of-concept application, along with the explicit version of the code. The simulation parameters are the same as those used previously, with the exception that the run is only 5.0 days long, and corrections are generated using the results from the last day of the simulation. The observations are the elevation results along the centerline of the 2D ADCIRC simulation with $G = 0.001$ s^{-1}. The correction, ΔG, is the mean of the nodal corrections using the elevation results to compute the errors.

The initial G value for this exercise is 0.0005 s^{-1}, and the convergence threshold for ΔG was set at 1.0×10^{-10} s^{-1}. As expected, specification of an initial value that is less than the target value resulted in each correction being in the appropriate direction (positive), with less than the optimal magnitude, as shown in Table 3. The target value is the value at which the sequential optimization finishes, 8.98×10^{-4} s^{-1} (however, it is close to the value of G used in the 2D model to create the observations, but in practice, this would not be known). The ratio of the correction to the optimal correction is notable; as the G value approaches the target value, the correction approaches the optimal correction. This is logical because as the difference between the current and target G values goes to zero, the instantaneous sensitivity to G given by the FSM gets closer to the average sensitivity over the range.

Table 3. Sequential optimization of G for the linear sloping domain compared to the 2D CG simulation with $G = 0.001\text{s}^{-1}$. The units for each of the columns, except for the fourth column, are s^{-1}. The ratios in the fourth column are dimensionless.

G Value	Mean Nodal Correction, ΔG	Optimal Correction, ΔG_{opt}	$\frac{\Delta G}{\Delta G_{opt}}$	New G Value, $G + \Delta G$
5.00×10^{-4}	2.24×10^{-4}	3.98×10^{-4}	0.564	7.24×10^{-4}
7.24×10^{-4}	1.39×10^{-4}	1.74×10^{-4}	0.801	8.63×10^{-4}
8.63×10^{-4}	3.28×10^{-5}	3.46×10^{-5}	0.948	8.96×10^{-4}
8.96×10^{-4}	1.78×10^{-6}	1.81×10^{-6}	0.983	8.98×10^{-4}
8.98×10^{-4}	3.10×10^{-8}	3.14×10^{-8}	0.984	8.98×10^{-4}
8.98×10^{-4}	4.81×10^{-10}	4.88×10^{-10}	0.986	8.98×10^{-4}
8.98×10^{-4}	7.02×10^{-12}	7.02×10^{-12}	1.000	8.98×10^{-4}

Additionally, tests were performed with an initial G value greater than the target value. As expected, specification of a value larger than the target, but still below the primitive threshold, results in an over-correction in the first step. For the explicit code with an initial value of $1.20 \times 10^{-3} \text{ s}^{-1}$, the mean correction for the first step is $\Delta G = -3.94 \times 10^{-4} \text{ s}^{-1}$, resulting in a new G value of 8.06×10^{-4}. From there, the corrections bring the G value up to the target value. However, if the initial specification is significantly higher than the target, the over-correction can result in negative G value. For instance, the mean correction with $G = 2.00 \times 10^{-3} \text{ s}^{-1}$ is $-2.38 \times 10^{-3} \text{ s}^{-1}$, which is larger than the previous G value. Thus, in practice, constraints on G would have to be put into the optimization algorithm.

5. Comparison of FSM to Dispersion Analysis

Kolar et al. [5] performed a dispersion analysis of the 1D shallow water equations using the GWCE for the Bight of Abaco, Bahamas. Kolar et al. noted that spurious $2\Delta x$ oscillations do not occur if the dispersion curve is monotonic. In their paper, they delineated the frequency for the M_6 tide [5] (p. 536) and found that the monotonic dispersion relations for this frequency exist as long as G does not exceed 0.075 s^{-1}. The frequency of the M_2 tide is one third the frequency of the M_6 tide, so G must be less than approximately 0.3 s^{-1} to ensure the solution remains free of spurious, short-wavelength oscillations for the M_2 frequency.

The dispersion analysis performed in Kolar et al. [5] used a bathymetry value of 2.0 m, an element size of 2700 m and a bottom friction value of 0.01 s^{-1}. For this study, these parameters were also used in 1D simulations with a flat bottom domain consisting of 21 nodes. The time step for the 1D simulations was 5.0 s. Larger time steps result in differences in the calculated sensitivities, whereas the sensitivities were consistent between simulations with time steps of 2.5 and 5.0 s. It should also be noted that dispersion analysis is restricted to interior nodes. The 1D simulations herein using the FSM include boundaries that are treated as stated previously (specified elevation on the left, zero velocity on the right).

For the 1D simulations using the M_6 tide, the dispersion analysis predicts spurious oscillations for G values greater than 0.075 s^{-1}. The elevation FSM sensitivity results are free of $2\Delta x$ oscillations with $G = 0.01 \text{ s}^{-1}$. With $G = 0.03 \text{ s}^{-1}$, the sensitivity results show $2\Delta x$ oscillations for the first four elements in from the left boundary. However, the interior of the domain is not impacted. Further increase of G results in oscillations in a greater percentage of the domain.

Using the M_2 tide, the dispersion analysis predicts spurious oscillations for G values greater than or equal to approximately 0.3 s^{-1}. Again, oscillations in the FSM elevation sensitivities to G do not occur with $G = 0.01$ s^{-1} and occur only near the ocean boundary with $G = 0.03$ s^{-1}. Similar to the case for the M$_6$ forcing, the oscillations become more prevalent as G increases, although the M$_2$ forced simulations generally have less prominent $2\Delta x$ noise than the simulations with the M$_6$ forcing. This is consistent with the results suggested by the dispersion analysis. With a G value of 0.1 s^{-1}, the entire domain experiences $2\Delta x$ oscillations.

The FSM sensitivities and dispersion analysis do not produce exactly the same values of G for the onset of $2\Delta x$ oscillations in the solution. Given the underlying differences in the analysis techniques (e.g., dispersion analysis is confined to interior nodes and continuous time), this is not an entirely surprising result. However, the similarity between the results for the two techniques points to FSM being a useful tool in the analysis of problems where dispersion analysis is not valid (e.g., non-linear equations, non-constant bathymetry, etc.).

6. Conclusions

The FSM was successfully applied to the linearized, 1D version of ADCIRC with constant G. The FSM is useful in determining the sensitivity, both in space and time, to G. In particular, the sensitivity of the elevation and velocity fields to changes in G varies greatly with G. The sensitivity is much greater at low values of G than at higher values, where the GWCE effectively approaches the primitive continuity equation. Additionally, as G increases, the sensitivities from the FSM show the $2\Delta x$ oscillations that plague the continuous Galerkin finite element solution when the primitive continuity equation is used instead of the GWCE. Furthermore, the maximum G threshold, above which the GWCE becomes "too primitive" and results in the generation of spurious $2\Delta x$ oscillations, can be identified through analysis of the FSM sensitivities. In that sense, FSM can be used as a tool like dispersion analysis to predict the folding of dispersion relations, with the advantage of being applicable to complex, real-world problems.

The corrections, ΔG, calculated in the data assimilation step of the FSM are intrinsically tied to the sensitivities. The change in sensitivity over the range of possible G values makes direct estimation of the optimal correction difficult using first-order methods. At high G values, the corrections are also hindered by the $2\Delta x$ oscillations in the sensitivities. However, sequential optimization should be possible as long as care is taken in the specification of the starting point for optimization. Specifically, use of a low initial value is optimal because the corrections are more stable, compared to higher values of G.

While this analysis was limited to the linearized, 1D SWE, the FSM has potential use in more complex systems. Additionally, while the analysis is focused on the sensitivity of the system to G, the method can be adapted to analyze other parameters of the model.

Acknowledgments: Funding for the project was provided, in part, by the National Oceanic and Atmospheric Administration—Integrated Ocean Observation System and the Department of Homeland Security Coastal Hazards Center of Excellence, which the authors gratefully acknowledge. Additional resources were provided by the University of Oklahoma. Any opinions, conclusions or findings are those of the authors and are not necessarily endorsed by the funding agencies.

Author Contributions: S.Lakshmivarahan developed the theory of the Forward Sensitivity Method (FSM) and helped advise E. Tromble (then a Ph.D. student) on that aspect of his dissertation work. R. Kolar and K. Dresback, advisor and member of E. Tromble's Ph.D. committee, respectively, provided guidance on the ADCIRC model and a historical perspective of the G-parameter. They also helped with the composition of the manuscript. E. Tromble carried out the details of the work as part of his dissertation.

Conflicts of Interest: The authors declare no conflict of interest. The funding sponsors had no role in the design of the study; in the collection, analyses or interpretation of data; in the writing of the manuscript; nor in the decision to publish the results.

Abbreviations

The following abbreviations are used in this manuscript:

FSM   Forward Sensitivity Method
GWCE   Generalized Wave Continuity Equation
WCE   Wave Continuity Equation
ADCIRC ADvanced CIRCulation
CG   Continuous Galerkin
1D   One-Dimensional
2D   Two-Dimensional

References

1. Kinnmark, I.P.E. The shallow water wave equations: Formulations, analysis and application. In *Lecture Notes in Engineering*; Brebbia, C.A., Orsszag, S.A., Eds.; Springer: Berlin, Germany, 1986; Volume 15, p. 187.
2. Lynch, D.R.; Gray, W.G. A wave equation model for finite element tidal computations. *Comput. Fluids* **1979**, *7*, 207–228.
3. Foreman, M.G.G. An analysis of two-step time discretizations in the solution of the linearized shallow water equations. *J. Comput. Phys.* **1983**, *51*, 454–483.
4. Gray, W.G. Some inadequacies of finite element models as simulators for two-dimensional circulation. *Adv. Water Resour.* **1982**, *5*, 171–177.
5. Kolar, R.L.; Westerink, J.J.; Cantekin, M.E.; Blain, C.A. Aspects of nonlinear simulations using shallow-water models based on the wave continuity equation. *Comput. Fluids* **1994**, *23*, 523–538.
6. Aldama, A.A.; Aguilar, A.; Kolar, R.L.; Westerink, J.J. A Mass Conservation Analysis of the Generalized Wave Continuity Equation formulation of the Shallow Water Equations. In Proceedings of the 13th International Conference on Computational Methods in Water Resources, Calgary, AB, Canada, 25–29 June 2000; Bentley, L.R., Ed.; A.A. Balkema Publishers: Rotterdam, The Netherlands, 2000; Volume 2.
7. Atkinson, J.; Westerink, J.; Hervouet, J. Similarities between the quasi-bubble and the generalized wave continuity equation solutions to the shallow water equations. *Int. J. Numer. Methods Fluids* **2004**, *45*, 689–714.
8. Luettich, R.A.; Westerink, J.J.; Scheffner, N.W. *ADCIRC: An Advanced Three-Dimensional Circulation Model for Shelves, Coasts, and Estuaries. Report 1. Theory and Methodology of ADCIRC-2DDI and ADCIRC-3DL*; Technical Report DRP-92-6; USACE Dredging Research Program, Department of the Army US Army Corp of Engineers: Washington, DC, USA, 1992.
9. Westerink, J.J.; Luettich, R.A. *ADCIRC: An Advanced Three-Dimensional Circulation Model for Shelves, Coasts, and Estuaries. Report 2. User's Manual for ADCIRC-2DDI*; Technical Report; Army Engineer Waterways Experiment Station: Vicksburg, MS, USA, 1994.
10. Luettich, R.A.; Westerink, J.J. Formulation and Numerical Implementation of the 2D/3D ADCIRC Finite Element Model Version 44.XX. Available online: http://www.unc.edu/ims/adcirc/adcirc_theory_2004_12_08.pdf (accessed on 3 November 2016).
11. Westerink, J.J.; Luettich, R.A.; Feyen, J.C.; Atkinson, J.H.; Dawson, C.; Roberts, H.J.; Powell, M.D.; Dunion, J.P.; Kubatko, E.J.; Pourtaheri, H. A basin- to channel-scale unstructured grid hurricane storm surge model applied to southern Louisiana. *Mon. Weather Rev.* **2008**, *136*, 833–864.
12. Dietrich, J.C.; Westerink, J.J.; Kennedy, A.B.; Smith, J.M.; Jensen, R.E.; Zijlema, M.; Holthuijsen, L.H.; Dawson, C.; Luettich, R.A.; Powell, M.D.; et al. Hurricane gustav (2008) waves and storm surge: Hindcast, synoptic analysis, and validation in Southern Louisiana. *Mon. Weather Rev.* **2011**, *139*, 2488–2522.
13. Bunya, S.; Dietrich, J.C.; Westerink, J.J.; Ebersole, B.A.; Smith, J.M.; Atkinson, J.H.; Jensen, R.; Resio, D.T.; Luettich, R.A.; Dawson, C.; et al. A high resolution coupled riverine flow, tide, wind, wind wave and storm surge model for Southern Louisiana and Mississippi: Part 1—Model development and validation. *Mon. Weather Rev.* **2010**, *138*, 345–377.
14. U.S. Army Corp of Engineers. Performance Evaluation of the New Orleans and Southeastern Louisiana Hurricane Protection System. Final Report of the Interagency Performance Evaluation Task (IPET) Force. 2009. Available online: https://ipet.wes.army.mil/ (accessed on 23 September 2016).

15. U.S. Army Corp of Engineers. Flood Insurance Study: Southeastern Parishes, Louisiana, Intermediate Submission 2: Offshore Water Levels and Waves, FEMA, US Army Corp of Engineers, New Orleans District. 2008. Available online: http://www.nd.edu/~coast/femaIDS2.html (accessed on 23 September 2016).

16. Dresback, K.M.; Fleming, J.G.; Blanton, B.O.; Kaiser, C.; Gourley, J.J.; Tromble, E.M.; Luettich, R.A.; Kolar, R.L.; Hong, Y.; van Cooten, S.; et al. Skill assessment of a real-time forecast system utilizing a coupled hydrologic and coastal hydrodynamic model during Hurricane Irene (2011). *Cont. Shelf Res.* **2013**, *71*, 78–94.

17. Hope, M.E.; Westerink, J.J.; Kennedy, A.B.; Kerr, P.C.; Dietrich, J.C.; Dawson, C.; Bender, C.J.; Smith, J.M.; Jensen, R.E.; Zijlema, M.; et al. Hindcast and validation of Hurricane Ike (2008) waves, forerunner, and storm surge. *J. Geophys. Res. Oceans* **2013**, *118*, 4424–4460.

18. Mewis, P.; Holtz, K.P. A quasi bubble-function approach for shallow water waves. In *Advances in Hydro-Science and Engineering*, Proceeding of the First International Conference on Hydro-Science and Engineering, Washington, DC, USA, 7–11 June 1993; Volume 1, pp. 768–774.

19. Lakshmivarahan, S.; Lewis, J. Forward sensitivity approach to dynamic data assimilation. *Adv. Meteorol.* **2010**, *2010*, 375615.

20. Rabitz, H.; Kramer, M.; Dacol, D. Sensitivity analysis in chemical kinetics. *Annu. Rev. Phys. Chem.* **1983**, *334*, 419–461.

21. Lewis, J.; Lakshmivarahan, S.; Dhall, S. *Dynamic Data Assimilation: A Least Squares Approach*; Cambridge University Press: Cambridge, UK, 2006.

22. Lakshmivarahan, S.; Lewis, J.M.; Jabrzemski, R. *Forecast Error Correction Using Dynamic Data Assimilation*; Springer: New York, NY, USA, 2016; in press.

23. Tromble, E.M. Advances Using the ADCIRC Hydrodynamic Model: Parameter Estimation and Aspects of Coupled Hydrologic-Hydrodynamic Flood Inundation Modeling. Ph.D. Thesis, University of Oklahoma, Norman, OK, USA, 2011.

Journal of
*Marine Science
and Engineering*

Article

Simulating the Response of Estuarine Salinity to Natural and Anthropogenic Controls

Vladimir A. Paramygin [1,*], Y. Peter Sheng [1], Justin R. Davis [1] and Karen Herrington [2]

1   Coastal and Oceanographic Engineering Program, University of Florida, Gainesville, FL 32611-6580, USA;
    pete@coastal.ufl.edu (Y.P.S.); davis@coastal.ufl.edu (J.R.D.)
2   Fish and Wildlife Biologist, Ecological Services Midwest Regional Office, U.S. Fish and Wildlife Service,
    Bloomington, MN 55437-1458, USA; Karen_herrington@fws.gov
*   Correspondence: pva@coastal.ufl.edu; Tel.: +1-352-294-7763

Academic Editor: Richard P. Signell
Received: 18 July 2016; Accepted: 8 November 2016; Published: 16 November 2016

Abstract: The response of salinity in Apalachicola Bay, Florida to changes in water management alternatives and storm and sea level rise is studied using an integrated high-resolution hydrodynamic modeling system based on Curvilinear-grid Hydrodynamics in 3D (CH3D), an oyster population model, and probability analysis. The model uses input from river inflow, ocean and atmospheric forcing and is verified with long-term water level and salinity data, including data from the 2004 hurricane season when four hurricanes impacted the system. Strong freshwater flow from the Apalachicola River and good connectivity of the bay to the ocean allow the estuary to restore normal salinity conditions within a few days after the passage of a hurricane. Various scenarios are analyzed; some based on observed data and others using altered freshwater inflow. For observed flow, simulated salinity agrees well with the observed values. In scenarios that reflect increased water demand (~1%) upstream of the Apalachicola River, the model results show slightly (less than 5%) increased salinity inside the Bay. A worst-case sea-level rise (~1 m by 2100) could increase the bay salinity by up to 20%. A hypothesis that a Sumatra gauge may not fully represent the flow into Apalachicola Bay was tested and appears to be substantiated.

Keywords: Apalachicola Bay; salinity; oysters; model

1. Introduction

For over two decades, the states of Georgia, Alabama, and Florida have been debating potential solutions to the management of shared water resources of the Apalachicola-Chattahoochee-Flint (ACF) River Basin. The ACF River Basin originates in northeast Georgia, crosses the Georgia-Alabama border into central Alabama, and follows the state line south until it terminates in Apalachicola Bay, Florida. The U. S. Army Corps of Engineers (USACE) operates five reservoirs on the Chattahoochee River and its water management operations impact fish and wildlife resources [1,2]. The river's water is used for various municipal, industrial, and agricultural users throughout the length of the system. As consumptive water use has steadily increased over the past several decades, reliance on the USACE's reservoirs to support river flows has also increased, and the amount of freshwater inflow into Apalachicola Bay has declined [1]. Reductions in freshwater inflow influence the salinity regime, which is critical to many marine species, including oysters and the threatened Gulf sturgeon. The USACE is currently updating their Water Control Plan for the ACF, which requires review under the Endangered Species Act and the Fish and Wildlife Coordination Act. Together, these laws attempt to assure that their proposed reservoir operations plan does not jeopardize the continued existence of endangered or threatened species, or destroy or adversely modify their critical habitat, and provides measures to mitigate impacts to fish and wildlife resources. Therefore, it is essential to develop a quantitative understanding of how freshwater inflow impacts salinity in Apalachicola Bay. Another factor that could have a significant effect on Apalachicola Bay is the potential sea-level rise. As the ocean levels rise, the salinity in the bay could increase [3,4]. Quantifying the effect of sea-level rise could help with planning and development of practical consumption scenarios for the ACF system that are mindful of the Apalachicola Bay well-being.

Apalachicola Bay is located along the Florida panhandle (Figure 1) and is well known for shrimp and oyster harvests. It produces about 90% of Florida's commercial oysters and is the only place in the United States where wild oysters are still harvested by tongs from small boats. The shallow (3–6 m) and flat bay is connected to the Gulf of Mexico via five openings counterbalancing the relatively large freshwater inflow from the Apalachicola River. Huang and Spaulding [5], using computer model simulations, found that the residence time in Apalachicola Bay typically ranges between three and nine days, with the daily inflow from Apalachicola River ranging between 177 m^3/s (drought season) and 4561 m^3/s (flood season).

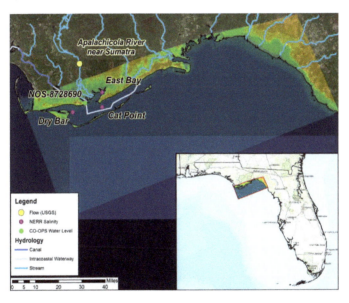

Figure 1. Apalachicola Bay system, data stations and Curvilinear-grid Hydrodynamics in 3D (CH3D) model grid (outlined in red).

The estuary receives over 90% of its freshwater from the Apalachicola River, which, combined with the Chattahoochee River, Flint River and Chipola River drain a watershed of over 20,000 m^2. The importance of the Apalachicola Bay system has been long recognized and the region has been designated as a National Estuarine Research Reserve (NERR), an Outstanding Florida Water, a State Aquatic Preserve, and an International Biosphere Reserve. Apalachicola NERR (ANERR) is the third largest reserve in the nation [2,3].

The importance of freshwater inflow has been recognized for years by managers and researchers alike, with the oyster population being particularly sensitive to the salinity regime in the bay. Livingston et al. [4] found that oyster production and mortality are correlated to bay salinity in the bay. High salinity can cause increased predation from invasive species such as stone crabs and oyster drills causing a significant drop in oyster production. Gulf sturgeon are also sensitive to changes in salinity. As an anadromous fish, the Gulf sturgeon is adapted to life in both fresh and saline waters; however, juvenile fish develop a tolerance to higher salinity gradually during the first year of life, and juvenile growth rates are highest when the salinity is 9 ppt [5]. Extended periods of salinity less than 10 ppt would likely limit feeding habitat availability [6,7], and availability of lower-salinity estuarine feeding habitats may influence recruitment [8–12].

Simulation of salinity and impact on oyster inside Apalachicola Bay has been conducted by Huang [13,14] and Wang et al. [15] using a coarse (~500–1000 m) grid hydrodynamic model and a relatively small model domain without the full influence of the ocean. In this study, the simulation of salinity is validated using a high-resolution coastal and estuarine hydrodynamic model, Curvilinear-grid Hydrodynamics in 3D (CH3D) [16–18] and a larger model domain coupled to an ocean model using observed river inflow rates during 1999–2008 (Scenario I). Once calibrated, the model is used to simulate the response of the system to four water management scenarios developed by the USACE. In these scenarios freshwater entering the system through the Apalachicola River is determined by: (I) the USACE's Hydrologic Engineering Center Reservoir System Simulation program, HEC-ResSim [19]; (II) The current reservoir operations in the ACF system; (III) and (IV) alternative reservoir operation plans with higher consumptive water usage. Simulated salinity is then analyzed as to its potential to affect the oysters' growth and/or mortality rates.

2. Materials and Methods

2.1. Observed Data for Model Validation

Water level data (relative to the North American Vertical Datum of 1988 (NAVD88) datum and with 6-min temporal resolution) was obtained from the NOAA (National Oceanic and Atmospheric Administration) CO-OPS (Center for Operational Oceanographic Products and Services) station NOS-8728690 located near the mouth of the Apalachicola River (Figure 1). NOAA also provides predictions of the tides based on the analysis of tidal constituents at the site, which is useful in identifying how well the model represents the tides. Regional tides are relatively low with three constituents (M2, S2 and K1) dominating the tidal signal.

The bay features several data collection sites that measure salinity, temperature and nutrient data. Salinity records are available at several locations near oyster bars: Cat Point, Dry Bar and East Bay (Figure 1) from 2002 to 2007. Near-surface salinity observations are available at 30-min and 15-min intervals depending on the time of collection.

2.2. The Integrated Modeling System—Description and Setup

The hydrodynamic modeling system used in this study is based on the CH3D (Curvilinear-grid Hydrodynamics in 3D) model [16,20]. CH3D had been used in numerous studies of complex shallow estuaries including Indian River Lagoon, Tampa Bay, Sarasota Bay, Roberts Bay, Florida Bay, Charlotte Harbor, West Florida Shelf, St. Johns River, Lake Okeechobee, and Lake Apopka, etc. (e.g., [21–27]).

CH3D uses a non-orthogonal horizontally boundary-fitted curvilinear grid and a vertically terrain-following sigma grid that accurately resolve coastal and nearshore waters with complex shoreline and bathymetry. The model contains a robust turbulence closure model [28] that enables accurate simulation of turbulent mixing and stratified flows. A fully integrated modeling system ACMS (Advanced Coastal Modeling System, formerly split into two subsystems: CH3D-IMS (Integrated Modeling System) and CH3D-SSMS (Storm Surge Modeling System)) has been developed and applied to several estuarine systems including the Indian River Lagoon [22,24], Tampa Bay [28], and Charlotte Harbor [23]. ACMS includes coupled models of circulation, wave, sediment transport, water quality, light attenuation and seagrass biomass. In addition, it has been used for simulations of storm surge and coastal inundation [26–28]. This modeling system is able to simulate 3D baroclinic flow with wetting and drying. It has the capability to use spatially and temporally varying wind fields such as tropical storms. It is also coupled to a wave model [27,29] and has the ability to obtain boundary conditions from a variety of sources including basin-scale models.

The computational grid developed for the bay and surrounding areas to simulate the salinity distribution is shown in Figure 2. The grid is 456 by 161 cells with the minimum cell size of 94 m and the average cell of 400 m. In vertical direction, the model uses 8 equally-spaced sigma layers (4-, 8- and 16-layer options were tested and it was found that 8 layers provide sufficient resolution with negligible differences compared to the 16-layer setup) The model uses a 60-s time step and simulated period for all scenarios spans from January 1, 1999 to December 31, 2008.

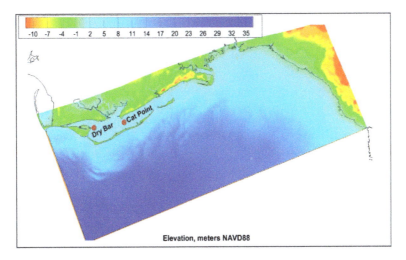

Figure 2. CH3D model grid bathymetry/topography, the orange lines at the south and west ends of the domain denote the model open boundary.

CH3D is coupled to the HYbrid Coordinate Ocean Model (HYCOM) [30,31] model for the entire Gulf of Mexico which provides time varying salinity at the open boundary. HYCOM is a generalized (hybrid isopycnal/σ/z) coordinate in vertical and curvilinear in horizontal direction ocean model. It is isopycnal in the open stratified ocean, but reverts to a terrain-following coordinate in shallow coastal regions, and to z-level coordinates near the surface in the mixed layer. This generalized vertical coordinate approach is dynamic in space and time via the layered continuity equation, which allows a dynamical transition between the coordinate types. The Gulf of Mexico model has $1/25°$ equatorial resolution and latitudinal resolution of $1/25°$ cos(lat) or ~3.5 km for each variable at mid-latitudes and uses 20 vertical layers.

The domain has two open boundaries at the west and south ends of the model grid (Figure 2) where tidal forcing is applied based on eight tidal constituents that are adjusted to match the predicted tidal water level at the NOAA station at that location. Open boundary salinity is obtained from the Gulf of Mexico HYCOM model for the period starting in 2003 and assumed as constant (34 ppt) before 2003 due to the lack of HYCOM data prior to that. Huang et al. [14] showed that the wind plays an important role on the dynamics of salinity in the bay, therefore in this study the wind forcing is based on atmospheric data from the NOGAPS (U.S. Navy's Operational Global Atmospheric Prediction System) Model [32].

2.3. River Flow Scenarios

Freshwater inflows are introduced at the Apalachicola River and the flows are based on the actual observed daily data from the Sumatra gage (Scenario I) and three different daily flow rates provided by the USACE ResSim (Reservoir System Simulation) model representing the ACF Basin hydrology and reservoir operations (Scenarios II–IV; Table 1). The model is initialized using observed values of water level and salinity in October 1998, and the three-month period from October–December of 1998 is used as a spin up period for the model followed by a 10-year simulation. As an example, flow rate at the Sumatra gage during 2004–2008 is shown in Figure 3.

Table 1. Characteristics for the flow rates (cfs) at the Sumatra gage.

Scenario	Mean	Mean (%)	Standard Deviation	Standard Deviation (%)	Minimum	Maximum
I	519.2	0.00	411.4	0.00	124.6	4700.6
II	514.4	0.92	391.3	4.89	136.4	3965.7
III	515.9	0.64	391.4	4.86	136.4	3965.7
IV	516.4	0.54	391.0	4.96	136.4	3965.7

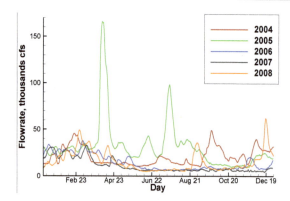

Figure 3. Observed flowrate (cfs) at Sumatra gage.

Scenario II represents the Corps' current reservoir operations, which are designed to provide for the authorized project purposes of flood damage reduction, hydroelectric power generation, and navigation, as well as for other authorized purposes or incidental benefits including fish and wildlife conservation, recreation, water quality, and water supply. For releases to the Apalachicola River, the Corps meets minimum flow targets [1] that vary by the amount of inflow into the reservoirs in the basin, the amount of storage available, and by season.

Scenario III represents a reservoir operation alternative that is similar to Scenario II but included changes in the amount of water storage available in each individual lake, a navigation season with increased minimum flows when storage is high, reduced releases for hydroelectric power during droughts at Lake Lanier (the upstream-most reservoir near Atlanta, Georgia), reduced releases from Lake Lanier for water quality and water supply, and a reduction in water supply withdrawals from Lake Lanier.

Scenario IV represents a reservoir operation alternative that is nearly identical to Scenario III but included slightly lower consumption (200 cfs) from the City of Atlanta. As shown in Table 1, the observed daily flows at the Sumatra gage (Scenario I) have the smallest minimum flow rate and the largest maximum flow rate of the four scenarios. The daily flows at the Sumatra gage in the remaining three scenarios vary only mildly relative to each other, which is not surprising since all three reservoir operation scenarios are similar.

Additional model scenarios were considered after an analysis, based on the concept of reach gain, was performed on the flow data from Sumatra gauge [33]. Observed flow data from Sumatra gauge is the main source of data that quantifies fresh water inflow into Apalachicola Bay. This analysis indicates that this data underrepresents actual total amount of fresh water flow coming into the system by 30%. Leitman argues that at flows over 15,000 cfs (a value that U.S. Geological Survey found to correspond with bank-full [34]) flow is entering the floodplain and then re-enters the river below Sumatra gauge therefore remaining uncaptured in data collected at the gauge. To test this hypothesis, we performed a simulation altering the measured flow and several other flow adjustments to see how the system would react to potentially more realistic, larger fresh water inflows. Table 2 shows the scenarios that were simulated and Table 3 list the characteristics for these scenarios.

Table 2. Flow adjustments for additional simulation scenarios.

Scenario	Flowrate Adjustment
V	90% (−10%)
VI	110% (+10%)
VII	130% (+30%)
VIII	150% (+50%)
IX	200% (+100%)
X	130% (+30%), when flow is over 15,000 cfs

Table 3. Characteristics for the flow rates (cfs) at the Sumatra gage for additional scenarios.

Scenario	Mean	Minimum	Maximum
I	519	124.6	4700.6
V	467	112.1	4230.5
VI	571	137.1	5170.7
VII	604	162.0	6110.8
VIII	778	186.9	7050.9
IX	1038	249.2	9401.2
X	1298	311.5	11,751.5

3. Results

3.1. Model Verification—Salinity during 2004

Simulated water level and salinity in 2004, a year during which four hurricanes (Dennis, Frances, Ivan and Jeanne) affected the area, are compared to observed data. Comparison of simulated water levels with 6-min data at the CO-OPS station at the mouth of the Apalachicola River gives a correlation value of 0.97. Simulated salinity values for Scenario I compare well with observed salinity data at several ANERR data stations inside the Bay (Figure 4). Values of the root mean square (RMS) error and the correlation coefficient can be found in Table 4. It is believed that the reason for poorer comparisons at the East Bay station is the lack of flow data in the smaller streams around the East Bay location as salinity at this stations tends to be overestimated by the model due to the lack of sufficient fresh water inflow.

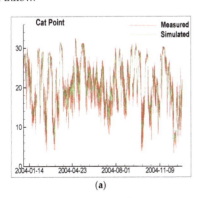 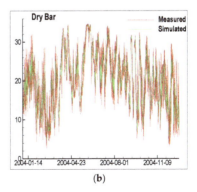

(a) (b)

Figure 4. Simulated salinity at (**a**) Cat Point; and (**b**) Dry Bar stations during 2004.

Table 4. Estimation of simulation error.

Station	Root Mean Square Error	Correlation Coefficient
Cat Point	1.3 ppt	0.87
Dry Bar	1.6 ppt	0.82
East Bay	2.4 ppt	0.71

Salinity at the ANERR stations shown in Figure 4 show salinity fluctuating between 3 ppt and 34 ppt. During the January and February periods salinity at both stations decreased due to the relatively large freshwater inflow from Apalachicola River. During the four major hurricanes, salinity initially decreased due to the increased precipitation and river inflow but quickly recovered to the pre-storm salinity values, due apparently to the good connectivity between the Apalachicola Bay and the ocean. In September of 2004 three tropical storms (Figure 5) had a significant effect on salinity in the Bay: Hurricanes Frances, Ivan and Jeanne. Simulated salinity in the bay around the time of the storm (Figure 6) indicates that it takes on the order of one to two weeks for the estuary to recover from the impact of the storm and restore the salinity regime established prior to the storm. This is consistent with the typical residence times of three to nine days found by [5] and can be attributed to a number of factors such as connectivity to the Gulf, large fresh water inflow from Apalachicola River and shallow depths in the bay. These results differ significantly from the response of other Florida estuaries to hurricanes. Tutak and Sheng [35] found that hurricanes had a much more significant effect on the salinity inside the estuarine system of the Guana-Tolomato-Matanzas (GTM) National Estuarine Research Reserve (NERR) at St. Augustine, FL, due to the relatively poorer connectivity of the estuarine system with the ocean.

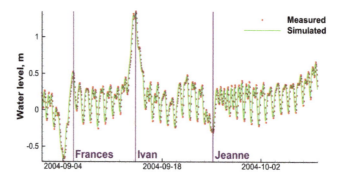

Figure 5. Water level before, during and after Hurricanes Frances, Ivan and Jeanne at Cat Point station.

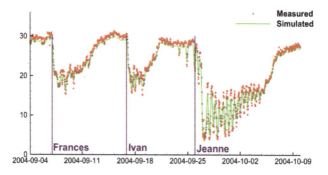

Figure 6. Salinity before, during and after Hurricanes Frances, Ivan and Jeanne at Cat Point station.

Model performance was recorded with approximate wall time of 12 min per day of simulation using a single CPU core and 84 s per day of simulation using 16 cores with OpenMP parallelization.

3.2. Model Results for the 1999–2008 Period

Four scenarios of Apalachicola River discharge are considered for model simulations. Scenario I, which uses the observed flow rates at the Sumatra gage provided by the USACE, serves as a base scenario and a reference for comparison. Scenarios II through IV use altered flows with statistics for the time series of flow rates are provided in Table 1. All other model parameters and forcing remained the same for all scenarios.

The above results showed that there is little difference in salinity inside the Apalachicola Bay among the current operation and two alternative operations (Scenarios II–IV). This is not a surprise given that the three different reservoir operation scenarios are all similar. However, the ResSim simulations of the current flow operation and two alternative flow operations result in higher salinity at the higher salinity range (15–35 ppt) while lower salinity at the low salinity range than the observed data from the gage. This difference is due to the consumptive demands used in ResSim. The three ResSim simulations (Scenarios II–IV) use demand data from 2007 in every year, but those demands were the highest on record, and higher than the actual demands observed over the years.

Using a relatively coarse grid hydrodynamic model, Huang [13] performed a study that featured several scenarios on riverine flow and attempted to analyze the changes in salinity response due to altered flow. He indicated that probability analysis can be useful in characterizing and summarizing the modification of historic flow pattern by a river flow scenario resulted from the changes of upstream reservoir operations and water demands. Huang [13] investigated how often a certain value of salinity (integer values from 0 to 34) occurs and calculated a probability density distribution to identify the maximum probable salinity values. It should be noted that Huang's analysis [13] of salinity in the bay during 1980–1989 revealed two distinct peaks in probability density curve for all stations, depending on the scenario and the location the first salinity peak occurs in the range from 4 to 9 while the second peak occurs in the range from 22 to 27. In most cases the second peak is more pronounced (means that the salinity from the second range is more likely to occur). Our simulations, however, did not produce two distinct peaks.

Impact of River Flow Scenarios on Bay Salinity

Exceedance probability curves are used in this study to analyze the differences between different simulated scenarios. The probability of exceedance is calculated based on the simulated salinity data (output at 1-min intervals) by ranking the data and calculating the number of data points that are larger than or equal to a value X at 0.05 ppt intervals forming the curve.

This study covers the ten-year period from 1999 to 2008. Probabilistic analysis (Figure 7) of results from this study produces curves that are a lot smoother than those in [13] and without the two distinct peaks shown in their study. These curves are verified by applying the probabilistic analysis to the observed data which produces similar curves. The reason for the double peaks in Huang's results could be due to the different hydrologic period or differences between the models, which require further investigation.

Exceedance probability curves (Figure 8) indicate that the Observed scenario has lower probability in the 15–25 ppt range and therefore the three scenarios using the Corps' simulated operations are more likely to result in higher bay salinity. Because the simulations in Scenarios II–IV use higher demand data than the observed data, this indicates that higher consumptive demands could adversely impact the oyster populations by resulting in higher bay salinities occurring more frequently. The salinity responses for the different flow scenarios show little difference, since the flow rates associated with these scenarios show little difference. However, if the freshwater consumption were to increase dramatically above those in the four scenarios, it is expected that the salinity in the bay could increase dramatically.

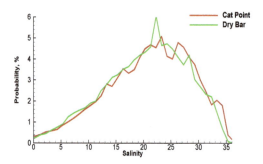

Figure 7. Probability distribution of salinity at Cat Point and Dry Bar.

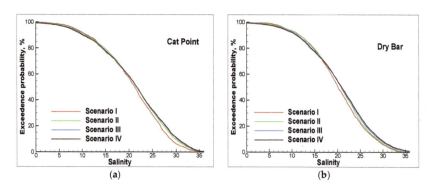

Figure 8. Exceedance rate of daily average salinity at (**a**) Cat Point; and (**b**) Dry Bar stations. Scenarios I–IV.

As expected, the additional scenarios that attempt to better capture high flow events yield a much more significant response (Figure 9). Furthermore, it is notable that adding 30% to the river flow does improve simulation results, slightly. Root mean square error improves from 1.3 to 1.1 ppt at the Cat Point station and from 1.6 to 1.5 ppt at the Dry Bar station.

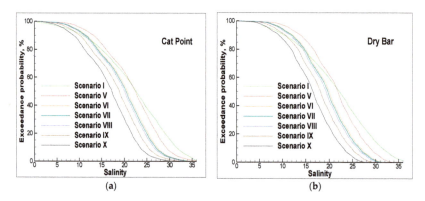

Figure 9. Exceedance rate of daily average salinity at (**a**) Cat Point; and (**b**) Dry Bar stations. Scenarios I, V–X.

As mentioned earlier, extreme storm events can significantly alter the salinity levels. Due to the relatively good connectivity of the Apalachicola Bay (relative to such estuary as the Guana-Tolomato-Matanzas National Estuarine Research Reserve estuary), salinity usually recovers quickly to the pre-storm values. Some of the impact factors that can affect the length of time required for the estuary to recover are duration and amount of rainfall, which often accompany the storm and can last significantly longer than the direct impact of the storm itself. Of course, there are others risk factors that can be brought in by hurricanes and affect oyster beds such as red tide bloom that was moved into the bay during Hurricane Katrina (even though the storm itself passed outside the domain and did not have a significant direct impact) or oil spill which almost entered Apalachicola Bay during the Deep Water Horizon spill in 2010. However, these are outside of the scope of this paper.

To better understand the impacts of the various flow scenarios, a statistical analysis was performed on simulated salinity values. shows the average number of days in a year where salinity exceeds 26 ppt at various locations, and Scenario III has the highest number of days when the salinity value exceeds 26 (Figure 10) making it the worst in terms of oyster production (US Fish and Wildlife Service determined 26 ppt as a cut-off value for optimal oyster growth, Wang et al, also show 26 ppt as an upper bound for the optimal oyster growth in Apalachicola Bay [15]).

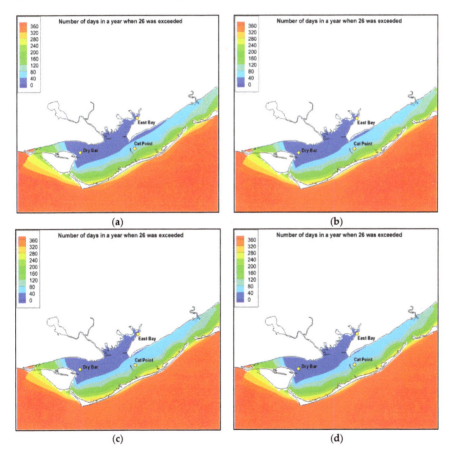

Figure 10. Average (over 1999–2008) number of days in a year when salinity exceeded 26 ppt. (**a–d**)—Scenarios I–IV, respectively.

3.3. Effects of Potential Sea Level Rise on Bay Salinity

So far, studies have focused on the impact of freshwater withdrawal on the salinity in the Apalachicola Bay, without considering the impact of global climate change and its impact on storms, sea level rise, and precipitation. A recent Intergovernmental Panel on Climate Change (IPCC) report [36] has predicted that sea level rise in the Panhandle area could reach 1 m by 2100. In this study, we analyze potential impact of a sea level rise of 1 m, while not taking into consideration other possible impacts of climate change, such as weather with subsequent changes in wind climate and rainfall (discharge into the Apalachicola River) and ignoring any potential geomorphological changes as well. The model simulation is run with the observed river flow data (Scenario II) and increased water level at the open boundary of the model by 1 m compared to all previous simulations.

Results of this simulation (as can be seen on Figure 10), show that salinity rises significantly (up to 20%) throughout the Bay, due to connectivity of the Bay to the ocean.

4. Discussion

Oyster growth rates and resultant population are sensitive to the salinity regime in the areas where oyster reefs are located. In particular, the number of oyster larvae recruited per spawn are minimal outside of moderately narrow temperature (27.5 °C–32.5 °C) and salinity (10 ppt–27.5 ppt) ranges [37]. Scenario III has the highest number of days when the salinity value exceeds 26 ppt (Figure 11) making it the worst in terms of oyster production. This is also confirmed by the exceedance probability curves that indicate that Scenario I is more likely to produce salinity in the 15 to 25 ppt range, while in the remaining three scenarios this range is likely to be lower. The difference between Scenarios II, III and IV is smaller and almost indistinguishable. Again, the relatively little difference in the bay salinity response for the different freshwater withdrawal scenarios is due to the relatively mild difference in the freshwater flow rates. However, if the flow rates were to reduce dramatically, the salinity response can be expected to increase dramatically as well.

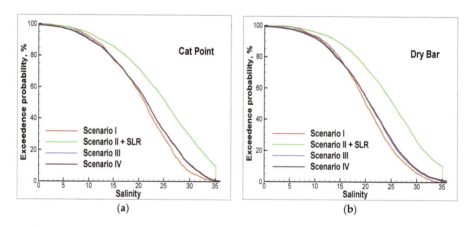

Figure 11. Exceedance rate of salinity at Cat Point (a) and Dry Bar (b) stations. Scenario 2 with sea level rise effects.

One notable observation is that the Apalachicola Bay system recovers relatively quickly from storms, due to shallow depths, strong riverine flow from Apalachicola River and good connectivity to the Gulf of Mexico. It takes on an order of one week to recover from an impact of the storm and this observation is consistent with earlier findings of [5] that note the typical residence time is between three and nine days, unlike in some other Florida estuaries such as the GTM-NERR [35], where it can take nearly three months for the estuary to recover from the impact of the storm.

J. Mar. Sci. Eng. **2016**, *4*, 76

The impact of various natural and anthropogenic (water management) controls on the bay salinity is summarized in the following:

- Apalachicola Bay salinity regime can quickly recover from extreme events such as hurricanes.
- Scenario I (observed) is more likely to create favorable conditions for oyster production.
- Scenarios II–IV, corresponding to higher (~1%) consumptive freshwater demand than in the observed scenario, are likely to result in slightly (~5%) higher salinities and unfavorable conditions for oyster production.
- Newer freshwater flow alternatives which may cause more significant changes to the bay salinity are being developed by the Corps.
- The worst case sea level rise scenario (~1 m by 2100) could significantly increase the bay salinity by up to 20%.

A more comprehensive study on the impact of natural and anthropogenic controls on the bay salinity may require more detailed investigation involving nutrient and sediment dynamics using an integrated physical-chemical-biological modeling system such as the one used in [15], which would also provide information on other factors that may affect oyster production such as temperature distribution in the Apalachicola Bay.

Acknowledgments: This work is sponsored by the Fish and Wildlife Service of the U.S. Department of Interior. Early support was provided by the University of Florida Water Institute. The findings and conclusions in this article are those of the author(s) and do not necessarily represent the views of the U.S. Fish and Wildlife Service.

Author Contributions: K.H. provided fresh water inflows and analysis, V.A.P. set up the model and performed hydrodynamic simulations, J.R.D. performed oyster analysis and modeling, Y.P.S., J.R.D. and V.A.P. wrote the paper.

Conflicts of Interest: Rick Luettich (UNC), Robert H. Weisberg (USF), Joannes J. Westerink (U of Notre Dame), and Scott Hagen (LSU). The funding sponsors had no role in the design of the study; analyses or interpretation of data; in the writing of the manuscript, or in the decision to publish the results except for providing data of ResSim model flows at Sumatra gauge.

References

1. US Army Corps of Engineers. 2015 ACF Water Control Manual Update and Draft Environmental Impact Statement. Available online: http://www.sam.usace.army.mil/Missions/Planning-Environmental/ACF-Master-Water-Control-Manual-Update/ACF-Document-Library/ (accessed on 15 September 2016).
2. US Fish and Wildlife Service. *Biological Opinion. Endangered Species Act Section 7 Consultation on the U.S. Army Corps of Engineers Mobile District Update of the Water Control Manual for the Apalachicola-Chattahoochee-Flint River Basin in Alabama, Florida, and Georgia and a Water Supply Storage Assessment*; USFWS Log No: 04EF3000-2016-F-0181; U.S. Fish and Wildlife Service Panama City Field Office: Panama City, FL, USA, 2016.
3. Huang, W.; Hagen, S.; Bacopoulos, P.; Wang, D. Hydrodynamic modeling and analysis of sea-level rise impacts on salinity for oyster growth in Apalachicola Bay, Florida. *Estuar. Coast. Shelf Sci.* **2015**, *156*, 7–18. [CrossRef]
4. Huang, W.; Hagen, S.C.; Bacopoulos, P.; Teng, F. Sea-Level Rise Impacts on Hurricane-Induced Salinity Transport in Apalachicola Bay. *J. Coast. Res.* **2014**, *68*, 49–56. [CrossRef]
5. Huang, W.; Spaulding, M. Modelling residence time response to freshwater input in Apalachicola Bay, Florida, USA. *Hydrol. Process.* **2002**, *16*, 3051–3064. [CrossRef]
6. Edminston, H.L. *A River Meets the Bay: A Characterization of the Apalachicola River and Bay System*; Apalachicola National Estuarine Research Reserve: Eastpoint, FL, USA, 2008.
7. Florida Department of Environmental Protection (FDEP); Apalachicola National Estuarine Research Reserve. Management Plan. October 2011. Available online: http://publicfiles.dep.state.fl.us/cama/plans/aquatic/ANERR_Management_Plan_2013.pdf (accessed on 14 November 2016).
8. Livingston, R.J.; Lewis, F.G.; Woodsum, G.C.; Niu, X.-F.; Galperin, B.; Huang, W.; Christensen, J.D.; Monaco, M.E.; Battista, T.A.; Klein, C.J.; et al. Modeling oyster population response to freshwater inputs. *Estuar. Coast. Shelf Sci.* **2000**, *50*, 655–672. [CrossRef]

9.   Altinok, I.; Grizzle, J.M. Effects of brackish water on growth, feed conversion and energy absorption efficiency by juvenile euryhaline and freshwater stenohaline fishes. *J. Fish Biol.* **2001**, *59*, 1142–1152. [CrossRef]

10.   United States Fish and Wildlife Service (USFWS). *Biological Opinion on the U.S. Army Corps of Engineers, Mobile District, Revised Interim Operating Plan for Jim Woodruff Dam and the Associated Releases to the Apalachicola River*; U.S. Fish and Wildlife Service, Panama City Field Office: Panama City, FL, USA, 2008; p. 225.

11.   Sulak, K.J.; Randall, M.T.; Edwards, R.E.; Summers, T.M.; Luke, K.E.; Smith, W.T.; Norem, A.D.; Harden, W.M.; Lukens, R.H.; Parauka, F.; et al. Defining winter trophic habitat of juvenile Gulf sturgeon in the Suwannee and Apalachicola rivermouth estuaries, acoustic telemetry investigations. *J. Appl. Ichthyol.* **2009**, *25*, 505–515. [CrossRef]

12.   Randall, M.T.; Sulak, K.J. Relationship between recruitment of Gulf sturgeon, Acipenser oxyrinchus desotoi, and water flow in the Suwannee River, Florida. In Proceedings of the Anadromous Sturgeon Symposium, Quebec City, QC, Canada, 11–13 August 2003.

13.   Huang, W. Hydrodynamic modeling and ecohydrological analysis of river inflow effects on Apalachicola Bay, Florida, USA. *Estuar. Coast. Shelf Sci.* **2010**, *86*, 526–534. [CrossRef]

14.   Huang, W.; Jones, W.K.; Wu, T.S. Modelling wind effects on subtidal salinity in Apalachicola Bay, Florida. *Estuar. Coast. Shelf Sci.* **2002**, *55*, 33–46. [CrossRef]

15.   Wang, H.; Huang, W.; Harwell, M.A.; Edmiston, L.; Johnson, E.; Hsieh, P.; Milla, K.; Christensen, J.; Stewart, J.; Liu, X. Modeling oyster growth rate by coupling oyster population and hydrodynamic models for Apalachicola Bay, Florida, USA. *Ecol. Model.* **2008**, *211*, 77–89. [CrossRef]

16.   Sheng, Y.P. Evolution of a Three-Dimensional Curvilinear-Grid Hydrodynamic Model for Estuaries, Lakes and Coastal Waters: CH3D. In *Estuarine and Coastal Modeling*, Proceedings of the Estuarine and Coastal Circulation and Pollution Transport Model Data Comparison Specialty Conference, Newport, RI, USA, 15–17 November 1989; American Society of Civil Engineers: New York, NY, USA, 1990; pp. 40–49.

17.   Sheng, Y.P.; Paramygin, V.A.; Zhang, Y.; Davis, J.R. Recent enhancements and application of an integrated storm surge modeling system: CH3D-SSMS. In Proceedings of the Tenth International Conference on Estuarine and Coastal Modeling, Newport, RI, USA, 5–7 November 2007; pp. 879–892.

18.   Sheng, Y.P.; Kim, T. Skill assessment of an integrated modeling system for shallow estuarine and coastal ecosystems. *J. Mar. Syst.* **2009**, *76*, 212–243. [CrossRef]

19.   Klipsh, J.D.; Hurst, M.B. *HEC-ResSim Reservoir System Simulation User's Manual, Version 3*; US Army Corps of Engineers: Washington, DC, USA, 2007.

20.   Sheng, Y.P. On modeling three-dimensional estuarine and marine hydrodynamics. In *Three-Dimensional Marine and Estuarine Hydrodynamics*; Nihoul, J.C., Jamart, B.M., Eds.; Elsevier: Amsterdam, The Netherlands, 1987; pp. 35–54.

21.   Sheng, Y.P. A framework for integrated modeling of hydrodynamic, sedimentary, and water quality processes. *Estuar. Coast. Model.* **2000**, *6*, 350–362.

22.   Sheng, Y.P.; Davis, J.R.; Sun, D.; Qiu, C.; Park, K.; Kim, T.; Zhang, Y. Application of an integrated modeling system for estuarine and coastal ecosystems to Indian River Lagoon, Florida. *Estuar. Coast. Model.* **2002**, *7*, 329–343.

23.   Kim, T.; Sheng, Y.P.; Park, K. Modelling water quality and hypoxia dynamics in Upper Charlotte Harbor, Florida, U.S.A. during 2000. *Estuar. Coast. Shelf Sci.* **2010**, *90*, 250–263. [CrossRef]

24.   Sheng, Y.P. An Integrated Modeling System for Forecasting the Response of Estuarine and Coastal Ecosystems to Anthropogenic and Climate Changes. In *Ecological Forecasting: New Tools for Coastal and Marine Ecosystem Management*; Valette-Silver, N., Scavia, D., Eds.; NOAA Technical Memorandum NOS NCCOS 1; 2003; pp. 203–210. Available online: http://oceanservice.noaa.gov/topics/coasts/ecoforecasting/ecoforecast.pdf (accessed on 14 November 2016).

25.   Sheng, Y.P.; Paramygin, V.A.; Alymov, V.; Davis, J.R. A Real-Time Forecasting System for Hurricane Induced Storm Surge and Coastal Flooding. In Proceedings of the Ninth International Conference on Estuarine and Coastal Modeling, Charleston, SC, USA, 2 September–31 October 2005; pp. 585–602.

26.   Sheng, Y.P.; Alymov, V.; Paramygin, V.A. Simulation of storm surge, waves, and inundation in the Outer Banks and Chesapeake Bay during Hurricane Isabel in 2003: The importance of waves. *J. Geophys. Res.* **2010**, *115*. [CrossRef]

27.   Sheng, Y.P.; Zhang, Y.; Paramygin, V.A. Simulation of Storm Surge, Wave, and Coastal Inundation during Hurricane Ivan in 2004. *Ocean Model.* **2010**, *35*, 314–331. [CrossRef]

28. Sheng, Y.P.; Villaret, C. Modeling the effect of suspended sediment stratification on bottom exchange process. *J. Geophys. Res.* **1989**, *94*, 14229–14444. [CrossRef]

29. Sheng, Y.P.; Liu, T. Three-dimensional simulation of wave-induced circulation: Comparison of three radiation stress formulations. *J. Geophys. Res.* **2011**, *116*, C05021. [CrossRef]

30. Bleck, R. An oceanic general circulation model framed in hybrid isopycnic-cartesian coordinates. *Ocean Model.* **2002**, *4*, 55–88. [CrossRef]

31. Chassignet, E.P.; Hurlburt, H.E.; Smedstad, O.M.; Halliwell, G.R.; Hogan, P.J.; Wallcraft, A.J.; Baraille, R.; Bleck, R. The HYCOM (HYbrid Coordinate Ocean Model) data assimilative system. *J. Mar. Syst.* **2007**, *65*, 60–83. [CrossRef]

32. Rosmond, T.E. The Design and Testing of the Navy Operational Global Atmospheric Prediction System. *Weather Forecast.* **1992**, *7*, 262–272. [CrossRef]

33. Light, H.M.; Vincent, K.R.; Darst, M.R.; Price, F.D. *Water-Level Decline in the Apalachicola River, Florida, from 1954 to 2004, and Effects on Floodplain Habitats*; U.S. Geological Survey Scientific Investigations Report 2006-5173; U.S. Geological Survey: Reston, VA, USA, 2006.

34. Leitman, S.; UF Water Institute, Gainesville, FL, USA. An explanation of the problems with flow data from the sumatra gauge. Personal communication, 2016.

35. Tutak, B.; Sheng, Y.P. Effect of tropical cyclones on residual circulation and momentum balance in a subtropical estuary and inlet: Observation and simulation. *J. Geophys. Res.* **2011**, *116*, C06014. [CrossRef]

36. Intergovernmental Panel on Climate Change (IPCC). *Climate Change 2013: The Physical Science Basis Working Group I Contribution to the Fifth Assessment Report of the Intergovernmental Panel on Climate Change*; Cambridge University Press: Cambridge, UK; New York, NY, USA, 2013; Available online: http://www.ipcc.ch/report/ar5/wg1/ (accessed on 10 May 2016).

37. Davis, H.C.; Calabrese, A. Combined effects of temperature and salinity on development of eggs and growth of larve of *M. Mercenaria* and *C. Virginica. Fish. Bull.* **1964**, *63*, 643–655.

Journal of
Marine Science and Engineering

Article

Model Development and Hindcast Simulations of NOAA's Gulf of Maine Operational Forecast System

Zizang Yang [1,*], Philip Richardson [1], Yi Chen [2], John G. W. Kelley [1], Edward Myers [1], Frank Aikman III [1], Machuan Peng [3] and Aijun Zhang [3]

[1] NOAA/National Ocean Service/Coast Survey Development Laboratory, 1315 East-West Highway, Silver Spring, MD 20910, USA; phil.richardson@noaa.gov (P.R.); john.kelley@noaa.gov (J.G.W.K.); edward.myers@noaa.gov (E.M.); frank.aikman@noaa.gov (F.A.)

[2] Earth Resources Technology (ERT) Inc., 6100 Frost Place, Suite A, Laurel, MD 20707, USA; yi.chen@noaa.gov

[3] NOAA/National Ocean Service/Center for Operational Oceanographic Products and Services, 1305 East-West Highway, Silver Spring, MD 20910, USA; machuan.peng@noaa.gov (M.P.); aijun.zhang@noaa.gov (A.Z.)

* Correspondence: zizang.yang@noaa.gov; Tel.: +1-301-713-2809

Academic Editor: Richard Signell
Received: 18 July 2016; Accepted: 24 October 2016; Published: 17 November 2016

Abstract: The National Ocean Service (NOS) of National Oceanic and Atmospheric Administration is developing an operational nowcast/forecast system for the Gulf of Maine (GoMOFS). The system aims to produce real-time nowcasts and short-range forecast guidance for water levels, 3-dimensional currents, water temperature, and salinity over the broad GoM region. GoMOFS will be implemented using the Regional Ocean Model System (ROMS). This paper describes the system setup and results from a one-year (2012) hindcast simulation. The hindcast performance was evaluated using the NOS standard skill assessment software. The results indicate favorable agreement between observations and model forecasts. The root-mean-squared errors are about 0.12 m for water level, less than 1.5 °C for temperature, less than 1.5 psu for salinity, and less than 0.2 m/s for currents. It is anticipated to complete the system development and the transition into operations in fiscal year 2017.

Keywords: Gulf of Maine; operational nowcast and forecast system; hydrodynamics; ROMS; water level; currents; water temperature; and salinity

---

1. Introduction

The Gulf of Maine (GoM) is a semi-enclosed coastal basin located along the coastline of the northeastern U.S. (Figure 1). It is surrounded by the New England coast to the west and to the north. It is adjacent to the Bay of Fundy (BF) to the northeast and is bounded by the coast of Nova Scotia to the east. To the south, the Gulf water communicates with the open ocean through a series of shoals, banks and channels, such as Nantucket Shoals (NS), the Great South Channel (GSC), Georges Bank (GB), the Northeast Channel (NEC), Brown Bank (BB), and the Cape Sable Channel (CSC).

The GOM/GB system demonstrates a broad variety of physical oceanography phenomena such as a complicated circulation system, intense tidal currents, fronts, internal tides, etc. Baroclinic hydrography, barotropic tidal dynamics, and meteorological factors are responsible for incurring their existence and modulating of their intensity. Their relative significance varies spatially as well as seasonally [1–5].

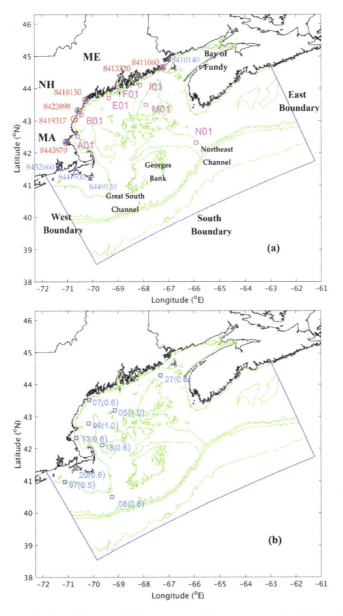

Figure 1. Map of the Gulf of Maine (GoM)/Georges Bank (GB) region and the GoMOFS model domain. Green lines represent the 50, 200, 500, 1000, and 3000-m isobaths. Blue lines denote the three open ocean boundaries of the model domain. (**a**) Map of observation stations: the CO-OPS water level stations (red circles) and water temperature stations (filled blue triangles), and the NeraCOOS buoys (magenta squares). The station IDs are labeled near the location markers. The measurement depths of the CO-OPS stations are 3.3 m (8410140), 2.4 m (8411060), 2.9 m (8413320), 4.9 m (8418150), 3.3 m (8419317), 2.9 m (8443970), 2.0 m (8447930), 1.2 m (8449130), and 1.8 m (8452660). The NeraCOOS depths are listed in Table 1; (**b**) Map of NDBC buoy stations. The station IDs are labeled near the location marks. Three leading digits "440" of each ID number are omitted for the clarity of illustration. The numbers in the parentheses following the IDs represent the measurement depths (in meters) relative to the sea surface.

The area is well known for its significant tidal fields. The tidal range is greater than 3 m along the northern and western coast and over 5 m in the BF. The tidal currents are as high as 0.5 to 1 m/s over the NS and GB. The tidal dynamics are heavily involved in forming the circulation, fronts, etc. [6]. Within the Gulf, tides are forced by ocean tides along the shelf break. Five tidal constituents, M_2, S_2, N_2, K_1, and O_1, account for 94% of the total tidal potential energy, while the M_2 constituent contributes over 80% of the total energy [7].

Researchers have explored the hydrodynamics of the area using various types of numerical models, such as the finite difference [8–10], finite element [4,11], and finite volume [12] models. Greenberg [8] and Naimie et al. [4] investigated the tidal dynamics of the M_2 astronomical constituent. Using the ADvanced CIRCulation (ADCIRC) model (ADCIRC), Yang and Myers [11] investigated the pathway and intensity of the barotropic M_2 tidal energy flux. Chen et al. [12] studied both barotropic and internal tidal dynamics in the region using the Finite Volume Coastal Ocean Model (FVCOM).

Several of the numerical studies focused on investigating the three-dimensional (3-D) hydrodynamics of the area. Naimie and Lynch [4] studied summer season stratification in the GB area using the unstructured-grid finite element model QUODDY. Chen et al. [9] used the modified Princeton Ocean Model (ECOM-si) to investigate the dynamics of the tidal currents rectifications and its impact on the formation of upwelling in the GB region. Xue et al. [5] simulated the seasonal circulations using the Princeton Ocean Model (POM). Gangopadhyay et al. [13] developed a multiscale feature model to study the characteristic physical circulation features. To support the Gulf of Maine Ocean Observing System (GoMOOS) operations, Xue et al. [10] developed the POM-based nowcasts/forecast system to produce real-time, 3-D distribution of circulation and water properties. More recently, Wilkin et al. [14] developed the data-assimilative "Doppio" real-time and reanalysis ROMS system to make the forecast of hydrodynamics for the broad Mid-Atlantic Bight and the GoM regions.

The National Ocean Service (NOS) of National Oceanic and Atmospheric Administration (NOAA) has recently been working on developing an operational oceanographic nowcast/forecast system for the Gulf of Maine (GoMOFS). The GoMOFS aims to produce real-time nowcast and short-range forecast guidance for water levels, 3-dimensional currents, water temperature, and salinity over the broad GoM region. It will support the GoM harmful algal bloom (HAB) forecast, marine navigation, emergency response, and the environmental management communities.

The GoMOFS uses the Regional Ocean Model System (ROMS) [15] as the hydrodynamic model. In developing the GoMOFS, we conducted a one-year hindcast simulation for the year of 2012 and evaluated the model performance using the NOS standard skill assessment software [16].

This article describes the model setup and skill assessment results of the hindcast simulation. It is organized as follows. This section reviews the general hydrodynamics in the Gulf, previous numerical studies, and NOAA's initiative in developing the GoMOFS. Section 2 describes the model setup of the 2012 hindcast simulation. Section 3 describes the observed data used for the skill assessment. Section 4 presents the model results. Section 5 describes the skill assessment results. Section 6 states the conclusion and summery.

2. Model Setup

The GoMOFS model has a nearly rectangular domain that goes from the eastern Long Island Sound in the west to the shelf of Nova Scotia in the east and extends to the deep ocean outside of the shelfbreak (see Figure 1). It has an orthogonal model grid with horizontal dimensions of 1177 by 776 and a uniform spatial resolution of 700 m. The grid resolved major coastal embayments including Cape Cod Bay, Boston Harbor, Casco Bay, Penobscot Bay, and the Bay of Fundy. However, the 700-m resolution prohibits the model from resolving small scale coastal features such as navigation channels and river courses, e.g., the Cape Cod Canal. The grid has three open ocean boundaries (see the blue lines in Figure 1): the western boundary in the western Long Island Sound, the southern boundary outside the shelfbreak to the southeast of the GoM, and the eastern boundary across the shelf of Nova Scotia.

The bathymetry of the model grid was populated by linearly interpolating the combined VDatum ADCIRC model grid bathymetry [17] and the bathymetry in the 2-min Gridded Global Relief Data (ETOPO2) [18]. Figure 2 displays the color coded bathymetry. The model grid resolves key bathymetric features such as Georges Bank, the Northeast Channel, the Great South Channel, etc.

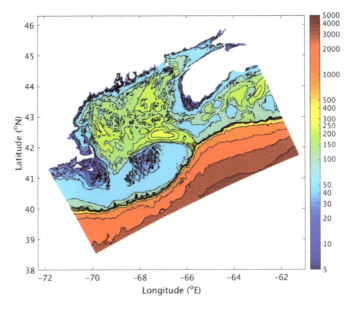

Figure 2. Bathymetry of the model grid. The color bar unit is meter.

The model is configured with 30 sigma layers. It uses the ROMS wetting and drying feature, a quadratic bottom friction scheme, and the two-equation model of the "revised" Mellor-Yamada Level 2.5 turbulence closure scheme (GLS/k-kl) implemented through the ROMS generic length scale (GLS) module.

For the open ocean boundary, we adopted the implicit Chapman condition for the free surface, the Flather condition for the 2-D momentum, and the radiation-nudging condition for the 3-D temperature, salinity, and velocity.

The hindcast simulation was driven with the complete suite of model forcing data including open ocean boundary forcing of the tidal and subtidal water level, 2-dimensional depth-averaged tidal currents, 3-dimensional temperature (T), salinity (S), and subtidal currents, river discharge, and the sea-surface meteorological forcing. It is noted that in the current setup the atmospheric pressure was not applied as a model forcing. Instead, we factored in the pressure effect by applying an inverse barometric pressure adjustment on the simulated water levels. In fact, we tested a setup with the air pressure forcing and the results appeared to be less satisfactory in terms of the model-data agreement.

The tidal water levels and currents on the open ocean boundaries were calculated using the tidal and currents harmonics of the TPXO 8.0-Atlas tidal database developed at the Oregon State University [19]. We chose eight tidal constituents (M_2, S_2, N_2, K_2, K_1, O_1, P_1, and Q_1) as the tidal forcing. The database was of the $1/30°$ horizontal resolution and was interpolated onto the GoMOFS grid. Some adjustment on the tidal amplitude and phase along the model's open ocean boundary was made to optimize the model-data agreement at the water level stations. The adjustment was made through a trial-and-error procedure. In quantitative details, the amplitude was altered by -7.0 cm for M_2, -1.5 cm for S_2, -0.5 cm for N_2, 1.0 cm for P_1, and 3.0 cm for K_1; the phase was altered by

8.0 degrees for M_2, 2.0 degrees S_2, 6.0 degrees for N_2, 6.0 degrees for K_2, 8.0 degrees for P_1, and 10.0 degrees for K_1.

The non-tidal open ocean conditions used the nowcast results from the Global Real-Time Ocean Forecast System (G-RTOFS) [20,21]. The G-RTOFS is being operated by the NOAA National Centers for Environmental Prediction (NCEP). It is based on the Naval Oceanographic Office's configuration of the $1/12°$ eddy resolving global Hybrid Coordinates Ocean Model (HYCOM). Its ocean model has 4500 by 3298 horizontal dimensions and 32 vertical hybrid layers (isopycnals in the deep, isolevel in the mixed layer, and sigma in shallow waters). The system assimilates in situ profiles of temperature and salinity from a variety of sources and remotely sensed SST, SSH and sea-ice concentrations. The G-RTOFS is forced with 3-hourly momentum, radiation, and precipitation fluxes from the operational NCEP Global Forecast System. It runs once a day and produces nowcasts and forecast guidance for sea surface values (SSH, SST, and SSS) at three hour intervals, and full volume parameters (3-dimensional temperature, salinity, currents, and mixed layer depths) at six-hourly interval. The nowcast outputs of the three-hourly water level and the six-hourly 3-D currents and T/S as the non-tidal forcing were spatially interpolated onto the model grid's open ocean boundaries and temporally interpolated across the hindcast period of the entire year of 2012.

It is noted that no adjustment on the G-RTOFS data were performed to improve the accuracy of the open ocean boundary conditions. Due to the lack of real-time observations at locations along the GoMOFS open boundary, it is not feasible to realize the adjustment during the GoMOFS operational practice. Considering that the hindcast simulation with the non-adjusted G-RTOFS forcing demonstrated skills meeting the NOS standard skill assessment criteria (Section 5), we decided to accept the "flawed" model configurations and the results therein in the forecast implementation. It is noted that data assimilation should ultimately be the methodology (being considered for future NOS OFS implementations) to solve this kind of input errors.

The river forcing includes discharges from nine rivers along the Gulf coast. From north to south they are: St. John River, St. Croix, Machias River, Penobscot River, Kennebec River, Androscoggin River, Saco River, Merrimack River, and Neponset River. The river discharge and water temperature data were the U.S. Geological Survey (USGS) river discharge observations [22]. Note that the river discharge data were available at locations usually far from the river mouths. In the hindcast setup, the magnitude of the discharge was increased by 20%. This factor was determined through a series of empirical trial-and-error experiments.

The salinity was specified to be zero for all nine rivers. The assumption of zero salinity was the recourse that was decided upon after considering factors such as data availability, the model grid configuration for the river course, and the skill of the hindcast run results. The GoMOFS model grid goes into the river course by four to ten kilometers for different rivers rather than defining the river entrance by the nodes immediately along the open coast. The distances from the open coast are not large enough to fully justify the zero salinity assumption. However, there is a lack of salinity observations of the river discharge. Hence, following the "informal" common practice, we specified the zero salinity values rather than choosing any other arbitrary value. As an ad hoc justification for the zero-salinity assumption and for the adjusted discharge, the hindcast salinity demonstrated reasonably good agreement with the observations (Section 5).

The hindcast made use of the 12-km resolution forecast guidance of the NOAA National Center for Environmental Predictions (NCEP's) North American Mesoscale Forecast Modeling System (NAM) for surface forcing. The ROMS model was forced with 10-m wind velocity to compute the surface wind stress, 2-m surface air temperature and relative humidity, total shortwave radiation, downward longwave radiation, and the ROMS bulk formulation to calculate the air-sea momentum and heat fluxes, evaporation and precipitation rate to calculate the net salinity flux across the air-sea interface.

Two scenarios of model simulations were conducted: a tidal forcing only simulation and a hindcast simulation of year 2012. The model configuration in both simulations remains the same except that the former was initialized with constant water temperature and salinity and forced with tidal water level and currents on the open ocean boundary, whereas the latter was driven with the total water level and currents on the open ocean boundary, sea-surface meteorological forcing, and river forcing. The purpose of the tidal only simulation was to verify the tidal open ocean boundary setup so as to ensure a favorable model performance in reproducing realistic water levels.

3. Observation Data

The observed data for the skill assessment are water levels from the NOS Center for Operational Oceanographic Products and Services (CO-OPS) water level stations, temperature (T) from the CO-OPS meteorological observation stations, the National Data Buoy Center (NDBC) buoys, and the Northeastern Regional Association of Coastal Ocean Observing Systems (NeraCOOS) buoys, and salinity (S) and currents from the NeraCOOS buoys.

The water level data in 2012 were downloaded from the NOS CO-OPS Web site [23]. Of the stations with the real time observations in 2012, the data from six stations (Figure 1a) were chosen for the model-data comparison by comparing the station location with the model domain and the grid layout. Some other stations located in the small estuaries, embayment, or inter-island channels which were not resolved by the model grid were excluded. They are the stations 8449130 (Nantucket Island, MA, USA), 8447930 (Woods Hole, MA, USA), 8447435 (Chatham, MA, USA), and 8410140 (Eastport, ME, USA).

The water temperature data were collected at five CO-OPS meteorological observation stations, ten NDBC buoys, and seven NeraCOOS buoys (Figure 1). All three data sets were downloaded from the NDBC online archive [24]. The CO-OPS and NDBC data were near surface observations. The depths of the CO-OPS and the NDBC measurements are shown in Figure 1a), respectively. The NeraCOOS measurement depths are listed in Table 1.

Table 1. Measurement depths of water temperature, salinity, and current velocity at the NeraCOOS buoys.

Station ID	Depth Relative to Mean Sea Level (m)		
	Temperature	Salinity	Current Velocity
A01	1, 2, 4 ,20, 50, 51	1, 20, 50	10, 22, 34, 46
B01	1, 2, 4, 20, 50	1, 20, 50	18, 30, 42
E01	1, 2, 4, 20, 50	1, 20, 50	18, 30, 42, 54, 66
F01	1, 2, 20	1, 20, 50	14, 26, 38, 50, 62, 74
I01	1, 2, 20, 50	1, 20, 50	14, 26, 38, 50, 62
M01	1, 2, 2.8, 20, 50, 150, 200	1, 20, 50, 200	34, 58, 82, 106, 130, 154, 178, 194
N01	1, 2, 20, 50, 100, 150,180	1, 20, 50, 100, 150, 180	24, 48, 72, 96, 104, 128, 152

Both the salinity and current velocity data were from the seven NeraCOOS buoys (Figure 1). Table 1 lists the corresponding measurement depths. The data were downloaded from the NeraCOOS website [25].

4. Results

4.1. Tidal Simulation

We computed the harmonic constants of tidal water levels using the outputs of the six-month, tidal forcing only simulation. Figure 3 displays the scatter plots of the model-data harmonics of four constituents: M_2, S_2, N_2, and K_1, respectively. The constituents represent the most prominent three semidiurnal and one diurnal constituents in the area. Table 2 lists the corresponding station IDs and the model-data differences at 24 NOS/CO-OPS water level stations encompassed in the GoMOFS domain.

For all the four constituents, the model-data discrepancy lies within the ten-percent lines at nearly all stations. A further detailed investigation indicated that the few outliers (see plots in Figure 3c,e,g,h) correspond to some coastal locations which were barely resolved with the current model grid. Over the 24 stations, the averaged root-mean-squared errors (RMSE) of the tidal amplitude are 4.3, 1.6, 1.7, 0.8 cm for M_2, S_2, N_2, and K_1, respectively; the corresponding RMSEs for tide phase are 3.8, 7.3, 4.5, and 3.3 degrees. Note that in obtaining the K_1 phase error of 3.3 degrees, three outlier stations (8455083, 8459338, and 8459479) were excluded from the calculation.

In general, the tidal simulation produced favorable model-data agreement with respect to both amplitude and phase. This helps the hindcast and the future nowcast/forecast system to reproduce realistic water levels.

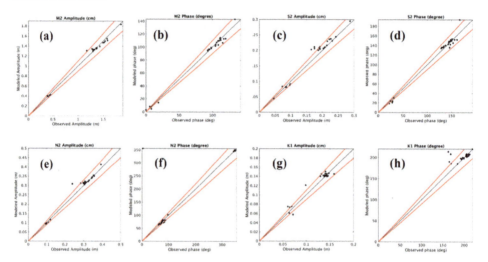

Figure 3. Scatter plots of the tidal harmonic constants (amplitudes and phases) of M_2, N_2, S_2, and K_1 constituents between model results and observations. The red lines on each plot outline the ten percent deviation from the perfect model-data match. (**a**) M_2 amplitude; (**b**) M_2 phase; (**c**) S_2 amplitude; (**d**) S_2 phase; (**e**) N_2 amplitude; (**f**) N_2 phase; (**g**) K_1 amplitude; and (**h**) K_1 phase.

4.2. Hindcast Simulation

The hindcast simulation ran from 1 January to 30 December 2012. It started from a still water state with the T/S fields initialized with the G-RTOFS results. Following an initial 5-day ramping up, the model run continued for another 10 days to ensure that an equilibrium state was reached. The time series of the ocean state variable (water level, currents, and T/S) were recorded at the 6-min interval from the 15th day to the end of the hindcast run. We then used the time series to evaluate the model performance using the NOS standard skill assessment software [16].

4.2.1. Water Levels

Figure 4 showed both the modeled and observed subtidal water level time series after applying a 30-day Fourier Transform low-pass filter to the total water level data. The model results demonstrated favorable agreement with the observations during both the event-free period (October) and the event period (early November). For instance, the model successfully reproduced the water level setup at stations 8423898, and 8443970 in early November (Figure 4e,f). At some stations, such as 8419317 and 8423898 (Figure 3d,e), the model slightly over-predicted the water levels in mid-October.

Table 2. The model-data comparison of harmonic constants for the M_2, S_2, N_2, and K_1 constituents, respectively. The stations are listed in the order of the total tidal range ranking from the largest to the smallest.

Station ID	Station Name	Differences between the Model Predictions and Observations							
		M_2 amp (cm)	M_2 Phase (Degree)	S_2 amp (cm)	S_2 Phase (Degree)	N_2 amp (cm)	N_2 Phase (Degree)	K_1 amp (cm)	K_1 Phase (Degree)
8411250	Cutler Naval Base, ME	−2.7	2.1	0.8	6.3	2.1	1.3	0.9	−2.7
8414721	Fort Pt., ME	−7.6	1.2	1	4	−0.5	4.4	−0.1	−7.6
8413320	Bar Harbor, ME	−3.4	1.7	0.1	5.5	0.3	1.1	0.6	−3.4
8413825	Mackerel Cove, ME	−4.1	1	1.4	3.9	0	−5.9	−1.4	−4.1
8414249	Oceanville, Deer Isle, ME	−4.5	2	−0.1	−10	−0.1	2.7	1.3	−4.5
8414888	Penobscot Bay, ME	−2.7	−0.5	1.4	3	−0.2	0	0.3	−2.7
8447241	Sesuit Harbor, MA	−3.9	1.4	0.2	3.9	0	2.1	0.4	−3.9
8446121	Provincetown, MA	−0.7	2.5	3.6	2.5	−0.2	3.7	0.6	−0.7
8446166	Duxbury Harbor, MA	0.2	−7.3	2	−9.1	1.6	−8.4	0	0.2
8444525	Nut Island, MA	−1.3	−0.5	0.2	2.1	0.5	1	0.2	−1.3
8446493	Plymouth Harbor, MA	0.2	−4.6	0.3	−4.3	1.4	−2.7	0.2	0.2
8444162	Boston Light, MA	0.6	0.9	0.3	4.1	0.8	0.5	0.2	0.6
8418606	Saco River, ME	2.5	−1.5	1.4	−0.6	1.3	−1.5	−0.5	2.5
8446009	Green Harbor River, MA	1.9	−1.9	1.3	−0.2	0.5	1.8	0.2	1.9
8441551	Rockport Harbor, MA	0.8	0.7	1.3	2	0.2	−0.1	−0.4	0.8
8418445	Pine Point, ME	4.6	−5.5	3.1	−5.2	2.8	−9.7	0.1	4.6
8417177	Hunniwell, ME	7.1	−3	1.9	2.9	1.7	−3.4	−0.1	7.1
8440452	Plum Island, MA	14.1	−9.1	3.8	−7.6	7	−10.9	1	14.1
8455083	Point Judith, RI	−3.3	−3.7	−0.8	−7.5	−0.9	−2.6	−0.3	−3.3
8447605	Hyannisport, MA	−3.1	8.8	−0.2	26.9	−0.5	2.4	2.2	−3.1
8459338	Block Island, RI	−2.5	−357	−0.9	−3.5	−0.2	1.7	1.4	−2.5
8459681	Block Island, RI	−0.8	2.2	−0.3	−1.4	−0.1	2.6	0.8	−0.8
8459479	Sandy Point, RI	−0.5	−0.5	−0.4	−5.6	0.1	−0.8	0.6	−0.5
8458022	Block Island Sound, RI	2.6	−5.3	1	−0.7	0	351.6	−1.4	2.6

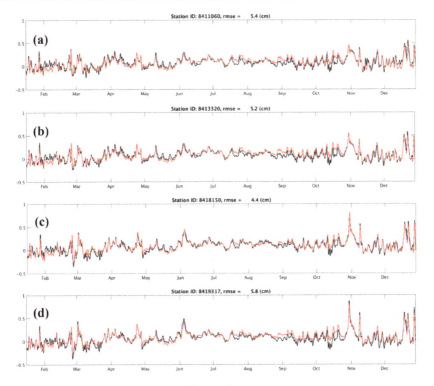

Figure 4. *Cont.*

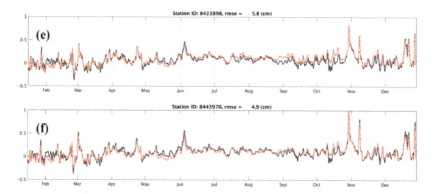

Figure 4. Subtidal water levels at six CO-OPS water level stations (Figure 1). The red and black lines represent the model results and observations, respectively. The six plots are for stations (**a**) 8411060; (**b**) 8413320; (**c**) 8418150; (**d**) 8419317; (**e**) 8423898; and (**f**) 8443970.

4.2.2. Currents

Figure 5 displays the (u, v) components of the modeled and observed subtidal time series at three measurement depths (10 m, 22 m, and 46 m) at buoy A. The subtidal data were extracted from filtering the model output with a 30-h low-pass Fourier filter.

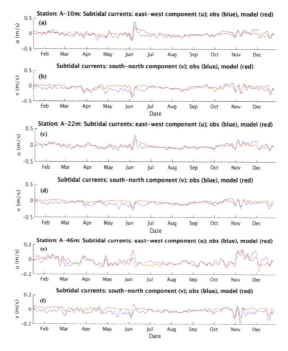

Figure 5. Comparison of the model (red lines) and the data (blue lines) time series of the current velocity (u, v) at the NeraCOOS buoy station A. The measurement depths are shown on the plots. (**a,b**) depict the u and v components at the 10 m depth; (**c,d**) depict the u and v components at the 22 m depth; and (**e,f**) depict the u and v components at the 46 m depth.

The hindcast simulation successful reproduced in the events taking place in early June and early to mid-November, respectively. During the events, the currents appeared to be more intense in shallow layers (at 10 m and 22 m) than in deeper layers (at 46 m). Comparison of the time series between the winds and the currents indicated that the enhanced currents speeds resulted from the intensified wind stress during the events.

4.2.3. Water Temperature

The modeled temperature time series were compared with the observations at the CO-OPS meteorological stations and the NDBC buoys, and NeraCOOS buoys. The model results demonstrate favorable agreement with the observations. As an example, the left panel in Figure 6 displays the monthly averaged temperature at six depths (1 m, 20 m, 50 m, 100 m, 150 m, and 200 m) at the NeraCOOS buoy M01. The plots illustrated that the model successfully reproduced both the magnitude and the annual cycle of the temperature. The near surface water temperature varied between 6 °C in the winter and the early spring and 20 °C in the mid-summer. In deeper water, temperature remained at a nearly constant value of 9 °C throughout the year. This suggests that an intense thermocline existed during the summer and completely faded away in the winter.

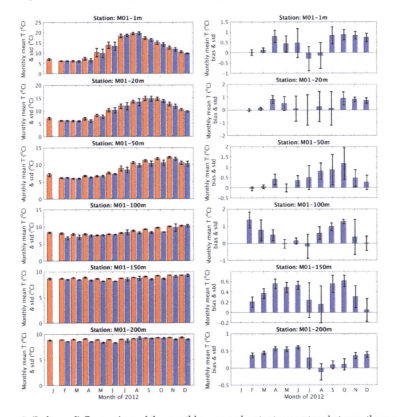

Figure 6. (Left panel) Comparison of the monthly averaged water temperature between the model (red bars) and the observations (blue bars) at the NeraCOOS buoy M01. The measurement depths are as shown on each plot. On some plots the observations do not appear due to the lack of data. **(Right panel)** Bias of the modeled monthly mean temperature. The thin lines on top of each bar plot represent the corresponding standard deviations.

The right panel in the figure displays the bias and the standard deviation (std) of the monthly averaged model temperature. The bias ranged from near zero to less than 1 °C and did not exhibit evident trend of seasonal variations. The std ranged between 0.03 and 1.2 °C and appeared to be greater in summer than in spring and winter.

4.2.4. Salinity

The modeled time series were compared with observations at the seven NeraCOOS buoys (Figure 1 and Table 1). The left panel in Figure 7 displays the monthly averaged salinity of at buoys A01 and M01. The corresponding measurement depths were 1 m, 20 m, and 50 m at buoy A01 and 1 m, 20 m, 50 m, 100 m, 150 m, and 200 m at buoy M01. The right panel displays the corresponding model bias and std.

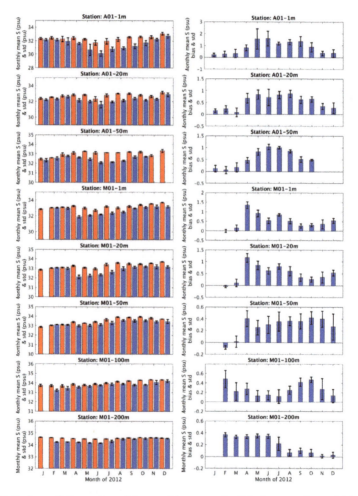

Figure 7. (Left panel) Comparison of the monthly averaged salinity between the model (red bars) and the observations (blue bars) at the NeraCOOS buoys A01 and M01. The station name and the measurement depths are as shown on each plot. On some plots the observations do not appear due to the lack of data. **(Right panel)** Bias of the modeled monthly mean temperature. The black lines on top each bar represent the corresponding standard deviations.

In general, salinity exhibited greater temporal variability near the surface than in deeper waters, especially during the late spring, summer, and early fall. The modeled salinity demonstrated positive biases with the typical magnitude of 0.5–1.0 psu at nearly each station throughout the year. This indicated that the hindcast tended to overestimate the salinity. However, this did not seem to be rooted from the specifics of the currently adopted turbulence closure scheme (TCS). In fact, the other TCS such as the k-ε, k-ω, and KPP models in the ROMS were also tested and they demonstrated similar model skills. Model bias might be attributed to inherent errors of various model forcing data.

During these periods, the model-data discrepancy appeared to be greater than in the winter. For instance, at buoy A01 the modeled surface salinity differed from the observations by 1.5 to 2 psu in the summer months, whereas the two exhibited close match in the winter months. Farther offshore at buoy M01, the model-data discrepancy appeared to be much smaller than at buoy A. The model agreed well with the observations in the fall and winter seasons. Even during the hydrodynamically active spring and summer seasons, the model-data differed by less than about 1 psu.

To examine the impact of the river discharges and rainfall forcings on the modeled salinity, we estimated the correlation coefficient, C_{SP}, between the sea-surface salinity (SSS) and the precipitation rate and the coefficient, and C_{SR} between the SSS and the discharge rates from the nearest river to each NeraCOOS station. It was found that the magnitude of C_{SP} was less than 0.06 at all stations. This seems to indicate that at the NeraCOOS stations the rainfall played a minor role in determining the modeled SSS compared with other forcing factors or ambient conditions.

C_{SR} was −0.42 and −0.46 at Stations B and F, respectively and was much less significant ($|C_{SR}| < 0.05$) at the other stations. Note that Stations B and F are relatively closer to the river entrance than the others and therefore demonstrated relatively higher C_{SR}. Figure 8a,b display the SSS and river discharge time series at Stations B and F to highlight the close correlation between the two properties at the stations.

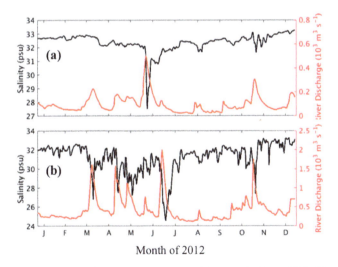

Figure 8. Daily time series of salinity (S) (black lines) and the river discharge (Q) (red lines): (**a**) S at station B01 vs. Q of the Saco River and (**b**) S at Station F01 vs. Q of the Penobscot river.

5. Skill Assessment

We evaluated the hindcast results using the NOS standard skill assessment software [16]. The model time series of water level, currents, temperature, and salinity were compared against the observed data (Section 2). In the following, we focused on reporting two key parameters, RMSE and the central frequency (CF). CF represents the fraction (percentage) of the model errors that are less than some prescribed criteria of RMSE. The NOS standard prescribes the criteria as 0.15 cm for water level, 0.26 m/s for the currents speed and 22.5 degree for the phase of currents, 3.0 °C for temperature, and 3.5 psu for salinity, as well as the constant value of CF equal to 90% for all the above ocean state parameters. The present skill assessment results demonstrated that the hindcast performance met the above criteria. It is noted that the one set value criteria are not region specific and may not reflect the regional variability of the concerned variables. Hence it poses limitations on the validity and applicability of the model skill metrics from the criteria.

We compared the criteria with the performance of the nowcast/forecast system of the Gulf of Maine Ocean Observing System (GoMOOS) [10] in terms of monthly averaged properties (i.e., T, S, and current speeds). In general, the GoMOOS model skill in all three variables meet the NOS criteria, especially for the 3 °C RMSE temperature criteria. The present results (reported in the following) also meet the criteria with large margins at nearly all stations. In this regard, the 3 °C criteria does not pose serious change to the model skill in the GoM region. This seems to indicate that the region specific criteria would be needed to closely reflect the model skill. Bearing this in mind, we adopted the constant criteria in this study before any regional dependent criteria are officially developed in the future.

5.1. Water Level

Figure 9 display the model RMSE and CF, respectively. The RMSE ranges nearly from 0.09 m (Station ID 8418150, Portland, ME, USA) to 0.13 m (Station ID 8411060, Cutler Farris Wharf, ME, USA). The CF ranges from 76.2% (Station ID 8411060, Cutler Farris Wharf, ME) to 89.6% (Station ID 8418150, Portland, ME, USA). With respect to the RMSE and CF, the hindcast demonstrated better skill at stations near the central western Gulf coast than that along the Massachusetts coast and the northern Maine coast.

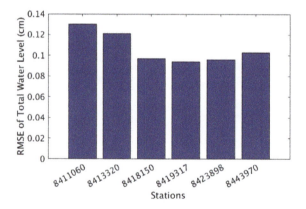

Figure 9. RMSE of the modeled water level.

The better model skill in the central domain stations might be attributed to their particular geographical locations. The stations are farther away from either the open ocean boundary (OOB) or the Bay of Fundy (BF) area compared with the other stations. The tidal range in the BF may reach up to nearly 7 m due to the tidal resonance effect (Section 1). The farther distance naturally made the central domain receive less adverse impact on the model skill due to the inherent inaccuracies in the OOB conditions or the errors in the model predicted tidal resonance effect in the BF.

5.2. Currents

Figure 10a,b displays the RMSE the currents speed and phase, respectively. In each figure, the station ID is named with the first letter denoting the buoy ID (Figure 1) and the following digits denoting the measurement depths in meter.

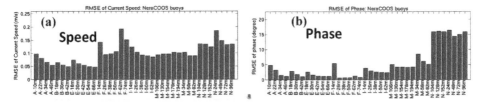

Figure 10. Skill assessment results of the currents speed and phase. (**a**) RMSE of speed and (**b**) RMSE of phase.

For the current speed, the RMSE ranges from 0.05 m/s at station E-66m to about 0.20 m/s at stations F-74m and N-24m. CF were mostly greater than 95% and lay between 80% and 90% at stations F-74m and N-24m. At buoys stations A, B, E, F, and M, RMSEs ranged between less than 2 degrees to 10 degrees and CFs were all above 95%. At station N01, RMSE was between 15 cm/s and 17 cm/s and CF was around 85% at all depths.

Note that the station N01 demonstrated significantly less favorable model skills than the other stations. This might be related to the complex hydrodynamics in the Northeast Channel where the station is located (Figure 1a). The channel has a sill depth of 230 m and is the major pathway for the water mass exchange between the Gulf and the open ocean. The deep ocean water flows into the central Gulf at depths and the Scotian water flows across the channel in the near surface layer. The channel also serves as a major route for tidal energy to propagate into the Gulf. The combined subtidal and tidal currents may reach a speed of 1 m/s or more. In contrast, hydrodynamics in the other areas of the Gulf appear to be much less complex. The complex hydrodynamics in the channel posed more serious challenges to realistically reproduce the local hydrography than elsewhere and contributed to the greater model errors at Station N01.

5.3. Water Temperature

Figure 11 illustrates the skill assessment results in three groups with respect to the sources of observed data, i.e., CO-OPS stations, the NDBC buoys, and the NeraCOOS buoys. In each figure, the abscissa represents the station ID. In particular, the NeraCOOS station IDs (Figure 11c) followed the same naming convention as shown in Figure 8. Both the CO-OPS and the NDBC buoy data corresponded to the near surface measurements and the NeraCOOS data correspond to both the surface and in-depth measurements. In addition, the CO-OPS stations are located in the nearshore area whereas the other two data sets (the NDBC and NeraCOOS buoys) correspond to the further offshore areas and even in the central Gulf and near the shelfbreak area. Therefore, the skill assessment results of the three groups represent the hindcast performance in different hydrodynamic regimes, e.g., nearshore vs. offshore areas as well as at the sea surface vs. the in-depth waters.

The RMSE at the seven CO-OPS stations ranged from 0.9 °C to 1.7 °C and CF was all above 95%. The RMSE at the NDBC stations was between 0.7 °C and 1.8 °C. Correspondingly CF was above 90%.

The RMSE at the NeraCOOS stations ranged from less than 1.0 °C at station M01 in the eastern Gulf to around 2.3 °C at stations N01-20m and −50 m. CF was above 90% except at stations N01-20m and −50 m for which CF equaled ~80%. Note that buoy N is located in the Northeast Channel (Figure 1).

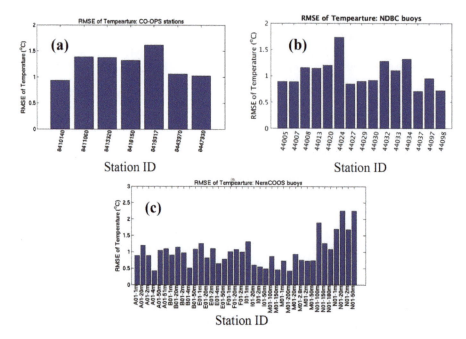

Figure 11. The RMSE of the modeled water temperature compared with three sets of observed data, (**a**) the CO-OPS stations; (**b**) the NDBC buoys; and (**c**) the NeraCOOS buoys.

5.4. Salinity

Figure 12 displays the RMSE of the salinity skill assessment results. In general, the RMSE ranged from 0.2 psu to 1.5 psu and the CF was close to 100%. At buoys A, B, E, F, I, and M, the RMSE of the near-surface salinity was around 1.0–1.5 psu, whereas the RMSE in the subsurface layer is much smaller, less than 0.7 pus in general. At buoy N, the RMSEs at all three depths (1 m, 20m, and 50 m) were between 1.0 psu and 1.4 psu.

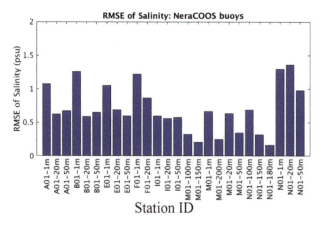

Figure 12. The RMSE of the modeled salinity.

J. Mar. Sci. Eng. **2016**, *4*, 77

6. Summary and Conclusions

The NOAA NOS is developing the Gulf of Maine operational nowcast/forecast system (GoMOFS) to aim for producing real-time nowcast and short-range forecast guidance for water levels, 3-dimensional currents, water temperature, and salinity over the broad GoM region. Following the routine procedure of the OFS development, we conducted a one-year period hindcast simulation of 2012. This manuscript described the model development, hindcast setup and the skill assessment results.

The model performance was evaluated using the NOS standard skill assessment software and the criteria by comparing the hindcast results with the observed time series of water level, T/S, and currents collected by both the NOAA agencies (including the CO-OPS and NDBC) and the NeraCOOS. In general, the hindcast results met the skill assessment criteria. The RMSE was about 0.12 m for water level, less than 1.5 °C for temperature, less than 1.5 psu for salinity, and less than 0.2 m/s for the currents speed and less than 15 degrees for the currents phase. The corresponding central frequency was between 80% and 90% for the water level and generally above 90% for the other properties.

The NOS is working on transitioning the hindcast setup into operations on the NOAA's Weather and Climate Operational Supercomputing System. The GoMOFS is anticipated to be in operations in fiscal year 2017.

Acknowledgments: John Wilkin, Hernan G. Arango, Julia Levin, Javier Zavala-Garay at the Rutgers University, Ruoying He at the North Carolina State University, and Dennis McGillicuddy at Woods Hole Oceanographic Institution provided valuable comments and data supports on the GoMOFS development. Three anonymous reviewers provided insightful comments and suggestions that substantially improved this paper. The authors would like to express our sincere gratitude for their help.

Author Contributions: All the authors contributed to the system development. Z.Y. conducted the hindcast simulation and the skill assessment.

Conflicts of Interest: The authors declare no conflicts of interest.

References

1. Chen, C.; Beardsley, R.C. Tidal mixing over a finite amplitude asymmetric bank: A model study with application to Georges Bank. *J. Mar. Res.* **1998**, *56*, 1163–1201. [CrossRef]
2. Chen, C.; Beardsley, R.C. A numerical study of stratified tidal rectification over finite-amplitude banks. Part I: Symmetric bank. *J. Phys. Oceanogr.* **1995**, *25*, 2090–2110. [CrossRef]
3. Naimie, C.E. Georges Bank residual circulation during weak and strong stratification periods: Prognostic numerical model results. *J. Geophys. Res.* **1996**, *101*, 6469–6486. [CrossRef]
4. Naimie, C.E.; Loder, J.W.; Lynch, D.R. Seasonal variation of the three-dimensional residual circulation on Georges Bank. *J. Geophys. Res.* **1994**, *99*, 15967–15989. [CrossRef]
5. Xue, H.; Chai, F.; Perrigrew, N.R. A model study of the seasonal circulation in the Gulf of Maine. *J. Phys. Oceanogr.* **2000**, *30*, 1111–1135. [CrossRef]
6. Wiebe, P.; Beardsley, R.; Mountain, D.; Bucklin, A. U.S. Globec Northwest Atlantic/Georges Bank program. *Oceanography* **2003**, *15*, 13–29. [CrossRef]
7. Zhang, A.; Wei, E.; Parker, B.B. Optimal estimation of tidal open boundary conditions using predicted tides and adjoint data assimilation technique. *Cont. Shelf Res.* **2003**, *23*, 1055–1070. [CrossRef]
8. Greenberg, D.A. Modeling the mean barotropic circulation in the Bay of Fundy and Gulf of Maine. *J. Phys. Oceanogr.* **1983**, *13*, 886–904. [CrossRef]
9. Chen, C.; Beardsley, R.C.; Franks, P.J.S. A 3-D prognostic model study of the ecosystem over Georges Bank and adjacent coastal regions. Part I: Physical model. *Deep Sea Res.* **2001**, *48*, 419–456. [CrossRef]
10. Xue, H.; Shi, L.; Cousins, S.; Pettigrew, N.R. The GoMOOS nowcast/forecast system. *Cont. Shelf Res.* **2005**, *25*, 2122–2146. [CrossRef]
11. Yang, Z.; Myers, E. Barotropic Tidal Energetics and Tidal Datums in the Gulf of Maine and Georges Bank Region. In *Estuarine and Coastal Modeling, American Society of Civil Engineers*, Proceedings of the 10th International Conference, Newport, RI, USA, 10–12 November 2007; Spaulding, M.L., Ed.; 2007; pp. 74–94.

12. Chen, C.; Huang, H.; Beardsley, R.C.; Xu, Q.; Limeburner, R.; Cowles, G.W.; Sun, Y.; Qi, J.; Lin, H. Tidal dynamics in the Gulf of Maine and New England Shelf: An application of FVCOM. *J. Geophys. Res.* **2011**, *116*, C12010. [CrossRef]

13. Gangopadhyay, A.; Robinson, A.R.; Haley, P.J., Jr.; Leslie, W.G.; Lozano, C.J.; Bisagni, J.J.; Yu, Z. Feature oriented regional modeling and simulations (FORMS) in the Gulf of Maine and Georges Bank. *Cont. Shelf Res.* **2003**, *23*, 317–353. [CrossRef]

14. Wilkin, J.; Levin, J.; Zavala-Garay, J.; Arango, H.; Hunter, E.; Robertson, D.; Fleming, N. ROMS 4DVar Data Assimilation: Mid-Atlantic Bight and Gulf of Maine. Available online: http://maracoos.org/sites/macoora/files/downloads/Wilkin-Rutgers-OMG.pptx (accessed on 8 July 2016).

15. Shchepetkin, A.F.; McWilliams, J.C. The Regional Ocean Modeling System: A split-explicit, free-surface, topography following coordinates ocean model. *Ocean Model.* **2005**, *9*, 347–404. [CrossRef]

16. Zhang, A.; Hess, K.W.; Wei, E.; Myers, E. *Implementation of Model Skill Assessment Software for Water Level and Current*; NOAA Technical Report NOS CS 24; U.S. Department of Commerce, National Oceanic and Atmospheric Administration: Silver Spring, MA, USA, 2006; p. 61.

17. Yang, Z.; Myers, E.P.; Jeong, I.; White, S.A. *VDatum for the Gulf of Maine: Tidal Datums, Marine Grids, and Sea Surface Topography*; NOAA Technical Memorandum NOS CS 31; U.S. Department of Commerce, National Oceanic and Atmospheric Administration: Silver Spring, MA, USA, 2013; p. 50.

18. National Geophysical Data Center (NGDC). 2-Minute Gridded Global Relief Data (ETOPO2v2). Available online: https://www.ngdc.noaa.gov/mgg/global/etopo2.html (accessed on 28 October 2016).

19. Egber, G.; Erofeeva, L. Efficient Inverse Modeling of Barotropic Ocean Tides. *J. Atmos. Oceanic Technol.* **2002**, *19*, 183204.

20. Mehra, A.; Rivin, I.; Garraffo, Z.; Rajan, B. Upgrade of the Operational Global Real Time Ocean Forecast System. Available online: https://www.wcrp-climate.org/WGNE/BlueBook/2015/individual-articles/08_Mehra_Avichal_etal_RTOFS_Upgrade.pdf (accessed on 29 October 2016).

21. Garaffo, Z.D.; Kim, H.-C.; Mehra, A.; Spindler, T.; Rivin, I.; Tolman, H.L. Modeling of ^{137}Cs as a tracer in a regional model for the Western Pacific, after the Fukushina-Daiichi Nuclear power plant accident of March 2011. *Weather Forecast.* **2016**, *21*, 553–579. [CrossRef]

22. U.S. Geological Survey (USGS). USGS Water Data for the Nation. Available online: http://waterdata.usgs.gov/nwis/ (accessed on 15 October 2013).

23. Center for Operational Oceanographic Products and Services (CO-OP). Water Levels—Station Selection. Available online: http://tidesandcurrents.noaa.gov/stations.html?type=Water+Levels (accessed on 28 October 2016).

24. National Data Buoy Center (NDBC). Archive of Historical Ocean Data. Available online: http://www.ndbc.noaa.gov/data/historical/ocean/ (accessed on 28 October 2016).

25. Northeastern Regional Association of Coastal Ocean Observing Systems (NeraCOOS). Graphing and Download. Available online: http://neracoos.org/datatools/historical/graphing_download (accessed on 28 October 2016).

Article

Tidal Datum Changes Induced by Morphological Changes of North Carolina Coastal Inlets

Jindong Wang [1,2,*] and Edward Myers [1]

[1]   Coast Survey Development Laboratory, National Ocean Service, National Oceanic and Atmospheric
     Administration, 1315 East-West Highway, Silver Spring, MD 20910, USA; edward.myers@noaa.gov
[2]   Earth Resources Technology, Inc., 14401 Switzer Lane, Suite 300, Laurel, MD 20707, USA
*   Correspondence: jindong.wang@gmail.com; Tel.: +1-301-713-2809

Academic Editor: Richard P. Signell
Received: 18 July 2016; Accepted: 12 November 2016; Published: 18 November 2016

Abstract: In support of the National Oceanic and Atmospheric Administration's VDatum program, a new version of a tidal datum product for the North Carolina coastal waters has been developed to replace the initial version released in 2004. Compared with the initial version, the new version used a higher resolution grid to cover more areas and incorporated up-to-date tide, bathymetry, and shoreline data. Particularly, the old bathymetry datasets that were collected from the 1930s to the 1970s and were used in the initial version have been replaced by the new bathymetry datasets collected in the 2010s in the new version around five North Carolina inlets. This study aims at evaluating and quantifying tidal datum changes induced by morphological changes over about 40 to 80 years around the inlets. A series of tidal simulations with either the old or new bathymetry datasets used around five inlets were conducted to quantify the consequent tidal datum changes. The results showed that around certain inlets, approximately 10% change in the averaged depth could result in over 30% change in the tidal datum magnitude. Further investigation also revealed that tidal datum changes behind the barrier islands are closely associated with the cross-inlet tidal flux changes.

Keywords: VDatum; tidal datums; morphological changes; inlets; North Carolina

---

1. Introduction

The software package VDatum, developed and maintained by the National Oceanic and Atmospheric Administration (NOAA), allows users to transform geospatial data among a variety of ellipsoidal, orthometric, and tidal datums [1]. For example, users can integrate the United States Geological Survey's elevation data referenced to the North American Vertical Datum of 1988 (NAVD88) with NOAA's sounding data referenced to Mean Lower Low Water (MLLW) to build a seamless bathymetry-topography Digital Elevation Model (DEM) dataset referenced to a common datum of Mean Sea Level (MSL) by using VDatum. The integrated DEM provides a basis for coastal inundation modeling and mapping [2].

As a critical part of VDatum, tidal datums are derived from water level time series simulated by a tide model. The tidal highs and lows from modeled water levels are used to calculate tidal datums: Mean Higher High Water (MHHW), Mean High Water (MHW), Mean Low Water (MLW), and Mean Lower Low Water (MLLW) [3]. Following the VDatum Standard Operating Procedures [4], we use the ADvanced CIRCulation (ADCIRC) model [5] to conduct tidal simulations for deriving tidal datums in VDatum. The ADCIRC model has been widely used for tidal simulations from the basin scale [6–8] to the regional scale [9–11].

The initial version of VDatum for North Carolina was released in 2004 [12]. An updated version has been developed to cover more areas and incorporate up-to-date tide, bathymetry, and shoreline data. Around five main North Carolina inlets (Beaufort, Barden, Ocracoke, Hatteras, and Oregon Inlet), the bathymetry datasets collected from the 1930s to the 1970s were used in the initial version for tide modeling to derive tidal datums. These old bathymetry datasets have been replaced by the datasets collected in the 2010s around five inlets in the updated version. Tidal datum changes induced by morphological changes of the inlets need to be quantified to provide NOAA guidance for future updating of VDatum, installing new tide gauges, and conducting new hydrographic surveys in this region.

Tidal inlets are typically dynamically active regions where tidal circulation and transport lead to continuous sediment movement and thus morphological changes. In general, the combination of tides and waves was considered to shape the inlet morphology into different types: flood-tidal delta and ebb-tidal delta [13–16]. Tidal distortion was found to affect net sediment transport [17,18]. Tidal prism and inlet cross-sectional area were also considered as important factors to affect the inlet morphology [19]. Around North Carolina's Beaufort Inlet, a nearshore jet in tidal circulation was identified and simulated and was considered to be associated with the net transport through the inlet [20,21]. Sediment deposition and erosion around North Carolina inlets was investigated with the local dynamics by Inman and Dolan [22]. These previous studies have mainly been focused on how hydrodynamics (e.g., tides and waves) affect the morphology of the inlets. Little attention has been paid to the feedback of tides to morphological changes of the inlets.

In this study, we aimed at evaluating and quantifying how morphological changes of the inlets affect tidal changes. This paper is organized as follows: following the introduction section, Section 2 describes the sources of a variety of tide, shoreline, and bathymetry data, as well as the tide model setup, numerical experiment design, and model validation. The results will be described in Section 3 followed by some discussions and conclusions in the last section.

2. Materials and Methods

2.1. Data Sources

The water level data [23] and the observed tidal datums [24] provided by the Center for Operational Oceanographic Products and Services (CO-OPS) of NOAA were used for model validation. CO-OPS typically publishes one single value for a particular tidal datum (e.g., MHW) at one station. The tidal datums were typically derived from the water level time series for a certain time period (from a couple of months to years). The observed tidal datums were referenced to the current National Tidal Datum Epoch (NTDE) (1983–2001) [24]. In this paper, the observed tidal datums at 31 tide stations were compared with the modeled tidal datums to evaluate the general model performance in North Carolina coastal waters. Since the identification (ID) numbers of all North Carolina stations begin with 865, the 865 will be ignored when we describe station IDs in the following discussions.

The locations of all 31 datum stations are shown in Figure 1. Among these stations, the 4 outside stations 1370, 4400, 6590, and 6937 are located on the Atlantic Ocean coast. The other 27 inside stations are located behind the barrier islands and within the sounds and estuaries. Among the 31 datum stations, tidal harmonic constituents are also provided for 16 stations [25]. In addition, the hourly water level data collected from 1967 to 2016 at Beaufort Station (ID: 6483), about 4 km behind the Beaufort Inlet and Duck Station (ID: 1370) on the Atlantic coast, were used to evaluate the temporal variation of MHW.

The development of the hydrodynamic model grid requires shoreline and bathymetry data. The National Geodetic Survey provided the up-to-date North Carolina shoreline data which combined NOAA Continually Updated Shoreline Product (CUSP) and the Office of Coast Survey (OCS) chart shoreline data [26]. The bathymetry data were mainly from three sources. The OCS sounding data collected from 1851 to 2012 were used for most of the North Carolina coastal regions. The particular areas covered by the datasets collected in a certain year can be found in a Bathymetry Data Viewer [27]. A global bathymetry-topography database SRTM30_PLUS from Scripps Institution of Oceanography was used for the far offshore region [28]. The sounding data collected since 2010 by the U.S. Army Corps Engineers' Wilmington District were used for coastal inlets and intra-coastal waterways [29]. All the up-to-date tide, bathymetry, and shoreline data have been applied to derive the updated tidal datums used by the currently available VDatum tool.

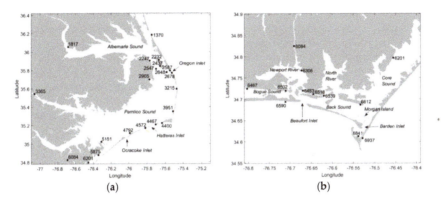

(a)   (b)

Figure 1. Map of North Carolina coastal waters and inlets and the locations of the National Oceanic and Atmospheric Administration (NOAA) water level stations (black dots): (**a**) Northern part; (**b**) Southern part. Please note that the scale in (**b**) is 4 times larger than (**a**).

2.2. Model Setup

The ADCIRC [5] Two-Dimensional Depth Integrated (2DDI) version was used in this study to solve the shallow water equations and simulate tidal water levels. The finite amplitude and convection terms and the wetting and drying option were activated. The lateral viscosity was set as a constant, 5.0 m·s^{-2}, throughout the model domain. The quadratic bottom friction scheme was used with a constant coefficient of 0.0025. The model was forced by a reconstructed tide at the ocean boundary (shown as blue lines in Figure 2a) using the harmonic constants of the five most significant tidal constituents (M_2, S_2, N_2, K_1, and O_1) from the EC2001 tidal database [7].

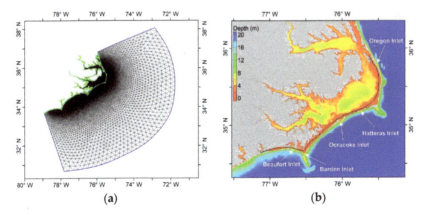

(a)   (b)

Figure 2. (**a**) The triangular model grid (the blue lines delineate the open ocean boundary; the green lines delineate the land boundary); (**b**) Model grid bathymetry in North Carolina coastal waters (the regions deeper than 20 m use the same blue color; the black line shows the location for longitudinal profiles in Figures 15 and 16).

The time step was set to be 1 s. Under this condition, the maximum Courant number is 0.67 over the smallest elements in the grid. This ensured model stability. The model simulations covered a time period of 40 days. The first 10 days were used for the tidal field to reach an equilibrium state. The 6-min water level time series at each node from the last 30 days of each simulation were then used to derive tidal datums and harmonic constants. The 15-min velocity time series at each node from the last 15 days of each simulation were used to calculate the flood and ebb fluxes across the inlets.

A triangular mesh (Figure 2a) has been developed with a spatially varying resolution from 30 km offshore to 10 m inland to resolve important geographical features such as inlets, channels, estuaries, and bays. We used this mesh as a basis to generate the model grids by interpolating the old (1930s–1970s) and the new (2010s) bathymetry datasets around five North Carolina inlets (Beaufort, Barden, Ocracoke, Hatteras, and Oregon Inlet) onto the mesh. In the following discussions, we will use the old-bathy grid to represent the model grid using the old (1930s–1970s) bathymetry data and use the new-bathy grid to represent the model grid using the new (2010s) bathymetry data around the inlets. The particular collection years for the old and new bathymetry datasets around each inlet have been listed in Table 1. For the old-bathy grid, we combined the patched bathymetry datasets collected in 1956 and 1962 around Ocracoke Inlet to represent the general morphology in this region in the mid-20th century. For the new-bathy grid, we combined the bathymetry datasets collected in 2014, 2015, and 2016 around Hatteras Inlet and the bathymetry datasets collected in 2014 and 2016 around Oregon Inlet to represent the recent morphology in these two regions. The detailed coverages of the old and the new bathymetry datasets are shown for Beaufort and Barden Inlet in Figure 3d, Ocracoke and Hatteras Inlet in Figure 4d, and Oregon Inlet in Figure 5d. Other than the inlet regions delineated by the polygons in Figures 3–5, the old-bathy grid and the new-bathy grid have the same depths interpolated from the same bathymetry datasets described in Section 2.1. Therefore, the only difference between the old-bathy grid and the new-bathy grid was the bathymetry around the five inlets.

Table 1. Bathymetric data and morphological parameters around five North Carolina inlets.

Inlet	Width (km)	Area with Changed Bathymetry (km²)	Collection Years of Old Bathymetry	Mean Depth of Old-Bathy (m)	Collection Years of New Bathymetry	Mean Depth of New-Bathy (m)
Beaufort	1.3	6.2	1953	5.0	2010	7.2
Barden	0.7	4.3	1955	1.7	2015	2.9
Ocracoke	2.4	8.8	1956, 1962	4.0	2013	4.9
Hatteras	2.2	8.7	1935	2.6	2014, 2015, 2016	2.7
Oregon	1.0	3.7	1975	3.6	2014, 2016	4.0

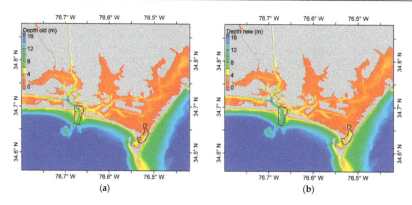

(a)   (b)

Figure 3. *Cont.*

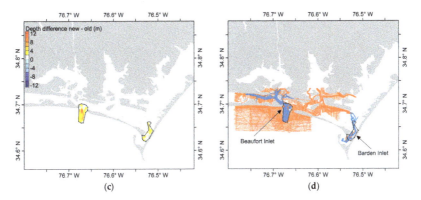

Figure 3. The morphological changes around Beaufort Inlet and Barden Inlet: (**a**) the old-bathy grid depths; (**b**) the new-bathy grid depths; (**c**) the depth difference between the new-bathy grid and the old-bathy grid; (**d**) the original bathymetry sounding data points (orange: data in 1953 around Beaufort Inlet and data in 1955 around Barden Inlet; blue: data in 2010 around Beaufort Inlet and data in 2015 around Barden Inlet). The black dotted polygons delineate the area with changed bathymetry.

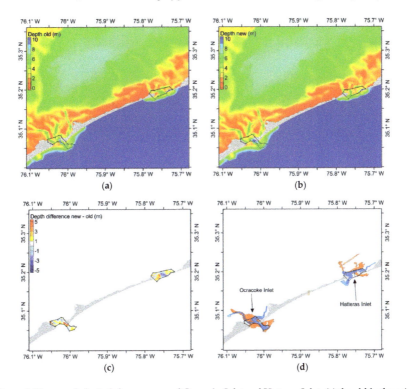

Figure 4. The morphological changes around Ocracoke Inlet and Hatteras Inlet: (**a**) the old-bathy grid depths; (**b**) the new-bathy grid depths; (**c**) the depth difference between the new-bathy grid and the old-bathy grid; (**d**) the original bathymetry sounding data points (orange: data in 1956 and 1962 around Ocracoke Inlet and data in 1935 around Hatteras Inlet; blue: data in 2013 around Ocracoke Inlet and data in 2014, 2015, and 2016 around Hatteras Inlet). The black dotted polygons delineate the area with changed bathymetry.

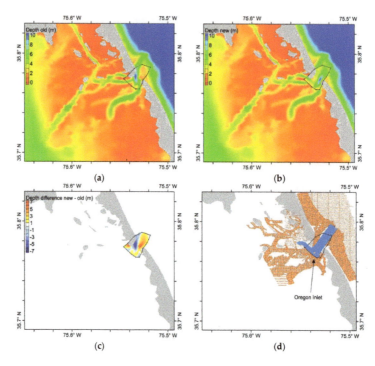

Figure 5. The morphological changes around Oregon Inlet: (**a**) the old-bathy grid depths; (**b**) the new-bathy grid depths; (**c**) the depth difference between the new-bathy grid and the old-bathy grid; (**d**) the original bathymetry sounding data points (orange: data in 1975 around Oregon Inlet; blue: data in 2014 and 2016 around Oregon Inlet). The black dotted polygons delineate the area with changed bathymetry.

The same model setup and tidal forcing were applied to the models using the old-bathy grid and the new-bathy grid. In the following discussions, we will use the old-bathy model and the new-bathy model to represent the models using the old-bathy grid and the new-bathy grid, respectively.

Since Beaufort Inlet and Barden Inlet are close to each other, we made another two grids new-bathy-BE and new-bathy-BA to evaluate the tidal datum changes induced by the morphological changes of each individual inlet. For the new-bathy-BE grid, the new bathymetry data were used around Beaufort Inlet and the old bathymetry data were used for the other four inlets. Similarly, for the new-bathy-BA grid, the new bathymetry data were used around Barden Inlet and the old bathymetry data were used for the other four inlets. We will use the new-bathy-BE model and the new-bathy-BA model to represent tidal simulations using the new-bathy-BE grid and the new-bathy-BA grid, respectively, in the following discussions.

The overview of the common area bathymetry is shown in Figure 2b. Most regions behind the barrier islands are shallower than 8 m. There are significant bathymetric differences between the old-bathy grid and the new-bathy grid around the inlets, as shown in Figures 3–5. For example, around Beaufort Inlet (Figure 3), the mean depth has increased by 44% from the old-bathy depth of 5.0 m to the new-bathy depth of 7.2 m. In addition, the recent deep channel became deeper and wider relative to about 60 years ago. These morphological changes around Beaufort Inlet should be mainly associated with historical dredging activities [30]. The mean depths increased by 70%, 22%, 4%, and 11% from the old-bathy grid to the new-bathy grid around Barden Inlet, Ocracoke Inlet, Hatteras Inlet, and Oregon Inlet, respectively. The morphological parameters for five inlets are listed in Table 1.

2.3. Model Validation

Computed tidal datums from both the old-bathy model and the new-bathy model were compared with the observed tidal datums at 31 stations. The root mean squared errors (RMSEs) of both models for four tidal datums have been listed in Table 2. In general, both models had decent performances relative to the observations. The new-bathy model had a little higher overall performance than the old-bathy model. It should be noted that the RMSEs of the new-bathy model are slightly higher than the uncertainty values published on the VDatum website [31]. This is mainly because the official VDatum tidal datums were calculated from longer time series of simulated water levels.

Table 2. The root mean squared errors of the modeled tidal datums relative to the observed ones.

Model	Mean Higher High Water (MHHW) (cm)	Mean High Water (MHW) (cm)	Mean Low Water (MLW) (cm)	Mean Lower Low Water (MLLW) (cm)
Old-bathy Model	6.1	4.6	4.5	6.0
New-bathy Model	4.8	3.5	3.3	4.5

Since the four tidal datums have similar trend and patterns, only MHW will be discussed as an example in the rest of the paper. The result for MHW is shown in Figure 6. The new-bathy model outperformed the old-bathy model at particular stations. At the inside stations not too far away from the inlets (e.g., 2678, 6084, and 6483), the new-bathy model matched the observations very well while the old-bathy model underestimated the observations by approximately 5% to 25%. This is because tidal datums at these stations had changed more dramatically than other stations and the new-bathy model simulation is closer to the current National Tidal Datum Epoch (1983–2001) conditions. At the outside stations and the inside stations far away from the inlets (e.g., 1370, 3365, and 6590), the MHW values from both models had very small differences.

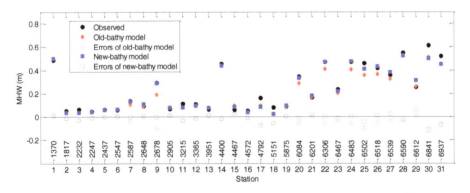

Figure 6. Comparison of MHW at 31 NOAA stations between the observations (black dots), the old-bathy model (red solid diamonds), and the new-bathy model (blue solid squares). The blank diamonds and squares indicate the model errors.

The amplitudes and phases of five principal tidal constituents (M_2, S_2, N_2, K_1, and O_1) from both models were also compared with the observations at 16 stations. As an example, the results for M_2 (Figures 7 and 8) indicate that the old-bathy model and the new-bathy model had decent performance. For some stations with small amplitude (e.g., 5875), the discrepancy between the modeled phase and the observed phase could be relatively high because the obscured tidal signals in the observed water level time series led to high uncertainty in the observed phase itself.

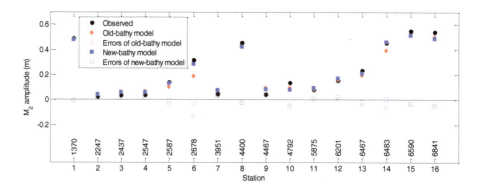

Figure 7. Comparison of the M_2 amplitude at 16 NOAA stations between the observations (black dots), the old-bathy model (red solid diamonds), and the new-bathy model (blue solid squares). The blank diamonds and squares indicate the model errors.

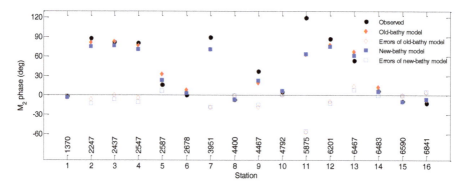

Figure 8. Comparison of the M_2 phase at 16 NOAA stations between the observations (black dots), the old-bathy model (red solid diamonds), and the new-bathy model (blue solid squares). The blank diamonds and squares indicate the model errors.

At the inside stations not too far away from the inlets (e.g., 2678 and 6483), the new-bathy model outperformed the old-bathy model. The old-bathy model had underestimated amplitudes and overestimated phases relative to the observations.

Tidal datum changes induced by morphological changes of Beaufort Inlet can also be observed from Beaufort Station (6483) about 4 km behind the Beaufort Inlet as shown in Figure 9a. The value of each black dot in the figure came from the monthly averaged MHW. In addition to the 18.6-year-cycle and seasonal variations, there was an obvious trend increasing from ~0.44 m in 1967 to ~0.49 m in 2016. The 18.6-year-cycle variation is due to the changing locations of the sun and the moon relative to the earth [2]. For the model results around the same location, MHW increased from 0.41 m of the old-bathy model to 0.47 m of the new-bathy model, which is largely consistent with the observed trend. As a comparison, for Duck Station (1370) on the Atlantic coast, MHW also showed the 18.6-year-cycle and seasonal variations and a slightly decreasing trend based on the analyzed data in 1978–2016 (Figure 9b). This trend is not reflected in the model results because Duck Station is approximately 50 km away from the nearest Oregon Inlet and thus is not affected by the inlet bathymetry changes.

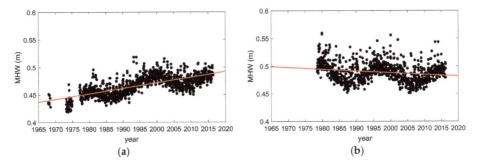

(a)   (b)

Figure 9. Temporal changes for the last few decades of the monthly averaged MHW at two NOAA stations: (**a**) Beaufort Station (ID: 6483); (**b**) Duck Station (ID: 1370). The red lines delineate the linearly best fit lines.

3. Results

3.1. Tidal Datum Changes Due to Morphological Changes of the Inlets

The MHW from the new-bathy model and the old-bathy model and their differences for the North Carolina coastal waters are shown in Figures 10–14. In general, MHW had higher values on the Atlantic Ocean side and lower values behind barrier islands. The MHW values were also higher behind Beaufort Inlet than those behind the other four inlets, indicating that it is much easier for the tides to propagate from the ocean into the sounds through Beaufort Inlet. In addition, the waters behind Beaufort Inlet have smaller areas and deeper depths relative to Pamlico Sound behind Ocracoke Inlet, Hatteras Inlet, and Oregon Inlet. Thus, tidal energy there is much less dissipated than that within Pamlico Sound.

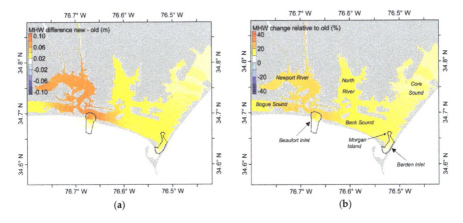

(a)   (b)

Figure 10. The MHW changes induced only by the inlet morphological changes around Beaufort Inlet: (**a**) the MHW difference between the new-bathy-BE model and the old-bathy model; (**b**) the MHW change in percentage relative to the old-bathy model MHW. The black dotted polygons delineate the area with changed bathymetry.

As shown in Figure 10, if the morphological changes only occurred around Beaufort Inlet (i.e., the new-bathy-BE model), MHW has increased behind Beaufort Inlet in three directions: Newport River, Bogue Sound, and Back Sound. MHW in the entire Newport River has increased by ~15% from ~0.4 m to ~0.46 m. The increased MHW becomes smaller where it is farther away from the inlet entrance in both the Bogue Sound and Back Sound directions. The percentage of the increased MHW relative to the old MHW drops to 10% about 10 km away from the inlet entrance in the Bogue Sound direction and about 5 km in the Back Sound direction. Thus, the inlet morphological changes have more influence on MHW in the Newport River direction than the other two directions. This is probably because Newport River is a more enclosed area.

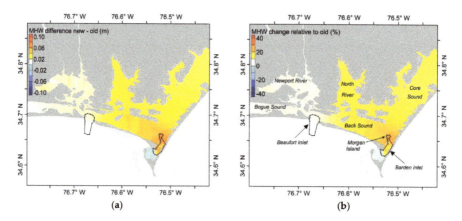

Figure 11. The MHW changes induced only by the inlet morphological changes around Barden Inlet: (a) the MHW difference between the new-bathy-BA model and the old-bathy model; (b) the MHW change in percentage relative to the old-bathy model MHW. The black dotted polygons delineate the area with changed bathymetry.

As shown in Figure 11, if the morphological changes only occurred around Barden Inlet (i.e., the new-bathy-BA model), the increased MHW has a maximum of 0.06 m (22% of the old MHW) around Morgan Island. The percentage of the increased MHW relative to the old MHW drops to 10% 7 km away from Morgan Island in the Back Sound direction and 3 km in the Core Sound direction. Thus, the inlet morphological changes have more influence on MHW in the Back Sound direction than in the Core Sound direction. This is probably because tidal changes induced by the inlet morphological changes are positively correlated with tidal range. Tidal range is larger due to less damped tidal energy in the deeper Back Sound relative to Core Sound (see depths in Figure 3a,b and MHW in Figure 12a,b).

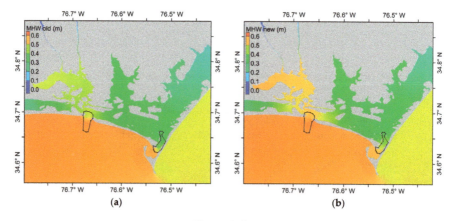

Figure 12. *Cont.*

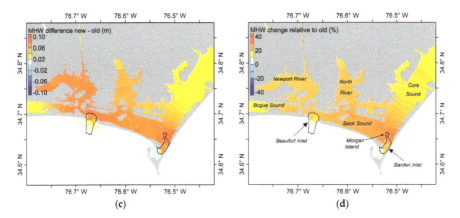

Figure 12. The MHW changes induced by the inlet morphological changes around Beaufort Inlet and Barden Inlet: (**a**) MHW from the old-bathy model; (**b**) MHW from the new-bathy model; (**c**) the MHW difference between the new-bathy model and the old-bathy model; (**d**) the MHW change in percentage relative to the old-bathy model MHW. The black dotted polygons delineate the area with changed bathymetry.

In fact, the morphological changes occurred around both Beaufort Inlet and Barden Inlet. As shown in Figure 12c, the increased MHW is almost the sum of that induced by individual inlet morphological changes. For example, the increased MHW in North River is about 0.04 m. About 0.02 m is from the morphological changes of Beaufort Inlet (Figure 10a). The other 0.02 m is from the morphological changes of Barden Inlet (Figure 11a). This is probably because the tides propagating through Beaufort Inlet interact with the tides propagating through Barden Inlet in the regions located in between both inlets. In the Core Sound direction, the location of the contour of 10% increase in MHW is 10 km (Figure 12d) away from Morgan Island, compared to 3 km in the new-bathy-BA model (Figure 11b). The extended part should come from the contribution of the Beaufort Inlet changes.

The influence range of the morphological changes around Ocracoke Inlet, Hatteras Inlet, and Oregon Inlet are shorter than the distances between itself and its neighbor inlets. Thus, the morphological changes of these three inlets have independent effects on local tidal datum changes.

For Ocracoke Inlet, water depths (Figure 4) have increased from ~4 m to ~9 m in the northeastern part of the ocean-side area of the inlet but have decreased from ~4 m to ~2 m in most sound-side areas of the inlet. As a result, MHW (Figure 13) has increased of ~20% from ~0.35 m to ~0.42 m in the middle of the inlet and the increased MHW is confined within the inlet. MHW has a sudden drop by ~20% from ~0.21 m to ~0.17 m on the northeastern side behind the inlet and the decreased MHW extends inside of Pamlico Sound. The percentage of the decreased MHW gradually drops to 10% about 6 km behind the inlet in the northeastern direction. Therefore the decreased water depths at the inside entrance play a key role in strengthening the tides within the inlet but weakening the tides behind the inlet.

For Hatteras Inlet, water depths (Figure 4) have decreased from ~5 m to ~2 m on the eastern side of the inlet, which leads to a MHW (Figure 13) drop of ~30% from ~0.25 m to ~0.17 m. The decreased MHW also extends inside of Pamlico Sound. The percentage of the decreased MHW gradually drops to 10% about 4 km behind the inlet in the northeastern direction. Water depths have increased from ~1 m to ~4 m on the western side of the inlet, which leads to a MHW increase of ~20% from ~0.23 to ~0.28. The extension of the increased MHW is confined within a small area inside the inlet and may be due to the decreased water depths in the western part of the inside entrance.

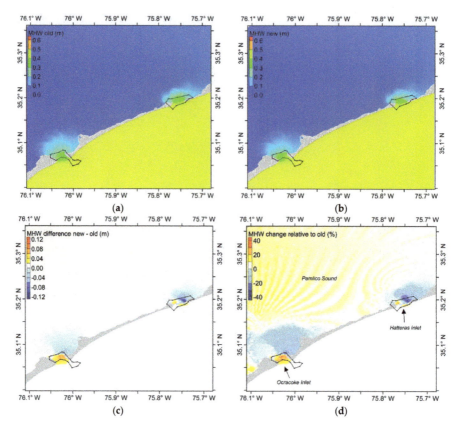

Figure 13. The MHW changes induced by the inlet morphological changes around Ocracoke Inlet and Hatteras Inlet: (**a**) MHW from the old-bathy model; (**b**) MHW from the new-bathy model; (**c**) the MHW difference between the new-bathy model and the old-bathy model; (**d**) the MHW change in percentage relative to the old-bathy model MHW. The black dotted polygons delineate the area with changed bathymetry.

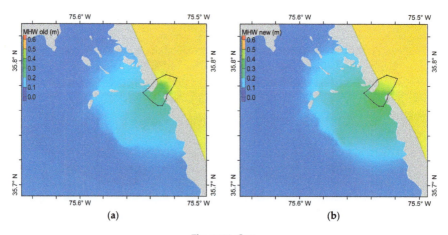

Figure 14. *Cont.*

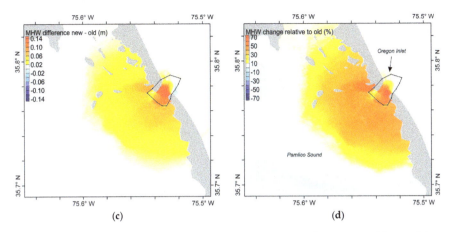

Figure 14. The MHW changes induced by the inlet morphological changes around Oregon Inlet:
(**a**) MHW from the old-bathy model; (**b**) MHW from the new-bathy model; (**c**) the MHW difference
between the new-bathy model and the old-bathy model; (**d**) the MHW change in percentage relative to
the old-bathy model MHW. The black dotted polygons delineate the area with changed bathymetry.

For Oregon Inlet, the inlet channel with ~8 m depth has shifted from the northwestern side in the
old-bathy grid to the southeastern side in the new-bathy grid (Figure 5). The average depth around
Oregon Inlet has increased from ~3.6 m of the old-bathy grid to ~4.0 m of the new-bathy grid. Unlike
Ocracoke Inlet and Hatteras Inlet, MHW (Figure 14) has increased by ~50% from ~0.25 m to ~0.37 m
across the interior of the inlet. The increased MHW extends inside of Pamlico Sound. The percentage
of the increased MHW gradually drops to 10% about 6 km behind the inlet in almost all directions. This
is probably because the presence of several deeper channels (Figure 5a,b) in Pamlico Sound behind
Oregon Inlet favors tidal propagation in all directions.

3.2. Tidal Harmonic Changes

The spatial pattern of the M_2 amplitude in North Carolina coastal waters is similar to that of
MHW because M_2 is the dominant component of tidal constituents in this region; consequently, the M_2
amplitude changes induced by the inlet morphological changes are also similar to the MHW changes.
Figure 15a,b show the M_2 amplitude and phase from the old-bathy model and the new-bathy model
along a line (shown in Figure 2b) approximately 1 km behind the barrier islands. The M_2 amplitude
has increased from the old-bathy model to the new-bathy model behind Beaufort Inlet, Barden Inlet,
and Oregon Inlet and has decreased behind Ocracoke Inlet and Hatteras Inlet. The M_2 phase has
slightly decreased from the old-bathy model to the new-bathy model behind Beaufort Inlet, Barden
Inlet, and Oregon Inlet and has changed very little behind Ocracoke Inlet and Hatteras Inlet. These
suggest that it becomes easier for the M_2 tide to propagate through Beaufort Inlet, Barden Inlet, and
Oregon Inlet relative to about 40 or 60 years ago. It becomes more difficult for the M_2 tide to propagate
through Ocracoke Inlet and Hatteras Inlet relative to about 50 or 80 years ago.

As shown in Figure 15c,d, the K_1 amplitude and phase changes induced by the inlet morphological
changes are similar to the M_2 amplitude and phase changes. However, when we compared the
percentage of the amplitude change relative to the old, we found that the K_1 changes are less dramatic
than the M_2 changes behind Beaufort Inlet and Barden Inlet (Figure 16). The K_1 changes in percentage
have similar magnitudes to the M_2 changes behind Ocracoke Inlet, Hatteras Inlet, and Oregon Inlet.

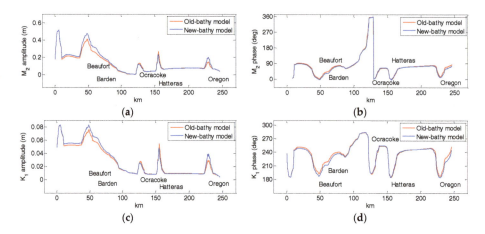

Figure 15. Longitudinal variations of: (**a**) the M_2 amplitude; (**b**) the M_2 phase; (**c**) the K_1 amplitude; (**d**) the K_1 phase along a line (shown in Figure 2b) about 1 km behind the barrier islands. The red lines indicate the results from the old-bathy model. The blues lines indicate the results from the new-bathy model.

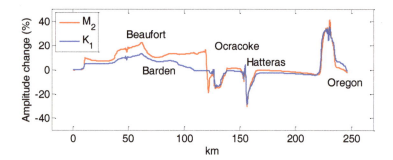

Figure 16. Comparison between the M_2 (red line) and K_1 (blue line) in amplitude change between the new-bathy model and the old-bathy model relative to the old-bathy model along a line (shown in Figure 2b) about 1 km behind the barrier islands.

4. Discussion and Conclusions

The model results validated with the observations show that tidal datums (represented by MHW) and harmonic amplitudes have increased by 10%–35% from the old-bathy model to the new-bathy model behind Beaufort Inlet, Barden Inlet, and Oregon Inlet. Tidal datums and harmonic amplitudes have decreased by 15%–30% from the old-bathy model to the new-bathy model behind Ocracoke Inlet and Hatteras Inlet. Compared with the other four inlets, tidal datums around Oregon Inlet experienced the most dramatic changes (35%) within a shorter time period (1975–2014). The reason needs to be further investigated. In addition, Beaufort Inlet has the largest range of influence probably due to the deeper waters behind it.

It should be noted that all four tidal datums (MHHW, MHW, MLW, and MLLW) are referenced to MSL. The MHHW, MLW, and MLLW changes induced by the inlet morphological changes are very similar to the MHW changes. Tidal range is an indicator of tidal energy. The morphological changes of the inlets affect the energy of the tides propagating through the inlets and thus tidal range behind the inlets. MHW and MLW are almost equal to half of the mean tidal range. MHHW and MLLW are almost equal to half of the diurnal tidal range. Therefore, all four tidal datums have similar changes in response to the morphological changes.

To evaluate these tidal changes induced by morphological changes of the inlets, we calculated the flood and ebb volumes and durations across the inlets based on the velocity and elevation outputs from the old-bathy model and the new-bathy model. The results have been summarized in Table 3. For Beaufort Inlet, the flood volume has increased by 18×10^6 m^3 (16%) while the ebb volume has increased by 8×10^6 m^3 (7%) from the old-bathy model to the new-bathy model, suggesting that more tidal energy and more water go into the sounds. Similarly, flood volumes have increased by 8×10^6 m^3 (38%) and 11×10^6 m^3 (15%) for Barden Inlet and Oregon Inlet, respectively. On the other hand, flood volumes have decreased by 5×10^6 m^3 (4%) and 7×10^6 m^3 (6%) for Ocracoke Inlet and Hatteras Inlet, respectively. These suggest that the cross-inlet tidal volume changes are closely related to tidal datum changes behind the inlets. The magnitude of the volume change is also positively correlated with the influence range.

Table 3. Flood and ebb volumes and durations across five North Carolina inlets from the old-bathy model and the new-bathy model.

Inlet	Flood Volume (10^6 m^3)	Ebb Volume (10^6 m^3)	Tidal-Cycle Residual (10^6 m^3)	Flood Duration (h)	Ebb Duration (h)
Beaufort (old)	111.31	−113.60	−2.29	5.95	6.53
Beaufort (new)	129.37	−121.43	7.95	5.99	6.48
Barden (old)	21.72	−18.76	2.96	5.92	6.56
Barden (new)	30.02	−27.67	2.36	5.96	6.51
Ocracoke (old)	132.47	−141.34	−8.87	5.79	6.71
Ocracoke (new)	127.09	−132.91	−5.81	5.77	6.73
Hatteras (old)	122.12	−122.90	−0.78	5.80	6.70
Hatteras (new)	114.87	−113.74	1.13	5.80	6.70
Oregon (old)	73.07	−73.63	−0.56	5.82	6.67
Oregon (new)	84.52	−84.30	0.22	5.84	6.66

As mentioned in Section 2.2, for the common regions other than the inlet regions, the old-bathy grid and the new-bathy grid used the same bathymetry sounding datasets [27]. For the shallow areas within the sounds, most sounding data were collected before the 1980s and very limited sounding data were collected after the 2010s. Tidal changes induced by morphological changes within the sounds will be evaluated in future work upon the availability of new sounding data in these regions.

Based on the numerical experiments in this paper, both the magnitude and geographical extension of the tidal datum changes behind the barrier islands can be easily evaluated by monitoring the inlet morphological changes induced by erosion or accumulation, dredging, or dumping. This can be used as a guidance for NOAA to make decisions on when to update VDatum tidal datums in this region and where to install new tide gauges. Furthermore, as the sea level may rise in the future, some new inlets may appear and the existing inlets may become wider and deeper. Under this circumstance, the spatial pattern of the tides behind the barrier islands may be dramatically changed, which will be evaluated in future work.

Acknowledgments: This study was supported by NOAA's VDatum program coordinated by three NOAA offices: the Office of Coast Survey, the Center for Operational Oceanographic Products and Services, and the National Geodetic Survey. We sincerely thank the anonymous reviewers for providing insightful comments and suggestions to help substantial improvements of this manuscript.

Author Contributions: J.W. and E.M. conceived and designed the experiments; J.W. performed the experiments and analyzed the data; J.W. and E.M. wrote the paper.

Conflicts of Interest: The authors declare no conflict of interest.

References

1. Parker, B.B.; Hess, K.W.; Milbert, D.G.; Gill, S. A national vertical datum transformation tool. *Sea Technol.* **2003**, *44*, 10–15.
2. Eakins, B.W.; Taylor, L.A. Seamlessly integrating bathymetric and topographic data to support tsunami modeling and forecasting efforts. In *Ocean Globe*; Bremen, J., Ed.; ESRI Press Academic: Redlands, CA, USA, 2010; pp. 33–86.
3. National Ocean Service. *Tidal Datums and Their Applications*; NOAA Technical Report NOS COOPS 1; Center for Operational Oceanographic Products and Services: Silver Spring, MD, USA, 2000; p. 112.
4. National Ocean Service. VDatum Manual for Development and Support of NOAA's Vertical Datum Transformation Tool, VDatum. 2012; p. 119. Available online: http://vdatum.noaa.gov/docs/publication. html (accessed on 20 September 2016).
5. Luettich, R.A., Jr.; Westerink, J.J.; Scheffner, N.W. *ADCIRC: An Advanced Three-Dimensional Circulation Model for Shelves Coasts and Estuaries, Report 1: Theory and Methodology of ADCIRC-2DDI and ADCIRC-3DL*; Dredging Research Program Technical Report DRP-92-6; U.S. Army Engineers Waterways Experiment Station: Vicksburg, MS, USA, 1992; p. 137.
6. Westerink, J.J.; Luettich, R.A.; Muccino, J.C. Modeling tides in the Western North Atlantic using unstructured graded grids. *Tellus A* **1994**, *46*, 178–199. [CrossRef]
7. Mukai, A.Y.; Westerink, J.J.; Luettich, R.A.; Mark, D. *Eastcoast 2001: A Tidal Constituent Database for the Western North Atlantic, Gulf of Mexico and Caribbean Sea*; Technical Report, ERDC/CHL TR-02-24; US Army Engineer Research and Development Center, Coastal and Hydraulics Laboratory: Vicksburg, MS, USA, 2002; p. 201.
8. Hench, J.L.; Luettich, R.A.; Westerink, J.J.; Scheffner, N.W. *ADCIRC: An Advanced Three-Dimensional Circulation Model for Shelves, Coasts, and Estuaries, Report 6: Development of a Tidal Constituent Database for the Eastern North Pacific*; Dredging Research Program Technical Report DRP-92-6; U.S. Army Engineer Waterways Experiment Station: Vicksburg, MS, USA, 1994; p. 21. Available online: http://acwc.sdp.sirsi.net/client/search/asset/ 1004166 (accessed on 20 September 2016).
9. Blain, C.A.; Rogers, E. *Coastal Tidal Prediction Using the ADCIRC-2DDI Hydrodynamic Finite Element Model*; Formal Report NRL/FR/7322-98-9682; Naval Research Laboratory, Stennis Space Center: Hancock County, MS, USA, 1998; p. 92. Available online: http://www.dtic.mil/dtic/tr/fulltext/u2/a358752.pdf (accessed on 20 June 2016).
10. Luettich, R.A., Jr.; Carr, S.D.; Reynolds-Fleming, J.V.; Fulcher, C.W.; McNinch, J.E. Semi-diurnal seiching in a shallow, micro-tidal lagoonal estuary. *Cont. Shelf Res.* **2001**, *22*, 1669–1681. [CrossRef]
11. Burrows, R.; Walkington, I.A.; Yates, N.C.; Hedges, T.S.; Wolf, J.; Holt, J. The tidal range energy potential of the west coast of the United Kingdom. *Appl. Ocean Res.* **2009**, *31*, 229–238. [CrossRef]
12. Hess, K.; Spargo, E.; Wong, A.; White, S.; Gill, S. *VDatum for Central Coastal North Carolina: Tidal Datums, Marine Grids, and Sea Surface Topography*; NOAA Technical Report NOS CS 21; the National Oceanic and Atmospheric Administration: Silver Spring, MD, USA, 2005; p. 46.
13. Hayes, M.O. General morphology and sediment patterns in tidal inlets. *Sediment. Geol.* **1980**, *26*, 139–156. [CrossRef]
14. Hubbard, D.K.; Oertel, G.; Nummedal, D. The role of waves and tidal currents in the development of tidal-inlet sedimentary structures and sand body geometry: Examples from North Carolina, South Carolina, and Georgia. *J. Sediment. Petrol.* **1979**, *49*, 1073–1092.
15. Komar, P.D. Tidal-inlet processes and morphology related to the transport of sediments. *J. Coast. Res.* **1996**, 23–45.
16. Cayocca, F. Long-term morphological modeling of a tidal inlet: The Arcachon Basin, France. *Coast. Eng.* **2001**, *42*, 115–142. [CrossRef]
17. Militello, A.; Zarillo, G.A. Tidal motion in a complex inlet and bay system, Ponce de Leon Inlet, Florida. *J. Coast. Res.* **2000**, *16*, 840–852.
18. Boon, J.D.; Byrne, R.J. On basin hyposmetry and the morphodynamic response of coastal inlet systems. *Mar. Geol.* **1981**, *40*, 27–48. [CrossRef]
19. Fitzgerald, D.M. Geomorphic variability and morphologic and sedimentologic controls of tidal inlets. *J. Coast. Res.* **1996**, 47–71.

20. Luettich, R.A., Jr.; Hench, J.L.; Fulcher, C.W.; Werner, F.E.; Blanton, B.O.; Churchill, J.H. Barotropic tidal and wind driven larvae transport in the vicinity of a barrier island inlet. *Fish. Oceanogr.* **1999**, *8*, 190–209. [CrossRef]

21. Churchill, J.H.; Blanton, J.O.; Hench, J.L.; Luettich, R.A., Jr.; Werner, F.E. Flood tide circulation near Beaufort Inlet, North Carolina: Implications for larval recruitment. *Estuaries* **1999**, *22*, 1057–1070. [CrossRef]

22. Inman, D.L.; Dolan, R. The Outer Banks of North Carolina: Budget of sediment and inlet dynamics along a migrating barrier system. *J. Coast. Res.* **1989**, *5*, 193–237.

23. NOAA Tides and Currents Website: Water Levels. Available online: http://tidesandcurrents.noaa.gov/stations.html?type=Water+Levels (accessed on 20 September 2016).

24. NOAA Tides and Currents Website: Datums. Available online: http://tidesandcurrents.noaa.gov/stations.html?type=Datums (accessed on 20 September 2016).

25. NOAA Tides and Currents Website: Harmonic Constituents. Available online: https://tidesandcurrents.noaa.gov/stations.html?type=Harmonic+Constituents (accessed on 20 September 2016).

26. NOAA Shoreline Website. Available online: https://shoreline.noaa.gov (accessed on 20 September 2016).

27. National Centers for Environmental Information (NCEI) Bathymetry and Global Relief. Available online: https://www.ngdc.noaa.gov/mgg/bathymetry/relief.html (accessed on 20 September 2016).

28. Becker, J.J.; Sandwell, D.T.; Smith, W.H.F.; Braud, J.; Binder, B.; Depner, J.; Fabre, D.; Factor, J.; Ingalls, S.; Kim, S.-H.; et al. Global bathymetry and elevation data at 30 arc seconds resolution: SRTM30_PLUS. *Mar. Geod.* **2009**, *32*, 355–371. [CrossRef]

29. US Army Corps of Engineering Wilmington District Website: Hydrographic Surveys. Available online: http://www.saw.usace.army.mil/Missions/Navigation/Hydrographic-Surveys/ (accessed on 20 September 2016).

30. Olsen Associates, Inc. Inlet Dredging and Disposal. In *Regional Sand Transport Study: Morehead City Harbor Federal Navigation Project Summary Report*; Olsen Associates, Inc.: Jacksonville, FL, USA, 2006. Available online: http://www.carteretcountync.gov/DocumentCenter/View/268 (accessed on 20 June 2016).

31. NOAA VDatum Website: Estimation of Uncertainties. Available online: http://vdatum.noaa.gov/docs/est_uncertainties.html (accessed on 20 September 2016).

Journal of
Marine Science and Engineering

Article

Modeling Water Clarity and Light Quality in Oceans

Mohamed A. Abdelrhman

Atlantic Ecology Division, National Health and Environmental Effects Research Laboratory, Office of Research and Development, United States Environmental Protection Agency, 27 Tarzwell Drive, Narragansett, RI 02882, USA; Abdelrhman.mohamed@epa.gov; Tel.: +1-401-782-3182

Academic Editor: Richard P. Signell
Received: 20 July 2016; Accepted: 18 November 2016; Published: 24 November 2016

Abstract: Phytoplankton is a primary producer of organic compounds, and it forms the base of the food chain in ocean waters. The concentration of phytoplankton in the water column controls water clarity and the amount and quality of light that penetrates through it. The availability of adequate light intensity is a major factor in the health of algae and phytoplankton. There is a strong negative coupling between light intensity and phytoplankton concentration (e.g., through self-shading by the cells), which reduces available light and in return affects the growth rate of the cells. Proper modeling of this coupling is essential to understand primary productivity in the oceans. This paper provides the methodology to model light intensity in the water column, which can be included in relevant water quality models. The methodology implements relationships from bio-optical models, which use phytoplankton chlorophyll *a* (chl-*a*) concentration as a surrogate for light attenuation, including absorption and scattering by other attenuators. The presented mathematical methodology estimates the reduction in light intensity due to absorption by pure seawater, chl-*a* pigment, non-algae particles (NAPs) and colored dissolved organic matter (CDOM), as well as backscattering by pure seawater, phytoplankton particles and NAPs. The methods presented facilitate the prediction of the effects of various environmental and management scenarios (e.g., global warming, altered precipitation patterns, greenhouse gases) on the wellbeing of phytoplankton communities in the oceans as temperature-driven chl-*a* changes take place.

Keywords: modeling; irradiance; oceans; phytoplankton

1. Introduction

The major factors affecting phytoplankton metabolism are nutrient availability, light and water temperature [1]. The maximum depth at which light intensity is adequate to maintain the plant is referred to as the depth of the photic (or euphotic) zone, which is referred to here as the "photic depth" [2]. Light intensity at this depth reaches 1% of its surface daylight value, which is enough for photosynthesis to sustain phytoplankton growth and reproduction. This depth can change as the incident solar irradiance changes with time during the day and throughout the year. The photic depth can also change in space as the concentrations of the various attenuators above it change.

The importance of light to phytoplankton has driven many researchers to develop quantitative methods to calculate light intensity in the water column. The complexity of this task arises from the variability not only in the spectral light intensity, but also in the water column due to turbidity. Bio-optical models are used to develop mathematical methods to calculate irradiance through the water column [3]. Optical models have to be calibrated based on field measurements of both water turbidity from phytoplankton, colored dissolved organic matter (CDOM) (also called yellow substances or Gelbstoff) and non-algae (non-pigmented) particles (NAPs), as well as associated spectral irradiance [4–9]. Abdelrhman [10] applied these methods to estuarine systems where both phytoplankton and total suspended solids (TSS) contribute to turbidity. In oceans, the major contributor to turbidity is phytoplankton [11,12]. The theoretical basis presented in [12] was further simplified here to accommodate numerical modelers' needs. Prieur and Sathyndranath [13] presented the optical classification of coastal and oceanic waters based on the specific spectral absorption curves of phytoplankton pigments, organic matter and other attenuators of light in the water column. A wide range of absorption and backscattering spectra for oceans was presented by the International Ocean Color Coordination Group (IOCCG) [3]. The IOCCG generated a wide range of synthetic data for use in testing remote sensing algorithms. This range was based on mathematical relationships that used measured phytoplankton concentration in ocean waters (Case 1 waters [14]) as a reference for absorption and backscattering by all other attenuators in the water column including NAPs and CDOM. These relationships are used here to calculate irradiance throughout the water column in the oceans.

The focus of this work is determining the available irradiance profile in the water column through the photic depth. The concentration of suspended solids and phytoplankton in the water column controls the amount of light that travels through it. The main objective of this work is to present a mathematical model, which can be included in numerical models, to resolve the coupling between irradiance and phytoplankton in the oceans. This objective is met by focusing on using available information from bio-optical methods, rather than developing them. Inherent optical properties of water (i.e., chl-*a* concentrations) [3] are used to meet the modeling objective.

2. Methods

The total concentration of chl-*a* is obtained from available field measurements and used to develop the mathematical methodology to estimate the irradiance throughout the water column at any location throughout the whole year. Figure 1 presents a definition sketch of the vertical structure for the mathematical model for irradiance, and Table 1 presents the definitions of all abbreviations and symbols. Attenuation of the incident irradiance through the water column is a function of absorption and scattering by the pure seawater and the dissolved and particulate materials therein.

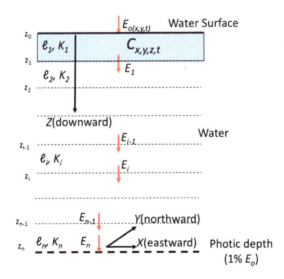

Figure 1. Definition sketch of the relation between the numerical model vertical structure and its utilization to study light intensity throughout the water column. Concentration of chl-*a* ($C_{x,y,z,t}$) should be provided by the numerical model at location (x,y) at every layer depth (z) and at every time step (t) during the year. E_{i-1} and E_i are the incident and departing downwelling irradiances through layer i (with thickness ℓ_i and extinction coefficient K_i) (Table 1).

Table 1. Definitions of all abbreviations and symbols.

Symbol	Definition	Dimension
Abbreviations		
CDOM	Colored dissolved organic material	
chl-a	Chlorophyll a	
IOCCG	International Ocean Color Coordination Group	
NAPs	Non-algal particles	
PAR	Photosynthetically-available radiation	
TSS	Total suspended solids	
Parameters		
a_w	Absorption coefficient of seawater	m^{-1}
a_c	Absorption coefficient of chl-a	m^{-1}
a_s	Absorption coefficient of NAPs	m^{-1}
a_g	Absorption coefficient of CDOM	m^{-1}
b_w	Backscattering [a] coefficient of seawater	m^{-1}
b_p	Backscattering [a] coefficient of phytoplankton particles	m^{-1}
b_s	Backscattering [a] coefficient of NAPs	m^{-1}
C	chl-a concentration	$\mu g \cdot L^{-1}$
E_0	Irradiance at the water surface	$W \cdot m^{-2}$
E_i, E_ℓ	Irradiance at the bottom of the i-th layer, ℓ_i	$W \cdot m^{-2}$
e	Exponentiation base ($e = 2.718281828459$)	dimensionless
f	Spectrum distribution function	dimensionless
g	CDOM concentration (not implemented)	$\mu g \cdot L^{-1}$
K	Downwelling [a] extinction coefficient	m^{-1}
ℓ_i	Layer thickness ($z_i - z_{i-1}$)	m
$P_{3,4}$	Calibration coefficients	dimensionless
$R_{1,2,3,4}$	Calibration coefficients	dimensionless
$RR_i(\lambda_j)$	Reduction ratio of wavelength λ_j at the i-th layer	dimensionless
S	NAPs concentration	$mg \cdot L^{-1}$
SS	Spectral slope	nm^{-1}
λ	Wavelength	nm
Subscripts		
i	Counter for the water layer,	
j	Counter for the wavelength λ	
t	Time	
x	Eastward spatial location (see Figure 1)	
y	Northward spatial location (see Figure 1)	
z	Vertical spatial location below the water surface (see Figure 1)	
Superscripts		
$+$	Normalized value (see Table 2 and Figure 2)	

[a] To avoid confusion in the subscripts presented in various equations, b is used for backscattering instead of the commonly used b_b, and K is used instead of K_d for the downwelling extinction coefficient.

There are seven major contributors to the loss of light intensity through the water column: (1) absorption by pure seawater; (2) absorption by phytoplankton (algae) pigment; (3) absorption by NAPs; (4) absorption by CDOM; (5) backscattering by phytoplankton particles; (6) backscattering by NAPs; and (7) backscattering by pure seawater [3,8,13,15]. While volume scattering exists in all directions, only backscattering is usually considered as a loss in the downwelling irradiance [2]. Although some methods combine some of these basic contributors, the following methodology provides calculations of these seven types of losses within the range of the photosynthetically-available radiation (PAR) (400 nm–700 nm).

The following equations define the mathematical values for the absorption and backscattering coefficients according to the basic relationships presented in [3] for Case 1 waters. These relationships use phytoplankton chl-*a* concentration ($\mu g \cdot L^{-1} = mg \cdot m^{-3}$) as a reference for the absorption relationships of phytoplankton pigment, NAPs and CDOM, as well as backscattering from phytoplankton particles and NAPs. Light absorption by phytoplankton, NAPs and CDOM uses reference absorption values of phytoplankton pigment at the wavelength $\lambda = 440$ nm, while light backscattering uses reference phytoplankton backscattering values at $\lambda = 550$ nm. Absorption coefficients for the whole visible range of the spectrum are calculated using the normalized spectral absorption values provided in the literature. Figure 2 and Table 2 present spectral distributions related to absorption by pure seawater, phytoplankton pigment, NAPs and CDOM; in addition to spectral distributions related to backscattering from phytoplankton, NAPs and seawater, as well as the derived spectral distribution function for the incident light [10].

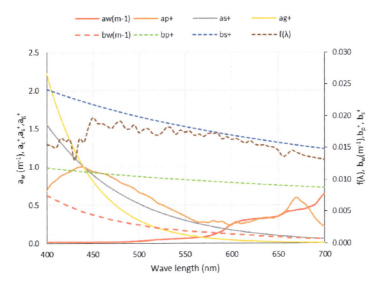

Figure 2. Spectral distributions of absorption by pure water and the normalized absorption coefficients for phytoplankton pigment, NAPs and CDOM (full lines read on left axis); in addition to backscattering from phytoplankton, NAPs and water, as well as the derived spectral distribution function for the incident light (broken lines read on right axis). Refer to Table 2 for the definitions of normalized absorption and backscattering coefficients.

Table 2. Spectral distributions of absorption, *a*, backscattering, *b*, and the shape function, *f*, for the PAR (see the footnotes for details).

1	2	3	4	5	6	7	8	9	10
i	λ_i	a_w (m^{-1})	a_c^+	a_s^+	a_g^+	b_w (m^{-1})	b_p^+	b_s^+	$f(\lambda)$
1	400	0.0180	0.6870	1.5530	2.2260	0.0076	1.1890	1.3250	0.0155
2	405	0.0180	0.7810	1.4700	2.0140	0.0072	1.1810	1.3100	0.0153
3	410	0.0170	0.8280	1.3910	1.8220	0.0068	1.1730	1.2960	0.0150
4	415	0.0170	0.8830	1.3170	1.6490	0.0065	1.1650	1.2820	0.0165
5	420	0.0160	0.9130	1.2460	1.4920	0.0061	1.1580	1.2690	0.0160
6	425	0.0160	0.9390	1.1790	1.3500	0.0058	1.1500	1.2560	0.0162
7	430	0.0150	0.9730	1.1160	1.2210	0.0055	1.1430	1.2430	0.0131
8	435	0.0150	1.0010	1.0570	1.1050	0.0052	1.1360	1.2300	0.0164
9	440	0.0150	1.0000	1.0000	1.0000	0.0049	1.1290	1.2180	0.0159
10	445	0.0150	0.9710	0.9460	0.9050	0.0047	1.1220	1.2060	0.0182
11	450	0.0150	0.9440	0.8960	0.8190	0.0045	1.1150	1.1940	0.0198

Table 2. *Cont.*

1	2	3	4	5	6	7	8	9	10
12	455	0.0160	0.9280	0.8480	0.7410	0.0043	1.1080	1.1820	0.0188
13	460	0.0160	0.9170	0.8030	0.6700	0.0041	1.1020	1.1710	0.0188
14	465	0.0160	0.9020	0.7600	0.6070	0.0039	1.0950	1.1600	0.0184
15	470	0.0160	0.8700	0.7190	0.5490	0.0037	1.0890	1.1490	0.0181
16	475	0.0170	0.8390	0.6800	0.4970	0.0036	1.0830	1.1380	0.0188
17	480	0.0180	0.7980	0.6440	0.4490	0.0034	1.0770	1.1280	0.0192
18	485	0.0190	0.7730	0.6100	0.4070	0.0033	1.0710	1.1170	0.0181
19	490	0.0200	0.7500	0.5770	0.3680	0.0031	1.0650	1.1070	0.0180
20	495	0.0230	0.7170	0.5460	0.3330	0.0030	1.0590	1.0970	0.0186
21	500	0.0260	0.6680	0.5170	0.3010	0.0029	1.0530	1.0880	0.0174
22	505	0.0310	0.6450	0.4890	0.2730	0.0028	1.0470	1.0780	0.0179
23	510	0.0360	0.6180	0.4630	0.2470	0.0026	1.0420	1.0690	0.0180
24	515	0.0420	0.5820	0.4380	0.2230	0.0025	1.0360	1.0600	0.0172
25	520	0.0480	0.5280	0.4150	0.2020	0.0024	1.0310	1.0510	0.0170
26	525	0.0500	0.5040	0.3930	0.1830	0.0023	1.0260	1.0420	0.0174
27	530	0.0510	0.4740	0.3720	0.1650	0.0022	1.0200	1.0330	0.0182
28	535	0.0540	0.4440	0.3520	0.1500	0.0022	1.0150	1.0250	0.0181
29	540	0.0560	0.4160	0.3330	0.1350	0.0021	1.0100	1.0160	0.0171
30	545	0.0600	0.3840	0.3150	0.1220	0.0020	1.0050	1.0080	0.0177
31	550	0.0640	0.3570	0.2980	0.1110	0.0019	1.0000	1.0000	0.0174
32	555	0.0680	0.3210	0.2820	0.1000	0.0019	0.9950	0.9920	0.0176
33	560	0.0710	0.2940	0.2670	0.0910	0.0018	0.9900	0.9840	0.0169
34	565	0.0760	0.2730	0.2530	0.0820	0.0018	0.9860	0.9770	0.0171
35	570	0.0800	0.2760	0.2390	0.0740	0.0017	0.9810	0.9690	0.0168
36	575	0.0940	0.2680	0.2270	0.0670	0.0017	0.9760	0.9620	0.0172
37	580	0.1080	0.2910	0.2140	0.0610	0.0016	0.9720	0.9540	0.0172
38	585	0.1330	0.2740	0.2030	0.0550	0.0016	0.9670	0.9470	0.0173
39	590	0.1570	0.2820	0.1920	0.0500	0.0015	0.9630	0.9400	0.0163
40	595	0.2010	0.2490	0.1820	0.0450	0.0015	0.9580	0.9330	0.0167
41	600	0.2450	0.2360	0.1720	0.0410	0.0014	0.9540	0.9260	0.0163
42	605	0.2680	0.2790	0.1630	0.0370	0.0014	0.9500	0.9190	0.0164
43	610	0.2900	0.2520	0.1540	0.0330	0.0013	0.9450	0.9130	0.0160
44	615	0.3000	0.2680	0.1460	0.0300	0.0013	0.9410	0.9060	0.0157
45	620	0.3100	0.2760	0.1380	0.0270	0.0012	0.9370	0.9000	0.0161
46	625	0.3150	0.2990	0.1310	0.0250	0.0012	0.9330	0.8930	0.0155
47	630	0.3200	0.3170	0.1240	0.0220	0.0011	0.9290	0.8870	0.0154
48	635	0.3250	0.3330	0.1170	0.0200	0.0011	0.9250	0.8810	0.0154
49	640	0.3300	0.3340	0.1110	0.0180	0.0010	0.9210	0.8750	0.0151
50	645	0.3400	0.3260	0.1050	0.0170	0.0010	0.9170	0.8690	0.0150
51	650	0.3500	0.3560	0.0990	0.0150	0.0010	0.9130	0.8630	0.0145
52	655	0.3800	0.3890	0.0940	0.0140	0.0009	0.9100	0.8570	0.0136
53	660	0.4100	0.4410	0.0890	0.0120	0.0008	0.9060	0.8510	0.0140
54	665	0.4200	0.5340	0.0840	0.0110	0.0008	0.9020	0.8460	0.0145
55	670	0.4300	0.5950	0.0800	0.0100	0.0008	0.8980	0.8400	0.0142
56	675	0.4400	0.5440	0.0750	0.0090	0.0008	0.8950	0.8350	0.0139
57	680	0.4500	0.5020	0.0710	0.0080	0.0007	0.8910	0.8290	0.0137
58	685	0.4750	0.4200	0.0680	0.0070	0.0007	0.8880	0.8240	0.0135
59	690	0.5000	0.3290	0.0640	0.0070	0.0007	0.8840	0.8190	0.0134
60	695	0.5750	0.2620	0.0610	0.0060	0.0007	0.8810	0.8130	0.0132
61	700	0.6500	0.2150	0.0570	0.0060	0.0007	0.8770	0.8080	0.0131

Column 1: wavelength counter, i; Column 2: wavelength (nm); Column 3: water absorption coefficient (m^{-1}) [13]; Column 4: $a_c^+(\lambda)$ is the normalized spectral absorption value at wavelength λ with respect to absorption at $\lambda = 440$ nm [13]; Column 5: NAPs relationship for absorption: $a_s^+(\lambda) = \exp(-SS_s(\lambda - 440))$ from [3]; Column 6: CDOM relationship for absorption: $a_g^+(\lambda) = \exp(-SS_g(\lambda - 440))$ from [3]; Column 7: water backscattering coefficient (m^{-1}) (modified from [15]); Column 8: example of phytoplankton backscattering relationship: $b_p^+(\lambda) = \tilde{b}_p \left(\frac{550}{\lambda}\right)^{n_1}$ from [3], with C = 0.4849 µg·L^{-1}; Column 9: example of NAPs backscattering relationship: $b_s^+(\lambda) = \tilde{b}_s \left(\frac{550}{\lambda}\right)^{n_1}$ from [3], with C = 0.4849 µg·L^{-1}; Column 10: spectral distribution shape function [10].

2.1. Overall Light Attenuation

The mathematical structure of the model to calculate irradiance in oceans is similar to that presented by [10] for estuaries. The only difference is the photic depth, which defines the lower bound for irradiance in the oceans rather than the bed in shallower systems. The intensity of light at any depth can be represented by the Beer–Lambert law. The following equations summarize this model.

Beer-Lambert law:

$$E_\ell = E_0 e^{-(a+b)\ell} \tag{1}$$

Spectral irradiance at the bottom of the first (surface) layer:

$$E_1(\lambda) = E_0(\lambda) e^{[-K_1(\lambda)\ell_1]} \tag{2}$$

with the incident irradiance:

$$E_0(\lambda) = E_0 f(\lambda) \tag{3}$$

and the spectral extinction coefficient:

$$K_1(\lambda) = a_w(\lambda) + a_c^1(\lambda) + a_s^1(\lambda) + a_g^1(\lambda) + b_p^1(\lambda) + b_s^1(\lambda) + b_w(\lambda) \tag{4}$$

Irradiance at the bottom of a general layer, i:

$$E_i(\lambda_j) = E_{i-1}(\lambda_j) \left[e^{-a_w(\lambda_j)\ell_i} \times e^{-a_c^i(\lambda_j)\ell_i} \times e^{-a_s^i(\lambda_j)\ell_i} \times e^{-a_g^i(\lambda_j)\ell_i} \times e^{-b_p^i(\lambda_j)\ell_i} \times e^{-b_s^i(\lambda_j)\ell_i} \times e^{-b_w(\lambda_j)\ell_i} \right] \tag{5}$$

Overall irradiance for numerical integration:

$$E_i = 5 \sum_{j=1}^{61} E_i(\lambda_j) = 5 \sum_{j=1}^{61} E_{i-1}(\lambda_j) \times RR_i(\lambda_j) \tag{6}$$

where:

$$RR_i(\lambda_j) = e^{-a_w(\lambda_j)\ell_i} \times e^{-a_c^i(\lambda_j)\ell_i} \times e^{-a_s^i(\lambda_j)\ell_i} \times e^{-a_g^i(\lambda_j)\ell_i} \times e^{-b_p^i(\lambda_j)\ell_i} \times e^{-b_s^i(\lambda_j)\ell_i} \times e^{-b_w(\lambda_j)\ell_i} \tag{7}$$

where E_0 is the incident irradiance just beneath the water surface $(W \cdot m^{-2})$, E_ℓ $(W \cdot m^{-2})$ is the irradiance at distance ℓ (m) from the incidence surface, a is the absorption coefficient (m^{-1}), b is the scattering coefficient (m^{-1}), $E_0(\lambda)$ is the spectral irradiance of the incident wavelength λ $(W \cdot m^{-2} \ nm^{-1})$ at the water surface, $E_1(\lambda)$ is the irradiance of wavelength λ $(W \cdot m^{-2} \cdot nm^{-1})$ at a downward distance $\ell_1 = z_1 - z_0$ (meters, m), $K_1(\lambda)$ is the extinction coefficient of the downwelling spectral irradiance (m^{-1}) and $f(\lambda)$ is the distribution function of the incident light between the various wavelengths within the PAR [10]. The subscripts w, c, s, g and p refer to water, chl-*a*, NAPs, CDOM (Gelbstoff) and phytoplankton, respectively; and the superscript i indicates the layer number. $RR_i(\lambda_j)$ is the reduction ratio (dimensionless) of the incident light within λ_j through layer ℓ_i. The subscript j refers to the discrete values of the normalized absorption coefficients at λ_j values representing PAR in 5-nm increments ($j = 1$–61; Table 2). According to Simpson's rule, only half of the first and last values can be used in each summation (i.e., at $j = 1$ and $j = 61$). Introducing the 5-nm increment in Equation (6) preserves the total irradiance within the PAR. The numerical integration procedure is executed for each layer within the water column. The superscripts and subscripts are sometimes dropped for convenience. The same consistent notation is used in the following descriptions of the various attenuators at the same discrete wavelengths considering λ and λ_j to be synonymous.

2.1.1. Light Absorption by Pure Seawater, a_w

Prieur and Sathyendranath [13] presented the absorption coefficient values, $a_w(\lambda_j)$, for pure seawater at discrete wavelengths, λ_j (Table 2, Figure 2).

2.1.2. Light Absorption by Algal Pigment, a_c

Light absorption by phytoplankton pigment is given by the following equations [16,17]:

$$a_c(\lambda) = a_c(440) \times a_c^+(\lambda) \tag{8}$$

$$a_c(440) = 0.05\,[C_{x,y,z,t}]^{0.626} \tag{9}$$

where $a_c(\lambda)$ is the absorption coefficient by phytoplankton pigment (m^{-1}) at any wavelength λ, $a_c(440)$ is the absorption coefficient by phytoplankton pigment (m^{-1}) at wavelength 440 nm, $a_c^+(\lambda)$ is the normalized spectral absorption value at wavelength λ with respect to absorption at $\lambda = 440$ nm [13] and $C_{x,y,z,t}$ is the concentration of chl-a $(\mu g \cdot L^{-1} = mg \cdot m^{-3})$ at the station location, (x-eastward, y-northward), and at the layer's vertical location z-below the water surface (m) and at the time, t, during the year. The coefficients 0.05 and 0.626 are based on observations from various regions including the North Atlantic, North Pacific, Gulf of Mexico, Mediterranean Sea, Arabian Sea and more. These coefficients can be site specific and can depend on λ [3,9,10,16]. For convenience, the stated values of the two coefficients are used in the methodology presented here. The normalized phytoplankton absorption values, $a_c^+(\lambda)$, from Prieur and Sathyendranath [13] (Table 2) provide a consistent parameterization for the modeling methodology presented here. As expected, at the normalization wavelength, $\lambda = 440$ nm, $a_c^+(440) = 1$ (Table 2). Gallegos [18] indicated that the values of Prieur and Sathyendranath [13] are adequate for use in his bio-optical methods. The calculated value of phytoplankton absorption, $a_c(440)$, is used in the following calculations of the other absorption and backscattering coefficients.

2.1.3. Light Absorption by NAPs, a_s

The following equations are from IOCCG [3]:

$$a_s(\lambda) = a_s(440)\,\exp\left(-SS_s\,(\lambda - 440)\right) \tag{10}$$

$$a_s(440) = P_1 a_c(440) \tag{11}$$

$$P_1 = 0.1 + \frac{0.5 R_1 a_c(440)}{0.05 + a_c(440)} \tag{12}$$

where $a_s(\lambda)$ is the absorption coefficient by NAPs (m^{-1}) at any wavelength λ, $a_s(440)$ is the absorption coefficient by NAPs (m^{-1}) at wavelength 440 nm and R_1 is a random value between 0.0 and 1.0. The randomness in R_1 controls the random values of P_1 makes the relationship between $a_s(440)$ and $a_c(440)$ not fixed and avoids extremely large $a_s(440)$ when $a_c(440)$ is small. The range of the random variable P_1 is 0.1–0.6, and its distribution is presented in [3]. SS_s is the spectral slope for NAPs (randomly valued between 0.007 and 0.015 nm^{-1} [3]). Recent studies indicate that the NAPs vs. the λ absorption curve has an exponential decay shape [19,20] similar to CDOM. However, understanding of the NAPs behavior is still very limited, and more detailed studies are recommended [20]. Until future values become available, this work assumes that the spectral slope for NAPs is in the middle of the above range (i.e., $SS_s = 0.011$ nm^{-1}). To eliminate the randomness, R_1 is calibrated as presented in the Calibration and Validation Section. Values of the spectral distribution $a_s^+(\lambda) = \exp(-SS_s\,(\lambda - 440))$ are presented in Table 2 and Figure 2.

2.1.4. Light Absorption by CDOM, a_g

The following equations are from IOCCG [3]:

$$a_g(\lambda) = a_g(440)\,\exp\left(-SS_g\,(\lambda - 440)\right) \tag{13}$$

$$a_g(440) = P_2 a_c(440) \tag{14}$$

$$P_2 = 0.3 + \frac{5.7 R_2 a_c\,(440)}{0.02 + a_c\,(440)} \tag{15}$$

where $a_g(\lambda)$ is the absorption coefficient by CDOM (m^{-1}) at any wavelength λ, $a_g(440)$ is the absorption coefficient by CDOM (m^{-1}) at a wavelength of 440 nm, SS_g is the spectral slope for CDOM between 0.01 and 0.02 nm^{-1} and R_2 is a random number between 0.0 and 1.0. The randomness in R_2 controls the random values of P_2, makes the relationship between $a_g(440)$ and $a_c(440)$ not fixed and avoids extremely large $a_g(440)$ when $a_c(440)$ is small. The range of the random P_2 values is 0.3–6.0, and its distribution is presented in [3]. To eliminate the randomness, R_2 is calibrated as presented in the Calibration and Validation Section. Values of the spectral distribution $a_g^+\,(\lambda) = \exp(-SS_g\,(\lambda - 440))$ are presented in Table 2 and Figure 2.

2.1.5. Light Backscattering by Phytoplankton, b_p

The calculations of backscattering for phytoplankton particles include the wavelength-dependent parameters for backscattering for the whole 400–700-nm spectrum, which are based on normalized values referenced to the wavelength $\lambda = 550$ nm [3].

$$b_p\,(\lambda) = \tilde{b}_p\, b_p\,(550) \left(\frac{550}{\lambda}\right)^{n_1} \tag{16}$$

$$b_p\,(550) = P_3 \left[C_{x,y,z,t}\right]^{0.57} \tag{17}$$

$$n_1 = -0.4 + \frac{1.6 + 1.2 R_3}{1 + \left[C_{x,y,z,t}\right]^{0.5}} \tag{18}$$

where $b_p\,(\lambda)$ is the backscattering of phytoplankton at wavelength λ, $\tilde{b}_p$ is the backscattering fraction, which depends on the phase function of phytoplankton (assumed 1% based on the Fournier-Forand phase function with respect to scattering angle [21]), P_3 is randomly valued between 0.06 and 0.6 for a given $C_{x,y,z,t}$ and R_3 is a random value between 0.0 and 1.0. The range of the random n_1 values is -0.1–2.0, and its distribution is presented in [3]. The randomness in R_3 controls the random values of n_1, makes the relationship between n_1 and $C_{x,y,z,t}$ not fixed and avoids extremely large n_1 when $C_{x,y,z,t}$ is small. The randomness in P_3 controls the random values of $b_p\,(550)$ and makes the relationship between $b_p\,(550)$ and $C_{x,y,z,t}$ not fixed. The range of the random values and distribution of n_1 are presented in [3]. To eliminate the randomness, R_3 and P_3 are calibrated as presented in the Calibration and Validation Section.

The original formulation in IOCCG [3] included the extra equation $(b_p^*\,(\lambda) = b_p\,(\lambda) - a_p\,(\lambda))$, which introduced superfluous error in b_p when $C_{x,y,z,t}$ was zero. This equation is not included here.

Examples of the values of the spectral distribution $b_p^+\,(\lambda) = \tilde{b}_p\left(\frac{550}{\lambda}\right)^{n_1}$ for an arbitrary chl-a concentration are presented in Table 2 and Figure 2. These values will change with depth according to the chl-a concentration (Equation (18)).

2.1.6. Light Backscattering by NAPs (Detritus, Minerals and Others), b_s

Similarly, the calculations of backscattering for NAP particles include the wavelength-dependent parameters for backscattering for the whole 400–700-nm spectrum, which are based on normalized values referenced to the wavelength $\lambda = 550$ nm. The following equations are from IOCCG [3]:

$$b_s\,(\lambda) = \tilde{b}_s\, b_s\,(550) \left(\frac{550}{\lambda}\right)^{n_2} \tag{19}$$

$$b_s\,(550) = P_4 \left[C_{x,y,z,t}\right]^{0.766} \tag{20}$$

$$n_2 = -0.5 + \frac{2.0 + 1.2R_4}{1 + \left[C_{x,y,z,t}\right]^{0.5}} \tag{21}$$

where $b_s\,(\lambda)$ is the backscattering of NAPs at wavelength λ, $\tilde{b}_s$ is the backscattering fraction, which depends on the average particle phase function of phytoplankton (assumed 0.0183 based on the Petzold phase function with respect to scattering angle [22]), P_4 is randomly valued between 0.06 and 0.6 for a given $C_{x,y,z,t}$ and R_4 is a random value between 0.0 and 1.0. The randomness in R_4 controls the random values of n_2, makes the relationship between n_2 and $C_{x,y,z,t}$ not fixed and avoids extremely large n_2 when $C_{x,y,z,t}$ is small. The randomness in P_4 controls the random values of b_s (550) and makes the relationship between b_s (550) and $C_{x,y,z,t}$ not fixed. The range of the random n_2 values is -0.2–2.2, and its distribution is presented in [3]. To eliminate the randomness, R_4 and P_4 are calibrated as presented in the Calibration and Validation Section. Examples of the values of the spectral distribution $b_s^+\,(\lambda) = \tilde{b}_s\left(\frac{550}{\lambda}\right)^{n_2}$ for an arbitrary chl-*a* concentration are presented in Table 2 and Figure 2. These values will change with depth according to the chl-*a* concentration (Equation (21)).

2.1.7. Light Backscattering by Pure Seawater, b_w

Buiteveld [23] presented the backscattering coefficient values, $b_w(\lambda)$, for pure seawater at 10-nm increments within the visible range. These values were linearly interpolated at 5-nm increments to fit within the same range of the numerical integration for the other coefficients (Table 2, Figure 2).

2.2. Data

Existing irradiance and chl-*a* data from the North Atlantic were used to calibrate and validate the presented methodology. Data were obtained through personal communication [24]. Details of the field methods, protocols and times are published in [25], and they are not repeated here. The data included incident surface irradiance ($W \cdot m^{-2}$) at the water surface for all wavelengths within PAR at 5-nm increments, profiles of the downwelling irradiance ($W \cdot m^{-2}$) at 2 m-depth increments and chl-*a* concentration profiles at various depth locations during various seasons. The data indicated that chl-*a* concentrations were always <3.5 $\mu g \cdot L^{-1}$. Data analysis indicated that the ship-based and the glider-based surface PAR agree [25]. Accordingly, the glider surface records were used here to represent the incident irradiance for the remainder of the corresponding downwelling profile.

Two sets of consistent data of incident irradiance, irradiance profile and chl-*a* profile were used to calibrate and validate the presented methodology. The major criteria to choose these data were: cloud cover does not obstruct incident irradiance during the period 10:00 GMT–14:00 GMT; the chl-*a* profile measurements are collected on the same day of the irradiance data; and the data extend to at least 100 m below the water surface. The collected chl-*a* concentrations were sparse throughout the monitored top part of the water column and had to be interpolated at the same depth increments as the irradiance profile (i.e., 2 m). Only fourteen chl-*a* data profiles reached depths $\geq$100 m. Two of these profiles with contrasting vertical distributions were used here.

2.2.1. The Spectrum Shape Function, f

For modeling purposes, Abdelrhman [10] suggested the use of the spectrum shape function at the top of the atmosphere to redistribute the incident irradiance, E_0, to its spectral values, $E_0(\lambda)$, within the PAR at the water surface (Table 2). The spectrum shape function alleviates the need to identify $E_0(\lambda)$ at each location throughout the simulation time. Instead, the overall incident irradiance, E_0, can be used with $f(\lambda)$ (Equation (3)). This simplification is tested with the incident irradiance of 339 $W \cdot m^{-2}$ on 11 June 2013 at 9:30 GMT. Figure 3a compares the shapes of the actual incident irradiance to that of the shape function, $f(\lambda)$ (Table 2). The difference between the calculated and observed values is $\pm$5% for most of the PAR (λ = 450 nm–650 nm) and <$\pm$15% outside that range. The scatter plot (Figure 3b) indicates that the correlation (slope) between calculated and observed shapes is 0.9981 (R^2 = 0.7068) with zero intercept, which indicates that the use of $f(\lambda)$ is adequate for modeling purposes. The spectrum shape function is used here to define the spectral distribution for the topmost near-surface record of the downwelling irradiance profile.

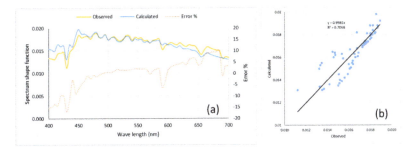

Figure 3. Comparison between observed and reconstructed spectrum shape functions on 11 June 2013 at 9:30 a.m.: (**a**) spectral distributions and the % error (100 (observed-calculated)/observed); (**b**) correlation between observed and calculated spectral values.

2.2.2. The Summer Dataset

The summer data used in this study were collected on 11 June 2013 (Figure 4). The concentration of chl-*a* showed a systematically decreasing trend with depth below the water surface (Figure 4a). This trend was used to calculate chl-*a* concentrations at 2 m-depth increments, which correspond to the measurements of the downwelling irradiance. The average of four irradiance profiles collected during midday (10:00 GMT–14:00 GMT) was used to represent the observed downwelling irradiance, *E*, on that day (Figure 4b). The topmost irradiance value was assumed to represent the incident irradiance, E_0. The distribution of the incident PAR was reconstructed according to Equation (3) (Figure 4c).

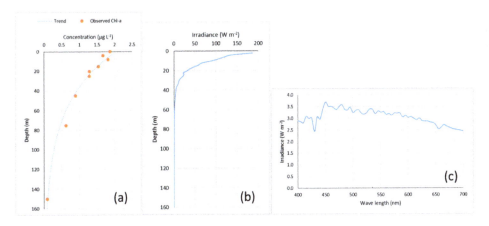

Figure 4. Summer data on 11 June 2013: (**a**) vertical distribution of ship-based measurements of chl-*a* concentrations and their vertical trend; (**b**) vertical distribution of glider-based average irradiance from 10:00 GMT-14:00 GMT; (**c**) spectral distribution of the near-surface average irradiance measurement.

2.2.3. The Fall Data Set

A subsurface maximum of chl-*a* concentration appeared in the fall season of 2013 at ~30–40 m below the water surface [25]. The data on 3 September 2013 consisted of the chl-*a* profile (Figure 5a), which demonstrated the subsurface maximum chl-*a* concentration. Two trends were used to interpolate chl-*a* concentrations at 2-m increments corresponding to the measured downwelling irradiance. The average of four irradiance profiles collected during midday (10:00 GMT–14:00 GMT) was used to represent the observed downwelling irradiance, *E*, on that day (Figure 5b). The topmost irradiance value was assumed to represent the incident irradiance, E_0. The distribution of the incident PAR was reconstructed according to Equation (3) (Figure 5c).

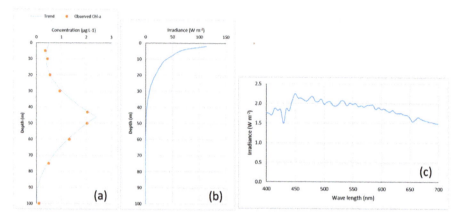

Figure 5. Fall data on 3 September 2013: (**a**) vertical distribution of ship-based measurements of chl-*a* concentrations and their vertical trend; (**b**) vertical distribution of glider-based average irradiance from 10:00 GMT-14:00 GMT; (**c**) spectral distribution of the near-surface average irradiance measurement.

2.3. Calibration and Validation

The following three important rules of thumb were observed in calibration: (1) any attenuation coefficient for any contributor at any wavelength (i.e., the exponentiation terms in Equations (5)–(7)) cannot exceed 1.0 at any depth; (2) any attenuation coefficient for any contributor except water should be correlated with chl-*a* concentration (the surrogate for all attenuations); and (3) observed irradiance should not exceed the irradiance in pure seawater.

2.3.1. Calibration with Fall Data

The main purpose of the calibration is to define non-random (fixed) values for R_1, R_2, R_3, R_4, P_3 and P_4. The measured topmost value of the downwelling irradiance represented E_0 on 3 September 2013; the recorded light intensity at each depth represented E_ℓ; depth increments (2 m) represented the layer thickness, ℓ; and the interpolated chl-*a* concentration within each layer represented $C_{x,y,z,t}$. The calibration started with the mid-range values of the parameter and proceeded to improve the fit with observations of the downwelling irradiance to find the correlation between predicted and observed values. A zero intercept was enforced in all of the correlation plots. For convenience, the *p*-values were assumed to be the same within their range of 0.06–0.6 (range = 0.54), and the *R* values were also assumed to be the same within their specified range of 0.0–1.0 (range = 1.0). Both *p* and *R* ranges were divided into 10 increments. Systematic iterations took place by fixing the *p*-values at each of the incremented values and checking the correlation between predicted and observed irradiances at each of the *R* incremented values. Figure 6a presents the calibrated irradiance profile with all of the *R* parameters calibrated to 0.3 and the *p* parameters calibrated to 0.438. The correlation scatter plot (Figure 6b) indicates that the calculated irradiance agreed with observed values ($R^2 = 0.9925$). The regression line slope was 0.9994, which is very close to unity for a one-to-one correlation.

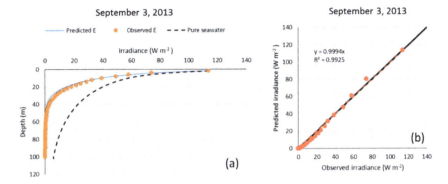

Figure 6. Calibration using fall data: (**a**) comparison between observed and predicted vertical irradiance profiles together with the expected irradiance in pure seawater; (**b**) correlation between observed and predicted irradiances.

2.3.2. Validation with Summer Data

Using the same calibration values for the R and p parameters, the summer irradiance profile on 11 June 2013 was checked against observations (Figure 7a). The scatter plot showed weaker linear agreement with the r^2 value of 0.8497 (Figure 7b). The regression line slope with zero intercept was 0.709, which reflects a one to-one correlation between predicted and observed profiles. The reason for the lower correlation was attributed to other factors (e.g., stratification). In addition, the reported irradiance measurements within the top 12 m coincided with the values of pure seawater (Figure 7a), which un-intuitively does not represent effects from other attenuators. Validation with other data is needed (see the discussion).

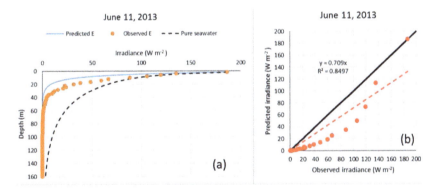

Figure 7. Validation using summer data: (**a**) comparison between observed and predicted vertical irradiance profiles together with the expected irradiance in pure seawater; (**b**) correlation between observed and predicted irradiances.

3. Results

The following results present a sample to illustrate the availability and quality of light in ocean waters. The availability of light is defined by the photic depth at which 1% of the incident irradiance exists. In addition, the presented methodology can identify the various depths where the spectral values reach 1% of their incident values. As some spectral bands will become extinct before others, the quality of light refers to the amount of energy remaining in each spectral band at any depth.

Figure 8 presents the percent change in the total downwelling irradiance with depth, which indicates a photic depth of 50 m on 3 September 2013. Figure 9 presents the penetration profiles of various wavelengths. The high wavelengths are attenuated heavily within the top 10–20 m, while the shorter wavelengths continue to deeper waters. The penetration depths of the whole PAR on the same day are shown in Figure 10. Wavelengths 485–500 nm reached a maximum depth of 46 m, while those close to 700 nm were almost extinct at an 8-m depth. Figure 11 presents the change in the spectral distribution of the PAR throughout the water column, which defines the light quality on that day. It is worth recalling that the shape and penetration depth of the various wavelengths will change throughout space and time as the chl-*a* concentration and incident irradiance change.

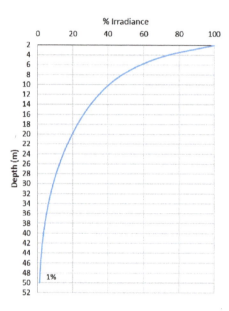

Figure 8. Change of the total downwelling irradiance with depth on 3 September 2013.

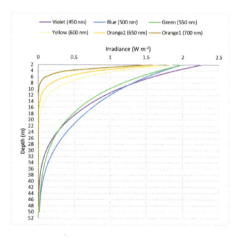

Figure 9. Profiles and penetrations of various wavelengths, which illustrates the change in light quality with depth.

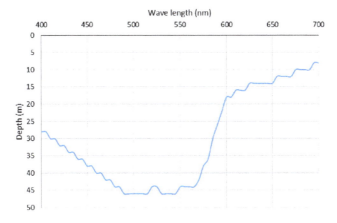

Figure 10. Penetration depth of the PAR on 3 September 2013.

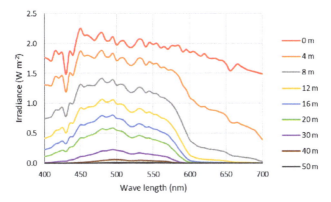

Figure 11. Change of the spectral distribution of the PAR throughout the water column on 3 September 2013.

4. Discussion

A mathematical approach was presented to calculate irradiance in ocean waters (Case 1 waters). The methodology is not site-specific, and it can be applied to any system. Nevertheless, proper calibration of the bio-optical model remains an essential factor for any site-specific application. The methodology presented here utilized relationships from a wide range of absorption and backscattering spectra that were presented by the IOCCG [3]. This range was based on mathematical relationships that used phytoplankton concentration in ocean waters as a reference to estimate all absorption and backscattering components in the water column. Employing numerical modeling with bio-optical modeling validates the use of the presented approach for predictions of future scenarios related to changes in environmental and anthropogenic conditions. For example, environmental impacts due to global warming may cause alterations to seasonal cycles in temperature, precipitation and wind patterns. Such alterations can impact ocean circulation and stratification, which directly impacts the transport, distribution and composition of phytoplankton groups and consequently their optical properties. Similarly, anthropogenic effects due to increased aerosols can alter the incident light, which affects the photic depth and the wellbeing of the phytoplankton communities.

It is argued here that the photic depth (at 1% irradiance) is an aggregate parameter for phytoplankton studies and that a more detailed representation of the "light quality" is more appropriate. As presented above, while the photic depth was 50 m, some wavelengths were extinct in much shallower depths (Figure 10). The resolved PAR distribution with depth (i.e., Figure 11) identifies light quality throughout the water column, which can provide useful information about the wellbeing of the phytoplankton communities at various depths. Such information can help in studies of primary productivity in the oceans. Most current numerical models calculate production (photosynthesis) based on total PAR only. In order for light quality to affect numerical models, they must compute the spectral photosynthesis of the competing dominant phytoplankton species and their adaptation to irradiance throughout the photic depth. An example of the complexity in this area is tackled for two coexisting phytoplankton species in [26]. Partial numerical implementation was presented using λ = 490 nm as a proxy to the PAR [27]. This topic needs more future studies to provide further guidance for implementing light quality and spectral photosynthesis in such models.

As indicated in the presented methodology, calibration is essential to reduce the level of uncertainty in the final irradiance predictions. Calibration of the bio-optical models eliminated the random processes that were incorporated in the original formulation [3]. Constant values for the relevant mathematical parameters and coefficients were calibrated using field observations [24]. The two physical parameters in Equation (9) can be site specific [3] and may have to be included in the calibration. Similarly, the spectral slopes (Equations (10) and (13)) have to be defined properly. Allowing such parameters to vary requires proper coupling between light and phytoplankton to account for the continually-changing parameterization (see the proposed numerical steps below). Validation of the presented methodology requires consistent high quality sets of data from various locations during various seasons. Figure 7 indicates that the observed downwelling irradiance failed to capture the attenuation within the top 12 m, which had the highest observed chl-*a* concentrations in the profile (Figure 4). Such inconsistency infers an unjustified increase in the observed downwelling irradiance. While physical effects (e.g., from density stratification) are beyond the scope of this work, they may have impacted the model and data shown. More data are definitely needed to improve the calibration and validation of the presented approach.

There are two major implications of the presented methodology: modeling implications and ecological implications. The methodology presented validates the coupling of bio-optical models with three-dimensional water quality models. The numerical implications of coupling phytoplankton to light in water quality models can execute the following general steps, which are recommended for relevant future work:

1. At time t
2. At location x,y
3. For layer ℓ_i
4. The numerical model provides $C_{x,y,z,t}$
5. Calculate $a_c(440)$ (Equation (9))
6. For every wavelength, calculate: $a_c(\lambda)$, $a_s(\lambda)$, $a_g(\lambda)$, $b_p(\lambda)$, $b_s(\lambda)$ (Equations (8), (10), (13), (16) and (19), respectively)
7. Calculate the spectral attenuation coefficient, $K_i(\lambda)$, for each λ (Equation (4))
8. Calculate attenuated irradiance for each λ, $E_i(\lambda)$ (Equation (5))
9. Calculate total irradiance, E_i, by numerical integration over all λ (Equation (6))
10. Move to the next layer down ($i + 1$) and repeat Steps 4–9
11. Move to next location and repeat Steps 3–10
12. For each layer, use E_i in the calculation of $C_{x,y,z,t+\Delta t}$, which fully couples light and phytoplankton at the next time level ($t + \Delta t$).

The ecological implications encompass the predictive ability of phytoplankton biomass and its primary productivity in the oceans. Coupling light quality to water quality models facilitates understanding the relationship between light quality and phytoplankton. Light quality impacts the

J. Mar. Sci. Eng. **2016**, *4*, 80

composition and health of phytoplankton communities in the water column, which, consequently, alter water clarity and irradiance levels. Water clarity is a major indicator used for many management decisions related to the health of estuarine, coastal and ocean waters. To the author's knowledge, such coupling is not present in most water quality models. However, recently, it was implemented in studies of primary productivity in the Pacific Ocean [27].

The presented approach is expected to work well in environments where phytoplankton particles are the major contributor to light attenuation through absorption by their chl-*a* pigment, their dead NAPs cells and their exudation of CDOM; as well as backscattering by the particulate phytoplankton cells and their dead NAPs. In other environments (e.g., with density stratification), the approach has to be augmented with additional considerations to account for such effects. Processes related to phytoplankton composition and dynamics (e.g., transport and vertical migration) should be covered by the water quality model. As the methodology is based on chl-*a* concentration, situations when phytoplankton cells and their chl-*a* content change may pose a challenge to this approach.

5. Conclusions

Predictive numerical models can use the presented methodology to couple light with phytoplnkton physiology throughout the photic depth. Not only light quantity but also its quality are essentisl for proper coupling. Nonetheless, numerical models have to accommodate the spectral photosynthesis of the competing dominant phytoplankton species and their adaptation to the spectral irradiance throughout the photic depth. The complexity of this coupling is still unresolved and needs more attention from both the numerical modeling community as well as the optical and bio-optical scientists.

Acknowledgments: The author wishes to thank Victoria S. Hemsley (Ocean and Earth Science, National Oceanography Center Southampton, University of Southampton, SO14 3ZH, U.K.) for providing all of the field data. The author also thanks the in-house reviewers of this manuscript, including Dan Campbell, Naomi Detenbeck and Henry Walker (USEPA-AED), as well as the journal's anonymous reviewers for their technical reviews, insights and constructive comments. Although the research described here has been funded by the U.S. Environmental Protection Agency, it has not been subject to agency-level review and, therefore, does not necessarily reflect the views of the agency, nor does mentioning trade names or commercial products endorse or recommend them. This manuscript is contribution No. ORD-017268 of the USEPA Office Research and Development, National Health and Environmental Effects Research Laboratory, Atlantic Ecology Division.

Conflicts of Interest: The author declares no conflict of interest.

References

1. Peterson, D.H.; Festa, J.F. Numerical simulation of phytoplankton productivity in partially mixed estuaries. *Estuar. Coast. Shelf Sci.* **1984**, *19*, 563–589. [CrossRef]

2. Topliss, B.J. Optical monitoring of coastal waters: Photic depth estimates. *Mar. Environ. Res.* **1982**, *7*, 295–308. [CrossRef]

3. Ocean Color Algorithm Working Group. Models, Parameters and Approaches That Are Used to Generate Wide Range of Absorption and Backscattering Spectra. International Ocean Color Coordinating Group, Ocean Color Algorithm Working Group. 2003, p. 11. Available online: http://www.ioccg.org/groups/lee_data.pdf (accessed on 30 July 2015).

4. Gallegos, C.L.; Kenworthy, W.J. Seagrass depth limits in the Indian River Lagoon (Florida, USA): Application of an optical water quality model. *Estuar. Coast. Shelf Sci.* **1996**, *42*, 267–288. [CrossRef]

5. Gallegos, C.L. Calculating optical water quality targets to restore and protect submerged aquatic vegetation: Overcoming problems in partitioning the diffuse attenuation coefficient for photosynthetically active radiation. *Estuaries* **2001**, *24*, 381–397. [CrossRef]

6. Gallegos, C.L.; Neal, P.J. Partitioning spectral absorption in case 2 waters: Discrimination of dissolved and particulate components. *Appl. Opt.* **2002**, *41*, 4220–4233. [CrossRef] [PubMed]

7. Keith, D.J.; Yoder, J.A.; Freeman, S.A. Spatial and temporal distribution of colored dissolved organic matter (CDOM) in Narragansett Bay, Rhode Island: Implications for phytoplankton in coastal waters. *Estuar. Coast. Shelf Sci.* **2002**, *55*, 705–717. [CrossRef]

8. Kenworthy, W.J.; Gallegos, C.L.; Costello, C.; Field, D.; di Carlo, G. Dependence of eelgrass (*Zostera marina*) light requirements on sediment organic matter in Massachusetts coastal bays: Implications for remediation and restoration. *Mar. Pollut. Bull.* **2014**, *83*, 446–457. [CrossRef] [PubMed]

9. Thursby, G.; Rego, S.; Keith, D. *Data Report for Calibration of Bio-Optical Model for Narragansett Bay*; United States Environmental Protection Agency Report Tracking Number EPA/600/R-15/211; U.S. Environmental Protection Agency: Washington, DC, USA, 2015; p. 25. Available online: https://cfpub.epa.gov/si/si_public_file_download.cfm?p_download_id=525010 (Accessed on 11 November 2016).

10. Abdelrhman, M.A. Quantifying contributions to light attenuation in estuaries and coastal embayments: Application to Narragansett Bay, Rhode Island. *Estuar. Coasts* 13 April 2016; under review.

11. Morel, A. Optical modeling of the upper ocean in relation to its biogenous matter content (Case I Waters). *J. Geophys. Res.* **1988**, *93*, 10749–10768. [CrossRef]

12. Sathyendranath, S.; Platt, T. The spectral irradiance field at the surface and in the interior of the ocean: A model for applications in oceanography. *J. Geophys. Res.* **1988**, *93*, 9270–9280. [CrossRef]

13. Prieur, L.; Sathyendranath, S. An optical classification of coastal and oceanic waters based on the specific spectral absorption curves of phytoplankton pigment, dissolved organic matter, and other particulate materials. *Limnol. Oceanogr.* **1981**, *26*, 671–689. [CrossRef]

14. Jerlov, N.G. Marine Optics. In *Elsevier Oceanography Series 14*; Elsevier: New York, NY, USA, 1976; p. 231.

15. Sathyendranath, S. Inherent optical properties of natural seawater. *Defense Sci. J.* **1984**, *34*, 1–18. [CrossRef]

16. Bricaud, A.; Babin, M.; Morel, A.; Claustre, H. Variability in chlorophyll-specific absorption coefficients of natural phytoplankton: Analysis and parameterization. *J. Geophys. Res.* **1995**, *100*, 13321–13332. [CrossRef]

17. Fischer, J.; Fell, F. Simulation of MERIS measurements above selected ocean waters. *Int. J. Remote Sens.* **1999**, *20*, 1787–1807. [CrossRef]

18. Gallegos, C.L. Refining habitat requirements of submersed aquatic vegetation: Role of optical models. *Estuaries* **1994**, *17*, 187–199. [CrossRef]

19. Bricaud, A.; Stramski, D. Spectral absorption coefficients of living phytoplankton and nonalgal biogenous matter: A comparison between the Peru upwelling area and the Sargasso Sea. *Limnol. Oceanogr.* **1990**, *35*, 562–582. [CrossRef]

20. Matsuoka, A.; Hill, V.; Hout, Y.; Babin, M.; Bricaud, A. Seasonal variability in the light absorption properties of western Arctic waters: Parameterization of individual components of absorption for ocean color applications. *J. Geophys. Res.* **2011**, *116*, 1–15. [CrossRef]

21. Fournier, G.; Forand, J.L. Analytic phase function for ocean water. In *Ocean Optics XII, Proceedings of SPIE—The International Society for Optical Engineering XII, Bergen, Norway, 13–15 June 1994*; Jaffe, J.S., Ed.; Society of Photo-optical Instrumentation Engineers: Bellingham, WA, USA, 1994; Volume 2258, pp. 194–201.

22. Morel, A.; Gentili, B. Diffuse reflectance of oceanic waters: Its dependence on sun angle as influenced by molecular scattering contribution. *Appl. Opt.* **1991**, *30*, 4427–4438. [CrossRef] [PubMed]

23. Buiteveld, H.; Hakvoort, J.H.M.; Donze, M. The optical properties of pure water. In *Ocean Optics XII, Proceedings of SPIE—The International Society for Optical Engineering XII, Bergen, Norway 13–15 June 1994*; Jaffe, J.S., Ed.; Society of Photo-optical Instrumentation Engineers: Bellingham, WA, USA, 1994; Volume 2258, pp. 174–183.

24. Hemsley, V.S.; University of Southampton, Southampton, UK. Personal communication, 2016.

25. Hemsley, V.S.; Smyth, T.J.; Martin, A.P.; Williams, E.F.; Thompson, A.F.; Damerell, G.; Painter, S.C. Estimating oceanic primary production using vertical irradiance and chlorophyll profiles from ocean gliders in the North Atlantic. *Environ. Sci. Technol.* **2015**, *49*, 11612–11621. [CrossRef] [PubMed]

26. Stomp, M.; Huisman, J.; de Jongh, F.; Veraart, A.J.; Gerla, D.; Rijkeboer, M.; Ibelings, B.W.; Wollenzien, U.I.A.; Stal, L.J. Adaptive divergence in pigment composition promotes phytoplankton biodiversity. *Nature* **2004**, *432*, 104–107. [CrossRef] [PubMed]

27. Xiu, P.; Chai, F. Connections between physical, optical, and biogeochemical processes in the Pacific Ocean. *Prog. Oceanogr.* **2014**, *122*, 30–53. [CrossRef]

Article

Development of the Hydrodynamic Model for Long-Term Simulation of Water Quality Processes of the Tidal James River, Virginia

Jian Shen *, Ya Wang and Mac Sisson

Virginia Institute of Marine Science, College of William & Mary, Gloucester Point, VA 23062, USA;
ricowang@vims.edu (Y.W.); Sisson@vims.edu (M.S.)
* Correspondence: shen@vims.edu; Tel.: +1-804-684-7359

Academic Editor: Rich Signell
Received: 2 August 2016; Accepted: 16 November 2016; Published: 24 November 2016

Abstract: Harmful algal blooms (HABs) have frequently occurred in the James River. The State has convened a Scientific Advisory Panel (SAP) to review the James River chlorophyll-a standards. The SAP will conduct a scientific study to review the basis for setting the chlorophyll-a standards. To support the SAP study of chlorophyll-a standards, the State of Virginia has decided to develop a numerical modeling system that is capable of simulating phytoplankton and HABs. The modeling system includes a watershed model, a three-dimensional hydrodynamic model and water quality models. The focus of this study will be on the development and verification of the hydrodynamic model. In order to simulate the complex geometry of the James River, a high-resolution model has been implemented. The model has been calibrated for a long-term period of 23 years. A series of model experiments was conducted to evaluate the impact of forcings on dynamic simulation and transport time. It was found that freshwater discharge is the most sensitive for an accurate simulation of salinity and transport time. The water age predicted by the model in the tidal freshwater region represents the fluctuation of transport processes, and it has a good correlation with the algal bloom, while at the downstream, the transport time simulation agrees with the delay of the HAB in the mesohaline of the James after the HAB occurred in the Elizabeth River due to the transport processes. The results indicate that the hydrodynamic model is capable of simulating the dynamic processes of the James and driving water quality models in the James River.

Keywords: estuarine dynamics; numerical model; transport time; James River

1. Introduction

The James River is a western tributary of the Chesapeake Bay (Figure 1). The unique geometry of the James River results in complex dynamic fields in both upstream and downstream portions of the James. The seasonal variation of the dynamic condition is believed to have a high influence on the frequent formation of harmful algal blooms (HABs) in the estuary.

In the tidal fresh portion of the James, the chlorophyll-a distribution is strongly influenced by hydrodynamic fields because of the limited mobility of phytoplankton. Bukaveckas et al. [1] found that the location of the chlorophyll-a maximum in the tidal freshwater James River is determined in part by the natural geomorphic features of the channel. The transition from a riverine-type (narrow, deep) cross-sectional morphology to a broad channel with shallow lateral areas provides favorable light conditions for the phytoplankton. The residence time increases during the low-flow period, which coincides with the summer period. Consequently, the phytoplankton bloom occurs frequently during summer in this region.

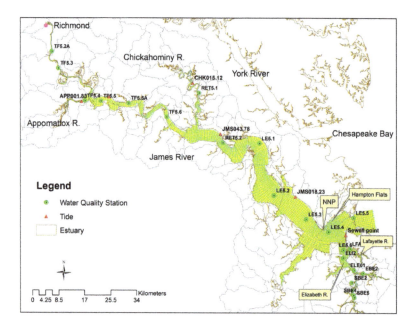

Figure 1. James River model grid and the location of observation stations for tide and water quality.

The downstream portion of the James River is distinguished by a meandering main channel. An abrupt bend in the river occurs at Newport News Point (NNP), approximately 10.5 km from its mouth, where the orientation of the river changes from northeast-southwest in the lower river to southeast-northwest in the upper river. Hampton Flats is the shoal flanking the northern side of the deep channel in the lower James River (Figure 1). Water depth over the Hampton Flats is less than 5 m. This unique geometry results in a strong circulation and topographic eddy [2], which contributes to both larval retention and the formation of the HAB in the mesohaline region of the James. Morse et al. [3] found that the Lafayette River inside the Elizabeth River, a sub-estuary of the James River, acted as the initiation region for the bloom of *C. polykrikoides* in the James River during the summers of 2007 and 2008. Although the bloom occurred initially in the Elizabeth River, *C. polykrikoides* was transported from the sub-estuary into the lower James River and a portion of the lower James due to this local estuarine circulation, and these form massive blooms over large portions of the tidal James River and the lower Chesapeake Bay.

The cause of the HAB in the James is attributed to the high nutrient input from both point and non-point sources. To improve the water quality condition of the estuary, nutrient reduction is needed for the upstream and lateral watersheds. Besides, the State has convened a Scientific Advisory Panel (SAP) to review and confirm or adjust the James River chlorophyll-a standards. The SAP will conduct a scientific study to review the basis for setting the chlorophyll-a standards. To support the SAP study of chlorophyll standards, a numerical model that is capable of simulating phytoplankton and harmful algal blooms is needed. The model system includes a watershed model, a three-dimensional hydrodynamic model and water quality models. The dynamic models have been often used for environmental studies and drive water quality models [4–10].

Considering the variations of tidal, wind and baroclinic forcings, water movement in the tidal James is truly multi-dimensional and quite complex. The accurate simulation of transport time and residence time in the James River is the key to the success of the water quality model of the James River. To accurately simulate the hydrodynamics of the James, we developed a numerical model, which is capable of simulating the circulation features that span timescales of hours to months, and simulate density circulation, geometry-induced circulation and residence time for a 23-year period. Although several models have been developed in the James River in the past, including the Chesapeake Bay water quality model [11], a model study of dynamics related to larval transport and an environmental assessment [2,3], none of the models have been verified for such a long period and for the correctness of the simulation of transport time. On the other hand, the traditional model skill assessment through comparison of the tide, salinity, etc., may not be sufficient to ensure correct simulations of algae and HAB, which require accurate simulation of residence time and transport time. These characteristics are very difficult to evaluate using the traditional method. The question as to what is the influence of external forcing on simulating dynamic fields and consequently affecting the transport of water quality state variables is not well-evaluated. Therefore, the variation of the external forcing on the uncertainty of the hydrodynamic model prediction skill is the focus of this paper. Several model sensitivity simulations were conducted with respect to the variation of the external forcings, and the influence of the forcing condition on model prediction are evaluated. In order to address the influence of the accuracy of model dynamics on transport processes, we will further evaluate the model through a comparison of key transport timescales, such as water age and residence time, to evaluate model performance.

2. Materials and Methods

2.1. Study Area

The James River is the southernmost tributary of Chesapeake Bay (Figure 1). It is about 160.0 km long, and the width ranges from 300 m at its upstream and 6 km at the downstream with a mean depth of 3.76 m. The tidal range is about 0.74 m at Sewells Point near the mouth. The mean freshwater discharge is about 226 $m^3 \cdot s^{-1}$. The monthly river discharge varies seasonally from 86 $m^3 \cdot s^{-1}$ in September to 365 $m^3 \cdot s^{-1}$ in March [2]. Salinity in the estuarine part of the James River varies seasonally, which is a common characteristic of estuaries in the mid-latitudes. Near the river mouth, the channel is more than 7 m deep, and salinity typically is around 25 parts per thousand (ppt). The horizontal salinity gradients are usually larger near the upper mesohaline of the river where the freshwater and saltwater converge. The denser, more saline bottom water enters the James River from the Chesapeake Bay and flows upstream, while the less dense surface waters, dominated by freshwater inflow, flow downstream toward the Bay [12,13].

2.2. Model Configuration

The three-dimensional Environmental Fluid Dynamic Code (EFDC) was used for simulations for the James River and its tributaries. The EFDC model is a general hydrodynamic model that solves three-dimensional, time-dependent flows governed by hydrostatic primitive equations [14,15]. The Mellor and Yamada [16] Level 2.5 turbulence closure scheme as modified by Galperin et al. [17] is implemented in the model. The model uses curvilinear, orthogonal horizontal coordinates and sigma vertical coordinates to represent the physical characteristics of a water body. A high-order transport scheme with an anti-numerical diffusion scheme is implemented in the numerical model, which is essential for simulating transport processes accurately in the Chesapeake Bay and its tributaries.

A Cartesian grid model has been applied to the James to study the eddy generated at the mesohaline and polyhaline regions of the lower James [2,18]. The model does not have sufficient resolution for the tidal freshwater region and Elizabeth River to simulate an algal bloom in these regions. A new model grid was developed for the long-term simulation of the dynamic fields. Because the water quality model simulation will span a 23-year period, the efficiency of computation needs consideration. We want to develop a model with sufficient spatial resolution for the simulation of all dynamic features, but maintaining a high efficiency of computation. The model grid cells were designed to follow the main channel of the James River. High resolution was placed on the main stem of the river to obtain the best representation of the topography in this area. The model grid is shown in Figure 1. There are a total of 3066 grid cells in the horizontal and eight layers in the vertical. The bottom bathymetry is interpolated using the NOAA coastal relief model with 90-m resolution (https://www.ngdc.noaa.gov/mgg/coastal/crm.html). For the Elizabeth River, data measured during a survey conducted by the Army Corps (Norfolk District) were used. For small creeks, NOAA charts were used to obtain depths in shallow areas. Eight evenly-spaced sigma layers were applied in the vertical.

The model simulation periods are from 1991 to 2000 and from 2007 to 2013. To allow the model spin-up, the model started from 1990 and 2006, respectively, a full year in advance of each simulation period. Therefore, the impact of the initial conditions can be efficiently removed. Daily river discharges from upstream and lateral watersheds are obtained from the James River watershed model developed by TetraTech, Inc., [19], which includes inflows from 87 sub-watersheds. The three main upstream freshwater discharges are from Richmond, the Appomattox River and the Chickahominy River, respectively. Hourly wind forcing data were obtained from the Norfolk and Richmond International Airports, which are located near the Sewells Point station at the mouth and near the fall line of the James, respectively. The open boundary conditions from 1990 to 2000 (which included hourly time-varying water level, temperature and salinity profiles) were obtained from the 3D model of the Chesapeake Bay Program [20]. Because the Chesapeake Bay Program (CBP) model does not simulate the period from 2006 to 2013, the tide boundary condition for this period used Sewells Point data with corrections of phase and amplitude. The mean differences of phase and amplitude were estimated based on CBP model outputs and measured tidal elevations at Sewells Point. The hourly salinity boundary conditions used for the 2006 to 2013 period are outputs from the large domain Chesapeake Bay model [21,22]. The temperature boundary condition used hourly measurements at Sewells Point at the surface and monthly temperature data measured at CBP Station CB8.1. Differences of surface and bottom temperatures at Station CB8.1 were interpolated in time and applied to the hourly surface temperature data to obtain an estimation of bottom temperature. Because the temperature is highly determined by the air-sea exchange and the open boundary has less impact on the temperature inside the James, this approach yields a good model-data agreement. The radiation boundary conditions are used for the tide, salinity and temperature. Hourly wind forcing, surface pressure, humidity and solar radiation obtained from the hourly meteorological data from Norfolk and Richmond Airports were used for temperature simulations.

2.3. Age Calculation

Any change of hydrodynamic conditions will result in a change of transport processes, which is more important for transporting both nutrients and phytoplankton [21,22]. Because it is difficult to evaluate the change of dynamic conditions (e.g., change of velocity, surface elevation) and their impact on algae and nutrient transport, we can use the transport timescale to evaluate the impact of dynamics on water quality because it shows a cumulative effect. Transport timescales, such as residence time and renewal time, are the first-order representatives of the dynamic conditions in the estuary, whereas the vertical transport time is directly related to DO exchange [21].

The timescales can be computed using the concept of water age [23]. Freshwater age is the elapsed time since a water parcel leaves the head of a tributary (or any origin), where it has a continual freshwater input. The age at location x is the mean time required for a water parcel to be transported from its discharge location to location x, regardless of its pathway [24]. Delhez et al. [23] provided a way to use a numerical model to compute the water age. Assuming there is only one tracer released to a system without internal sources and sinks, the transport equation for computing the tracer concentration $C(t, \vec{x})$ and the age concentration $\alpha(t, \vec{x})$ can be expressed as [24]:

$$\frac{\partial C(t, \vec{x})}{\partial t} + \nabla[\vec{u}C(t, \vec{x}) - K\nabla C(t, \vec{x})] = 0 \tag{1}$$

$$\frac{\partial \alpha(t, \vec{x})}{\partial t} + \nabla\left[u(t, \vec{x})\alpha(t, \vec{x}) - K\nabla\alpha(t, \vec{x})\right] = C(t, \vec{x}) \tag{2}$$

The mean age can be calculated as follows:

$$a(t, \vec{x}) = \frac{\alpha(t, \vec{x})}{C(t, \vec{x})} \tag{3}$$

where $a(t, \vec{x})$ is water age, $\nabla = \vec{i}\frac{\partial}{\partial x} + \vec{j}\frac{\partial}{\partial y} + \vec{k}\frac{\partial}{\partial z}$ and K is the diffusivity tensor. To simulate age, the tracer was continuously released at the upstream or at Elizabeth River. The radiation boundary condition was applied at the mouth [18]. Because the upstream of the James River is very narrow, the age has minor variation laterally and vertically. Therefore, the difference of the cross-section average age between its upstream and downstream for a control volume is a good estimate of the local residence time for that control volume.

3. Results

3.1. Tidal Elevation and Current

Model validation for the tide was conducted for the entire simulation period. The surface elevations were compared to the observations at six stations. There is only one NOAA tidal station at Sewells Point. Another five stations are maintained by Virginia Estuarine and Coastal Observing System (VECOS, http://web2.vims.edu/vecos/), which measure water depth using pressure sensors. The bottom roughness height was adjusted to make the tidal propagation correct in the estuary. A constant roughness height of 0.33 cm was used. The statistics of model performance are summarized in the Taylor diagram. The Taylor diagram provides a concise statistical summary of how well patterns match each other in terms of their correlation, their root-mean-square difference and the ratio of their variance [25,26].

Figure 2 shows the model results of tidal elevation. There are three axes shown in the diagram that represent correlation coefficients, the centered root-mean-square difference and standard deviation. All data (both modeled and observed) are normalized by the observed standard deviation at a reference station (APP001.83). The correlation axis shows the correlation between model results and observations. The standard deviation axis indicates the deviation of model results from measurements measured by the standard deviations. The circle of root-mean-square difference shows the root-mean-square difference (RMSD). The value used to normalize the RMSD is 0.3 m.

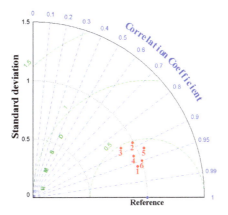

Figure 2. Taylor diagram representing model-data comparisons for surface elevation (1 = JMS043.78, 2 = JMS073.37, 3 = APP001.83, 4 = JMS018.23, 5 = JMS002.55, 6 = Sewells Point, reference RMSD value = 0.3 m).

The modeled surface elevations are within 0.5 RMSD, which is less than 0.15 m. The RMSD is relatively low, and the simulation variations are close to observations based on the measure of the standard deviation, which is close to the reference site as observations. The correlation is larger than 0.86. It can be seen that the tide is well simulated.

In recent years, NOAA has conducted surface current observations in the lower James. The model-simulated currents at a station near EL5-4 are compared to the NOAA observations. Figure 3 shows the scatter plot of observations against the model simulations. The model skill, which is defined as $SS = 1 - \sum (A_{model} - A_{obs})^2 / \sum (A_{obs} - \overline{A_{obs}})^2$, was used to evaluate the model performance. Performance levels are categorized by the SS value as: >0.65 excellent; 0.65 to 0.5 very good; 0.5 to 0.2 good; <0.2 poor [25]. It can be seen that the model simulations vary each year. Overall, the simulations agree with observations with model correlation ranges from 0.6 to 0.82 and skill between 0.24 and 0.65, indicating that the current simulation is satisfactory. For detailed model results, the readers are referred to the James River Chlorophyll Study Modeling Report [19].

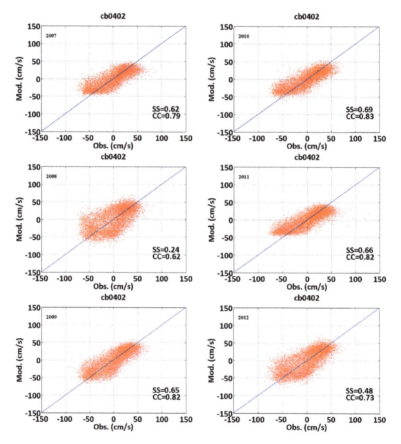

Figure 3. Scatter plots of comparisons of modeled versus observed current (SS is the model skill and CC is the correlation coefficient).

3.2. Salinity

The long-term transport processes are driven by sub-tidal circulation [12]. Correct calibration of salinity is important for accurate simulation of sub-tidal circulation. The calibration of salinity is focused on stratification and salinity intrusion. We used monthly data (measured once a month) to conduct the salinity calibration. The salinity calibration was conducted from 1991 to 2000, and the validation was conducted from 2007 to 2013. Although the data do not have high temporal resolution, these can be used to evaluate a long-term simulation of salinity for seasonal and inter-annual variations. Unlike the model calibration of surface elevation, there are no model parameters to calibrate salinity for the 3D model. The discrepancy of salinity between modeled and observed is mainly caused by the freshwater discharge, boundary condition(s), the wind and bathymetry (which will be discussed in later sections). Both the transport scheme and turbulent scheme used in the model play important roles. EFDC uses a second-order transport scheme with anti-numerical diffusion; it can simulate salinity well in general. The summary of model prediction skill is shown in Figure 4 as a Taylor diagram, in which salinity is compared at seven monitoring stations along the James River (locations are shown in Figure 1). The value used to normalize the root-mean-square difference is 2.39 psu. It can be seen that the model has a high correlation with a low root-mean-square difference at each station. The model performance for the second period is better than that for the first period.

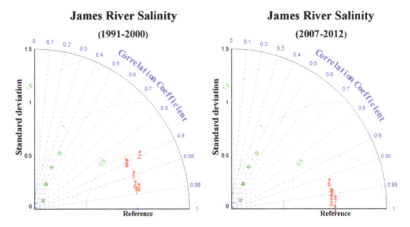

Figure 4. Taylor diagrams representing model-data comparisons at seven monitoring stations in the James River. Three axes represent correlation coefficients (blue lines), the centered root-mean-square difference (green lines) and normalized standard deviation (black lines) (station location: 1 = LE5.5, 2 = LE5.6, 3 = LE5.4, 4 = LE5.3, 5 = LE5.2, 6 = LE5.1, 7 = RET5.2, reference RMSD value = 2.39 psu).

Important characteristics of the salinity simulation are the stratification and salinity intrusion, which are the key parameters that determine gravitation circulations. Examples of salinity stratification (difference between bottom and surface) are shown in Figure 5 for Stations LE5.1, LE5.2, LE5.3 and LE5.4, respectively, for 2008 and 2010. We compared the salinity difference between bottom and surface layers. It can be seen that the model simulated the salinity stratification during this period rather well. The model simulation of salinity intrusion is shown in Figure 6, for surface and bottom salinity. We compared mean, minimum and a maximum of salinity for a three-day window of observations along the James River from the mouth to the salinity intrusion limit and compared it to the observations and their range. It can be seen that the simulation of modeled salinity intrusion agrees well with the observations. The model performance to simulate salinity is satisfactory.

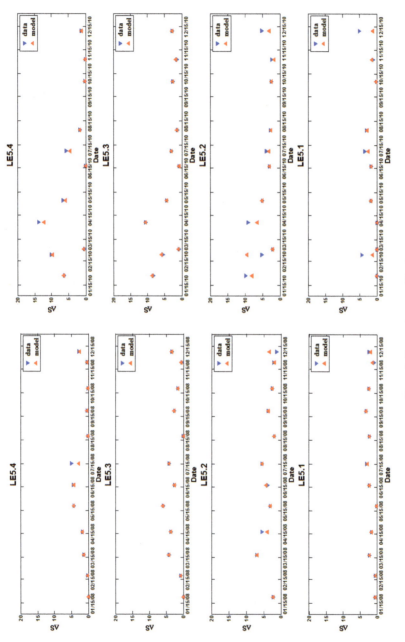

Figure 5. Comparison stratification.

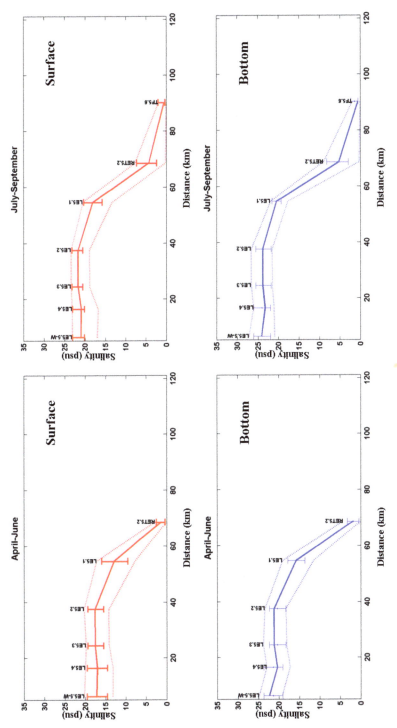

Figure 6. Comparison of salinity intrusion (the bar represents one standard deviation, and the upper and lower bounds are the maximum and minimum salinity).

3.3. Temperature

Temperature is a key parameter for the eutrophication model, as all kinetic parameters depend on temperature, which varies from 5 to 30 °C. The observations are monthly (one observation each month at each location). A summary of model prediction skill for temperature simulation is shown in Figure 7 as a Taylor diagram, in which temperature is compared at ten monitoring stations along the James River. It can be seen that the model results include a high correlation at each station with a low root-mean-square difference. There is no difference for all stations statistically for model calibration and validation. The model results are satisfactory.

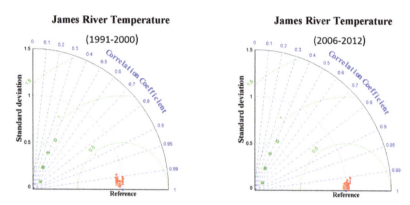

Figure 7. Taylor diagrams representing model-data comparisons at seven monitoring stations in the James River. Station locations: 1 = LE5.5, 2 = LE5.6, 3 = LE5.4, 4 = LE5.3, 5 = LE5.2, 6 = LE5.1, 7 = RET5.2, 8 = TF5.6, 9 = TF5.5, 10 = TF4.5 (reference RMSD value = 8.69 °C).

3.4. Sensitivity Tests

For a three-dimensional model of the EFDC, the logarithmic wall function is used for shear stress. The only model parameter to be calibrated is the bottom roughness height, which determines the model simulation of the tide. However, the external forcing and open boundary conditions are critical for the accurate simulation of salinity, which is important for estuary dynamics and estuarine circulation. A series of model sensitivities is conducted to test the model performance and help understand the impact of external forcing on model performances.

3.4.1. Freshwater Discharge

Estuarine stratification is a competition between barotropic and baroclinic forcings. The large buoyant forcing is from freshwater discharge, which flows out of the estuary on top of the salty, dense water. It can be expected that a change of freshwater discharge can cause a change in salinity. For the current 3D model configuration, we used a watershed model output to drive the model. The model predictive skill is very high, but some discrepancy can be expected, as shown in Figure 8, upstream of Richmond. A sensitivity run was conducted to replace three freshwater discharge input records from locations upstream of Richmond, Appomattox River and Chickahominy River with United States Geological Survey (USGS) flows (USGS02037500, USGS020416500 and USGS02042500). These three stations account for the majority of the flow.

Figure 9 shows the comparison of the salinity difference when using watershed runoff and USGS flow. It can be seen that the model is very sensitive to the flow. The salinity can differ by 2 to 4 psu, which is on the same order as the root-mean-square error of the model calibration. Therefore, some discrepancy during salinity calibration can be expected when using flow from the watershed model.

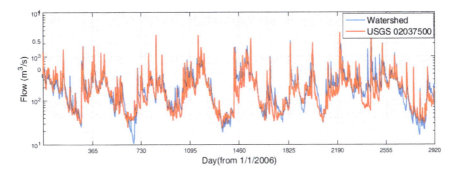

Figure 8. Comparison of freshwater discharge between USGS data (USGS02037500) and watershed model simulation output at Richmond.

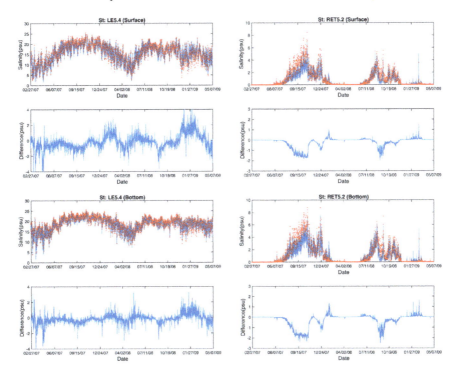

Figure 9. Sensitivity tests for flow at Stations RET5.2 and LE5.4 (red lines show the results of a model simulation using watershed flow, and blue lines show results of a simulation using USGS flow at three upstream stations; the difference shows the difference of runs between USGS flow and watershed flow).

It is interesting to know if the change of salinity, which is within the accepted error range due to flow or other forcings, will affect the long-term transport or export of nutrients, as the retention of nutrients and eutrophication are highly determined by the residence time [27–29]. The transport property of a substance can be quantified by the transport timescales, such as residence time and water age [21–24]. The age of water is defined as the time elapsed since it leaves the headwaters. The age at each location indicates the time required for the water or conservative substance to travel from the headwaters to a specified location [18]. The age and the residence time are often sufficient to characterize the motions of a conservative substance. We computed the freshwater age along the James River using different flows and compared the results in Figure 10. It can be seen that the transport process is very sensitive to the flow condition. The difference can be about five days for a given period for this example or at a particular day during the high-flow period. The change of flow can affect short-term transport processes. However, the annual mean water age does not change much as shown in Figure 11, especially at the downstream. As the watershed model simulated flow is slightly lower than the USGS flow, even if it is higher during some high-flow periods, the transport slows slightly. However, the results indicate that it will not affect the long-term transport of nutrients in the estuary.

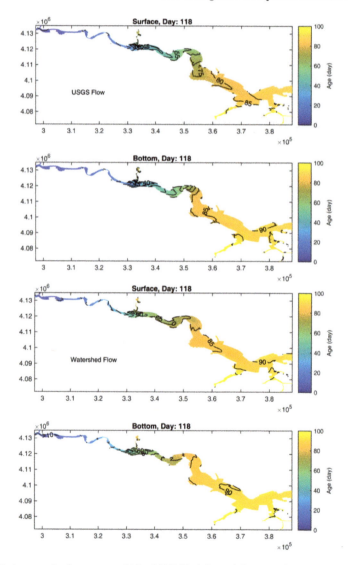

Figure 10. An example of water age at 16 April 2008 (the left panel shows results using watershed flow, and the right panel shows results using USGS flow).

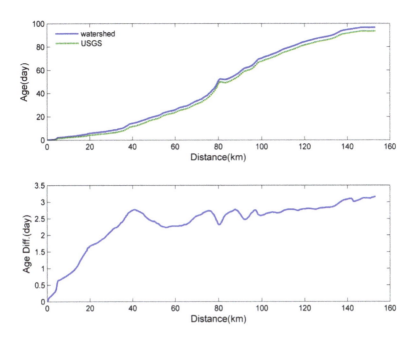

Figure 11. Mean water age and difference along the James River for the period of 2002 to 2008 with respect to different freshwater discharge.

3.4.2. Wind

Wind is a very important forcing to change estuarine circulation. Downstream wind can enhance the estuarine circulation, while upstream wind can increase mixing in the estuary. The wind plays an important role in the modulation of hypoxia in the Chesapeake Bay [30,31]. A sensitivity test to determine the influence of the wind on salinity was conducted. It is unknown if the wind will have a large impact on salinity for this relatively small estuary. We reduced wind forcing by 10%, ran the model from 1990 to 1992 and compared the salinity at Stations LE5.4 and RET5.2, which represents the range of salinity intrusion in the estuary. The sensitivity results are shown in Figure 12. It can be seen that a 10% reduction of wind can change salinity up to 2 psu at Station LE5.4, but causes less than a 0.5-psu change at Station RET5.2. Because the wind-forcing fluctuation has a frequency of three to five days in Chesapeake Bay, the short-term change of the wind on long-term transport appears not to be important for this narrow estuary. We compared water age (not shown here), as well, and found that there is no difference in water age. The results suggest that a 10% error in wind forcing will not affect the long-term transport of nutrients in the James River.

3.4.3. Open Boundary Condition

We used the output of salinity from the large model as the open boundary condition. The influence of the open boundary condition of salinity on the model was evaluated by running the model with a reduction of 5% of the salinity at the open boundary. Comparisons of model results at Stations LE5.4 and RET5.2 are shown in Figure 13. The salinity decreases by about 1.5 psu at Station LE5.4, but only decreases up to 1 psu at Station RET5.2. It can be seen that the salinity simulation is sensitive to the open boundary specification near the mouth. Based on the sensitivity runs, the calibration results are satisfactory, although there are errors in the salinity open boundary condition.

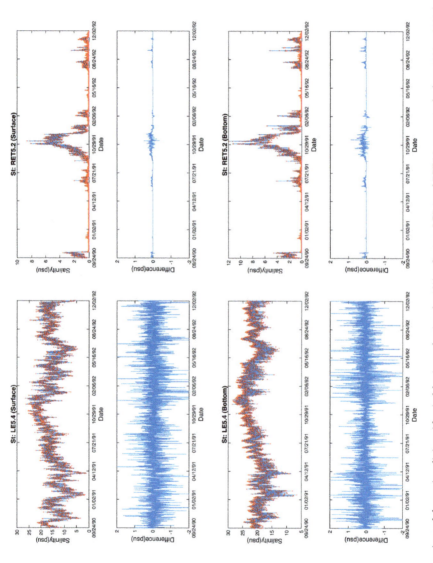

Figure 12. Comparison of change in salinity with wind forcing reductions by 10% at Stations LE5.4 and RET5.2, respectively, from 1990 to 2002 (red lines are the baseline condition; blue lines are the sensitivity run; the difference shows the difference between the sensitivity run and the baseline run).

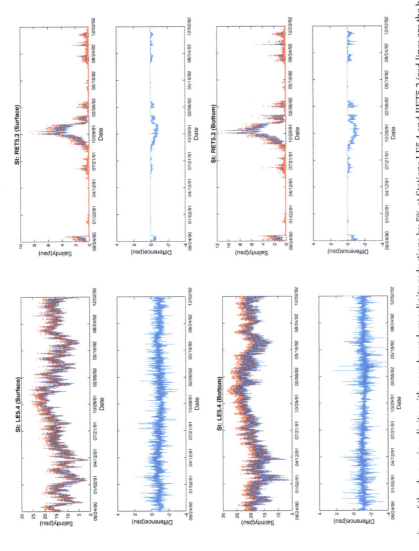

Figure 13. Comparison of the change in salinity with open boundary salinity reductions by 5% at Stations LE5.4 and RET5.2 (red lines are the baseline condition; blue lines are the sensitivity run; and the difference shows the difference btween the sensitivity run and the baseline run).

4. Discussion and Summary

The location of an algal bloom not only depends on light and nutrients, but also depends on residence time [28,29]. A correct simulation of transport processes and residence time is critical for the algal bloom. To evaluate the model performance, we computed residence time in the tidal freshwater region and compared the results to the Chl-a observations at Stations TF5.5 and TF5.5A. It can be seen that the peak algal bloom corresponds to the low residence time at that region with a good correlation ($R = 0.64$, $p = 0.001$) (Figure 14). Because of the impact of available nutrients and light, it does not match all of the variation as expected. The results indicate that the model simulation transport process is satisfactory and can be used to simulate the HAB.

HABs have occurred almost every year in summer in the mesohaline region of the James, and they are believed to be caused by the HAB bloom initiated in the Lafayette River, a tributary of the Elizabeth River [3]. After a HAB has occurred in the Elizabeth River, the bloom will occur in the James after 10 to 15 days. To verify the transport time for algal transport from the Elizabeth River to the James River, we computed the water age from the Elizabeth River to the James River. The tracer is released from the Elizabeth River; a water age at any location represents the time required for any dissolved materials to be transported from its source to the location. Figure 15 shows the age distribution. It can be seen that it takes about 10 to 15 days to reach the mesohaline region during spring and neap tides. The surface water moves upstream faster during spring tide than during neap tide. The bottom water moves 5–10 days faster upstream than surface water, which is due to the unique front and eddy system near the mouth of the James River [2]. A portion of the ebb flow will turn to the north and flood into the Hampton Flats, where a frontal system is well developed, and surface water will dive to the bottom through this frontal system and be transported upstream along the deep channel near the northern shore. Meanwhile, the flood tide will move surface water upstream [2]. The transport time for water to move from Elizabeth River to the mesohaline region of the James River agrees well with the time delay of the occurrence of the HAB in the James River after the HAB occurred in the Elizabeth River.

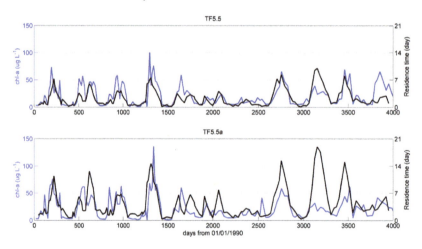

Figure 14. Comparison of residence time and Chl-a concentration at Stations TF5.5 and TF5.5a.

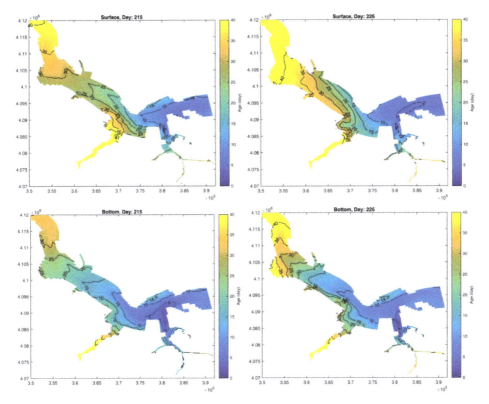

Figure 15. Travel time (age) corresponding to the dissolved substances released from the mouth of the Elizabeth River at Day 215 (**left**, spring tide) and Day 220 (**right**, neap tide). The travel time is relative to the releasing day.

In summary, a three-dimensional hydrodynamic model has been developed for the James River. The Environmental Fluid Dynamics Computer Code (EFDC) is used for developing the James River hydrodynamic model. The model was calibrated for surface elevation over the period from 2006 to 2008, for current over the period from 2007 to 2012 and for salinity and temperature from 1991 to 2000. Furthermore, it is validated from 2007 to 2013 for salinity and temperature. The model validation results indicate that the model is robust; it adequately simulates the hydrodynamics and temperature; and it is suitable for the water quality model development for the James River.

Acknowledgments: The funding for this project was supported by Virginia Department Environmental Quality through Chesapeake Environmental Communications. Many people provided help and advice during the course of the model development. We thank Nikolai Gurdian of TetraTech for providing watershed model results for our model simulation. We thank J. Fitzpatrick, H. Wang, P. Wang and D. Jasinski for providing help and advice and for reviewing the model results. We thank J. Kennedy of DEQ for providing leadership of the project.

Author Contributions: The authors collaborated closely on this work. Ye Wang is the key modeler for conducting hydrodynamic model calibration and verification. J. Shen served as co-PI on the project. J. Shen and M. Sisson conducted simulations of the time scale and model sensitivity test. M. Sisson edited the manuscript.

Conflicts of Interest: The authors declare no conflict of interest.

References

1. Bukaveckas, P.; Barry, L.E.; Beckwith, M.J.; David, V.; Lederer, B. Factors determining the location of the chlorophyll maximum and the fate of algal production within the tidal freshwater James River. *Estuar. Coasts* **2011**, *34*, 569–582. [CrossRef]

2. Shen, J.; Boon, J.; Kuo, A.Y. A numerical study of a tidal intrusion front and its impact on larval dispersion in the James River estuary, Virginia. *Estuaries* **1999**, *22*, 681–692. [CrossRef]

3. Morse, R.E.; Shen, J.; Blanco-Garcia, J.L.; Hunley, W.S.; Fentress, S.; Wiggins, M.; Mulholland, M.R. Environmental and physical controls on the formation and transport of blooms of the dinoflagellate *Cochlodinium polykrikoides* Margalef in the lower Chesapeake bay and its tributaries. *Estuar. Coasts* **2011**, *34*, 1006–1025. [CrossRef]

4. Sheng, Y.P. *A Three-Dimensional Mathematical Model of Coastal, Estuarine and Lake Currents Using Boundary-Fitted Grid*; Technical Report No. 585; Aeronautical Research Associates of Princeton: Princeton, NJ, USA, 1986.

5. Cheng, R.T.; Casulli, V.; Gartner, J.W. Tidal residual intertidal mudflat (TRIM) model and its applications to San Francisco Bay, California. *Estuar. Coast. Shelf Sci.* **1993**, *36*, 235–280. [CrossRef]

6. Cerco, C.F.; Cole, T. *Three-Dimensional Eutrophication Model of Chesapeake Bay, Volume I: Main Report*; EL-94.4; U.S. Army Corps of Engineers Waterway Experiment Station: Vicksburg, MS, USA, 1994.

7. Wool, T.A.; Ambrose, R.B.; Martin, J.L.; Comer, E.A. *Water Quality Analysis Simulation Program (WASP)*; version 6.0; Draft User's Manual; United States Environmental Protection Agency: Atlanta, GA, USA, 2001.

8. Wan, Y.; Ji, Z.; Shen, J.; Hu, G.; Sun, D. Three dimensional modeling of a shallow subtropical estuary. *Mar. Environ. Res.* **2012**, *82*, 76–86. [CrossRef] [PubMed]

9. Testa, J.M.; Kemp, W.M.; Boynton, W.R.; Hagy, J.D. Longterm changes in water quality and productivity in the Patuxent River estuary: 1985 to 2003. *Estuar. Coasts* **2008**, *31*, 1021–1037. [CrossRef]

10. Chen, C.; Liu, H.; Beardsley, R.C. An unstructured, finite-volume, three-dimensional, primitive equation ocean model: Application to coastal ocean and estuaries. *J. Atmos. Ocean. Technol.* **2003**, *20*, 159–186. [CrossRef]

11. Cerco, C.F.; Kim, S.; Nole, M.R. *The 2010 Chesapeake Bay Eutrophication Model*; A Report to the US Environmental Protection Agency Chesapeake Bay Program and to the US Army Engineer Baltimore District; US Army Engineer Research and Development Center: Vicksburg, MS, USA, 2010.

12. Pritchard, D.W. The dynamic structure of a coastal plain estuary. *J. Mar. Res.* **1956**, *15*, 33–42.

13. Kuo, A.Y.; Neilson, B.J. Hypoxia and salinity in Virginia estuaries. *Estuaries* **1987**, *10*, 277. [CrossRef]

14. Hamrick, J.M. *A Three-Dimensional Environmental Fluid Dynamics Code: Theoretical and Computational Aspects*; VIMS SRAMSOE #317; College of William and Mary, Virginia Institute of Marine Science: Gloucester Point, VA, USA, 1992; p. 63.

15. Park, K.; Kuo, A.Y.; Shen, J.; Hamrick, J.M. *A Three-Dimensional Hydrodynamic Eutrophication Model (HEM-3D): Description of Water Quality and Sediment Process Submodels*; Special Report in Applied Marine Science and Ocean Engineering No. 327; Virginia Institute of Marine Science: Gloucester Point, VA, USA, 1995; p. 102.

16. Mellor, G.L.; Yamada, T. Development of a turbulence closure model for geophysical fluid problems. *Rev. Geophys. Space Phys.* **1982**, *20*, 851–875. [CrossRef]

17. Galperin, B.; Kantha, L.H.; Hassis, S.; Rosati, A. A quasi-equilibrium turbulent energy model for geophysical flows. *J. Atmos. Sci.* **1988**, *45*, 55–62. [CrossRef]

18. Shen, J; Lin, J. Modeling study of the influences of tide and stratification on age of water in the tidal James River. *Estuar. Coast. Shelf Sci.* **2006**, *68*, 101–112. [CrossRef]

19. Chesapeake Environmental Communications (CEC). Modeling Support for the James River Chlorophyll Study: Modeling Report, prepared by CRC, HDR, Tetra Tech, and Virginia Institute of Marine Science for Virginia Department of Environmental Quality: Richmond, VA, USA, February 29, 2015.

20. Cerco, C.; Noel, M. *The 2002 Chesapeake Bay Eutrophication Model*; EPA 903-R-04-004; US Army Engineer Research and Development Center: Vicksburg, MS, USA, 2004.

21. Du, J.; Shen, J. Decoupling the influence of biological and physical processes on the dissolved oxygen in the Chesapeake Bay. *J. Geophys. Res. Oceans* **2015**, *120*, 78–93. [CrossRef]

22. Hong, B.; Shen, J. Linking dynamics of transport timescale and variation of hypoxia in the Chesapeake Bay. *J. Geophys. Res.* **2013**, *118*, 6017–6029. [CrossRef]

23. Delhez, E.J.M.; Campin, J.M.; Hirst, A.C.; Deleersnijder, E. Toward a general theory of the age in ocean modeling. *Ocean Model.* **1999**, *1*, 17–27. [CrossRef]
24. Deleersnijder, E.; Campin, J.M.; Delhez, E.J.M. The concept of age in marine modeling: I. Theory and preliminary model results. *J. Mar. Syst.* **2001**, *28*, 229–267. [CrossRef]
25. Wilmott, C.J. On the validation of models. *Phys. Geogr.* **1981**, *2*, 184–194.
26. Taylor, K.E. Summarizing multiple aspects of model performance in a single diagram. *J. Geophys. Res.* **2001**, *106*, 7183–7192. [CrossRef]
27. Nixon, S.W.; Ammerman, J.W.; Atkinson, L.P.; Berounsky, V.M.; Billen, G.; Boicourt, W.C.; Boynton, W.R.; Church, T.M.; Ditoro, D.M.; Elmgren, R.; et al. The fate of nitrogen and phosphorus at the land-sea margin of the North Atlantic Ocean. *Biogeochemistry* **1996**, *35*, 141–180. [CrossRef]
28. Lucas, L.V.; Thompson, J.K.; Brown, L.R. Why are diverse relationships observed between phytoplankton biomass and transport time. *Limnol. Oceanogr.* **2009**, *54*, 381–390. [CrossRef]
29. Peierls, B.L.; Hall, N.S.; Paerl, H.W. Non-monotonic responses of phytoplankton biomass accumulation to hydrologic variability: A comparison of two coastal plain North Carolina estuaries. *Estuar. Coasts* **2012**, *35*, 1376–1392. [CrossRef]
30. Scully, M.E. Wind modulation of dissolved oxygen in Chesapeake Bay. *Estuar. Coasts* **2010**, *33*, 1164–1175. [CrossRef]
31. Shen, J.; Hong, B.; Kuo, A.Y. Using timescales to interpret dissolved oxygen distributions in the bottom waters of Chesapeake Bay. *Limnol. Oceanogr.* **2013**, *28*, 2237–2248. [CrossRef]

Journal of
Marine Science and Engineering

Article

Effect of Coastal Erosion on Storm Surge: A Case Study in the Southern Coast of Rhode Island

Alex Shaw [1], Mohammad Reza Hashemi [1,*], Malcolm Spaulding [1], Bryan Oakley [2] and Chris Baxter [1]

[1] Department of Ocean Engineering, University of Rhode Island, Narragansett, RI 02882, USA; alex_shaw@my.uri.edu (A.S.); spaulding@egr.uri.edu (M.S.); baxter@egr.uri.edu (C.B.)

[2] Environmental Earth Science Department, Eastern Connecticut State University, Willimantic, CT 06226, USA; oakleyb@easternct.edu

* Correspondence: reza_hashemi@uri.edu; Tel.: +1-401-8746217

Academic Editor: Richard P. Signell

Received: 26 July 2016; Accepted: 22 November 2016; Published: 7 December 2016

Abstract: The objective of this study was to assess the effect of shoreline retreat and dune erosion on coastal flooding in a case study located in the southern coast of Rhode Island, USA. Using an extensive dataset collected during 2011, an ADCIRC model was developed to simulate the propagation of storm surge in the coastal areas, including coastal inlets and ponds. A simplified methodology, based on the geological assessment of historical trends of the shoreline retreat and dune erosion in this area, was incorporated in the model to represent coastal erosion. The results showed that for extreme storms (e.g., a 100-year event), where coastal dunes are overtopped and low-lying areas are flooded, the flooding extent is not significantly sensitive to coastal erosion. However, failure of the dunes leads to a significant increase of the flooding extent for smaller storms. Substantial dampening of the storm surge elevation in coastal ponds for moderate and small storms was associated with coastal inlets connecting to coastal ponds which are often not resolved in regional surge models. The shoreline change did not significantly affect the extent of flooding. It was also shown that the accuracy of a storm surge model highly depends on its ability to resolve coastal inlets, which is critical for reliable storm surge predictions in areas with inlet-basin systems.

Keywords: dune erosion; coastal ponds; storm surge; coastal flooding

1. Introduction

The northeast of the US, including the coastal regions of Rhode Island, have been impacted by hurricanes in the past, most recently Hurricane Sandy in 2012. Climate change is expected to change the strength and frequency of these events, putting more coastal areas at risk [1]. Further, it is estimated that sea level will rise between 0.2 and 2 m by 2100 in the northeast of the US, which also magnifies the impacts of coastal flooding [2]. As coastal flooding is sensitive to changes in bathymetry and topography of a region, coastal erosion can potentially affect the storm surge propagation. Storm surge and coastal erosion interact in two ways: (1) storm surges (and wave forces) lead to coastal erosion; (2) coastal erosion affects the propagation of storm surge and consequently alters the extent of flooding. While it is possible to examine the two-way interaction processes using morphodynamic models (e.g., [3,4]), which incorporate sediment transport and bed level changes, validating morphodynamic models is very challenging, and developing those models is costly. Alternatively, assuming worst case scenarios (complete dune erosion, shoreline retreat at specified rate, etc.) is an alternative method which allows understanding the effect of coastal erosion on flooding for extreme scenarios (e.g., [5]).

Our case study is located in the southern coast of Rhode Island (Figure 1), which consists of several coastal ponds and barriers. The shorelines are retreating at a rapid rate, in some areas up to

1.15 m per year [6]. The coastal dunes are also eroded during major storm events (Figure 2). The failure of dunes can affect the dynamics of the inlet-basin/pond system.

Figure 1. Overview of the the study area in the southern coast of Rhode Island. Other details include save points (blue crosses) from the North Atlantic Coast Comprehensive Study (NACCS) (see Section 2), Woods Hole Group Inc. water level gauge locations (orange dots), and a red box around the study area. Transects in the dark blue area were used to apply erosion scenarios (Figure 8).

Figure 2. Failure of dunes protecting Ninigret Pond after Hurricane Carol (1954); source: Rhode Island (RI) Coastal Resources Management Council.

The objective of this study is to investigate the effects of dune erosion and shoreline retreat (together and separately) on storm surge. The study was carried out using numerical modeling, and analysis of the field data.

Section 2 describes several sources of data (observed/hindcast) which have been used in this study; in particular, the hydrodynamic data, which have been collected during 2011, and other relevant storm surge modeling studies in the region are presented. Section 3 explains the simplified methodology which has been used to simulate shoreline retreat and dune erosion. Details of the ADCIRC (ADvanced CIRCulation) model of the study area are provided in Section 4. Several scenarios of coastal erosion and storm surge are discussed in Section 5. Discussions and summary of the results are presented at the end.

2. Data

From July 2010 to September 2011, Woods Hole Group carried out an extensive data collection program [7], for the US Army Corp of Engineers (USACE) New England District, entitled "Wave, Tide and Current Data Collection, Washington County, Rhode Island". The primary purpose of that work was to collect site-specific data to support a RI Regional Sediment Management Study, and included a collection of water elevation, currents, wave, and meteorological data. Their study included measurement of water elevations inside coastal ponds (Figure 1), as well as waves and currents offshore. This data provided a unique source for understanding the effect of inlet-pond systems on water elevation in this area. Hurricane Irene, which impacted this area during the observation period, was also used for model validation.

For simulation of synthetic storms (i.e., 100-year event), the North Atlantic Coast Comprehensive Study (NACCS; [8,9]) was used. NACCS is based on a system of numerical models including ADCIRC [10], WAve Model (WAM), and STeady state spectral WAVE model (STWAVE) [11]. It has simulated hydrodynamic and wave fields of 1050 synthetic tropical storms as well as 100 extratropical historical storms over the Atlantic Coast. The model was based on a relatively high resolution unstructured mesh (30 m–50 m near the coast). The synthetic storms were generated based on the statistical analysis of past storms. The NACCS provides model results at the save points (Figure 1), including time series of the wind, wave and water levels for the events and return period analyses for the tropical storms. These data were used to force the model at the boundary for a synthetic storm representing a 100-year event. It should be added that some of the save points of the NACCS are located inside the coastal ponds which may be inaccurate, as will be discussed later. For the 100-year event, all synthetic storms simulated in NACCS were examined, and a storm surge event which generated the water levels of around 100-year storm surge at Newport (8452660) and Providence (8454000) National Oceanic and Atmospheric Adminstration (NOAA) water level stations was selected. This storm had a maximum surge of 3.20 m (Mean Sea Level (MSL)) at Newport (Figure 3), which is close to 3.35 m (MSL) or 2.7 m (Mean Higher High Water (MHHW)) for the 100-year event, considering the 100-year event at the upper 95% confidence level.

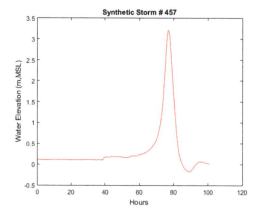

Figure 3. The time series of storm surge for synthetic storm 457—from NACCS—which approximately produces 100-year storm surge (at the upper 95% confidence level) near the Newport NOAA water level station.

Since coastal erosion occurs during major storms, several hurricanes were considered in this study. For validation, Hurricane Irene (late August 2011) was selected as observed data was available during this hurricane in several locations inside the model domain. A larger storm event, Hurricane Bob, a strong tropical storm which occurred on 19 August 1991 was chosen. Hurricane Bob provides a good representation of large storms in the area, but it was not large enough to overtop the barriers. Also, two synthetic storms from NACCS including a storm representing the 100-year event (which is important for planning purposes) were simulated.

For the surge model, both bathymetry and topography of the domain (a digital elevation model: DEM) were necessary due to wetting and drying. A DEM with a resolution of 10 m was used based on the National Geography Data Center (NGDC) Bathymetry Data and the USACE 2010 coastal Light imaging, Detection, And Ranging (LiDAR) survey. The LiDAR survey focused on the south coast and extended about 1 km offshore (Figure 4).

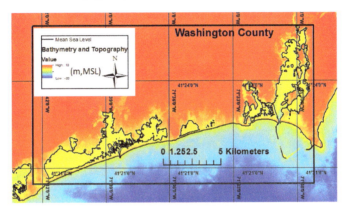

Figure 4. The Digital Elevation Model (DEM) around the study area.

Wind data (for forcing the ADCIRC model) were extracted from the USACE Wave Information Study (WIS) hindcasts near the domain. The WIS data covers a period from 1980 to 2012. For this study, the wind fields from large storm events were of interest. It should be mentioned, as the model domain covered just the southern coast of RI, the spatial variability of wind was considered negligible in this small area. For this 30-year period, Hurricane Bob which made land fall in RI on 19 August 1991, was chosen. Hurricane Bob gives a good representation of large storms in the area [9]. It is the fifth largest storm recorded at the NOAA tide gauge at Newport RI, and approximately corresponds to a 20-year event, according to the extremal analysis for the site (Figure 5). The Newport water elevation station is the closest station to the study area (71.33 W, 41.51 N) and has a long record including major hurricanes. The wind field for Hurricane Bob extracted from WIS is plotted in Figure 6.

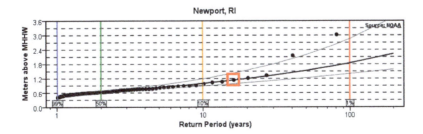

Figure 5. Extremal analysis of water elevation (MHHW = MSL + 0.65) for Newport NOAA station (8452660); the red box shows Hurricane Bob.

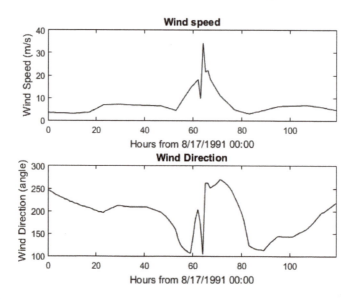

Figure 6. Plots of the wind speed and direction for Hurricane Bob at WIS station number 63079, which is located near the region (71.22 W, 41.25 N).

3. Coastal Erosion Scenarios

Coastal erosion scenarios were based on shoreline retreat and dune erosion during large storm events. The past shoreline retreat rates were used to estimate erosion rates for erosion scenarios, and the DEM was changed according to these rates. It should be mentioned that the rate of erosion is expected to rise due to Sea Level Rise (SLR); nevertheless, this assumption was made to simplify the analysis. Further research is necessary to include the effect of SLR on the rate of erosion. The shoreline retreat rates were calculated using aerial photographs from 1939 to 2014 (Figure 7; [6]). It should be added that shorelines retreat in severe storms and recover during fair weather; however, there is a consistent trend of shoreline retreat over past decades in this region.

Figure 7. A sample shoreline change map for a beach in the study area [6].

The projected shoreline retreat over the next 25 years was considered. The shoreline was divided into the cross-shore profiles shown in Figure 8. In the selected area, the beach profiles consist of an offshore beach slope, a near shore beach slope, and a dune system. The offshore beach slope was extended horizontally to the corresponding 25 years erosion (Figure 9). The same near shore profile and dune system was then assumed at the end of each profile. This method retreats the shoreline while keeping the same beach profile geometry. Once the transects were modified, they were linearly interpolated to modify the DEM of the model.

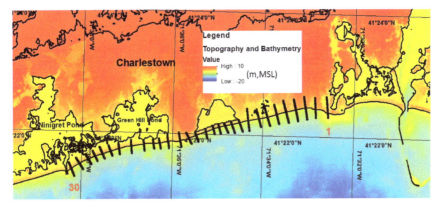

Figure 8. Crossshore transects made to implement coastal erosion between Charlestown Beach and Matunuck Beach (Numbered 1–30).

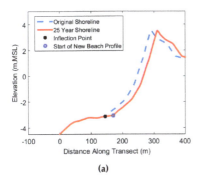 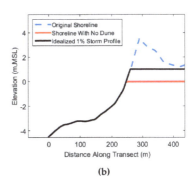

(a)   (b)

Figure 9. The simplified method which was used to estimate the shoreline geometry after erosion in future. Transect 30 (as an example; Figure 8), with the original shoreline (blue), 25-year shoreline (red), and intersection point (star) are shown. The vertical axis is exaggerated for better clarity. (**a**) shoreline geometry after erosion; (**b**) erosion of the dunes.

Coastal erosion during large storms can lead to failure of dunes as well as retreat of the shoreline. During storm events, the combined action of storm surge and waves erode the dune and create surge channels and wash-over fans (Figure 2). To implement dune erosion in the DEM, it was assumed that the dunes were eroded or simply cut off at an elevation Mean High Water (MHW) with a horizontal line (Figure 9). The elevation of the post storm profile was determined by examining the washover fans deposited after past hurricanes in this area, including 1938 Hurricane, the Ash Wednesday storm (1962), and Hurricane Sandy. The elevations of the washover fans were estimated using LiDAR; the slope of 0.003 cm/m was measured for washover fans after Hurricane Sandy, which can be assumed horizontal for the model resolution used in this study.

4. Numerical Modeling

For surge modeling, the ADCIRC model was used. ADCIRC is based on the finite element method and unstructured mesh discretization, allowing areas such as coastal inlets to be resolved with a reasonable computational cost. ADCIRC has been coupled with Simulating WAves Nearshore (SWAN), and can simulate the wave-surge interactions [12]. This model has been extensively used to predict storm surge flooding (e.g., [10,13]).

A mesh was created, resolving coastal inlets, using the Surface water Modeling System Software (SMS) with a resolution of 30 m near the coastline, 150 m farther offshore, and 2 km near the open boundaries. The mesh is plotted in Figure 10. The model was forced along the open boundaries by water elevation, and by wind stress/pressure over the domain. The model was run in the 2-D mode, with a Manning friction coefficient of 0.018 (below MSL), and up to 0.06 in land areas. For the tidal case, the model was forced using five harmonic constituents for tides including M2, N2, K1, S2, and O1 which can be extracted from tidal databases [14]. M4 and other overtide constituents were neglected. M4 is generated in shallower regions by friction, and causes tidal asymmetry. Neglecting the M4 component can change the water level by around 6 cm, which can be neglected during a major storm surge event. These constituents represent the main components of tide for this area (Table 1).

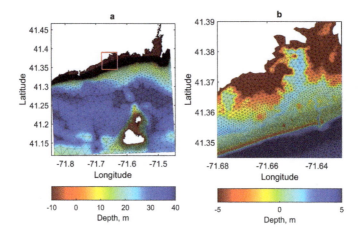

Figure 10. An overview of the mesh used for surge modeling in the southern coast of RI. The model domain is larger than the study area and includes Block Island near the southern boundary. Subfigure (**b**) shows a magnified view of the rectangular area in Subfigure (**a**) around Ninigret Pond.

Table 1. Harmonic constituents at the Newport and Providence NOAA water elevation stations.

Harmonics	Newport Amplitude (m)	Newport Phase (degrees)	Providence Amplitude (m)	Providence Phase (degrees)
M2	0.505	2.3	0.643	9.5
S2	0.108	25.0	0.138	33.6
N2	0.124	345.8	0.152	354.6
K1	0.062	166.1	0.073	169.4
M4	0.057	35.8	0.103	202.2
O1	0.047	202.0	0.027	312.7
M6	0.0005	220.1	0.027	312.7
MK3	0.0008	19.5	0.016	39.3
S4	0.0007	5.1	0.014	23.8
MN4	0.026	347.9	0.014	12.7

5. Results

5.1. Model Skill Assessment

To test the performance of the model for tides and storm surge, the Woods Hole Group Inc. data were used [7]. The observed data were compared with the model results during a spring-neap cycle (for tides), and during Hurricane Irene (for storm surge). For tides, the model was run for 30 days from 14 May 2011 until 13 June 2011 with a one day ramping period. This time period is within the duration of the Woods Hole Group data collection campaign. The model and observed water elevation data were analysed by T_Tide code to compute tidal constituents [15]. Table 2 shows the comparison between the modeled results and the observed data at the two stations inside Ninigred Pond. As this table shows, the modeled and observed data, in general, are in good agreement. In particular, the performance of the model for the phase and amplitude of the dominant M2 component is good. The model underpredicts the amplitude of S2, but as this component is very small, its effect is not that significant inside the pond. The overall RMSEs (Root Mean Square Error) for amplitude and phase are 0.015 m and 25°, respectively, which are convincing.

Table 2. Skill assessment of the numerical model for tidal predictions inside Ninigret Pond; see Figure 1 for location of the stations. RMSE for amplitude and phase are 0.015 m and 25°, respectively.

	NW				NN			
	Model		Observation		Model		Observation	
Constituents	amp (m)	Phase (deg)	amp (m)	Phase (deg)	amp (m)	Phase (deg)	amp (m)	Phase (deg)
O1	0.022	277	0.018	283	0.022	271	0.017	277
K1	0.024	217	0.019	223	0.024	210	0.019	216
N2	0.021	48	0.017	71	0.020	34	0.017	56
M2	0.083	82	0.081	89	0.075	69	0.077	75
S2	0.008	114	0.021	106	0.007	98	0.021	101

For the storm surge case, Hurricane Irene was simulated, a category 3 storm that occurred in late August 2011. The comparison of the model results and observations are depicted in Figure 11. The performance of the model for both stations is very good with an RMSE of 0.065 m and 0.041 m for NN and NW respectively; however, the model slightly overestimates the surge. Overall, given the magnitude of errors, the performance of the model was considered satisfactory.

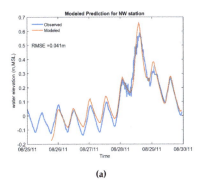

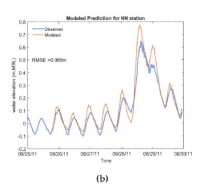

(a)   (b)

Figure 11. Comparison between the model predictions and the observed data for Hurricane Irene (see Figure 1 for location of the stations). (**a**) NW station; (**b**) NN station.

5.2. Propagation of Tides/Storm Surge in Coastal Ponds; Effect of Coastal Inlets

As mentioned previously, the southern coast of RI consists of several coastal ponds and barriers, and the failure of dunes can affect the inlet-basin/pond system. At first, a simplified analysis was carried out based on the previous research about the dynamics of inlet-basins, and the collected data in this area. This analysis helped interpret modeling results. Figure 12 shows the comparison of water elevation inside and outside Ninigret Pond using observed data for a duration of one month. A dramatic reduction of the amplitude can be observed in this figure. A coastal inlet, in general, causes a reduction of water elevation amplitude and a phase-lag or a delay inside coastal ponds relative to offshore. This is mainly associated with the energy dissipation by high velocity currents in an inlet. Simplified analytical methods have been introduced in the literature to compute the reduction of the amplitude, and the phase lag, based on the geometry and physical characteristics of the inlet-basin system. A detailed analytical analysis of inlet-basin hydrodynamics can be found in the Coastal Engineering Manual [16]. Considering a long wave (e.g., tide or surge), with an amplitude of a_o, and a period of T, the effect of a coastal inlet on tide/surge signal as it propagates from the ocean to the pond can be written as,

$$[R, \phi_l] = f(A_i/A_b, R_h, L, T, \mathbf{F}); \quad R = 1 - a_i/a_o \tag{1}$$

where R is the reduction in the amplitude, a_i is the amplitude inside the basin/pond, ϕ_l is the phase lag, A_i is the cross sectional area of the inlet, A_b is the area of a basin or a pond, R_h is the hydraulic radius of the inlet, L is the length of the inlet, and $\mathbf{F}$ represents the frictional coefficients for the entrance, exit and channel friction losses. For Ninigret Pond, $A_b = 7.5$ km², $A_i = 45$ m², $L = 1.7$ km, $R_h = 1.5$ m. Using these parameters, and assuming entrance, and exit loss coefficients of 0.1 and 1.0, respectively (recommended by the Coastal Engineering Manual [16]), leads to $R = 80\%$ and $\phi_l = 90°$. The impact of inlets on tidal signal was also assessed using observed data. By performing a tidal analysis using T_Tide [15] inside (Wood Holes Group Station) and outside this pond (NOAA, Weekapaug Point 71.76 W, 41.33 N), R for the M2 tidal component was found to be 76% for the NW station (Figure 1), with phase lags of 90.5° or about 3 h and 6 min. These values which are based on the observations are very close to the analytical method predictions (i.e., $R = 80\%$ and $\phi_l = 90°$). Considering that some storm surge events have similar (or longer) periods, if coastal barriers for this pond fail, this reduction of the amplitude no longer exist. Consequently, dune erosion can lead to a significant increase in the flooding area.

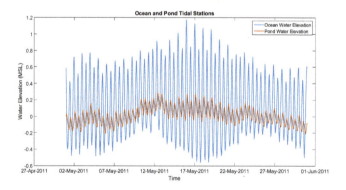

Figure 12. Comparison of observed water elevation data inside and outside Ninigret Pond (NW Gauge, Figure 1).

Further, the geometry of a coastal inlet has a controlling effect on the reduction of the amplitude of water elevation signal. Considering the three coastal ponds in this area (Figure 1; Ninigret Pond, Trustom Pond, and Point Judith Pond), the effect of coastal inlet geometry can be further examined. Point Judith Pond has a wide and deep inlet with a width of 80 m and a depth of around 7 m. Trustom Pond, on the contrary, has no permanent connection to the ocean for tides, but during large storm events, part of its barrier is overtopped or breached (for example in Hurricane Sandy) causing some flooding. Ninigret Pond has a relatively narrow inlet (35 m), protected by hard structures. The water elevations in the three ponds are plotted for a tidal cycle, and for a storm event (Hurricane Bob) in Figure 13 using the ADCIRC model. As this figure shows, the water elevation signal for tide inside and outside of the Point Judith Pond is almost the same due to its wide inlet, but the peak of storm surge slightly attenuates during the storm event. For Trustom Pond, the barrier is not overtopped for tides or the storm surge scenario. Ninigret Pond shows a significant reduction for tides ($R = 80\%$) and for Hurricane Bob ($R = 68\%$) due to its narrower inlet. Therefore, if a storm surge does not overtop or erode coastal dunes, coastal inlets can significantly decrease the magnitude of a storm surge (inside a coastal pond).

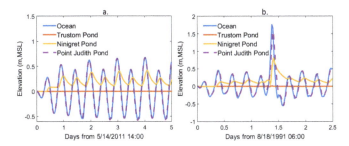

Figure 13. Effect of coastal inlet geometry on surge inside three coastal ponds in the study area; comparison of water elevation in Ninigret Pond, Trustom Pond, and Point Judith Pond for (**a**) Tides; (**b**) Hurricane Bob.

The above analysis shows a significant dampening of tide and surge signal caused by coastal inlets. However, the frequency/period of a water elevation signal and the geometry of an inlet are the two important factors which control this dampening [17–19]. Figure 14 shows the reduction of amplitudes of various water elevation signals assuming different periods for Ninigret Pond. The analysis was performed using the simplified analytical method mentioned earlier [16]. As this figure shows, frequencies of 1, 2, and 2.5 days lead to 0.65, 0.38, and 0.25 reductions, respectively. Therefore, a storm surge which has a long period (more than 2 days) will be less effected compared to a tidal signal with a period of 12 h. It should be added that the total water level during a storm surge is due to the combination of tide and surge signals. In addition, the geometry of an inlet, as discussed above, is another important factor, which should be always considered before generalizing these results.

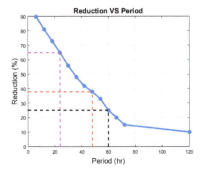

Figure 14. Effect of water elevation signal period on reduction of the amplitude for Ninigret Pond.

5.3. Effect of Erosion on Storm Surge

Two erosion scenarios were considered: shoreline change in 25 years, and dune erosion. As mentioned, the erosion of dunes is a common consequence of large hurricanes in the study area as can be seen in Figure 2, which shows the partial failure of the dune system of Ninigret Pond during Hurricane Carol in 1954. Several scenarios considering the two storm cases (100-year synthetic storm and Hurricane Bob) were considered.

For Hurricane Bob, the flooding areas assuming eroded (retreated) shoreline and the current shoreline were examined. Table 3 shows the summary of results. Considering a retreated shoreline in 25 years, the flooding extent slightly increases by 0.22 km^2, which is 20% of the original flooded area (1.12 km^2). This increased flooding area is approximately the advance of the sea (about 30 m) due to coastal erosion; therefore, the shoreline retreat does not significantly increase the extent of flooding. However, when the dunes are eroded, the flooding extent increased by 2.33 km^2, which is a 207% increase. When dunes erode, the coastal inlets of the ponds can no longer dampen the surge signal, and therefore a much larger area within coastal ponds are flooded. For this scenario, the flooding extent advanced up to 500 m in some areas. Figure 15 shows the flooding extent for existing dunes, and eroded dune profile scenarios.

Table 3. Differences in flooded areas near the eroded shoreline for Hurricane Bob assuming erosion scenarios.

Erosion Scenario	Current Flooded Area, km^2	Changed Flooded Area, km^2	Difference, km^2	Percentage Increase
Shoreline retreat in 25 years	1.13	1.35	0.22	19.7%
Eroded dunes	1.13	3.5	2.33	207%

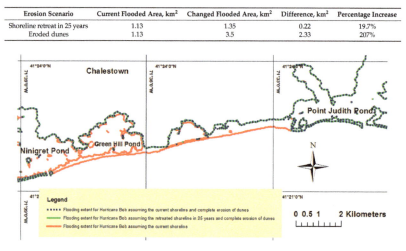

Figure 15. Comparison of Hurricane Bob flooding extent assuming current condition (red) and current shoreline with no dune system (blue), and the 25-year retreated shoreline as well as complete dune failure (black).

For the 100-year event, the erosion scenarios (shoreline retreat and dune erosion) did not lead to a significant change in flooded areas as shown in Figure 16. This is because for this event, the storm surge is large enough to overtop the dunes (the dune top elevation is about 3 m, MSL in this area); therefore, even if the dunes were solid structures and could resist the erosion during storm surge, they could not protect the coastal ponds. It should be noted that the failure of dunes may significantly affect wave propagation for the 100-year event (waves can break over dunes, due to decreased water depth).

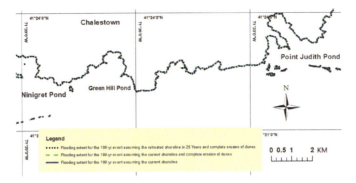

Figure 16. Comparison of 100-year flooding extent assuming the current shoreline (blue), current shoreline with eroded dune system (green), and the 25-year retreated shoreline plus complete dune failure (black). Lines overlap for this scenario.

SLR, in general, leads to an increase of the flooding extent [20]. A very simple way of investigating the impact of SLR on flooding is the bathtub approach or adding the magnitude of SLR to elevations predicted by a storm surge model; this methods neglects the nonlinearity of the storm surge propagation. A more accurate method includes changing the DEM, and simulating the storm surge assuming a SLR scenario. Consistent to our analysis which assumed a 25 years shoreline retreat, 30 cm or 1 foot SLR was assumed, corresponding to projected values by NOAA (High) for 25 years [21]. Figure 17 shows that the extent of flooding, as expected, increases in some areas. The flooding area increased from 4.72 km^2 to 6.80 km^2, leading to a 44% increase.

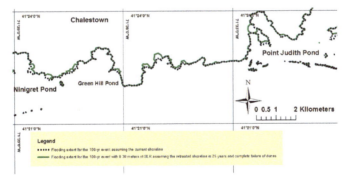

Figure 17. Comparison of flooding extend of the 100-year storm event, assuming 30 cm SLR, and coastal erosion.

6. Discussion

The geometry of coastal inlets controls the storm propagation for moderate storms in areas with inlet-basin systems. Some regional modeling studies such as NACCS have not resolved these inlets, and their predictions inside coastal ponds may not be reliable beyond barriers and inside ponds. Figure 18 is an example showing the poor resolution of the NACCS mesh around Ninigret Pond inlet. In Figure 19, the prediction of storm surge for a moderate synthetic storm (220, which has a peak elevation of 1.67 m, MSL in Newport [8]), near two save points (see Figure 18b) located inside and outside Ninigret Pond, has been compared with that from our model. The surge event was channeled through the inlet, but given the poor resolution of the NACCS model, water levels are overestimated. It should be noted that NACCS results, unlike the ADCIRC model developed in this study, have not been validated inside coastal ponds and very near shore in RI. Also, waves for this storm are not that significant inside the pond; therefore, wave-surge interaction cannot be associated with higher storm prediction in the NACCS model. The results are identical at the boundary (Point A), as the ADCIRC model was forced by NACCS at the open boundary.

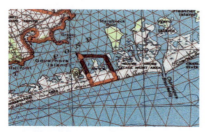

(a) NACCS model resolution around Ninigret inlet

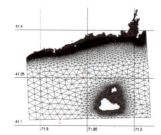

(b) Comparison points: A, B, and C

Figure 18. Effect of model resolution on the results; Subfigure (**a**) shows an example of low resolution NACCS mesh in a coastal inlet; Subfigure (**b**) shows the locations of comparison for NACCS results and those obtained in this study.

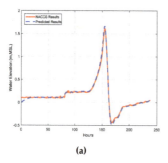

(a)

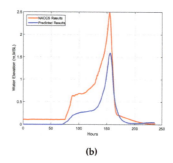

(b)

Figure 19. Comparison of NACCS results and ADCIRC model of this study for synthetic Storm 220. See Figure 18b for locations of comparison. (**a**) Comparison at B: outside Ninigret Pond; (**b**) Comparison at C: inside Ninigret pond.

The dunes along the entire southern coast of RI have an average height of 3.39 m above MSL, but in some areas they are as low as 1.1 m. This means that a storm with a magnitude of 100-year (3.35 m, (MSL) considering the 100-year event at the upper confidence level curve) can potentially overtop all of the dunes. A hurricane such as Carol, which had a surge height of 2.7 m, MSL at Newport RI can breach the dunes (Figure 2), and have a similar but lesser effect on flooding (increasing the flooding extent). Various factors are associated with the erosion of dunes [22], including the geotechnical properties of dunes, the elevation of dunes compared to surge, wave-induced forces, and wave runup/overtopping. Therefore, it is a challenging task to specify a threshold for a storm which leads to dune failure. Morphological modeling (e.g., [4]) along with data collection during and after large storms around coastal dunes can improve our understanding of this process for this area, for future studies.

The analysis carried out in this study was based on two extreme scenarios: complete dune erosion, and no dune erosion. In reality, dunes are partially eroded during major storms (Figure 2), and gradually recover during calmer months. Therefore, a storm cluster can lead to more damage compared with isolated events. The effect of erosion on storm surge is overestimated by assuming complete erosion of dunes. However, the results show the significant impact of dune erosion on flooding, and quantify this impact for this extreme scenario.

7. Conclusions

We explored the effect of dune erosion and shoreline retreat on coastal flooding in an area which consists of coastal ponds protected by dunes and connected to the ocean by narrow inlets. A storm surge model was developed/validated with a unique dataset, which included water elevation data inside coastal ponds during 2011 and measurements during Hurricane Irene. The conclusions are summarized as follows:

1. The results showed that erosion of dunes has more effect on flooding extent compared with retreat of shorelines.
2. For storms which do not overtop or erode the coastal dunes, the inlets of coastal ponds can significantly decrease the storm surge elevation. This can be explained using the concepts of inlet-basin hydrodynamics. However, for very extreme storms such as a 100-year event where coastal dunes are overtopped, and low-lying areas are flooded, the flooding extent did not significantly change.
3. Assuming complete erosion of the dunes and for the scenario of Hurricane Bob, simulations showed a more than 200% increase in the flooding extent. Several sources of uncertainty can affect these estimations. For instance, in many cases, dunes are partially eroded. Coupled hydrodynamic and morphodynamic models which can simulate dunes erosion more accurately, can lead to more realistic estimations.
4. Numerical surge models which do not fully resolve coastal inlets (e.g., NACCS model in RI) lead to significant errors in the prediction of surge in coastal ponds. Accurate bathymetric and topographic measurement of coastal inlets is essential for storm surge modeling in areas with inlet-basin systems.

Acknowledgments: This work was under taken with funding support from a Rhode Island Community Development Block Grant (4712) from the U.S. Department of Housing and Urban Development and the State of Rhode Island Division of Planning Office of Housing and Community Development. Thanks to US Army Corps of Engineers (USACE) for sharing the North Atlantic Coastal Comprehensive Studies' dataset. Thanks to National Hurricane Center (NHC) and Center for Operational Oceanographic Products and Services from NOAA for supplying hurricane and water level data. Thanks to Woods Hole Group Inc. for providing the water elevation data. Thanks to Marissa Torres for her comments on the paper.

Author Contributions: Alex Shaw developed the numerical models, and analysed the results. Mohammad Reza Hashemi initiated and led the research, and helped in discussion of the results. Malcolm Spaulding advised the research in many aspects, including analysis of the results and development of the models. Bryan Oakley contributed in coastal erosion and general discussions. Chris Baxter helped in the discussion of the results.

Conflicts of Interest: The authors declare no conflict of interest.

References

1. Wahl, T.; Jain, S.; Bender, J.; Meyers, S.D.; Luther, M.E. Increasing risk of compound flooding from storm surge and rainfall for major US cities. *Nat. Clim. Chang.* **2015**, *5*, 1093–1097.
2. Parris, A.; Bromirski, P.; Burkett, V.; Cayan, D.R.; Culver, M.; Hall, J.; Horton, R.; Knuuti, K.; Moss, R.; Obeysekera, J.; et al. *Global Sea Level Rise Scenarios for the United States National Climate Assessment;* NOAA Technical Report OAR CPO-1; NOAA: Silver Spring, MD, USA, 2012
3. Roelvink, D.; Reniers, A.; van Dongeren, A.; de Vries, J.V.T.; McCall, R.; Lescinski, J. Modelling storm impacts on beaches, dunes and barrier islands. *Coast. Eng.* **2009**, *56*, 1133–1152.
4. McCall, R.T.; de Vries, J.V.T.; Plant, N.; van Dongeren, A.; Roelvink, J.; Thompson, D.; Reniers, A. Two-dimensional time dependent hurricane overwash and erosion modeling at Santa Rosa Island. *Coast. Eng.* **2010**, *57*, 668–683.
5. Kurum, M.O.; Edge, B.; Mitasova, H.; Overton, M. Effects of coastal landform changes on storm surge along the Hatteras Island breach area. *Coast. Eng. Proc.* **2011**, *1*, 25.
6. Boothroyd, J.; Hollis, R.; Oakley, B.; Henderson, R. *Shoreline Change from 1939–2014, Washington County, Rhode Island. 1:2,000 scale, 45 maps;* Technical Report; Rhode Island Geological Survey: Kingston, RI, USA, 2016.

7. Woods Hole Group. *Wave Tide and Current Data Collection Contract No. W912WJ-09-D-0001-0026*; US Army Corps of Engineers: New England District, MA, USA, 2012.
8. Cialone, M.A.; Massey, T.C.; Anderson, M.E.; Grzegorzewski, A.S.; Jensen, R.E.; Cialone, A.; Mark, D.J.; Pevey, K.C.; Gunkel, B.L.; McAlpin, T.O. *North Atlantic Coast Comprehensive Study (NACCS) Coastal Storm Model Simulations: Waves and Water Levels*; Technical Report, DTIC Document; The U.S. Army Engineer Research and Development Center: Vicksburg, MS, USA, 2015.
9. Hashemi, M.R.; Spaulding, M.L.; Shaw, A.; Farhadi, H.; Lewis, M. An efficient artificial intelligence model for prediction of tropical storm surge. *Nat. Hazards* **2016**, *82*, 471–491.
10. Luettich, R., Jr.; Westerink, J.; Scheffner, N.W. *ADCIRC: An Advanced Three-Dimensional Circulation Model for Shelves, Coasts, and Estuaries*; Report 1. Theory and Methodology of ADCIRC-2DDI and ADCIRC-3DL. Technical Report, DTIC Document; US Army Corps of Engineers : Washington DC, USA, 1992.
11. Smith, J.M.; Sherlock, A.R.; Resio, D.T. *STWAVE: Steady-State Spectral Wave Model User's Manual for STWAVE*, version 3.0; Technical Report, DTIC Document; US Army Corps of Engineers: Washington DC, USA, 2001.
12. Dietrich, J.C.; Tanaka, S.; Westerink, J.J.; Dawson, C.; Luettich, R., Jr.; Zijlema, M.; Holthuijsen, L.H.; Smith, J.; Westerink, L.; Westerink, H. Performance of the unstructured-mesh, SWAN + ADCIRC model in computing hurricane waves and surge. *J. Sci. Comput.* **2012**, *52*, 468–497.
13. Westerink, J.J.; Luettich, R.A.; Feyen, J.C.; Atkinson, J.H.; Dawson, C.; Roberts, H.J.; Powell, M.D.; Dunion, J.P.; Kubatko, E.J.; Pourtaheri, H. A basin-to channel-scale unstructured grid hurricane storm surge model applied to southern Louisiana. *Mon. Weather Rev.* **2008**, *136*, 833–864.
14. Mukai, A.Y.; Westerink, J.J.; Luettich, R.A., Jr.; Mark, D. *Eastcoast 2001, a Tidal Constituent Database for Western North Atlantic, Gulf of Mexico, and Caribbean Sea*; Technical Report, DTIC Document; US Army Corps of Engineers: Washington DC, USA, 2002.
15. Pawlowicz, R.; Beardsley, B.; Lentz, S. Classical tidal harmonic analysis including error estimates in MATLAB using T_TIDE. *Comput. Geosci.* **2002**, *28*, 929–937.
16. US Army Corps of Engineers. *Hydrodynamics of Tidal Inlets*; EM 1110-2-1100 ed.; US Army Corps of Engineers: Washington DC, USA, 2008.
17. Wong, K.C.; DiLorenzo, J. The response of Delaware's inland bays to ocean forcing. *J. Geophys. Res. Oceans* **1988**, *93*, 12525–12535.
18. Chuang, W.S.; Swenson, E.M. Subtidal water level variations in Lake Pontchartrain, Louisiana. *J. Geophys. Res. Oceans* **1981**, *86*, 4198–4204.
19. Aretxabaleta, A.L.; Butman, B.; Ganju, N.K. Water level response in back-barrier bays unchanged following Hurricane Sandy. *Geophys. Res. Lett.* **2014**, *41*, 3163–3171.
20. Woodruff, J.D.; Irish, J.L.; Camargo, S.J. Coastal flooding by tropical cyclones and sea-level rise. *Nature* **2013**, *504*, 44–52.
21. Sweet, W.V. *Sea Level Rise and Nuisance Flood Frequency Changes around the United States*; NOAA Technical Report NOS CO-OPS 073; National National Oceanic and Atmospheric Administration: Silver Spring, MD, USA, 2014.
22. Judge, E.K.; Overton, M.F.; Fisher, J.S. Vulnerability indicators for coastal dunes. *J. Waterw. Port Coast. Ocean Eng.* **2003**, *129*, 270–278.

Article

Multi-Layered Stratification in the Baltic Sea: Insight from a Modeling Study with Reference to Environmental Conditions

Bijan Dargahi [1,3,*], Venkat Kolluru [2,*] and Vladimir Cvetkovic [3]

1   Division of Hydraulic Engineering, School of Civil and Architectural Engineering, KTH Royal Institute of
    Technology, 10044 Stockholm, Sweden
2   Environmental Resources Management, Inc., 75 Valley Stream Parkway, Suite 200, Malvern, PA 19355, USA
3   Division of Water Resource Engineering, School of Civil and Built Environment, KTH Royal Institute of
    Technology, 10044 Stockholm, Sweden; vdc@kth.se
*   Correspondence: bijan@kth.se (B.D.); venkat.kolluru@erm.com (V.K.); Tel.: +46-484-913-0393 (B.D.)

Academic Editor: Richard P. Signell
Received: 18 July 2016; Accepted: 7 December 2016; Published: 7 January 2017

Abstract: The hydrodynamic and transport characteristics of the Baltic Sea in the period 2000–2009 were studied using a fully calibrated and validated 3D hydrodynamic model with a horizontal resolution of 4.8 km. This study provided new insight into the type and dynamics of vertical structure in the Baltic Sea, not considered in previous studies. Thermal and salinity stratification are both addressed, with a focus on the structural properties of the layers. The detection of cooler regions (dicothermal) within the layer structure is an important finding. The detailed investigation of thermal stratification for a 10-year period (i.e., 2000–2009) revealed some new features. A multilayered structure that contains several thermocline and dicothermal layers was identified from this study. Statistical analysis of the simulation results made it possible to derive the mean thermal stratification properties, expressed as mean temperatures and the normalized layer thicknesses. The three-layered model proposed by previous investigators appears to be valid only during the winter periods; for other periods, a multi-layered structure with more than five layers has been identified during this investigation. This study provides detailed insight into thermal and salinity stratification in the Baltic Sea during a recent decade that can be used as a basis for diverse environmental assessments. It extends previous studies on stratification in the Baltic Sea regarding both the extent and the nature of stratification.

Keywords: Baltic Sea; hydrodynamics; modeling; vertical structure; stratification; dicothermal; GEMSS

---

1. Introduction

The Baltic Sea is a brackish sea located in northern Europe from 53° N to 66° N latitude and from 20° E to 26° E longitude. It is connected to the Atlantic Ocean via the Danish Straits. The Baltic Ice Lake was born 13,000 years ago and its present brackish state emerged 7000 years ago. For 2000 years, the salinity has been close to the present level (mean salinity: 7 parts per thousand). The Baltic Sea borders nine coastal countries with a total population of 85 million people (see Figure 1, [1]). The maximum length and width are 1600 km and 193 km, respectively. The surface area is 377,000 km², with an average depth of 55 m and a water volume of 20,000 km³. Its maximum depth is 459 m, which is located between Stockholm and the Island of Gotland. The Baltic Sea is a shallow sea that consists of a series of basins interconnected through narrow sills (Figure 2).

In spite of the Baltic Sea HELCOM agreement signed in 1974, the state of the Baltic Sea has worsened (http://www.helcom.fi). Nutrient levels in the water and sediments are high, and poor oxygen conditions and "dead bottoms" exist in large archipelago areas of both Sweden and Finland [2].

However, during the past few decades there have been considerable efforts towards better and more sustainable management of the Baltic Sea. Here, the hydrodynamics of the Baltic Sea, which has been the subject of intensive research since the 1930s, plays a major role. The number of available journal articles and other publications exceeds several hundred. The foci of these studies are exchange processes, especially salt transport from the North Sea, and water age. Some of the main contributors are Meier [3], and Lehman and Hinrichsen [4]. Here, the work of Omstedt et al. [5] should be mentioned as it presents the state of knowledge on various hydrodynamic features of the Baltic Sea. There are also several excellent books covering many different aspects, including Feistel et al. [6], Leppäranta and Myrberg [7], and Harff et al. [8]. For a general literature review, the interested reader is referred to the comprehensive review given by Dargahi and Cvetkovic [9].

Figure 1. The Baltic model region and the model open boundary location [1].

The present study concerns the hydrodynamics of the Baltic, with a focus on the details of stratification, which is the primary feature of the sea. The novel features of the work are the relatively long simulation period of 10 years and the use of a complete set of external boundary conditions with maximum spatial and temporal resolution, in combination with highly accurate bathymetry. The main objectives were to create an accurate and validated 3D hydrodynamic model for investigating specific stratification characteristics that have not been addressed in the previous studies. In the following paragraph we present a short summary of previous research works on stratification.

The Baltic Sea is highly stratified by strong vertical salinity and temperature gradients. The stratification is commonly referred to as a two-layer structure that consists of an upper and a lower layer. A transitional middle layer exists between the upper and lower layers, which are known as halocline and thermocline, respectively. There is a significant variation in the depth of the halocline, from 40 m to 80 m in deeper regions to 10 m–30 m in shallower regions [7]. The lower values are found in the Gulf of Riga (mean value = 25 m), and Arkona Basin, with a mean value of 25 m for both regions [10,11]. The surface salinity varies in the north with a mean value of 3 ppt (parts per thousand) to 8 ppt to the south, i.e., the Arkona Basin. The corresponding mean value at the lower layer is in the range of 4–12.5 ppt. However, the salinities are considerably higher in the open sea. The mean values in the Kattegatt (the region in which the Baltic Sea drains through the Danish strait) are 22 ppt and 31 ppt, respectively (same references). Suominen et al. [12] studied surface salinity gradients and their temporal fluctuations in the Archipelago Sea of the northern Baltic Sea based on field salinity data for the time period July 2007–August 2008. They identified a broad scale gradient from low salinity in the shallow inner bays to the high salinity in the open sea areas towards the Baltic proper. The steepest gradients were observed in the semi-closed part of the archipelago. One important result was that the use of temporal mean values of salinity was insufficient for coastal management purposes in the region.

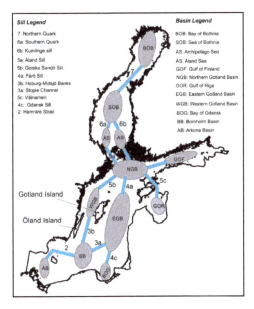

Figure 2. The Baltic Sea basin system, redrawn from an interpolated figure by Leppäranta & Myrberg [7].

The halocline depth is controlled by wind-induced mixing and advection, which appears to change little over time. Väli et al. [11] looked into variations of the halocline during 1961–2007. Two periods were identified with shallow halocline during 1970–1975, and with deep halocline during 1990–1995. The main conclusion was that the freshwater content and absolute wind speed control the halocline depth in the Baltic Sea. However, they found the wind speed to have a moderate impact on the mean halocline depth in the Baltic proper due to the low impact of runoff.

An important issue is the effect of fresh water on stratification in the Baltic Sea. Hordoir and Meier [13] studied the dynamics of fresh water, which is released during spring into the Baltic proper. They showed that the fresh water only reaches the center of the Baltic proper after late summer. A small amount of fresh water may reach the entrance of the Baltic Sea during one season. The arrival of fresh water increases vertical stratification, which can in turn trigger the onset of the spring blooms. They also found that the seasonal changes in the fresh water outflow were closely connected with those of the zonal wind. An important result was the correlation of the annual variability of the seasonal freshwater outflow maximum with the North Atlantic Oscillation.

The temperature stratification in the Baltic Sea has a mean three-layer structure in analogy to the salinity stratification. The layers are commonly referred to as the epilimnion (upper layer), thermocline (middle layer), and hypolimnion (lower layer). In similarity with the other large water bodies, there is a seasonal stratification cycle, which is driven by the variations in the energy balance. However, in the case of the Baltic Sea there are two specific features. First, fall and spring overturns are not well defined, and second, the hypolimnion has a nearly constant temperature, with few seasonal variations. During the winter periods, the epilimnion layer has a lower temperature than the hypolimnion layer. The Baltic Sea is monitored using 22 stations, as shown in Figure 3. A typical temperature difference at the gauge station BY15 is about 5 °C. In the spring, following the ice melt, a thin warmer surface layer rapidly develops and sets up the thermocline. The thickness of the layer varies considerably from north to south, but a mean value of about 15 m can be used. The temperature gradient is high within the epilimnion layer. For instance, at BY15, the temperature can vary from 1.5 °C to 5 °C within a depth of 60 m. Below this depth, the temperatures increase rapidly to reach the constant temperature of the hypolimnion layer (about 5 °C). The layer with transitional temperature is known as the dicothermal layer, which is a cold layer sandwiched between two layers with higher temperatures (dicothermal). The dicothermal layer was first discovered by the Ekman expedition of 1877 to the Baltic Sea (see Fonselius [14]). The layer appears to originate from the vertical convection of the surface water in the winter. It is further explained that this cold surface water from the previous winter was preserved between the thermocline and halocline (see Fonselius [14]). The dicothermal layer develops at high latitudes with cold climates. Peter [15] reports the development of a layer with a thickness of 100 m in the Indian Ocean region of the Antarctic. The reported thickness in the Baltic Sea is in the range of 5–30 m, which persists during the summer and disappears during the autumn [7]. Here, we note that the measured temperature profiles in the southern basins confirm the formation of the dicothermal layer even during the spring.

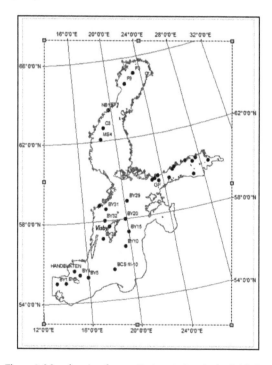

Figure 3. Map showing the monitoring stations in the Baltic Sea.

The stratification is strongest during the summer due to high solar radiation input and warm air temperatures. The surface layer thickness increases to about 20 m during the summer period due to wind induced vertical mixing The temperature within the layer is nearly constant. Below the surface layer, a strong thermocline develops that has a sharp temperature drop of about 10 °C over a depth of about 10 m (e.g., temperature profile at BY15). There is also a dicothermal layer below the thermocline, which has a thickness of about 30 m at BY15. The hypolimnion layer has a relatively constant temperature of 4–5 °C, which is close to the temperature of maximum density of water. The layer thickness varies considerably, from about 30 m in shallow regions to 100 m in the deeper region. The negative effect of the strong stratification limits the exchange between the epilimnion and hypolimnion layers.

During autumn, the surface heat losses start to increase and the thermocline depth deepens. For instance, in the Eastern Gotland Basin, the thermocline reaches a depth of about 40 m. The lower temperatures cause the temperature gradient to decrease, which in turn weakens the thermocline. The temperature changes in the thermocline cause a weak positive temperature gradient to develop in the hypolimnion layer (e.g., 1 °C over 100 m).

2. Materials and Methods

The materials used to model the Baltic Sea consisted of basic geometrical and various flow and meteorological data for the period 2000–2009 as listed below.

- The shoreline and the bathymetry in GIS format.
- Daily flow discharges for 24 Swedish rivers, 38 Finnish rivers, and five Eastern European rivers (i.e., the Daugava, Neman, Neva, Odra, and Vistula).
- Monthly mean flow discharge for four Eastern European rivers (i.e., Lielupe, Narva, Pärnu, and Narva). The daily records were not available.
- Water temperature for all the rivers.
- The forcing meteorological data (air temperature, dew point, cloud cover, pressure, wind speed, and wind direction) at 3-h intervals as grid data.
- Precipitation as rain intensity at 19 stations at daily intervals.
- Water quality data at 15-day intervals for 22 different stations spread across the sea. The data included water temperature, salinity, dissolved oxygen, and phosphorous.
- Wave heights and sea and water levels at several stations across the sea.

The main data sources were the Swedish Meteorological and Hydrological Institute, SMHI [16], and the Finnish Meteorological Institute, FMI [17]. The gridded meteorological data were obtained from http://www.smhi.se/en/research/research-departments/analysis-and-prediction, computed based on actual measurements. Among the many variables that affect the hydrodynamics of a large water body, the bathymetry and inflow of freshwater are the most important. So, special attention was paid to improving the quality and reliability of the bathymetry data.

The digitized bathymetry data for the Baltic Sea were obtained from the Leibniz Institute for Baltic Sea Research [18]. This dataset was frequently used in previous models of the Baltic Sea and also agrees well with published bathymetry maps. This dataset performed poorly in resolving the various channels along the coastlines of Finland, and in the Stockholm archipelago. The Åland Sea and its archipelago were also poorly reproduced. The latter problems caused a significant flow blockage in the forenamed areas. To resolve the foregoing issues, the bathymetry had to be refined using several different resolutions ranging from 50 m to 400 m that depended upon the model regions. The focus was on the areas along the coastlines and the interconnected channel systems. The modifications were done by a combined method using published maps and other databases in ARCGIS. The final bathymetry was analyzed using standard statistical methods to gain an understanding of the depth distribution and its relationship for resolving the vertical layers for the study domain. It was observed that depths less than 100 m cover 80% of the sea. This is an important result since it indicates the need for finer vertical grid resolution within the depth of 0–100 m.

2.1. Model Description

A three-dimensional, time-dependent hydrodynamic model, GEMSS® (Generalized Environmental Modelling System for Surface waters), was used. GEMSS was developed and maintained by Environmental Resources Mangement, Inc., Malvern, PA, USA. GEMSS is an integrated system of 3D hydrodynamic and transport models embedded in GIS. GEMSS is in the public domain [19] and has been used for similar studies throughout the United States and worldwide. Edinger and Buchak [20,21] first presented the theoretical basis of the model. The model was enhanced by implementing higher-order transport schemes, construction of various constituent modules, incorporation of various supporting software tools, GIS interoperability, visualization tools, graphical user interface (GUI), and post processors [22–26].

The hydrodynamic and transport relations are developed from the horizontal momentum balance, continuity, constituent transport and the equation of state. A detailed mathematical formulation of the model both in the hydrostatic and non-hydrostatic forms is described in [17,19] so will not be repeated here. The hydrodynamic equations are semi-implicit in time, have the advantage of computational stability, and are not limited by the Courant condition. The vertical momentum dispersion coefficient and vertical shear are evaluated from a Von Karman relationship modified by the Richardson number. Higher-order turbulence closure schemes (two-equation model, and second-moment closure model by Mellor and Yamada [27] are also included. The Two-Equation model used in GEMSS is based on the Generic Length Scale (GLS) model proposed by Umlauf and Burchard [28], and by Warner et al. [29]. The longitudinal and lateral coefficients are scaled to the dimensions of the grid cell using the dispersion relationships field developed by Okubo [30] and modified to include the velocity gradients using the Smagorinsky [31] relationship. The wind stress and bottom shear stress are computed using quadratic relationships with appropriate friction coefficients.

The transport module can run in fully explicit to fully implicit modes in a vertical direction while performing explicit computations in a horizontal direction [32]. GEMSS uses a curvilinear variably spacing horizontal staggered finite difference grid, which is based on control volume, with the elevation and constituent concentration computed at cell centers and velocities through a cell interface. Z-level with variable thickness is used for defining the grid in the vertical direction. Additional details of the model can be found in the technical documentation of GEMSS [32–35].

The wave dynamic module of GEMSS has two wave models, i.e., a steady state linear and a non-linear model. In the present investigation, the non-linear model was used. The model accounts for the wave influence on the bottom shear stresses by using the Madsen and Grant [36] equation. In the current study, a simplified linear ice model that relates the growth of ice thickness to the temperature differences between water and melting ice, and ice in equilibrium was used. Based on sensitivity studies, the linear ice model is a reasonably good model for the present study, which was run for a long period of time to understand the hydrodynamic characteristics. In addition, the particle tracking module of GEMSS was used for the current study to understand the travel time, water age [37] and vertical mixing processes at various basins in the Baltic Sea using the current persistency index defined in [38].

The GEMSS model was recently used by the first author to investigate the hydrodynamic and related water quality characteristics of Saltsjo [33] and Lake Tana in Ehiopia [34].

2.2. Model Setup

The model setup involved several main steps of creating the model grid, interpolating the bathymetry into the grid, defining the boundary conditions that include river inflow, water levels, precipitation, and forcing meteorological conditions.

The model grid was created using the grid generator tool of GEMSS®. A non-uniform boundary-fitted curvilinear grid in a horizontal plane (x-y) with a non-uniform z-layering in the vertical plane was created for the study domain and is shown in Figure 4. The grid dimensions are 195×200, with an approximate cell size of 4.8 km. The final bathymetry described in the previous section was used to interpolate the depths for each grid cell in the study domain. Since depths less than

100 m cover almost 80% of the Baltic Sea, the vertical layers were designed to have a finer resolution within this depth. The total number of vertical layers used in the current study was 47, with thicknesses varying from 1.5 m to 12 m.

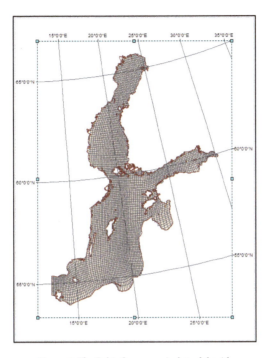

Figure 4. The Baltic Sea numerical model grid.

2.2.1. Input Data

The model boundary conditions consisted of discharge, head (water levels), precipitation, and meteorological forcing conditions. The true dynamic character of the input data is an important issue that directly affects the results of any hydrodynamic simulations. Here, the input data are the river discharge hydrographs and the forcing meteorological conditions. The amplitude and frequency of the data control various hydrodynamic properties such as stratification and mixing processes. The control file generator tool of GEMSS was used to define all forcing data needed for the current study.

The discharge boundary conditions were defined for 69 rivers out of 72 that enter the modeled region. To define the exact locations of the rivers, a GIS file was used. The river data included the flow discharge, water temperature, and salinity. We assumed that the rivers enter through the water surface grid in the model.

The water level was set at the open boundary with the North Sea, as shown in Figure 1 with a red line (≈104 km wide). The GPS coordinates are 54°28′ N 12°50′ E and 55°22′ N 13°03′ E in the south and north directions, respectively. To set the water level, the data at the gauge station Skanör (55°26′ N 12°50′ E) were used. At the open boundary the water temperatures and salinity profiles from monitoring station BY1 (see Figure 3) were used.

The precipitation data in mm/day were applied regionally by dividing the Baltic Sea surface into 19 regions, each with its corresponding rain intensity. Both point and gridded data were used for meteorological forcing conditions. The gridded data cover the whole Baltic drainage basin with a grid of (1° × 1°) squares. The grid extends over the area: Latitude 49.5°–71.5° N, Longitude 7.5°–39.5° E. The gridded data covers 32 years, starting in 1970. The gridded meteorological data represent geostrophic wind and were converted to the open surface wind speed needed for the model using the 2/3 power law. The second set was point data, which are available mainly along the coastlines.

2.2.2. Initialization

The model initialization is an important part of any hydrodynamic simulation, especially in the case of large water bodies such as the Baltic Sea. The long residence times make the model output sensitive to the choice of method. In the present study, we initiated the model using the data available at all the monitoring stations for water temperature and salinity. A total of 22 monitoring stations (see Figure 3) were used to interpolate temperature and salinity for the entire model grid at the start of the model simulation on 1 January 2000.

2.3. Simulations

In the present study we used the following setups for both partial and complete simulations, i.e., one year and 10 years.

- Vertical dispersion: Two-Equations with Mellor–Yamada formulation.
- Mixing dispersion: Okubo formulation.
- Transport diffusion: Prandtl method.
- Surface heat exchange: term by term, defining all the heat source and sink terms with atmospheric interaction.
- Transport model: Quick.
- Vertical momentum: Non-hydrostatic.
- Coriolis force: Using model grid.

The maximum time step used in the model simulations was 360 s. The auto time step feature available in GEMSS® was used so that the model time step goes only below the maximum time step due to extreme forcing conditions such as large wind speeds and river discharges. The calibration and verification simulations were carried out on a 4.8-km model grid shown in Figure 4. The model was run for the year 2000 for calibration. The model validation was done for the full 10 years using the restart files created by the calibration run.

3. Results

3.1. Model Calibration & Validation

A detailed description of model calibration and verification is available in [9] and will not be repeated here. Instead, it will be briefly described here using some relevant plots and tables.

The model calibration for year 2000 was done using all the 22 monitoring stations shown in Figure 3. The temperature, salinity, and water levels field data were used. It involved a systematic two-step approach with a focus on temperature and salinity profiles. The first step was initiating the model using the data available at all the monitoring stations for water temperature and salinity. The RMS (Root Mean Square) errors of temperature and salinity were then evaluated. In Step 2 the model was re-run with new sets of initial data that were successively adjusted to lower the RMS values. The procedure significantly improved the agreement with the measurements, with a relative error range of 10%–20% for both temperature and salinity. During the calibration procedure, the bottom friction coefficient, wind drag coefficient, and coefficients related to surface heat exchange processes were adjusted to lower the RMS values with respect to field observations. The coefficient values used for the calibration matched reasonably well with similar modeling exercises completed for the Baltic Sea. Based on all the calibration adjustments we have done for various model parameters, we found that establishing the appropriate horizontally and vertically varying initial condition was the most important precursor to achieve low RMS values on model results. The model successfully captured the seasonal variations in water temperature and salinity profiles as well as the stratification across the entire Baltic Sea. Here, we have chosen only some typical results for a few stations. Figures 5 and 6 show the combined temperature and salinity profiles at the monitoring stations F3, GF, BY15, and BY5. Table 1 summarizes the absolute and mean relative errors at these monitoring stations. The range of the error is 4%–10%, which is acceptable considering the large volume of the Baltic Sea and its complex hydrodynamics.

Table 1. Calibration error summary for temperature and salinity.

	Absolute Error								Mean Relative Error %	
Time	14 January 2000		28 May 2000		18 August 2000		9 November 2000			
Station	T (°C)	S (ppt)	T (°C)	S (ppt)	T (°C)	S (ppt)	T (°C)	S (ppt)	T	S
F3	0.15–0.6	0.1–0.2	0.1–1.5	0.1–0.2	0.1–0.2	0.1–0.2	0.1–0.2	0.1–0.2	10	3
Time	14 January 2000		28 May 2000		22 August 2000		25 October 2000			
BY15	0.1–0.57	0.1–0.8	0.1–1.3	0.1–0.8	0.1–0.9	0.1–0.7	0.1–1.6	0.1–1.2	4	4
Time	14 January 2000		28 May 2000		22 August 2000		25 October 2000			
BY5	0.1–0.2	0.1–0.2	0.1–0.5	0.1–0.3	0.1–0.5	0.1–0.3	0.1–1.6	0.1–2	5	6
Time	2 January 2000		6 June 2000							
GF	0.1–1	0.1–0.7	0.1–1	0.1–0.2					9	8

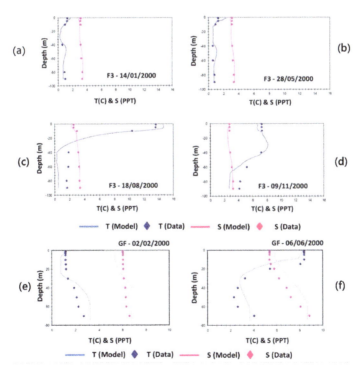

Figure 5. Comparison of model predicted vertical temperature and salinity profiles at the monitoring stations F3 (Bay of Bothnia) and GF (Gulf of Finland) with field measurements for the year 2000. (a) Station F3—14/01/2000; (b) Station F3—28/05/2000; (c) Station F3—18/08/2000; (d) Station F3—09/11/2000; (e) Station GF—02/02/2000; Station (f)—06/06/2000.

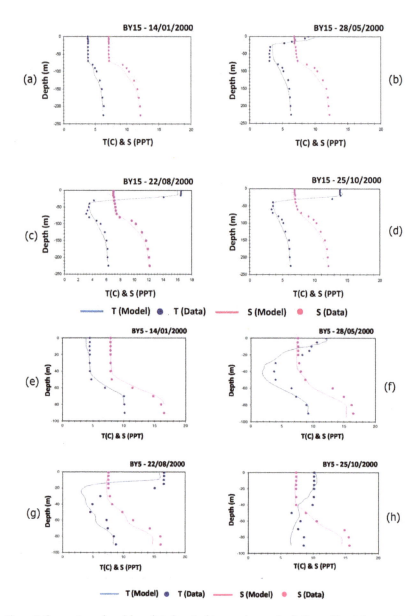

Figure 6. Comparison of model predicted vertical temperature and salinity profiles at the monitoring stations BY15 (Eastern Gotland Basin) and BY5 (Arkona Basin) with field measurements for the year 2000. (**a**) Station BY15—14/01/2000; (**b**) Station BY15—28/05/2000; (**c**) Station BY15—22/08/2000; (**d**) Station BY15—25/10/2000; (**e**) Station BY5—14/01/2000; (**f**) Station BY5—28/05/2000; (**g**) Station BY5—22/08/2000; (**h**) Station BY5—25/10/2000.

Model validation was done for the whole 10 years using the restart files created by the calibration simulation for the year 2000. For this purpose, the complete sets of field data at all the monitoring stations were used (Figure 3). These data were considered independently from the simulation results as only the first day records were used in the calibration simulations.

The model predictions of water temperatures and salinities were satisfactory at all the monitoring stations. Here, we have chosen some representative results for only a few stations. The time history plots in Figures 7 and 8 compare the model predicted temperature and salinity with the field data at stations F3 and BY29 at water surface and 40 m depth.

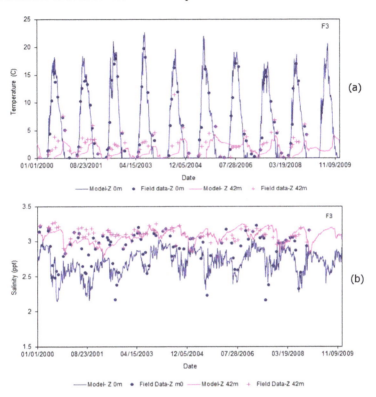

Figure 7. (a) Comparison of model predicted and measurements of temperature in the Baltic Sea at the Station F3 surface and 42 m depth for the time period 2000–2009; (b) Comparison of model predicted and measurements of salinity in the Baltic Sea at the Station F3 surface and 42 m depth for the time period 2000–2009.

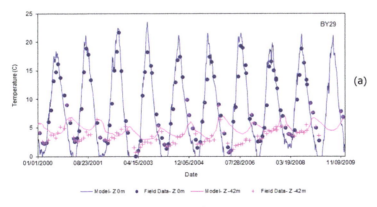

Figure 8. *Cont.*

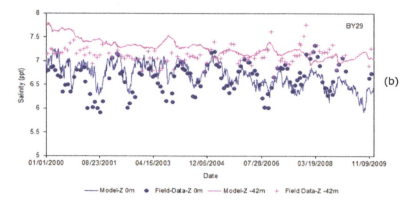

Figure 8. (a) Comparison of model predicted and measurements of temperature in the Baltic Sea at the Station BY29 surface and 42 m depth for the time period 2000-2009; **(b)** Comparison of model predicted and measurements of salinity in the Baltic Sea at the Station BY29 surface and 42 m depth for the time period 2000–2009.

The time history plots in Figure 9 compare the model predicted salinity with the field data at stations BY15 and BY5. The comparisons are shown at the water surface and at the deepest points in the basins. The agreements for these stations are better than the other stations as they are closer to station BY1, which defines the model boundary condition.

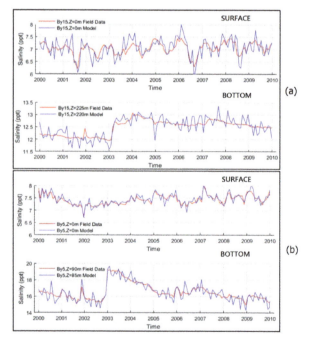

Figure 9. (a) Comparison of model predicted and measurements of salinity in the Baltic Sea at the Station BY15 surface and bottom for the time period 2000–2009; **(b)** Comparison of model predicted and measurements of salinity in the Baltic Sea at the Station BY5 surface and bottom for the time period 2000–2009.

The range of Nash–Sutcliffe coefficients [39] calculated for all the monitoring stations was 0.72–0.83, respectively, also suggesting close agreement. One other important feature is the ability of the model to capture the 10-year seasonal variations of water temperatures and salinities. The conclusion is that the model is reasonably validated over a considerable period, with a maximum relative error of 10%.

3.2. Stratified Vertical Structure

We used the validated model to investigate the stratified structure within all the basins of the Baltic Sea for the time period 2000–2009. The complete sets of numerical results are too extensive to be reported here. We will present and discuss some general results that are illustrated using a few plots (i.e., temperature and salinity) in both horizontal and vertical sections. The latter were investigated along several cross sections shown in Figure 10 that were selected to cut through all the basins (see Figure 2 for basin names) included in this study. The structure concerns thermocline and halocline stratifications, which are controlled by the hydrodynamic variables, forcing meteorological parameters, the topography, the shorelines, and the exchange processes with the North Sea.

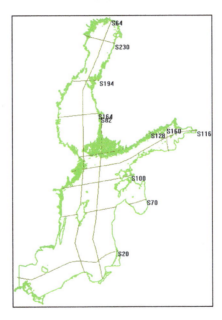

Figure 10. Selected cross sections in the Baltic Sea for vertical structure analysis.

Examples of simulation results for temperature and salinity are presented seasonally for winter (15 January), spring (15 May), summer (15 August), and autumn (15 October). Figures 11 and 12 show the surface and bottom contour plots of temperature for the year 2000, respectively. The typical cross-sectional plots of temperature are given for sections S64 and S116 for the year 2000 are given in Figures 13 and 14. The basins' abbreviated names are also given in the foregoing figures. It should be noted that the plotting scales were adjusted to show the full range of the hydrodynamic variables. This is particularly important for insuring that the stratification features are not obscured by the choice of the color scales. The summary results for all nine basins are presented in Tables 2 and 3. In these tables the layer thicknesses are normalized (L_n) with mean depth.

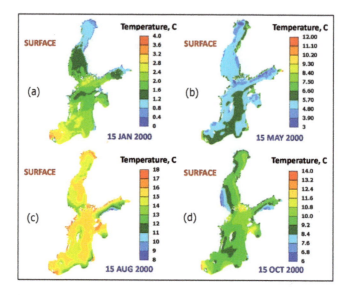

Figure 11. Seasonal surface temperature contour plots for the year 2000. (**a**) Winter; (**b**) Spring; (**c**) Summer; (**d**) Autumn.

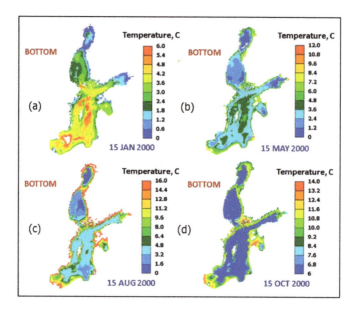

Figure 12. Seasonal bottom temperature contour plots for the year 2000. (**a**) Winter; (**b**) Spring; (**c**) Summer; (**d**) Autumn.

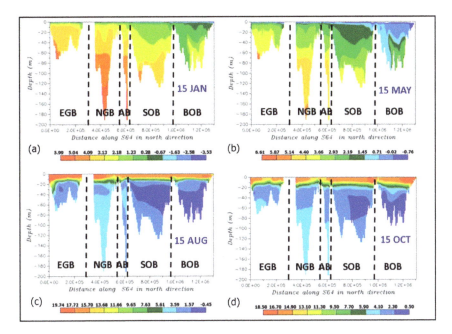

Figure 13. Seasonal thermal stratification plots in the Baltic Sea at cross section S64 for the year 2000. (**a**) Winter; (**b**) Spring; (**c**) Summer; (**d**) Autumn.

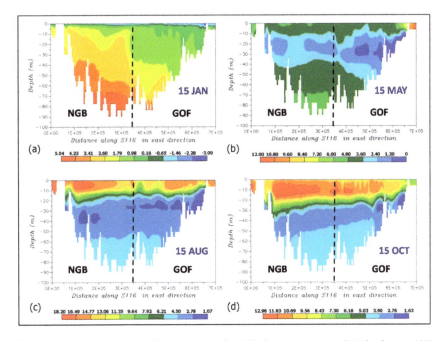

Figure 14. Seasonal thermal stratification plots in the Baltic Sea at cross section S116 for the year 2000. (**a**) Winter; (**b**) Spring; (**c**) Summer; (**d**) Autumn.

The temperature development at the Baltic Sea is affected by the intrusion of the warmer water masses from the North Sea and cold low salinity river water masses that flow into the Bay of Bothnia. The northern part of the Baltic Sea is covered by ice during winter and spring, which reduces the water temperature well into the summer. Figure 11 shows the seasonal variations of water temperature at the surface and bottom layers. The surface temperatures are in good agreement with the SMHI measurements available in [40]. The surface temperatures vary in the range of 0 °C to 18 °C. In the winter, the bottom temperatures are higher than the surface temperatures by several degrees. The spring is marked by higher surface temperatures, with the exception of the Bay of Bothnia and the eastern Gulf of Finland. The surface temperatures increase significantly during the summer and are about 2 °C higher than the bottom layer temperatures. The autumn shows a transitional behavior, with a decreasing temperature differences between the two layers. This marks the start of the cooling of surface water due to increased mechanical and thermal convection.

In summary, the thermal stratification in the Baltic Sea shows a considerable variation among the different basins with a clear seasonal feature. During the winter period, the lower water layers are warmer than the upper layers. The ice starts to melt in late spring but still maintains a higher water temperature in the bottom layers. The temperature of the upper water layers starts to increase as the end of the summer approaches. By then, the upper water layers have a higher temperature and the stratification is reversed.

The common thermal stratification features in the Baltic Sea are obtained by analyzing the transient plots along all the cross sections:

1. The number of the stratified layers varies from two to five.
2. There are two distinct layers, one with lower surface temperature, i.e., winter stratification and a reversed summer-type stratification with higher surface temperatures. These two types prevail during winter–spring and summer–autumn, respectively. Typical transitional behavior may begin in late autumn, when the wind speed increases, but does not last more than a couple of weeks. These stratification features dominantly occur in shallower regions of the Baltic Sea.
3. The surface layer has a transient structure composed of two to three minor thermoclines with a mean thickness of about 10 m. It is often difficult to distinguish between these layers. Here, the thermocline layer is considered as a layer with temperature variations more than 0.4 °C, which gives negligible density difference (i.e., 0.01 kg/m^3). The thermocline is located at a depth of 10–30 m.
4. The summer stratification has a dicothermal character in the northern basins of the Baltic Sea. This implies the existence of a colder layer sandwiched between two layers of higher temperatures. The layer is stable since the upper layer has a lower salinity than the deep underlying layer.

The foregoing features are shown in Figures 13 and 14 at two typical cross sections of S64 and S116, respectively. The former crosses most of the major basins in the Baltic Sea. This plot does not do justice to the complexity of the stratification in the Baltic Sea. The intention is to provide support to the results and the discussion. For thermal stratification, the layers are numbered in descending order from the surface (Table 2). The division was needed due to the complex nature of the multilayered thermal stratification. Layer 1 is defined as the surface or the top layer and the last layer refers to the bottom layer. It is not very useful to list the absolute values due to the significant geometric variations within and among the basins (size, volume, and depth).

In the Bay of Bothnia, there is a significant seasonal variation regarding the number and thickness of the layers. The stratification in the Aland Sea is dominated by a three-layer structure, with the exception of a four-layer structure during the spring period. The stratified structure in the Gulf of Finland consists of three layers with significant variations in both thickness and temperature. The multilayered stratification structure for the Northern Gotland Basin is composed of top and bottom layers with constant temperatures. The Western Gotland Basin shows a sustained three-layered structure from the winter to summer period. The Eastern Gotland Basin stratification is similar to the northern basin except that the water temperatures are higher by 1 °C during the spring and autumn periods. The Bornholm Basin features are similar to the Eastern Gotland Basin. The Arkona Basin has a clear three-layer structure and during the winter and summer periods, the temperatures are constant in the 10-m thick upper layer, i.e., 4 °C and 16.5 °C, respectively. A short summary of each basin is reported in this paper. A detailed description of each basin's stratification is given in Dargahi and Cvektovic [9]. The foregoing results are summarized in Table 2.

Table 2. Characteristics of thermal stratification in the basin system of the Baltic Sea, 2000–2009.

Basins	Layers	Winter		Spring		Summer		Autumn	
		T °C	L_n %	T °C	L_n %	T °C	L_n %	T °C	L_n %
Bay of Bothnia	1	0.5	65	1.2	5	11	10	13.5	5
	2	0.5–1.5	23	1.2–0.8	5	11–3	30	13.5–3	35
	3	1.5	12	0.8	80	3–2	50	3–2	50
Sea of Bothnia	1	1.5	12	4.5	4.5	14–11.2	3	12	10
	2	1.5–3	33	4.5–1	13.5	11.2–3.2	25	12–2.5	20
	3	3	55	1.3	82	3.2–1.5	9	2.5–2	10
	4					1.5–3	40	2–3	47
	5					3	23	3	13
Gulf of Finland	1	0.2–0.25	42	7.5–1.5	42	16.2	21	13–12.8	21
	2	0.25–2.6	42	1.5	16	16.2–2.6	50	12.8–3.5	50
	3	2.6	16	1.5–4.2	42	2.6–4.2	29	3.5	29
Sea of Åland	1	0.5–4	25	4	10	14.2	10	10	10
	2	4–4.3	35	4–2.4	27	14.2–6.5	27	10–9	18
	3	4.3–4.8	40	2.4	27	6.5–3.9	63	9–5	72
	4			2.4–2.9	36				
Northern Gotland	1	4.2	43	6	8	16.2	5	13.5	10
	2	4.2–5.2	10	6–3.2	12	16.2–16.8	5	13.5–14.2	10
	3	5.2	47	3.2–2.8	11	16.8–16	10	14.2–3.5	20
	4			2.8–4.8	29	16–3	20	3.5–5	15
	5			5.5	40	3–4.8	16	5	35
	6					4.8	42		
Western Gotland	1	2	3	7–2.6	12	16–3.2	12	13.5	8
	2	2–5	20	2.6–5	18	3.2–5	11	3.5	4
	3	5–5.2	77	5–5.2	70	5–5.2	77	3.5–5	11
	4							5–5.2	77
Eastern Gotland	1	3.8	28	9–3	19	16.5	10	14	9
	2	3.8–6	33	3	13	16.5–3.7	10	14–3.7	9
	3	6–6.3	39	3–6	35	3.7–3	12	3.7–3	9
	4			6–6.3	33	3–6	26	3–6	28
	5					6–6.2	42	6–6.2	45
Bornholm Basin	1	4.5	55	12–4	33	17–16.5	28	15–14.8	18
	2	4.5–10	22	4	22	16.5–4.7	28	14.8–4.7	27
	3	10	23	9	33	7–6.2	16	4.7–7.8	22
	4			9–9.2	12	6.2–8	28	7.8–8.5	33
Arkona Basin	1	4	25	13.2–5.2	76	16.5	25	17–16.2	50
	2	4–4.5	25	5.2–4.8	23	16.5–8.5	25	16.2–8.8	25
	3	4.5–6	50			8.5–10.7	50	8.8–10.5	25

The seasonal variation in surface and bottom layer salinities is shown in Figures 15 and 16, respectively. Figures 17 and 18 show salinity contours for the years 2000 and 2006 as two typical years in the 10-year simulation period of 2000–2009. The general features are an outgoing surface flow with low salinity that is diluted by the fresh water from the rivers and a denser incoming bottom flow from the North Sea. The surface salinity varies from 1.6% to 9% and the bottom salinity in the range 3%–16%, moving southwards from the Bay of Bothnia to the Arkona Basin. The corresponding salinity gradients are 0.0042%/m and 0.0054%/m, respectively. The intruded high salinity water from the North Sea propagates like a plume as far as the Northern Gotland Basin, with a mean advection velocity of 6 cm/s. The feature is apparent from Figures 13, 14, 17 and 18, which show the dense water settling mainly in the deep regions of the Northern and Eastern Gotland Basins. The salinity stratification has a multi-layer structure similar to the thermal stratification shown in Figures 13 and 14. The general features are two thick (i.e., >30 m) surface and bottom layers with a transition layer in-between. The stratification is complicated by its temporal and spatial variations both within and among the basins. A detailed discussion on salinity stratification is provided by Dargahi and Cvektovic [9] for all basins and so will not be repeated here. As an example, salinity stratification is briefly discussed for the Gulf of Finland and the Northern Gotland Basin.

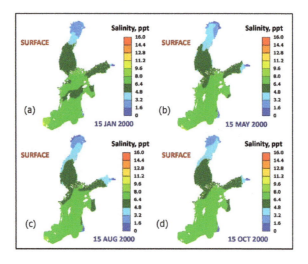

Figure 15. Seasonal plots of surface salinity in the Baltic Sea for the year 2000. (**a**) Winter; (**b**) Spring; (**c**) Summer; (**d**) Autumn.

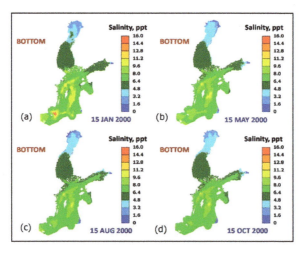

Figure 16. Seasonal plots of bottom salinity in the Baltic Sea for the year 2000. (**a**) Winter; (**b**) Spring; (**c**) Summer; (**d**) Autumn.

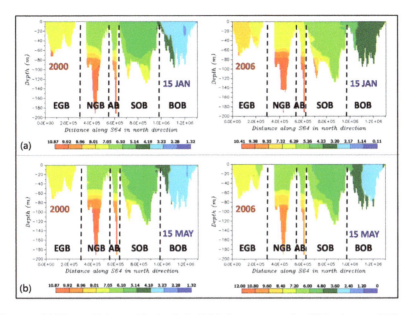

Figure 17. (a) Winter salinity stratification in the Baltic Sea at cross section S64 for the years 2000 and 2006; (b) Spring salinity stratification in the Baltic Sea at cross section S64 for the years 2000 and 2006.

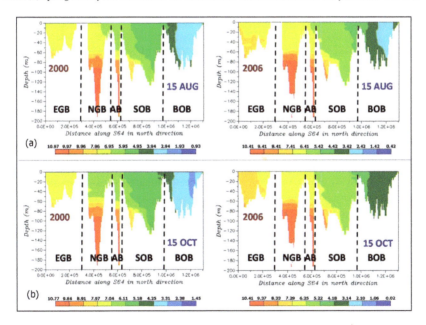

Figure 18. (a) Summer salinity stratification in the Baltic Sea at cross section S64 for the years 2000 and 2006; (b) Autumn salinity stratification in the Baltic Sea at cross section S64 for the years 2000 and 2006.

4. Discussion

The understanding of stratification in large water bodies is of significant environmental importance due to its direct coupling with water quality dynamics. Severe thermal stratification can have a number of adverse effects, among which are reduced water quality and the spatial distribution of fish [41]. Any prolonged stratification can reduce oxygen solubility, which leads to oxygen depletion in deep water masses. The deeper water masses in the Baltic Sea are particularly vulnerable to eutrophication below the halocline or in regions affected by thermal stratification [42]. We know that eutrophication is the most serious and challenging environmental problem for the Baltic Sea [1]. Consequently, accurate knowledge of stratification dynamics is required for the management of eutrophication in the Baltic Sea.

The river Neva, the most voluminous river entering the Gulf of Finland (referred as Gulf in the foregoing discussion) from the eastern coastline (2500 m^3/s), significantly affects the stratification in the Gulf. The zero-salinity water from the river creates a permanent plume that propagates westwards to a distance of 50–150 km. The plume salinity varies from 0% to 5% and extends to a depth of about 15 m. The maximum extension occurs during early spring periods. The seasonal cross section plots are shown in Figure 14 at S116 for the year 2000. The stratification in the Neva region appears to have a permanent multi-layer structure with few seasonal variations. The characteristic three-layer structure is found in the inner Gulf region. The stratification characteristics in the Northern Gotland Basin are similar to those in the inner Gulf region. It is interesting to note the significant salinity increase to 9.5% that is confined to the Northern Gotland Basin and the bottom layer.

The model prediction of three-layered salinity stratification in all basins of the Baltic Sea is in general agreement with previous studies [8]. Salinity stratification has a strong seasonal variability but is much weaker than the corresponding variability in temperature. The summary of model-predicted salinity data for the entire 10-year period into seasonal normalized layer thicknesses is shown in Table 3. The normalized values are more applicable than the absolute values given in the literature as the layer thicknesses could be estimated as a function of depth. The latter vary significantly within and among the basins. To examine the validity of the generalization, we compared the model and measured salinities at all stations and found good agreement between the data. An example is given in Table 4, which compares model results with measurements at station C3 (located in the Sea of Bothnia; see Figure 3) for the year 2000. Evidently, the predicted mean thicknesses are within the range of the measured data that supports our generalization.

The detailed investigation of thermal stratification for a 10-year period (i.e., 2000–2009) revealed some new features. The current study revealed a multilayered structure that contains several thermocline and dicothermal layers. The statistical analysis of all simulation results made it possible to derive the mean thermal stratification properties, expressed as mean temperatures and the normalized layer thicknesses (Table 2). The three-layered structure reported by Leppäranta and Myrberg [7] appears to be oversimplified.

The thermocline layer has a sharp temperature gradient that connects the upper and lower two layers. We have found the three-layer model to be valid only during the winter. In the northern basins, the vertical temperature gradients are significantly lower than for the southern basins (a factor 3). We attribute the difference to the formation of an ice cover during winter and spring in the northern basins (i.e., Northern Gotland Basin and above), which affects the surface heat transfer and its exchange with the overlying cold air. The ice layer acts as a thermal barrier preventing further heat losses due to the action of wind and convective transport. Consequently, the upper layer is rather thick and can occupy up to 65% of the depth in these basins. Following the winter, the three-layered structure is decomposed into several layers with increasing or decreasing temperature gradients. The process takes place in all the basins in the Baltic Sea. Here, we believe the primary driving force is the increased mixing processes between the basins during the ice-free periods. The high-momentum fresh water inflows from the rivers contribute to higher surface water temperatures, thus increasing the temperature gradients. On average, the thickest layer is the bottom layer ($\approx$50%) with a small temperature gradient, except in the Bornholm and Arkona basins. We believe the low gradients are due to low-intensity exchange processes in the northern basin of the deep water regions.

Table 3. Characteristics of salinity stratification in the basin system of the Baltic Sea, 2000–2009.

Basins	Layers	Winter L_n %	Spring L_n %	Summer L_n %	Autumn L_n %	Salinity ‰
	Upper	18	34	31	22	3
Bay of Bothnia	Halocline	33	15	22	66	3.2
	Bottom	49	51	41	12	4
	Upper	50	15	5	15	5
Sea of Bothnia	Halocline	35	65	70	70	5.5
	Bottom	15	20	25	15	6.5
	Upper	15	10	10	10	5.9
Sea of Åland	Halocline	35	50	46	40	7.6
	Bottom	50	40	44	50	10
	Upper	25	32	25	30	4.7
Gulf of Finland	Halocline	30	38	50	40	6.5
	Bottom	45	40	25	30	8.3
	Upper	35	38	20	25	5
Northern Gotland	Halocline	30	32	55	45	42
	Bottom	35	30	25	30	28
	Upper	35	50	55	50	6.9
Western Gotland	Halocline	50	40	30	30	8.1
	Bottom	15	10	15	20	10
	Upper	30	20	25	20	6.8
Eastern Gotland	Halocline	35	50	50	55	9.3
	Bottom	35	30	25	25	11.5
	Upper	45	35	50	50	7.8
Bornholm Basin	Halocline	10	30	35	30	12.5
	Bottom	45	35	15	20	15.5
	Upper	35	60	38	60	8
Arkona Basin	Halocline	50	25	50	25	9
	Bottom	15	15	12	15	12

Table 4. Comparison of modeled and measured salinity stratification at station C3 (Sea of Bothnia), 2000.

Period	Upper Layer (m)		Halocline (m)		Bottom Layer (m)	
	Measured	Model	Measured	Model	Measured	Model
Winter	60–90	100	50–90	62	10–40	30
Spring	10–20	18	100–125	135	20–50	30
Summer	10–15	10	110–140	140	20–50	33
Autumn	15–30	22	100–130	127	20–45	22

The Bornholm and Arkona basins are shallower and more influenced by the exchange of warmer and more saline waters with the North Sea. This is reflected by the increased temperature gradients in these basins (from ≈0.02 °C/m to ≈0.5 °C/m). Our simulations indicate a wide spectrum in the layering properties among the basins. However, a few generalizations appear to be possible based on the results listed in Table 2. The thermocline occupies about 25% of the water depth in each basin. The deep bottom layer is about 40% of the water depth with temperatures of about 3 °C and 5 °C in the northern and southern basins, respectively. Our mean results on the properties of thermal stratification agree well with the results reported by Leppäranta and Myrberg [7]. Here, the reported annual averaged halocline thickness is 10–20 m. For example, in the Bay of Bothnia we get an averaged normalized depth of 35% from Table 2. The mean depth is 40 m, which yields a thickness of 14 m—well within the range given by Leppäranta and Myrberg [7].

There is also some evidence of upwelling and downwelling along the coastlines across the Baltic Sea [3,6,39,43]. The existence of the dicothermal layer is an indication of upwelling. The two features occur as wind causes surface water to diverge (Ekman transport) or converge (downwelling). During both processes, water is either replenished from the deep region or forced downwards [44]. Consequently, the salinity variations, which are mainly controlled by the water balance, are further modified.

We will also examine the validity of having normalized layer thicknesses (Table 2) in each basin that only vary seasonally. We start by examining the measured vertical temperature profiles for two extreme locations of F3 (Bay of Bothnia) and BY5 (Bornholm Sea). Figure 19 shows the measured vertical temperature profiles at F3, and BY5 for the years 2000, 2008, and 2009. Note that the data were rather limited and thus the lines are only illustrative and do not necessarily show the correct trends. The good agreement with the simulated summary results listed in Table 2 is apparent. For example, Table 2 predicts a thick top layer in the winter period (red line) at both stations that agrees well with the plots for F3, on 27 January 2000, and BY5, on 19 January 2000. We can also note that the profile shapes are preserved during the simulation period. However, the magnitudes of the temperatures show some significant variation. In conclusion, we believe the normalized layer thicknesses give reasonable estimates, with a standard deviation of ±15%.

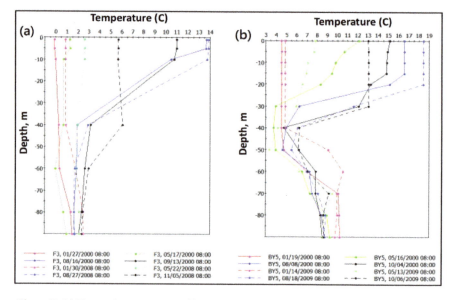

Figure 19. (**a**) Measured temperature profiles at F3 in 2000, 2008 and 2009; (**b**) Measured temperature profiles at BY5 in 2000, 2008 and 2009.

An interesting feature is the extreme inflow event of January 2003. According to Lehmann et al. [45], a massive salt intrusion of cold and oxygen-rich water from the North Sea took place at Darss Sill, which is a few kilometers west of the open sea boundary used in the model domain (see Figure 1). They consider the event as "the most important inflow from 1993". Their results indicate significant changes in both salinity and temperature distributions in the deeper basins of the Baltic Sea. In the present study, we have investigated the reported event by comparing the surface and bottom salinities at all the stations (see Figure 3). We present the results in Figure 20, illustrating the salinity time series at stations BY1, BY5, and BY15 at the surface and bottom layers. The curves at BY1 are measured field data but the curves at BY5 and BY15 are model results. The model results are plotted at seven-day intervals for ease of comparison with the field data. Several important features are evident from this figure:

1. The event took place on 18 January 2003 with a salinity of 29%.
2. It took nearly a month for the peak salinity to reach station BY5, which dropped to 19%.
3. The peak salinity was reduced to 12.5% at station BY15 after almost five months.

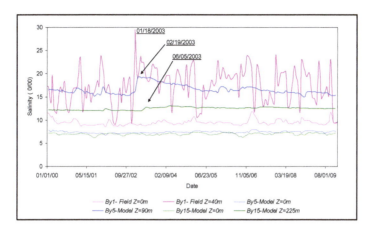

Figure 20. Time series of surface and bottom salinities at stations BY1, BY5, and BY15.

We computed the horizontal diffusive $\left(\vartheta_D \frac{\partial C^2}{\partial x^2}\right)$ and advective transports $\left(U_m \frac{\partial C}{\partial x}\right)$ using the foregoing information and the distances between the three stations (Table 5). A representative diffusion coefficient (ϑ_D) for the Baltic Sea is 10^3 m^2/s [7]; the advective velocity is typically 0.1 m/s in the Arkona and Bornholm basins (present study). We can conclude that the diffusive transport is much faster than the advective transport. There is a significant reduction in the Eastern Gotland Basin in both modes of transport. It is interesting to note that the temporal variations in the bottom salinity appear to be random as opposed to the surface salinities. The surface salinities have lower amplitudes with no corresponding peaks as the bottom salinity. We believe the outgoing freshwater plays a significant role in lowering the salinity amplitude.

Table 5. Estimates of salinity transport in the southern basins.

Transport of Salt	BY1 (Arkona)-BY5 (Bornholm)	BY5-BY15(Eastern Gotland)
Diffusive (‰/day)	17×10^{-3}	5×10^{-3}
Advective (‰/day)	86×10^{-8}	1.12×10^{-8}

5. Conclusions

An integrated 3D modeling system was developed for the Baltic Sea using a public domain model called GEMSS®. The model was calibrated and verified using 10 years of data covering 2000–2009. We have incorporated boundary conditions and bathymetry with as high an accuracy as possible, to serve as an improvement over previous studies. The model was then used to investigate the vertical structure of the Baltic Sea to understand the stratification and exchange processes across various basins. This paper addressed in detail both the thermal and salinity stratifications, with a focus on the structural properties of the layers.

The hypothesis was that the layer properties could be expressed as dimensionless numbers valid for all seasons. In particular, the detection of cooler regions (dicothermal) within the layer structure has been an important finding. The detailed investigation of thermal stratification for a 10-year period (i.e., 2000–2009) revealed some new features. A multilayered structure that contains several thermocline and dicothermal layers prevails. Statistical analysis of the simulation results made it possible to derive the mean thermal str atification properties, expressed as mean temperatures and the normalized layer thicknesses.

The three-layered structure reported in the literature appears to be rather simplified. The current study found that the three-layer model is valid only during the winter.

The layering properties vary significantly among the basins whereby the layered structure could not be generalized. Nevertheless, a few generalizations appear to be possible. The thermocline occupies about 25% of the water depth in each basin. The deep bottom layer is about 40% of the water depth, with temperatures of about 3 °C and 5 °C in northern and southern basins, respectively.

Three-layered salinity stratification prevails in all basins of the Baltic Sea, in general agreement with previous studies. Salinity stratification has a strong seasonal variability but this is much weaker than the corresponding variability in temperature. We have succeeded in generalizing the seasonal normalized layer thicknesses for the entire 10-year period. The use of normalized values is advantageous compared to the absolute values given in the literature, enabling estimation of layer thickness as a function of depth.

This study provides detailed insight into thermal and salinity stratifications in the Baltic Sea during a recent decade and can be used as a basis for diverse environmental assessments (e.g., anoxia and reduced nutrient mixing between layers [1]). It extends previous studies on stratification in the Baltic Sea regarding both the extent and the nature of stratification.

Acknowledgments: This study was initiated and the first stage financed by the Central Baltic Interreg IV Programme as part of the project "Phosphorous from the seabed and water quality in archipelagos—modeling attempt (SEABED)". The second stage of this study was funded by KTH Royal Institute of Technology, Division of Water Resources Engineering and Division of Hydraulic Engineering. The third and final stage of this study was funded by the project "The Baltic Sea Region System (BALSYS)".

Author Contributions: The Baltic Sea hydrodynamic modeling study was done entirely by Bijan Dargahi. The original manuscript was prepared by Bijan Dargahi. The GEMSS model was developed by Venkat Kolluru. He also provided GEMSS model training tor this study. The subsequent manuscript revisions and refinement of graphics were prepared by Venkat Kolluru. The project management and funding from three different sources were managed by Vladimir Cvetkovic.

Conflicts of Interest: The authors declare no conflict of interest.

References

1. World Atlas. Available online: http://www.worldatlas.com/aatlas/infopage/balticsea.htm (accessed on 12 December 2016).
2. Elmgren, R.; Larsson, U. *Himmerfjajrden: Changes in a Nutrient-Enriched Coastal Ecosystem in the Baltic Sea*; Report 4565; Swedish Environment Protection Agency: Naturvårdsverket, Stockholm, Sweden, 1997.
3. Meier, M. On the parameterization of mixing in three-dimensional Baltic Sea models. *J. Geophys. Res.* **2001**, *106*, 30997–31061. [CrossRef]
4. Lehmann, A.; Hinrichsen, H.H. Water, heat and salt exchange between the deep basins of the Baltic Sea. *Boreal Environ. Res.* **2002**, *7*, 405–415.
5. Omstedt, A.; Elken, J.; Lehmann, A.; Piechura, J. Knowledge of the Baltic Sea physics gained during the BALTEX and related programmes. *Progress Oceanogr.* **2004**, *63*, 1–28. [CrossRef]
6. Feistel, R.; Nausch, G.; Wasmund, N. *State and Evolution of the Baltic Sea, 1952–2005: A Detailed 50-Year Survey of Meteorology and Climate, Physics, Chemistry, Biology, and Marine Environment*, 1st ed.; John Wiley & Sons, Inc.: Hoboken, NJ, USA, 2008.
7. Leppäranta, M.; Myrberg, K. *Physical Oceanography of the Baltic Sea*, 1st ed.; Springer: Berlin, Germany, 2009.
8. Harff, J.; Björck, S.; Hoth, P. *The Baltic Sea Basin*, 1st ed.; Central and Eastern European Development Studies; Springer: Berlin, Germany, 2011.
9. Dargahi, B.; Cvektovic, V. *Hydrodynamics and Transport Characterization of the Baltic Sea 2000–2009*, 1st ed.; TRITA-LWR REPORT 2014:03; KTH Royal Institute of Technology, School of Architecture and the Marine Environment: Stockholm, Sweden, 2014.
10. Bock, K.H. Monthly salinity maps of the Baltic Sea for different depths. *Deustsche Hydrogr. Z.* **1971**, *12*, 1–147.

11. Väli, G.; Meier, H.E.; Elken, J. *Simulated Variations of the Baltic Sea Halocline during 1961–2007*; Report Oceanography; Swedish Meteorological and Hydrological Institute (SMHI): Stockholm, Sweden, 2012; No. 44; pp. 1–37.

12. Suominen, T.; Tolvanen, H.; Kalliola, R. Geographical persistence of surface-layer water properties in the Archipelago Sea, SW Finland. *Fennia* **2010**, *188*, 179–196.

13. Hordoir, R.; Meier, H.E.M. Effect of climate change on the thermal stratification of the Baltic Sea: A sensitivity experiment. *Clim. Dyn.* **2012**, *38*, 1703–1713. [CrossRef]

14. Fonselius, S. History of hydrographic research in Sweden. *Proc. Estonian Acad. Sci. Biol. Ecol.* **2001**, *50*, 110–129.

15. Peter, B. Dicothermal Layer Characteristics—A Case Study in the Antarctic Zone of Indian Ocean. *Proc. Indian Natl. Acad. Sci. USA* **1993**, *59*, 439–447.

16. SMHI. Swedish Meteorological and Hydrological Institute. Available online: http://www.smhi.se/en (accessed on 25 February 2012).

17. FMI. Finnish Meteorological Institute. Available online: http://en.ilmatieteenlaitos.fi/ (accessed on 10 April 2012).

18. Leibniz Institute for Baltic Sea Research Warnemunde. Available online: http://www.io-warnemuende.de/topography-of-the-baltic-sea.html (accessed on 20 September 2012).

19. GEMSS®. Available online: http://www.gemss.com (accessed on 10 August 2011).

20. Edinger, J.E.; Buchak, E.M. Numerical hydrodynamics of estuaries in estuarine and wetland processes with emphasis on modeling. In *Estuarine and Wetland Processes with Emphasis on Modeling*; Hamilton, P., Macdonald, K.B., Eds.; Plenum Press: New York, NY, USA, 1980; pp. 115–146.

21. Edinger, J.E.; Buchak, E.M. Numerical waterbody dynamics and small computers. In Proceedings of the ASCE Hydraulic Division Specialty Conference on Hydraulics and Hydrology in the Small Computer Age, Lake Buena Vista, FL, USA, 13–16 August 1985; American Society of Civil Engineers: Reston, VA, USA, 1985; pp. 13–16.

22. Kolluru, V.S.; Buchak, E.M.; Edinger, J.E. Integrated Model to Simulate the Transport and Fate of Mine Tailings in Deep Waters. In Proceedings of the Tailings and Mine Waste '98 Conference, Fort Collins, CO, USA, 26–29 January 1998; pp. 599–610.

23. Kolluru, V.S.; Buchak, E.M.; Wu, J. Use of Membrane Boundaries to Simulate Fixed and Floating Structures in GLLVHT. In Proceedings of the 6th International Conference on Estuarine and Coastal Modeling, New Orleans, LA, USA, 3–5 November 1999; Spaulding, M.L., Butler, H.L., Eds.; pp. 485–500.

24. Kolluru, V.S.; Edinger, J.E.; Buchak, E.M.; Brinkmann, P. Hydrodynamic Modeling of Coastal LNG Cooling Water Discharge. *J. Energy Eng.* **2003**, *129*, 16–31. [CrossRef]

25. Kolluru, V.S.; Fichera, M. Development and Application of Combined 1-D and 3-D Modeling System for TMDL Studies. In Proceedings of the Eighth International Conference on Estuarine and Coastal Modeling, Monterey, CA, USA, 3–5 November 2003; American Society of Civil Engineers: Reston, VA, USA, 2003; pp. 108–127.

26. Kolluru, V.S.; Prakash, S. Evaluation of Urbanization and Impacts on Water Quality in Nottawasaga Bay Using an Integrated 3-D Modeling Framework. In Proceedings of the 7th International Congress on Environmental Modelling and Software, San Diego, CA, USA, 15–19 June 2014; Ames, D.P., Quinn, N.W.T., Rizzoli, A.E., Eds.; Available online: http://www.iemss.org/society/index.php/iemss-2014-proceedings (accessed on 25 January 2013).

27. Mellor, G.L.; Yamada, T. Development of a turbulence closure model for geophysical fluid problems. *Rev. Geophys. Space Phys.* **1982**, *20*, 851–875. [CrossRef]

28. Umlauf, L.; Burchard, H. A generic length-scale equation for geophysical turbulence models. *J. Mar. Res.* **2003**, *61*, 235–265. [CrossRef]

29. Warner, J.C.; Sherwood, C.R. Performance of four turbulence closure methods implemented using a generic length scale method. *Ocean Model.* **2005**, *8*, 81–113. [CrossRef]

30. Okubo, A. Oceanic diffusion diagrams. *Deep-Sea Res.* **1971**, *18*, 789–802. [CrossRef]

31. Smagorinsky, J. General circulation experiments with the primitive equations. *Mon. Weather Rev.* **1963**, *91*, 99–164. [CrossRef]

32. Prakash, S.; Kolluru, V.S. Implementation of higher order transport schemes with explicit and implicit formulations in a 3-D hydrodynamic and transport model. In Proceedings of the 7th International Conference on Hydroscience and Engineering, Philadelphia, PA, USA, 10–13 September 2006; Available online: http://web.abo.fi/seabed (accessed on 10 June 2013).

33. Dargahi, B.; Cvetkovic, V. Hydrodynamic and transport properties of Saltsjö Bay in the inner Stockholm Archipelago. *J. Coast. Res.* **2010**, *27*, 572–584. [CrossRef]

34. Dargahi, B.; Setegn, S. Combined 3D hydrodynamic and watershed modelling of Lake Tana, Ethiopia. *J. Hydrol.* **2011**, *398*, 44–64. [CrossRef]

35. Environmental Resources Management. *GEMSS Software Technical Documentation*; ERM: Malvern, PA, USA, 2006.

36. Madsen, O.S.; Grant, W.D. Quantitative description of sediment transport by waves. In Proceedings of the 15th International Conference on Coastal Engineering, ASCE, Honolulu, HI, USA, 11–17 July 1976; pp. 1093–1112.

37. Myrberg, K.; Andrejev, O. Modelling of the circulation, water exchange and water age properties of the Gulf of Bothnia. *Oceanologia* **2006**, *48*, 55–74.

38. Palmen, E. Untersuchungen über die Stromungen in den Finnland umgebenden Meeren. *Soc. Sci. Fennica Comment. Phys. Math.* **1930**, *12*, 1–94.

39. Harmel, R.D.; Smith, P.K.; Migliaccio, W.; Chaubey, I.; Douglas-Mankin, K.R.; Benham, B.; Shukla, S.; Muñoz-Carpena, R.; Robson, B.J. Evaluating, interpreting and communicating performance of hydrologic/water quality models considering intended use: A review and recommendations. *Environ. Model. Softw.* **2014**, *57*, 40–51. [CrossRef]

40. SMHI Oceanography. Available online: http://www.smhi.se/klimatdata/oceanografi/havsis (accessed on 7 March 2012).

41. Lackey, R.T. Response of physical and chemical parameters to eliminating thermal stratification in a reservoir. *Water Resour. Bull.* **1972**, *8*, 589–599. [CrossRef]

42. Baltic Marine Environment Protection Commission. *The Baltic Marine Environment 1999–2002*; Baltic Sea Environment Proceedings, No. 87; HELCOM: Helsinki, Finland, 2003.

43. Myrberg, K.; Andrejev, O. Main upwelling regions in the Baltic Sea a statistical analysis based on three-dimensional modelling. *Boreal Environ. Res.* **2003**, *8*, 97–112.

44. Lehmann, A.; Krauss, W.; Hinrichsen, H.H. Effects of remote and local atmospheric forcing on circulation an upwelling in the Baltic Sea. *Tellus* **2002**, *54*, 299–316. [CrossRef]

45. Lehmann, A.; Lorenz, P.; Jacob, D. Modelling the exceptional Baltic Sea inflow events in 2002–2003. *Geophys. Res. Lett.* **2004**, *31*, 1–4. [CrossRef]

Article

Towards the Development of an Operational Forecast System for the Florida Coast

Vladimir A. Paramygin, Y. Peter Sheng * and Justin R. Davis

Coastal and Oceanographic Engineering Program, University of Florida, Gainesville, FL 32611-6580, USA;
pva@coastal.ufl.edu (V.A.P.); justin.r.davis@essie.ufl.edu (J.R.D.)
* Correspondence: pete@coastal.ufl.edu; Tel.: +1-352-294-7764

Academic Editor: Richard P. Signell
Received: 18 July 2016; Accepted: 5 January 2017; Published: 13 January 2017

Abstract: A nowcasting and forecasting system for storm surge, inundation, waves, and baroclinic
flow for the Florida coast has been developed. The system is based on dynamically coupled CH3D
and SWAN models and can use a variety of modules to provide different input forcing, boundary and
initial conditions. The system is completely automated and operates unattended at pre-scheduled
intervals as well as in event-triggered mode in response to Atlantic-basin tropical cyclone advisories
issued by the National Hurricane Center. The system provides up to 72-h forecasts forward depending
on the input dataset duration. Spatially, the system spans the entire Florida coastline by employing
four high-resolution domains with resolutions as fine as 10–30 m in the near-shore and overland to
allow the system to resolve fine estuarine details such as in the Intracoastal Waterway and minor
tributaries. The system has been validated in both hindcast and nowcast/forecast modes using water
level and salinity data from a variety of sources and has been found to run robustly during the test
periods. Low level products (e.g., raw output datasets) are disseminated using THREDDS while a
custom defined web-based graphical user interface (GUI) was developed for high level access.

Keywords: forecasting; storm surge; baroclinic; Florida

1. Introduction

Coastal zones in the U.S. and throughout the world are subject to increasing hazards including
storms and storm surge, sea level rise, and harmful algal bloom. Tropical cyclones and associated
surge and inundation along the southeastern US coastline area major concern for coastal communities
and their economies. Coastal waters in the southeastern US support ecologically and economically
significant ecosystems, providing tourism, boating, fishing, and other recreational opportunities with
an annual economic benefit of $675+ billion. With 73.5% of the population living in the coastal zone and
77.1% of GDP coming from shore-adjacent counties, this concern about tropical cyclones is particularly
important to the State of Florida as it ranks in the top five of US states in the total ocean economy for
its reliance on coastal tourism, recreation, and transportation sectors for employment [1,2]. Florida's
battle with tropical cyclones is notorious as it has been affected by more hurricanes than any other
state. For example, between 1900 and 2010, Monroe County, located along the southwest Florida coast
was affected by 32 hurricanes, which is more than any other county in the United States [3].

Management of the Floridian coastal environment is a challenging task for several state and local
agencies including Florida Department of Environment Protection, Florida Division of Emergency
Management, Water Management Districts, and coastal counties as well as local governments. The work
of these agencies is heavily dependent on information made available by such federal agencies as
National Oceanic and Atmospheric Administration (NOAA), Federal Emergency Management Agency
(FEMA), U. S. Geological Survey (USGS), etc. Within NOAA (the primary agency associated with
surge and inundation hazards), the National Weather Service (NWS), National Ocean Service (NOS),

as well as the U.S. Integrated Ocean Observing System (IOOS) provide a multitude of data on the national scale. However, data at physical scales relevant to regional and sub-regional management can be scarce, which makes coastal zone management difficult.

There are several operational and/or quasi-operational forecasting systems for the Florida coast. The National Hurricane Center (NHC) provides the official tropical cyclone surge forecasts, based on the SLOSH [4] and ADCIRC [5] model forecasts. These forecasts provide information for emergency operations and evacuation along the U.S. Atlantic and Gulf coasts. However, both SLOSH and ADCIRC forecasts are based on two-dimensional barotropic models. SLOSH is further constrained in that it uses a coarse grid resolution (on the order of a kilometer) and lacks such important processes as tides, waves, and nonlinear inertia. The Center for Ocean Atmospheric Prediction Studies (COAPS) of Florida State University operates a HYCOM-based 3D forecasting system [6] which possesses robust physics (such as atmospheric-ocean interaction) and 3D baroclinic ocean processes. However, the HYCOM forecasting system uses a relatively coarse grid (>500 m) which is inadequate to resolve the complex coastal and estuarine processes. Similar issues can be found in other Florida forecasting systems based on implementations of the ROMS model [7] and the NCOM model [8] which use relatively course grid resolutions along the Florida coast.

To address the need for a high-resolution forecasting system which can simulate water levels, waves, salinity, and baroclinic circulation along the Florida coast the Advanced Coastal Modeling System (ACMS) was developed. This system can provide forecast information which could be used by the state and local agencies to enhance management of coastal ecosystems and coastal communities in the state of Florida.

Example applications of ACMS forecast information include improved protection of coastal communities from coastal inundation; improved coastal and marine planning and decision-making; improved public health advisories; improved storm surge and rip current warnings; safer and more efficient marine operations and emergency response; advanced decision-making regarding commercial, recreational fisheries and shoreline erosion; improved planning to enhance climate resiliency; improved operational management of water control structures and utility infrastructure by Water Management Districts and utility companies, respectively; and improved emergency operations and management during tropical cyclones via information provided to Weather Forecasting Offices (WFOs) and National Estuarine Research Reserves.

The ACMS is based on the dynamically-coupled CH3D [9–13] and SWAN [14] models which account for wave effects (such as wave-induced wind stresses, wave-current interaction which includes radiation stresses throughout the water column and wave-current bottom stresses) and can incorporate a variety of input forcing functions and boundary and initial conditions for driving these models. The system is automated and can be run at pre-scheduled intervals or be triggered by such events as tropical storm advisories by the National Hurricane Center.

Another significant issue to be considered for operational modeling is computational efficiency. Multiple (often over ten) forecasting model runs with high grid resolutions every day require significant computing resources. A forecasting system must be able to produce timely forecasts, since the value of forecast products declines quickly with the time it takes to produce them.

In the remainder of this paper, ACMS is first described, followed by a description of the model setup, and example model validations.

2. Materials and Methods

2.1. The ACMS Modeling System

2.1.1. CH3D

CH3D (Curvilinear Hydrodynamics in 3D) is a hydrodynamic model originally developed by Sheng [9,10]. The model can simulate 2-D and 3-D barotropic and baroclinic circulation driven by tide, wind, density gradients, and waves. CH3D uses a boundary-fitted non-orthogonal curvilinear grid in the horizontal direction and a terrain-following sigma grid in the vertical direction. As such, the model can accurately represent complex shoreline and geometries in coastal regions. It uses a robust turbulence closure model to represent vertical turbulent mixing [15] and a Smagorinsky type model for horizontal turbulent mixing. The model uses bathymetry and topography which are referenced to the NAVD88 vertical datum for all domains to accurately simulate the coastal inundation. CH3D has been applied to such water bodies as Charlotte Harbor, Biscayne Bay, Apalachicola Bay, Florida Bay, Indian River Lagoon, Lake Okeechobee, Lake Apopka, Sarasota Bay, St. Johns River, Tampa Bay, Naples Bay, and Rookery Bay in Florida, as well as Chesapeake Bay, New York Bight, Long Island Sound, and the Gulf of Mexico.

2.1.2. CH3D-IMS

CH3D has been coupled to models of wave, sediment transport, water quality, light attenuation, and sea grass dynamics to produce CH3D-IMS [16], an Integrated Modeling System for simulating the response of estuarine and coastal ecosystems to anthropogenic (e.g., increased nutrient loading) and natural (e.g., sea level rise) changes.

2.1.3. CH3D-SSMS

CH3D-SSMS (Storm Surge Modeling System) is a modeling suite that features coupled CH3D and SWAN models for coastal dynamics and large scale surge-wave models that are used to extract boundary conditions for the coastal model [11,17], which has been used extensively to simulate storm surge and inundation due to various tropical cyclones including Hurricanes Charley (2004), Dennis (2005), Isabel (2003), Frances (2004), Ivan (2004), Jeanne (2004), Katrina (2005), Wilma (2005), Katrina (2005), Ike (2009), Sandy (2012), Matthew (2016), and others [11–13,17–19]. Details of the CH3D model, including equations of motion and boundary and initial conditions, are described in [11]. CH3D-SSMS contains a robust flooding and drying scheme which is an extension of that developed by Davis and Sheng [20].

In a regional storm surge and coastal inundation model Testbed [21], CH3D-SSMS was compared with ADCIRC [5], CMEPS [22], FVCOM [23], and SLOSH [4]. Detailed comparisons of models were made in terms of simulated storm surges during historic storms as well as coastal inundation maps including the surge atlas and the 1% annual chance coastal inundation maps which is also known as the Base Flood Elevation (BFE) according to the Federal Emergency Management Agency (FEMA) of the US [24]. The results of CH3D-SSMS were found to compare well with observed water level data and was as accurate as other models. The computational efficiency of CH3D-SSMS is only inferior to the extremely efficient SLOSH model which uses a very coarse grid (~1 km) and has simpler physics. The model Testbed results demonstrated that, to obtain accurate model results efficiently, it is feasible to use a highly efficient coastal surge-wave model, e.g., CH3D-SWAN, with high resolution in the coastal region, and couple it to large-scale surge-wave models with coarser resolution in the offshore region. Alternatively, one can use an unstructured grid surge-wave model for the coastal and offshore domains with a single grid, but a high-resolution grid in the coastal region often results in stringent computational time step limitation and requires dramatically more computational resources.

CH3D suites continue to be improved as new research enables incorporation of more dynamic features, e.g., vegetation effects on storm surge, into the models. For example, Lapetina and Sheng [25] recently used the vegetation-resolving ACMS to simulate the effects of vegetation, three-dimensionality, and onshore sediment transport on complex storm surge dynamics during Hurricane Ike which inflicted major damage to the Texas coast in 2009. Results of the 3D model are found to be more accurate than 2D model results.

2.2. ACMS

The cornerstone of the ACMS modeling system includes the CH3D (shallow water hydrodynamics) and SWAN (wave) models, running on four domains (Figure 1) that span the entire Florida coast.

The two models are dynamically coupled, which enables representation of complex physics such as vertically varying wave-current interaction. ACMS is essentially the integration of CH3D-SSMS and CH3D-IMS which was described in the previous section.

Figure 1. Advanced Coastal Modeling System (ACMS) Florida coast domains: Northern Gulf (NG) of Mexico (pink), Southwest (SW) (blue), Southeast (SE) (green), and East Coast (EC) (yellow).

SWAN is a third-generation phase-averaged wave model that can be applied to nearshore wave modeling. The model can use a variety of computational grid arrangements including non-orthogonal regular, curvilinear, and unstructured triangular grids. SWAN accounts for wave propagation in time and space, shoaling, refraction due to currents and depth, frequency shifting due to currents and dynamic depth, wave generation by wind, energy dissipation by bottom friction, depth-induced breaking and transmission through and reflection from obstacles (full or partial reflection can be considered). SWAN represents waves using a two-dimensional wave action density energy spectrum and the evolution of the spectrum is described by the spectral action balance equation in which a local rate of change of action density in time is related to the propagation of action in geographical space, shifting of relative frequency due to currents and depths, depth-induced and current-induced refraction balanced by the source term in terms of energy density representing the effects of energy generation, energy dissipation and nonlinear wave-wave interactions.

ACMS can use a variety of wind fields such as

- Hurricane Research Division's H*Wind [26];
- Navy's NOGAPS [27];
- GFDL [28];
- NAM (North American Mesoscale) that uses WRF (Weather Research and Forecasting model [29]) and is run by the National Centers for Environmental Prediction [30]; and

- Several synthetic parametric wind models driven by storm parameters that are derived from National Hurricane Center (NHC) predictions.

2.3. ACMS Modules and Workflow

ACMS consists of four main modules (Figure 2): (1) data acquisition and pre-processing module; (2) simulation setup (staging/running/etc.) and job management module; (3) post-processing module; and (4) visualization module. These modules provide automation of such processes as input data acquisition, archiving and cataloging of data and model results, data pre-processing, setting up model simulations, running and monitoring jobs, post-processing of model results, and visualization. Some of the most important properties of the ACMS are full automation, compliance with existing standards for ocean data, and efficient use of available computational resources. Previous implementation of the system showed that it can perform both 3D baroclinic and storm surge simulations simultaneously during tropical cyclones [18], as well as ensemble forecasting of storm surges based on an ensemble of storm tracks generated from the probability distribution of previous track forecasting errors [31].

The data acquisition module is responsible for data acquisition and consists of monitors that poll the data providers for new data and acquires the data as it becomes available. Monitors for a variety of datasets are available: NOAA NHC advisories, the U.S. Navy's Automated Tropical Cyclone Forecasting System (ATCF [32]) forecast products, atmospheric inputs (NAM, NOGAPS, GFDL, etc.), boundary and initial conditions for circulation from such models as HYCOM [33] and ROMS, and boundary and initial conditions for waves from wave models such as WaveWatch III (WWIII) [34]. River flow measurements and predictions, salinity measurements, etc. are also collected where available from USGS, National Estuarine Research Reserves, and the National Weather Service River Forecast Center. All the data are obtained as they become available, processed (with QA/QC, subsetting, and necessary format conversions), archived, and cataloged (using a MySQL database).

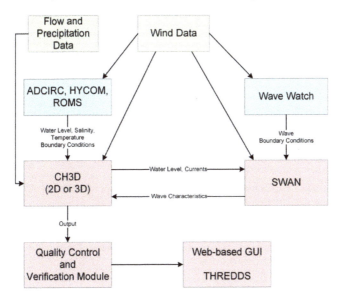

Figure 2. ACMS workflow diagram.

ACMS supports two modes of operation:

- Event triggered, where a model instance is created as a response to an event (such as an NHC-issued tropical cyclone advisory) or

- Preset cycles, where a model is initiated at fixed times, which usually follow the standard 4-cycles per day scheme (model initialized at 00:00, 06:00, 12:00 and 18:00 UTC).

The job management module initiates the simulation and polls the data acquisition module. Once all the data necessary for model input is collected, the module generates the necessary input files, sends the job to the computing cluster via HTCondor job management system [35] and monitors the job status for potential computing resource failures in which case the jobs are resubmitted to alternate resources.

The post-processing module extracts output from completed forecast runs, generates aggregate products, calculates statistics, and places products and outputs in the archive. ACMS currently uses NetCDF with CF-1.5 conventions as a data format of choice and Unidata's THREDDS Data Server [36] as the main platform for data distribution. Visualization module (mostly client-based) is written in JavaScript and uses THREDDS server (via WMS feeds and NetCDF subsetting) as a data provider to display data in a user-friendly manner (Figure 3).

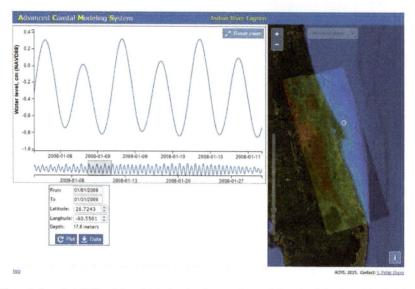

Figure 3. Sample ACMS web-based interface for data preview and download developed for St. Johns River Water Management District with focus on the Indian River Lagoon on the east coast of Florida.

Data availability is the limiting factor for initiating a new forecast cycle. A complete data set such as wind, the waves at the open boundary, the surge at the open boundary, and the flow rates at rivers should be available from the archive for the forecast cycle to be initiated. Data is pulled from the archive by the Data Processing Module and all necessary input files are generated for all the simulations that are scheduled to run within that cycle. Completion of this process triggers the start of the cycle at the Core Module which is responsible for setting up the boundary conditions for all the models involved in the cycle, scheduling, and submitting the simulation to one of the available computational resources. There are mechanisms that enable forecasts even when some of the data is missing. Certain data such as missing atmospheric snapshots or relatively short gaps in time-series data can be reconstructed, interpolated or extrapolated based on available data.

2.4. ACMS Model Setup

Two implementations of ACMS are discussed in this paper:

1. 2D implementation—The 2D barotropic CH3D model is coupled with SWAN and CH3D receives open boundary conditions from a large-scale ADCIRC model running on a coarse grid ~2–5 km, while SWAN receives open boundary condition from WWIII. Despite the coarseness of the grid, ADCIRC produces satisfactory results along the offshore CH3D boundary and runs very quickly to allow syncing with the CH3D model. This implementation is event-triggered by NHC tropical cyclone advisories. ACMS downloads NHC advisories and, whenever it contains forecasted tropical cyclone track coming within 100 miles of a CH3D domain, creates a model instance for that advisory. This implementation is used to quickly forecast storm surge and inundation during tropical storms. Not only do 2D model simulations complete quicker, but all the inputs required for the model are also contained in the advisory, because the surge and wave models are driven by a synthetic parametric model for atmospheric wind and pressure. In most cases, the amount of time between the advisory time stamp and prediction is less than two hours.

2. 3D Implementation—The 3D baroclinic CH3D model is coupled with SWAN, and CH3D receives boundary conditions from a large-scale HYCOM or ROMS model, while SWAN receives open boundary condition from WWIII. The model runs four times a day at 6-h intervals starting at 00:00 UTC. This implementation is intended to provide more comprehensive forecasts including water levels, waves, baroclinic circulation, and salinity. However, this increased fidelity comes at a cost: not only the model runtime increases to 4–6 h (depending on domain and conditions such as networking and transfer speeds, etc.), but the time required to fetch all the inputs (including open boundary conditions from HYCOM or ROMS, atmospheric predictions from NAM, and river flows, etc.) can be twice as long. The model has the capability to simulate temperature, however, due to limited data available for boundary conditions and verification, current forecasting implementation does not include temperature simulation.

2.4.1. Atmospheric Forcing

Atmospheric forcing in ACMS includes atmospheric pressure, wind, and precipitation. The system can use a variety of wind fields as well as several synthetic parametric models. The 2D implementation uses the parametric model of Xie et al. [37]. Model parameters such as location of the storm, maximum wind, and radii to 34 kt, 50 kt, and 64 kt winds are based on the NHC predicted storm parameters. The 3D implementation is driven by the atmospheric forcing predicted by the NAM model.

2.4.2. Surge-Wave Coupling

In ACMS, the CH3D model is dynamically coupled to the SWAN wave model [14]: wave results obtained by SWAN are passed to CH3D and water depths and currents obtained by CH3D are passed onto SWAN. This accounts for wave setup and wave-current interaction within the CH3D model, which features several formulations for calculating wave stresses [38], including vertically varying formulations (e.g., Mellor [39]) as well as the vertically uniform formulation of Longuet-Higgins and Stewart [40,41]. The 3D implementation of the model uses the formulation by Mellor [39] as it was found to produce more accurate results [38].

The time step used for CH3D simulation is 60 s and time step used for SWAN simulation is 5 min, which is when the two models exchange information.

2.4.3. Coastal-Offshore Coupling

Both coastal CH3D and SWAN models use the same non-orthogonal curvilinear model grid and are dependent upon open boundary conditions provided by larger scale ocean models. ACMS interfaces enable it to receive boundary conditions from a variety of large-scale models such as HYCOM, ROMS, CH3D, and ADCIRC for CH3D, and larger-scale SWAN or WWIII for SWAN.

In the 2D implementation, CH3D obtains open boundary conditions (elevation at the open boundary) from a coarse-grid (~2–5 km) ADCIRC model which is run simultaneously with the CH3D model. Large-scale SWAN model produces boundary conditions for the coastal SWAN model.

In the 3D implementation, CH3D obtains open boundary conditions (vertically varying currents and salinity) from a HYCOM, while SWAN derives its boundary conditions either from a WWIII model or a large-scale SWAN model.

2.4.4. ACMS Model Domains and Forecast Cycles

The four domains used by ACMS span the entire Florida coastline (Figure 1) and extend 50–100 km offshore (Table 1). The forecasts range from 48 h up to 72 h, depending on the configuration and available input. Each cycle is initialized from the previous cycle, and a 6-h nowcasting is performed to fill the 6-h gap between cycles, followed by a forecast.

ACMS model domains use NAVD88 as a vertical datum of choice, which makes computing surge, inundation, and flooding a simple and transparent process since all the topography data is generally referenced to NAVD88. The 3D implementation of the model typically uses six equally spaced sigma layers in vertical—this number was determined by comparing simulations obtained with 4, 6, 8, 16 layers, which found that 6 layers were sufficient to resolve the pycnocline and that going from 6 to 8+ layers provides negligible differences in simulation results.

Table 1. Characteristics of Advanced Coastal Modeling System (ACMS) model domains.

Domain	Minimum Resolution (m)	Approximate Grid Cell Count	Average Offshore Extent (km)
East Coast (EC)	32	339,000	55
Southeast (SE)	21	607,000	60
Southwest (SW)	29	366,000	65
Northern Gulf of Mexico (NG)	47	404,000	75

2.4.5. Boundary Conditions

The water level at the open boundary of CH3D domain is prescribed by combining the water level predicted by a regional ocean circulation model and spatially varying tidal constituents which include M2, S2, N2, K2, K1, O1, P1, Q1, SA, and SSA. These tidal constituents were determined to be important for the Florida coast based on the NOAA tidal gauge data, while other constituents generally are estimated to have an amplitude of less than 1 cm. The constituents at the open boundary are developed via an iterative process in which phases and amplitudes at the open boundary are adjusted during tide-only simulations to provide the best possible fit with observed tides at the coastal stations. Salinity at the open ocean boundary is interpolated from a 1/12 degree HYCOM or ROMS (provided at 6-h intervals).

Open boundary conditions for SWAN are wave height and period obtained from the results of a 0.25 degree WWIII model.

River flow measurements/forecasts and salinity measurements are gathered from a variety of sources such as NOAA Advanced Hydrologic Prediction Service, Florida DEP, Florida Water Management Districts, and National Estuarine Research Reserves. These data serve as boundary conditions for flow and salinity upstream of rivers and creeks and are crucial to accurate predictions of currents and salinity in estuaries, inlets, and near-shore zone. River flow and salinity data used for boundary conditions in estuaries are extrapolated in time based on the trend identified in previous data for stations where flow forecasts are unavailable or the forecasted period is shorter than the length of ACMS forecast. The extrapolation is based on identifying a linear trend during the last 7 days and using it to extrapolate the flow (subject to a maximum increase/decrease of 2 ppt in a 7-day period). This was found to produce slightly better results compared to using the last available value for the entire forecast period.

3. Results

3.1. Model Validation

Using the model setup described in the previous section, a series of validation tests were performed by hindcasting non-storm events (lighter wind speeds, tidally-dominated flow) as well as several tropical cyclones including Andrew (1992), Jeanne (2004), Wilma (2005), and Fay (2008). The storms are selected to represent different hurricanes ranging from slow moving Tropical Storm Fay, which became almost stationary for about a day just off the east coast of Florida near Jacksonville, to fast-paced Hurricane Wilma that went across the entire state in less than six hours with significant variation in intensity and size. Some forecast results are also presented since the ACMS system has been running in the quasi-operational mode since 2012. Only a select few stations (Figure 4) per domain are shown here as it would be impossible to show model-data comparisons for all of them in the scope of this paper.

Figure 4. Location of select data stations used for ACMS validation.

3.1.1. Non-Storm Conditions

Simulation of tides is a key feature of a forecasting system because water levels and currents are very important for safe navigation and recreation as well as the increasing coastal inundation during high tides. Under calmer weather conditions, tides usually dominate and determine the coastal circulation. Hence, the ability to accurately predict tidal water level and flows is crucial. Data during 2008–2014 were used for validation purposes and the criterium for tidal validation is to achieve an average RMS error of 7 cm per domain. The total number of stations used for validation of tides is: nine for the EC domain, five for the SE domain, five for the SW and six for the NG domains. Vilano Beach (Figure 5) and Melbourne (Figure 6) stations are examples of tidal simulations on the EC domain.

Data from a NOAA station at Naples, FL (Figure 7) on the west coast was used to validate the tides for the SW domain.

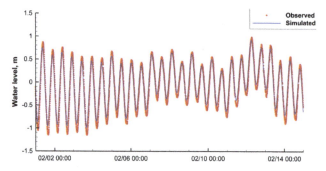

Figure 5. Comparison of simulated (hindcast) and observed water levels at Vilano Beach station for tidally-dominated flow.

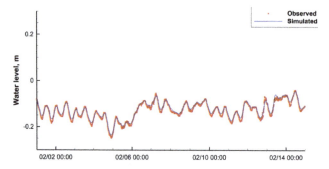

Figure 6. Comparison of simulated (hindcast) and observed water levels at Melbourne station for tidally-dominated flow.

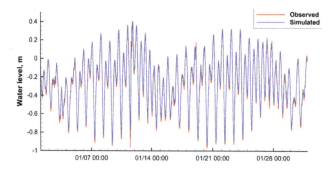

Figure 7. Comparison of simulated (hindcast) and observed water levels at Naples station for tidally-dominated flow.

Tidal Simulation

Overall, ACMS predicted amplitudes and phases of select tidal constituents (M2, S2, N2, K2, K1, O1, P1, Q1, SA, and SSA) are very close to the observed values at all stations with the average RMS error being under 5%.

Nuisance Flooding

The ACMS was used to forecast "king" tides (astronomically high tides) near Miami Beach (Figure 8), and the results were provided to the city of Miami Beach. During a "king" tide, numerous South Florida communities (Miami Beach, Fort Lauderdale, Key West, and Naples, etc.) experience nuisance flooding with streets inundated of 30 cm or more. Nuisance flooding is occurring more frequently as the sea level continues to rise. By 2050 some communities (e.g., Key West) are expected to have nuisance flooding during more than 100 days per year. The City of Miami Beach installed 20 pumps in 2015 to mitigate nuisance flooding during king tides.

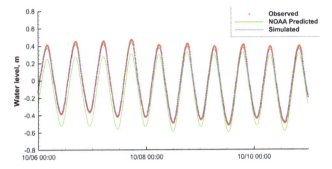

Figure 8. Forecast of "king" tides and comparison with National Oceanic and Atmospheric Administration (NOAA) observed and predicted water levels at Virginia Key station in October 2014 (initialization time: 6 October, 2014 00:00Z).

Salinity Simulation

Limited salinity data was available for validation with just two stations for the EC and SE domains, five stations clustered inside the Naples/Rookery Bay region on the west coast of Florida and a few in the Apalachicola Bay maintained by the Apalachicola National Estuarine Research Reserve (ANERR). The quality of salinity predictions can vary drastically depending on availability and accuracy of river flow predictions. However, most stations show satisfactory agreement. The RMS error in the SW domain during September and October 2014 varied between 2 ppt and 7 ppt with a correlation coefficient (r^2) between 0.52 and 0.9. The NG domain comparisons (Figure 9) show slightly better agreement with the RMS error between 2 ppt and 5 ppt. The RMS errors for stations in the EC domain vary between 3 ppt and 9 ppt, most likely due to the inaccuracy and limited availability of river flow data that provides fresh water inflow into the model domains.

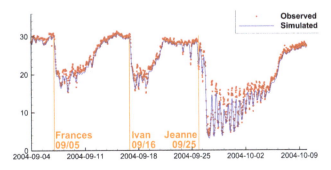

Figure 9. Comparison of simulated and observed salinity Cat Point station (NG domain), orange vertical lines indicate land fall times of the three storms: Frances, Ivan, and Jeanne.

Surface Current Simulation

There exist limited datasets of observed surface currents collected by the high frequency radar (HF Radar, [42,43]) along the southeast coast of Florida near Biscayne Bay. The ACMS simulated currents in the central part of the coastal domain appear to be comparable (Figure 10) with the observed data. However, it should be noted that these currents data have not been fully analyzed to remove errors associated with interference of the radar signals.

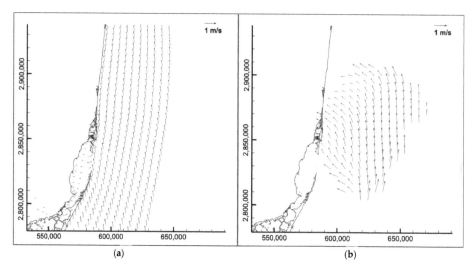

Figure 10. Comparison of estimated surface currents (**a**) vs. surface currents measured by the HF Radar (**b**) east of the Biscayne Bay (SE domain, 20 March 2014 12:00Z). Coordinate space is UTM zone 17N (m).

3.1.2. Simulation of Surge, Wave, and Inundation during Tropical Cyclones

Model validations for tropical cyclone conditions were carried out in a hindcast mode for the following four storms: Hurricane Andrew (1992), Hurricane Jeanne (2004), Hurricane Wilma (2005), and Tropical Storm Fay (2008).

Hurricane Andrew

Andrew was a small but ferocious hurricane that brought unprecedented economic devastation to the southern Florida peninsula. Overall damage in the U.S. is estimated at ~$26.5 billion (1993 USD) making it one of the five costliest storms in U.S. history. The tropical cyclone struck southern Dade County, Florida (Figure 11) especially hard, with violent winds and storm surges characteristic of a category 5 hurricane [44] on the Saffir/Simpson Hurricane Scale, and with a central pressure of 922 mb. Unfortunately, the amount of data available for Andrew is limited to a single station at Haulover Pier, but the model predicted water level at this station compared very well with the observed data (Figure 12), especially when the wave model is coupled to the surge model in the simulation.

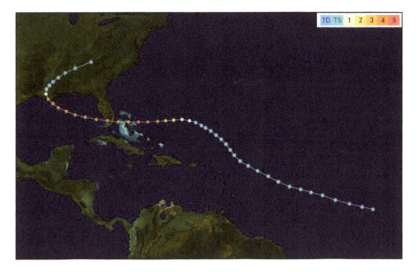

Figure 11. Track of Hurricane Andrew (1992).

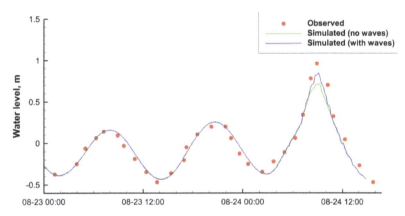

Figure 12. Comparison of observed and simulated (hindcast) water levels at the Haulover Pier station during Hurricane Andrew (1992). "No waves" curve shows results based on CH3D model that does not include wave effects and "with waves" shows results based on the coupled CH3D-SWAN model.

Hurricane Jeanne

Hurricane Jeanne (Figure 13), while known as a very deadly storm claiming more than 3000 lives in Haiti alone, weakened significantly before making its landfall on the east coast of Florida near Stuart [45]. After which, it further weakened to a tropical cyclone making its way across Florida peninsula towards Tampa. Because of its smaller size (about 50 miles at landfall) the area affected by it was relatively small. As such, a very limited amount of data is available for comparison. The water level response predicted by ACMS at Trident Pier (Figure 14) matches the observed data well, both in terms of the peak water level and phase.

Figure 13. Track of Hurricane Jeanne (2004).

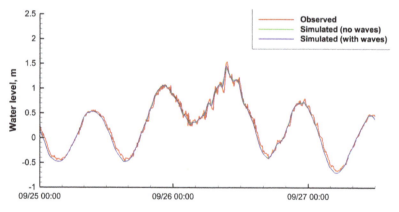

Figure 14. A comparison between simulated (hindcast) and measure waver levels at the Trident Pier Station during Hurricane Jeanne (2004).

Hurricane Wilma (2005)

Hurricane Wilma (Figure 15) was the most intense tropical cyclone ever recorded in the Atlantic basin. In the U.S. it made landfall near Cape Romano, Florida with winds of 120 mph [46] and quickly crossed Florida emerging on the east coast just 5 h later. There is significant amount of data available for Wilma, including over 20 storm gauges that were installed along the west coast of Florida by the USGS. Below is a comparison of peak surge heights at these gauges (Figure 16) and comparison of simulated and observed data at Trident Pier station on the east coast that was affected by the storm after Wilma crossed the Florida peninsula (Figure 17). Maximum storm surge during Wilma was also compared to a number of high water marks and the correlation coefficient between recorded and predicted water marks was 0.78.

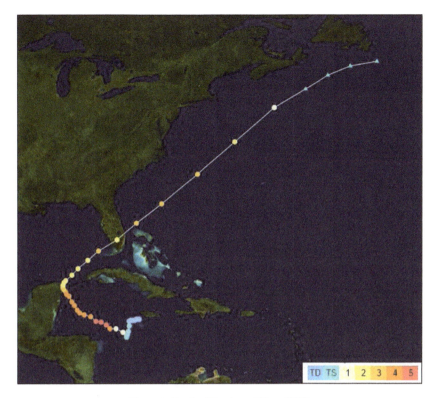

Figure 15. Track of Hurricane Wilma (2005).

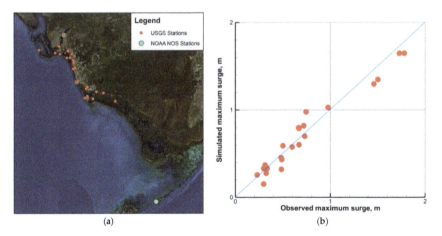

(a)   (b)

Figure 16. Map of data stations with observed data (**a**) and comparison between observed and simulated (hindcast) and peak surges during Hurricane Wilma (**b**).

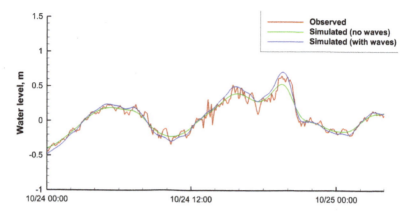

Figure 17. A comparison between simulated (hindcast) and observed water levels at the Trident Pier Station during Hurricane Wilma (2005).

Tropical Storm Fay

The last storm presented for validation purposes is Tropical Storm Fay [47], (Figure 18). It is the weakest storm of the four presented, however, one notable feature of this storm is that it was slowly moving just off the east coast of Florida zigzagging across the coastline over a period of about 24 h making a total of four landfalls in Florida. Fay produced torrential rainfall dropping as much as 27 inches of rain near Melbourne, Florida. The rainfall significantly affected the river flows and salinity making it an interesting case study. Water level comparison at I-295 bridge station (Figure 19) near Jacksonville and salinity comparison at Pine Island station (Figure 20) show that predicted values compare quite well with observed data. It is worth noting that, even though the semidiurnal variations in salinity are only partially captured, the observed significant drop in salinity over the 3-day period was well captured by the model simulation.

Figure 18. Track of Tropical Cyclone Fay (2008).

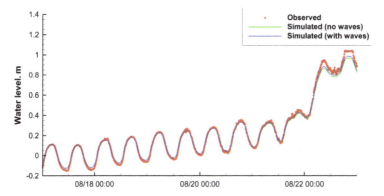

Figure 19. A comparison between the simulated (hindcast) and observed water levels at the I-295 Bridge Station (EC domain) during Tropical Storm Fay (2008).

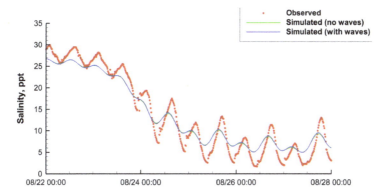

Figure 20. A comparison between simulated (hindcast) and observed salinity at the Pine Island Station (EC domain) during Tropical Cyclone Fay (2008).

3.2. 2015 Hurricane Season Forecasting

ACMS was tested in a quasi-operational mode during the 2015 hurricane season spanning from 1 June 2015 to 30 November 2015. Unfortunately, arrangements for hardware location, networking, etc. are such that it is currently impossible to guarantee a 24/7 uptime for the system as it is located in a research rather than an operational environment and is subject to power and network outages, hardware failures, etc. The system was functioning about 85% of the time. Several statistics were calculated (Table 2) based on these forecasts: root mean square error (RMSE), central frequency (CF), and positive/negative outlier frequency (POF/NOF). These are some of the criteria that are used by NOS for model skill assessment [48]. The error calculations are for the 0–24 h forecast window. Acceptable error limits used for calculation of CF are 15 cm for water level and 3 ppt for salinity and acceptable error limits used for calculation of POF/NOF are 30 cm for water level and 6 ppt for salinity [48].

Table 2. Errors statistics calculated based on ACMS forecasts during 1 June 2015–30 November 2015. Units for root mean square error (RMSE) are cm for water level data and ppt for salinity. Green indicates that the errors are within acceptable limits (>90% for CF and <1% POF/NOF), red indicates otherwise.

Data Station	ACMS Domain	Data Type	Source	RMSE cm/ppt	CF %	POF/NOF %
8728690 Apalachicola	NG	WL	NOAA	7	92.4	0.1/0.3
8727520 Cedar Key	NG	WL	NOAA	6	93.2	0.2/0.3
8726724 Clearwater Beach	SW	WL	NOAA	6	92.0	0.1/0.1
8720219 Dames Point	EC	WL	NOAA	6	93.8	0.2/0.2
8720030 Fernandina Beach	EC	WL	NOAA	5	94.6	0.2/0.1
8725520 Fort Myers	SW	WL	NOAA	4	97.2	0.1/0.0
8720357 I-295 Bridge	EC	WL	NOAA	4	95.6	0.1/0.2
Key West	SE	WL	NOAA	5	95.6	0.1/0.1
Lake Worth Pier	SE	WL	NOAA	6	94.1	0.2/0.2
Mayport	EC	WL	NOAA	4	97.8	0.1/0.0
Mckay Bay	SW	WL	NOAA	5	96.2	0.1/0.1
Naples	SW	WL	NOAA	4	98.2	0.0/0.0
Old Port Tampa	SW	WL	NOAA	5	96.7	0.4/0.2
Panama City	NG	WL	NOAA	5	95.7	0.2/0.7
Pensacola	NG	WL	NOAA	7	93.3	0.4/0.9
Port Manatee	SW	WL	NOAA	6	94.8	0.3/0.2
Racy Point	EC	WL	NOAA	12	86.8	1.4/0.8
Red Bay Point	EC	WL	NOAA	10	91.2	1.1/0.8
S. Riverwalk	EC	WL	NOAA	7	94.0	0.2/0.6
St Petersburg	SW	WL	NOAA	6	94.4	0.3/0.2
Trident Pier	EC	WL	NOAA	5	93.4	0.3/0.3
Vaca Key	SE	WL	NOAA	5	94.8	0.2/0.3
Virginia Key	SE	WL	NOAA	5	96.2	0.2/0.1
Bing's Landing	EC	WL	FLDEP	6	93.2	0.2/0.3
Binney Dock	EC	WL	FLDEP	6	94.7	0.2/0.3
Dry Bar	NG	WL	FLDEP	5	95.3	0.2/0.2
East Bay	NG	WL	FLDEP	6	92.2	0.3/0.6
Gordon River Inlet	SW	WL	FLDEP	5	94.4	0.3/0.1
Melbourne	EC	WL	FLDEP	4	96.6	0.2/0.1
Naples Bay	SW	WL	FLDEP	4	96.3	0.1/0.1
Pilot Cove	NG	WL	FLDEP	7	92.0	0.3/0.5
Ponce de Leon	EC	WL	FLDEP	6	94.5	0.3/0.2
St. Lucie Inlet	EC	WL	FLDEP	5	95.8	0.2/0.2
Tolomato River	EC	WL	FLDEP	7	93.3	0.1/0.3
Vilano Beach	EC	WL	FLDEP	7	94.0	0.1/0.2
Bing's Landing	EC	S	FLDEP	2.1	94.1	0.6/0.4
Dry Bar	NG	S	FLDEP	6.2	77.5	1.7/3.3
Melbourne	EC	S	FLDEP	2.7	88.2	0.7/0.9
Tolomato River	EC	S	FLDEP	1.8	92.9	0.7/0.4
Cat Point	NG	S	ANERR	2.8	87.0	0.8/0.6
Henderson Creek	SW	S	RNERR	1.7	93.7	0.3/0.3
Fakahatchee Bay	SW	S	RNERR	2.3	90.2	0.5/0.4
Faka Union Bay	SW	S	RNERR	2.6	88.2	0.6/0.4
Pellicer Creek	EC	S	GNERR	4.1	81.5	1.5/0.9
San Sebastian	EC	S	GNERR	3.1	86.7	0.8/0.6
Pine Island	EC	S	GNERR	3.3	81.1	1.3/0.8

NOAA—NOAA Tides and Currents [49]; FLDEP—Florida Department of Environmental Protection [50]; ANERR—Apalachicola Bay NERR [51]; RNERR—Rookery Bay NERR [51]; GNERR—Guana-Tolomato-Matanzas NERR [51]; Data types: WL—Water level, S—Salinity.

3.3. Computational Efficiency and Timing

One notable feature of ACMS is its computational efficiency. Currently, model codes run in parallel (implemented via OpenMP) on Intel-based machines running Red Hat Linux (RHEL6/7) with quad-core CPUs (Intel i5-4690 CPU @ 3.50 GHz). Computers are not shared by simulations of different domains or with any other resource-intensive tasks (i.e., each simulation is assigned to a dedicated quad-core machine). The wall times for the full ACMS setup described earlier in this paper for each domain are shown in Table 3.

As noted previously, given the computational efficiency of ACMS provides good balance between the provided accuracy and required resources. In order to run in real time, ACMS needs only 1–4 processing cores, compared to other systems which often require a high-performance computing system with hundreds or thousands of processors. Current ACMS setup uses a single quad-core system (as described above) per model domain. The codes within the system are effectively parallelized and the wall time can be reduced by using more CPU cores. For example, using 32 CPU cores yields approximately 30–40 min wall times (Table 3).

Table 3. Average wall-clock time for ACMS simulations (a simulation consists of a 6-h hindcast/nowcast and a 72-h forecast) per domain. Times can vary from cycle to cycle, depending on conditions and number of wetted grid cells.

| | Wall Clock Time (Hours:Minutes) | | | |
| Domain | 4 CPU Cores | | 32 CPU Cores | |
	2D	3D	2D	3D
East Coast	0:58	3:40	0:22	00:28
Southeast	1:45	5:42	0:37	00:43
Southwest	1:10	4:11	0:29	00:32
Northern Gulf of Mexico	1:29	5:04	0:34	00:37

As such, the 2D and 3D implementations of ACMS differ significantly in wall time required to perform the model simulations, however, this difference only slightly affects the total forecast cycle time. The amount of data required and time needed to fetch these data is significantly different for the 2D and 3D implementations. It can take up to 12 h to obtain all the required boundary conditions for the 3D implementation. The only external data required for the 2D model is a hurricane track as it uses a synthetic parametric wind model to generate wind and pressure fields, which generally takes only minutes to obtain. Pre/post-processing steps take 2–5 min and hence the entire forecast cycle using a 2D model can be completed in less than two hours using the current computational setup.

4. Discussion and Future Work

This paper details how the ACMS was setup, tested, and validated in tidal and hindcast scenarios. The system is shown to be robust and results match well with data for hindcasting. Simulated water levels and salinity for hindcasted periods match well with data and 24-h forecasts that were performed during the 2015 hurricane season are within acceptable limits for most stations. RMS errors for water levels are found to vary between 4 cm and 12 cm. Additional efforts will be undertaken to analyze the sources of error for stations that do not satisfy the criteria (e.g., two stations located upstream the St. Johns River: Racy Point and Red Bay Point) and attempt will be made to reduce the errors. The computational performance of the system is also discussed. Model efficiency allows the production of robust forecasts in a limited-resource environment and choice of NetCDF-based data standards gives flexibility in distributing the data using a THREDDS server and derived products using in-house web-based user interface. The system will be tested in operational settings (completely unattended) and operational performance, uptime, etc. will be a subject of a future publication.

Data availability and its accuracy significantly affect the results of simulations. It is especially important for salinity, as missing river flow or salinity boundary conditions can drastically change the quality of predictions inside an estuary. Additional quality control and data extrapolation methods will be explored along with an option to include a watershed model into ACMS suite for more robust predictions of upstream river flows and subsequently salinity inside estuaries. Temperature is another important variable. While ACMS is capable of simulating temperature, such simulations are currently in the preliminary phase. Feasibility of accurate temperature predictions constrained by limited data is being explored. The key to this is data availability with very little data available for use as boundary conditions and for validation. Efforts will be made to obtain such data, and setup and validate the temperature model.

Forecasting results from the 2016 hurricane season will be analyzed using more statistical categories and NOS criteria, including maximum duration of positive and negative outliers and worst case outlier frequency, as well as timing of maximums and minimums.

Sheng et al. [52,53] developed a vegetation model which incorporates the effects of vegetation on mean flow and turbulence in the water column. The vegetation resolving model showed that, during hurricanes, total inundation volume can be reduced by up to 40% due to the presence of vegetation. The reduction of storm surge and coastal inundation depends on the characteristics (type, distribution, height, and density, etc.) of vegetation as well as hurricane characteristics (intensity and forward speed, etc.). The vegetation module will be added to the ACMS, however, additional efforts are needed to optimize the algorithms and ensure that this addition does not hinder the efficiency of ACMS.

Acknowledgments: This work was sponsored by the Southeast Coastal Ocean Observing Regional Association (NOAA/NOPP, IOOS.11(033)UF.PS.MOD.1), St. Johns River Water Management District, South Florida Water Management District, and U.S. Fish and Wildlife Service.

Author Contributions: V.A.P., J.R.D. and Y.P.S. conceived and designed model simulation, developed various parts of the model. V.A.P. setup, performed the model simulation, and wrote the paper with Y.P.S.

Conflicts of Interest: The authors declare no conflict of interest. The founding sponsors had no role in the design of the study; in the collection, analyses, or interpretation of data; in the writing of the manuscript, and in the decision to publish the results.

References

1. NOEP (National Ocean Economics Program). Coastal and Ocean Economic Summaries of the Coastal States. 2014. Available online: http://www.oceaneconomics.org/download (accessed on 17 July 2015).
2. NOEP (National Ocean Economics Program). State of the U.S. Ocean and Coastal Economies Coastal States Summaries—2016 Update. 2014. Available online: http://www.oceaneconomics.org/download (accessed on 17 July 2015).
3. NOAA Hurricane Research Division. Detailed List of Continental United States Hurricane Impacts/Landfalls, 1851–1960, 1983–2015. Available online: http://www.aoml.noaa.gov/hrd/hurdat/UShurrs_detailed.html (accessed on 25 August 2016).
4. Jelesnianski, C.P.; Chen, J.; Shaffer, W.A. *SLOSH: Sea, Lake, and Overland Surges from Hurricanes*; US Department of Commerce, National Oceanic and Atmospheric Administration, National Weather Service: Washington, D.C., USA, 1992.
5. Luettich, R.; Westerink, J.J.; Scheffner, N.W. *ADCIRC: An Advanced Three-Dimensional Circulation Model for Shelves Coasts and Estuaries, Report 1: Theory and Methodology of ADCIRC-2DDI and ADCIRC-3DL*. DRP-92–6; U.S. Army Engineers Waterways Experiment Station: Vicksburg, MS, USA, 1992; p. 137.
6. Bleck, R.; Benjamin, S. Regional weather prediction with a model combining terrain following and isentropic coordinates. Part I: Model description. *Mon. Weather Rev.* **1993**, *121*, 1770–1785. [CrossRef]
7. Shchepetkin, A.F.; McWilliams, J.C. The regional oceanic modeling system (ROMS): A split-explicit, free-surface, topography-following-coordinate oceanic model. *Ocean Model.* **2005**, *9*, 347–404. [CrossRef]
8. Barron, C.N.; Kara, A.B.; Hurlburt, H.E.; Rowley, C.; Smedstad, L.F. Sea surface height predictions from the Global Navy Coastal Ocean Model (NCOM) during 1998–2001. *J. Atmos. Ocean. Technol.* **2004**, *21*, 1876–1894. [CrossRef]
9. Sheng, Y.P. *A Three-Dimensional Numerical Model of Coastal and Estuarine Circulation and Transport in Generalized Curvilinear Grids*; Technical Report No. 587; Aeronautical Research Associates Of Princeton: Princeton, NJ, USA, 1986.
10. Sheng, Y.P. *Evolution of a Three-Dimensional Curvilinear-Grid Hydrodynamic Model for Estuaries, Lakes and Coastal Waters: Estuarine and Coastal Modeling I*; ASCE: Reston, VA, USA, 1990; pp. 40–49.
11. Sheng, Y.P.; Paramygin, V.A.; Alymov, V.; Davis, J.R. A Real-Time Forecasting System for Hurricane Induced Storm Surge and Coastal Flooding. In Proceedings of the Ninth International Conference on Estuarine and Coastal Modeling, Charleston, SC, USA, 31 October–2 November 2006; pp. 585–602.

12. Sheng, Y.P.; Alymov, V.; Paramygin, V.A. Simulation of storm surge, waves, and inundation in the Outer Banks and Chesapeake Bay during Hurricane Isabel in 2003: The importance of waves. *J. Geophys. Res.* **2010**, *115*, C4. [CrossRef]

13. Sheng, Y.P.; Zhang, Y.; Paramygin, V.A. Simulation of Storm Surge, Wave, and Coastal Inundation during Hurricane Ivan in 2004. *Ocean Model.* **2010**, *35*, 314–331. [CrossRef]

14. Ris, R.C.; Holthuijsen, L.H.; Booij, N. A third-generation wave model for coastal regions: 2. Verification. *J. Geophys. Res.* **1999**, *104*, 7667–7681. [CrossRef]

15. Sheng, Y.P.; Villaret, C. Modeling the effect of suspended sediment stratification on bottom exchange process. *J. Geophys. Res.* **1989**, *94*, 14429–14444. [CrossRef]

16. Sheng, Y.P.; Kim, T. Skill assessment of an integrated modeling system for shallow coastal and estuarine ecosystems. *J. Mar. Syst.* **2009**, *76*, 212–243. [CrossRef]

17. Sheng, Y.P.; Paramygin, V.A. Forecasting storm surge, inundation, and 3D circulation along the Florida Coast, Estuarine and Coastal Modeling. In Proceedings of the 11th International Conference ASCE, Fort Lauderdale, FL, USA, 20–22 May 2010.

18. Sheng, Y.P.; Paramygin, V.A.; Zhang, Y.; Davis, J.R. Recent enhancements and application of an integrated storm surge modeling system: CH3D-SSMS. Estuarine and Coastal Modeling. In Proceedings of the Tenth International Conference ASCE, New Orleans, LA, USA, 9–12 March 2008; pp. 879–892.

19. Sheng, Y.P.; Tutak, B.; Davis, J.R.; Paramygin, V. Circulation and flushing in the lagoonal system of the Guana Tolomato Matanzas National Estuarine Research Reserve (GTMNERR), Florida. *J. Coast. Res.* **2008**, *55*, 9–25. [CrossRef]

20. Davis, J.R.; Sheng, Y.P. Development of a parallel storm surge model. *Int. J. Numer. Meth. Fluids* **2003**, *42*, 549–580. [CrossRef]

21. Sheng, Y.P.; Davis, J.R.; Figueiredo, R.; Liu, B.; Liu, H.; Luettich, R., Jr.; Paramygin, V.A.; Weaver, R.; Weisberg, R.; Xie, L.; et al. A Regional Testbed for Storm Surge and Inundation Models. In Proceedings of the 12th International Conference on Estuarine and Coastal Modeling, St. Augustine, FL, USA, 7–9 November 2011.

22. Peng, M.; Xie, L.; Pietrafesa, L.J. A numerical study of storm surge and inundation in the Croatan–Albemarle–Pamlico Estuary System. *Estuar. Coast. Shelf Sci.* **2004**, *59*, 121–137. [CrossRef]

23. Chen, C.; Cowles, G.; Beardsley, R.C. *An Unstructured Grid, Finite Volume Coastal Ocean Model: FVCOM User Manual*, 2nd ed.; SMAST/UMASSD TR-06-0602; MIT: Cambridge, MA, USA, 2006; p. 315.

24. National Academy of Sciences. *Mapping the Zone—Improving Flood Map Accuracy*; Committee on FEMA Flood Maps, National Research Council: Washington, DC, USA, 2009.

25. Lapetina, A.; Sheng, Y.P. Simulating complex storm surge dynamics: Three-dimensionality, vegetation effect, and onshore sediment transport. *J. Geophys. Res. Oceans* **2015**, *120*, 7363–7380. [CrossRef]

26. Powell, M.D.; Houston, S.H.; Amat, L.R.; Morisseau-Leroy, N. The HRD real-time hurricane wind analysis system. *J. Wind Eng. Ind. Aerodyn.* **1998**, *77*, 53–64. [CrossRef]

27. NOGAPS. Available online: http://coaps.fsu.edu/woce/html/models/fnoc.htm (accessed on 8 January 2017).

28. About the GFDL Hurricane Model Ensemble. Available online: http://data1.gfdl.noaa.gov/hurricane/gfdl_ensemble/about.html (accessed on 8 January 2017).

29. Michalakes, J.; Dudhia, J.; Gill, D.; Henderson, T.; Klemp, J.; Skamarock, W.; Wang, W. The Weather Reseach and Forecast Model: Software Architecture and Performance. In Proceedings of the 11th ECMWF Workshop on the Use of High Performance Computing In Meteorology, Reading, UK, 25–29 October 2004.

30. NAM Products. Available online: http://www.nco.ncep.noaa.gov/pmb/products/nam (accessed on 8 January 2017).

31. Davis, J.R.; Paramygin, V.A.; Forrest, D.; Sheng, Y.P. Towards the probabilistic simulation of storm surge and inundation in a limited resource environment. *Mon. Weather Rev.* **2010**, *138*, 2953–2974. [CrossRef]

32. Miller, R.J.; Schrader, A.J.; Sampson, C.R.; Tsui, T.L. The Automated Tropical Cyclone Forecasting System (ATCF). *Weather Forecast.* **1990**, *5*, 653–660. [CrossRef]

33. Halliwell, G. Evaluation of vertical coordinate and vertical mixing algorithms in the HYbrid Coordinate Ocean Model (HYCOM). *Ocean Modelling.* **2004**, *7*, 285–322. [CrossRef]

34. Tolman, H.L. *User Manual and System Documentation of WAVEWATCH III Version 3.14. NOAA/NWS/NCEP/MMAB Technical Note 276*; National Weather Service: Camp Springs, MD, USA, 2009; p. 194.

35. HTCondor—Home. Available online: https://research.cs.wisc.edu/htcondor (accessed on 1 July 2016).

36. THREDDS Data Server. Available online: http://www.unidata.ucar.edu/software/thredds/current/tds (accessed on 15 June 2016).

37. Xie, L.; Bao, S.; Pietrafesa, L.J.; Foley, K.; Fuentes, M. A Real-Time Hurricane Surface Wind Forecasting Model: Formulation and Verification. *Mon. Weather Rev.* **2006**, *134*, 1355–1370. [CrossRef]

38. Sheng, Y.P.; Liu, T. Three-dimensional simulation of wave-induced circulation: Comparison of three radiation stress formulations. *J. Geophys. Res.* **2011**, *116*, C05021. [CrossRef]

39. Mellor, G.L. The depth dependent current and wave interaction equations: A revision. *J. Phys. Oceangr.* **2008**, *38*, 2587–2596. [CrossRef]

40. Longuet-Higgins, M.S.; Stewart, R.W. Radiation stress and mass transport in gravity waves with application to 'surf beats'. *J. Fluid Mech.* **1962**, *13*, 481–504. [CrossRef]

41. Longuet-Higgins, M.S.; Stewart, R.W. Radiation stresses in water waves: A physical discussion with applications. *Deep-Sea Res.* **1964**, *11*, 529–562. [CrossRef]

42. Parks, A.B.; Shay, L.K.; Johns, W.E.; Martinez-Pedraja, J.; Gurgel, K.-W. HF radar observations of small-scale surface current variability in the Straits of Florida. *J. Geophys. Res.* **2009**, *114*, C08002. [CrossRef]

43. Shay, L.K.; Cook, T.M.; Peters, H.; Mariano, A.J.; Weisberg, R.; An, P.E.; Soloviev, A.; Luther, M. Very High Frequency Radar Mapping of Surface Currents. *IEEE J. Coast. Eng.* **2002**, *27*, 155–169. [CrossRef]

44. Landsea, C.W.; Franklin, J.L.; McAdie, C.J.; Beven, J.L., II; Gross, J.M.; Jarvinen, B.R.; Pasch, R.J.; Rappaport, E.N.; Dunion, J.P.; Dodge, P.P. A reanalysis of hurricane Andrew's intensity. *Am. Meteorol. Soc.* **2004**, *85*, 1699. [CrossRef]

45. Lawrence, M.B.; Cobb, H.D. *Tropical Cyclone Report Hurricane Jeanne 13–28 September 2004*; National Hurricane Center: Miami, FL, USA, 2005.

46. Pasch, R.J.; Blake, E.S.; Cobb, H.D., III; Roberts, D.P. *Tropical Cyclone Report Hurricane Wilma. 15–25 October 2005*; National Hurricane Center: Miami, FL, USA, 2006.

47. Stewart, S.R.; Beven, J.L., II. *Tropical Cyclone Report Tropical Cyclone Fay (AL062008) 15–26 August 2008*; National Hurricane Center: Miami, FL, USA, 2009.

48. Kelley, J.G.W.; Zhang, A.; Chu, P.; Lang, G.A. *Skill Assessment of NOS Lake Huron Operational Forecast System (LHOFS)*; NOAA Technical Memorandum NOS CS 23: Silver Spring, MD, USA, 2010.

49. NOAA Tides and Currents. Available online: https://tidesandcurrents.noaa.gov (accessed on 8 January 2017).

50. Florida Department of Environmental Protection/Division of State Lands/Bureau of Survey and Mapping. Available online: http://www.fldep-stevens.com (accessed on 8 January 2017).

51. Centralized Data Management Office. Available online: http://cdmo.baruch.sc.edu/get/landing.cfm (accessed on 8 January 2017).

52. Sheng, Y.P.; Lapetina, A.; Ma, G. The reduction of storm surge by vegetation canopies: Three-dimensional simulations. *Geophys. Res. Lett.* **2012**, *39*, L20601. [CrossRef]

53. Lapetina, A.; Sheng, Y.P. Three-dimensional modeling of storm surge and inundation including the effects of coastal vegetation. *Estuaries Coasts* **2014**. [CrossRef]

MDPI AG

St. Alban-Anlage 66

4052 Basel, Switzerland

Tel. +41 61 683 77 34

Fax +41 61 302 89 18

http://www.mdpi.com

JMSE Editorial Office

E-mail: jmse@mdpi.com

http://www.mdpi.com/journal/jmse

www.ingramcontent.com/pod-product-compliance
Lightning Source LLC
LaVergne TN
LVHW071356070326
832902LV00028B/4626